CLARA SCHUMANN

Clara Schumann, age 38, Munich. Photograph by Franz Hanfstaengl, 1857. Robert-Schumann-Haus, Zwickau.

CLARA SCHUMANN

The Artist and the Woman

Revised Edition

NANCY B. REICH

Cornell University Press

ITHACA AND LONDON

First edition published 1985 by Cornell University Press
First printing, Cornell Paperbacks, 1987
Revised edition published 2001

Printed in the United States of America

Library of Congress Cataloging-in-Publication Data

Reich, Nancy B.
Clara Schumann : the artist and the woman / Nancy B. Reich.—Rev. ed.
p. cm.
"Catalogue of Works": p.
Includes bibliographical references (p.) and index.
ISBN 0-8014-3740-7 (cloth : alk. paper) — ISBN 0-8014-8637-8 (pbk.: alk. paper)
1. Schumann, Clara, 1819–1896. 2. Pianists—Germany—Biography. I. Title.
ML417.S4 R4 2001
786.2'092—dc21
00-011932

Cornell University Press strives to use environmentally responsible suppliers and materials to the fullest extent possible in the publishing of its books. Such materials include vegetable-based, low-VOC inks and acid-free papers that are recycled, chlorine-free, or partly composed of nonwood fibers. Books that bear the logo of the FSC (Forest Stewardship Council) use paper taken from forests that have been inspected and certified as meeting the highest standards for environmental and social responsibility. For further information, visit our website at www.cornellpress.cornell.edu.

Cloth printing 10 9 8 7 6 5 4 3 2 1
Paperback printing 10 9 8 7 6 5 4 3 2 1

In memory of
Haskell A. Reich,
1926–1983

Contents

Illustrations

Preface to the Revised Edition

In the fifteen years since the first edition of this biography was published, interest in Clara Schumann has exploded. Performances, editions, and recordings of her music, films, dramas, radio and TV programs inspired by her life, piano competitions in her name, dissertations, scholarly papers, articles in the scholarly and popular presses, program notes, publication of letters, biographies in several languages and revisionist biographies, all attest to the significance of and fascination with Clara Wieck Schumann as an artist and as a woman.

Some part of the fascination was generated by the feminist movement, which stirred the demand for courses in women's studies, women's history, and gender studies now found in universities around the globe. Clara Schumann—career woman and single mother—was an ideal subject for students interested in women, history, and music. Indeed, many of the lecture invitations I received the first few years after the publication of the book were from groups more interested in women's issues than in music history. As awareness of her accomplishments grew, however, she increasingly came to be seen not only as a symbol of women achievers but as an acknowledged composer of the new romantic school of the early Romantic period and a towering influence on pianists in the nineteenth century.

The need for a new edition has grown more pressing as a result of the publication of a variety of significant documents—letters, medical reports, and music—that were in private hands and unavailable when I was working on the first edition. The publication in 1994 of excerpts of the medical log kept by Robert Schumann's physicians in Endenich, Clara Schumann's correspondence with Dr. Härtel of the publishers Breitkopf & Härtel (published in 1997) and with the List family (published in 1996), and the letters and diaries of her granddaughter Julie (published in 1990) were among the documents that, though they did not change my basic conceptions of the character and personality of Clara Schumann, have informed this revised edition and enriched my understanding and admiration of this remarkable woman.

Preface to the Revised Edition

The many new publications of the music of Clara Wieck Schumann, especially the editions by Gerd Nauhaus, Janina Klassen, and Joachim Draheim, and the increasing number of genuinely artistic performances of her works have led to a reassessment of her as a composer. Though I do not analyze her works in this book, it is my hope that the extended Catalogue of Works, which lists new editions, and the citations to the scholarly literature will enable performers and listeners to locate her compositions and the new studies they have inspired.

The centenary of the death of Clara Schumann in 1996 was the occasion for many festivals and conferences at which scholars, young and old, presented the latest findings on the multifaceted musician. The publications that ensued (cited in the bibliography) have also facilitated this edition, and it is hoped they will dispel the myths and legends that continue to proliferate.

To the frequent comments about the "lovely romantic" story of Clara and Robert Schumann, I can answer that it was indeed a romantic story, but it was only one aspect of a long and difficult life. Too often the tragedies endured by Clara Schumann are forgotten: the final heartbreaking years of Robert Schumann's life; the pressures of carrying on a public career to pay for the hospitalization of a mentally ill husband and to support a family; the burdens of a widow raising and educating seven children ranging in age from two to fourteen; the deaths and illnesses of four adult children. In 1985 I wrote of a life of triumph and tragedy, but now I recognize that the tragedies suffered by this courageous woman far outweighed the triumphs, and that her life can more accurately be described as a story of great talent, struggle, and survival.

Political events of the past decade have greatly aided the preparation of this revised edition. Almost all the sources used for the first edition were in the libraries and archives of the former German Democratic Republic, and though I was granted entree to them on my many research trips to that country and found librarians and archivists universally friendly and cooperative, the same could not always be said of the agencies that governed study and research. Photocopying was unavailable, so documents and music had to be copied by hand. Searches at border crossings became explanatory ordeals. For this edition, I had the great privilege of accessing Clara Wieck's girlhood diaries (*Jugendtagebücher*) on my computer, a luxury unthinkable in the early 1980s. The access to sources and the publication of the Robert Schumann *Tagebücher* and the first two volumes of the Robert and Clara Schumann *Briefwechsel* also have made the task of correcting errors and filling gaps much easier.

My own research after the publication of the first edition has contributed to this revision a greater awareness of the impact of class and gender on music history, of Clara Wieck Schumann's relationship with the Mendelssohn family, and of the enduring influence of Clara Schumann on pianists and pianism throughout the world.

I was fortunate to have many doors opened to me after the publication of *Clara Schumann: The Artist and the Woman* in 1985 and its publication in England in 1985 and 1987 (Gollancz and Oxford University Press), in Japan in 1987

(Ongaku No Tomo Sha), and in Germany in 1991 (Rowohlt Verlag). I met Schumann relatives, scholars, and music lovers from four continents who have shared with me their knowledge of and experiences with Clara and Robert Schumann and their music. Their help and the generosity of friends and colleagues whose interest continually rekindled my enthusiasm and excitement for this project have enabled me to present a more complete portrait of Clara Schumann.

NANCY B. REICH

Hastings-on-Hudson, New York

Preface to the First Edition

Though much has been written about Clara Schumann, she is still, more than 165 years after her birth, known to us only through the eyes and minds of her own era. She is viewed even today as her nineteenth-century contemporaries saw her—as a saint or "priestess," as a dedicated wife, mother, and musician. In seeking a modern approach to this great artist, I have examined new sources and reexamined the old. This study has deepened my regard for the artist and woman; it has also convinced me that she is worthy of the truth. Such a quest calls for the tools of musicological scholarship, the insights of psychology, and sensitivity to the history of women and their place in nineteenth-century musical history.

All of her biographies, even the most recent (published in English, French, German, Danish, and several other languages—testimony to the continuing interest in Clara Schumann), have been based on Berthold Litzmann's *Clara Schumann: Ein Künstlerleben,* published between 1902 and 1908, and on her correspondence with Johannes Brahms, which was published in 1927.

Litzmann's three-volume, 1,459-page biography, written under the supervision of Marie, the eldest Schumann daughter, and authorized by the Schumann family, is a major source for scholars of nineteenth-century music, and indeed has been a major source for my own book. Litzmann, a literary scholar and friend of the Schumann family, sifted through thousands of letters and all of the diaries of Robert and Clara Schumann as well as court orders, travel notebooks, household books, old programs, music autographs—all the papers that Robert Schumann meticulously filed and treasured. The two volumes of letters exchanged by Clara Schumann and Brahms between 1853 and 1896, to which Litzmann alone was granted access, remains a precious record of the lives of two great musicians. Litzmann's objectivity, understanding, and warmth were in no way reduced by the Teutonic thoroughness with which he performed his task. The many English admirers of the art of Clara Schumann eagerly awaited translations of the letters and of Litzmann's biography; they were published almost simultaneously with the German editions. Unfortunately, Grace Hadow's admirable translations of the biography (1913) and letters (1927) are sharply abridged versions of the originals and thus omit many details vital to a complete understanding of the woman and her time.

A review of the original sources, moreover, reveals many nuances overlooked by Litzmann, who omitted much information, perhaps to protect the persons involved or perhaps because he believed it was not worth consideration. The translations suffer even more, less from the language conversion than from the shortening of the biography by one-third and of the correspondence by half. Hadow hews close to the facts, but so much is omitted that serious readers cannot depend on the translations. The same can be said of many other translations of Schumann sources. For these reasons, I have used only the German publications and provided my own translations for all material quoted. All citations are to the German works. (The *Memoirs* of Eugenie Schumann are the only exception, for reasons made clear in the bibliography.) I was most fortunate in being able to consult the first volume (1832–38) of the recently published critical edition of the letters of Clara and Robert Schumann, edited by Eva Weissweiler. Wherever possible, I have referred to this volume rather than to Litzmann's edition, as it offers an unabridged transcription of the correspondence. The volumes covering the later years are not yet available, and as I was unable to consult the surviving original letters, I have relied (cautiously) on Litzmann and on Wolfgang Boetticher's *Robert Schumann in seinen Schriften und Briefen* for quotations from letters after 1838.

A remarkable series of scholarly publications of Schumann documents from the archives of Robert-Schumann-Haus, Zwickau, has been appearing since 1971. These documents, meticulously edited according to contemporary scholarly procedures, have changed the course of Schumann research. Readers are no longer limited to family-authorized publications or to studies flawed by the prejudices of their editors. Through the courtesy of Martin Schoppe and Gerd Nauhaus of Robert-Schumann-Haus, I have had the good fortune to study many of the documents—the household books and "marriage diary," for example—before publication, and to read others, including the diary of Clara Wieck and the Wieck and Schumann family papers, whose publication is scheduled many years hence. I have also examined many hundreds of letters stored in archives in Europe and the United States, as well as published collections of correspondence involving the Schumanns. As a consequence I have gained an enormous respect for Litzmann but also an added dimension of understanding of the woman who was artist, wife, mother, teacher, editor, and a creative partner of Friedrich Wieck, Robert Schumann, and Johannes Brahms.

Since the reader may obtain from Litzmann (or the Hadow translation) a day-by-day chronology of Clara Schumann's life, I have not attempted to duplicate this detail or repeated many of the legends familiar to readers of the Schumann literature. Although Part I is organized chronologically, I have focused on what I see as key issues in the life of Clara Schumann—her close bond with her father, her relationship with her mother, her education and the development of her unparalleled career, her agonizing struggle for independence, the choices she was forced to make between family and career, her responses to motherhood, the changing balance in her family life, and her strategies for coping with the illness, suicide attempt, and hospitalization of her husband. During the forty years left to her after his death she built and maintained a career in Europe and England second to none. This rich life I have treated in Part II, where four major areas of her life are explored in detail: her friendships, her creative work, her life on the concert stage, and her activities as a teacher. In each of these chapters I have attempted to answer the many questions raised by musicians in regard to her contributions and influence, to offer information that has not previously been available, and to place Clara Schumann in perspective in the musical life of the nineteenth century. Readers may be surprised to see Brahms relegated to one chapter in her life; it was a most significant chapter, to be sure, but it was not the consuming central relationship that so many people have suspected.

My search for materials for this biography began inadvertently: in 1973 I came across the unpublished correspondence (1858–96) between Clara Schumann and Ernst Rudorff, who had been her student for a short time and who later taught her daughter Eugenie. There were many ties between Frau Schumann and the younger man. As head of the piano department of the Berlin Hochschule für Musik, Rudorff was a member of the inner circle of musicians and friends on whom she most depended. The Rudorff correspondence was a starting point; from there other collections of published and unpublished correspondence gave me insights to the personality and character of Clara Schumann not yielded by Litzmann.

Major sources for this study are listed in the bibliography, but a few documents, published and unpublished, which have been particularly meaningful must be mentioned here. All the papers and materials in Robert-Schumann-Haus, Zwickau, particularly the unpublished diaries of Clara Wieck, offer the researcher a wealth of previously unknown information—names, places, dates—as well as a new perception of the character and personality of Clara and of Friedrich Wieck, her father. The letters of Friedrich Wieck, edited by Käthe Walch-Schumann and not available in their entirety until 1968, provide a clearer picture of the man, a figure not treated with particular sympathy by Litzmann and never revealed in his true light. Joseph Joachim's correspondence with Brahms, Rudorff, and Clara Schumann, the letters of the Joachim family, the Schumann family correspondence, the Ferdinand Hiller correspondence, and the correspondence between Clara Schumann and Ernst Rudorff have illuminated music and concert life of the nineteenth century as well as the personal relationships of all involved.

Some of the letters that proved most significant to me appeared in articles in long-forgotten German music periodicals: the wonderful letters of Clara Schumann to Emilie Steffens (Chapter 6), for example, and her letter to Selmar

Bagge (Chapter 10). Other writings from well-known volumes overlooked by previous biographers—a description of Clara in 1854 by Hedwig Salomon (Chapter 7), a letter of Clara to Emilie List about her sixteenth birthday party (Chapter 4), an indignant letter to Hiller about her treatment in Düsseldorf (Chapter 7), a letter from Amalie Joachim to her husband in 1872 (Chapter 8), and entries from Ruppert Becker's diary (Chapter 7)—reveal a more human Clara Schumann, a woman who comes to life through her own words. These documents have been translated, most for the first time, and many are given in their entirety.

Students of women's history know that female influences, even in the lives of prominent women, are usually overlooked. This has certainly been the case in studies of Clara Schumann. Robert Schumann plays an inordinately large role in most biographies of Clara Schumann written by both men and women; and the place of Clara Wieck's mother, Marianne, and her significance in the life of the young pianist has never been explored. Indeed, Marianne is virtually ignored by Litzmann once she has borne Wieck's children and left his home. Perhaps the early divorce was an embarrassment to the Schumann family and thus to Litzmann. It is my hope that with this study Marianne Bargiel has been restored to her rightful place in the story of her daughter's life. In this task I was aided by Herma Stamm-Bargiel, who kindly shared pictures and family documents of the Bargiel family with me.

Locating the compositions of Clara Schumann has not been an easy task, but here, too, the archives at Robert-Schumann-Haus have provided valuable materials. The collection of autographs and prints of Clara Schumann's music in Zwickau and the exciting discovery in the Staatsbibliothek, Berlin, of her song autographs collected into one notebook (listed in the Catalogue of Works), as well as Robert Schumann's instrumentation of the last movement of her concerto, enabled me to date her works and prepare a more complete catalogue of her works than any that has appeared previously.

Musical examples in Chapter 11 are taken from the first editions of Clara Schumann's works and from the Dover reprint (1972) of *Robert Schumann's Werke,* edited by Clara Schumann (Leipzig: Breitkopf & Härtel, 1879–93). Example 7 is from *Johannes Brahms: Sämtliche Werke,* edited for the Gesellschaft der Musikfreunde, Vienna, by Hans Gál and Eusebius Mandyczewski (Leipzig: Breitkopf & Härtel, 1926–28). Examples 8 and 10 are from Schumann, *Impromptus,* edited by H. J. Köhler (Leipzig: Peters, 1979), 29.

The spellings of names and musical titles varied considerably in the nineteenth century. Clara Schumann, for example, always spelled her name with a *C* whereas Robert Schumann used both *C* and *K* in writing his wife's name. I have attempted to establish consistency in the spelling of names by using the spelling given by the individual himself or herself or in official documents of the period.

In their search for great women of the past, feminists have rallied round the figure of Clara Schumann. It must be pointed out, however, that she was not a feminist in the modern sense of the word. She had little interest in women's rights or the struggle for recognition that other creative German women were just beginning to launch in the mid–nineteenth century. She concentrated on her own career and her many obligations as she endeavored to reconcile the conflicts that inevitably arise when a woman steps out of her conventional place.

Clara Schumann was always her own person, perceiving herself as an artist who was a woman, and eternally grateful for the art that was to sustain her through a lifetime of tragedy and triumph.

NANCY B. REICH

Hastings-on-Hudson, New York

Acknowledgments to the Revised Edition

I am grateful to the friends and colleagues who were so helpful when I was preparing the first edition and were there for me as I began the task of assembling new material for this revised edition.

Gerda Lederer, Herbert Weber, and Josef Eisinger have generously offered expert assistance with transcriptions and translations. I am especially grateful to Dr. Eisinger for his translations of the reviews in the Catalogue, a task I could not have undertaken without his help.

My thanks to the staff of the Music Library of Columbia University; Special Collections, Oberlin College Library; Theodore Finney Music Collection, University of Pittsburgh; Rigbie Turner of the Pierpont Morgan Library; Bernhard Appel and Matthias Wendt of the Robert-Schumann-Forschungsstelle, Düsseldorf. Inge Hermstrüwer of the Heinrich-Heine-Institut and Martin Schoppe, former director of Robert-Schumann-Haus, both scholars who were unfailingly helpful, have died in recent years; they are sorely missed.

It is a pleasure to acknowledge the kindness of Gerd Nauhaus and the staff of Robert-Schumann-Haus, Zwickau. I also wish to express my appreciation to Gustav Abel, John Daverio, James Deaville, Claudia De Vries, Joachim Draheim, Valerie Goertzen, Helma Kaldewey, Janina Klassen, Claudia Macdonald, Margit McCorkle, Monica Steegmann, and Maria Zduniak for their comments, suggestions, and generosity in sharing information. Again, many thanks to Mi-Won Kim for her readiness to undertake still more musical examples and to Barbara Salazar, who edited both editions with skill and patience.

Friends and family have been supportive and encouraging. My thanks to Anna Burton, M.D., for her wise counsel; to Styra Avins for many stimulating discussions; to Adrienne Fried Block and Judith Tick for advice, hope, and confidence; to my daughter Susanna for loving interest and concern; and to Maurice M. Rapport for his patient understanding during the many months of work on this edition.

N. B. R.

Acknowledgments to the First Edition

My profoundest gratitude goes to Anna Burton, M.D., for her friendship, continuing support and sympathy, and the stimulating and fruitful collaboration we have had over many years. An accomplished musician and practicing psychoanalyst, she was a true silent partner in the creation of this book. Dr. Burton never spared herself in helping me think through and understand problematical situations and questions that arose during the course of my research. Her wisdom and penetrating insights have informed every page of this book.

I gratefully thank the many colleagues in both Europe and the United States who have aided this endeavor: Martin Schoppe and Gerd Nauhaus, who generously opened the archives at Robert-Schumann-Haus, Zwickau, to me and who have been helpful in every possible way; Hans Joachim Kohler, Leipzig, and Renate and Kurt Hofmann, Hamburg, for enlightening conversation; R. Klaus Müller, Käte Pittasch, Leipzig; Brigitte Berenbruch, Bonn; Helga Heim, Hamburg; Maike Holling-Suhl, West Berlin, whose friendship and devoted interest have made my research in Europe so gratifying and productive; Janina Klassen, Kiel; Maria Párkai-Eckhardt, Budapest; and Peter Cahn, Frankfurt, who have generously shared information with me; and Eva Weissweiler, Cologne, who kindly sent me her transcriptions of Clara Schumann's letters to Bettina von Arnim.

I thank also Imogen Fellinger, whose family connections with the Schumanns go back several generations, for her guidance and assistance, and Herma Stamm-Bargiel, who provided me with copies of unpublished sketches of the Tromlitz family, shared information about her Tromlitz and Bargiel descendants, and kindly gave me permission to reproduce the picture of Marianne Tromlitz.

I am very appreciative of the hospitality and kindness of Johannes von Gottberg, who granted me access to the Rudorff archives and gave me permission to quote excerpts from letters of Clara Schumann to Ernst Rudorff.

Among friends and colleagues in the United States, warmest thanks to Marianne von Recklinghausen Bowles and Gabriele Wickert for their expert assistance with translations, and to Adrienne Block, Gary Golio, Mary Ann Joyce, Gladys Krasner, Karen Miller, Susanna Reich, Judith Tick, and Rachel Wade for unflagging encouragement, counsel, and assistance over many years. I have had stimulating and provocative conversations with Dr. Peter Ostwald, who was writing his Robert Schumann biography during the years I was working out ideas about Clara Schumann, and I thank him for his interest and encouragement.

I am grateful to Rufus Hallmark, Mildred Parker, and my colleagues at the Stanford Center for Research on Women, especially Susan Bell, Karen Offen, and Marilyn Safir, for helpful suggestions. To Ralph Locke and Jurgen Thym for information about the Dickinson Collection, many thanks.

I have used the facilities of many libraries and archives and appreciate the gracious assistance of the following individuals and music libraries in the United States: Ruth Hilton and the New York University Music Library; Rigbie Turner and the Pierpont Morgan Library, New York; Bernard Wilson and the Newberry Library, Chicago; and the staffs of the music libraries of Columbia University, the Eastman School of Music, Harvard University, the Library of Congress, the New York Public Library, Queens College, Stanford University, the University of California at Berkeley, and Yale University.

I thank colleagues in European libraries who have been kind and helpful: in England, the staff of the Music Division of the British Library; in West Germany, the Stadtgeschichtliche Sammlungen, Baden-Baden; the library of the Hochschule der Künste, West Berlin; the Staatsbibliothek Preussischer Kulturbesitz, Musikabteilung und Handschriftenabteilung, West Berlin; the Staatliches Institut für Musikforschung, Preussischer Kulturbesitz, West Berlin; the Musikbücherei Schumannhaus and the Stadtarchiv, Bonn; the Musikwissenschaftliches Institut der Universität, Cologne; the Heinrich-Heine-Institut and the Universitätsbibliothek, Düsseldorf; the Stadt- und Universitätsbibliothek, Frankfurt am Main; the Staats- und Universitätsbibliothek, Hamburg; the Kestner-Museum, Hannover; the Bayerische Staatsbibliothek, Munich; and the Landesbibliothek, Stuttgart. In the German Democratic Republic, I have had kind and patient assistance from the staffs of the Deutsche Staatsbibliothek, Musikabteilung, Berlin; the Universitätsbibliothek, Leipzig; and Robert-Schumann-Haus, Zwickau. I also thank the staffs of the archives of the Gesellschaft der Musikfreunde, Vienna, and the Biblioteka Jagiellońska, Kraków.

Many thanks to Margit McCorkle and the staff of the Brahms Cataloging Project for placing their library and working papers at my disposal in Vancouver.

I am deeply grateful to Barbara Salazar of Cornell University Press for her patience and expert guidance. To Alan Lippert and Michael Lippert for technical assistance, and to Mi-Won Kim for preparing the musical examples, much appreciation.

Portions of Chapters 1 through 4 have appeared in substantially different form in *The Musical Quarterly*, Summer 1984. I am also grateful for the cooperation of Breitkopf & Härtel, Wiesbaden, publishers of Berthold Litzmann's biography of Clara Schumann and his edition of the letters of Clara Schumann and Johannes Brahms, and I thank the following institutions for permission to publish excerpts from letters and to reproduce pictures in their possession: Deutsche Staatsbibliothek, Berlin/DDR, Musikabteilung; Robert-Schumann-Haus, Zwickau/DDR; Staatsbibliothek, Preussischer Kulturbesitz, Musikabteilung, West Berlin; Schumannhaus, Bonn; Heinrich-Heine-Institut, Düsseldorf; the Newberry Library, Chicago; and the Pierpont Morgan Library, New York.

I acknowledge with thanks a grant for college teachers from the National Endowment for the Humanities, travel grants from the Deutscher Akademischer Austauschdienst, and the Penrose Fund of the American Philosophical Society, and assistance from the Faculty Service Committee, Manhattanville College.

This book could not have been written without the steadfast encouragement, faith, and devotion of my late husband, Haskell A. Reich.

N. B. R.

Chronology

1785 Birth of father, Friedrich Wieck, August 18.
1797 Birth of mother, Marianne Tromlitz, May 17.
1810 Birth of Robert Schumann in Zwickau, June 8.
1816 Marriage of Marianne Tromlitz and Friedrich Wieck, June 23.
1817 Birth of Adelheid Wieck, August 10 (d. May 12, 1818).
1819 Birth of Clara Josephine Wieck, September 13.
1821 Birth of Alwin Wieck, August 27.
1823 Birth of Gustav Wieck, January 31.
1824 Birth of Victor Wieck, February 22 (d. January 2, 1827).
Mother leaves Wieck and children, takes infant, May 12.
Clara spends summer with mother; returns to father September 17.
Clara begins formal piano lessons, October 27.
1825 Divorce of Marianne and Friedrich Wieck, January 22.
Marriage of Marianne Wieck and Adolph Bargiel, August.
1828 Robert Schumann arrives in Leipzig; studies with Wieck.
Marriage of Friedrich Wieck and Clementine Fechner, July 3.
Clara plays at Gewandhaus as assisting artist, October 20.
1829 Robert Schumann leaves Leipzig to study in Heidelberg, July 4.
1830 Clara gives private concerts in Dresden, March 6–April 7.
Schumann returns to Leipzig; studies and boards with Wieck family.
Clara gives first Gewandhaus concert as solo artist, November 8.
1831 Clara and father begin concert tour to Paris, leaving Leipzig end of September and returning May 1, 1832.
1832 Birth of Marie Wieck (half sister), January 17.
Solo concerts in Leipzig, July and September.
Local concert tours with father to Altenburg, Zwickau, Schneeberg, November. Schumann joins them in Zwickau.
1833 Concerts in Leipzig, January, February, April, and local tours to Chemnitz, Karlsbad, and Schneeberg.
1834 Schumann becomes editor and publisher of *Neue Zeitschrift für Musik*.
Ernestine von Fricken arrives in Leipzig; studies and boards with Wieck.
Birth of Cäcilie Wieck (half sister), July.
Concert tour with father and Carl Banck to northern Germany (Halle, Magdeburg, Braunschweig, Hamburg, Hannover, Bremen, Berlin), November 11–April 1835.
1835 Robert Schumann begins courtship of Clara Wieck.
Clara and Wieck begin December tour to Zwickau, Plauen, Glachau, Chemnitz.

1836 Death of Schumann's mother. Robert meets Clara secretly in Dresden, February 7–11.
Tour with father to Breslau, February–April.
Tour with father to Naumburg, Jena, Weimar, September.
1837 Secret engagement of Clara and Robert, August 14.
Concert tour with father to Berlin, Hamburg, Bremen, February–May.
Clara meets with mother in Berlin.
Schumann asks Wieck for Clara's hand, September 13; suit rejected.
Concert tour with father to Vienna, October 15–May 15, 1838.
1838 Clara named Royal and Imperial Virtuosa, March 15.
Schumann leaves Leipzig for Vienna, September 27.
1839 Clara leaves for Paris without father, January 8. In Paris, February 6–August 14.
Clara petitions Court of Appeals for permission to marry without father's consent, June 15.
1840 Clara in Berlin with mother from September 1839 till marriage.
Concerts in Berlin and tours with mother in north Germany.
Court consents to marriage, August 1.
Banns posted, August 16.
Last concert as Clara Wieck in Weimar, September 5.
Marriage of Robert Schumann and Clara Wieck, September 12, one day before her 21st birthday.
1841 Death of Adolph Bargiel, February 4.
First concert as Clara Schumann, Gewandhaus, March 31.
Birth of Marie, September 1.
1842 Concert tour to Hamburg with Robert, February 14.
Robert returns to Leipzig; Clara to Copenhagen, returns April 26.
1843 Birth of Elise, April 25.
1844 Concert tour to Russia with Robert, January 25–May 30.
Clara named honorary member, St. Petersburg Philharmonic Society, March 5.
Robert and Clara to Dresden, October.
Family resettles in Dresden, December 13.
1845 Birth of Julie, March 11.
1846 Birth of Emil, February 8.
Vacation trip with Robert to Norderney, July 6–August 25; miscarriage.
Concert tour to Vienna with Robert and two eldest daughters, November 23–February 4, 1847.
1847 To Berlin for performances of Schumann's oratorio *Das Paradies und die Peri* and several concerts, February and March.
Death of Emil, June 22.
To music festival in Zwickau with Robert, July.
1848 Birth of Ludwig, January 20.
1849 May revolution in Dresden.
Birth of Ferdinand, July 16.
1850 Concerts in Leipzig, Hamburg, and Bremen with Robert, February 5–March 29.
Decision to leave Dresden for new employment in Düsseldorf made March 31.
Genoveva premiere and concerts in Leipzig, May 18–July 10.
Arrival in Düsseldorf, September; many concerts.
1851 Birth of Eugenie, December 1. Clara continues concertizing and teaching.
1852 "Schumann Week" in Leipzig; many concerts at Gewandhaus.

Concerts in Düsseldorf and neighboring cities.
Vacation in Scheveningen, August 12–mid-September; miscarriage.
1853 Concerts at Lower Rhine Music Festival, May.
Brahms arrives in Düsseldorf, meets Schumanns, September 30.
Robert leaves position as music director of Düsseldorf orchestra.
Concert tour to Holland with Robert, November 24–December.
1854 Concerts in Hannover with Robert, January 21–30; visits with Joachim and Brahms.
Robert Schumann attempts suicide, February 27. To hospital at Endenich, March 4.
Birth of Felix, June 11.
Clara Schumann begins concert tours, October–December.
1855 Concert tours, January–July and October–December.
1856 Concert tours to Vienna, Prague, Budapest, January–March.
First concert tour to England, April 18–July 6.
Clara sees Robert for first time in two years and five months, July 27.
Death of Robert Schumann, July 29.
Clara begins concert tours, October 28–December 25.
1857 Continues concert tours. Resettles family in Berlin, October.
1863 First season in summer home, Baden-Baden.
1869 Marriage of Julie to Count Radicati di Marmorito, September 22.
1870 Ludwig pronounced incurably ill; institutionalized in Colditz.
Ferdinand called up to serve in army during Franco-Prussian War, returns September 1871.
1872 Death of mother, Marianne Bargiel, March 10.
Death of Julie, November 10.
1873 Marriage of Ferdinand to Antonie Deutsch, August 13.
Baden-Baden house sold. Resettles at 11 In den Zelten, Berlin.
Friedrich Wieck dies, October 6.
1877 Marriage of Elise to Louis Sommerhoff, November 27.
Begins work as editor of Robert Schumann's collected works.
1878 Resettles in Frankfurt; begins work on faculty of Hoch Conservatory.
Fiftieth jubilee as concert artist celebrated in Frankfurt and Leipzig, October 24.
1879 Death of Felix, February 16.
1883 Begins work as editor of Instructive Edition of Robert Schumann's piano works.
1885 Death of Alwin, October 21.
1887 Ferdinand hospitalized. Clara assumes responsibility for his six children.
1888 Final concert tour to England, February–March.
Sixtieth jubilee celebrations in Frankfurt, October 26.
1891 Final public concert in Frankfurt, March.
Death of Ferdinand, June 6.
1893 Death of Clementine Wieck, December 27.
1896 Clara Schumann suffers stroke March 26 and dies May 20.
1897 Death of Johannes Brahms, April 3.
1899 Death of Ludwig, January 9.
1916 Death of Marie Wieck, November 2.
1928 Death of Elise, July 1.
1929 Death of Marie, November 14.
1938 Death of Eugenie, September 25.

Abbreviations and Sources

Abschriftenbuch	"Abschriften verschiedener Gedichten zur Composition," RSH 4871/VIII, 4-5977-A3. A notebook into which RS and CS copied poems they deemed suitable for song texts. The second section of the notebook is inscribed in CS's hand, "Gesammelt von Robert und Clara Schumann vom Jahre 1839 an," but it is likely that RS began entering poems even before that date. See Kaldewey.
AfMw	*Archiv für Musikwissenschaft.*
AmZ	*Allgemeine musikalische Zeitung,* Leipzig.
Appel/Katalog	Appel, Bernhard, and Inge Hermstrüwer, eds. *Robert Schumann und die Dichter: Ein Musiker als Leser. Katalog zur Ausstellung.* Düsseldorf: Droste, 1991.
Avins	Styra Avins. *Johannes Brahms: Life and Letters.* Trans. Josef Eisinger and Styra Avins. Oxford: Oxford University Press, 1997.
B&H	Breitkopf & Härtel.
Boetticher/1942	Boetticher, Wolfgang. *Robert Schumann in seinen Schriften und Briefen.* Berlin: Hahnefeld, 1942.
Briefwechsel	Schumann, Clara, and Robert Schumann. *Briefwechsel.* Ed. Eva Weissweiler. Vol. 1, *1832–1838.* Vol. 2, *1839.* Basel: Stroemfeld/Roter Stern, 1984, 1987.
Chissell	Chissell, Joan. *Clara Schumann: A Dedicated Spirit.* London: Hamish Hamilton, 1983.
CS	Clara Schumann.
CS/Goebels	Schumann, Clara. *Romantische Klaviermusik.* Ed. Franzpeter Goebels. 2 vols. Heidelberg: Willy Müller Süddeutscher Musikverlag, 1967, 1977. (Now Kassel: Bärenreiter.)
CS/JB Briefe	Schumann, Clara, and Johannes Brahms. *Clara Schumann–Johannes Brahms Briefe aus den Jahren 1853–1896.* Ed. Berthold Litzmann. 2 vols. Leipzig: Breitkopf & Härtel, 1927.
CS/Piano Works	Schumann, Clara. *Pianoforte-Werke.* Leipzig: Breitkopf & Härtel, 1879.
CW	Clara Wieck.

CW/Diary — Clara Wieck Tagebücher, RSH 4877-A3. Nine unpublished diaries bound into four volumes covering the years 1819–40. Transcriptions by Gerd Nauhaus; publication forthcoming. My translations.

CW/Early Works — Wieck, Clara. *Frühe Klavierwerke*. Ed. Joachim Draheim and Gerd Nauhaus. Hofheim: Hofmeister, 1996, 1997. (Opp. 1-6, op. 7, based on first editions.)

Da Capo — Schumann, Clara Wieck. *Selected Piano Music*. New York: Da Capo, 1979.

Daverio — Daverio, John. *Robert Schumann: Herald of a "New Poetic Age."* New York: Oxford University Press, 1997.

De Vries — De Vries, Claudia. *Die Pianistin Clara Wieck-Schumann: Interpretation im Spannungsfeld von Tradition und Individualität.* Mainz: Schott, 1996.

Draheim/Höft — Schumann, Clara. *Sämtliche Lieder für Singstimme und Klavier*. Ed. Joachim Draheim and Brigitte Höft. 2 vols. Wiesbaden: Breitkopf & Härtel, 1990, 1992.

Dwight's — *Dwight's Journal of Music.*

FW — Friedrich Wieck.

Grove — *The New Grove Dictionary of Music and Musicians.* Ed. Stanley Sadie. 20 vols. London: Macmillan, 1980.

HHI — Heinrich-Heine-Institut, Düsseldorf.

HHI/Dickinson — Heinrich-Heine-Institut, Dickinson Collection. Manuscripts, prints, and personal effects of Clara Schumann acquired by HHI in 1984 from the collection assembled by June and Edward Dickinson. See Inge Hermstrüwer and Joseph A. Kruse, "Treue Freunde sind gar selten," *Katalog*, 171–77.

Hohenemser — Hohenemser, Richard. "Clara Wieck-Schumann als Komponistin." *Die Musik*, 5 (1905–6), 113–26, 166–73.

JJ/*Briefe* — Joachim, Joseph. *Briefe von und an Joseph Joachim*. Ed. Johannes Joachim and Andreas Moser. 3 vols. Berlin: Julius Bard, 1911–13.

Jugendbriefe — Schumann, Robert. *Jugendbriefe von Robert Schumann: Nach den Originalen mitgetheilt.* Ed. Clara Schumann. 2d ed. Leipzig: Breitkopf & Härtel, 1886.

Kalbeck — Kalbeck, Max. *Johannes Brahms.* 4th ed. 4 vols. Berlin: Deutsche Brahms-Gesellschaft, 1921.

Kaldewey — Kaldewey, Helma. "Die Gedichtabschriften Robert und Clara Schumanns." In *Robert Schumann und die Dichter: Ein Musiker als Leser,* ed. Bernhard Appel and Inge Hermstrüwer. Düsseldorf: Droste, 1991.

Katalog — Bodsch, Ingrid, and Gerd Nauhaus, eds. *Clara Schumann, 1819–1896: Katalog zur Ausstellung*. Bonn: Bonn Stadtmuseum, 1996.

Klassen/1987 — Klassen, Janina, ed. *Clara Wieck-Schumann Ausgewählte Klavierwerke.* Munich: Henle, 1987.

Klassen/1990 — Klassen, Janina. *Clara Wieck-Schumann: Die Virtuosin als Komponistin.* Kassel: Bärenreiter, 1990.

Liederbuch — SBPK/CS5: Mus. Ms. Autogr. C. Schumann 5. Songs of CS collected in a music notebook in 1842. Title page has inscription in RS's hand, "Lieder/mit Begleitung d. Pianoforte/von/Klara Schumann./1842."

Below the title is a table of contents in which 16 songs written between 1840 and 1846 are listed in the order in which they were composed. In right margin, in CS's hand vertically from bottom to top: "Verzeichniss von Robert geschrieben." On p. 2, another list in the hand of Marie Schumann(?), in which the six songs of op. 23 and "Das Veilchen," all composed in 1853, are listed. Each song in the Liederbuch is written in CS's hand with date of composition in top left corner, author of text in top right corner. Only a few of the songs are titled, and the title written by CS is not always identical to that written by RS in the table of contents. The songs have been numbered (by librarian or Marie Schumann?) in top center and conform with the numbers written on the title page by RS.

Litzmann — Litzmann, Berthold. *Clara Schumann: Ein Künstlerleben nach Tagebüchern und Briefen*. 3 vols. Leipzig: Breitkopf & Härtel, 1902–8.

Marciano — Schumann, Clara. *Drei kleine Klavierstücke*. Ed. Rosario Marciano. Vienna: Doblinger, 1979.

Memoirs — Schumann, Eugenie. *The Schumanns and Johannes Brahms: The Memoirs of Eugenie Schumann.* Trans. Marie Busch. New York: Dial, 1927.

MGG — Blume, Friedrich, ed. *Die Musik in Geschichte und Gegenwart.* 14 vols. Kassel: Bärenreiter, 1949–68.

ML — *Music and Letters.*

MQ — *The Musical Quarterly.*

MT — *The Musical Times.*

NBMz — *Neue Berliner Musikzeitung.*

Niecks — Niecks, Frederick. *Robert Schumann.* London: J. M. Dent, 1925.

NZfM — *Neue Zeitschrift für Musik.*

Norderval — Schumann, Clara. *Seven Songs*. Ed. Kristin Norderval. Bryn Mawr, Pa.: Hildegard, 1993.

PN — Plate number.

PS — Programm-Sammlung, RSH 10463. A collection of five scrapbooks containing 1,299 programs (1828–91) of concerts in which Clara Wieck Schumann played. They are numbered and the city in which the performance took place is noted on each. The collection was begun by FW in 1828 and continued by CS.

Quellenwerk — Georg Eismann, ed. *Robert Schumann: Ein Quellenwerk über sein Leben und Schaffen.* 2 vols. Leipzig: Breitkopf & Härtel, 1956.

Rehberg — Rehberg, Paula, and Walter Rehberg. *Robert Schumann: Sein Leben und sein Werk.* 2d ed. Zurich: Artemis, 1969.

RSH — Robert-Schumann-Haus, Zwickau.

RS/Jansen — Schumann, Robert. *Robert Schumanns Briefe. Neue Folge* Ed. F. Gustav Jansen. Leipzig: Breitkopf & Härtel, 1904.

RS/Tgb 1 — Schumann, Robert. *Tagebücher.* Pt. 1, *1827–1838*. Ed. Georg Eismann. Leipzig: Deutscher Verlag für Musik, 1971.

RS/Tgb 2 — Schumann, Robert. *Tagebücher.* Pt. 2, *1836–1854*. Ed. Gerd Nauhaus. Leipzig: Deutscher Verlag für Musik, 1987. Includes marriage diaries and other entries of RS and CS.

RS/Tgb 3	Schumann, Robert. *Tagebücher.* Pt. 3, *Haushaltbücher (1837–1856).* Ed. Gerd Nauhaus. 2 vols. Leipzig: Deutscher Verlag für Musik, 1982.
Rudorff-Archiv	Rudorff-Archiv: Privatarchiv v. Gottberg.
SATB	Soprano, alto, tenor, bass.
SBPK	Staatsbibliothek zu Berlin Preussischer Kulturbesitz, Musikabteilung mit Mendelssohn-Archiv. CS autographs listed as "Mus. ms. autogr. K. Schumann" and number.
Steegmann	Schumann, Clara. *". . . dass Gott mir ein Talent geschenkt": Clara Schumanns Briefe an Hermann Härtel und Richard und Helene Schöne*. Ed. Monica Steegmann. Zurich: Atlantis Musikbuch-Verlag, 1997.
Wendler	Wendler, Eugen, ed. *"Das Band der ewigen Liebe": Clara Schumanns Briefwechsel mit Emilie und Elise List*. Stuttgart: J. B. Metzler, 1996.
Wieck/*Briefe*	Wieck, Friedrich. *Briefe aus den Jahren 1830–1838*. Ed. Käthe Walch-Schumann. Cologne: Arno Volk-Verlag, 1968.
WCMA	Glickman, Sylvia, and Martha Furman Schleifer. *Women Composers: Music through the Ages*. Vols. 6 and 7. New York: G. K. Hall, 1999–2000.
Wgm	Gesellschaft der Musikfreunde in Wien.

PART I

The Life of Clara Schumann

CHAPTER 1

Prelude: The Wiecks of Leipzig

On January 9, 1838, a poem, "Clara Wieck und Beethoven," appeared in the *Wiener Zeitschrift für Kunst*.[1] Written by Franz Grillparzer, Austria's leading dramatic poet, the verse linked the name of the great composer with that of a young woman who had just given her third Viennese recital at the age of eighteen. Grillparzer's response to her performance of Beethoven's Piano Sonata op. 57, the "Appassionata," reflected the wild enthusiasm the young pianist aroused in Vienna.

Clara Wieck had arrived in the Austrian capital from her native Leipzig with her father, Friedrich, in December 1837. From her first concert on the fourteenth in the Musikvereinsaal to her last appearance in April, when she played for the emperor in the Burg, she was greeted with the kind of adoration the Viennese reserved for artists of the rank of Niccolò Paganini and Sigismund Thalberg.[2] Music lovers fought to buy seats in the overcrowded halls where she played; critics vied with one another in expressions of admiration. At her fourth concert, frenzied applause recalled her to the stage thirteen times. Princes and barons invited her to play at their palaces and showered her with jewels and treasure. The empress herself let her deepest satisfaction be known with a gift of fifty gold ducats.[3] Recalling Clara's reception, Eduard Hanslick, the Viennese critic and music historian, described her as "not a wonderchild—and yet still a child and already a wonder."[4]

On March 15, 1838, she received the greatest honor Austria could bestow: she was named *Königliche Kaiserliche Kammervirtuosin* (Royal and Imperial Chamber Virtuosa), a distinction without precedent for an eighteen-year-old who was, moreover, a Protestant, a foreigner, and a female. The emperor had agreed to make an exception for Clara Wieck. On March 21 the emperor dubbed her *Wundermädchen* and assured her that he had made the award with great personal satisfaction.[5]

Who was Clara Wieck? How did this slender, oval-eyed daughter of an unknown Leipzig piano teacher and music dealer manage to reach such heights of artistry? The question is still more intriguing when we consider that this girl, born in an age when musical talent in a female was generally regarded only as an asset in the marriage market, subsequently built a glorious career that spanned over sixty years, a career that influenced the concert and musical life of the nineteenth century. Acknowledged as the peer of Franz Liszt, Thalberg, and Anton Rubinstein, she was a thorough professional and a working wife and mother, managing the manifold problems of career, household, husband, and children. At twenty-one she was married to a major composer; at thirty-seven, a widow with seven children, she became involved in a lifelong friendship with another major composer. Furthermore, the indefatigable Clara composed music (twenty-three published opus numbers and an equal number without opus numbers),* taught, and was responsible for the authoritative edition of the *Collected Works of Robert Schumann.*

This remarkable woman was a creative partner of three men: Friedrich Wieck, Robert Schumann, and Johannes Brahms. The first, her father, sole teacher, and concert manager, much maligned for the role he was later to play in the romance between his daughter and Robert Schumann, was a self-made man and self-trained musician, obsessive and ambitious. Convinced that gender was no handicap in the race for artistic greatness, he gave Clara the instruction and musical understanding that carried her beyond the ranks of the merely gifted to a position in the constellation of the great nineteenth-century virtuosi. His discipline and pride in her achievements provided the practical sense and stability that sustained her through personal and artistic crises. Wieck firmly believed that his pedagogical genius alone was responsible for the creation of the young pianist who generated such excitement in Vienna in 1838, overlooking entirely the role of Clara's mother, the girl's own remarkable talents, and the series of circumstances, at once tragic, auspicious, fortuitous, and predictable, which went into the making of the "Queen of the Piano." Wieck was at first, of course, the dominating figure in her life, but Clara soon grew to be the more significant, and he eventually shone only in the reflected glory of her light.

FRIEDRICH WIECK, 1785–1873

Friedrich Wieck, the youngest son of a merchant in Pretzsch, a small town about forty-five kilometers from Leipzig, was born in 1785 into a family with declining fortunes and very little interest in music.[6] Always passionately fond of the art, he studied where he could. At age thirteen he was given the opportunity to attend the Thomas-Schule in Leipzig, but was forced to return home after six weeks because of illness. A weak and sickly youngster, he remained in

*All her known works are listed in the Catalogue of Works.

Pretzsch until 1800, when he went to the Torgau gymnasium to prepare for the university and his eventual goal, the ministry. In Torgau and later at the University of Wittenberg, where he matriculated in 1803, his musical education was haphazard. His only formal piano lessons were some six hours with Johann Peter Milchmeyer, who was in Torgau for a short time to give lessons to the wife and children of a well-to-do townsman.*

When Wieck completed his theological studies at the university and had preached the obligatory trial sermon in Dresden, he left theology and turned to the traditional occupation of the German university graduate who had neither money nor connections: he became a *Hauslehrer,* a private tutor in the home of a wealthy family. Over the next nine years he worked for several aristocratic families in Thuringia. His first position was with a baron von Seckendorff in Querfurth, where Adolph Bargiel, the music teacher of the Seckendorff children, became a close friend. Bargiel will appear again at a critical point in Wieck's life.

Conscientious, observant, and intelligent, Wieck was a perceptive teacher. He understood the latest thought in educational psychology (dominated, at that period, by Jean-Jacques Rousseau and his *Emile* and such educators as Johann Basedow and Johann Pestalozzi) and applied it successfully to his students. The young teacher speculated on such concepts as individualized learning and the critical role of motivation in teaching. And, like other progressive educators of his time, he placed great importance on regular physical exercise in the open air. His daughter's musical education, which was to begin in 1824, was influenced by his reading and experiences as a *Hauslehrer.*

In keeping with the rationalist spirit of the time, the young man insisted that the goal of moral training should be to educate the child to be a good person. Religion should not be a matter for the mind but should come from the heart, he wrote. He was particularly concerned with *Ehrtrieb* (which can be loosely translated as a striving for a higher state) and how it could be used as a positive force by the teacher. He cautioned that great care had to be exercised so that *Ehrtrieb* would not degenerate into mere ambition, a passion for glory, vanity, boastfulness, and malicious pleasure in denigrating others. Consistency, however, was not one of Wieck's virtues. In view of his later preoccupation with his daughter's musical career and bitter anger at her, his own *Ehrtrieb* seems to have been easily sullied by ambition.

Wieck came to music late. During his years as a tutor, he had little exposure to events in the musical world; his experience was limited to small-town musicians and church choirs, perhaps a performance of a neighboring nobleman's

*It was a fortunate meeting: Milchmeyer (1750–1813), pianist and teacher, was a figure of considerable prominence to be teaching in Torgau. In addition to a treatise published in 1797, *Die wahre Art, das Pianoforte zu spielen,* he was the editor of a collection of piano works. He held the title of *Hofmechanikus* to the elector of Bavaria because of a specially constructed piano he invented. See Ernst Ludwig Gerber, *Neues historisch-biographisches Lexikon der Tonkünstler,* 4 vols. (Leipzig: Kuhnel, 1812–14), 3:428–29.

Kapelle. He did not attend a large-scale public concert until he was well into his twenties.

Since symphonic and choral works were performed only in a few large German cities in the early years of the nineteenth century, opportunities to hear a Beethoven symphony or a Haydn oratorio simply did not exist in the provincial centers where Wieck was working. In 1811 the young tutor heard, probably for the first time in his life, orchestral works by Beethoven, Louis Spohr, and Mozart, and the Haydn oratorio *Die Schöpfung* (The Creation). His copy of the program, preserved by his family, testifies to his attendance at the second German *Musikfest,* a two-day music festival in which forces from a number of Thuringian towns joined to play large works.[7]

Where and when Wieck learned enough theory to compose and enough about piano technique to set himself up as a teacher are still not clear. Yet by 1815 he was confident enough to dedicate and send a group of his songs to Carl Maria von Weber. To Wieck's delight, the composer took the time and trouble to write a detailed criticism of the works.[8] After publication, the songs were reviewed in a Leipzig journal, the *Allgemeine musikalische Zeitung*.[9] Some shortcomings were noted, and Wieck was advised to study voice because his vocal lines were "unnatural" and hard to sing. At the same time, however, the critic noted that the songs showed "some indications of talent." Wieck must have been gratified to see that his work was taken seriously and that a career in music appeared to be possible.

Wieck left his tutorial post and, applying his keen intelligence, energy, soaring ambition, and native talents to music, undertook a new vocation at the age of thirty. In 1815 he was established in Leipzig—with the financial help of a friend—as a piano teacher and owner of a piano store and music shop.

Although the actual date of his settling in Leipzig is not known, it must have been well before the April 19, 1815, issue of the *Allgemeine musikalische Zeitung,* which referred to him as "the popular Leipzig music teacher." Wieck's business—which he kept going until 1840, when he moved to Dresden—was called a *Piano-Fabrik,* usually translated as "piano factory." The enterprise was not a piano factory, however, but a store in which he rented and sold pianos, and tuned and repaired them as well. The term *Fabrik* was justified in part by his explanation that he stood behind every piano he sold.[10]

Leipzig was the natural place for an ambitious man to establish himself. Located in a flat basin at the confluence of several rivers and the crossroads of ancient north-south and east-west roads, the city had no natural beauty to recommend it, but from the time of its founding in the twelfth century it had been an important trading and cultural center. Though situated in Saxony and subject to its ruler, Leipzig was governed by a town council of middle-class citizens, mostly merchants and manufacturers, which had considerable political and fiscal independence. The semi-annual trade fairs that for more than five centuries had drawn buyers and sellers from all over Europe gave the city a cosmopolitan air and international renown. Leipzig's musicians were always particularly busy during the fair, for visitors enjoyed musical interludes in their business affairs. The founding of the university in 1409 and the establishment of the printing industry in 1480 contributed to the city's importance as an intellectual and cultural center.

In settling in Leipzig in 1815, then, Wieck had established himself in the right place at the right time. It not only was a metropolis with a strong commercial and middle-class tradition but one in which music had always had a special position and musicians a favored status. In 1841 a citizen wrote, "In our Leipzig, music . . . the interpreter of all human feelings, was held in high esteem and cultivated with an unmistakable preference."[11]

An active musical life had been recorded in the city since the thirteenth century. Music composed for daily and ceremonial events and performed by town-appointed musicians was described as early as the fifteenth century, and by the seventeenth century private citizens and university students had joined together in a *collegium musicum*, one of the first in Germany. Cultivation of the musical art was well established when Johann Sebastian Bach was employed by the town council in 1723. Unlike Dresden, the nearest large city and the royal seat of Saxony, with a courtly musical tradition and court-sponsored musical activities, Leipzig was a commercial center whose musical life served the needs of middle-class families.

The unusual interest and pride in church music, the traditions associated with the university (where music had been taught as a discipline since its founding), and the musical activities of the middle class encouraged the growth of such institutions as the Grosse Concert, a concert organization created by merchants in 1743, and its successor, the Gewandhaus Concerts, founded in 1781. The Gewandhaus Concerts, in which Clara Wieck was to play more frequently than any other pianist, was governed by a directorate of twelve townspeople, six from the learned professions and six from the mercantile community. In an age when most European musicians were household servants who performed for their aristocratic patrons and invited friends, the establishment of a concert hall in a commercial building and the administration of the concert organization by a group of middle-class citizens was an augury of the coming century, when concerts would be open to all who could afford the price of tickets.* From its inception the Gewandhaus was the leading musical organization in Leipzig. Other musical groups performed in the city, but the Gewandhaus concerts were and remain a unique Leipzig institution.

Theater and opera productions had never flourished in the serious Leipzig

*In *Geschichte der Gewandhausconcerte zu Leipzig vom 25. November 1781 bis 25. November 1881* (Leipzig, 1884), 15, 251, Alfred Dörffel points out that the name of the building in which the concerts were held reflects the fact that cloth (*Gewand*) was sometimes stored there, but that it actually was a multipurpose building that also housed the city library, with its magnificent collection of manuscripts.

community as they did in the court cities of Dresden and Weimar. Until a Leipzig city theater in which both dramas and operas were produced was founded in 1817, audiences in the commercial center were entertained by visiting troupes from Dresden. But Wieck attended the theater regularly, and saw to it that his daughter knew the great dramas of Lessing, Goethe, and Schiller as well as the popular operas of the day. The young girl heard an astonishing number of operas; by the time she was twelve she had seen almost every work presented in Leipzig, including operas by Mozart, Beethoven, Weber, and Rossini.*

Printing establishments had existed in Leipzig since the invention of type. At the end of the eighteenth century, eighteen general presses, each employing seventy to eighty people, affirmed the status of literacy and education in this region.[12] A typical Leipzig event that Clara attended was the *Gutenbergfeyer,* on June 24, 1840. Processions, music (by Felix Mendelssohn), speeches, fireworks, a great dinner for 3,000 people, and the unveiling of Johann Gutenberg's statue celebrated the four hundredth anniversary of Gutenberg's invention of movable type. Toasts were drunk while music was printed on presses set up in the great square.[13]

In 1815, the year Wieck came to Leipzig, the city, which then had a population of 35,000, was recovering from the upheavals of the Napoleonic Wars. Parts of Saxony had been occupied by French troops, but at the so-called Battle of the Nations, fought on the flat meadowlands surrounding the city, the French were decisively defeated. Peace was restored and commercial life resumed.

Several concerns in Leipzig were already catering to the prosperous musical amateurs but there was always room for another aspiring dealer. In his store in the Hohe Lilie, not far from the main square, Wieck taught, kept his shop, and lived from 1818 to 1821.† An enterprising businessman, he sold and lent music, music books, and periodicals. In addition to pianos, he sold a keyboard instrument known as the physharmonica and such contraptions as the *Handleiter* (wrist guide), trill machines, finger stretchers, silent fingerboards—all devices intended to speed up music learning and teach correct habits to the large numbers of eager middle-class keyboard amateurs.

By the 1820s Wieck was traveling to Vienna regularly to buy pianos. He became friendly with the piano manufacturers Conrad Graf and Andreas Stein, corresponded with the pianist Carl Czerny, and met Beethoven.[14] Wieck impressed Leipzigers with his energy and ambition, and it was assumed he would go far.

Acting with his customary confidence and optimism, Johann Gottlob Friedrich

*According to entries in her diary, Clara heard, among other works, Weber's *Oberon* and Spohr's *Der Berggeist* in 1826, Mozart's *Die Zauberflöte* in 1827, and Spohr's *Faust* in 1828. In 1831 she heard Beethoven's *Fidelio,* three operas by Rossini, and operas by Weigl and Auber. All in all, she heard at least thirty operas between 1826 and 1838.

†The house, built in 1695, had originally been a guesthouse and later housed a wineshop. It was still standing before World War II but no longer exists.

Wieck made a practical and desirable marriage on June 23, 1816. The bride was his student Marianne Tromlitz, the high-spirited nineteen-year-old daughter of Christiana Friederike, née Carl, and Georg Christian Gotthold Tromlitz (1765–1825), the cantor in Plauen, a town in southeast Saxony. Marianne's grandfather, Johann George Tromlitz, a leading flutist, composer, teacher, and flutemaker, had played solo flute in the Grosse Concert and was well known in Leipzig and other German musical centers.[15]

Marianne Tromlitz Wieck Bargiel, 1797–1872

It is clear that Marianne Tromlitz was an uncommonly talented young woman. In the first year of her marriage, Madame Wieck was singing solos at the weekly concerts in the Leipzig Gewandhaus. A review of Mozart's *Requiem,* which had been performed on December 15, 1816, referred to the soprano soloist, Madame Wieck, as the young wife of a local piano teacher, and praised her voice and "skill, confidence, and diligence." On March 13, 1817, she sang a solo at a Gewandhaus performance of the Beethoven Mass in C, and she performed in other works on March 27 and April 6, 1817.[16] Wieck was already acquiring a reputation through the talents of a family member. His prestige as a businessman and piano teacher rose with each performance Marianne gave.

To achieve and maintain a successful career, Marianne could not neglect the piano. She continued to study (perhaps with their friend Adolph Bargiel), supervised the household, and assisted Wieck by taking on students in voice and piano. Since she was the skilled pianist in the family, she taught the advanced students. Between household tasks and concert engagements (she was the first of Wieck's students to perform at the Gewandhaus)[17] she gave birth to five children. The first, Adelheid, was born in 1817, a few months after Marianne's first Gewandhaus appearance. Her second child, Clara, was born September 13, 1819, some sixteen months after the death of Adelheid in Plauen. Marianne continued her career after Clara's birth, and on October 18, 1821, appeared with the Gewandhaus Orchestra, this time as a pianist, playing Ferdinand Ries's Concerto in E-flat. Her work was not interrupted by the birth of a third child, Alwin, on August 27, 1821, and of still another son, Gustav, on January 31, 1823. Marianne performed at the Gewandhaus in October 1822 and November and December 1823. Her November performance of John Field's Second Piano Concerto was reviewed in the *Allgemeine musikalische Zeitung* in July 1824.[18] By the time the review appeared, Madame Wieck had had one more child, Victor, born February 22, 1824, and had departed the bed and board of Friedrich Wieck.

On May 12, 1824, Marianne Tromlitz Wieck returned to her father's home in Plauen, taking with her her infant son of three months (who did not survive his third year) and her oldest child, Clara, then not quite five years old. Saxon law assigned the three older children to the custody of the father, since they were legally his property.[19] Wieck permitted Marianne to keep Clara until her fifth

Marianne Tromlitz, June 7, 1816, shortly before her marriage. Drawing, inscribed to a cousin. Courtesy of Herma Stamm-Bargiel.

birthday, but four days after that date, on September 17, the child was returned to her father in Leipzig. An appeal from the heartbroken Marianne begging Wieck to meet her in September so that Clara could be delivered "from my hands to yours" was ignored.* Johanna Strobel, Friedrich's maid, was sent to fetch the child in Altenburg, a town halfway between Plauen and Leipzig. A sobbing mother and grandmother accompanied Clara to Altenburg, and there she said good-bye.

Marianne Tromlitz Wieck and Friedrich Wieck were granted a divorce on January 22, 1825, and within a few months she was the wife of Adolph Bargiel, the piano teacher who had been Wieck's colleague in his first tutorial position. That she had been in contact with Bargiel through the years is clear from a letter from Marianne's father to Wieck.[20] Tromlitz acknowledged that his daughter might have behaved dishonorably, but chided Wieck for leaving Marianne alone with Bargiel so much. Wieck's driving ambition, vanity, and exploitation of his young wife never came into question.

The Bargiels remained in the vicinity of Leipzig for more than a year after their marriage, and Marianne was permitted to see her children during that time. Clara already dominated the family scene; there is no mention of her brothers in the querulous letter Wieck addressed to the mother of his children:

> Madam! I am sending you the dearest thing in life still left to me, with the proviso, however, that you say nothing, if possible, about what has happened, or that you express yourself simply, truthfully, and at the same time clearly, so that this guiltless, innocent, and natural creature hears nothing that could arouse her suspicions. Furthermore, you will give the child little pastry and make sure you do not condone any naughtiness. . . . When she practices, do not allow her to rush. I expect the most rigorous adherence to my wishes; if not, my anger will be incurred. 7 Nov. 1825.[21†]

Soon after this document was delivered, the Bargiels established themselves in Berlin, where Adolph took over the Logier Institute, a piano school established by Johann Bernhard Logier, a piano pedagogue who had a brilliant and influential but short-lived career in Berlin. The move to Berlin further limited Marianne's contact with Clara and her two sons. In December 1825 Clara suffered another blow. Johanna Strobel, the nursemaid who had been with the family since before Clara's birth, was dismissed and a new housekeeper installed. Thus within a year the five-year-old girl lost the two women to whom she was closest. Both were fre-

*The letter reproduced in Litzmann, 1:3–4, is identical to Marianne's note in RSH (5966-A2) except for one phrase (italicized here), which for some unknown reason was omitted. The mother wrote, "Du bestehst darauf die Clara jetzt zu haben, nun sei es, in Gottesnamen, ich habe Alles versucht dich zu erweichen, *mag das Herz mir brechen,* Du sollst sie haben; jedoch meiner Mutterrechte begabe ich mich nicht" (You insist on having Clara now, so be it, in God's name, I have tried in every way to soften your stand, and *though my heart may break,* you shall have her; but at the same time, I do not renounce my rights as a mother).

†Wieck addresses his wife in the formal manner, as *Sie.*

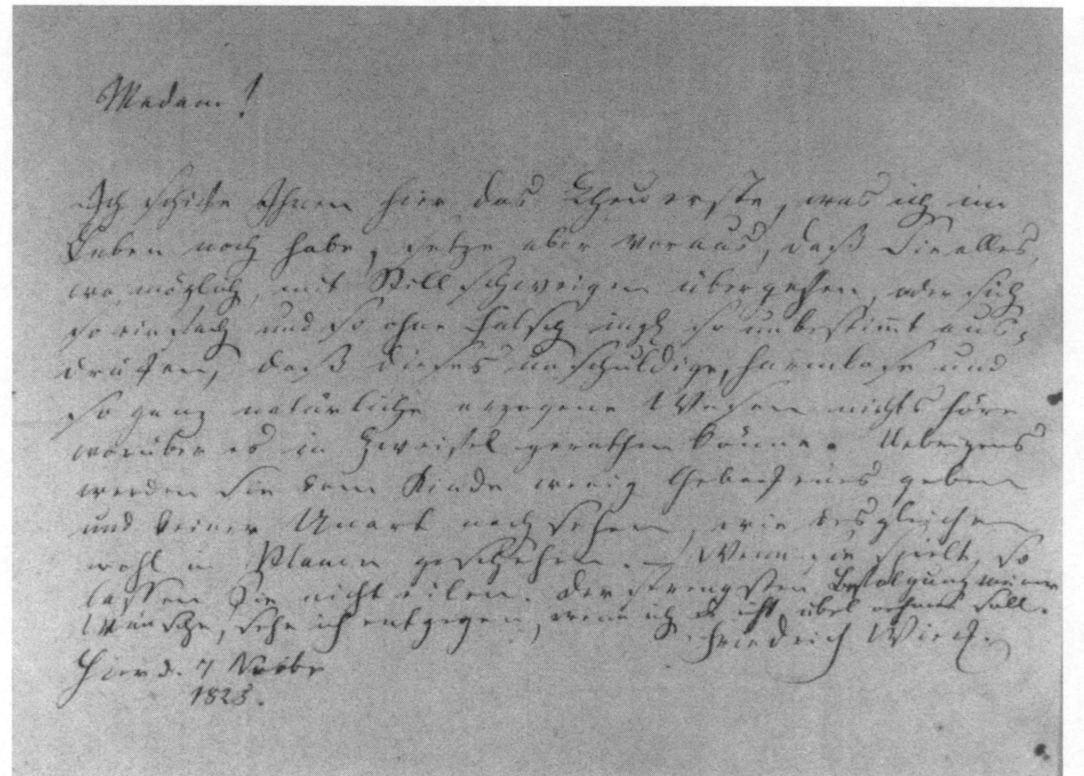

Madam!

Friedrich Wieck's letter to Marianne Wieck. Robert-Schumann-Haus, Zwickau.

quently vilified by Wieck; in later years he blamed any misbehavior on Clara's part on "contrariness" inherited from her mother and reinforced by Johanna.[22]

Clara corresponded with her "Berlin mother" and saw her from time to time, usually for short visits when Frau Bargiel was passing through Leipzig on her way to Plauen.* Life was not easy for Frau Bargiel. Divorce was uncommon and always threw a shadow on the woman. The young mother knew that she would lose her children if she left Wieck, but desperation forced the choice; the pressures of living with Wieck must have been unbearable. Though there is little written evidence about tensions or discord in the marriage, enough is known about Wieck to enable us to reconstruct the situation of his young wife. In the seven years of their marriage, she bore five children, practiced under his supervision, sang and played professionally, assisted him with piano pupils, helped with the business, and entertained his friends and business associates. Despite his rationalist education, Wieck's emotions often prevailed over reason. Harsh and stubborn, he dominated, controlled, and used those closest to him. His customers and students valued him and his skills because—it is very clear—he was a man of uncommon intellect and talent. There must have been a bond between the nineteen-year-old Marianne and Wieck at their marriage in 1816, but his demands and expectations, coupled with insensitivity, crudeness, and a cruel temper, drove her to flight. One surviving portrait of the young Marianne depicts a woman of strong character and determination, traits that Clara inherited in full.

Adolph Bargiel, the man to whom Marianne fled, was very different from Wieck, gentle, affectionate, and evidently undemanding.† Though he had more musical education and background than Wieck, he had less business acumen, and he suffered a series of blows in Berlin. The Logier Institute, which had been prospering, was forced to close in 1830 because of a cholera epidemic (all the students left the city). Soon thereafter he suffered a stroke from which he never fully recovered. He died on February 4, 1841, leaving Marianne with their four children. She was able to maintain the family by giving piano lessons in Berlin after his death and enlisting the aid of friends. (Robert Schumann was one of those who helped support her during those difficult years.) One of the children of her second marriage achieved musical prominence: Woldemar Bargiel, a composer, pianist, and conductor, later became a close friend and confidant of his half sister, Clara.

Intimacy between Clara and her mother was resumed only when she broke with her father, in 1839. Robert Schumann, who had enjoyed a close relationship with his own mother, got in touch with Marianne Bargiel. Thus Clara, at age twenty, rediscovered her mother and her mother's love. At that time she

*Biographers have assumed that Clara definitively lost her mother when she went to live with her father. Her diary entries make it clear that they maintained contact with each other.

†August Adolph Bargiel was born in Silesia on November 1, 1783. I am indebted to Herma Stamm-Bargiel for information about him and the Bargiel family.

lived with her mother's sister when she was in Leipzig and with her mother when she was in Berlin. Thereafter she turned to her mother for help at crises throughout her life, and Marianne always responded warmly, immediately, and unselfishly.*

Clara: The Earliest Years

When Clara was born, in September 1819, her father chose her name. He fully expected that Clara—meaning light, brilliance—would be a great virtuosa, trained by him from birth. And indeed, both hereditary and environmental conditions favored such a development. The sounds of piano music were heard continuously in the Wieck house as customers tried out the instruments in the shop. Piano students came and went, and Marianne spent hours preparing for her performances.

The daily routine in the Wieck household included a walk of several hours, in which Clara joined when she was three. Wieck took it for granted that his daughter would keep up with the adults; fortunately, this sturdy child was able to do so. It was a routine that Clara loved and observed all her life; it was a daily necessity for her. Indeed, she attributed her health and longevity to this regular habit.

Aside from the musical activities of the elder Wiecks and the daily walks, very little is known about the first five years of Clara's life, but much can be inferred. An entry on Page 2 of her diary, which her father began for her when she was seven, reports the extraordinary fact that she did not speak—not even single words—until she was over four years old. Her father also recorded that she understood very little. Even when she finally began to speak, her parents assumed she was hard of hearing because she was so self-absorbed and appeared unconcerned with what went on around her. The myth that she was deaf and "slow" arose at this time, and seemed to be common talk in Leipzig.[23]

In the spring before she left home to spend the last few months with her mother, Wieck began, despite the "deafness," to teach her some little pieces by ear. She learned the music without difficulty; it was speech—words—that she could not hear. Soon after she returned from Plauen to live with her father, formal piano lessons with two other girls of her age commenced. At this time she began to speak full sentences, but the "deafness" did not totally disappear until she was eight.†

*That Clara ultimately understood her mother's tragedy is clear from the attitudes she held as a mature woman toward divorce and the custody laws. In May 1895, she wrote Brahms that a recently divorced woman acquaintance had fled the country in order to keep her eldest son; Clara Schumann approved (*CS/JB Briefe*, 2:583).

†In view of the abilities that Clara manifested later, this may have been what Dr. Anna Burton terms "selective mutism," caused by emotional conflicts.

We may assume that there was a great deal of either angry talk or tense silence during Clara's early years. Wieck was not a man given to self-control. He characterized himself as caustic and blunt; indeed, he gloried in his "unceremonious" behavior.[24] His treatment of Gustav and Alwin was often cruel and physically abusive.[25] When Clara defied him, his bitter anger was never modulated. When she refused to give up plans to marry Robert Schumann, Wieck sought revenge by sending defamatory letters about her to Berlin and Hamburg, where she was about to perform. The letters, which circulated among influential musicians and music lovers, described Clara as a "demoralized, shameless girl who has opposed her father in the most unnatural and shocking manner," and warned that other girls should be guarded lest they be "poisoned" by her.[26] And his efforts to besmirch the name of Schumann continued even after Clara had become Frau Schumann.

In view of Wieck's documented conduct toward his children, we may assume that Marianne, too, suffered his anger if she deviated from his expectations. And his expectations were onerous: his wife was to be artist and teacher as well as mother and wife, and was to submit to his will in all things. Considering Wieck's domineering personality and Marianne's tasks, the probability of normal and friendly communication between them in the eight years of their marriage seems small indeed. Johanna Strobel, the housemaid in whose care Clara was left and with whom she formed a close attachment, was described by Wieck himself as "not talkative."[27] Thus Clara did not hear much speech, the first requirement for learning to talk. And in all likelihood, her mother was not only overwhelmed by all her duties but probably too angry for the kind of patient exchange children need in order to develop speech. Clara's "deafness" and "self-absorption" may well have served as a buffer against the tensions in the house: it would be more comfortable to shut out words than to endure the sounds of displeasure and disapproval. Music, on the other hand, was not angry or threatening. It was safe. All her life it was to be a solace from which she could gain relief from pain and tragedy.

Left without a wife, Wieck turned to his five-year-old daughter as the instrument of his musical ambition. She was to show the world what Friedrich Wieck could do. The girl responded nobly.

Wieck did not remarry for some time. For four years Clara and her brothers lived in a motherless home under the care of her father and servants. During this time she studied with her father and rapidly gained attention as a child prodigy. Her brothers had neither her aptitude nor her compliant personality, and were largely ignored while Clara, the eldest child and only daughter, dominated the household. When she was nine, Wieck at last decided to marry again. On July 3, 1828, in the presence of his three children, he married Clementine Fechner, the twenty-three-year-old daughter of a pastor, Samuel Traugott Fechner.[28] Three days after the wedding, on what presumably was their honeymoon, Wieck, Clementine, and Clara visited Dresden, where the child gave some private performances.

At the time of Wieck's second marriage, his business was firmly established and, thanks to his daughter (and his first wife), he already had a considerable reputation as a piano teacher. Clementine Wieck faced a formidable adversary in the person of her nine-year-old stepdaughter. To the two motherless boys she may have been a welcome addition to the household, but to Clara she was a rival, and for the most part an unsuccessful one. Clementine was in an unenviable position. Clara never relinquished her position as the star. The stepmother remained at home with the other children and ran Wieck's business while he was off touring with Clara. All his energy and skills were devoted to his eldest child, the most gifted of his and Marianne's three surviving children. For years the household revolved about her and her needs: the silk gowns necessary for concerts, her own room, special pianos brought from Vienna. All the father's expectations centered on this daughter. The two boys, in contrast, having already lost their mother at the ages of one and three, were virtually booted out of the house as soon as they were old enough to survive on their own.

Clementine and Friedrich Wieck had three children. Marie, born in 1832, was groomed by her father to emulate Clara. She also played at the Gewandhaus and had a fairly successful career as a pianist, eventually receiving the title of *Fürstliche Hohenzollern Hof- und Kammervirtuosin* (Court Pianist to the Prince of Hohenzollern). She never achieved the fame and brilliant success of her older half sister, and her jealousy and hostility were poorly concealed in the book she wrote after Clara's death, *Aus dem Kreise Wieck-Schumann* (From the Wieck-Schumann Circle). Marie Wieck never married. Her father was her hero, and, unlike her half sister, she never withdrew her loyalty from him. The other two children of the second marriage had sad fates: one, Clemens, died at age three; the other, Cäcilie, lived to 1893 but was mentally ill.

Clementine Wieck was not a musician and from all accounts was possessed of great patience—two facts that undoubtedly contributed to the success of the marriage, which endured forty-five years. The relationship between her and her stepdaughter, on the other hand, was, as might be expected, always strained. With Clementine, Clara acted out emotions she controlled in her father's presence. (Clementine is rarely mentioned in the diary by either Friedrich or Clara, and when her name does appear, it is not always in a complimentary context. Clara commented on October 24, 1833, for example, "My little sister Marie seems to be a born singer since she screams when Mother—who sings off-key—sings. When I sing, she laughs and listens happily.") Wieck's letters to his wife in 1830,[29] when he and Clara embarked on the first of many tours that were to take them away from home for several months at a time, indicate that Clementine Wieck was a woman of intelligence, culture, and capabilities. She managed the piano business during his absence, handled the correspondence, and above all, remained completely obedient.

The letters also reveal another side of Wieck; he had a sense of humor—

earthy, at times even coarse—and no hesitation about expressing it. His humor, vivacity, and practical common sense, combined with his self-confidence and generally acknowledged talent as a teacher, explain how this otherwise formidable man could charm and gain the respect of the musical circles of Leipzig. His pedagogical principles, published in 1853 in a small book, *Clavier und Gesang*, were successfully applied to his docile and willing pupil Clara, and gained him worldwide fame.

CHAPTER 2

Clara's Career Begins

The girlhood diaries of Clara Wieck are an unparalleled source of information about her education, career, and the musicians and musical life she knew. Most significant, however, is what they reveal about Friedrich Wieck and the nature of the relationship between father and daughter. Until she was eighteen years old, almost every diary entry was written or supervised by her father. The title page reads: "My diary, begun by my father, the seventh of June 1827, and continued by Clara Josephine Wieck."* Thus Clara was seven years old when the diary, which was to be the "dearest companion" of her life, began.[1] The diary is visible evidence of Wieck's domination.† On May 24, 1831, he wrote in Clara's name, "From now on, I will write in my diary myself, whenever I have the time." But he made certain that she had very little time. Those sections that were written by Clara were examined by her father; he frequently made emendations and comments in the margins. Many of the entries in her hand were painstaking copies of the acerbic letters he wrote to associates, friends, and enemies, letters in which he made demands, threatened, castigated, denigrated, and denounced. Clara copied angry letters to the Gewandhaus directorate regarding her fees, letters to editors complaining about her reviews, arguments over money owed her father.

Wieck used the diaries as a way of communicating with and educating his child; he preached and philosophized. Information, praise, reproach, condemnation, exhortation are all clearly seen in his black, bold handwriting, but he

*Litzmann (Vorwort, v) gave the wrong date, May 7, 1827, on the title page of vol. 1 and omitted mention of other information that appeared on that page. On the lower part of the page is an inscription signed by Friedrich Wieck in Dresden, dated March 1859, which reads, "Notebooks 1–6 were given by me to my daughter Clara Schumann and belong to her." On the verso of the title page is a note written by Clara Schumann in Frankfurt on June 6, 1889: "At my death, I should like my daughter Marie to have all my diaries, since she is the eldest of all the sisters and brothers, and was always the most faithful and truest friend to me."

†Though Litzmann's biography is based on the diaries, he rarely distinguishes between the entries made by Wieck and those written by Clara. Diary entries quoted hereafter indicate the writer by the initials FW or CW.

Cover of Clara's *Tagebuch* (diary), with handwriting of Friedrich Wieck and Clara Wieck. Robert-Schumann-Haus, Zwickau.

persisted in using the first person throughout, as though Clara were writing; he even referred to himself as "Father." Most startling is the way he seemed to be taking over her personal identity.

A revealing entry written by Wieck in Dresden on June 17, 1834, reads: "Father arrived by coach at seven in the evening. I flew into his arms and took him right to the [Hotel] Stadt Frankfurt." On February 28, 1833, he noted, "I played the "Bravour" Variations of Herz (without rehearsal) and Hummel's D-Minor Septet in the 18th subscription concert. Everything was received with great applause." A few months later, on April 29, 1833 (Clara was then almost fourteen years old), we find, "My own concert in the Gewandhaus. . . . There was a fine article about me in the *Tageblatt*." On the rare occasions on which he wrote as Friedrich Wieck, his daughter is referred to as "my Clara."

Only when Clara left home at the age of nineteen did the diary finally become her own. The last notebook, begun on April 20, 1838, accompanied her to Paris on her first independent tour and ended the day after her marriage—September 13, 1840, her twenty-first birthday. Wieck retained possession of all her other childhood diaries until March 1859, when he finally handed them over to her. By the time he was able to part with this record of her early years, she was a forty-year-old widow with seven children.

A not unintended effect of this kind of diary keeping was a practical education: by copying his letters and reading his entries in her diary, Clara learned how to manage a correspondence and arrange a concert tour. She also absorbed—through her eyes, ears, and fingers—her father's attitudes toward money and success and something of his competitive personality and controlling spirit.

The diary for 1838–40 is unique in that it furnishes an intimate record of her thoughts without her father's intervention. After her marriage and until 1844, the couple kept a joint diary, which is extant. And though, like many nineteenth-century diarists, Clara considered her journal a part of herself—it was at once a means of communication, a confessional, and a catharsis—the later ones, those from 1844 to 1896, cannot be found.*

In an 1831 letter to his wife, written during Clara's first extended tour, Wieck described a scene with a Frau Schmidt, the influential wife of a Weimar government official. She reproached him for allowing Clara to perform so much and not giving her time to play with other children. He replied angrily, "I have thought about education for twenty-five years and put my theories into practice. For the last seven years I have lived only for the education of my daughter. If, however, I still need advice, I will ask for it at the right time—and until then I decline to accept any." She, of course, felt insulted, and said she would not give him the letters of introduction prepared by her husband. Though he begged her pardon for his rude words, he could not refrain from ending the

*Martin Schoppe, late director of Robert-Schumann-Haus, Zwickau, believed that the later diaries were destroyed after Litzmann used them, presumably by order of Marie Schumann.

encounter by saying: "I must tell you, however, that I would rather not accept advice and pedagogical precepts, especially from a woman, until I ask for it."[2*]

Wieck was justly proud of his skill in teaching. He had developed pedagogical theories during his years as a tutor, and his approach to his daughter's instruction was carefully considered; it was a planned program that included supervision of her every waking hour. From the moment Clara was returned to her father's home, a few days after her fifth birthday, she was in training.

Wieck began to work with her alone in the spring of 1825. She did not learn to read music during her first year of instruction (though she learned to write notes). Small pieces, written expressly for her, encouraged her to concentrate on position, musical phrasing, and a "singing" tone, and provided a familiarity with the keyboard that accounted for the facility and ease she kept to the end of her life. At the age of seven she was at the piano for three hours a day—one hour for a lesson and two for practice.

Her meager general education was squeezed into the hours between the piano and the daily walks. For six months beginning in January 1825 she attended a neighborhood primary school run by a Demoiselle Marbach, and then she was sent to the Noack Institute, a larger establishment, for perhaps another year. Wieck deliberately limited her hours of school attendance; he gave her a lesson every morning before school and often an additional one in the afternoon. The months at the two primary schools constituted her only formal education. Thus she lacked the usual opportunities for social intercourse with her contemporaries, obviously not an important consideration for her father.

In *Clavier und Gesang*, the treatise Wieck wrote in 1853, he explained:

> My daughters always had a special tutor with whom I worked so that with just a few hours a day, their general education could keep pace with their artistic training and still leave enough time to exercise outdoors and strengthen their bodies, while other children have to sweat for nine hours a day on school benches and pay for this with the loss of their health and a happy childhood.[3]

Wieck's goal was to create a virtuosa. To achieve this goal, he wrote, "the whole education from the earliest youth must be planned accordingly."[4†] Clara learned what her father thought she needed to know—reading, writing, and, with private tutors, French and English, the languages required for the concert tours Wieck expected to arrange for her. In addition there were private lessons

*Tactless and often insensitive, Wieck was respected but not liked. Louis Spohr, for whom Clara played several times, referred to Wieck as a braggart and windbag ("Der Vater Wieck prahlte und windbeutelte wie gewöhnlich") in his *Lebenserinnerungen,* ed. Folker Göthel, 2 vols. (Tutzing: Hans Schneider, 1968), 2:171.

†From the unpublished diary we learn more details: lessons in score reading and instrumentation began in February 1831 (when Clara was eleven) and violin lessons with a Herr Prinz started about the same time. She began taking two lessons a week in counterpoint with Heinrich Dorn on June 20, 1832, and in April 1833 a daily fifteen-minute voice lesson with her father. That same month, she sang with the chorus in a performance of Handel's *Samson*.

in theory and harmony with Christian Theodore Weinlig, cantor of the St. Thomas Church, and composition with Heinrich Dorn, director of the Leipzig Opera; she had lessons with outstanding teachers in the cities where she toured, studying counterpoint with Siegfried Dehn in Berlin, for example. She was sent to Dresden to study orchestration with Carl Reissiger, the kapellmeister, and voice with Johann Aloys Miksch, the renowned voice teacher. Wieck had her take violin lessons and study score reading with Leipzig teachers, and provided some sessions in religion to prepare her for confirmation at age fourteen. These lessons rounded out her education as Wieck conceived it. There was not much time for childish play or reading, but enough for many evenings of concerts, opera, and drama. Beginning at the age of six, she saw almost every opera mounted in Leipzig, and Wieck made a point of attending the opera in every city in which they toured. She prepared for these performances by studying the scores at the piano with her father.

Before she was nine, Clara was a member of the music circle that met at the Wiecks'.[5] In 1828 the group included Friedrich Hofmeister and Heinrich Probst, music publishers; Heinrich Marschner, composer; Dr. Ernst August Carus, a physician and music lover; and Gottfried Fink, editor of the *Allgemeine musikalische Zeitung*. A visitor recalled many years later, "Wieck's home was always the gathering place for local and visiting musicians and friends of music. Every composer and virtuoso who came to Leipzig found that the morning or evening gatherings there offered the best opportunity to play and to hear new things. The soul of the entire proceedings was Father Wieck, who, when he was in a good mood, sparkled with humor."[6] Robert Schumann, who arrived in Leipzig for a permanent stay in 1830, joined the Wieck circle and saw the family almost every day.

Frau Wieck did not take part in these musicales, but Clara, who was a more skillful pianist than her father, was very much in evidence, playing old and new works. The artist Johann Lyser, a friend of Schumann, remembered, "What could match those evenings when Francilla Pixis [singer and daughter of the composer Johann Pixis] and that *Wundermädchen* Clara sang and played together?"[7] Wieck deliberately slowed the pace of public appearances. Clara played with professional musicians, but the first performances were at home and for Leipzig and Dresden friends. On December 26, 1829, for example, Wieck made this entry in the diary: "We had guests for whom I played my own variations and then, with Alwin (violin) and Gustav (glockenspiel), performed my three waltzes for the three of us. And with Herr C. Kraegen, who was visiting from Dresden, I played his polonaises for four hands."

With her first appearance at the Gewandhaus, on October 20, 1828, Clara, like her mother before her, brought Wieck into the public eye. Although her part in the concert was minor (she played a duet with Emilie Reichold, another Wieck student), she—along with her father—was mentioned in the *Allgemeine musikalische Zeitung*'s review of the concert:

Clara Wieck, age 8, one year before her first appearance at the Leipzig Gewandhaus. Colored miniature on ivory, artist unknown. Robert-Schumann-Haus, Zwickau.

> It was especially pleasing to hear the young, musically talented Clara Wiek [*sic*], just nine years old, perform . . . to universal and well-earned applause Kalkbrenner's Variations on a March from Moses. We may entertain the greatest hopes for this child who has been trained under the direction of her experienced father, who understands the art of piano playing so well and teaches with devotion and great skill.[8]

Clara's first appearances outside the familiar circles of her home took place in Dresden between March 6 and April 7, 1830. The ultimate purpose of the trip was clearly set forth by Wieck in letters to his wife: they were there to make connections that would enable them to play at court and to obtain introductions to the larger and more prominent Berlin and Vienna courts.

Father and daughter performed perfectly; Clara won all hearts and Wieck was besieged by requests to give lessons and share the secrets of his success. Moreover, he wrote his wife, the cognoscenti found it very "noble" of him to reject offers of public concerts. He was biding his time.

Clara was invited everywhere; aristocratic ladies vied with each other in bestowing rings, chains, and earrings on the ten-year-old child; older girls and titled ladies came to fix her hair. Wieck was careful to see that her head was not turned by the praise and compliments. "If I notice anything the least bit damaging, I will leave immediately, so that she can be in proper middle-class surroundings. I am too proud of her unpretentiousness to exchange it for any worldly honors."[9]

So successful was the trip that Wieck seriously considered moving to Dresden, where he felt more appreciation would be shown for his talents. On March 19, 1830, he wrote to his wife:

> The sensation the two apes from the Leipzig menagerie are making here is not to be described. In Leipzig, they are too amazed and too nasty to understand the unique qualities of this goose among so many geese, to realize what an extraordinary child Clara is, and even less that your Fritz from Pretzsch could possess and educate this very same Clara. Everyone assures us that your two apes are the talk of the court and the town. It seems to have only the best effect on Clara because she is playing with a self-assurance that she has never shown before and she is, and remains, the Clara of old.[10]

The summer of 1830 was spent in preparation for her first solo concert in Leipzig, but the events of the year caused more than one change in plans. Repercussions of the July Revolution in Paris, the uprisings in Poland, and the subsequent disturbances in Dresden reached Leipzig; Clara's concert, originally scheduled for September, was postponed to November. Meanwhile, another event that was to have profound significance in Clara's life took place: in October a new pupil-boarder named Robert Schumann moved into the Wieck household. Schumann had returned to Leipzig after a short interlude in Heidelberg, where he had gone ostensibly to study law; now he intended to devote himself to music.

Piano (Andreas Stein) used by Clara Wieck at her first Gewandhaus concert, October 20, 1828. The piano was rebuilt in 1996. Robert-Schumann-Haus, Zwickau.

IM SAALE DES GEWANDHAUSES.

CAROLINE PERTHALER,

Pianoforte - Spielerin aus Grätz in Steyermark,

macht ergebenst bekannt, dass sie ein

CONCERT

im Saale des Gewandhauses

Montag, den 20sten October 1828,

geben wird.

Anfang halb 7 Uhr. Oeffnen des Saales halb 6 Uhr.

ERSTER THEIL.

Ouverture von Onslow, aus dem Colporteur.

Schottisches Lied, von C. M. v. Weber, mit Quartettbegleitung, gesungen von Dem. Henriette Grabau.

Grosses Concert von Kalkbrenner, Nr. 2. E moll, gespielt von der Concertgeberin.

ZWEITER THEIL.

Schottisches Lied, von C. M. v. Weber, mit Quartettbegleitung, gesungen von Dem. Henriette Grabau.

Variationen von Kalkbrenner, für das Pianoforte, vierhändig, über einen Marsch aus Moses, gespielt von Clara Wiek und Demoiselle Emilie Reichold.

Die Forelle, Lied von Fr. Schubert, mit oblig. Pianoforte-Begleitung, gesungen von Dem. Henr. Grabau, begl. von Dem. Emilie Reichold.

Grosse Concert-Variationen von Pixis, gespielt von der Concertgeberin, mit Orchesterbegleitung.

Billets à 16 Gr. sind bei Friedrich Hofmeister und an der Casse zu haben.

Program, October 20, 1828, Leipzig. Clara Wieck's first concert at the Gewandhaus. Robert-Schumann-Haus, Zwickau.

Political events and even the handsome new boarder were of lesser importance than Clara's first solo concert, which took place at the Gewandhaus on November 8, 1830. Wieck gave the Leipzig audience what was expected of a virtuoso artist, and secured the financial returns and the reviews he hoped for. Clara, "the eleven-year-old daughter of a local piano dealer and expert piano teacher," was hailed for her talent, industry, and excellent instruction.[11]

The success of the Gewandhaus concert and additional Dresden appearances spurred Wieck's ambitions. Convinced that Clara was ready for Paris, the center of the musical world at that time, he prepared to leave his pregnant wife and other children, his pupils, and his business and devote himself wholly to Clara's career.

His not unwilling daughter was set to studying new music and French to prepare for the big concert tour that would take her to Paris and, her father hoped, international renown. Father and daughter departed at the end of September 1831. Traveling night and day (Wieck would not part with an extra groschen merely for comfort), they jolted through Thuringia to Kassel and Frankfurt and thence through Darmstadt and Mainz to Paris, not to return until the following May.

Their first stop, only a day's trip by coach, was Weimar, where, through the efforts of a music-loving official, Clara played at private homes and stirred Johann Wolfgang von Goethe's interest. The great poet, who had heard many child prodigies in his day, was more than cordial and gave them an accolade Wieck had hardly dared hope for: a medal with his portrait and a note inscribed: "For the gifted artist Clara Wieck." Her father's talents were not overlooked. In a written dedication, the great poet thanked him for his "masterly musical entertainment."[12*]

Wieck believed that no musician had ever been so highly honored by Goethe (he was obviously unaware of the impact on the poet of the twelve-year-old Mendelssohn some ten years earlier), and asked his wife to be sure to tell Friedrich Hofmeister, the music publisher, that Clara had played at the Weimar court and *twice* for Goethe. He continually reminded her of the need to have Clara's success mentioned in the newspapers and requested that Hofmeister and Robert Schumann (already involved in musical journalism) do what they could about publicity.

They succeeded. A review from the Weimar correspondent appeared in the *Allgemeine musikalische Zeitung* in March 1832:

> Even in her first piece, the artist who is still so young reaped thundering approval that mounted to enthusiasm in the works that followed. And indeed, the great skill, assurance, and strength with which she plays even the most difficult movements so easily is highly remarkable. Even more remarkable is the spirit and feeling of her performance; one could scarcely wish for more.[13]

*"Der kunstreichen Clara Wieck" and, to Wieck, "Für meisterlich musikalische Unterhaltung verpflichtet." Weimar, 9 October, 1831. J.W. Goethe.

The journey progressed through Erfurt, Arnstadt, and Gotha with alternating fortunes. In some towns they found decent concert halls, good pianos, appreciative and knowledgeable audiences; others lacked one or more of these elements. In each situation, good or bad, however, Wieck had to perform the same chores—find lodging, provide himself and his child with food, cajole prospective patrons, make the proper contacts, rent the halls, try out the pianos, calculate which piece would have the best effect, publicize the event, and collect the money. And in each town Clara dutifully copied into her diary Wieck's letters to friends and foes, excoriating the provincial audiences and unresponsive patrons, commenting on fees, complimentary tickets, programs, and instruments. She was learning how to manage a concert tour; this practical education formed the basis of her own managerial skills later on.

In Frankfurt the Wiecks learned that Clementine had given birth to a daughter in January 1832. The new father responded by asking his wife what the child would be named (it was Marie) and remembered to express his concern for the health of mother and child in a few affectionate sentences. The bulk of the letter, however, described Clara's triumph at a concert of the Museum, the leading Frankfurt concert society. This was the sixteenth such event of their journey. She played so beautifully, he wrote, that the orchestra applauded at the rehearsal and at the performance, indicating their approval by tapping their bows on the stands, a real tribute from her older colleagues.

Though Wieck, feeling the strain of incessant travel, complained long and loudly of the lack of appreciation accorded his twelve-year-old treasure on this trip, she actually received glowing notices in almost every town. The girl herself seemed to flourish despite the tiring journey, and they pushed on.

As Clara made her way toward Paris, she practiced, studied new works, performed, composed, and took her daily walk. Still the dutiful daughter, she copied her father's letters into her diary, ostensibly to improve her handwriting. She studied French to prepare for Paris, but she was no longer a child—and perhaps never had been in the usual sense.

Wieck's boast when he told Frau Schmidt that Clara did not have time to play with dolls or other children reflected his sincere belief that his training gave her more happiness than the usual pleasures of childhood. Though he insisted that he cherished her childishness, her naturalness, her innocence, he exploited her musical gifts, treating her as a professional. Even in her first concerts, Clara played with the tone and musical understanding of an adult musician.

The impression she made on perceptive onlookers in Weimar was described in a letter by the tutor of the duke of Weimar:

> We heard the little Wieck of Leipzig—she's a veritable marvel; for the first time in my life I caught myself admiring with enthusiasm a precocious talent: perfect execution, irreproachable measure, force, clarity, difficulties of all sorts successfully surmounted—here are rare things at any age—but still one encounters them occasionally, and if little Clara had offered nothing more, I

> should have said that she was a machine, to play so remarkably, and I would have remained cold as a stone; but she is a musician, she feels what she plays and knows how to express it; under her fingers the piano takes on color and life; one takes an interest in her without wanting to, and if she does not succumb early to some lingering illness, she will not have much need of beauty in order to become a tempting siren. Poor child! She has a look of unhappiness and of suffering, which distresses me; but she owes perhaps a part of her fine talent to this inclination to melancholy; in examining closely the attributes of the Muses, one could almost always find there some traces of tears.[14]

The portrait of Clara sketched by her stepmother's brother in Paris in 1832 shows a girl with a thin heart-shaped face and enormous dark eyes, her hair swept into a kind of chignon topped by a large, fluttering ribbon. Her head, held slightly to one side, seems too small for the elaborate off-the-shoulder gown with huge puffy sleeves. A filmy net covers the décolletage and a frilly collar accentuates the neck and thin sloping shoulders. The waist is tightly cinched with a wide belt. Clara is wearing long, dangling earrings. Most striking is the wistful expression about her mouth and the unusual, slightly exotic eyes. The sharp, pointed chin betrays the child.

Within a year after her return from Paris, a description of Clara was published in the Hamburg journal *Caecilia*, edited by Johann Peter Lyser, a friend of Robert Schumann. A prominent feature of this short-lived publication was a six-page essay on Clara Wieck. Whether Lyser wrote the following description or whether, as Wieck speculated, it was based on a letter by Heinrich Heine is not known. That it was written by an astute observer, however, is clear:

> At first glance Clara seems to be a quite lovable thirteen-year-old girl . . . and one thinks no more about it—but, observed more closely, everything seems quite different! The delicate, pretty little face with the somewhat strangely shaped eyes, the friendly mouth with the touch of sentiment that now and then draws up in a somewhat mocking or wistful way, particularly when she answers. And the mixture of grace and carelessness in her movements—not studied, but it goes far beyond one of her years. All this—I confess it openly—stirred a quite peculiar feeling in me when I saw it. I know of no better way to describe it except as "an echo of Clara's mocking-painful" smile. It seems as though the child could tell a long story, a story woven out of joy and pain—and yet—what does she know? Music.[15]

Wieck was pleased, as always, by the references to his child, apparently disregarding the allusions to melancholy, tears, and pain.

The time spent in Paris—February 15 to April 13, 1832—gave Clara the cachet of a Parisian concert, and it exposed the girl to new music, new manners, and new values, all of which she quietly absorbed. Yet she hardly made the impact on Parisian musical life her father seems to have envisioned. Though she and a Frenchwoman shopped hurriedly for the requisite new dresses and hats,

Clara Wieck, age 12, in Paris. Lithograph based on a portrait by Eduard Fechner, 1832. Robert-Schumann-Haus, Zwickau.

the serious child with the awkward, aggressive father could not conquer the glamorous French capital. He wrote to his wife:

> You should see me at the soirées in yellow gloves and white neckband, speaking half German and half French and half despairing, hat in hand, from 10 in the evening till 2 in the morning, always pricking up my ears to make sure I will not miss anything. Child, you won't recognize your Friedrich again. You have never seen a more interesting sight.[16]

Wieck was determined to display Clara's talent and was willing to ignore the discomforts and financial costs of a Paris stay. But even the redoubtable Friedrich Wieck quailed at the thought of having to make himself understood in French. One senses from his letters that he is feeling distinctly uncomfortable in this center of Gallic fashion and grace.

"Our French doesn't help us at all, on pauvre allemand ne comprend pas un mot à Paris," he complained. "Everything is different here—everything! . . . One sleeps, eats, drinks differently." Worst of all, he had not been able to smoke in his carriage for four days on the way to Paris, and once there he could smoke only in his room. "Clara can never compensate me for what I am doing for her," he wrote.[17] This complaint may have been written half-mockingly, as far as the smoking was concerned, but it was a motif that ran through his relationship with Clara from that time on.

Wieck lamented that in Paris everything was done for superficial reasons, for the sake of appearances. Clara had to be dressed entirely in white and had to wear a new dress at each appearance—but the Parisians didn't care about cleanliness. "One small napkin is used for the whole week, and one glass of water is provided in the morning for washing." And, he adds, reminding us that he was traveling with an adolescent, "That suits our Clara just fine." He was overwhelmed by French customs; his pen failed him, and he promised he would have tales to tell when he returned to Leipzig. "You should see the life here. Ce n'est pas dire!"[18]

Without Eduard Fechner, Wieck's brother-in-law, they never could have made their way. He arranged Clara's first appearances at the Parisian salons of two wealthy German-born music lovers, Madame Valentin and Madame Leo.[19] Through the latter, a patroness of many musicians, they met many eminent composers living in Paris that winter. Giacomo Meyerbeer presented them with tickets to his *Robert le Diable,* the spectacular audience-pleaser then reigning at the opera. Felix Mendelssohn, ten years older than Clara and later to become her fast friend, was already a sophisticated, well-traveled young man, not to be compared with the provincials from Saxony. Friedrich Kalkbrenner, the composer and pianist, admired the girl's playing but fell into a dispute with the quarrelsome father. Johann Pixis and Heinrich Herz, composers whose works Clara played, remained kindly but distant; Niccolò Paganini, who remembered them from Leipzig, and Pierre Erard, the piano manufacturer, were friendlier and more helpful.

In Paris it was customary to play at soirées in the lavish homes of aristocrats or wealthy music lovers, await a newspaper mention, and then, at the right moment, schedule a public concert. Unfortunately, the right moment never came. First a Paganini concert at which Clara had the opportunity to be an assisting artist was canceled because of the violinist's illness. A concert at the music school of a friend, Franz Stoepel, on March 19 was a success, but the big concert arranged for April 9 at the Hôtel de Ville had to be held at Stoepel's small auditorium instead because of a cholera epidemic and few people attended. The Wiecks left Paris almost immediately after the last recital and arrived in Leipzig on May 1, 1832.

The Young Artist

Friedrich Wieck, an astute businessman, prepared for Clara's appearances with great care. Although he believed in a dignified approach, he was not averse to capitalizing on the public interest in the young girl. At her concerts he peddled lithographs of the portrait painted by Fechner, his Parisian brother-in-law. The lithographs sold well and new ones were received in August 1832. Copies were sent to Robert Schumann and to her "Berlin mother," among others.[20]

Wieck never forgot the poverty of his childhood and never scorned an opportunity to make a taler. For him money was a powerful source of security and he impressed its importance on his young daughter, conveying in many ways the lesson that money could be equated with love. From her earliest years Clara was rewarded with money for her playing and for learning quickly. All sums earned from concerts were noted in her diary by her or her father; he also recorded the costs of gifts he gave her, as on April 24, 1834: "Father bought me a large beautiful gold chain at Herr Struve for 45 reichstaler; it is worth 32 reichstaler in gold."

Wieck's interest in money was well known to everyone in Leipzig (Schumann referred to him as "Meister Allesgeld"—Master All-for-Money); businessmen appreciated his shrewdness. He worked out barter arrangements so that Clara could take French or theory lessons in exchange for the loan of a guitar or piano from his shop. Her father had contempt for payments in jewelry for his artist daughter; such gifts were usually appraised and turned into cash. Those patrons who did not deliver the expected fees were roundly berated in letters that the child copied into her diary.

The money Clara earned at concerts was collected by Wieck (quite literally collected—he often stood at the door as the audience poured in) and invested in state bonds and in all likelihood in his business as well. From these funds Clara received rewards from her father when she played particularly well and small sums, perhaps eight groschen, after a concert—enough for a treat in a café. She paid for her own lessons if he was unable to arrange a trade with another teacher. As her father, teacher, and concert manager, Wieck believed he was entitled to the money she earned, and told her so in later years when Clara requested the return of money for which she had worked. The money was legally his not only because he was her father but also because of Clara's gender: social and economic restrictions on women remained in force longer in Germany than in most Western countries.[21] Wieck claimed, moreover, that he had a moral right to this money, since—as he pointed out in her diary and in the letters she copied—he had neglected the education of her siblings and given up other pupils so that he could devote himself entirely to her education and career. Though Clara may have felt some guilt over the treatment of her brothers, she was led to accept the situation as quite normal and natural. The attentions received, the marks of preference shown by her father, the applause of the audiences were gratifying. The realization that she might have been exploited occurred to her only in 1839, when the father she had loved and trusted refused her the thousands of taler she had earned through her talents—and which he had, in the meantime, saved and invested. When she persisted in plans to marry Robert Schumann, she was informed that she owed Wieck money for the lessons he had given her. He also demanded that she share her earnings with her brothers and other family members. During the battle she told Robert, with some bitterness, that she had never received so much as a pin from her stepmother; she was always told to use her own money.[22] Even after a court had ruled in favor of her marriage and the banns were announced, Wieck kept the proceeds of her concerts. She was forced to bring suit to recover the money for which she had labored—even the piano that had been given to her as a gift—but the matter did not go to court. After her marriage, it was finally settled through an intermediary, Major Friedrich Serre.[23]

Clara's wistful, "mocking-painful" smile was the only outward manifestation of childhood unhappiness. The docile daughter occasionally exhibited "willful" or "contrary" behavior, which Wieck attributed to her mother and the influence of the maid Hanne. (Thus the two women she loved in her early years were similarly censured.) Her conduct was easily controlled by her father. For this child, to whom music and playing the piano were indispensable—perhaps even equivalent to love—prohibitions against playing or practicing were terrifying. Wieck punished infractions of behavior by withholding lessons or favorite pieces. Nine days after her first public appearance at the Gewandhaus (October 20, 1828), the following entry was made in her diary:

> My father, who has long hoped for a change in my behavior, remarked again today that I am just as lazy, careless, disorderly, stubborn, disobedient, etc. as ever, and that I show all these traits in my piano playing and in my studies. And because I played Hünten's new Variations op. 26 for him so badly, and did not take the repeats in the first variation, my father tore up the music before my eyes, and will not give me any lessons beginning today, and I may not play anything but scales, Cramer's Etudes, Book I, and Czerny's Trill Exer-

cises. My brothers will take my place in the 8 o'clock morning lesson and my father will start with them tomorrow.[24]

On November 5 the instruction was resumed, after the "lazy and stubborn" child solemnly promised to change.

Possibly because of her gender and her moneymaking ability, Clara was never subjected to the abuse that Wieck unleashed on his sons. Robert Schumann, whose own family life had been quiet and affectionate, described one episode in his diary on August 21, 1831:

> Yesterday I saw a scene whose impression will be indelible. Meister Raro [Wieck] is surely a wicked man. Alwin had not played well: "You wretch, you wretch—is this the pleasure you give your father"—how he threw him on the floor, pulled him by the hair, trembled and staggered, sat still to rest and gain strength for new feats, could barely stand on his legs anymore and had to throw his prey down, how the boy begged and implored him to give him the violin—he wanted to play, he wanted to play—I can barely describe it—and to all this—Zilia [Clara] smiled and calmly sat herself down at the piano with a Weber sonata.

The horrified Robert added: "Am I among humans?"[25]

As a close observer of the Wieck family scene, Schumann also noted the interplay among daughter, stepmother, and father. When Clara was almost twelve, he wrote that he discerned "a trace of peevishness, capriciousness, and even a semblance of ill will in her conduct toward her stepmother." A year later he wrote, "Clara displays great obstinacy toward her stepmother, who is certainly a woman worthy of respect. The old man rebukes Clara, but nevertheless he is coming under her thumb more and more. She is giving orders like a señora—but she can also beg and cajole like a child."[26]

At fifteen Clara actively began to defy her father. On a concert tour to Magdeburg, Hannover, and other northern cities in 1834–35 the baffled father had a rebellious adolescent on his hands:

> Clara now is often so inconsiderate, domineering, full of unreasonable opposition, careless, totally disobedient, rude, prickly, blunt, monstrously lazy, capriciously vain about rags [clothes] (we cannot even speak of other kinds of vanity because she no longer has the slightest interest in her art—and certainly no time to study—since she gets up at nine o'clock and isn't ready till half past ten, then receives visitors, is invited to dinner at noon, and in the afternoon is desperately unhappy if she should have to play, because then she is thinking only of the theater and—the gentlemen). In short, what is to become of her, God only knows—she certainly cannot remain at home. I will be irritated with her for the rest of my life; I can hardly enjoy anything about her without grief. A day doesn't pass when she doesn't vex me with all the things I mentioned. If I were not here, she would not perfect one single piece. She is so distracted that as a rule she doesn't even know if she is playing and her obstinacy about it

> all distorts her face. I will not be able to sell the pianos because she is so heedless that she is continually finding fault with them, complaining to other people about how hard they are to play and giving them a bad reputation.[27]

One can almost feel sorry for the father, surprised by the treacherous vagaries of the adolescent. She had not only been the proverbial apple of his eye; she had reigned over the entire household, and understandably so. Her concerts brought a sizable income; her labor attracted pupils and publicity for his business. Her talents gave him status and prestige, the means to travel, and opportunities to mix with great musicians, the rich, and the noble. Her concerts were his concerts, her reviews his. He shared in the tension, the mishaps, the success, the applause. A letter he wrote to his wife from Magdeburg tells part of the story:

> Listen, it is a miracle that the anxiety and anger I had last night didn't finish me off. Just think, there were 600 people in the hall, unbelievably full because of Clara; the piano keys began to stick . . . in the Finale of the Chopin Concerto; fortunately, everything turned out well but it took much worry and lots of sweat to get through it. During the intermission I had to take the keyboard out in full view of the audience and fix the keys. It was all right—but when the staccato variations came in the second part, the whole damper mechanism and ten single keys stuck. What was I to do? Clara played, did not dare lift the damper (because it would not fall back down again), and so I pressed the single pedal during her performance, maybe 100 times, in full view of the whole audience. Yet Clara played like a god with unprecedented applause and unanimous bravos. I was bathed in sweat and had to rush back to the house, a half hour away, to change my clothes. Isn't it dreadful to have to live through something like that—especially after I had sworn to the music lovers here that I would have everything fixed and running as Graf and Bayer [well-known piano makers] did?[28]

Not the least of the shocks on this trip was Clara's developing sexuality. Wieck had asked Carl Banck, a young Leipzig composer and voice teacher, to accompany them, ostensibly because he was a native Magdeburger and could help with arrangements in that city. The primary purpose, however, was to divert Clara's mind from Robert Schumann, in whom she was showing unmistakable signs of interest. The lure worked. Clara flirted with Banck and with every other young man she met. For the first and probably only time in her life, she acted the coquette. The girl whose portrait was painted in Hannover has a mischievous glint in her eye—she looks out at us as if she knows her power. In Halberstadt she opened a ball and danced with an older man, who, she reported, was a great admirer of beautiful women.[29] A day earlier, she gleefully reported in her diary that two men were fighting over her.

The tour continued for several months despite Wieck's overwrought condition. They returned home in April to face greater battles.

Clara Wieck, age 15, in Hannover. On the piano is the solo part of the third movement of her concerto, op. 7. Lithograph by J. Giere, 1835. Robert-Schumann-Haus, Zwickau.

CHAPTER 3

Robert Schumann and the Wiecks

When Clara and her father returned from Paris in 1832, they were eagerly awaited by Clementine, Alwin, Gustav, the four-month-old baby, Marie, whom the father had never seen, and the former boarder, Robert Schumann. The young composer noted in his diary that Alwin and Gustav had run over to his rooms the instant Clara and Wieck returned.[1] In the days following, Clara's name appears in his diary with increasing frequency.

Born in Zwickau, a town of about 4,000 people in Saxony, some forty miles south of Leipzig, Robert was the youngest (and a late) child of a devoted family. The father, August Schumann, was a literary man who had prospered; beginning as the son of a poor country minister, he built a successful small-town career as bookseller, writer, publisher, translator, editor, and compiler of dictionaries and reference works. His wife, Johanne Christiane, née Schnabel, the daughter of a surgeon, doted on Robert. He showed musical talent early, and the parents turned to Johann Gottfried Kuntsch, a local music teacher, who offered much encouragement to the boy. Quickly outgrowing Kuntsch's knowledge, Robert continued on his own, composing songs and piano works, directing, improvising, entertaining his family and friends, and making a local reputation as a musical talent.

His father, the major supporter of his musical and literary interests, died when Robert was sixteen, and although he had three older brothers—Eduard and Julius, in the family business in Zwickau, and Carl, a publisher and printer in nearby Schneeberg—he was placed under the guardianship of Gottlob Rudel, a friend and local merchant, who administered his share of his father's estate and advised Frau Schumann about Robert's future.* The two formed an alliance for a "practical" life based on the study of jurisprudence.

*An older sister, Emilie, born in 1796, had died in 1825 of a "nervous stroke," according to the death certificate in the family papers in RSH. It was known, however, that she was mentally ill and had actually committed suicide.

Soon after his graduation from the Zwickau Lyceum—where he had been an outstanding student, highly praised for his industry and intellectual gifts—Robert arrived in Leipzig on a preliminary trip to enroll at the university and find lodgings. But the study of law was merely a cover for Schumann's real passions: music and literature. Friends reported that he rarely even approached the buildings where law lectures were held. His time was spent with music—playing and improvising on the piano, studying and listening to the music of Schubert and Beethoven—and walking and reading with friends.

One of the families in Leipzig with whom he was on visiting terms was that of Dr. Ernst August Carus, a physician whom he had known when Carus was director of a mental hospital in nearby Colditz. It was probably at a musical evening at Carus's home on March 31, 1828, that Robert Schumann met Friedrich Wieck and heard Clara play. Impressed by the child's musicality and technical prowess, he applied to Wieck for piano lessons, and studied with him until the following year. The Carus home remained the center of his musical and social life. The doctor's wife, Agnes, was an attractive young woman, with whom Robert frequently made music and with whom he was certainly in love. At eighteen, Robert was in love with every pretty woman he saw, including his three sisters-in-law. His letters and diaries chronicle adolescent enthusiasms for girls, poetry, music—all the emotions fervidly recorded.* He also enjoyed drinking (often to excess) and smoking, and, to add to the list of adolescent misdemeanors, was totally irresponsible about money. His letters to his mother and brothers are the typical calls for help of the impecunious student.

Robert convinced his mother that Heidelberg would be a better place to study law than prosaic, flat, and ugly Leipzig, but there, too, Schumann devoted more time to music than to law. Handsome, charming, gifted, spoiled, Robert played at studying law for two years before he eventually persuaded his mother to allow him to devote himself totally to music. In a well-thought-out letter he explains himself:

> My entire life has been a twenty-year struggle between poetry and prose, or if you like, call it music and the law. . . . Now I am standing at the crossroads, and the question "Which way?" frightens me, if I follow my guardian angel, he points to art, and, I believe, to the right way.[2]

Frau Schumann reluctantly agreed, but only after a correspondence with a man she felt she could trust: Friedrich Wieck, Robert's Leipzig piano teacher. At Robert's suggestion, she asked for Wieck's opinion of her son's chances:

> At the request of my dearly beloved son, Robert Schumann, I am taking the liberty to turn to you about his future. I am beset by trembling and deep anxiety as I write to ask you if you like Robert's plan, which is explained in the

*Eugenie Schumann quotes from a letter of Robert: "The first thing I will look for in Heidelberg is a girl" (*Robert Schumann: Ein Lebensbild*, 91).

enclosed letter. They are not my opinions and I tell you openly that I am anxious about Robert's future. To *excel* in this art and be able to earn one's bread, much is necessary, as far too many artists before him have discovered—and even if his talent were truly outstanding, it would still be uncertain whether he could win approval and took forward to a secure future.

He has now studied almost three years, and needed many things—many; and now, just when I believed that he would soon reach his goal, I see him take a step backward to begin all over again; I see this just when he has reached the point when he could show what he could do, when his small inheritance is gone and he is still dependent on other people, and I wonder if he will get the approval he needs. Ah, I can't describe how depressed and unhappy I am when I think of Robert's future. He is a good person; nature has given him intellectual gifts for which others must strive with great difficulty; not an unpleasant exterior—enough capital so that he could study without cares—and of which enough could remain to live on respectably—and now he suddenly wants to enter upon a profession he should have begun ten years ago. Since you, honored sir, are a father yourself, you can well feel that I really am right and my cares are not without foundation. My other three sons are unhappy about this and all agree that I should not give in. I am the only one who does not want to force him to do something when his feelings lead him in another direction—because it is certainly not honorable—after three vanished years—to begin again as an apprentice and throw away his few taler on something *unknown.*

Everything depends on your answer, the peace of a *loving mother, the entire happiness* of a young, inexperienced person who lives solely in higher spheres and does not wish to enter practical life. I know that you love music—do not let your feelings about Robert speak, but judge his years, his fortune, his strength, and his future. I beg you, I beseech you as a husband, a father, and a friend of my son, treat this as an honest man would and tell me frankly your opinion—what he has to fear—or to hope.

Please excuse the distractedness of my letter. I am so deeply affected by everything that I feel sick to my very soul, and have never found a letter more difficult to write than this one.[3]

Wieck's later attitude toward Robert Schumann when he presented himself as a prospective son-in-law was doubtless colored by this emotional letter from Frau Schumann. But for the moment he took the opportunity to expand on his prowess as a teacher, to boast a bit about his daughter, and to assure Frau Schumann that in three years he could turn her son "into one of the greatest pianists now living." The hardheaded teacher understood the weaknesses of the young Schumann; he raised realistic questions and included some conditions for taking Schumann on as a student. First of all, Robert would have to follow Wieck's advice about practicing. He reviewed the history of the lessons Robert had already taken with him, in which Wieck had succeeded only "after hard struggles . . . in convincing Robert of the importance of a pure, precise, equal, smooth, clear, rhythmically distinctive and elegant touch." He complained of the irregularity of Robert's lessons and his propensity for excuses. "Has our

Robert changed?" he asked. "Has he become more prudent, firmer, stronger, and may I say calmer and more manly? His letters do not bear this out."

Robert would have to take a lesson with him every day for a year. He pointed out that this requirement might pose a problem, since he would be out of town for varying periods on concert tours with his daughter. Would Robert be able to work alone? Wieck seemed doubtful, given the young man's previous lack of discipline.

Wieck declared that every virtuoso had to supplement his income by giving lessons, and he was even preparing Clara for that eventuality. Would Robert consent to live in this way?

Could Robert resolve, he asked, to study "cold theory" for two years and would he be able to work at exercises (as Clara did for several hours a day)? Admittedly, exercises stifle the imagination, he added, but that was one quality Robert had in plenty.

If Robert would not follow Wieck's advice, he could guarantee nothing. But, he assured Frau Schumann, if Robert succeeded in erasing Wieck's doubts—and he would give him six months to do so—he ought to be given the opportunity to try.[4]

Why would such a busy and ambitious man as Wieck undertake to work with a young man of such doubtful character? It is possible that the older man admired, even envied Robert. Robert's gifts appealed to the tough old teacher, and he was clearly eager for the opportunity to work with the imaginative young man, not only because he was a paying pupil or one who might bring him some renown, but because he relished Schumann's fantasy and playfulness, so alien to the serious, plodding young tutor that Wieck had been at the same age. Even during the early days of the struggle over Clara, when Schumann and Wieck had become adversaries, the father valued the composer and his gifts though he scorned the suitor.

Back in Leipzig, in the autumn of 1830, Robert was jubilant. He agreed to everything, moved into two rooms in the Wieck house, and became a member of the household. During the following eight or nine months he and eleven-year-old Clara took lessons daily and practiced intensely—she to prepare for her solo debut at the Gewandhaus and Robert to work toward a career as a performing musician. In the biography of her father, Robert Schumann, Eugenie Schumann described those autumn days as her mother recalled them:

> Now a glorious life began. The mornings belonged to work, to serious study under Wieck's direction. . . . Evenings were the nicest time. Robert would fetch the children—Clara and her two brothers, Alwin and Gustav—to his room, and here he would become a child again with the children. He told them his best stories and played charades with them; he teased and frolicked and had the little boys taking turns standing on one leg—the one who could hold out the longest received a prize. Or he appeared clothed as a ghost, so that they ran from him shrieking; told the fearful Clara about doppelgänger, and about the pistol that he always carried with him, and she was the kind of child who believed everything he told her. . . . So, in this way, Robert was the biggest child of all and brought something of the sunshine of childishness to the serious life of his little friend. One can imagine how she loved him.[5]

Robert was soon dissatisfied with Wieck's tutelage and wrote his mother that he would like to go to Weimar to study with Johann Nepomuk Hummel. This was not a mere caprice; Hummel was a leading musical figure of the day—a student of Mozart, a rival of Beethoven, and kapellmeister at the Weimar court from 1819 to 1837. The name and reputation of the master undoubtedly lured Schumann, but he was also irked by his slow progress and by Wieck's insistence that he begin with finger exercises, "like a beginner."[6] His irritation was exacerbated by the daily example of the little virtuosa who achieved everything so effortlessly. He compared his playing with hers: "This whole morning everything went miserably. . . . Wieck sides against me, says I play the Herz variations like a dog . . . with Clara it just comes pouring out."[7] But when he mentioned his plans to Wieck, "in a light and casual way,"[8] a violent quarrel ensued; Wieck was threatening and ugly. Robert reported to his mother soon afterward that they were friendly again, but his diaries tell a different story. The Weimar plans had evaporated; the resentment lingered. Schumann treated Wieck with his customary respect, confided in him, worked with him, accepted his advice and hospitality; his true feelings were reserved for his journal. Here he recorded that Wieck was often hateful: "Meister Allesgeld has been gone with Zilia [Clara] for fourteen days now. His letters to his wife are the height of arrogance." He described his horror at the way Wieck mistreated his son, and on another occasion noted, "Wieck seems more dull, insipid, and arrogant every day."[9]

The contradictions that were to mark Schumann's relationship with his piano teacher began early. Wieck was more than a father figure; in Robert's eyes he seemed almost superhuman, and Robert desperately wanted this man's affection and approval. From Heidelberg, after only a few months of study, he wrote Wieck long poetic letters about himself, his music, and his enthusiasms (Franz Schubert and the novelist Jean Paul), and begged him to answer soon. And when he finally received his mother's permission to leave law and devote himself to music, his letter to Wieck, his "most venerated teacher," was glowing and exalted: "Take my hand and guide me. I follow wherever you wish. . . . Trust in me; I will earn the right to be called your student."[10] In 1832, when Clara and her father had left Leipzig for a concert trip, Robert wrote: "You can hardly believe how I long for her [Clara] and both of you. I must always be among people who are above me. Among people who are my equals, or especially with people I cannot permit to judge me, I easily get proud and cynical." And in June 1832 he wrote to Wieck, "Every day in which I cannot speak with you or Clara is a blank in my Leipzig life."[11]

Many years later, in the midst of the battle with Wieck over Clara, Robert wrote a soul-searching letter to his beloved. He confided that he had "terrible hours of self-doubt" because of the way Wieck treated him: he had been "repulsed, insulted, slandered." But, he admitted, "I love and honor your father for his many great and noble qualities, more than anyone else can, except for you. It is a primitive, innate attachment on my part, a submission I feel toward him, as I do toward all energetic natures."[12]

If Robert could write these words in 1838, when he was already an established editor, critic, and composer, his need for Wieck must have been stronger still in 1831. Robert, at twenty-one, was still "finding himself." His indecision and unrest lasted well into his twenties, and the cyclic, seemingly unpredictable alternations of mood that remained with him to the end of his life had already made their appearance. Torn between his desires to perform, compose, write, and direct, continually running out of funds, reminded daily by Clara's skill of his late start as a pianist, he still turned to his mother for money, comfort, and security. Thus, when he was considering study with Hummel in 1831, he proposed that she leave her home in Zwickau and her other children and grandchildren to live with him in Weimar.[13]

He was also suffering from a "wound" of some kind during this time. Whether this was the trouble that affected his finger and ultimately forced him to abandon a career as a performer or some other illness is not clear.[14] Robert was overwrought much of the time. In September 1831 he wrote his brother Julius that he was in such a state of restlessness and indecision that he almost wished to put a bullet through his head. In a fit of hypochondria triggered by the cholera epidemic that was sweeping Europe in the early 1830s, he confided in his already nervous mother that he had written a will, "principally for your sake."[15]

Throughout this tumultuous year, Schumann was composing. His earliest attempts had been in Zwickau and Heidelberg, well before he had acquired any substantial formal training. In July 1831 he began to study counterpoint and thoroughbass (basic skills that he had avoided up to that time for fear they might inhibit his creativity) with Heinrich Dorn, director of the Leipzig opera, a man only six years his senior. (Twelve-year-old Clara began studies with Dorn in 1832.) The "dull" lessons, providing a discipline to which Robert had never before submitted (and sometimes lightened with champagne, according to his teacher), were not appreciated at the time: "I will never be able to get together with Dorn; he has no feelings, and what's more, has that East Prussian tone." But he admitted later that the theoretical studies were a good influence.[16] Dorn's recollection of Schumann was that he was an avid student and always produced more than was required of him. Robert was distressed when Dorn discontinued the lessons, but pursued theoretical and analytical studies on his own.

With the publication of his first compositions, the ties between Schumann and the little girl grew stronger. On Clara's return from Paris, he brought his *Papillons,* his second published work, to Wieck, who thought the music piquant and original and immediately gave it to Clara to learn. Disappointed at her first readings, Schumann described her playing as uncertain and wanting in understanding; he felt that the thirteen-year-old did not have full control over the work. Despite the "soulfulness" and "healthy enthusiasm" of her performance, he complained he missed a certain tenderness. But finally, on May 27, he wrote, "I have never yet heard Clara play as she did today—everything was played masterfully and also beautifully."[17]

For his twenty-second birthday, on June 8, Clara played two of his Paganini

Caprices (op. 3) for him and also gave him a small gift she had brought from Paris. He was pleased by her attention but valued her performance above all, for by the time *Papillons* came out, Robert had given up the thought of a concert career, resolved to become a composer, and was turning to the young girl for performances of his work.

From this time on, Clara was the foremost interpreter of his piano works. A touching reminder of this dependence is a letter he wrote from Vienna a few years later:

> I am sometimes unhappy, particularly here, because I have an injured hand. And I want to tell you it is getting worse. I have often cried to heaven and asked, "God, why did you do this to me—of all people?" It would have stood me in such good stead, especially here; music is so complete and alive within me that I ought to be able to exhale it like a whispered breath. But now I can scarcely play at all and one finger stumbles over the other. It is really terrible and has already given me so much pain. Now, you are my right hand and you, you must take care of yourself so that nothing happens to you. I often think of the happy hours you will give me through your art.[18]

In contrast to Clara, who lived in a household of regular routines and controlled stability and concentrated on the career laid out so carefully by her father, Robert, nine years older, changed career plans several times, and suffered physical and mental crises that Clara was never to experience. He was haunted by the thought of insanity; fear of heights forced him to leave his fourth-floor room and move in with a friend on the first; he asked a companion to stay with him during the night. The deaths of his brother Julius and, soon afterward, his beloved sister-in-law Rosalie deepened his anguish and fears, and he referred to the night of October 17–18, 1833, as "the most frightful" in his life.[19]

By December the mental anguish was over, possibly alleviated by a new and close friendship with Ludwig Schunke. In the new year, 1834, described by Schumann as "the most significant of my life,"[20] he began working on plans for a new musical journal, a project in which his musical and literary talents would be united. He and a group of friends, dubbed the *Davidsbündler,** founded the *Neue Zeitschrift für Musik,* a weekly journal intended to counteract the conservative, "Philistine" tendencies of the musical world and the reactionary influence of such journals as the *Allgemeine musikalische Zeitung.* Only one of a group of editors during the first year (the others were Julius Knorr, Ludwig

*May be translated as "Davidites." The term was chosen in celebration of the biblical hero. Included as members of the *Davidsbund* were friends, colleagues, and several mythical figures: Florestan, Eusebius, and Master Raro (characters who had appeared in 1831 in his essay on Chopin), who represented various aspects of Schumann himself. Florestan was bold and impetuous, Eusebius dreamy and gentle, and Master Raro mature and reflective. The latter name, which may have been a synthesis of Cl*ara* and *Ro*bert, also represented their teacher, Wieck. Many other *Davidsbündler* appeared under various pseudonyms in the essays and reviews Schumann wrote. Clara, for example, was known as Zilia, Chiara, or Chiarina; F. Meritis stood for Felix Mendelssohn; and Jeanquirit was Stephen Heller, the composer and the Paris correspondent for Schumann's journal.

Schunke, Wieck, and Christian Ferdinand Hartmann, the publisher), Schumann was the busiest, conducting most of the correspondence, contacting potential contributors, editing articles, writing reviews, negotiating and planning. He continued to compose as well. A new phase of his life began when he decided to buy the journal and run it himself. (Schunke died in December 1834 and Schumann had a falling out with Knorr and Hartmann, but Wieck remained an associate for several years.) In 1835, after much maneuvering, he became the sole owner and director of the journal, which he was to edit for ten years.[21]

During these busy years, Schumann was briefly engaged to a young woman who had come to Leipzig to study with Wieck. Schumann announced her arrival in a letter to his mother dated July 2, 1834:

> Two glorious creatures of the fair sex have recently joined our circle. One of them, Emilie . . . is the sixteen-year-old daughter of the American consul List, an Englishwoman [*sic*] through and through with keen sparkling eyes, dark hair, firm step, full of intellect, dignity, and life.* The other, Ernestine. . . ."[22]

When Ernestine von Fricken first came to Leipzig to study and board with Wieck, in April 1834, Clara enjoyed the thought of another friend close to her age.† Wieck, however, had evidently decided months earlier, in accordance with his grand plan for his daughter's career, that she was to go to Dresden to work on French and English, study instrumentation with Kapellmeister Carl Reissiger, and take voice lessons from Johann Aloys Miksch. Clara viewed this arrangement as banishment from Leipzig and her friends. The letter she wrote Robert on his birthday, June 8, reveals her state of mind:

> Is this permitted, H. Schumann, to pay so little attention to a friend and not write to her even once? Every time the mail arrived, I hoped to receive a little letter from a certain Herr—Enthusiast, but alas, I was disappointed. I comforted myself with the thought that at least you would come here, but my father just wrote that you would not be coming because Knorr is ill.[23]

When she came home from Dresden at the end of July for the christening of her half sister Cäcilie, she saw Robert and Ernestine together and realized something was going on but tried to ignore it. An entry in her diary (written by Wieck) dated July 24, 1834, refers only to two young men she met in Leipzig. One was Carl Banck, "a highly cultivated musician and song composer and

*Emilie List, one year older than Clara, was one of the daughters of Friedrich List, a German political economist. Forced to leave Germany for political reasons, he had taken his family with him to the United States, acquired U.S. citizenship, and returned to Leipzig in 1833 as the U.S. consul. See Wendler.

†Both girls celebrated birthdays in September. Ernestine would be eighteen that year and Clara only fifteen, but Clara's experiences as a touring artist made her mature for her age.

teacher, who has made my stay here very pleasant." Robert was perceptive enough to note in his diary that she returned to Dresden "sadly."[24]

Four years later she wrote to Robert, "When I returned to Leipzig, I was torn from my paradise. Ernestine barely spoke to me—she was mistrustful—for which I had truly given her no cause; Mother told me about a beautiful letter you had written her on Cäcilie's christening—and then I heard you were betrothed."[25]

Robert was convinced that he was in love with Ernestine von Fricken, who has been described as "physically luxuriant, emotionally strongly developed, and intellectually insignificant."[26] With a little aid from Henriette Voigt, an older, married woman of whom he was fond, and who evidently enjoyed matchmaking, he quickly persuaded Ernestine of his affection. Rumors reached her father, who wrote from his home at Asch to ask Wieck in alarm what was going on. Wieck's reply brought the baron von Fricken to Leipzig, and his arrival seemed to bring the affair to a head. When Ernestine left Leipzig on September 6 with her father, who was ill, it was clear that she and Robert had an "understanding," and that in Leipzig she was regarded as his fiancée. Clara was not unhappy to see her go.

Eugenie Schumann, the youngest of the Schumann daughters, has told of a comment written by her mother in the margin of Philipp Spitta's 1882 biography of Robert Schumann. Spitta had written, "As far as we know, a special affection [between Robert and Clara] first was apparent in the spring of 1836." Clara corrected the entry: "Already in 1833."[27] With the advantage of hindsight and awareness of the girl's preadolescent longings, we might date it even earlier.

Clara's relationship with Robert, whom she had first met when she was nine, had many elements: a mutual ongoing childish fantasy based on his stories, music they improvised and played together, shared memories and experiences, motherly concern, and girlish coquettishness. She was eleven when Robert lived at her house and she first enjoyed his attentions, his stories, and the childish games he played with her and her brothers—pleasures she had never before experienced. She placed his name on her list of those who were to receive copies of her opus 1, published in 1831. Opus 3, her *Romance variée,* was dedicated to him (presumably with her father's permission) and sent off with this playful letter:

> Much as I regret having dedicated the enclosed trifle to you, and much as I wished that these variations not be printed, the evil has already come to pass and cannot be altered. Therefore, I ask your forgiveness for the enclosed. Your ingenious setting of this little musical thought will redeem the errors in mine.* I would like to request yours; I can hardly wait to make a closer acquaintance with it.[28]

When Robert left for a visit to Zwickau in 1832, Clara sent him news of Leipzig's musical life with the explanation "I just want to make you curious so that you will long for Leipzig." She needled the young composer: "Listen, Herr

*Schumann had used a motif from her work in his op. 5. Her op. 3 is discussed in Chapter 11.

[Richard] Wagner has outdistanced you. A symphony of his was performed; it is as like Beethoven's A-Major Symphony as it is possible to be." She teased him about leaving his laundry in a carriage and wrote of saving a Christmas cake for him (which was not yet baked). The letter closed with a cautious neutrality: "Your friend, Clara Wieck."[29] A childish letter? Perhaps, but this playful girl was asking for attention, chiding the man, toying with him. Coming from Clara Wieck, already a recognized artist, the reference to Wagner's success must have been like a twisting knife. But who could take her seriously? She was only thirteen.

By the time Ernestine von Fricken arrived in Leipzig, Clara viewed Robert as her special friend; when she realized the extent of the relationship between Robert and Ernestine, her reaction was typically adolescent. She flirted with Banck and let it be known (through her father) that she had fallen in love with a cellist in Magdeburg, knowing full well that this news would reach Schumann. His affections for Ernestine were cooling rapidly, however, and by the summer of 1835 the engagement, never formalized, was over as far as Robert was concerned. In the spring, while the ties were loosening, he was again seeing Clara daily. During this transition from Ernestine to Clara, Robert Schumann seems to have been emotionally attached to both young women. After receiving a birthday gift from Clara, he set off for Zwickau and Asch, Ernestine's home.

Early in the fall of 1835 Clara celebrated her sixteenth and, according to her diary, "most brilliant" birthday with a group of her father's friends, all men, and several of them, to her joy, young. In a letter to Emilie List, after listing her many birthday presents (including "the complete works of Bulwer" from Schumann), she described the great day:

> In the early morning, about half past six, I received my things, and when I had looked at everything, I urged Father to get going, otherwise it would get too late. (We had, as you know, proposed to go to the Kuchengarten.) But Father said, "Just wait a little while longer. The others [men] will be coming soon in order to go with us." . . . Just then, as I wanted to go out, . . . a servant girl came. She carried a beautiful wreath on a glass plate. I recognized her as Schumann's servant, took the plate from her, looked inside, and, imagine my surprise, found a basket with a porcelain handle within, and, in the basket, a golden cylinder watch. You cannot imagine my astonishment as well as my joy. You must certainly be wondering—as I was—the watch could not possibly be from Schumann alone? No, that was not the case. Indeed, it was from Schumann, [Dr. Moritz] Reuter, [Wilhelm] Ulex, [Louis] Rakemann, [Ernst] Wenzel, and [Ernst] Pfundt. Immediately afterward we went—I with the golden watch—to the Kuchengarten, and there were the Stegmayers, who had placed a huge bouquet on the table. We weren't sitting long when the above-mentioned watch givers came, all adorned with "burning love" [the flower pelargonium].
>
> You can imagine my embarrassment. I couldn't utter a word. . . . (The porcelain basket was from Herr Schumann alone.)
>
> At twelve o'clock, the six gentlemen (and Felix Mendelssohn as well) re-

> turned and dined with us. Now imagine my heroic courage: as we were drinking champagne, I stood up with the glass in my hand. Everyone was amazed, and I began and said, "Gentlemen, I cannot refrain from expressing my warmest thanks for the beautiful gift." Was that not lovely? The gentlemen still can't forget it. . . . I must have seemed quite stupid. . . . After we ate, I played for Mendelssohn and he played also. Everyone left at 5 o'clock, but at 6, Dr. Reuter and Schumann came round to fetch us for a walk. However, we danced until 8 and then went out walking.
>
> That was the famous sixteenth birthday. Oh, Emilie, if you only had been here. It was marvelous. I will not forget this day soon. We are saving a little post-party celebration until you and Herr Banck are here again.[30]

Except for Felix Mendelssohn, the newly appointed director of the Gewandhaus Orchestra, the guests were old friends of Wieck's and associates of Schumann on the *Neue Zeitschrift für Musik.* We may assume that Frau Wieck was present as hostess, but, as usual, she is not mentioned. Clara, though so often surrounded by adult men—friends, students, and walking companions of her father*—evidently still found it easier to communicate with them through the piano than through speech. Her characteristic shyness in speaking explains her pride in finally being able to thank the gentlemen properly.

Schumann abandoned all principles soon after Clara's birthday; he assured her that all was over between him and Ernestine, that Ernestine was engaged to someone else. (She was not.) Recalling those months several years later, he wrote in his diary:

> Clara's birthday on September 13. . . . Clara's eyes and her love. . . . The first kiss in November. Then her trip to Zwickau at the end of November. I follow. Our meeting. . . . Break with Ernestine. . . . Clara's return to Leipzig. The poor Rakemann [another suitor of Clara's]. Lovely hours in her arms in the evenings in the Wieck house. Christmas 1835—New Year's Day 1836—break with Wieck. Complete separation from Ernestine.[31]

Clara was deliriously happy. She wrote to him later, "When you gave me that first kiss, I thought I would faint; everything went blank and I could barely hold the lamp that was lighting your way out."[32]

The kisses continued when they met in Zwickau in December on a concert tour Wieck had arranged. The engagement to Ernestine was over—although Ernestine did not know it until January 1836. (In 1838 she married the baron von Zedtwitz, to the great relief of Robert and Clara, and she was later generous enough to come to their aid in the legal proceedings between Wieck and Robert.) Lulled by Robert's attachment to Ernestine, Wieck did not realize what was happening for some time, but when his suspicions were at last

*Note that Clara's guest list, presumably drawn up by her father, was all male. Guests at her fourteenth and fifteenth birthday celebrations were also chiefly men, friends of her father's. Even Clara's birthday parties were not her own.

aroused, his first reaction was to remove his daughter from Leipzig. He took her to Dresden on January 14 and remained there with her until February 7, when he had to leave on business. (Wieck was still renting and selling pianos.) Clara stayed on in Dresden with friends.

In the first flush of love, Robert persisted in the naive belief that Wieck would approve their marriage. Since Wieck admired Robert's compositions, had treated him as a friend, and had been a respectful collaborator on the *Zeitschrift,* he assumed Wieck would be happy to see his daughter and the promising young composer united. He went so far as to convince himself that he had been "chosen" and educated to be Clara's husband.[33] In ordinary circumstances, Robert Schumann was perceptive and showed unusual depths of sensibility and self-understanding for a young man, but in this situation he misjudged Wieck completely. Forgetting, or perhaps suppressing, his memories of Wieck's temper, jealousy, and possessiveness, he was astonished and hurt at Wieck's fury when the father learned that Robert and his friend Wilhelm Ulex had visited Clara in Dresden between February 7 and 11, while he was away. During that time promises had been exchanged and letters arranged. By the time Wieck returned, Robert was on his way to Zwickau to pay belated respects to his mother, who had died on February 4, and to take care of the will and other legal matters. (Unable to bring himself to attend the funeral, Robert had gone to see Clara instead.)

The struggle between Wieck and Robert for Clara that began after this incident was complicated by the fact that Clara and Robert both needed Wieck at this point in their lives. Schumann wanted to be both son and son-in-law to his old teacher. Yearning for the stability and firmness of an association with Wieck, he was shocked to find he could not have Clara and Wieck too. Clara knew she was in love with Robert but understood her father well enough to suppress Schumann's name in her diary; it appears occasionally and only in an offhand way in Clara's handwriting during the next few months. Music, her career, and the daily routines organized by her father still remained the center of her life. Within the next two years, however, she was to take the first faltering steps on her own. Wieck, supremely insensitive to those around him, proceeded impulsively and irrationally toward the estrangement that was to embitter his life.

Now, in February 1836, Wieck's rage erupted at Clara for the first time. He threatened to shoot Schumann if she should meet him again. He entered his thoughts on their deceitful behavior in her diary. All the insults, threats, and fury that she had seen visited on her brothers (and perhaps, in the dim past, on her mother) burst upon her now. From beloved pupil and protégée, source of all Wieck's artistic and personal gratification, she had suddenly become the enemy.

Wieck scheduled another long concert trip to keep her away from Leipzig and, except for a maid, was her sole companion on a concert tour to Dresden, Görlitz, and Breslau from February to April. It was a miserably unhappy tour, with Wieck in a rage from beginning to end. In Clara's diary he fumed at the miserly Dresden audiences, the inadequate pianos, weak orchestras, and dirty lodgings.[34] He sent Schumann an insulting letter informing him that all connections between him and the Wieck household were severed. For almost a year and a half Clara and Robert, for so long daily companions, did not meet or communicate in any way. Friends kept him informed of Clara's whereabouts and doings. Johann Peter Lyser, a close friend, described a concert he had attended in Dresden:

> February 24, 1836
>
> There is not much more to tell you about Clara's last concert except what is expected: it was jammed, a Beethoven overture opened the concert, then Clara appeared—stormy reception—Now she played "Là ci darem la mano"—You know how! *Lieder ohne Worte* by Felix (give him three kisses for it), a Bach étude, and variations by Herz.
>
> The audience applauded madly, the Old Man had a full money chest, Clara made her bows. . . .[35]

Since Clara's diary was still in large part her father's, we have no direct knowledge of her feelings. Touring with her father, shut up with him for days on end in slow coaches and rehearsal halls, closeted in uncomfortable inns, she was forced to endure his attacks on Robert just at the point where a love long cherished and secretly hoped for had seemed possible. Yet Wieck expected his daughter to carry on her concert career as she had always done, and she acquiesced. Her only contact with Robert was through his music; she played his Toccata and First Piano Sonata (in manuscript) for small private musical circles in Dresden and Breslau at every opportunity. Wieck apparently had no objection.

During this first, long separation, Schumann threw himself into work—composing, studying, writing—and an active social life. Among his close friends and companions were Mendelssohn, Ferdinand David (concertmaster of the Gewandhaus Orchestra), the wealthy musical Voigt family, Dr. Moritz Reuter, Wilhelm Ulex (a music teacher), and the greatly admired English pianist and composer William Sterndale Bennett, who arrived in Leipzig at the end of October 1836. Schumann let his sorrows be known to all Leipzig and points south. To his sister-in-law, Therese, he revealed his soul: "Come soon and be a good sister to me; I have no one to give me womanly care." He described briefly what was happening between the Wieck family and himself. "I am in a critical situation and lack the calm and clear sight that would enable me to pull out of it. The way it stands now is that either I can never speak with her again or she will be mine entirely." Though he had many male friends, he missed a woman in his life. In December 1836 he wrote to Therese, "Oh, remain true to me. In the deadly anxiety into which I sometimes fall, I have no one but you to turn to, to hold me by the arm and support me."[36]

These were the years when Schumann was creating his best-known works, those impassioned piano pieces that include the *Davidsbündlertänze,* the *Fantasiestücke,* the Fantasie in C Major, and the three piano sonatas. A published copy of his Sonata in F-sharp Minor, "dedicated to Clara by Florestan and Eusebius," was sent to her in May 1836. Clara was not permitted to acknowledge receipt of the sonata, and soon thereafter Wieck insisted that all Robert's letters be returned. She obeyed.

In contrast to the festivities of the year before, Clara's seventeenth birthday, in 1836, passed under a cloud. It was the first such celebration in many years at which Schumann had not been present. While anticipating the next big concert trip to Berlin and northern Germany, planned for the spring of 1837, she toured in the small nearby towns of Naumburg, Jena, and Weimar. At home she endured the close supervision of her father and stepmother.

The trip north, a prelude to even longer international tours, began on February 7, 1837, in Berlin, where Clara's mother, now Marianne Bargiel, lived. Immediately upon her arrival, Wieck took Clara to see her. "Here, Madam, I bring you your daughter," he announced.[37] The fact that Wieck himself recorded the words in Clara's diary tells us much about the man: he gloried in his power as he permitted a reunion between mother and child.

The two Wiecks saw Clara's mother and her ailing husband several times. Bargiel, recovering from a stroke, is mentioned briefly; Wieck's anger and contempt were reserved for Marianne. She was, he recorded in his daughter's diary, "far more rude, mean, deceitful, petty, and presumptuous than she had ever been." Unforgivably, moreover, she tried to "meddle" with the arrangements for Clara's concerts.[38]

In Wieck's correspondence there is no mention of Clara's feelings or reactions to her mother (or, indeed, about her relations with anyone else). Nevertheless, this must have been a time of thought and reconsideration for Clara. Though she had seen her mother briefly from time to time over the years, she had always been returned to her father and his influence. Now, almost adult herself and at odds with her father, she could begin to understand what had happened in Leipzig in 1824 and why Marianne had been forced to abandon her children. The Berlin visit gave her an opportunity to rediscover her mother, as it were, and from that time a genuine relationship developed between the two women. Within a few years Clara was able to turn to her mother for love and support.

Wieck's letters to his wife, Clementine, tell us much about the vicissitudes of touring in the 1830s, a great deal about Wieck, and very little about Clara.[39] His complaints were many: the high cost of food (which he partially circumvented by sending Nanny, the maid, out for dry rolls that they could eat for breakfast in their high-priced hotel room); the vast numbers of free tickets that Berlin concertgoers expected; the poor seats they were given for concerts; the problems with the censors and the bureaucracy; the surly Berlin serving classes; the supporting musicians who refused to cooperate on his terms in Clara's concerts; and not least, the high cost of postage.

His earthiness and vulgarity make themselves evident in the letters. Clara was taking lessons from Siegfried Wilhelm Dehn, a "formidable contrapuntist"—the kind of "fellow" (he wrote *Kerl*) for whom he had been looking a long time. "He will bring her to the point of writing circle canons; in a word, after twelve lessons, when she spits, she will spit up fugues." He damned the assisting artists, Carl Möser (the leading chamber musician in Berlin) and his "cursed" quartet, for having the temerity to ask for fifteen free tickets. He was proud of the way he outmaneuvered Möser and wanted all Berlin to know of his behavior.

Most striking in Wieck's letters is his attitude toward Clara: she is discussed as though she were an object on display. He was concerned about her health—but largely because a canceled concert would cause great inconvenience. The morning after her last Berlin concert, a triumph played in a hall filled to capacity, he sarcastically referred to "the queen," still sleeping at 6:30 A.M.

Wieck took great delight in routing his foes; the struggle with the "enemy" often seemed more important than Clara's playing. He was, of course, proud of her artistry and her talent at composition. He informed Clementine that publication of Clara's collected works would be announced in the papers; that three publishers had bid for her Variations (op. 8) and Clementine was to ask Friedrich Hofmeister, their Leipzig publisher and close friend, how much he would give for them; Gasparo Spontini, the grand master of music in Berlin, not only wanted Clara to play privately for him but considered the Bellini Variations "the grandest and most beautiful piece of bravura music in recent times." But above all, Wieck felt successful because Clara's triumphs had "destroyed all the cabals."

Again and again we read of "victories"—victories over those who plotted against them, victories over the jealous Berlin dogs who would have done them in, victories over the poisonous music critics who doubted his daughter's genius. The reports of praise for Clara are laced with comments on the enemy. "Clara is the talk of the town and the other artists are butting their heads together in despair." After her first concert, on February 24, he boasted, "Triumph, triumph, Clara created a furore last night. Her masterly playing was rewarded by an hour and a half of thunder and formidable bravissimos—all the cabals have been destroyed . . . the public has decided—and *how* they have decided! Even Paganini did not have such accolades here."

All the concert arrangements were in Wieck's hands: he made the required rounds of visits to impress important people; he secured the permission of the police; he rented the concert halls; he borrowed or rented the pianos for practice and performance; he had posters and programs printed; he prepared publicity for the newspapers; he paid a visit to Mendelssohn's mother. "The amount of work is frightful," he wrote, but he did not forget to mention the many contacts he was also making for his piano business. Reviewers were commenting on his pianos along with Clara's performances. "Berlin will be a gold mine for us—and my business too," he wrote.

They moved on to Hamburg, where the "glorious Clara" was eagerly awaited. By the end of the concert trip, which closed in Bremen, both were exhausted. The weary travelers returned home on May 3 and were greeted by stepmother and Carl Banck at the outskirts of Leipzig.

Banck's proximity to Clara and her family plus the continued silence of the girl he loved drove Schumann wild. In the autumn of 1836 he began to have strong doubts. He wrote to his sister-in-law, Therese, "C. loves me as warmly as ever, but I am completely resigned [to giving her up]."[40] During 1837 Schumann's spirits rose and fell in an alarming way. He wrote to Clara in January 1838:

> The darkest time, when I knew nothing of you and tried to force myself to forget you, was about a year ago. Did you not think of me then? Our spirits must have been estranged at that time. I had resigned myself. But then the old pain broke out again—and I wrung my hands—and then I said to God on many a night—"Let but this one thing mercifully pass away, without my going mad." . . . I hurled myself to the ground and cried aloud—then I wished to cure myself, to compel myself to fall in love with a woman who had already half drawn me into her net.[41]

Several writers have speculated on the identity of this woman. Although musicians are mentioned (the British pianist Robena Laidlaw, for example, who passed through Leipzig about this time), he may have been referring to the Christel (or Charitas) whose almost daily visits to his room were noted in his diary. Robert certainly never entertained any idea of marriage to her, but she must have provided the female comfort and sexual gratification he craved, particularly at this time, when he was estranged from the woman he loved.

Banck's presence in the Wieck home and Wieck's persistent criticism of Robert almost succeeded in alienating the lovers. The possessive father, however, became characteristically agitated at Banck's friendly relationship with Clara, and, acting angrily and impulsively, he banished the young man from the house. Soon afterward Banck left Leipzig. Robert's diary notes, "Banck's departure from here—happier mood."[42] Within a few months the relationship between Clara and Robert was secretly resumed, this time on Clara's initiative.

While spending the summer of 1837 at the home of friends near Dresden, Clara was informed by her father that he had arranged a concert for her on August 13 in Leipzig. A few days later a conversation with Ernestine von Fricken, who was visiting in the area, evidently stilled her doubts concerning Schumann's previous relationship. Clara agreed to the concert but insisted on including three of Schumann's Symphonic Etudes in the program.* She then

*In the first (1902) edition, Litzmann mistakenly names the Sonata no. 1 in F-sharp Minor.

plucked up the courage to ask Ernst Adolph Becker, a mutual friend and a great admirer of Schumann's music, to convey a message to Robert, thus breaking the enforced silence of eighteen months. A swift and passionate exchange of letters through Becker followed. On August 13, the day of the concert, Robert wrote:

> Are you still *firm* and true? As indestructible as my belief in you* is, yet even the strongest spirit loses confidence when nothing is heard of the one who is loved more than anyone else in the world. And you are that to me. I have thought it all over a thousand times, and everything says to us, "It must be, if we wish it and if we act." Write me just a simple "yes" if you will give your father a letter from me on your birthday [September 13]. Just now he is well disposed toward me and will not reject me if you add your pleas to mine.[43]

Her answer, simple, beautiful, and positive, sealed the bond with Robert. For the remainder of their lives, they considered the following day, August 14, the day of their betrothal. In his diary Robert wrote, "A union for eternity."[44]

Clara Wieck had declared her intention to move away from her father and to the man she now hoped to marry. But a long struggle with herself and with her father lay ahead.

The famous courtship began with surreptitious meetings and secret letters. Their hopes were pinned on the formal proposal, written with Ernst Adolph Becker's help and advice, which was to be presented to Wieck on Clara's eighteenth birthday. With the letter Robert requested an interview and enclosed notes to Frau Wieck and to Clara. The interview was granted but Clara was never given the note. In a touching letter Robert formally asked for Clara's hand and implored Wieck, "with the utmost seriousness of which an anxious, loving heart is capable: bless us, be once more a friend to one of your oldest friends, and the best father to the best child!"[45]

Robert's self-confidence had been restored by Clara's yes and he was buoyed by the admiration and love of his many friends. To Robert's anxious queries, Becker replied:

> I do not know to whom I would rather have my daughter betrothed than a man whose heart is as true as yours, and who can write such études. I received them [the Symphonic Etudes] yesterday. . . . One cannot find anything more beautiful; I have reveled in them, undisturbed, all day.
> . . . For majesty and grandeur of thought, I know of no living person who can stand at your side.[46]

Despite Becker's confidence, it was another tear-soaked birthday for Clara, and Robert's interview with Wieck was a bitter and humiliating experience.

*The two were still addressing each other as *Sie*. It was not until October that the intimate *du* was used by both Robert and Clara.

"This coldness, this ill will, this confusion, these contradictions—he has a new way to destroy, he thrusts blade and hilt into my heart," he wrote to Clara.[47]

Robert believed that Wieck's interest in money was at the root of his opposition. Knowing what we do about Wieck, we can hardly doubt that he regarded Clara as a financial asset, but in all fairness we must acknowledge that other factors, many of them legitimate doubts that any responsible father might have, also figured in Wieck's resistance to the match. Gradually Schumann perceived that a great battle was beginning. "Eventually he must accept the idea of losing you. His obstinacy will shatter itself against our love. . . . Convince your father that his views are distorted."[48]

Wieck could have chosen several courses of action, but, oddly enough, he began, and continued, a weak, often irrational offense. His behavior repelled many of their mutual friends, all of whom sided with the young lovers. His only ally was his wife. Though not a man of financial substance, Schumann had inherited a moderate legacy, had a growing reputation as a composer, was owner and editor of a successful music journal, and was a man of intellect and undeniable genius, respected and loved by many. Wieck knew all this and, more than many other musician of his generation, understood and valued Robert's gifts and adventurous musical spirit. But he doubtless recalled the revealing letter from Robert Schumann's mother and knew the undisciplined and sometimes erratic early youth, the drinking and extravagance with money; he must have had an inkling of Robert's experience with women—Leipzig was a small town—and he was aware of the cyclic depressions and family history.* Yet in the battle over Clara, he chose to concentrate on insignificant details (poor handwriting, inaudible voice, social maladroitness) and accusations about drinking to excess—a charge that may have been true in Schumann's earlier years but could no longer be substantiated. Wieck insisted that Robert did not have the money to support Clara in the style to which she was accustomed and that marriage would mean the end of her glorious career. The second argument shook Clara and created doubts that were to surface over the next two years. For the time being, however, she was in love and remained unconvinced by her father's arguments.

The letters exchanged between the lovers in the next few weeks are beautiful. Clara's letters, so prosaic in her later years, are here filled with poetry and warmth, tenderness and beauty. Robert's letters, always a joy to read, rise to new heights as the two pledge themselves to each other, even as Wieck is leading Clara off to Vienna and new triumphs on the concert stage.

*In "Schumann's Hand Injury," *MT*, 112 (1971), 1156-59, Eric Sams speculates that Wieck was aware that Schumann had sought treatment for syphilis and that this was the major (and unnamed) reason he objected to their marriage. In view of Wieck's character and the steps he took to prevent the marriage, however, it hardly seems possible that he would have failed to mention the disease if he had had even a faint suspicion that Schumann had it.

CHAPTER 4

The Break with Wieck

After the travails of the trips to Paris, Dresden, and Berlin, the success in Vienna was sweet indeed. Little was heard from Wieck about plots and cabals, and though he issued occasional curses at conditions and foes in the Austrian capital, his letters reflected less anger and hostility than did those from Berlin. Viennese charm had softened the old man—but not to the point of changing his mind about Robert. He had given permission for them to correspond while Clara was on tour, but she was so fearful that her father would read her correspondence that she secretly scribbled a few words at a time to her lover while standing at her bureau after long days of wearying performances.

The eighteen-year-old young woman had firmly declared her love for Robert but was still dependent on her father, emotionally, financially, and above all artistically. The effort to break with her father engendered extreme anguish. The situation was as monumentally difficult for her as any of the later crises of her tragedy-filled life, and in fact may have served to armor her against the impact of the devastating events to come. For Clara, the conflict between father and lover continued to the eve of her marriage, and even beyond.

Friedrich Wieck, the parent of this virtually motherless girl, was also the developer of her art and provider of the self-esteem that nourishes the artist. From the beginning, at a time when middle-class girls were expected to learn to tickle the piano keys prettily enough to amuse a husband but not to attract public attention, Wieck envisioned Clara as a musician—a great performer—and insisted that she could do anything a boy could do (and certainly do it better than his sons). He quoted with pride Goethe's remark, "She plays with as much strength as six boys."[1]

Yet during the trip to Vienna which began in October 1837, a psychological separation from her father began to seem possible. Robert was more insistent; she had given him her word and her ring; the Vienna press and public accorded her more recognition than she had ever received before; and though Wieck's letters still refer to "our concerts" and "our feelings," Clara was gaining an independent identity. If a question remained in her mind about her future with Robert, she did not allow it to sully the triumphal days in Vienna during the winter of 1837–38.

Wieck viewed the trip to Vienna as his greatest artistic and financial triumph. Clara's success exceeded anything he had ever dreamed of. She was so immensely popular that Wieck worried through sleepless nights whether she could maintain her position and keep Vienna's hysteria at the high pitch her artistry had inspired. "All Vienna is saying that no artist has ever made a sensation like this," he wrote to his wife.[2] He marveled at the way the money rolled in. The Viennese were storming the box office and police had to be called in to restore order. Newspapers reported a new confection, "torte à la Wieck." In a letter to Robert on January 30 Clara described it: "Just imagine. They are serving 'torte à la Wieck' in the restaurants, and all my enthusiasts go and eat the cake. It was recently advertised in the *Theaterzeitung* with the comment that it was an ethereal, light dessert that played itself into the mouth of the eater. Isn't that a laugh?"[3]

In his usual fashion, Wieck gloried over the blows dealt to Sigismund Thalberg, the famed virtuoso, and other rivals. The triumphant Clara, he reported, aroused keen jealousy among other artists, who were losing their audiences to her, and among teachers, who were exploding with anger at her (his?) triumphs. "We have been vegetating in Leipzig," he wrote to his wife in the letter in which he enclosed the Grillparzer poem "Clara Wieck und Beethoven."* "Now comes the reward—now the whole world shall know there is only one Clara, a Clara at whose feet all Vienna lies."

The honors flowed so copiously that the reader (and Wieck himself) can barely keep up. He couldn't think of leaving; "Vienna would weep." The prospect of years of glittering success was exciting, but we sense that Wieck was beginning to feel some strain. While waiting to hear whether or not Clara would receive the emperor's award, he wrote, in an unexpectedly pessimistic mood, that it wouldn't help Clara in any case, because this was the last trip he would make. His health was affected by the rigors of concert life: the obligation he felt to stay in one place as long as money could be made, Clara's contrariness and obstinacy, the endless burdens and constant anxieties of concertizing—he could not take it much longer.

Once Clara received the imperial honor, however, Wieck cried for joy and hailed it as a vindication of all he had suffered:

> What a letter of recommendation this is! What a lesson to the envious pianists who have made a public spectacle of all my aspirations. We have borne it humbly and continued to strive—here is the reward. . . . Haven't I always, and rightly, soothed Clara by saying, "Have patience"? Now she has the highest title; it is the greatest guarantee of safe-conduct in all of Europe. Now she understands the kind of steadfast resolution that is responsible for this. Would we be in Vienna if I had not battled the boors?

*Described at the beginning of Chapter 1.

Clara was honored by musicians as well as by royalty: she received an autograph of Schubert's "Erlkönig" from a friend of the composer; editions were dedicated to her.[4] Publishers fought for the privilege of publishing her works, and she was named an honorary member of the prestigious Gesellschaft der Musikfreunde.[5]

The Viennese reception was immensely gratifying to Wieck, and possibly as a result, his letters expressed more concern about his family; he teased Clementine, he sent kisses to his children. Feeling more secure and expansive, he directed Clementine to get bigger and better lodgings for the family. Clara, of course, was to have a room of her own in the new apartment; his children were to have rugs on the floor so they wouldn't be cold. But he spoke only of the two little girls—the children of his second marriage. Alwin and Gustav had not turned out well, he said, and would have to leave. His attitude toward the boys was unequivocal; he would not support them any longer. Gustav, just turned fifteen, was to be apprenticed to a piano maker. And if Alwin did not improve, Wieck wrote, he would be sent to an instrument maker in Pressburg. He warned that if either tried any "dumb tricks," they would go straight to prison (despite the fact that their sister was a Royal and Imperial Chamber Virtuosa).

The crimes of these dreadful youngsters were never spelled out, but it is obvious that, unlike Clara, who was earning "unheard-of" sums, they remained financial burdens. Clementine received her orders: "His [Alwin's] fate is irreversible—he must go—take the first opportunity [to ship him off] during the first week of the fair. He will never see his family home until he becomes a useful person." As for Gustav, Clementine was ordered to find an old suitcase for the boy so that he could set out on his journeys; "their father's home no longer exists for these bad boys."*

Wieck's thoughts also went out to Robert, whose talents as editor, publisher, and composer he enlisted in Clara's interests. Since it was necessary to keep in touch with Leipzig musical life, he requested every word printed in Schumann's *Zeitschrift.* Clementine was to ask Schumann to reprint the Vienna reviews, to publish the Grillparzer poem, to print up copies of reviews and the poem and send them all to Wieck for the Viennese press. Near the end of the trip it occurred to him that a sketch of Clara's life would also make good copy for the local papers. He directed (through his wife) that Robert write such a sketch and send fifty copies for distribution on concert trips. At the same time, he expressed resentment because Schumann had not thought to do so himself.

It seemed to Wieck that Schumann was not writing enough about Clara while she was busy playing Robert's works and building his reputation. "His *Carnaval* was performed by us for the great connoisseurs and created a great furor; since there is so much speaking, gossip, explaining, running, visiting, etc.

*Gustav was apprenticed to and became an instrument maker. Alwin eventually became a professional violinist and played in orchestras in Reval and St. Petersburg before he settled in Dresden in 1859.

here, his name as a composer will quickly become known. Clara also played the sonata [F-sharp minor] but it was not so well understood."

Though Wieck was clearly pleased with Clara on this trip, he made no mention of her feelings or reactions. Apparently she existed for Wieck's purposes, and as far as he was concerned, the triumphs were his.

Meanwhile, Clara and Robert, considering themselves engaged, carried on their clandestine correspondence. Elaborate plans were made so that she could receive his letters. To allay Wieck's suspicions, Robert was to address his letters to fictitious characters—now "BCDE," now "Herr Kraus"—in care of friends who were to send them on in fresh envelopes addressed to her, since Wieck knew his handwriting. Nanny, Clara's maid, was a firm ally, and picked up the letters for her at the post office. Robert did not understand why she did not write more frequently, and she explained that the only time she had to write was in the evenings when she was half dead with fatigue. Wieck would fly into a rage if he found her door locked.

There was much discussion of their future. Robert was dreaming, and Clara, the practical, experienced performer, sharply brought him back to earth, as she was to do often:

> I had to laugh at the place in your letter where you write, "and so we will return to our little house, laden with treasure." Oh, my God, what are you thinking of? Treasures cannot be acquired by instrumental art *any more.* How much one has to do in order to leave a town with a few taler! While you are sitting at Poppe's [a Leipzig coffeehouse] at 10 o'clock in the evening, or are going home, I, poor thing, am just arriving at a party, where I have to play to people for a few pretty words and a cup of warm water, and arrive home, dead tired, at 11 or 12 o'clock, have a sip of water, lie down and think, "Is an artist much more than a beggar?"

"Yet," she went on, in an impressive statement of faith from such a young artist—a statement that was to form the motto of her life—

> art is a beautiful gift. What is more beautiful than to clothe one's feelings in sounds, what a comfort in sad hours, what a pleasure, what a wonderful feeling, to provide an hour of happiness to others. And what a sublime feeling to pursue art so that one gives one's life for it.[6]

The covert correspondence was not entirely free of the conflicts that were agitating the girl. Clara's indecision tormented Schumann and undoubtedly contributed to his insecurities. At one point she wrote to Robert that she could sympathize with her father: "I am terribly upset when I see how miserable Father is when he thinks of losing me someday—I know my duty toward him and yet I love you endlessly." During all this time she was subjected to her father's continual threats of disinheritance if she married Schumann and began to react to them: "I no longer am so fond of my father, ah God, I cannot be as wholeheartedly loving as I should like to be—it is my father, after all, that I have to thank for everything."[7]

Many of her letters reflected her father's influence. The tone of this letter, for example, is strangely like Wieck's:

> I have also considered the future *very seriously* and I must tell you one thing: I cannot be yours before circumstances have entirely altered. I don't want horses, I don't want diamonds, I am happy to be yours, but I want to lead a life free of worry and I can see that I would be unhappy if I could not always be working with my art. . . . I need much, and I realize that much is needed for a respectable life. Robert, test yourself. Are you in a position to offer me a life free from care? Consider that though I have been brought up simply, I have never had a care. Must I bury my art now? Love is all very beautiful, but, but—[8]

Robert was beside himself, but he managed to point out with dignity that she should have brought up these objections before he asked her father for her hand. Though he recognized her father's pressure in her letter, he was hurt:

> And now, since you value my ring so little, I care no longer for yours, since yesterday, and wear it no longer. I dreamed that I was walking by deep water—and an impulse seized me and I threw the ring into the water—and then I was filled with a passionate longing to plunge in after it.[9]

His dark words were a foreboding of the future: just before Schumann attempted suicide by leaping into the Rhine in 1854, he removed his wedding ring and threw it into the water. But in 1838 he was able to recover from the blow and gathered the strength to advise and comfort her. He was aware of the daily nagging and verbal assaults to which she was exposed. But Wieck, too, according to Clara, vacillated. On March 3 she wrote that she and her father had spoken of Schumann and that Wieck seemed to be prepared to accept him once more as a friend of the house. She optimistically assured her lover that her father was "quite kind." "He sees very well that I will *never* give my heart to another—and a father like mine would never consent to give my hand without my heart."[10]

Clara had misinterpreted her father's comments, perceiving them in her own way. She pointed out that it would be difficult to earn an adequate living in Leipzig and went on to sketch a glorious life in Vienna, where Robert could continue to compose and edit his journal and she could earn perhaps 2,000 taler through concerts and teaching. These earnings, added to his income of 1,000 taler a year, would enable them to live comfortably.

This was not exactly the way Wieck saw the situation. What he actually wrote in her diary on March 3, 1838, was:

> . . . spoke with Clara about Sch. and told her I will never give my consent to Leipzig, and Clara quite agrees with me, and assures me her view will also

> never alter. Sch. can maneuver, philosophize, enthuse, idealize as much as he likes; it is settled that Clara can never live in poverty and obscurity—but must have over 2,000 taler a year to spend.

Robert was happy to hear of a rational conversation, and his answer recalls his longing for a father:

> Now if only I could win the love and confidence of your father—whom I would so gladly call Father, whom I have to thank for so much of the happiness in my life, for his teaching—and also for grief—and to whom I should like to give nothing but joy in his old age, so that he should say, "They are good children."

Yet he was suspicious and added, "There can be no happiness in this relationship until your father . . . considers me the future son of the house."[11]

The constant rise and fall of their hopes did not weaken Robert's resolve, and before she returned to Leipzig she received a firm letter from him, asking her to set a date for their marriage and expressing grave doubts that Wieck would ever give his consent: "Since he has taken back what he promised so many times, he will do it again—in a word, I expect nothing from him, *we must act for ourselves.*" And he concluded, in a long letter written over about a week in April 1838, that they should settle on Easter 1840 for their marriage.[12]

The return to Leipzig, on May 15, 1838, marked the final period of the courtship but the conflicting emotions only became more intense. Though she never considered giving up Robert, doubts about the continuation of her career and guilt over separation from her father tormented Clara, and the reverberations of these feelings shook Robert again and again.

"If anyone asks if I have already seen you," she wrote to Robert in May 1838,

> tears spring to my eyes. You are so near and yet I cannot see you. . . . I am suspended in heaven and immediately afterward am so unhappy because I cannot embrace you right away, you who are everything to me, you who have opened another world to me. . . . You are the ideal of a man, an ideal I have always carried in my heart.[13]

And on June 2, 1838, she wrote:

> It would be lovely if Therese could be with us the first weeks after our wedding. She could teach me many things that I cannot learn at home because my father does not want to see me anywhere but at the piano. How I would like to concern myself with household tasks now and then, but I would just be laughed at.[14]

In April, while Clara was still away, Robert had written that although they were going to be in the same city for the summer, it might be best if they did not meet. He wanted a wife, not a girl for secret meetings and kisses. He had endured the situation for two years, he wrote, and he could hold out for two more years. The strain of plotting, of stealing a few minutes in order to have a couple of distracted words together, was too much to bear. "I am no longer a moonlight knight," he wrote. "If you yearn for me terribly, I will gladly come; otherwise let it go; it leads to nothing." But Clara could not restrain herself and they met frequently in the weeks she was in Leipzig. She even suggested visits to his room, but Robert decided it was too risky. "If anyone were to see you at my house, your father might do something dreadful. I cannot have you visit me now." Their notes indicate that they met often, however, perhaps daily.[15]

Complicated operations were set in motion for a visit of a moment or two. On June 8, Robert's twenty-eighth birthday, Clara wrote: "Be at our window at *exactly* 9. If I signal with a white cloth, walk slowly toward the old Neumarkt. I will follow soon after and go with you, since I have to fetch Mother at her mother's. *If I don't signal, it means she hasn't gone.*"[16]

Robert to Clara, an agonizing letter, June 20:

> I have such an urgent desire to see you, to press you to my heart, that I am sad—and sick as well. I don't know what is absent in my life, and yet I do know: you are absent. I see you everywhere, you walk up and down with me in my room, you lie in my arms and nothing, nothing is real. I am ill. And how long will this all endure?[17]

She could give no response. Visiting friends in Dresden from July 3 to August 7, however, she could write more freely. From the carriage that took her to Dresden she had seen Robert standing by, waiting to follow the carriage with his eyes.

> I saw you, two steps away from me, and could not get out of the carriage to throw myself into your arms. . . . As you came toward me, I felt as though I would fall into a faint because of the pain; everything turned black, and when I could see you no longer, my heart opened and the tears flowed so that I could not hide them. The feeling was indescribable.[18]

In the long August and September evenings of that year, 1838, Robert stood across the street from the Wieck home and watched the window for a glimpse of her shadow or listened for a few measures of his music as she practiced. She knew he was there.

Clara was beginning to be frightened by her feelings about her father:

> It has already come to this: I sometimes have frightening thoughts that I no longer love my father as I should. And when my beloved Robert is derogated, ridiculed, insulted, this arouses bitter feelings, this is the deepest wound. . . . The parting from Father will be difficult for me. I will have to struggle mightily, but *love will give me strength for everything.* When the time comes, *I will*

> *come too.* Father may perhaps disown me, oh my God, how dreadful, will it really go so far? God in heaven will forgive me then—it is indeed only love.[19]

Clara never accepted the anger she felt; guilt haunted her for many years. In July she wrote from Maxen, a suburb of Dresden:

> I forgive your anger at Father because I know you would forgive everything just as quickly if he would be friendly toward us. Your heart is so good that I cannot take [your anger] badly. I am his daughter and though at times I am bitter, yet I still love Father so much. Believe me, he is good and believes he is doing this for my best interests. . . . He is very hard at times, and does not know the love that we cherish for each other, nor does he understand delicacy of feeling in such a situation, but believe me, when I am finally with you, he will gradually become favorably disposed toward me—he loves me too much to cast me aside. Be calm, my Robert, he loves you too; he just will not admit it.[20]

All his life Robert was to face the fact that Clara never really gave up her father, even in the face of the bitterest hostility, even when Wieck's behavior seemed insane. On the whole, Robert bore the situation well; his attitude indicated concern and understanding for Clara's need. But despite his surface dignity, he was frightened, shaken, and easily depressed. On August 1, 1838, he wrote, "You are attached to your father with great love and I respect you all the more for it. But Clara, if you were to give me up on his account! My blood runs cold. Forgive me. I am still so sick." On August 21 he complained, "Your father embitters my whole life, our entire love. He tramples everything underfoot; he worships only Mammon. What lies has he been telling Becker again? And you don't defend me at all? Enough of this . . . but all these slanders haunt me even in my dreams."[21]

Because of Wieck's rigidity and obduracy, the lovers were forced to resort to lies and deception. Even their friends were caught in the web. Ernst Adolph Becker, the courier of their secret letters, was put in one compromising position after another. While enjoying Wieck's hospitality in Leipzig between August 11 and 26, he was carrying notes between the daughter of the house and Robert. The Wiecks never suspected him, but they did suspect Moritz Reuter, the physician who was a friend of Schumann and of Wieck. Clara had to suffer the indignity of being searched for letters after Reuter visited the house. The lovers lived in constant fear of having their correspondence discovered. Her stepmother had warned Nanny that they had ways and means of finding out if Clara were writing to Robert. Clara begged him not to leave her letters lying around and not to mention anything that she had written. "For God's sake," she wrote, "*be careful;* the unfortunate consequences would be dreadful."[22]

Again, as in Vienna, Clara's anger at her father was entwined with her need and gratitude for his teaching. She felt she was indebted to him even for her love for music, her only solace when she was made miserable by his nagging and unreason. From Dresden in August she wrote:

> How love makes one so receptive to everything beautiful. Music is now quite another thing for me than it used to be. How blissful, how full of longing it sounds; it is indescribable. I could wear myself out now at the piano, my heart is eased by the tones and what sympathy it offers! . . . Oh, how beautiful music is; so often it is my consolation when I would like to cry. Yet we have my father to thank for this and will *never* forget this.[23]

In early September 1838, a few days before her nineteenth birthday, Wieck arranged a Gewandhaus concert, her first after the Viennese triumph. The next issue of Robert's journal brought a poem titled "Dream Picture," in which he praised Clara's playing as the acme of romanticism; it evoked images of Schubert songs: of the "Erlkönig" and "Mignon," of knights of old, of a pious nun. Robert pictured Clara as an elusive "angel child."[24] The poem was for the public. Privately, the concert aroused in Robert a sense of the anguish he would experience many times as the husband of a concert artist, and for the first time he expressed ambivalence over his situation. To begin with, he had found it uncomfortable to attend because he resented having to share his glimpses of her with so many others. He sat quietly in a corner, watching his ring on her finger sparkle for him as she played, and felt completely left out. His true feelings are revealed in his letter of September 9, 1838:

> You played magnificently. The people don't deserve your [playing]. . . . You are too dear, too lofty for the kind of life your father holds up as a worthy goal; he thinks it will bring true happiness. What difficulties, what a long way, how many days—and just for a few hours! . . . No, my Clara will be a happy wife, a contented, beloved wife. I consider your art great and holy. I hardly dare think of the happiness you will give me with it; but if we don't consider it necessary, you won't lift a finger if you don't want to, for people who aren't even worth playing scales for, isn't that so, my girl? Don't misunderstand me: you know I am an artist who believes you can preserve art without our having to make long concert tours, indeed you will find in me a truly ardent musician, to whom it is all the same if you rush a little or hold back or play a little more elegantly—as long as it always comes from within—and it does with you.[25]

Soon after that concert, Robert left for Vienna. This trip had been conceived a few months earlier, when it occurred to Clara that it might be advantageous for Robert to visit the Austrian capital and perhaps eventually to move his journal there, particularly in view of her success there and Wieck's insistence that they could not remain in Leipzig if they married. Robert concurred and wrote to Vienna immediately. His plan was to enlist the help of Joseph Fischhof, the Vienna correspondent for his *Neue Zeitschrift* and professor of piano in the conservatory, and some of the influential people Clara had met in steering the project through the bureaucracy and intrigues of the music-loving capital. This was no easy task in a city where censorship was of a virulence unknown in Leipzig. As it turned out, the Vienna trip came to nothing as far as the journal was concerned but was of great importance in other ways: Schumann met Ferdinand Schubert, brother of the composer he had idolized, and discovered the great C-Major Symphony, which had been laid away with other priceless music manuscripts; he had more opportunities to hear vocal music, particularly opera, than had been possible in Leipzig; and he created a number of works in which the Viennese influence on both his emotional and musical life are evident. "Arabesque," op. 18; "Blumenstück," op. 19; "Humoresque," op. 20; and "Faschingsschwank," op. 26, were among the piano works composed in Vienna.[26]

Dreading his departure, Clara clung to him, begging for just one more meeting and still another, until finally Robert concocted an elaborate plot so that they could spend some time alone. He announced to his friends and landlady that he would be staying in Zwickau for two weeks before embarking on the final stages of the trip to Vienna. He did remain in Zwickau—but only until he received a message from Clara that Wieck had left town on a business trip. He then slipped back into Leipzig and stayed two days with a friend so that he and Clara could be together. Finally he left for Dresden on his way to Vienna.[27]

This separation engendered much anxiety and tension, and the letters between the lovers carried the seeds of a misunderstanding that was to break out in full force when Clara was in Paris. Moreover, Wieck was furious when he learned that the two were carrying out plans to meet the conditions he himself had laid down a few months before: that Robert was to leave Leipzig and establish his paper in Vienna and that Clara was to go to Paris alone. New conditions were established: Nanny, who was known to be sympathetic to Clara and Robert, was to be dismissed; Clara was to go on no more tours; and if she married, she was to "fulfill her duties to her mother" by sending Frau Bargiel the interest on her capital.[28] The demands were puzzling, as Wieck had previously forbidden her to send anything to her mother.* More puzzling still was the announcement that he would not accompany her to Paris. Fearful, she turned to Schumann, who assured her that if worse came to worst and she had to leave her father's home, he would provide (indeed, had already provided) a fund on which she could draw. Yet despite Schumann's generosity and forethought and her father's senseless demands, Clara still wavered and Robert had to endure constant fluctuations in her mood.

"You are, forgive me, like a pair of children," he wrote on October 24, 1838. "You cry, he scolds, and it is still the same as ever. . . . You can't belong to him and to me at the same time. You will have to leave one, him or me."[29]

Though she protested that Robert was the one who mattered, Wieck's influence remained stronger. Without realizing the effect her words might have on Robert, Clara wrote of waiting until after 1840 for their marriage, if necessary,

*Clara did send her mother money from time to time, since she knew that her need was great. After her September 1838 concert, for example, she sent her six louis d'or.

so they would be on firmer financial ground. Schumann's despair was so intense that Dr. Reuter had to remind her to be careful about what she wrote. Finally, on November 25, she wrote what he was longing to hear: "For your sake I will give up my father, whom I love more than anyone except for you. I will follow you without my father's consent. . . . That is a great deal for a feeling heart to do, difficult, but *I trust you,* my life will lie in your hands and by loving me you will make me happy."[30]

Alas, this was not to be her last word.

The trip to Paris became both a private and a public testing ground for Clara's independence, a frightening thought for her. Even Robert was hesitant at first and had to be convinced of the advantages to be gained from such a trip. As late as August he was writing to her: "About Paris, if I were in your place I would not act as if it means too much, nor would I talk about it too much either. Your father will certainly not stay home all winter. You cannot travel alone; I won't permit it."[31]

During the next few months Clara began to recognize the depth of her father's hostility. He would permit her to go to Paris without him, but he hoped for her failure and counted on her return from what he predicted would be an ignominious defeat. Fury at her defiance and independent spirit outweighed pride in her success; this man would be vindicated at any cost. But in counting on her need for him as teacher, father, protector, Wieck ignored all she had learned from that same source: practicality, self-confidence, and a particular hardheaded stubbornness. And so she decided to go.

Nanny, her only confidante, was not permitted to accompany her, and Wieck hired as chaperone Claudine Dufourd, a Frenchwoman whom Clara did not know. She left Leipzig with the stranger on January 8, 1839, heading toward Nuremberg in a heavy snowfall. She planned to earn money by giving concerts along the way, as she had done on her previous trip with her father in 1832, and was gratified that despite her father's absence, her concerts in Nuremberg, Stuttgart, and Karlsruhe went well. Though she told herself that her father would come as soon as his business would allow, she was beginning to realize how well she had learned to carry on a career without him.[32] There were, of course, anxious moments as she sat in the carriage, writing to Robert. Addressing him now as Eusebius, now as Florestan, she described her headaches, her sleepless nights, and the responsibilities of the concert arrangements that were now hers.

The journey yielded two happy events: in Asch she learned that Ernestine was married and was willing to help Clara and Robert in any way; and in Stuttgart she found a traveling companion, Henriette Reichmann, a young woman of her own age who wished to study with her and was prepared to go to Paris to be with her. Henriette remained a friend for life.

The Paris the two young women and their chaperone were timorously approaching was still the musical capital of Europe: nineteen theaters and at least three concert salons presented opera, drama, vaudeville, ballet, revues, recitals, and other events daily. Giacomo Meyerbeer, one of many German composers Clara and Wieck had met on her earlier trip, was now the most admired composer in Paris, tsar of the opera, and, fortunately for Clara, a man easy to know. She was able to turn to him for advice, and although later Robert despised and castigated his music, he proved to be a reliable friend to Clara. She met other composers as well—Friedrich Kalkbrenner, Daniel Auber, Georges Onslow, and Jacques Halévy—but made little impression on them, nor did she care for the French composers (except for Onslow, of whom she became fond). Among the musicians she encountered were Charles Alkan, Pierre Baillot, Adolphe Adam, Luigi Cherubini, Johann Baptiste Cramer, and Anna de Belleville-Oury (a former competitor whom she branded "the most abhorrent woman in the world"), as well as Princess Cristina Belgiojoso, a wealthy patroness. Through the Erard family, makers of musical instruments, she was introduced to many distinguished writers, including Alexandre Dumas and Heinrich Heine.

Hector Berlioz, whose *Symphonie Fantastique* had been analyzed, reviewed, and praised by Schumann in 1835, was introduced to her at the home of the Bertins, an influential Parisian publishing family. She described the meeting in a letter to Robert:

> He is quiet, has uncommonly thick hair, and is always looking at the floor, casting his eyes downward. He will visit me tomorrow. At first I didn't know it was he and wondered who this man was who continually spoke about you; finally I asked him his name, and when he told me I reacted with such happy astonishment that he must have been flattered. His new opera [*Benvenuto Cellini*] has been a complete failure.[33]

Berlioz, still struggling for a foothold on the perilously political musical paths of the French capital and burdened with an ill and incompatible wife and young child, had little time or inclination to help the young German pianist. She was not happy with his review in the *Journal des Débats* of her concert on April 16; he acknowledged her gifts as a pianist but damned her Scherzo with faint praise. Although she professed modesty about her creative abilities, she was accustomed to critical acclaim. She was taken aback by Berlioz's words, felt he was hostile, and in her diary entry of April 18, 1839, described his review as "extremely malicious." In a letter to Robert she called him her "secret enemy," repeated some slanderous gossip about his activities as a music critic, and accused him of engaging in cabals against her.[34]

On her arrival in Paris on February 6, 1839, Clara had found good friends: Emilie List was there with her parents, and the mezzo-soprano Pauline García (later Viardot), whom she had met in Dresden the previous summer, was settled in the French capital with her mother and brother-in-law, the Belgian violinist Charles de Bériot, and making a great sensation.* Erard and Pleyel, the leading piano manufacturers, both pressed pianos on Clara, placing her in a predicament that she found difficult to handle: how was she to use the Pleyel (which she preferred) without insulting Pierre Erard?[35]

*Bériot was Clara Wieck's assisting artist at the April 16 concert.

There were many difficulties and disappointments in the big foreign city. It was several weeks before she was able to retrieve Robert's letters from the post office; she received no word from her father for even longer. Feeling completely cut off from her former life, she lamented to Robert that she was really alone for the first time in her life. But when Heinrich Probst, a friend and business associate of her father, and Eduard Fechner, her stepmother's brother, urged her to return home, she refused to leave and arranged to give concerts at the Conservatoire and the Erard salon. She wrote to Robert that she was considering touring in England for several months and returning to Paris in the summer to give lessons. She weighed the possibility of a tour in the French provinces before returning to Leipzig to marry at Easter 1840, with or without her father's permission.

She and Henriette Reichmann, accompanied by Claudine Dufourd (soon to be dismissed), took lodgings in the Hôtel Michadière, where Pauline García was also staying, but within a few months Clara and Henriette moved again, this time to share lodgings with the List family. Besides practicing, teaching, making her own concert arrangements, and playing in the right places, she and Henriette saw everything to be seen in Paris: the Tuileries, Nôtre Dame, the Palais Royal, the Invalides, the Panthéon, the stock exchange; they were caught on the streets during a political uprising (excitedly described in great detail to Robert); they attended operas, concerts, and ballets at every opportunity. Clara was not isolated in Paris and she managed to make her way, although it cannot be said that her presence was strongly felt. She found, probably for the first time in her life, much competition, and told Robert with some trepidation that all the pianists, male and female, were playing in Paris. But in March and April she arranged and gave several successful concerts, which were well reviewed in the Paris journals as well as in the Leipzig *Allgemeine musikalische Zeitung.*[36]

The triumphs and praise, however, were not enough to sustain her. She needed her father's approval. Soon after she reached Paris, on February 14, she tearfully wrote to Robert:

> Just look, I have only you; you shall be my support. I have a father whom I love infinitely, who loves me, and yet I do not have the kind of father my heart requires. You must be all to me, my father as well, isn't that so, Robert? True, I have received letters since I have been here, but they are letters of a different sort. Not one loving word, like those that I so like to hear from you; they contain only cold advice, reproaches; my father is unhappy and that hurts me; I cannot feel any differently. I firmly believe that my father's heart will still yield, and in this belief, may our goal come closer and closer; when he sees us happy, he too will be happy.[37]

Within a few weeks Wieck read the reviews, heard from friends, and realized to his dismay that Clara was doing well without him. In an angry letter to Emilie List he declared his intention to deprive Clara of her inheritance, including the money she herself had earned, unless she gave Robert up, and threatened to begin a lawsuit against them both.

Robert's reactions to her reviews were ambivalent. He was proud of her (all of his letters to Paris are addressed to the "Royal and Imperial Chamber Virtuosa Clara Wieck"), and his advice demonstrated his confidence in her: "Don't leave Paris before you've had a *total* triumph. . . . Don't go to London before you're certain that your Parisian reputation has reached there. Those cities are the largest in the world. You are actually appearing in those places as a fully developed artist for the first time."[38]

But he sent quite another message when, in the same letter, he wrote:

> I am musing about our first summer in Zwickau as married folks. . . . First (another kiss), young wives must be able to cook and to keep house, if they want satisfied husbands, and you can have fun learning that from Therese; and then young wives may not make long journeys right away, but must take care of themselves and spare themselves, especially one who has spent the entire previous year working and sacrificing for her husband; third, we want to free ourselves from boring and curious visitors; fourth, we want to be able to take walks and I will show you all my boyhood haunts; fifth, your father could do us no harm. . . .[39]

Then the young man again reversed himself and wrote, "Write often and write long letters. Use your time to compose, play. *Don't be so retiring,* let them know what kind of artist they have in Paris."[40] A few days later he was still attempting to resolve his conflicting aims:

> I have just read the letter in which you write, "If I remain in Dresden for one year I will be forgotten as an artist." . . . Clärchen, you are not really serious—and if you were to be forgotten as an artist, would you not be beloved as a wife? . . . The first year of our marriage you *shall* forget the artist, you *shall* live only for yourself and your house and your husband, and wait . . . just see how I will make you forget the artist—because the wife stands even higher than the artist and if I only achieve this much—that you have nothing more to do with the public—I will have achieved my deepest wish. Yet you still remain an artist. The bit of fame in the contemptible paper that your father considers the greatest happiness in the world—I despise it. Forgive this outburst.[41]

Robert's frustrations and ambivalence about her career continued. Even more threatening to his peace of mind was her protracted clinging to her father. Notwithstanding Wieck's threats, she urged Robert to placate him. In answer to Robert's reproach that she was too weak with her father, she replied on April 22, "My father . . . is to be pitied, and in my heart I often grieve over it; yet I cannot change it in any way. . . . Oh, Robert, forgive me if in the future a sudden melancholy sometimes overcomes me when I think of my father—but it is so painful."[42] Schumann may have found it even more difficult to accept

Clara's reaction to a second and softer letter from her father, a letter from which the peremptory tone had vanished. Grasping at what she perceived as warmth, she wrote deeply and passionately to him of her feelings for Robert, what their relationship meant for her, and her longing for her father's blessing. She begged him to come to Paris, offering Emilie's help with the language for a trip to England.

Then in May, forgetting all her promises, she asked Robert to postpone their marriage, saying, in effect, "Father is right." She had just enough sensitivity to realize that Robert would have a right to be angry, but not enough tact to understand that the closing remark, "You are a man, Robert, are you not, and will not surrender to grief?" was equally insulting.[43]

Emilie List contributed to the hurt Schumann must have suffered. Attempting to be objective, she sent him a letter presenting Wieck's side but also describing Clara in a precarious condition, physically and mentally. If Clara wanted to keep her position as a virtuosa secure, Emilie wrote, she could give no more than one lesson a day, which might not suffice to support a household. Clara, she said, had two choices: she must either neglect her art and accept the cares of a housewife or have the means to survive without those petty cares and lead a free, independent life. "Therefore," she wrote, "I feel it would be far better if Clara gathered a small capital before she married." She ventured so far as to propose that Robert become a book dealer and publisher and take over the business of his recently deceased brother, Eduard. "Your art would not suffer," the young lady advised him, "and you would make enough money to satisfy Wieck."[44]*

The thought of taking over Eduard's business had already crossed Robert's mind, but to receive such advice from Clara's friend infuriated him and might have caused a serious rift had he not received a letter almost immediately from Clara begging him to forgive her. "Tell me, my good, beloved Robert, what am I to do to restore your tender feelings toward me? Please tell me, I cannot be at ease when I know you are angry with me," she wrote when the full realization of what she had done struck her.[45]

Robert replied, "Just promise me not to entertain any more unnecessary fears, trust and obey me; after all, men are above women."[46] And Clara fervently agreed. Robert then sent her two letters, the first a dignified appeal to Wieck for permission to marry, the second a joint letter that was to be submitted to the Court of Appeals in Leipzig after she had signed it if Wieck withheld his consent. She did not hesitate; on June 15, she went alone to a notary in Paris, signed the letter, and sent it off.†

*Emilie List, only one year older than Clara, was a perceptive and mature young woman who was a loyal friend throughout Clara's life. Robert perceived her letters to him as meddling until she convinced him that she was primarily concerned about Clara's and his happiness.

†Saxon law required the consent of the parents of both parties for any marriage, regardless of the age or rank of the children. (As an orphan, Robert was not obliged to obtain consent. Clara's mother gave her consent immediately.) If such consent could not be obtained, it was customary to appeal to the court.

Robert Schumann, age 29, in Vienna. Lithograph by Josef Kriehuber, 1839. Robert-Schumann-Haus, Zwickau.

Clara's wavering seemed to be at an end, and as before, her decision was probably due to a blunder on Wieck's part. Just before she received the legal document from Robert, she had received a harsh letter from her father enclosing a list of conditions to which she was to agree. The conditions were absurd; Wieck had gone too far. She replied:

> Allow me to answer but one thing. I have not signed my agreement to your conditions and I tell you, I will never sign them, I have too much pride for that; besides, how could you think that I would sign a paper in which nothing but evil things are written of the man I love? You were not serious, and if you were serious, then I must say to you, you will never bring me to do such a thing.[47]

Robert's letter to Wieck read:

> Honored Sir:
>
> Clara writes that you yourself desire that we should come to a conclusion; I gladly offer my hand in peace. Let me know your wishes; I am happy and ready to fulfill them in any way I can. If by a week from today I have no word from you, I will assume that your response to my inquiry is a negative one.[48]

The answer, written by Frau Wieck, was brief: "Wieck does not choose to have any connection with Schumann."[49]

Robert forthwith presented the document with both signatures to the court and sent Clara money for a return trip to Leipzig, because a personal appearance was required.[50] Clara and Henriette left Paris the second week of August; they parted company a few days later in Stuttgart.

The months in Paris had not brought Clara the great reputation she had sought, but they were of inestimable importance for her growth. Here she had lived, found and made friends, arranged, performed, negotiated, and maneuvered in the muddy waters of Parisian musical life, composed, taught, survived—all without her father, and in a state of emotional turmoil that might easily have felled a lesser spirit.

On August 18, 1839, Robert met Clara in Altenburg, the city in which she had parted from her mother many years before. The lovers were together for a few days but entered Leipzig separately. Clara was apprehensive of her father's anger, but found that that problem had been taken out of her hands: her father's house was no longer open to her. She stayed with friends and relatives but soon left Leipzig to live with the Bargiels in Berlin. All her possessions—her clothing, music, piano, even her childhood diary—remained at her father's home.

The next year was to be the most difficult she had endured, even though her mother and Robert were nearby. To witness the genteel poverty of the Bargiels was a frightening experience. Marianne was obliged to give piano lessons while caring for four children, nursing a sick husband, and supervising a home. Clara realized that her presence, however much her mother welcomed her, was an additional burden for the Bargiels. Though Schumann gave Clara 400 taler in Prussian state bonds on September 3 (since Wieck had left her penniless), she felt helpless.* To add to her anxiety, she received several pitiful begging letters from Ernestine von Fricken, now widowed and also penniless.[51] Her discomfort turned to despair when she realized that Robert was experiencing a serious depression after the months of acting boldly and taking the initiative. He made no effort to disguise it in his letters to her:

> I beg you to whisper my name to the Almighty now and then that he protect me, because I can tell you that I am so depressed and worn out with pain that I can hardly pray. I am carrying a great burden of guilt—I separated you from your father—and this often torments me.[52]

On a visit to Zwickau in July, he was tortured by thoughts of death. "I feel as if I must lie down here, where so many of those I have loved are lying. . . . There is no longer any joy here for me."[53]

Although Clara had endured many difficult moments, she had never known this kind of mental anguish. In Paris and now in Berlin, she reacted to emotional strain with such physical symptoms as pain in her fingers, shoulders, or arm, but even this discomfort rarely prevented her from practicing or performing. In January 1840 she gave a number of concerts in Berlin while suffering depression, aches and pains, fainting spells, and neuralgia, and found, to her surprise, that her audiences were unaware of her problems, that she played just as well as ever and received the same tumultuous applause. She was aware of Robert's history of depression but had never fully comprehended that she would have to deal with it. The realization was frightening, particularly now that she was dependent on him for emotional and moral support. It was easier to bear when he wrote and described his state: "I am often silent for days on end—without thoughts—merely muttering to myself."[54] But frequently he did not write or wrote coldly. She was in despair over one letter and wrote in her diary on January 15, 1840:

> Today a letter from Robert caused me to suffer one of the most painful hours of my life. He confirmed the fact that the court case may not be over before Michaelmas [September] and at the same time wrote that he would not prevent my returning to Father if I wished, etc. That was worse than a stab—at

*From entries in Schumann's household books for 1839–40, we know that Schumann supported her for the entire year before their marriage. He sent money for all her needs—concert dresses, living expenses, and gifts for her mother, her stepfather, and even her brother Alwin.

> first it put me in a state of insensibility but then the tears came and flowed without ceasing. Oh, Robert, what an injustice you have done me.

On January 17 she wrote:

> My state of mind is indescribable—I cannot forget the words in Robert's last letter—they torture me. I have endured everything, I have lost my father, I have stood up to him in a court of law, what battles have I fought with myself, but Robert's love made up for all this. I believed his faith was immovable, and now he hurts me so much. I can barely calm myself.

She could not know at the time that Schumann was reacting to a "declaration" that Wieck had presented in court on December 14, 1839. It was too painful for him to describe the impassioned eleven-page document, which was both malicious and libelous.* Although Schumann was able to prove the charges false, the situation was humiliating and expensive, and necessitated a further postponement.

The case dragged on, as court cases do. Wieck followed his declaration with a formal five-page paper to which Schumann responded in an equally formal, lengthy, reasoned reply refuting Wieck's charges. Schumann's response was accompanied by supporting documents: an honorary doctorate from the University of Jena, an accounting of his income, letters from Ernestine von Fricken's father and other influential friends. The court was convinced and by July Wieck was finished, though he refused to acknowledge defeat. The court's consent for the marriage was conferred by default.

Schumann had answered Wieck's accusations with a suit of his own. On June 1, 1840, a "denunciation" was sent to Dresden, the city to which Wieck had moved, charging Wieck with slander and suing for the money Clara had earned on her tours. The suit for Clara's money was settled out of court but the slander charges were tried and resulted in a judgment against Wieck in April 1841. He was ordered to pay court costs and a considerable amount to the Schumanns.[55] In addition to the legal maneuvers, Wieck made several last-moment attempts to bring Clara to her knees. In April 1840 he sent Alwin to demand that she pay for his violin lessons; soon afterward Wieck spread word throughout Leipzig

*The eleven heated pages still seem to smoke with Wieck's unreasoning fury. He included nasty comments on Schumann's capabilities as a musician and composer, as journalist and editor; he wrote that Schumann could not help Clara with her career, since he was socially inept—could not speak clearly or write legibly; that he crippled his finger through his own stupidity; that he lied about his income; that he had been badly brought up and displayed an indescribable egotism and unlimited vanity; that he was a solitary drinker and drank to excess; and that he did not really love Clara—he wanted to use her for his own purposes and live off the money she earned as an artist. His daughter, he wrote, having been trained as an artist, was unfit to run a home; moreover, her special needs as an artist required her to have more money than a woman in ordinary circumstances would need. The document is in the Staatsarchiv, Dresden; a transcription by Georg Eismann is in RSH (5725-A3c).

Clara Wieck, age 20, shortly before her marriage. Colored drawing by Johann Heinrich Schramm, 1840. Robert-Schumann-Haus, Zwickau.

that she would soon come begging at his door and sent maligning letters to Hamburg and Berlin just as she was about to appear there in concert. The foulest blow was his declaration that she was not playing well and would ruin any piano she used.[56]

He continued the assault on Schumann as well, spreading stories throughout Leipzig. The attacks were so virulent and his actions so irrational that Clara and many others thought he was losing his mind.[57] All the charges were lies, distortions, or half-truths, and thus easily disproved—but at a terrible emotional cost to the young composer.

In September 1839, Clara had asked her father for some of her earnings to serve as a dowry, but he refused, saying that if Robert really loved her, he would contrive to give her the money she asked for. The courageous young woman then resolved to provide her own dowry by giving concerts. Besides performing in Berlin, she traveled with her mother to Stettin and Stargardt, and later to Hamburg, Bremen, and Lübeck. By March 1840 she was able to write to Schumann, "I will tell you, though I don't like to speak about it, that I earned 970 taler, of which some went to travel expenses, purchases for me and Mother and the household, so that I now have 490 taler left. Are you satisfied? I am very happy about it and realize that in five weeks one could hardly ask for more."[58]

The tour brought her more than money; it was exhilarating to be on stage once more. She was distressed at Schumann's desire that she remain home during the first year of their marriage, and pointed out—as she was to do many times during their marriage—that she should earn money "now that I am young and have all my strength." There were some further uneasy moments in the months before her marriage when Clara proposed concert tours to England and to St. Petersburg, but Robert would not agree. She was quite prepared to face a lengthy separation, pointing out, in her practical way, that she could not make as much money as a married woman as she had made as a girl. Clara was dissuaded from the Russian tour only when she learned that Liszt would be there at the same time. She was not prepared to compete with him for audiences.[59]

Clara was clearly concerned about solvency. The possibility of having to use Robert's capital to set up housekeeping, she wrote in her diary on April 2, 1840, "pains me; I cannot look forward to the marriage in a happy frame of mind." But although she attributed all her anxiety to worries about money, other thoughts were undoubtedly troubling her. The attachment to her father had not lost its grip and the trauma of this separation was overwhelming. Outpourings of love for Wieck found their way into the diary during all the trials, both legal and emotional:

> [August 24, 1839] I think his fatherly love will triumph over his unreason.
>
> [August 31] My filial love and thankfulness can never cease.
>
> [September 20] Today I was overwhelmed by melancholy as I thought of my

Friedrich Wieck, ca. 1853. From Marie Wieck, *Aus dem Kreise Wieck-Schumann* (Dresden: v. Zahn & Jaensch, 1914).

> father. I pity him so much, and yet was he not cruel? Nonetheless I feel such an unextinguishable love for him—one friendly word from him and I would forget all the pain he caused me.
>
> [October 1] Above all, I feel such great pity for Father, I cannot describe it. In losing me, he has lost all his hopes.
>
> [November 11] I would like to forget him (heaven forgive me), and yet cannot. I cannot suppress the childlike love I feel, and if I ever do, it breaks through stronger than ever and then I must weep. Yet it is a quieting thought to know that the feeling for my father has not disappeared and that is something I also want to preserve. On the one hand, he is to be pitied, even though, on the other hand, he has treated me so terribly.

Clara's letters during the months of touring in the winter of 1839–40 reveal patterns of behavior that were not to change. Like many other artists, she was nervous before a concert, rarely satisfied with her performance, and often depressed after the event. She often suffered lapses of self-confidence and physical symptoms. Schumann had little patience with her laments, pointing out that these reactions might have been deliberately encouraged by her father so that she would feel helpless without his presence. In a letter of February 1840 Robert also attributed to her father her fear of being forgotten if she married and stopped playing publicly.[60] As soon as Clara read this analysis, she realized how right he was; her mood changed instantly and she was ready to compete again. Lapses in self-confidence, however, were to occur again and again. By May, she had another mild crisis, clearly expressed in her diary on May 23, 1840: "Oh God, I get so little encouragement when Robert is not with me. Who else says a kind little word to me? Mother, *never!* and I don't believe those praises from strangers. Encouragement from others is always a necessity; it gives you resolve and the ability to perform at a higher level than you could almost never expect from yourself."*

The conflicts of 1838–40 intensified Clara's jealous and suspicious disposition. The success of other artists troubled her. Camilla Pleyel, a beautiful and accomplished French pianist just a few years older than Clara, was in Leipzig while Clara was touring in the north with her mother. It was upsetting to learn that her father fawned on the coquettish young woman, worse when the Hamburg musicians sang her praises, unbearable when Robert praised Pleyel in his letters and in his journal reviews.

When, during one of Robert's very creative periods ("February is always a good month for me," he wrote),[61] he began to send her the songs he was composing, the first of the rich harvest of 1840, Clara's appreciation was clouded by

*This need of Clara's may well have been one of the reasons she stopped composing at Robert's death.

suspicions she could not control. "How wonderful that you are composing so diligently," she wrote, "but as for the songs, it has occurred to me—is there perhaps some young nightingale in Leipzig who is inflaming you?" There was no reply to this question, but the letter that accompanied the songs should have been reassuring: "The songs are my first published ones, so don't criticize them too much. As I composed them, I thought only of you. Your eyes, you romantic girl, follow me everywhere, and I often think one cannot make such music without such a bride."[62]

Clara was never completely convinced, despite the passionate letters and the need for her he expressed in this letter of December 1, 1838:

> It is from you that I receive all life, on whom I am wholly dependent. Like a slave, I should often like to follow you from afar at a distance, and await your slightest bidding. Ah! let me say it once more, come what may—I will whisper it even to whoever closes my eyes, "One alone has ruled my life completely, drawn me into her inmost being, and it is she that I have ever honored and loved above all."[63]

The young artist always had a lingering fear that she wasn't pretty enough or intelligent enough to keep Robert happy. During the last month before her marriage, other doubts assailed her. On June 17, 1840, she wrote in her diary:

> Oh, how I tremble, how my heart pounds—I have an unhappy character. Even my great love for Robert gives me unhappy hours—I often ask myself, can I make him as happy as I would like to, as he deserves? Won't family responsibilities eventually put too much pressure on him? Will he be recognized? Oh, my God! These and so many thoughts torment me—if I were only his wife already!

Schumann was also tense during the summer. Like Clara, he had never been altogether free of jealousies and suspicious. His often vicious references to Wieck in the correspondence of 1839, his violent hatred of Carl Banck, and his fierce anger at the men who courted her in Vienna indicate his all-too-human fears. His continuing envy of Clara's friendship with Mendelssohn plagued him for years. His letters during the summer of 1840, filled with criticisms, recriminations, and admissions of jealousy even toward such old friends as Johann Verhulst, reveal the strains he felt.[64]

The times Clara and Robert spent together in Berlin and Leipzig were the happiest during the long months of 1839 and 1840. They made music together, they walked, they talked—but not too much. Both found it easier to communicate through music or pen. They kissed and reveled in their physical proximity.

The court's decision came in July 1840, and though they had to wait ten more days to learn if Wieck would appeal, they began to look for an apartment in Leipzig. By July 16 they found one on Inselstrasse, and she began shopping for furnishings. They decided on September 12 for their wedding day—while she was still twenty years old, she wrote in her diary on July 19—but she added, "I am trembling and quivering about the coming day with both joy and anguish. I have hardly any mind left; I feel continuous anxiety and have never felt more exhausted. If only heaven preserves my health!"

By August they learned that the court had ruled entirely in their favor. A concert tour to nearby Thuringian towns was planned just before the first banns were published. Her last concert as Clara Wieck took place on September 5 in Weimar.

Her mother came from Berlin to join a group of loyal friends for the wedding, which Clara described as

> the most unforgettable day of my life. . . . My entire being was filled with thanks to Him who had finally brought us to one another over so many rocky barriers and chasms. My most fervent prayer was that He would preserve my Robert for me for many long years to come; oh, when the thought that I might lose him sometime comes over me, I feel I could go crazy. Heaven protect me from such a misfortune, I could not bear it.[65]

The wedding on September 12, the day before her twenty-first birthday, settled the conflict between father and lover. Filled with both joy and trepidation, she was now the wife of Robert Schumann.

On September 13, 1840, she made the last entry in her diary:

> Now a new life is beginning, a beautiful life, a life in which love for him is greater than all else, but difficult duties are nearing as well. Heaven grant me the strength to fulfill them faithfully, as a good wife should—He has always stood by me and always will. I have always had great faith in God and will preserve that faith forever.

CHAPTER 5

The Marriage

The marriage between Robert and Clara Schumann was unique in musical history. They were drawn together and remained together not only because of common musical experience, mutual emotional dependency, and physical attraction, but because their musical and creative needs complemented each other.

The early months of their marriage were the most joyful Clara had ever experienced. Her husband was both mother and father to the woman who had lost both: his tender, Eusebius side (the one she preferred) provided maternal warmth; his brilliant mind, creative genius, and sharp critical talent stimulated and inspired the young artist. And finally, her sexual fulfillment, after so many years of postponement, must have been an overwhelmingly joyful experience; the diaries and letters of this prudish age are silent on the subject.

Now that they were at last together, they began a journal, the *Ehetagebuch* (marriage diary), in which they vowed to write, alternating weekly. Diaries and journals were common, joint diaries less so but not unusual. Felix and Cécile Mendelssohn and Liszt and the countess d'Agoult were among other musicians who kept such chronicles. For the Schumanns, however, such a venture was particularly apt, since both had difficulty expressing their feelings in speech. Clara's reticence may have stemmed from her early years of silence. Robert's inarticulateness probably began as social diffidence, awkwardness, lack of confidence, but it continued past adolescence, gradually worsened, and during his later years became at times total speechlessness. He always spoke best with his pen; writing was his mode of expression, for words as well as music, and the marriage diary was to be the primary avenue for intimate communication between the two. It remains an important source of information about their daily life in Leipzig and about their visitors, providing a record of the vicissitudes of their emotional life, their thoughts on the music they composed, played, and heard, and "character studies of significant artists with whom we are in close contact."[1] Problems, complaints, fears—all were shared on the pages of the marriage diary.

For the next few months they kept to the plan of writing in alternate weeks, but as Robert became absorbed in his composing, the task became Clara's. Robert, who was extremely orderly, also kept household books—notebooks in which he entered household accounts and recorded his income, Clara's earnings, appointments, comments on music and people, and brief notes on his compositions and their dates. Over the years his note taking became increasingly compulsive. In 1846 he even began to record the dates on which he and Clara had sexual relations.

On December 5, 1840, Clara declared in the marriage diary, "We have been married a quarter of a year today, and it is the happiest quarter of a year of my life." There was, however, one "but" expressed: her sadness about the continued break with her father. The only contact between the two families was through lawyers, courts, and go-betweens. The slander suit (denunciation) initiated by Schumann on June 2, 1840, was not settled until April 1841, when the court ruled against Wieck.[2] On February 27, 1841, Clara's piano was delivered to her—the result of distressful negotiations conducted by a go-between.[3*] In August 1841, however, just before her first child, Marie, was born, Clara was forced to ask their old friend Ernst Adolph Becker to intercede in order to collect the 43 taler Wieck had agreed to pay for the shipping of the piano.[4]

Wieck had given up his Leipzig piano business and resettled as a voice and piano teacher in Dresden almost a year before his daughter's marriage, ostensibly because he wished to work with Johann Aloys Miksch, who was nearing the end of his long career as a voice teacher.[5] The healthier air in that city may also have figured in his decision to move. It is more than likely, however, that he felt he had to get away from Leipzig, which seemed to be filled with Schumann's friends. Wieck ignored the birthday greetings Clara sent him in August 1841; the note announcing the birth of his granddaughter was answered with a rude letter.[6] He continued to spread rumors about Schumann and his daughter; during Clara's solo trip to Copenhagen in March and April 1842, he told people that they had separated.[7] They feared he would return Clara's money in worthless notes, if at all. Wieck had no compunctions about making public his contempt for Schumann (even at the risk of another libel suit) and referred to his son-in-law's "Spring" Symphony as the "Symphony of Contradictions" (*Widerspruchssymphonie*).[8] Clara was all too aware of her father's behavior. In her report to Emilie List of the March 31 concert she wrote, "My husband's symphony [the "Spring" Symphony, no. 1 in B-flat major] triumphed over all the cabals and intrigues of Father. I have never heard a symphony receive such applause."[9]

In May 1842, however, after premieres of both the First and Second (the

*Major Serre, an old friend who lived near Dresden, took on this task.

latter was published in 1853 as the Fourth) symphonies, Wieck initiated efforts toward a rapprochement. Wieck had always considered the creation of a symphony to be the mark of a *real* composer (one of his complaints was that Schumann had been talking about a symphony for years but had not yet produced one); perhaps he weakened after Schumann composed two such works.

On a visit to Leipzig in May 1843, Wieck presented to a mutual friend a proposal for mediation of the differences between Schumann and himself. Schumann, finding his tone offensive and no doubt recalling the gossip Wieck had spread during Clara's Copenhagen visit, did not reply.

Well before the unsuccessful attempt in May, Wieck had tried again to effect a reconciliation with Robert. In a letter that Clara received on January 13, 1843, he said he was writing at the instigation of Clementine, his wife, "your best, noblest, truest, etc. friend." He admired Robert's diligence and creativity, he said, and hoped they would both visit him in Dresden, where his music studio and any other rooms in his home would be placed at their disposal for a performance of Robert's quintet. "The Dresdeners will come," he assured Clara, "if one attracts them with food or drink or music." He asked her to bring the baby along, reminding her that she would not have to pay for the baby on the train. Offering to meet them all at the railway station,* he assured her that there need be no discussion of the previous four years. "We have many other things to talk about." Wieck evidently wanted to wipe out the whole history of the conflict. He was so eager to see her, he wrote, that he would come to Leipzig if she could not get to Dresden. And he indicated some sensitivity about the reaction of other people to the Wieck-Schumann affairs. "Your husband will agree with me that we should not speak to anyone about all this. When people see us together, they will assume everything is all right."[10]

Robert's career was well under way; Clara, now a mother, was continuing to make headlines as a performer; and Wieck seems to have feared that he would be left out of their lives and successes. Clara grasped eagerly at this offer of reconciliation. She wrote a long and affectionate reply, dated two days after his letter, asking about his health and about her stepmother and stepsisters, describing her activities and Robert's new compositions.[11] Wieck visited her on February 3, 1843, and soon thereafter, on February 11—two months before Elise was born—she went to Dresden, alone, to see her family.[12]

This was the first of many short trips she made that year. After a private performance of the Schumann Quintet in Dresden on February 14, Clara wrote, "Father is now heart and soul [*Feuer und Flamme*] for Robert's compositions." Though she expressed great joy at the reconciliation, she was sick for three days on her return, possibly the result of the excitement and tensions of the Dresden visit.[13]

*A railroad line between Leipzig and Dresden, one of the first in Germany, was established in 1839.

Clara met with her father during a visit he made to Leipzig in May 1843 and saw him with new eyes:

> I didn't see much of Father; he was busy from morning till evening with instruments and Marie, who had to test them all. I am so used to a quiet, peaceful life with Robert that I could no longer be with Father, even for a short time. This frightful agitation, this restlessness of mind and body doesn't permit him—or anyone around him—to secure any kind of tranquil enjoyment of life.[14]

Schumann grumbled about Clara's visits to Dresden. Several times he was tempted to join her, but pride and memories held him back. A letter to his friend Johann Verhulst on June 19, 1843, sets out his feelings: "A reconciliation between Kl. and old W. has taken place; which I am glad of for Klara's sake. He is also trying to resume ties with me. But the man has no feelings; otherwise he would not attempt it. You can see, however, that the skies are gradually clearing and I am glad on Klara's account."[15]

The success of his oratorio *Das Paradies und die Peri* and its forthcoming Dresden production brought a note from Wieck (December 15, 1843) directly to Robert:

> Tempora mutantur et nos mutamur in eis.* With Clara and the world to consider we can no longer remain at a distance. You are yourself the father of a family—why do we need long explanations? We were always agreed as far as art is concerned—I was even your teacher—my verdict decided your career. I don't have to assure you of my appreciation of your talent and your fine and genuine endeavors. I await you in Dresden with joy. Your father.[16]

Finally, in December 1843, more than a year after Clara's reunion with her father, Schumann reluctantly agreed to meet with him, and after the *Peri* performances in Dresden, Clara and Robert spent Christmas with the Wiecks. The reunion was cool, however, and the relationship remained perfunctory. Clara never regained her trust in her father, and both she and Robert suspected bad faith for years after the reconciliation.

One other conflict ruffled the idyllic early months of the marriage, and the emotions aroused led to much discomfort and suppressed anger. Clara craved and for the most part received from Robert love, warmth, approval, and musical and intellectual inspiration, but he could not give her what had been part of her life for many years—full participation in the musical world, the opportunity for self-expression that making music provided, the adoration and admiration of an audience. Robert would have been happy to live quietly, to have Clara perform for him and perhaps some friends and provide a comfortable nest, like a conventional *Hausfrau.* For Clara, however, such a life was impossible, and the

*Times are changing and we are changing with them.

conflict permeated their married life. They rarely acknowledged this aspect of their relationship openly, but their children and friends were aware of it, and it is clearly revealed in their letters and diaries.

Schumann was, by and large, a devoted and thoughtful husband. He was generous and left the administration of the household to Clara: his household books record gifts and "extra" money for his wife almost every month; he registered his love and great pride in her playing and musicianship in the diary and in letters to friends. Yet her discomfort expressed itself in many ways: she was jealous of Robert's attentions to Amalie Rieffel, a student of his and the daughter of a friend; she was annoyed by her aunt Emilie Carl, her mother's sister, who she felt interfered in the running of the Schumann household; most distressing, and in the face of all evidence to the contrary, she had recurrent fears of losing Robert's love. In an entry beginning October 24, 1841, she wrote in their diary:

> I have had several unhappy days in which I really tormented my poor husband—I thought he didn't love me as much as he had during the first year [of our marriage]. I know very well that he has many things on his mind that vex him. I was very irritable and because of this gave myself many troubled hours.[17]

A year later, in November 1842, she wrote:

> An indescribable melancholy has taken hold of me for the last few days. I think you don't love me the way you used to. I often feel so clearly that I cannot satisfy you and at times it seems to me—when you are tender—that it is only because of your good heart, which does not wish to hurt me.[18]

The diary contains no response to these fears, and they seem to have subsided as her career took on larger dimensions.

During the Leipzig years they lived in the apartment on Inselstrasse, one flight up. Clara spent her time studying music, reading, playing (when it did not interfere with Robert's composing), entertaining visiting musicians, and keeping house with the help of several servants.* Almost every musician of note who passed through Leipzig visited them during the first year of their marriage. The list of visitors included Mendelssohn; the Dutch composer Johann Verhulst; their old friends Ernst Becker, Ernst Wenzel, and Moritz Reuter; the English composer William Sterndale Bennett; Walther von Goethe, the grandson of the poet; such local composers and publishers as Moritz Hauptmann and Robert Friese; the pianist and composer Adolph Henselt; the Norwegian violinist Ole Bull; the young pianists Amalie Rieffel and Harriet Parish, with their families;

*The wages of servants were exceedingly low. In the household books, we read that Schumann reckoned on a little over 3 taler (plus frequent tips) for three months' wages for the serving girl. In comparison, the wedding ring cost 6 taler, two bottles of champagne cost 4 taler, the bookbinder's fee for the special binding for *Myrthen,* the songs that were his wedding gift to Clara, was 3 taler, and rent for the apartment from September to Easter was 65 taler.

Heinrich Lichtenstein, a Berlin zoologist and music lover, with his family; and many others.

In a letter to her friend Dr. Adolph Keferstein, dated October 22, 1840, Clara described her situation:

> Allow me to send you a greeting and to present myself as a young married woman. Yes, we have finally achieved our greatest desire and enjoy great happiness. We love each other more every day and live only for each other. . . . We have so many musical pleasures now that our life is truly blissful. Moscheles was here last week and was honored by Mendelssohn in the Gewandhaus and by David, Kistner, etc., and we gave soirées in our homes.* It was a frantic time—something different every day. Now he has gone and we are awaiting Ole Bull, about whom I am very curious. He is an artist about whom many differing opinions prevail. Our Gewandhaus concerts have begun and have already given us two wonderful symphonies of Beethoven—the Eroica and the Fourth. Today there will be a Mozart symphony. In the soirée Mendelssohn gave to honor Moscheles, the Bach Triple Concerto was one of the works performed—played by Mendelssohn, Moscheles, and me.[19]

For a time the novelty of her situation satisfied her. In February 1841, the twenty-fourth week of her marriage, she wrote in the diary, "We are enjoying a happiness that I never knew. My father always mocked at the so-called domestic bliss. How I pity those who do not know it; they are only half alive."[20] Clara valued, too, the intellectual and musical growth of this period. The two musicians analyzed Bach fugues together, read Shakespeare and Goethe together, and composed, Clara with many reservations. Her first Christmas gift to her husband was a group of three songs on texts by Robert Burns and Heinrich Heine, composed at odd moments when her husband was out of the house and she could use the piano freely.

But another nagging problem disturbed the domestic bliss. In addition to Robert's responsibilities as editor of the *Neue Zeitschrift*, he was so engrossed in his composing that Clara made this plaintive entry at the end of January 1841:

> Robert has been very cold toward me the last few days. It is true that there may well be a happy basis for it, and no one can appreciate all he undertakes as much as I do, yet at times this coldness, which I have not deserved in the least, hurts me. Forgive me, dear Robert, for the complaint.[21]

More and more she began to feel shut out of his creative life. The frustration was intensified, of course, because she was not herself performing and could not even use the piano when Robert was working. Even a room and a piano of her own could not meet her needs.

*Ignaz Moscheles was a leading piano virtuoso and composer who had taught Mendelssohn and was his lifelong friend. Ferdinand David was a violin virtuoso, composer, teacher, and concertmaster of the Gewandhaus Orchestra. Friedrich Kistner was a Leipzig music publisher.

Robert, aware of the cost to her of his intense absorption, was not unappreciative. In February 1841 he wrote in the marriage diary:

> I could never say enough about all the love shown to me with such a willing heart by Clara during this time [while he was composing the First Symphony]. I could have sought among millions [without finding one] who, like her, treats me with so much forbearance and consideration.

But this was only an interlude; he shifted from self-absorption to gratitude again and again during the years to come.[22]

Today Schumann's early piano pieces are considered to be his greatest works: they were innovative, even revolutionary, a bold and exciting affirmation of the new romantic spirit; technically brilliant without mere superficiality, they explored new harmonies, colors, and metric patterns, opening the way to the new German romanticism. Yet Schumann (and Clara) firmly believed that it was necessary to prove oneself as a composer by writing orchestral works in the larger, extended forms.* The new head of household may also have been moved by practical considerations: recognition as a composer of symphonies would bring financial rewards as well as status. Whatever the reasons were—and he may have had many—he began sketches of symphonic works in the final months of his "year of song," and on January 23 threw himself into the creation of the B-flat "Spring" Symphony. She heard nothing of this symphony, which was composed and completed in a virtual frenzy—sketched in four days, orchestrated in ten—until it was performed for her and two old friends, Ernst Wenzel and Ernst Pfundt, on February 14, 1841.

Some of her frustration is evident in this two-edged diary entry of January 1841: "I must admit, my dear husband, I had not given you credit for such skill—you continually inspire me with new awe."[23] This backhanded compliment must have irked the composer, who had been exposed to similar tactless comments from Clara in the past. In 1838, for example, Clara had responded to his expressed intention of writing string quartets with the question ". . . do you really know the instruments well enough?"[24]

At the completion of the symphony, Schumann forgot his irritation and paid homage to Clara's understanding:

> Now, many sleepless nights are followed by exhaustion; what is happening to me is what might happen to a young woman who has just been delivered of a child—so light, so happy, and yet ill and weak. My Clara knows this very well, and is attending to me with doubled tenderness, which I will repay later.[25]

*In a letter of September 28, 1840, to Camille Stamaty, a French pianist and admirer, Schumann described his *Kinderscenen* as "mere bagatelles," not to be compared with works in the larger forms (Boetticher/1942, 347–48).

A concert on March 31, 1841, her first solo appearance since her marriage, was the great reward for her care and patience: it generated public acknowledgment of her husband as an important composer and—probably most important for her—provided the contact with the public that was so essential for her and that she had been craving. The occasion was a benefit concert conducted by Mendelssohn for the Gewandhaus Orchestra pension fund. In the history of music, this date is remembered as the premiere of Robert Schumann's First ("Spring") Symphony, but in Leipzig the orchestral masterpiece was only one of many works on the program and was overshadowed by Clara's reappearance in her native town.

Robert considered it an "unforgettable evening," and added, "My Clara played everything like a master and in such an inspired mood that everyone was enchanted."[26] Clara described the concert in a letter to her friend Emilie List:

> I was received with such enthusiasm that I went pale and red; it did not cease even when I had already seated myself at the piano. (I have never yet heard anyone received like this, not even Thalberg.) You can imagine that this gave me courage since I had been shaking all over with anxiety. I played as I can hardly ever remember having played. The applause after each piece did not end.[27]

Even before the March 31 concert, Schumann was deeply involved in new works, among them the Overture, Scherzo, and Finale, op. 52, the Phantasie in A Minor for piano and orchestra (later the first movement of the Piano Concerto), and the first version of the Symphony in D Minor. Plans for the oratorio *Das Paradies und die Peri* were under way, and once again Clara could not disturb him by practicing. "The more Robert involves himself with his art, the less I can do as an artist, Heaven knows! There are always interruptions, and small as our household is, I always have this and that to do and that robs me of my time," she wrote in the diary in May 1841.[28] She was unhappy, he felt guilty, but both agreed that his work had to take precedence.

Clara was not involved in the creation of any of his works, not even the works for piano that she later premiered. She was in a fever of anticipation and a little resentful on May 31, when she wrote:

> Yesterday he began a symphony once more. . . . I have not yet heard anything of it, but I see Robert's [creative] energy and often hear D minor sounding wildly from afar so that I already know it is a work created from the depths of his soul. Heaven is good to us. Robert cannot be any happier in composing than I am when he shows me such a work. Do you believe me, my Robert? You could well believe it.[29]

Complaints were confided (and probably confined) to the diary. On June 2, 1841, she wrote:

> My piano playing is falling behind. This always happens when Robert is composing. There is not even one little hour to be found in the whole day for myself! If only I don't fall too far behind. Score reading has also been given up once again, but I hope that it won't be for long this time. . . .[30]

She may have taken some comfort in the knowledge that the Phantasie was revealed to her first; she played it with the Gewandhaus Orchestra at a closed rehearsal on August 13, a week or two before Marie's birth. The occasion was a prepublication run-through of the "Spring" Symphony. She was so agitated with excitement and joy over the symphony, the Phantasie, and the opportunity to play that she reported in the marriage diary on August 14 that she was ill for days.

Almost exactly one year after their marriage, Clara gave birth to her first and best-loved child, Marie. The delivery was not difficult, and the firstborn was joyfully welcomed by both parents. In the next thirteen years Clara was to give birth to seven more children, but later ones did not receive the wholehearted reception conferred upon Marie. Clara conceived very easily, generally had uncomplicated pregnancies, and evidently made no attempt to prevent conception, though her husband must have been aware of some of the contraceptive methods in use at the time.

Schumann may have harbored some hopes that babies would put a halt to Clara's performances, but he did not reckon with her determination. The year 1842 brought a full-scale renewal of Clara's solo career. Once she realized that wetnurses were available, that the baby could be boarded with relatives, that an additional maid could be hired for a pittance, that motherhood did not necessarily tie her down, she wasted no time.* Clara composed, toured, played, and was feted as in the old days before marriage and childbearing. The schedule took its toll, but she knew she had to establish herself as Clara Schumann, pianist, as soon as possible. There was no lack of pianistic talent in the 1840s, and the twenty-two-year-old performer was already mindful of younger artists making their way to fame. Clara's fears of other artists were quite realistic. Notwithstanding the glowing comparisons of her playing with that of Franz Liszt, Sigismund Thalberg, and Camilla Pleyel, and the musical growth during her marriage, she could not compete with these virtuosi unless she remained in the public eye. Nor was she any longer a child prodigy or young girl. She greeted the news of the mushrooming career of the eleven-year-old Anton Rubinstein politely but with some trepidation. In January 1842 she wrote to Emilie List that she had heard he was "supposed to be the greatest genius born in a long time."[31]

Conscious of such rivals' threats to her career, she accepted all invitations to perform. In all she gave at least fifteen concerts between January 1 and April

*A wetnurse was hired for about six months for each Schumann baby. The expenditures are noted in the household books.

25, 1842. And all this activity created a grave crisis. In those years a woman, even a married woman, could not travel alone. Robert had to accompany her on most of the tours. He did not relish the role of traveling companion and manager, and though his works for both piano and orchestra were always performed on her programs, he was uncomfortable about leaving home and child, his editorial responsibilities, and the peace and quiet required for creative work. He was almost always ill in the weeks preceding their tours—a possible consequence of his conflicting emotions.[32]

The concerts in nearby Weimar in November 1841, in which Clara played solos in the first half and his new symphony was performed in the second, were gratifying to both. In accepting the invitation, Robert proudly wrote to the conductor, "My wife requests that her maiden name be omitted from the announcement of the concert; she wants to be called by my name, once for all, and I love her all the more for it."[33] But the decision to accept invitations from Bremen and Hamburg involved more problems. This would be a longer journey, and plans had to made for care of Marie, now six months old (she was sent to stay with Schumann's brother in Schneeberg) and for a replacement at the *Neue Zeitschrift*. Schumann was pleased with the conducting of Friedrich Wilhelm Grund, the leader of the Hamburg Philharmonische Gesellschaft, and he enjoyed his status as a recognized composer. An incident in Oldenburg, however, a duchy about seventy-five kilometers from Bremen, unnerved him. Robert's entry in the marriage diary tells the story: "February 26. Clara rode to the court and returned, overjoyed at her reception. The thought of my undignified position in such situations did not permit me to feel any pleasure."[34] In short, she was the only one to be invited.

The difficulty was compounded by Clara's decision to accept a long-deferred invitation to play in Copenhagen, though her husband could not accompany her. Even Clara felt uncomfortable about the situation. Many months later, her guilt still had not subsided when she wrote, on May 30, 1842, a long explanation to her friend Emilie List:

> Yes, I really did go to Copenhagen alone (that is, without Robert, but with a lady from Bremen)*, separated from him, but this shall never happen again, God willing. I will explain the whole thing to you so that you will understand. . . . As the time approached, Robert realized more and more the impossibility of leaving his paper in strange hands for perhaps another two months; the three weeks for which he had arranged were over, and so we decided to give up the journey; but I weighed the whole thing—I am a woman, am not neglecting anything at home, earn nothing, why shouldn't I use my talent for once to contribute my mite to Robert? Could anyone blame me for this? Or my husband for going home to his child and his business?[35]

Copenhagen was an overnight journey over the water—a frightening prospect for the landbound Leipzigers. Clara had many misgivings, particularly

*Marie Garlichs, niece of Emma Eggers, née Garlichs.

when illness and a storm forced a postponement of her journey from Kiel to Copenhagen. While she waited for the right weather for the boat, concerts were quickly arranged in Lübeck, Kiel, and Hamburg. Her Hamburg friends were astonished at her determination, she wrote in the marriage diary:

> Several times my courage deserted me; I thought that heaven had sent me all these troubles [illness, storms etc.] to dissuade me from my plans, but I thought of Robert, and my wish to contribute my mite through my talents and the joyful reunion after a successful journey. . . .[36]

The reception in Copenhagen more than made up for her frustrations. She was there from March 20 to April 18 and performed seven times. She met Hans Christian Andersen, the composer Niels Wilhelm Gade, and the Danish royal family, enjoyed great acclaim, and earned large sums of money.

In all the marital disputes over her career, the question of money loomed large. "We need more than we earn," Robert wrote in February 1843.[37] They both knew she could earn more in one three-week concert tour than Schumann obtained from composing and editing in a year. Glorying in her skill as a performing artist and manager, this daughter of Friedrich Wieck never considered that her husband's pride might suffer. Independent, proud, and determined, she persisted in her professional career and savored both the money and the fame.

Robert's letters from Leipzig were melancholy, but she did not receive them until she was well into the Copenhagen triumphs. Though she wrote to Schumann daily, the separation proved to be an almost unbearable strain for him. The diary and household books are filled with such comments as "Miserable life," "Drank a frightful amount," "Leading a bad life."[38] He drank too much, borrowed money from friends, and wrote his wife:

> Leipzig, March 13 [1842]
> My dear Clara, do you still recognize this handwriting? What a mood I am in. I already regret having allowed you to part from me and I have to listen to the most unkind judgments about it. Your father is here now and running all over town. Early this morning Dr. Reuter told me about it—at first I was quite beside myself, now I have collected my thoughts and know that I have behaved as a proper family man and businessman. . . . You are probably arriving in Copenhagen this very hour. The weather here is mild, yet I am fearful; was it rough during your crossing? . . . It is really sad in our home; everything seems to ask me, "Where is your good Clara?," even the flowers at the window. . . . Otherwise, nothing much has happened. . . . I found many letters when I came, but nothing of significance. My symphony is supposed to be given in Breslau on the seventh . . . and also in Dresden, just about now. . . . I am thinking of America again; you consider it too. Your mother in Berlin was very much in favor of it.

Leipzig, March 16
Still no news from you, my Clara. Have you forgotten me already? Yesterday I could hardly bear the melancholy that overwhelmed me. This desolation in the house; this emptiness in me! *Letting you go was one of the most foolish things I ever did* in my life and it certainly won't happen again. Nothing tastes good or right. On top of that, I am really not well at all—and am tormented by the worst cold—and without music. But if a letter came from you, I would be better. Reuter acts very peculiarly toward me, as if I had committed a crime in letting you go alone. So I scold him. . . . And then the dummies here think that one must travel over icebergs to get to Copenhagen and that you are traveling by reindeer. . . . I will not let you go to Stockholm . . . or at least only if I can come with you. Do you play for small groups sometimes? That always makes an artist popular. . . . I intend to make up my mind about America by the end of April. Reuter urges it strongly. It depends on you.

March 24
. . . I am calmer now and a little bit more used to our lonely life. . . . May the sacrifice be worth it and bring you satisfaction as an artist. You are still so young and I can scarcely blame you for not wanting to be forgotten as an artist after working so hard in your youth—in a word—you can still enjoy giving people pleasure through your lovely talent. . . . What about America? It must be decided by the end of April.

Leipzig, April 1
I read your letters three, four times over, and know them by heart. Your handwriting looks so firm and steadfast . . . otherwise everything is quite still in our household. Emilie [the maid] is a diligent and unassuming girl . . . we really speak very little. She may very well consider me severe and morose. . . . I am rejoicing at the coming of spring. . . . Then we will discuss the future too. . . . Yesterday I laid out our whole position clearly for myself . . . on paper—with figures. . . . We don't have to worry at all; we still have enough money. But a change must take place this year. Don't write to Emilie [List] about America. The thought just occurred to me to write an acquaintance there who is also very musical. I shall get some information and wait for an answer. The step is too enormous. . . . Write to me right away about your concert, what you played, how you were received, send me the newspapers that have some words about you. I would like everyone here to know about it. . . . *I have to scold you, however: you write so little about yourself as an artist, where you have played and whether you were understood.*

April 14
Perhaps you are on the sea now. . . . The sky here is somewhat overcast, yet the weather is gentle and there is no strong wind. I hope it is the same on your boat. May our loving heaven lead us to each other soon. Your last letter with the news from the papers delighted me immensely, as do all your and my joys. It cheers me up, which I need. A few days ago I was frightfully angry. I'll tell you about it later. Listen, [August] Cranz [a music publisher] in Hamburg is a

miserable fellow and a gossip. . . . He reported the dumbest blather to Hofmeister—who then told it to David—and now it is making the rounds, e.g., that I left you in Hamburg *sick*—that we ran up debts in Hamburg, that nobody liked you there, and all sorts of things like that. I was beside myself. . . . When you get to Hamburg now, . . . go to his wife and tell her calmly, but with all the pride of which you are capable, your and our opinions [of such talk]. Cläre, I beg you, play with all imaginable care and genius so that such shameful gossip will be disproved. Your honor as an artist is as dear to me as your honor as a woman, and I must and can rely on you in all things. . . .

April 22
I wanted to write to you yesterday, but was so sick with a horrible anger that I could not. Your father has told all of Dresden that we *were separated*. On many days, like today, for example, which is so wonderfully blue, one can laugh at such baseness, but on others it can embitter the heart and I have had many days like that.[39]

America seemed to offer solutions to many of their problems. By 1842 the New World had become both a refuge and a land of plenty for Europeans. Many Germans had already emigrated to the United States; others hoped to go for a short time, make a fortune, and then return. The Schumanns were toying with the latter idea, since many friends and acquaintances had already braved the Atlantic and returned prosperous and safe. Emilie List's father, for example, had fled with his family for political reasons and acquired U.S. citizenship. As a child, Pauline García had lived in New York City, where her parents established the first Italian opera company in the New World. And well before the big German emigration of 1848, European artists were enthusiastically received and highly paid in New York, Boston, Philadelphia, Charleston, New Orleans. Reports of events in the United States appeared regularly in the German newspapers. In just a few years, Jenny Lind, introduced to the New World by the great showman Phineas T. Barnum, was to be paid close to $1,000 a concert plus expenses for a staff that included companion, secretary, two servants, and a carriage.[40]

The Schumanns began to think about America during their trip to Hamburg and Bremen (the port from which many émigrés left). An American tour of a year or two, they thought, might enable them to earn enough money to live well for the rest of their lives. By March 6, 1842, however, Robert wrote his friend Theodor Töpken, "The American plans have receded into the background somewhat. The gulf that separates it from home is just too enormous."[41] But they continued to think about America as they searched for solutions to the problems of finances and competing careers.*

*Although Clara and Robert Schumann never made the journey across the Atlantic, their daughter Elise lived in New York for several years after her marriage, and three of her children were born here and thus were U.S. citizens. Several other grandchildren and great-grandchildren also settled in the United States. Many descendants still make their home in this country.

Schumann was happiest when Clara could settle down for a few months, as she did on her return to Leipzig in April 1842, to the life he had envisioned before their marriage: *Hausfrau*, mother, hostess, student (with Robert she began to study the string quartets of Haydn and Mozart). The housewife grumbled a bit to Emilie List about Robert's unwillingness to have her leave home to perform while he stayed home. She repeated again to Emilie that she wanted to use her talent to help out financially, but Robert would not hear of it.[42]

Robert was working again, with feverish intensity and speed, in still another genre: this was his year for chamber music. Within a few months he wrote three string quartets and two works for strings and piano: the piano quartet and the piano quintet, both premiered by Clara. But, as before, Clara heard only faint and frustrating glimmerings of the music as he worked on it, and she was unable to practice or compose while he did so.

Almost always a period of intense creation was followed by a depression, during which Robert was unable to work. He referred to such episodes as "weakness of the nerves." On February 17, 1843, he wrote in the diary that Clara was giving him "tender care," though she was once again pregnant, expecting a child in April 1843.[43] Robert's depression, of short duration, was followed by another phase of violent activity. He accepted a position as professor of piano and score reading in the newly established Leipzig Conservatory of Music and took up his duties there in April 1843. At the same time he began work on *Das Paradies und die Peri* (completed in a few short months) and continued his writing and editorial work on the *Zeitschrift*.

By 1843 Schumann was gaining some recognition for his orchestral works in European musical circles. His works were played in several German cities, and champions in Paris, Brussels, Amsterdam, Copenhagen, and Vienna saw to it that his pieces were performed for connoisseurs, if not for the general public. His status as a writer and critic was recognized as well. Despite this success, however, money was still a problem, and a teaching position represented a certain amount of financial security.

The Leipzig Conservatory was from its inception a school of the first rank. Founded by Mendelssohn during the period that saw the spread of professional music education, it drew students from the entire musical world. Edvard Grieg was one of the hundred Norwegian students who attended, and Arthur Seymour Sullivan was an early representative from Great Britain.*

Professional music training in Europe developed in the aftermath of the French Revolution. The Paris Conservatoire, founded in 1795, became the model for similar institutions in Milan, Bologna, Prague, and London. Up until the establishment of the Leipzig Conservatory, the first modern school of its

*The roster of foreign students is truly impressive. In the period 1843–68, for example, there were 109 students from Great Britain (73 male, 36 female), 90 from Russia (67 male, 23 female), 85 from North America (68 male, 17 female), and one from South America and California (grouped together). See Emil Kneschke, *Das Conservatorium der Musik in Leipzig: Seine Geschichte, seine Lehrer und Zöglinge* (Leipzig: Breitkopf & Härtel, 1868), 69–70.

kind in Germany, professional training was not organized. Most musicians learned from family members, were apprenticed to musicians, or studied privately with a succession of teachers. Clara Wieck's education, for example, with teachers from Leipzig, Dresden, and Berlin, was not unusual. (It *was* remarkable, of course, for a girl to undertake such systematic instruction in so many branches of the art, but she had her father's ambition and good pedagogical sense to thank for that.)

Schumann had joined in many of the preliminary discussions about the conservatory, but the moving force was Mendelssohn, who poured his time and organizational talents into the new venture. Schumann noted its founding in the marriage diary on February 17, 1843:

> The establishment of the music school . . . will certainly be productive for us too. I look forward to its beginning as a musician and doubtless it will also be a support for good music and will have a significant influence on the entire education of German youth. The teachers who have been named are Mendelssohn, [Ferdinand] David, [Moritz] Hauptmann, [Christian August] Pohlenz, [Carl Ferdinand] Becker, and me. Later Clara will also teach when she can, as they say, offer lessons with some degree of regularity.[44]*

Schumann hoped to teach composition as well as piano, but apparently he was not a successful teacher. When he was depressed or "melancholy," as he put it, he found it difficult to speak. Even at his best he was not a talker. Students complained that he would sit through a lesson or rehearsal and rarely say a word, even when there was a clear need for a comment or criticism.[45]

The premiere of *Peri* in December 1843 entailed additional responsibilities for the Schumanns. Though Clara did not hear the work until it was completed (she complained in the diary in April 1843, "Robert has completed the second part of *Peri* but shared little of it with me"),[46] she was called on to arrange the piano-vocal score and be with him at rehearsals. Rehearsals and the first performance were conducted by Schumann, making his debut as a conductor. Though he had avoided such positions in the past—probably because of his inexperience with the orchestra—he could not always refuse, and after accepting the challenge of conducting *Peri,* he was satisfied with his work. Gradually he accepted more offers and eventually assumed the musical directorship of several musical organizations. He could handle performances without difficulty but his inability to communicate during rehearsals was a continuing handicap. Clara's first inkling of this problem came in a letter from her friend Livia Frege, the leading soprano in the premiere of *Peri:* "If only your dear husband could resolve to scold a little and to demand greater attention, everything would go better right away."[47] It was the first of many such appeals to Clara.

Though Clara did not take her place at the conservatory until later, her own

*Clara was in an advanced state of pregnancy at the time.

professional activities did not cease. Maternal cares and pregnancy had not prevented her from performing at the Gewandhaus on October 2, 1842; on January 8, 1843, at a special Schumann matinee; and on February 2 and 9. After Elise's birth in April, she played twice more in Leipzig, and gave several concerts in Dresden. Though the trip to Dresden was short—only a few hours on the new railway that linked Leipzig and the capital—Robert's daily letters during her absences indicate his constant need for her and dependence on her:

> [February 12, 1843] There is a strange silence in the house, but it seems to me that your dear spirit is everywhere. . . . I was very sorry for the poor papa; he was depressed. Marie is well; when she hears the word "Mama" she waves her hand sadly as if she knew you were gone.[48]

In September both children were with her, and the "poor papa" wrote:

> The weather was so beautiful. I thought of you often, especially last night at 6:30. When I don't have you, I bring out old diaries and read them. Yesterday I read yours from the Paris days until late at night. What an exciting life we led then—it often sounds like a novel to me. But there are also many beautiful memories, are there not? . . . Otherwise, everything is quiet around me. The sun shines full into the window, but the air is cool, the sky wonderfully blue. Today I finally wrote to Herr von Bielke [of the Weimar court] and the grand duchess and am glad to be free of that matter. I would have preferred to dedicate the quintet to you, but, I thought, princely roses are also not to be despised.* However, I intend the first opera to be yours.[49]
>
> [November 14, 1843] Dr. Härtel was just here and offered me the editorship of the *Allgemeine musikalische Zeitung*. . . . I did not reject it right off because there is much to be said for it—but I did ask for time to think it over. . . . I just told Dr. Härtel that in any case I would not want to take over the editorship between New Year and July 1844, since I was going to be traveling with you and wanted to have a half year for myself, just for once.[50]

A letter of November 19 shows his need for her counsel: "If only you were here! . . . Drop me a line tomorrow, so I will know exactly where I am and how long I can put off Härtel because I *absolutely* must talk it over with you." A few days later he wrote, "I must consult with you about so many things: about Härtel, about my plans for the future, about *Peri*."[51]

Occasionally Schumann expressed some guilt about depriving his wife of a full career as a musician. On February 17, 1843, he wrote in the diary that she had composed some fine songs and piano works. After she presented him with a number of songs on his thirty-third birthday, he noted on June 28, 1843, that she seemed melancholy and added that he suspected it was because she could

*The quintet was dedicated to her after all.

not buy him fine gifts. At the same time, however, he expressed the conviction that she was happiest in her role as a mother. And in the marriage diary, at least, Clara did not contradict him.

On January 25, 1844, the Schumanns started on another great journey to the north, the journey to which Robert referred in November when he was negotiating with Härtel. After initial reluctance and much vacillation, he agreed to a Russian concert tour, not only for Clara's sake and the extra income it might bring but because he mistakenly thought it would give him time to compose and the opportunity to refresh himself after the hectic activities of the previous year. He felt unwell almost until the day they left, and he had such ambivalent feelings about the trip that Clara, at her wits' end, went to see Mendelssohn for advice.[52] Evidently Mendelssohn was able to persuade Robert, for on January 6 he finally agreed to go. Marie and Elise were left with Robert's brother and sister-in-law in Schneeberg.

For Clara this trip was no sudden fancy. Clara had longed to tour Russia even before her marriage. In the fall of 1840 Schumann had announced Russian plans in a letter to Liszt, but Robert's work, Clara's ill health in the months immediately following the wedding, and above all the news that Liszt's Russian tour would coincide with theirs caused a postponement. In November 1840, Count Aleksei Fedorovich Lvov, director of the Russian Imperial Chapel, offered his help in any trip they should undertake, but advised against an attempt to compete with Liszt, an established favorite in Russia.[53]

Historically, St. Petersburg had always been a mecca for Western European artists. In the late eighteenth century Catherine the Great, herself a German princess, inaugurated a "glorious epoch" by inviting such Italian composers as Baldassare Galuppi, Giovanni Paisiello, Giuseppe Sarti, and Domenico Cimarosa to St. Petersburg. The Russian aristocrats, raised by English, German, and French governesses, denigrated Russian culture and depended on Italian, French, and German troupes for concerts, dance, and opera. Even during the repressive regime of Nicholas I (1825–55), literature and the arts flourished, and foreigners were greeted with passionate enthusiasm. Vladimir Stassov, a Russian writer on music, reminisced, "In those days, the Russian ruble had a very good clink to German ears; it was customary for such musical luminaries as Liszt, Thalberg, [Giuditta] Pasta, [Pauline García] Viardot, . . . and others to come."[54] Ferdinand David, the Leipzig concertmaster and a good friend of the Schumanns, had spent six years in Dorpat, a Germanic outpost in what was then Livonia, now Estonia, as the first violinist of a resident string quartet at the estate of a wealthy baron (whose daughter he later married). Pauline Viardot had made a smashing debut with an Italian opera company just a few weeks before the Schumanns arrived in St. Petersburg. Clara's brother Alwin, later employed in a St. Petersburg theater orchestra as a violinist, was living in Reval, on the Gulf of Finland. And during their tour the Schumanns were assisted by two old friends, Adolph von Henselt and Heinrich

Romberg, both well-known German musicians who had established themselves in Russia.

Clara, with her amazing stamina, had no difficulty with the rigors of a Russian tour in midwinter. She described several weeks of cold, exhausting travel by coach and sleigh through forests, over frozen rivers, huddled under furs and rugs, and stopping at uncomfortable and dirty inns. Arising at three o'clock in the morning in order to be under way by four, she gave solo concerts without supporting artists day after day in Königsberg, Tilsit, Riga, Mitau, and Dorpat (and intended to continue in this way, she wrote to her father).[55] They almost froze, but Clara, exhilarated and fulfilled, pressed on.

Robert did not fare so well. He fell ill in Dorpat and during the entire trip never fully recovered. Suffering from cold, fever, aches, and pains, from anxiety and melancholia, he did not consider the tour a success, despite several charming letters to his father-in-law. Three doctors who were consulted in Dorpat diagnosed "nerve fever." Clara described him as weak, sick, sad, and angry. He was insulted by a gesture of the baron von Liphardt, who had invited them to dinner in Dorpat. After Clara had played for the assembled guests, Liphardt pressed 150 rubles into his hand. Schumann was furious and Clara had to convince him it would be best not to return the money.[56]

He recovered somewhat and they went on to St. Petersburg, but there he was unable to accompany her on her rounds of visits to ministers, officials, and the court. (She went with Henselt.) On their way to Moscow they detoured to Tver to visit Schumann's uncle, a seventy-one-year-old surgeon who had emigrated to Russia forty years earlier. The journey to Tver was extraordinarily difficult and more than once Robert thought he would faint. He was still weak and suffering from attacks of vertigo when they arrived in Moscow. The worst of his physical sufferings gradually subsided, but not before one frightening episode when he could not see and believed he was going blind. While he rested in their hotel room and wrote poetry (composing music was out of the question), his wife, animated and energetic, visited institutions and potential patrons, practiced, and gave several concerts.

Clara earned a great deal of money—close to 6,000 taler, of which almost 3,000 was clear profit—and was much acclaimed on the Russian tour.[57] She performed for the tsar and tsarina in the Winter Palace (which seemed like a "fairy tale in the Thousand and One Nights"),[58] gave many brilliant concerts, and on March 5, 1844, was made an honorary member of the St. Petersburg Philharmonic Society.

Though Schumann traveled to Russia primarily for Clara's sake, he was gratified to find that he was greeted respectfully by such influential connoisseurs as Count Mikhail Wielhorski and the princess Elena Pavlovna, and letters and documents hint that he would have been welcome to stay on and continue his career there. But the flattering attention and compliments did little to overcome his severe depression.

A man who met the Schumanns at a soirée given by the composer and conductor Count Aleksei Fedorovich Lvov described them as he saw them that evening:

> Schumann was, as usual, silent and withdrawn the whole evening. He spoke very little and just murmured incomprehensibly to the questions put by Count Wielhorski and the host, A. F. Lvov. Something like a conversation developed with the famous violinist [Wilhelm Bernhard] Molique, who had just arrived in St. Petersburg a few days earlier, but it was carried on in whispers, without life and vivacity. Most of the time Schumann sat in a corner near the piano . . . with a sunken head, his hair hanging in his face; he had a pensive expression on his face, and it looked as if he were about to whistle to himself. That night Schumann looked to me exactly like the life-size statue by Donndorf.* Clara Schumann was a little more talkative; she answered all the questions for her husband. In her playing, she proved herself to be a great artist with masculine energy and feminine instinct in interpretation and execution, although she was only twenty-five or twenty-six years old.† But one could hardly characterize her as a gracious or sympathetic woman. They both spoke French with Saxon accents and German like true Leipzigers.[59]

It seems clear that Robert was in serious trouble, certainly the worst since his marriage—aptly described by John Daverio as in "a debilitated physical and psychological state."[60] And it is equally clear that Clara did not face up to the situation. Practicing, performing, visiting, sightseeing, she was a self-absorbed concert artist on tour, and considered it her primary duty to carry on with her commitments. He, of course, could not bring himself to articulate his despair, and so, on their return, she was surprised to find that Robert had written in his travel diary: "Almost unbearable suffering and Clara's conduct!" She recorded this line in the marriage diary and added:

> I know of nothing, but it seems to me now, as I read through the notebooks, that I frequently provoked Robert's anger though it was certainly never done intentionally, but only because of my own awkwardness and because I am slow. It often takes quiet deliberation on my part to understand what other, wiser souls may see in a moment.[61]

A few days later, however, she seemed to have forgotten she had ever written this as she related to Emilie List the triumphs she had enjoyed and the money she had earned. Robert's illness was not even mentioned.[62]

As Robert's illnesses and depressions became more frequent, it was difficult to overlook his obviously disquieting behavior. For a long time Clara simply assumed more responsibilities without acknowledging the situation. A few

*Adolph Donndorf created a statue of Schumann for his tombstone.
†She was in fact only twenty-three.

months after their return from Russia, Robert was so ill that he took to his bed, and she had to recognize that drastic action was necessary.

The return to Leipzig and reunion with the children brought mixed feelings to Clara. She had left the heady world of the glamorous star and had to function as wife, homemaker, and mother once more. Schumann had to make a decision about the journal. Ten years old, it had achieved international recognition and even some financial success, but the composer realized that his own creative work was suffering. His hopes, standards, and goals for the *Neue Zeitschrift* had remained high, and he put it aside with some reluctance but also with relief. In June 1844 Oswald Lorenz became the editor of the *Neue Zeitschrift* and Schumann severed his connections with the periodical.

In August 1844 Clara joined Robert on the faculty of the Leipzig Conservatory, but their teaching was interrupted when Robert suffered a severe physical and mental breakdown. They took a short trip to the Harz Mountains. Several other cures were attempted, but Robert became so weak that he could barely walk across the room. It was no longer simply a "nervous" condition; he had pains, he trembled, he wept, he could not sleep. Clara, by this time pregnant with her third child, abandoned plans for another concert trip and devoted herself to Robert and his health. They decided to visit Dresden, perhaps for better air, perhaps for diversion. He was very weak on the journey and in Dresden "there were eight terrible days. Robert didn't sleep at night, his imagination created the most frightening pictures, in the mornings I usually found him bathed in tears, he gave up completely," she wrote in the diary. Wieck's presence in Dresden must have exacerbated the situation, as he tried to "rouse Robert forcibly."[63] They moved from a hotel to private lodgings and then took an apartment.

Clara fulfilled some concert engagements in Halle and Leipzig. After a rather precipitous decision to leave Leipzig permanently and settle in Dresden, events moved quickly. Their friends arranged a farewell musical evening for them. The Mendelssohn Octet was performed (twelve-year-old Joseph Joachim, Ferdinand David's prize pupil, was one of the players); Livia Frege, the first Peri, sang; and Clara played duets with Mendelssohn. After a public performance at the Gewandhaus on December 5 and a farewell matinee a few days later, the Schumanns bade farewell to Leipzig, the city where Clara was born, where her talent had been recognized and nurtured, the city where she had first faced the world as a concert artist.

CHAPTER 6

The Dresden Years

Why Dresden? The Schumanns must have asked themselves this question often; certainly their friends puzzled over the move from Leipzig, the musical capital, to the baroque court city of Dresden. The years in the Saxon capital began in sickness and anxiety and continued through many illnesses and disappointments. During those years Schumann composed many of his great works, but the feverishly exalted creative periods were interspersed with serious depressions that forced his wife to take on increasing responsibilities. Clara's health and stamina carried her forward as she continued her own concert career, aided her husband artistically, emotionally, and financially, bore four more children during the five years they lived in Dresden, supervised a household that included three servants, and composed her best works. In a letter of May 15, 1848, to Emilie List, she apologized for not writing because

> every minute of the day was taken up with giving 2 or three lessons (an hour each), practicing (one hour), writing in the diary, working on a piano arrangement [for Robert], walking for at least an hour with Robert, providing for the children, studying English with a student from Plymouth, not to mention the visits that must be made and received.[1]

Clara Schumann's basic character changed little after adolescence, but the Dresden years fixed firmly the conscientious, dutiful seriousness mixed with some bitterness (and doubtless some resentment) with which she performed her duties.

The move from Leipzig, the city they both loved, is difficult to comprehend. During the years Schumann had lived in Leipzig, the Gewandhaus Orchestra had been brought to the highest level in Europe, the conservatory was off to a triumphant start, the Leipzig music journals circulated throughout the world, and Leipzig's music publishing houses maintained their reputation as the most prestigious in Europe. The libraries and multitude of readers were matters of pride for Leipzig's citizens. Schumann boasted, "Liszt, the spoiled darling of the aristocracy, arrived and complained continually of the absence of fine dresses and of countesses and princesses, so that I was annoyed, and told him that we too had our own aristocracy here, namely, 150 bookstores, 50 printing establishments, and 30 newspapers."[2]

Henry F. Chorley, an English traveler, described Leipzig as a quaint, cheerful, friendly town that had no court "to stiffen its social circles into formality, or to hinder its presiding spirits from taking free way. . . . It possesses a University to stir its intelligences, a press busy and enterprising, and a recurrence of those gatherings which bring a representative of every class in society in Europe together."[3] From Dresden, in October 1844, Schumann wrote a friend, "Leipzig remains the most important city for music and I would advise every young talent to go where one hears so much good music."[4]

The reasons for the hurried move were ostensibly related to Robert's health; Dresden was generally considered to have a salubrious environment. Situated on the broad and beautiful Elbe, ringed by gently rolling hills, it had better air and more scenic beauty than Leipzig. There was little commerce, industry, or manufacturing in Dresden in the 1840s. One has only to recall the imposing baroque churches and palaces, the royal galleries, the gardens and promenades, all vividly portrayed in Canaletto's paintings, to see instantly why Dresden, the seat of a kingdom for many hundreds of years, was known as "the Florence of Germany."

Schumann's doctor had originally recommended a trip to Dresden because other treatments had failed. And though Robert was ill and depressed during his first few weeks there, he decided to remain. It has been suggested that Schumann was offended because he had not been considered for the post of Gewandhaus director while Mendelssohn was away in Berlin, but as Schumann had never indicated any desire to take over a position that required so much administrative work and so many public appearances, this conjecture seems unlikely. Moreover, he had just given up the *Zeitschrift* (undoubtedly a traumatic decision) so that he could devote all his time to composition.

One can speculate on another reason for the move. Robert was ill, could not make decisions, was unable to conduct, teach, or even compose. Clara was pregnant again. Father Wieck was in Dresden. The recent reconciliation had obscured the bitter memories and they remembered only the father, the man of strength and character. At this juncture in their lives, they may have entertained the illusion that Wieck would serve as a protector in the new sanctuary.

Dresden had, of course, many pleasant associations for them. As a ten-year-old, Clara had given her first concerts outside the home circles here and had attracted the attention of influential and wealthy music lovers among the court circles. The estate of Major Serre and his wife, Friederike, at Schloss Maxen, near the city, had long been a refuge for the Wieck family; Clara had spent many vacations there. Other friends in Dresden included the Kaskels, whose home she had been visiting in 1836 during the first major conflict with her father over Robert; Carl Kraegen, a pianist, an old friend of her father and a great admirer of Robert's work; Wolf August von Lüttichau, the intendant of the court theater; and Carl Gottlieb Reissiger, now the kapellmeister, with whom she had been sent to study the summer Robert and Ernestine were engaged.

In Dresden, stylishness and luxury were highly valued; and though in the past Dresden had had its share of musical luminaries—Heinrich Schütz and Johann Adolph Hasse, for example—the Schumanns found that music took second place to literature and the plastic and graphic arts. Moreover, musical life was dominated by the tastes of the aristocracy, who traditionally patronized the court chapel and opera. Dresden was proud of the reputation of Carl Maria von Weber, who had been appointed kapellmeister in 1817 and was the first to develop German opera in that Italianate city. Richard Wagner, who joined the opera staff in 1842, was in Dresden during the first few years the Schumanns lived there, but Clara saw little of him.

The Schumann circle was small; it included Ferdinand Hiller, composer and conductor, their closest friend among the musicians; Wilhelmine Schröder-Devrient, a singer greatly admired by both Clara and Robert; and Franz and Friedrich Schubert, the Dresden concertmaster and his cellist brother, with whom Clara later instituted a regular series of chamber concerts. Aside from Hiller, however, they were neither welcomed by nor felt comfortable with the local musicians. Their closest friends were artists, painters, and sculptors. Schumann's music—romantic and "modern"—had few adherents in Dresden, and he made no secret of his low opinion of his musical colleagues.

Fortunately, Leipzig was only a four-hour train ride away, and Clara took frequent advantage of the proximity to her native town. Thoughts of Leipzig were always with them. A year after the move to Dresden, when they visited Leipzig for a concert, Robert wrote to Hiller, "The life and people here certainly do cheer us up considerably. Sooner or later, I really think we shall settle down here again."[5] They never did.

The Schumanns began a joint study of fugue and counterpoint in January 1845, after Robert's illness of the autumn, and continued through the next few months, ignoring the doctor's advice to stay away from music. During these few months his "nervous illness" waxed and waned. "Gloomy demons possessed me," he wrote to the Dutch composer Johann Verhulst on May 28, 1845. "Now it is better and I am working again, something that had been quite impossible for months."[6] But in that same May, Clara wrote in the diary, "Robert's nerve trouble will not lessen," and in July he himself wrote to Mendelssohn, "I have so much to tell you. What an awful winter I had with a terrible nervous languor accompanied by a host of terrible thoughts that nearly brought me to despair; but things look better now—music is again beginning to sound within me, and I hope to be recovered soon."[7]

From the beginning of the Dresden years to 1849, the Schumanns' letters and diaries read like catalogues of misery. He was not self-conscious about his illness or averse to Clara's discussing it. Indeed, much of our information about his mood variations comes from Robert's letters to friends. In September

1845 he wrote to Mendelssohn, "Hofrath [Dr.] Carus has recommended early-morning walks, which do me a great deal of good but I am not yet myself, and every day I suffer . . . in a hundred different places. A mysterious complaint—when the doctor tries to take hold of it, it seems to disappear."[8]

On December 3, 1849, during the negotiations for a position in Düsseldorf (which he accepted in 1850), he wrote to Hiller, "All this time I have been suffering from headaches, which kept me from working or thinking." And he added, in an oblique reference to Düsseldorf's insane asylum, "I have to be careful to guard against all melancholy impressions."[9]

Despite the ill health, the Dresden years were in fact very productive. Many of Robert's best-known works—the Piano Concerto, the C-Major Symphony, the Song Album for the Young, the Concert Piece for Four Horns and Orchestra—stem from this period. Other great works of the Dresden years are not so well known today, but Schumann regarded them highly, pouring into them his talents and mastery—indeed, as he wrote, his "life's blood": *Genoveva,* his only opera; Scenes from *Faust;* and *Manfred,* the melodrama based on a poem by Byron. In April 1849 Schumann wrote Hiller, "This has been my most fruitful year."[10] By this time Schumann had eliminated all his literary work and other distractions, and with Clara's help was concentrating solely on composition except for the few hours a week devoted to a choral society he had organized.

Clara's public career slowed down somewhat during the Dresden years. There were many reasons: Robert's health and her obligations as wife and mother, her continuous pregnancies (five in all; one resulted in a miscarriage) during their five years in Dresden, the musical and political situation there, and her unfailing presence at and support of all Schumann's activities.

For most of 1845 and 1846, her concertizing was limited to Dresden and Leipzig, but the concerts she gave were outstanding events and she premiered works of great significance. She performed Schumann's Piano Concerto for the first time in Dresden under Hiller on December 4, 1845, and in Leipzig under Mendelssohn on January 1, 1846, the final month of her fourth pregnancy. (Emil was born on February 8.) Two months earlier she had premiered Adolph Henselt's new concerto (October 5, 1845), and in October 1846 she played Beethoven's Fourth Piano Concerto with cadenzas she had composed. All in all, she gave some twelve concerts in these two years. It is astonishing to read in the household books that on a vacation on the island of Norderney—a North Sea resort—she underwent "a change in her condition" (a miscarriage) on July 26, yet played publicly there on July 27, 1846.[11]

She put her entrepreneurial skills to use by organizing a trio in Dresden, and in October 1847 inaugurated a chamber music concert series, probably the first of its kind in that city. She also gave benefit concerts for friends and various causes.

Clara's income from tours and concerts during the Dresden years was not 17inconsiderable and helped pay for their rent and other basic family needs. There is no doubt that the profits from the Russian trip were a comfortable cushion during the first years in Dresden, when Robert was so ill; her concerts continued to be an important source of income. She earned 120 taler from the Norderney and Leipzig concerts in 1846, 320 taler (after travel costs) from the Vienna-Brünn-Prague tour in 1846–47, and 482 taler from two Berlin concerts in 1847.[12] In the years 1845–47, her husband's only income consisted of small amounts from his capital, from music publishers, and from occasional teaching. By 1849, however, Schumann was earning substantial amounts from the sale of his compositions (1,223 taler in one year),[13] so that her earnings were a proportionately smaller share of the family income.*

Both Clara and Robert began giving lessons in piano and composition soon after they settled in Dresden. Teaching grew into a satisfying source of income, so that by 1847 Clara could write, "I give two lessons nearly every day. . . . It is certainly quite a pleasant feeling to earn something daily."[14]

The first two Dresden years were also productive for Clara Schumann the composer. It was during this stressful period that her Preludes and Fugues and the Trio in G Minor were completed.

At the close of 1846 the Schumanns and their two oldest children left on an ill-fated tour to Vienna. Distasteful arguments with Wieck, who was in Vienna at the same time, and empty halls for their concerts created discomfort and anxiety. The critics were unsympathetic to Schumann's music, although Clara's playing was not faulted. On their return home, they found their youngest child, Emil, ill, but they had to leave him and the other children with servants and take off almost immediately to prepare for a performance of *Peri* and several concerts in Berlin for which Clara was scheduled.

Probably the most remarkable incident of the Dresden years was Clara Schumann's heroic behavior during the May 1849 uprising. The insurgents expected that every able-bodied man would join them. Schumann's sympathies lay with the rebels but he was in no condition to fight. Clara hid him as long as she could, then had to flee through the back door with him and their eldest child, leaving the other children behind with the servants. She returned in the middle of the night with another woman, courageously walking through open fields to the embattled city, seven months pregnant (Ferdinand was born on July 16), facing squadrons of armed men, to rouse her children—ranging in age from a year and a half to six years old—and lead them to safety in the suburbs. The family remained away for about a month.

Curiously enough, this was a time of great activity for Schumann. While wife and children were sheltered by friends, he was writing feverishly (in a *Schreibfeuer*, as he put it), completing the Song Album for the Young, Songs from *Wilhelm Meister*, songs for men's voices, and a motet, and planning the cathedral scene for his *Faust.* Many other works originated in the months during and just after the May uprising, an event in which Richard Wagner took

*The figures in RS/Tgb 3:669–83 indicate the continuously growing popularity of Schumann's music during his lifetime. Though the audiences were small, the music was selling.

Clara and Robert Schumann in Vienna. Lithograph by Eduard Kaiser, 1847. Robert-Schumann-Haus, Zwickau.

such an active part that he was exiled from the Saxon kingdom. Political statements in the diary and letters during these months indicate that both Schumanns sided with the insurgents, but Schumann, unlike the extroverted, outspoken Wagner, was not a fighter. He remained a spectator and composed his music.

During his "nervous" times, Robert depended on his wife for psychological as well as artistic and financial support. When she went to Leipzig for the opening of the season in October 1845, he remained behind because, as he put it to Mendelssohn, "any disturbance in the simple order of my life throws me off balance and into a nervous and irritable condition. That is why I preferred to stay at home when my wife was with you in Leipzig—much to my regret. Wherever there is fun and excitement, I must still keep my distance."[15] And the troubled composer wrote to his wife while she was in Leipzig for the premiere of the Henselt concerto, "I am getting along tolerably well, yet I am in a perpetual state of agitation because I think of you continuously. . . . Did you arrive safely? . . . Do you feel strong?"[16]

Another letter to his absent wife shows dramatically his need for her:

> I had a bad night. I always feel so strained but this always gets better when you are with me again. Yet I feel how much I am lacking in health; I cannot tolerate anything. All the pains and joys of life disconcert me; it is an overexcited state of mind—if only it would change soon. I *cannot* work at all; all peace has left me and I search for it everywhere.[17]

In good times, too, he depended on her, not only as a wife but as a musician. Clara's superb skills and training were exploited in the arrangements for piano of his Overture, Scherzo, and Finale, the C-Major Symphony, the *Faust* scenes, and *Genoveva,* and she served as assistant conductor and accompanist for his Dresden choral group. She coached at rehearsals of his *Peri, Mignon,* and *Faust,* and, as we have noted, premiered all his great piano solos and vocal and chamber works in which the piano had a part.

Looking back almost fifty years, Marie von Lindemann, one of the women who sang in the Choral Society, described the close collaboration of the two Schumanns:

> I still can remember the influence that the superlative artist Frau Clara Schumann exerted on us as she accompanied our singing and developed our understanding of the music through her wonderful, thoroughly intelligent playing. One can imagine how, under this double leadership, all the powers we possessed would grow. . . . In each gathering, it was clearly seen that one spirit dwelled in both and this was even more evident when it was our lovely task to bring a new creation of Robert Schumann to the ears of the public. With what calm, with what confidence he turned to his Clara to bring us

closer to an understanding of his ideas through stressing every important tone, through intensifying the nuances. And how we saw her eyes flash with enthusiasm when the beauty of his music was appreciated![18]

Emilie Steffens, a favorite piano student of Clara's, spent much time with the family, in a sense filling the role of "wife" for Clara. According to Steffens, Clara practiced during the hours Schumann was away from the house, usually from 6 to 8 P.M., when he took his customary beer at a neighborhood tavern. Practicing ceased when he returned for supper. Steffens remained in Dresden in charge of the children when the Schumanns went to Leipzig in June 1850 for the *Genoveva* premiere. The letters she received from Clara Schumann tell most eloquently of this woman's responsibilities and the conscientious manner in which she carried them out:

Monday, June 17, 1850

Dear Emilie,

The children are coming tomorrow afternoon at 2:30 and I would ask that either you or Pauline [the maid] wait for them at the train station; from there take a droshky and go with them to the house.* Take the suitcases with you in the droshky. You will find some things in the suitcases that I have sent back and in the dirty laundry there are some of my things. Please throw them in the big laundry. I am enclosing ten taler so that you will have enough money. I should very much like you to make out a small extra bill for the expenditures that I do not have my husband settle, such as the tailor, the seamstress, the handkerchiefs, etc. The laundry likewise.

Today I am asking you to send two things by return mail, namely, the book for which I have already asked; it is lying on my piano in a yellow paper cover and inside are some songs that I have written and also some small pieces of music paper, which naturally you should not send; then go into my husband's room, sit down at his piano, and stretch your right hand out toward the other package of music that is underneath in his music cabinet. There you will find copies of his *Lieder-Album für die Jugend.* Look for a clean copy and send it along, carefully packed, of course, so that it won't be damaged. Both things *right away*, please! . . .

June 24

About the opera . . . I believe that it is best that you come early Monday, in any case, since it is very possible that it will be performed on Monday though this will not be decided on before Sunday. Would you tell the others and write once more how many tickets I should order? . . . I hope Pauline is well again so that you will not have to bring a stranger into the house—that would be a very big nuisance to me. Lock everything up, lock up the key to the laundry room. . . .

*The two oldest children had been taken to Leipzig for their father's birthday and were returning home.

> June 29, 1850
> I am writing today with a joyful heart after the second performance of the opera, which took place yesterday. I wished you could have been there. The performance was far better than the first. . . . God grant that the children remain healthy—I am worried about Ferdinand. Write to me again right away. . . . What does Julie want? I have ordered a charming baby doll for her—will she like that? Ludwig is getting soldiers and a nice picture book. . . . Also give Pauline notice for August 1 as soon as you get this letter. Don't neglect to do this before July 1.[19*]

In their painstaking attention to detail and their peremptory tone, these letters are reminiscent of Wieck's, with their exacting instructions and admonitions to his wife. In contrast to Wieck's arrogance, however, consider the selflessness exhibited by Clara. There is no trace of the narcissism one associates with a concert artist, a woman who was once the spoiled darling of the Viennese aristocracy. Her concerns are her children, her husband, the routines of a household that she manages with efficient determination. Here, writing from Leipzig, she is the wife of a composer, dependent on the skills of others to do justice to her husband's music, suffering through the endless wrangles, temperamental outbursts, and intrigues of an opera premiere, awaiting the rising of the curtain with beating heart.

It is clear that Clara's career took second place to that of her husband during the Dresden years. She was apparently not aware of any resentment toward Robert, but her outbreaks of anger and bitterness over the reception of his music may have been sharpened by this buried frustration. The Vienna concerts of 1846–47 were a great disappointment to Clara, not because her playing was criticized (it was in fact praised) but because Schumann's symphony and concerto were coolly received. Eduard Hanslick, who was present, described the scene after a concert:

> The minutes passed in an uncomfortable silence, since each of us was depressed by the cool reception of the marvelous evening of music. Clara broke the silence first, complaining bitterly of the coldness and thanklessness of the public. The more we tried to soothe her, the more audible her despondency became. Then Schumann spoke the unforgettable words: "Calm yourself, Clara dear. In ten years it will all be different."[20]

And indeed, a change was evident in less time than that. By 1849, publishers were vying for his work. *Peri* was performed as far away as New York. On September 18, 1849, Schumann could write to Franz Brendel, who had taken over the editorship of the *Neue Zeitschrift*, that he was "quite content with the recognition" he had been receiving.[21] But the composer, feted and honored in so many other places, was virtually ignored in Dresden. Clara fumed and raged at the lack of respect received in their hometown. She referred to the Dresden

*The Schumanns were planning to move to Düsseldorf in August.

audiences as *Klötze* (klutzes) with no spark of life—dull, boring, conservative people. When the attendance of the men in the Choral Society dropped, she wrote angrily, "That is the Dresden feeling for art—now that there are only a few more Wednesdays that we will be here, they have stopped attending." And a few days later she wrote, "It isn't a taste for art that drives people here to make music, but, at the most, an interest in people, or just ordinary curiosity." She saw the Dresden musicians as hypocrites: "This is altogether a fine group—first they embrace each other as 'dear colleague' and 'darling' and then they would like to scratch each other's eyes out."[22]

Her father's presence in the town must have added to the discomfort of living in Dresden. Wieck, now well established as a piano and voice teacher, had been helpful when they first arrived in the difficult autumn of 1844, but Clara soon found she could manage better without him and was angered by his arrogance. When her father criticized Robert, she defended her husband, who still was unable to express verbally his deep-seated anger at his father-in-law. They spent the first Christmas in Dresden together but the two families still found themselves far apart on many issues. Clara concertized with her half sister Marie several times but had misgivings about her talent: "She plays well, but not exceedingly well."[23]

An argument with Wieck in Vienna in 1846 aggravated their relationship. The major difficulty seemed to lie in Wieck's prodigious self-assurance and egoism; he could permit no contradictions and could not acknowledge Schumann's success as a musician. The disagreement centered on his voice students, and culminated in his refusal to allow Marie and Minna Schulz, a favorite student, to participate in Schumann's Choral Society. The animosity grew so extreme that they even suspected he had a hand in some unfavorable reviews in Vienna. By 1850 his name had all but disappeared from the Schumanns' diary and letters. He was not invited to the premiere of *Genoveva* in June, whereas Marianne Bargiel was a frequent and welcome visitor. Clara never broke completely with her father, but by the time they left Dresden, the emotional attachment had withered.

During the Dresden years Clara gradually assumed a new role, that of Schumann's defender and protector. Both husband and wife were probably unaware of the extent of his growing dependency. Because of his recurring illnesses and his total self-absorption when he was working, she began by participating in and then taking over many of his responsibilities, a situation he seemed to accept willingly, though it is difficult to imagine he did not feel some resentment. He was not unappreciative of her help and praised her openly and publicly. Though he doubtless preferred to think her principal role was that of mother and wife, Schumann encouraged her professional activities and took pride in her talents and achievements. Twice he went to great lengths to have her compositions published as a birthday surprise for her. He informed Heinrich Dorn, their old teacher, that Clara had published a volume of fugues, and added that he wished Dorn could get to know them. To the pianist and composer Ferdinand Hiller he wrote in 1847 that when he visited he would hear Robert's new trios and Clara's as well.[24]

His letters to friends are filled with expressions of tenderness for his wife and family: "She is a gift from above," he wrote to Mendelssohn in October 1845. "There is no doubt that she really deserves affection and encouragement as an industrious and hard-working artist, and indeed as a woman too." "My two girls are dear angel-children, my wife the same old dear," he wrote to Verhulst in 1844, and to Mendelssohn in 1845, referring to his own poor health, "But I daresay better times are coming, and when I look upon wife and children I have joy enough."[25]

Whenever he was able, he acted as manager and made concert arrangements—the role once filled by her father. In a letter outlining his considerations before accepting a job offer in Düsseldorf he asked Hiller, "Would there be anything for my wife to do? You know her, and that she cannot be inactive."[26]

Robert understood his wife. No matter how busy she was with her husband and his work, with her children and their needs, she required her own artistic activity to be truly content. At the end of July 1847, after a year that included concert tours to Vienna and Berlin, a Schumann festival in Zwickau, the death of her youngest child, and the start of a new pregnancy, this woman wrote in her diary: "I am lazy, but I cannot help it because I am always ill and terribly weak. Oh, if I could only work, that is my one sorrow."[27]

CHAPTER 7

Düsseldorf and the Death of Robert Schumann

Clara Schumann's conduct during the last years of her marriage raises many questions. Did she become overly directive during the years in Düsseldorf? Did she neglect her husband during his hospitalization? Why did she wait more than two years before visiting him in the institution where he died? An examination of newly available material permits us to view these difficult years in perspective and goes far toward understanding her actions.*

The position offered Robert in Düsseldorf—music director of the Municipal Orchestra and Chorus, with responsibility for ten concerts and four church music services yearly—was accepted with many reservations. The warm greeting in the Rhenish city dispelled their doubts, but the good feelings were of short duration on both sides.[1] In contrast to the reception in Dresden, the Schumanns were treated with great respect, but objections to the composer's conducting style arose almost at once; discipline in the chorus was lax, attendance at rehearsals dropped, critics murmured, and by the end of the first season it was evident that there was general dissatisfaction with the new director, though esteem for his creative work had not lessened. Clara was defensive and raged in her diary and in letters to friends about the loose character of the Rhinelanders, their lack of taste, and the "intrigues" against their music director. As early as April 1851 she complained to her sister-in-law that Robert was unappreciated and announced their plans to leave Düsseldorf.[2] Throughout the three remaining years they made frequent futile inquiries about other positions. There were no offers, no places to go—and so they remained. The Düsseldorf years saw Schumann's deepening mental illness, his suicide attempt, and the tragic closing of his life; for Clara it was a time of unending worries about her children, the beginning of a forty-year widowhood, the inauguration

*The release in 1994 of excerpts from the daily log in Endenich has given an authoritative medical picture of Robert Schumann's final years. See notes 32 and 55.

of close friendships with Joseph Joachim and Johannes Brahms, and a renewal of her concert career.

From the outset of their arrival in the new city, Clara Schumann was honored not only as Schumann's wife but as an artist in her own right. She was Düsseldorf's premiere pianist and played with the orchestra under Schumann's direction as well as in solo and chamber music concerts. As the soloist in the first orchestra subscription concert on October 24, 1851, Clara, like her husband, was greeted with a flourish of trumpets. She was delighted by her enthusiastic welcome but dismayed by Robert's angry reaction after the concert, when Ferdinand Hiller chivalrously proposed a toast to her rather than to him. This incident signaled the start of many misunderstandings. Tensions grew and many bitter tears were shed, but they never prevented her from continuing either her full support of her husband or her own professional career.

During their first season in Düsseldorf Clara appeared as soloist only occasionally, but letters and newspaper reports reveal that she was not forgotten; her influence and reputation as a musician were growing. There was ample professional recognition during the Düsseldorf years: a glorious Schumann Week in Leipzig honored both husband and wife in March 1852, a few months after the birth of their seventh child, Eugenie; the post brought urgent invitations to perform in England; Clara gave brilliant performances at the Lower Rhine Music Festival in May 1853, in which her long-lasting association with Joseph Joachim, now a mature artist, began; gala concerts with Robert launched her popularity in Holland, where she gave twelve concerts between November 26 and December 20, 1853, and appearances in Hannover in January 1854 strengthened her relationship with Joachim. She gave concerts on every trip she took, even those that were officially vacations. Visits to and from old rivals—Camilla Pleyel in Brussels in August 1851 and Liszt, who came to Düsseldorf in September—were reminders of her days on the stages of Europe. And within a few months she had a "little colony" of students who came from all over Germany to study with her.[3] Finally, in September 1852, the Schumanns moved into a new apartment on Bilkerstrasse, in which she had her own piano in a room where she could practice without disturbing her husband. In this room she began to compose again, and within three months in 1853 she wrote pieces that were to be her last published works: Variations on a Theme by Robert Schumann, Three Romances for Piano, Three Romances for Violin and Piano, and Six Songs from *Jucunde,* opp. 20–23.

Although long concert tours were not possible because of the many young children and the continuing pregnancies (one pregnancy between the births of Eugenie and Felix ended in a miscarriage in September 1852), Clara performed in Düsseldorf and the neighboring cities of Bonn, Cologne, and Krefeld as frequently as she could. The scheduling and arranging of the concerts were entirely her responsibility, and the details she attended to were staggering. Why did she undertake these additional tasks?

A letter to Wilhelm Joseph von Wasielewski, a friend and violinist with whom she often played, tells part of the story:

> January 20, 1853
> I have another question to ask of you today, dear friend, about which Robert knows nothing, and I ask that you frame your answer in such a way that it seems like more of an inquiry from you, or, if something stands in the way of realizing my wish, then just do not answer at all. It concerns a soirée in Bonn, about which we once spoke last summer and for which I have had a great desire because, first, it would give us the pleasure of playing with you and Reimers* again (I am thinking, naturally, of the *Quintett* [op. 44]), and then it would also perhaps yield a small income. You know well that there is not very much here and our household requires much! (This is between us, dear J. v. Wasielewski, is it not?)[4†]

In addition to her own professional activities and the obligations to her growing family, her diary shows an increasing involvement with her husband and his duties, an involvement that Robert Schumann both encouraged and resented. Though it was customary in Düsseldorf for the conductor to accompany the chorus at rehearsals, for example, Clara took over this task, partly because of Robert's finger injury but mainly because his difficulties with speech obliged him to depend on her support at the piano.

Clara Schumann identified completely with her husband and took any criticism of his work as a personal affront. To her letter to Wasielewski she added a postscript: "Excuse my terrible writing, but I am so agitated today, unfortunately again by an insult that was directed at Robert, that my hand is trembling. But don't let Robert know that I mentioned it to you." Frederick Niecks, who personally knew many of their Düsseldorf colleagues, writes, "She watched over him, she placed herself between the outside world and him, and prevented, as far as possible, those rubs which tortured his sensitive mind."[5]

In March 1852, after describing a rehearsal of the Choral Society at which the behavior of the women singers was so undisciplined that it made her "blood boil," she wrote in her diary, "I would like nothing better than for Robert to withdraw entirely from the Choral Society, for the position is not worthy of a man of his stature."[6] But she participated willingly in each rehearsal of the chorus and never suggested that the hackwork at the piano during rehearsals hardly befitted her rank as a concert artist.

Her responsibility for the family and her greater personal strength were

*Christian Reimers, cellist.

†These and other confidences paved the way for Wasielewski's 1858 biography of Schumann, which Clara disavowed and refused to read. Perhaps she felt some guilt for having undermined the image of Schumann as master of the house. Wasielewski, a violinist in the Gewandhaus Orchestra in Leipzig, had been brought to Düsseldorf by Schumann in 1850 to serve as concertmaster. He left for Bonn in 1852 to work as choral director.

recognized on November 7, 1853, when a committee from the city administration informed Clara (not Robert) that in the future Robert would conduct only his own works; all other conducting responsibilities would be taken over by Julius Tausch, the assistant director. Clara reacted violently in her diary:

> This was an infamous intrigue and an insult to Robert, which forces him to give up his position entirely, as I told the gentlemen immediately, without having spoken to Robert. . . . I cannot say how angry I was and how bitter it was for me not to be able to spare Robert this outrage. Oh, they are low-minded people here! Vulgarity rules, and those men who mean well . . . draw back, condemning but doing nothing. What would I not have given to pick up and leave immediately with Robert, but when one has six children, it is not so easy.[7]

Though she reacted to the insult as any loyal wife would have done, she did not perceive that the manner in which it came—through her—was equally insulting.

Schumann had never been an effective conductor, should never have been offered the position, and should not have accepted it. Friends always knew he had problems in this kind of executive post, but neither he nor Clara (who must have been aware of his problems) acknowledged any weakness on the podium.* After his first attempt at leading an orchestra in Leipzig, he proudly wrote Clara of what he perceived as success, but she received his letter at the same time as the gentle admonition from Livia Frege, "If only your dear husband could resolve to scold a little. . . ."† Schumann gave up the Men's Chorus in Dresden ("I found too little real musical aspiration, and did not feel suited to it, nice people though they were"),[8] and despite some critical enthusiasm for the Dresden Choral Society, it was known that he had difficulty holding that group together. He depended increasingly on Clara, who would communicate the conductor's wishes to the chorus from her place at the piano.

The conducting responsibilities in Düsseldorf were heavier and his weaknesses more severe and more visible; the strain on him and his wife was correspondingly greater. When Schumann was away or ill, Julius Tausch, his deputy, took over. At first this arrangement suited Schumann, and he asked that Tausch continue with preliminary rehearsals because, as he wrote to the committee, "for a creative artist, after his day's work, it is too great an irritation to direct the preliminary studies of an amateur choir."[9] But when the chorus preferred

*In a letter to the Austrian critic Eduard Hanslick written from Brünn on January 19, 1859, she was still resolutely denying that Schumann had any special problems as a conductor and blaming his difficulties in Düsseldorf on his illness and "intrigues." The letter, published in Hanslick, *Aus neuer und neuester Zeit,* 3d ed. (Berlin: Allgemeiner Verein für deutsche Literatur, 1900), 320–21, is in the Theodore Finney Music Library of the University of Pittsburgh. I am grateful to James Cassaro for sending me a copy of the letter, which Hanslick published almost exactly as written.

†Quoted in Chapter 5, p. 94.

Tausch for all rehearsals, Clara, who had never liked Tausch (and who was displaced as pianist by him), took the new arrangement as a personal affront. Her suspicions were aroused and she saw it as a "plot."

In 1852 Schumann's condition deteriorated rapidly. He suffered great physical and mental anguish during the 1852–53 season, and although he conducted one concert at the Lower Rhine Music Festival in May 1853, it seemed clear to everyone—except his wife—that he did not have the energy to continue as municipal music director and certainly did not have the strength to withstand the accusations and counteraccusations, threats of dismissal, and charges of intrigue that were flying back and forth. His symptoms were alarming: he was more taciturn and withdrawn than ever, he had attacks that resembled mild strokes, he had no strength or stamina, and worst of all, he suffered from auditory hallucinations in which certain tones sounded incessantly—torture to anyone and a special horror for a musician. Effective conducting was out of the question, though he continued to compose and write. Litzmann refers to "a certain apathy and dreaminess" as well as "a peculiar and noticeable difficulty, from time to time, with verbal expression."[10] Wasielewski, more specific, describes a noticeable increase in difficulty with speech. "More than ever, all musical tempi seemed too fast. . . . His physical bearing had something weighed down about it, and despite declarations of friendliness, a real apathy was evident in his intercourse with others."[11] Other problems were insomnia and an embarrassing (for Clara) fervor for table tapping—a parlor game in which spirits from the other world were supposed to manifest their presence by rapping on a table. Ten-year-old Elise was expected to assist with this new enthusiasm.[12]

One cannot help wondering how a musician of Clara's stature could defend Schumann's conducting when his incapacities were so obvious. Perhaps she harbored the natural (but vain) hope that if she ignored the signals of mental illness, they might disappear. Burdened with six children and a household, teaching, and performing, the thirty-three-year-old woman probably avoided thinking about the situation; to acknowledge it would have been to acknowledge the need for action. Berthold Litzmann, her greatest apologist, wrote, "The warding off of each and every criticism that was directed against him was the only protection against critical or skeptical agitation in her own soul."[13]

The situation was made even more difficult by a change in Schumann's behavior toward her. He was now frequently nervous and irritable and increasingly critical of her playing. Frederick Niecks reports two incidents in which he denigrated her, both times as a woman artist: once Schumann asked Tausch to replace Clara in playing his quintet because, Schumann explained, "a man understands that better," and on another occasion he had Tausch "relieve her" as the accompanist of the chorus, "since the pianoforte drumming tired her too much and was more suitable for a man."[14] As early as November 9, 1850, Schumann blamed her playing for the cool audience response to his D-Minor Trio, faulted her performance of Beethoven's "Appassionata" Sonata (a work she had made her own as early as 1838), and told her that her accompaniment of the singer was "terrible."*

To her diary she poured out her feelings after that evening in November:

> What grieved me so frightfully was that I had played with all my strength, given it my best, and thought to myself that it had never gone so well, and so it was even more bitter to hear, instead of a friendly word, only the most bitter, discouraging reproaches. I hardly know any more how I should play. Though I took great pains to accompany the singer in the most sensitive and responsive way, Robert said my accompanying was terrible! If I did not have to use my playing to earn some money, I would absolutely not play another note in public, for what good is it to me to earn the applause of the audience if I cannot satisfy him?[15]

We may wonder at this artist's desperate need for her husband's approval; her history gives some insight into the problem. From childhood on, Clara equated approbation of her playing with love. Her early performances had secured the love and attention of her father, the one parent who was left to her. During the early years of the courtship, audience approval compensated for the lack of her father's support. Her performances in Berlin revived the opportunities to regain her mother's attention and love. Thus, for Clara, Robert's criticism was tantamount to a withholding of love. As far as we know, however, she never acknowledged to herself or revealed to her husband any resentment of his criticism. Tears fell, but the anger she was probably feeling (and suppressing) was directed at the ungrateful Düsseldorf audiences rather than at the man who was causing it. She treasured every bit of praise he gave and guarded him more zealously than ever.

Despite the illness and strains generated by the official position, Schumann was composing throughout the Düsseldorf years. Clara's diary describes the joy his music gave her: "I have no peace; I must try Robert's new sonata immediately"; "I am burning with impatience for it"; "overpowering"; "sweeps one away to the wildest depths"; "It has been a long time since I have been so affected by music."[16]

Many of her comments, however, reveal a curious conflict of emotions. She reported in her diary that while Schumann was composing this Trio in G Minor, op. 110, which made a "powerful impression" on her, he allowed her to hear nothing at all of his work. When, on October 27, 1851, she was finally permitted to listen to it, she wrote:

> How wonderful is such an incessantly creative, powerful spirit; how I glory in the fortune that heaven has granted me sufficient intellect and feeling to comprehend this heart and soul so completely. Often a terrible anxiety comes

*It is possible that this criticism was a projection of his own inability to function well, as reviewers and friends reported no diminution of her artistry.

> over me when I think that I, among millions of wives, am the one who is so blessed, and then I ask heaven if it is perhaps too much happiness. The shadows cast by material cares cannot compare with the joys and the blissful hours that I enjoy through the love and work of my Robert.[17]

The months that began in September 1853 were fateful. Clara's birthday—her thirty-fourth—and their thirteenth wedding anniversary were celebrated in great style. After elaborate preparations, Schumann, who was feeling particularly well at this time, arranged an excursion and the following day presented his wife with a new piano, piled high with newly composed music. Again her "hunger" for his music was appeased, though she had "a feeling akin to sadness." She was frightened by the frenzied pace at which he had been working and by the great expense of the new piano. In her diary she wrote, "I cannot express very well what I feel, but my heart was filled with love and respect for Robert and thanks to heaven for the great happiness that overwhelms me. It may be presumptuous to say it, but is it not really true that I am the happiest wife on earth?"[18]

At the end of that month, however, the "happiest wife on earth" found she was pregnant again and that a long-awaited trip to England would have to be postponed once more.* This time she was able to express her feelings quite plainly; on September 30 she lamented, "My last good years are passing, my strength too. . . . I am more discouraged than I can possibly say."[19]

On the same day Schumann wrote in his diary: "Herr Brahms from Hamburg," and the following day, "Visit from Brahms, a genius."[20]† The arrival of the twenty-year-old composer was described, many years later, by Marie, the Schumanns' eldest daughter, at that time twelve years old:

> One day—it was in the year 1853—the bell rang toward noon; I ran out, as children do, and opened the door. There I saw a very young man, handsome as a picture, with long blond hair. He asked for my father. My parents went out, I said. He ventured to ask when he could come again. Tomorrow, at eleven, I said; my parents always go out at twelve. The next day at eleven o'clock—we were in school—he came again. Father received him; he brought his compositions with him and Father thought that as long as he was there, he could play the things for him then and there. The young man sat down at the piano. He had barely played a few measures when my father interrupted and ran out saying, "Please wait a moment, I must call my wife." The midday meal that followed was unforgettable. Both parents were in the most joyful excitement—again and again they began and could not speak of anything but the gifted young morning visitor, whose name was Johannes Brahms.[21]

Brahms had turned up at the Schumann home at the urging of Joseph Joachim. The impact of the Hamburg musician on the Schumann family was

*The Schumanns' last child was born June 11, 1854.

†Two days later, on October 3, he added, "Clara's certainty": Clara was pregnant again.

stunning. In words befitting an oracle, Schumann described Brahms as a "young eagle . . . a mighty Niagara . . . the true Apostle."[22] By October 13, Schumann, who had not written a literary essay in ten years, completed "Neue Bahnen" (New Paths) for the *Neue Zeitschrift,* in which he hailed the young composer as "springing forth, fully armed, like Athena from the head of Zeus; a young man over whose cradle graces and heroes have stood watch."[23*] He urged Breitkopf & Härtel to publish the young composer's first efforts.

Schumann had always given generously of his time, talents, and advice to other composers, but never before had he reacted so enthusiastically. "Robert loves him and takes great pleasure in him, both the man and the artist," wrote Clara in her diary on October 30, and added, "Robert has written a nice article about him, 'Neue Bahnen.' It appeared in Brendel's Zeitschrift." They saw Brahms almost every day during October, playing music, walking, talking, reading together. Although Clara had not always shared Schumann's enthusiasms, this time she took equal delight in the young man's music. The sonatas that Brahms brought with him had a masterful sweep and freshness that captured the imagination of both Schumanns. Brahms's presence may have helped the couple recapture the joy and excitement of their early days in Leipzig, when they were at the center of new musical thought. For a moment, perhaps, they were able to reclaim a sense of the sureness of their musical direction and forget the troubles in Düsseldorf. Brahms, who referred to Schumann as "the Master," may have been embarrassed, but he accepted the praise gratefully. He left Düsseldorf on November 2, a few days before the delegation visited Clara to announce the reduction of Robert's responsibilities.

The Schumanns did not devote themselves exclusively to Brahms during October 1853. Throughout the month they had critical confrontations with committees from the orchestra society. On October 19 Schumann noted in his household book, "Conference. Shameless people."[24] He conducted several disastrous rehearsals and concerts in the church and for the orchestral subscription series. They entertained many out-of-town visitors, including the French artist Jean-Joseph-Bonaventure Laurens and his family (Laurens sketched portraits of Brahms and Schumann at this time); Bettina von Arnim and her daughter, Gisela; Joachim, who came briefly on October 14 and then again at the end of the month to play with the Düsseldorf orchestra and give a recital with Clara. There was much music making with Albert Dietrich and Ruppert Becker, young local musicians, as well as with Brahms. Throughout this time, Clara, pregnant again, continued to concertize locally, teach, practice, write letters for

*Schumann may have had second thoughts about his overenthusiastic response. He wrote to Georg Wigand, the publisher of his *Gesammelte Schriften* (Collected Writings), on February 2, 1854, requesting that "Neue Bahnen" be omitted from the collection. The article did not, in fact, appear in the first edition published by Wigand in 1854, although it has appeared in subsequent editions of the book. See Gerd Nauhaus, "Nachwort," in Robert Schumann, *Gesammelte Schriften über Musik und Musiker,* 4 vols. (Leipzig: Wigand, 1854; rpt. Leipzig: Breitkopf & Härtel, 1985), 4:319.

Robert, make the necessary arrangements to play in Cologne on November 8 (Beethoven's Fifth Concerto) and Bonn on November 12 (chamber works), and supervise her six children and the household.

The difficulties that culminated in the delegation's meeting with Clara on November 9 were never officially resolved;[25] the Schumanns did not remain in Düsseldorf to attempt to work anything out. After a rather high-handed letter to the concert committee dated November 19,[26] they left on November 24 for a concert tour in Holland that turned out to be a heartwarming success. In Düsseldorf the arguments and discussion over a possibly broken contract continued, but in the end the mayor, Ludwig Hammers, in a noble gesture insisted that Schumann's salary for 1854 be paid whether or not he conducted. Hammers was also instrumental in ensuring that Schumann's salary was continued even after he was hospitalized.[27]

Clara gave ten highly appreciated concerts in the three weeks of the Dutch tour. Her husband received a laurel wreath and the couple was serenaded. A short tour in January 1854 to Hannover, where they were welcomed by Joachim and Brahms, was a pleasant contrast to their uncomfortable position in Düsseldorf. Schumann was cheerful and talkative, Clara noted in her diary, but she added that Brahms seemed unusually quiet and Joachim more serious than usual.[28] Could they have noticed something disquieting in Schumann's behavior?*

By February 10, when the final breakdown began, they were back in Düsseldorf. With great alarm Clara noted increasingly frequent auditory hallucinations, headaches, and sufferings beyond anything she had ever seen. Dr. Richard Hasenclever, a friend and member of the chorus, attended him until it was thought necessary to consult another physician, a military doctor named Böger.

A witness to Schumann's last days in Düsseldorf was Ruppert Becker, Wasielewski's successor as concertmaster of the Düsseldorf orchestra. The young violinist—the son of their old friend Ernst Adolph Becker, their confidant and adviser during the battle with Wieck—described the situation in his diary:

> February 14
>
> Today Schumann spoke about a peculiar phenomenon that he has noticed for several days now. It is the inner hearing of beautiful music in the form of entire works! The timbre sounds like wind music heard from afar, and is distinguished by the most glorious harmonies. Even as we were sitting at Junge's [a restaurant], his inner concert began and he was forced to stop reading his newspaper! God grant that this doesn't mean the worst. He spoke of it, saying, This is what it must be like in another life when we have shed our corpo-

*A letter to Joachim dated February 6, 1854, in which Schumann wrote of a "secret message between the lines," could not have allayed Joachim's fears that Schumann was disturbed. See JJ/*Briefe*, 1:153–54.

real selves. Most significant that these strange phenomena appear now, at a time when Schumann has not composed for eight weeks or more.

February 21
What I had not dared to think would happen has happened! Schumann has been insane for several days now, I learned it first yesterday from Dietrich, who told me that Frau Schumann would like someone to come in order to free her from the continuous watching. So I visited him today but it would not have occurred to me to think he was ill if Dietrich had not assured me of it. I found him quite as usual. I conversed with him for a half hour and then took my leave. Frau Schumann looks as if she is suffering as she never has before. If the situation doesn't change, the worst is to be feared. She is in the eighth month of pregnancy [actually the fifth or sixth] and has not closed an eye since his illness. The poor, unfortunate woman! During the night she sits by his bed and listens for every movement.

February 24
I visited him at noon and Frau Schumann asked me to go walking with him. During the hour I spent with him he spoke quite rationally, except when he told me that the spirit of Franz Schubert had sent him a wonderful melody that he had written down and on which he had composed variations.[29]

By the night of February 26 Schumann was insisting that he must go to an insane asylum, "as he could no longer control his mind and could not know what he might do during the night." Doctors and assistants were summoned, and for the first time in ten days and nights Clara did not sit with him. "The next morning," she wrote in her diary, "he got up but was so profoundly melancholy that I cannot possibly describe it. When I merely touched him, he said, 'Ah, Clara, I am not worthy of your love.' *He* said that, he to whom I had always looked up with the greatest, deepest reverence."[30]

That day Marie was given the task of keeping an unobtrusive eye on her father while Clara spoke with Dr. Hasenclever in another room. Marie later told what happened:

The last time I saw my father was on the day on which he left the house to take his life. I had been called, since my mother had to speak with the doctor. I was supposed to sit in my mother's little room and pay attention if my father, who was in his room nearby, needed anything. I sat at my mother's writing table for a while when the door of the next room opened and there stood my father in his long, green-flowered dressing gown. His face was quite white. As be looked at me, he thrust both hands in front of his face and said, "Oh, God." And then he disappeared again. I sat as if spellbound for a short time, and then I realized what I was supposed to be doing. I went into Father's room. It was empty, and the doors, those to my parents' bedroom and those that opened from there to the hall, were wide open. I rushed to my mother, the doctor was still there, and then all the rooms in the house were thoroughly searched. It

> was clear my father was gone. Now they sent people out for him, but my mother told me to go to Fräulein Leser, to tell her what had happened.* When I went out to the street I saw a large noisy crowd of people coming toward me, and as I came closer I recognized my father, supported by two men under his arms, and with his hands in front of his face. I was terrified, and sobbing aloud I ran through the streets to Fräulein Leser, to whom I told everything and who immediately arranged that she and Fräulein Junge [her companion] would come back with me. We found my mother in the greatest anxiety. She had seen Father coming, the doctor and Fräulein Leser attempted to calm her, and then the doctor insisted that she go to Fräulein Leser. An attendant was obtained for my father and a few days later he was taken away in a carriage. We children stood upstairs at the window and saw him get in. The carriage was driven into the courtyard to avoid being seen out in the street. Dr. Hasenclever and the attendant climbed in after him. We children were told that our father would soon return to us quite recovered, but the household servants who were standing near and watching cried.[31]

They were never to see him again, although he lived on for two and a half more years at a hospital in Endenich, a suburb of Bonn, a short train journey from Düsseldorf. Periods of peace and clarity alternated with episodes of anxiety, depression, and psychotic behavior.

By the time Schumann's rescuers got him back to his house after his suicide attempt, Clara was no longer there. The doctor had urged her to go to the home of her friend Rosalie Leser, for her own sake as well as Schumann's, and she did not see him during the five days he remained in Düsseldorf, though she sent him flowers and messages. In her diary she described his departure in the carriage but she herself did not witness it. She remained at Rosalie Leser's home until after he left. The doctor's injunction against seeing him continued throughout the years of Schumann's hospitalization, and we learn with astonishment that she did not see her husband until two days before his death, when he was so weak he could neither move nor speak.

Once Schumann was at Endenich, the doctors forbade her to visit him, partly to shield her from the acute distress she might suffer at seeing him in a psychotic state and partly because they feared that reminders of the past would provoke renewed anxiety and agitation on his part. We know now, from the recently released medical log, that Schumann was far more ill than Clara was told.[32] For much of the time in Endenich his moods were unpredictable and shifted wildly within seconds. He was guarded twenty-four hours a day by attendants with whom he seemed to be on good terms. Friends and relatives visited but were permitted only to observe him. They then reported back to Clara. For many months Schumann did not even ask for or about her (though he knew she was pregnant), and the doctors believed it best to prohibit all communication be-

*Rosalie Leser, blind friend of Clara Schumann.

tween them. Brahms, who had spoken with the doctors in August, suggested that her letters to the doctors might be too "overexcited." He advised her to tone them down so that the physicians could see that she was stable and realistic and so might permit direct contact with Schumann.[33] Finally, in September 1854, Dr. Peters, assistant to Dr. Franz Richarz, the institution's director, asked Clara to write to her husband, who seemed somewhat improved and had begun asking about his family. She wrote immediately and as frequently as possible thereafter, always assuming that their correspondence would be read by the staff.

Between September 1854 and May 1855, Schumann wrote eight letters to Clara. They varied greatly: some were warm, loving, and rational, others brief, enigmatic, and confused.[34] Then the letters ceased. In September 1855 Dr. Richarz wrote her saying there was no hope for a complete recovery. If she continued to write to her husband, the letters have not survived.

For the first ten months in the hospital Schumann saw no one other than the hospital staff. Clara received weekly reports from the doctors but was told not to visit. Finally, in December 1854, Joachim was permitted to speak with him, and thereafter Schumann had some face-to-face visits with Brahms and the writer Bettina von Arnim as well. Frau von Arnim, sister of Clemens Brentano and wife of Achim von Arnim, had met the Schumanns through Joachim, and Clara was flattered by her offer to visit Robert. In an emotional letter dated April 13, 1855, Clara thanked her in advance and told her that she had written to prepare Schumann for the visit.[35] The visit, which took place in late April or early May, actually caused Clara much grief. The older woman described a desolate, cheerless place and recommended that the patient be returned home to his family. This advice contradicted everything Clara had been told by the doctors, and in great alarm she sent Joachim to assess the situation. He reported that Schumann was very agitated and no change was made.*

Dr. Richarz had a reputation for being humane and progressive; he followed the precepts of the English psychiatrist John Conolly, who argued against the use of restraint in the treatment of psychiatric patients.[36] Moreover, Schumann seems to have been given special attention, probably because of his reputation. He had his own room with the use of a piano in a nearby common room, and after his initial recovery he walked daily in the garden. By April 1854 he was taking long walks, accompanied by his nurse-attendant, into Bonn and the surrounding area. Richarz's hospital was a private institution in a parklike setting. From the large, pleasant rooms that are presumed to have been Schumann's, mountains can be seen.

Despite Dr. Richarz's excellent reputation, Schumann's friends and family

*Bettina von Arnim, a writer and composer, was a revered figure though she was known to exaggerate. She obviously saw Schumann at a relatively quiet period. Joachim's appraisal of the situation after Bettina's visit is described in Johannes Brahms and Joseph Joachim, *Johannes Brahms im Briefwechsel mit Joseph Joachim*, ed. Andreas Moser, 2 vols. (Berlin: Deutsche Brahms-Gesellschaft, 1908), 1:105–8.

always felt some uneasiness about the treatment and regime at Endenich. There were times during the course of the two and a half years he spent there when Schumann seemed quite well. Bettina von Arnim evidently saw him during one of those periods.

To add to Clara's uncertainties about Endenich, Schumann himself made several troubling remarks about his stay there. In a letter to Joachim and during a visit from Brahms, Schumann whispered that he would like to get away—"away, away from here."[37] Everyone offered advice. Brahms's mother ventured to say she thought Schumann would be better off at home with his family, or at the very least should try another doctor or cure.[38] In the spring of 1855 and again in March 1856 Brahms made several trips to inspect other hospitals but was disappointed in both the institutions and the doctors he investigated.[39] At Joachim's urging, Clara went to speak with Dr. Richarz in May 1855 to discuss the possibility of a move, but he convinced her that the patient was in no condition to make a change.*

Because Clara Schumann never challenged the doctor's position regarding visits, she has been accused of being unfeeling and worse. Clara Schumann had many reasons for making no attempt to visit Endenich. First, she was basically a dutiful and conscientious woman; the thought of questioning the orders of a physician would never have occurred to her—or to many of her contemporaries, for that matter. True, she had defied her father to marry Robert, but the decision was, as we know, extraordinarily difficult for her, and she vacillated for many years before she was able to disobey her father. Her ordinary mode was to follow the instructions of those who were in positions of authority. Then too, after her husband was hospitalized, she was forced to acknowledge the extent of his illness, something she had always avoided. "Melancholia," headaches, rheumatic pains, dizziness, ringing in the ears, hallucinations had been noted for years but never faced squarely. Though she had doubts from time to time about the doctors at Endenich and always entertained hopes that he would recover, she did not question their authority and accepted the ban on visiting.

We can speculate on other reasons. Relatives of mental patients, particularly those who are suicidal, frequently feel guilty. Though Clara was not officially informed of the suicide attempt, she suspected it almost immediately. The news had spread rapidly throughout the musical world.† Everyone knew. Albert Dietrich, a close friend in Düsseldorf, wrote Joachim that he was sure she knew the truth.[40]

*They met in Brühl, some fifty kilometers north of Bonn.

†In far-off Boston, the suicide attempt was reported on April 22, 1854, just two months after the event, in a sympathetic statement:

> The melancholy report of the insanity of this great composer appears to be confirmed, although we get no direct and full accounts. Foreign papers contain a paragraph, under the head of Düsseldorf, his last place of residence, to the effect that he had escaped his keepers and thrown himself into the Rhine, but that he was saved. His case, however, was considered hopeless. . . . Probably the overexcitement of an active brain, always intensely busied with the conception and execution of new musical creations, was the true secret of his lamentable state. (Dwight's, 5 [1854], 22.)

Schumann's depression was so deep and his sense of isolation so extreme that Clara was undoubtedly apprehensive about seeing him. The man she knew was no longer there. Moreover, the fear, expressed in her diary and in letters to friends, that in a moment of insanity he might, as he himself had suggested, harm her or the children or himself was not unrealistic, as we now know. Added to the fear were the anger and resentment she must have felt when she found he did not ask after her or their children or want to see them.

The growing relationship with young Brahms originally brought her relief from engulfing melancholy and then gradually brought her a happiness she had not experienced for many years. It was inevitable that some feelings of guilt emerged when she realized what was happening.

Added to these considerations was the certainty that she received a sense of comfort, exhilaration, and power from the successful concert life she had resumed—indeed, felt she was forced to resume, in order to pay for Schumann's hospitalization and support her family.

During the first few weeks of his hospitalization, Clara was desperately anxious to see her husband and get some information about him. She begged Wasielewski, at that time choral director in Bonn, to inquire after him daily and send her news about Robert's condition. On March 10 she wrote:

> Oh, dearest friend, what are you inflicting upon me by not writing a word about my husband! Today is the sixth day that he is in Endenich and I know nothing, not a word! Oh, what a sorrow this is for me! My heart breaks when I have no idea of how he is living, what he is doing, if he still hears the voices, in short, every word about him is balm for my wounded heart! I don't ask for any kind of decisive word, just how he sleeps, what he does during the day, and whether or not he asks after me, *that* I am certainly entitled to know. Oh, my dear friend, don't do this to my heart—leaving me so completely without news. If you yourself cannot go . . . pay someone, charging it to me, and have them go to ask.[41]

She poured out her feelings on paper but made an effort to control herself in front of her children. On May 7, 1854, Brahms's twenty-first birthday, Hedwig Salomon, an acquaintance from Leipzig, stopped in to see her and later recorded her impressions:

> My longing to see Clara Schumann prevailed over my shyness toward this celebrated artist. We came to Schumann's kitchen first, from there went to the children's room, where the nurse asked us to wait because "the Frau Doktor" was playing just now but we could listen from outside. The playing sounded grand, serious and powerful; we could not understand how she could play like that at this time. When the piece was over (I didn't recognize it though it was familiar), she came out; she looked so pathetic that it was difficult not to embrace her immediately. She was altered, looked old and jaundiced, but not broken or tearful. We avoided talking about the misfortune;

> she asked after friends and why her father had not written for so long. Then she . . . struggled against tears and burst out in bitter sobs. "If I didn't have the firm hope that my husband would be better soon, I wouldn't want to live anymore. I cannot live without him. The worst is that I may not be with him and he has not yet asked for me, not even once during the whole time." She could barely bring out these words, they were interrupted by convulsive sobs and her lovely eyes looked at me in an unspeakably sorrowful way. "But don't think," she continued, "that my husband is so bad. You would hardly notice that he was ill, he can carry on the deepest conversations, and is totally lucid about his situation; he went to the institution voluntarily so he could return to us all the sooner."

Two young men were at the piano in Schumann's room. Brahms had been playing his C-major sonata for Clara and Julius Otto Grimm. As he played, Hedwig Salomon noted, Clara became cheerful, appeared transfigured and young. It seemed to do her heart good, but she praised Brahms only with smiles and a handshake.[42]

On April 2 Clara asked Wasielewski to suggest that the doctor write on Mondays rather than Sundays because, she wrote,

> on Monday mornings I give piano lessons at court early and always receive his letter just before I go there, and that is terrible because I am always so upset after the letter that I break out in audible sobbing, and that is awful for me. If he cannot write regularly on Monday, then let it go and better not say anything about it because I would rather endure it all than lose a word.[43]

In the terrible days after February 27, Clara turned to friends for support: her blind friend Rosalie Leser and Leser's companion, Elise Junge, were at her side from the beginning; Clara's mother came posthaste from Berlin; the young Düsseldorf musicians Albert Dietrich and Julius Otto Grimm and the two young men who had been closest to Schumann in the last few months, Brahms and Joachim, arrived almost immediately. Brahms came on March 3, announcing he was there to help her in any way he could.

Clara's greatest solace was music and her piano. The presence of the young musicians and Brahms's unwavering loyalty supplied sorely needed support. She did not have the heart to give public concerts immediately (pregnancy alone would never have stopped her), but she did resume teaching two days after Schumann left, and she played with Brahms and Dietrich or Grimm daily, first only her husband's music and then that of other composers. In the course of the next two years she saw Brahms almost every day when she was at home and corresponded with him when she was touring. Brahms stayed on in Düsseldorf, composing a bit, trying to make some money by teaching, and helping Clara's housekeeper and the servants with her children. The friendship with Brahms sustained her during the two and a half years Robert Schumann was in Endenich; only gradually did she perceive that it had turned to love.

Clara Schumann remained in Düsseldorf with her children until after the birth of Felix, her eighth and last child, in June. She wrote Emilie List that she worked as much as possible, teaching, playing, supervising the children, and then, exhausted, retired to Robert's workroom, where she sat at his desk, looked at his belongings and picture, and mourned. She added that though people might wonder how she could contemplate giving concerts at such a time, she did it because she believed she could earn the money needed to pay all the expenses of the illness. When he returned, she wrote, there would be no financial loss to remind him of his illness.[44] (This was an illusion, of course, but it enabled her to avoid falling into a depression.)

Soon after Felix's birth, a period of touring and concertizing began. The staggering extent of her activities can be seen in her schedule for the last six months of 1854:

July	Berlin	Julie brought to stay with Marianne Bargiel
August	Ostend	Vacation; Clara plays several concerts in Brussels and Ostend
October 16	Hannover	Concert at court
October 19	Leipzig	Gewandhaus concert
October 23	Leipzig	Gewandhaus concert
October 27	Weimar	Concert under Liszt's direction
November 3	Frankfurt am Main	Concert
November 4	Frankfurt am Main	Concert
November	Düsseldorf	Short visit to see children
November 13	Hamburg	Three concerts with Philharmonic
November 15	Altona	Concert
November 16	Hamburg	Concert
November 18	Lübeck	Concert
November 21	Bremen	Concert
November 23	Berlin	Concert
November 29	Breslau	Concert
December 1	Breslau	Concert
December 4	Berlin	Concert with Joachim
December 7	Frankfurt an der Oder	Concert
December 10	Berlin	Concert with Joachim
December 14	Potsdam	Concert
December 16	Berlin	Concert with Joachim
December 20	Berlin	Concert with Joachim
December 21	Leipzig	Concert with Joachim
December 22	Düsseldorf	Home for Christmas

The year 1855 opened with eight concerts in the Netherlands in January; ten concerts in Danzig, Berlin, and Pomerania in February and March; and at the music festival in Düsseldorf in May. A tour to England had been arranged but was canceled when she heard better news from Endenich and decided to remain in Germany in case word came that she would be able to see Robert.[45] During the autumn of that year she toured with Joachim again. In 1856 she made even more extensive tours: Vienna, Budapest, and Prague early in the year, and from May to June the long-postponed trip to England, where she gave twenty-six concerts in two and a half months.[46]

She could not remain at home; her disquiet was not assuaged by the concert tours, and she took frequent trips: to hear Beethoven's *Missa Solemnis* in Cologne, to attend a performance of her husband's *Manfred* in Hamburg, short vacations alone, with women friends, and with Brahms and a woman companion. Often weak, exhausted, prone to attacks of anxiety about Robert, she was buoyed by the enthusiastic reception of her audiences and by Brahms's adoration (though they were rarely, if ever, alone). Obsessed by her pain and by her need to support her family, she rejected all offers of financial aid from friends and set out again and again, despite pleas from Brahms and others to stop. Her need to keep moving was desperate; she felt relief from grief only when she was working.

Her art gave her more than solace: performing for audiences provided the love Schumann had withheld in the last years, and though his letters from Endenich were now filled with praise and admiration for her playing, actual applause was more gratifying. Mixed with the pleasures of concertizing was the ambivalence she confided to her diary and in letters to friends. On the one hand, she desperately wanted her husband back again; on the other, she could not face seeing him mentally ill. After hearing from Dr. Richarz on September 10, 1855, that Schumann's situation was hopeless, she wrote in her diary:

> What a thought, to see him, the most zealous of artists, mentally weakened, perhaps, or far more likely, prey to the most terrible melancholy! Do I want to have him *like this*? And yet, should I not want to have, most of all, the person back again? Oh, I don't know what to think any more; I have thought it all over thousands upon thousands of times, and it always remains just terrible.[47]

She was proud that she could earn the money to pay the doctors' bills promptly but found them a heavy burden and briefly considered sending Robert to a less expensive state institution.[48] The news that Robert was again composing and writing letters to his friends was welcome, but she and Brahms were concerned that his letters would reveal his mental condition.[49] She responded immediately to his requests for music paper but knew that the work in Endenich was not worthy of him and later suppressed much of it. For those closest to him—Brahms, Joachim, and Clara—the image of Robert as a man revered, respected, and loved slipped gradually into that of a pitiable figure and a source of embarrassment.

In 1854 there was no real financial necessity for Clara to go on tour. Schumann's salary continued until 1855, and offers of help from wealthy friends and music lovers in Leipzig and Hamburg came pouring in. She rejected Härtel's offer to give a benefit concert in Leipzig for her and her children, saying, "I will never allow anyone to give a concert for me. That I will do for myself when it is necessary."[50] The only aid she accepted was from Paul Mendelssohn Bartholdy, her banker and brother of Felix. He sent her a note as soon as he heard of the events of February 1854:

> When my wife and I received the news of the indescribable misfortune that fate has inflicted upon you, our first thought and wish was to be able to be helpful and useful to you in some way. . . . It has occurred to me that peace and quiet will be a necessity for your physical and spiritual condition for a considerable time and that such an interruption of your professional activities may be detrimental to your household situation. In this case, just let me know with a word and *what you would like* and I am ready and willing to do whatever I can for you. And if my assumption is incorrect, I beg you again, if there is any opportunity for me to be useful in any other ways, treat me as you would have treated my brother, in whose spirit I turn to you!
>
> About the misfortune itself, I will say nothing more. That I have ventured to write this letter to you may indicate to you how I feel about it. May God be with you in your difficult life's task.[51]

Mendelssohn Bartholdy enclosed a letter of credit for 400 taler.

The offer was so generous and put forth with such sympathy and sensitivity that she accepted the money and consented to hold it in case of need. She was able to return it within a few months. Between 1854 and 1856, Clara added 5,000 taler to the Schumann family capital, more than Robert's Düsseldorf salary over a four-year period.[52]

Schumann never learned of the full extent of her professional activities. She was just completing an English tour in June 1856 when a telegram from Endenich reached her. Schumann was totally debilitated, though he was still conscious. Before the final days, Clara went to Endenich twice—on July 14 and July 23—but was dissuaded from seeing her husband. Though she was prepared to see him on the twenty-third, Brahms (who had accompanied her) and the doctors persuaded her not to go into his room because his appearance was so shocking.* Only when they realized that he had no more than a day or two to live was she permitted to see him. Clara spent July 27 and 28 and the morning of July 29 with her husband; she was calm and controlled and able to describe in her diary what she saw: "For weeks he had had nothing but wine and gelée—today I gave it to him—and he took it with the happiest expression and in haste, licking the wine from my fingers—ah, he knew that it was I."[53]

On the afternoon of July 29 she and Brahms slipped out to meet Joachim at the railway station. The three returned about an hour later to find that he had

*Brahms described it to Joachim as "moving and pitiful." He added, "Schumann is very wasted, there is no question of his talking or being conscious" (*Johannes Brahms im Briefwechsel mit Joseph Joachim,* 1:158).

died in his room, quite alone. She could feel only relief at his release. She wrote in her diary:

> His head was beautiful in death, the forehead so transparent and gently rounded. I stood at the body of my dearly loved husband and was calm; all my feelings were of thankfulness to God that he was finally free, and as I knelt at his bed I had such a holy feeling. It was as if his magnificent spirit hovered above me, oh—if he had only taken me with him! I saw him today for the last time—I placed some flowers on his brow—he has taken my love with him![54]

Schumann's illness and the cause of his death have been subjects of much controversy. The symptoms he presented were puzzling and the medical diagnosis was as difficult in 1956 as it was in 1856. The release of the long-lost medical record in 1994, however, threw much light on the tragic final two and a half years of his life.[55] The document contains excerpts from the log kept by Dr. Franz Richarz, the psychiatrist and director of the private institution to which Schumann had been sent. Dr. Richarz or his assistant, Dr. Peters, saw Schumann daily and noted his pulse, digestion, pupils, temperature, eating habits, medication, mental condition, and behavior. Visitors—Brahms, Joachim, Marianne Bargiel, Bettina von Arnim—were permitted at times when Schumann was relatively calm, but the physician obviously believed that visits from Clara at any time would be too upsetting for both husband and wife.

The record reveals that the patient was often agitated and unruly, screamed, was hostile and aggressive, lost control of bodily functions, had seizures, and hallucinated. Eventually he lost the power of speech and could barely swallow. Richarz wrote on September 12, 1855—without comment—that Schumann told him he had contracted syphilis in 1831 but that he had been given arsenic and was considered cured. (Arsenic was one of the heavy metals used to treat syphilis at that time.) Dr. Richarz could not (or would not) give a diagnosis of tertiary neurosyphilis; tests to determine the presence of that disease were not yet available and many of the symptoms resembled other mental illnesses. Both the symptoms and the treatments Richarz described, however, were typical of those of patients in the tertiary stage of syphilis. The disease was widespread in the nineteenth century; Franz Franken writes that it is almost impossible for us to imagine how common it was.[56] Richarz had a roster of eminent patients with similar medical histories.

It was known that Robert Schumann had also suffered cyclical variations in mood (often viewed as an expression of bipolar or manic-depressive disorder) and that he suffered from many physical problems and psychological stresses from late adolescence on. He made no attempt to conceal these episodes and recorded them in his diaries and in letters to friends. But in view of the suicide attempt, increasing psychotic behavior, information about an early bout of syphilis, and partial paralysis, Richarz could not have ignored the possibility that Schumann's later illness was tertiary syphilis and treated him accordingly.*

Clara was carefully shielded from any hint of syphilis. She and her family believed what Drs. Richarz and Peters reported: that Robert Schumann's death was caused by a nervous condition aggravated by overwork and that an inflammation of the lungs dealt the final blow.

*Schumann's exposure to syphilis occurred in 1831 (according to his own admission), and was undoubtedly treated in accordance with the medical precepts of that time. These treatments would have eliminated his primary symptoms and rendered him noninfectious. Thus the contagious stages were past by the time of his marriage in 1840, and his wife and children were not infected. However, these treatments were inadequate to stop the internal progress of the infection. It is not uncommon for decades to pass before the final stages of syphilis are manifested. My thanks to Anna Burton, M.D., who reviewed the medical reports and helped me understand this and other illnesses suffered by Robert Schumann.

CHAPTER 8

The Later Years

In her place of prominence, the young widow seemed to provoke either great loyalty or downright hostility. Despite her modesty, simplicity, and unpretentiousness, she seemed to her children, friends, and audiences to be larger than life. On stage and off, she had a sense of self that never deserted her: as mother, teacher, and pianist she rarely lost her dignity and self-possession.

Throughout her lifetime she was described as a "priestess," and the appellation seems appropriate not only because of her consecration to her art but because of her characteristic solemnity. Sober and earnest, she was often teased for her serious demeanor. Dressed almost always in dark colors, she did not condescend to court her audiences by cultivating an appealing stage personality, by personal display, or by playing popular music. There were periods when the once slender woman gained weight, but she never seemed bulky or awkward; her erect, dignified bearing made her appear taller than she was.* Although she had an expressive, pleasant face with large, beautiful dark-blue eyes, she never thought of herself as attractive. At the age of eighteen she made derogatory comments on her appearance, writing to Robert from Vienna that she could not understand why all the lovesick swains came flocking round.[1] In 1842, when she was compared with a leading Danish actress whom she resembled, she declared, "We have similar features and figures, but she is pretty whereas I am ugly."[2] Even as a young unmarried woman she found it difficult to act playful, coy, or flirtatious, and though her father urged her to put on a pose, if necessary, for box office considerations, she was incapable of emulating the flirtatious Camilla Pleyel, for example, about whom she wrote, "At this point, half of her art consists of coquetry; now I really understand why Father was

*In her autobiography, Adelina de Lara describes her first conversation about Clara Schumann with Fanny Davies, an older Schumann student: "What is she like?" "Very regal." "Like the Princess of Wales?" "No, not quite. How can I describe her? She is a big woman; there is a 'presence' about her. She is not good-looking but there is a lovely calmness in her face. You see, Adelina, she has suffered a good deal" (*Finale* [London: Burke, 1955], 35).

always so unhappy that I was not coquettish." But she comforted herself with the thought that the real connoisseurs "will like me as I am."[3*]

Her students found her fussy about details, very strict, but capable of real warmth and generosity. She demanded no more of them than she did of herself, and when she insisted on conscientious rehearsals for each concert, even if her students had played the music in public only a few days earlier, they knew this was her own practice. In his memoirs the baritone and conductor Sir George Henschel wrote:

> Her art she took very much in earnest. . . . Whenever Madame Schumann and I, as was frequently the case, were the soloists at the same concert and she accompanied me in her husband's songs, we would invariably have a rehearsal of the songs some time before the concert, even though perhaps we had done the same songs only a week before, somewhere else.[4]

To her friends—male and female—she was often peremptory, demanding, and even controlling, but her open mind, integrity, stability, and rectitude won their loyalty. These qualities were inherent in her performances. Amy Fay, a young American who studied piano in Berlin in 1869, wrote home after she first saw Madame Schumann, "Such *noble* playing I have never heard."[5] Reviews of Clara Schumann's concerts always stressed her solidity and objective "classical" playing.

Despite her many triumphs and brilliant career, observers always noted the sadness that seemed to pervade her spirit. Even when she was a child, her melancholy look struck those who observed her. And during the years of artistic triumph and marital happiness, a lingering remnant of sadness remained visible. During Robert's final illness and after his death, friends and children often saw her in tears. Liszt's description after she played in Weimar in 1854 was published widely: "To the moist, youthful lustre of her eyes, there has succeeded a fixed and anxious look. The flower crown, once so loosely woven in her hair, now scarcely hides the burning scars which the holy circlet has impressed so deeply on her brow."[6]

It was on this occasion that George Eliot met Clara Schumann. Later she described Clara as "a melancholy, interesting creature. Her husband went mad a year ago and she has to support eight children."[7]

The young Clara had met tragedy early in life; her defenses against loss evolved in early childhood as she learned to cope with the loss of her mother and nurse, the divorce of her parents, and the tyranny of her father. During her adolescence she was rarely granted the opportunity for normal carefree times,

*In the same entry, Clara noted that she had heard from Frau Mendelssohn, Felix's mother, that Pleyel "had bewitched all the men in Leipzig . . . she had accompanied [Wilhelmine] Devrient in 'Erlkönig' [Schubert's song] so beautifully that the singer was completely eclipsed. . . . Each movement she made was contrived: at the end of a work, she remained with the orchestra, spoke with the musicians, bowed again and again in a childlike way as though she could not understand why she received so much applause and then sat herself down at the piano and played another piece."

high spirits, and laughter. She often expressed regret that her letters to Brahms were too often recitals of woe and sorrow, and she resolved many times to "ban sad thoughts to avoid making life so hard for the children."[8]

On August 20, 1869, she wrote in her diary that she admired and envied the "lightheartedness" of Pauline Viardot, and she added, "Everything is always so merry there [in the Viardot home], as if there were no sorrows in the world."[9] An observer described her appearance after Schumann's hospitalization as "careworn and sad" and added, "she appeared just so years ago when she was a young girl. She never had a childhood. Her father was determined to make a virtuoso of her, and she never knew the joyousness of youth. Even then her countenance showed her secret sorrow."[10]

As she was buffeted by continuing disasters, the melancholy was transformed into a relentless sobriety and severe self-discipline. Doing one's duty, she once told Eugenie, is what brings happiness.[11]

Making music was, as always, her solace. Without it she would not have had the strength to endure the illnesses, deaths, and tragedies that were the regular companions of her life. Ever thankful for the professional activities that could relieve her sufferings, she wrote, after Julie's death, to Avé-Lallement, a conductor and old friend in Hamburg: "It often seemed to me—and still does—that when I played, my overburdened soul was relieved, as if I had truly cried myself out."[12]

Motherhood

Her children took great pride in their mother but also suffered from the divided life she led. The triumphant star, the renowned teacher, the successful editor and composer was unable to give her children the emotional environment they needed. In part, this was the result of her own childhood experiences—a deprivation of which she was well aware. She wrote Robert, "Father loved me very much, and I loved him too, but I did not have what a girl needs so much—a mother's love . . . and because of that was never really happy."[13] By the time she "found" her mother, she was already an adult.

Even before Robert Schumann died, his children were dispersed—as they were to be for many years. Marie and Elise, aged fifteen and thirteen, were at boarding school in Leipzig; Julie was in Berlin with her grandmother; Ludwig, Ferdinand, Eugenie, and Felix were in the Düsseldorf apartment in the care of Bertha, the housekeeper. Brahms, who occupied a room in the same apartment house, helped with the children while Clara was away on tour. The arrangements Clara made for the welfare of her children after Schumann's hospitalization were not unusual in nineteenth-century Germany, odd as they may seem to the modern reader. Wealthy families frequently sent young children to boarding schools for a proper upper-class education. Middle-class parents generally entrusted the care of their children to servants—to wet nurses when they were infants and to a *Kindermädchen* or governess when they were older.

Mothers were expected to spend some part of each day with them, partly to instill proper moral and ethical values and partly to set an example of proper feminine behavior for the girls. The father provided the financial support, and, occupied with this important duty, spent little time with his children except for formal occasions or by prearrangement. Families celebrated such occasions as Christmas, birthdays, name days, and confirmations together but might not dine or vacation together. The child-centered family was the rare exception in the nineteenth-century German middle class.

Like many other families in their situation, the Schumanns had two or three servants—a maid, a cook, and usually a general housekeeper who took major responsibility for the household under Clara's supervision. During Schumann's lifetime—and for his time, Robert Schumann was an unusually devoted father—the parents frequently left the children with friends, relatives, and servants when they went on tour and on vacation trips. This was not at all unusual.

In those few European families in which the mother was a performing artist, the experience of the children differed little from that of the Schumann children. Occasionally they were taken along on tours with servants to care for them; more often they were sent to boarding schools. The younger children of Pauline Viardot, for example, generally accompanied her and her husband on their rounds of European opera houses, but the eldest daughter, Louise, was often left home in the care of a grandmother or maid—and resented it.[14] The six children of Margarete Stockhausen, a singer and the mother of Julius Stockhausen, Clara's "glorious singer," occasionally toured with her and their harpist father, but beginning at the age of seven, Julius spent most of his childhood in boarding schools with his younger siblings.

Clara's own mother departed from the traditional mothering role not only by her ultimate surrender of her three children in order to divorce their father but also by cultivating her musical career, teaching, and supporting her children. The second and more conventional Frau Wieck was never a model for her stepdaughter. As a child, Clara knew her primary task was to play the piano, the activity that brought her her father's love and admiration. She returned to this priority when her husband died. She had, of course, never given up the piano but simply added household tasks and motherhood to what she considered her basic responsibility.

During the fourteen years of their marriage, the Schumanns lived four years in Leipzig, six years in Dresden, and four years in Düsseldorf. In each of these cities Clara Schumann established a home with the needs of children, composer-husband, and performer-wife in mind. In each home she practiced, performed, composed, and taught—as a professional—despite the demands of her children, the illnesses of her husband, and the discomforts of childbearing. Between 1840 and 1854 Clara Schumann gave at least 139 public concerts, and during those years she was pregnant almost continuously. At a time when respectable women were expected to remove themselves from public view when their pregnancy became obvious, Clara continued, like her mother before her, to teach, practice, and perform, sometimes up to one week before the birth of a child. Though she had several servants and a wetnurse for each child, the pressures on the artist-mother must have been immense.

Clara Schumann's feelings about motherhood progressed from enthusiasm to ambivalence. Marie, born in 1841, was welcomed wholeheartedly and greatly loved,[15] as was Elise, born in 1843, and perhaps Julie, born in 1845. By the time there were four children, however, Clara began to express grave doubts about her role as a mother. In May 1847, when she may have just become aware of a fifth pregnancy, she wrote in her diary:

> What will become of my work? Yet Robert says "children are blessings" and he is right, because without children there is indeed no happiness, and so I have decided to face the difficult time that is coming as cheerfully as possible. Whether it will always be like this, I don't know.[16]

As the family grew, she became increasingly resentful. Ludwig's birth, following the death of the infant Emil, may have offered the grieving mother some consolation, but the prospect of still another child (Ferdinand was born eighteen months after Ludwig) caused her some distress.[17] The Schumanns evidently did not practice birth control, and comments in the household book gradually change from "great blessing" to "Clara's new fear" and "frightening expectations." Entries in the household book ("change in Clara's condition and her joy—good effect of the bathing") suggest that the termination of the pregnancy in Norderney in 1846 was welcome.[18]

For the most part, Robert Schumann enjoyed the role of paterfamilias. In September 1845 he wrote to Mendelssohn to congratulate him on the birth of a second child. "We are looking forward to a similar event, but I always say to my wife, 'One cannot have enough.' It is the greatest blessing we can have on earth." To Verhulst he wrote in November 1848, "I possess great treasures in my own home, such a dear wife, such satisfactory children. We have got a boy now too; his name is Ludwig and he is the delight of his mother." To his friend Eduard Krüger he wrote in November 1849, "Our house is very merry. Five children are running about and already beginning to listen to Mozart and Beethoven."[19] His *Jugendalbum, Liederalbum,* and the three sonatas of op. 118 were written with his children in mind. Characteristically, he kept detailed notes on their growth and progress in his "Little Book of Memories."[20]

Though Robert Schumann was aware of his wife's need to continue her professional activity, it did not occur to him to alter his daily pattern to give her the time she needed. He did not, of course, participate in child rearing and household management, and it is certain that Clara Schumann, a woman of her time, would not have expected him to do so. Always conscientious, she never shirked what she regarded as the woman's responsibilities, but she must have felt underlying resentment as she went about her homemaking duties and practiced only when her husband, the composer, would not be disturbed. Once Schumann became ill, however, and the household had a clear need for funds, his wife assumed the combined burden of career and financial responsibility more than willingly.

In July 1856, on tour in England after more than two years without sight of her husband, Clara received the telegram that notified her of Schumann's extreme weakness. On July 4 she returned to the Continent, but instead of rushing directly to Endenich or proceeding immediately to Düsseldorf to see her children, she detoured from Antwerp, where Brahms met her, to Ostend in order to show her young friend the North Sea. On July 6 she returned to Düsseldorf, where her four youngest children were waiting for her. As we know, Schumann died on July 29, two days after Clara was finally permitted to see him.

After the funeral in Bonn, the two eldest children were informed of their father's death in a letter from Clara. Two weeks later, Clara took Ludwig and Ferdinand along on a month's vacation in Switzerland with Brahms and his sister, Elise. But by October there was further dispersal: Ludwig and Ferdinand, eight and seven years old, were sent to a boarding school in Bonn. "I felt terrible, but it is certainly in their best interests," Clara wrote in her diary on October 18, 1856.[21] The two youngest children, five and three, remained with the housekeeper. Brahms left Düsseldorf in October, just as Clara Schumann began her round of concerts for the new season.

In the years that followed, the health and well-being of her children were constantly in her thoughts; one might even describe her as being consumed with worry about them. In every letter to friends—Emilie List, Brahms, even Theodor Kirchner—she dwelt on her anxieties about her children. She devoted much time and energy to their school and living arrangements. "You wouldn't believe how difficult it is to bring up so many children so that each one is educated to be a capable human being," she wrote to Emilie List in 1860.[22] No detail was too small for her concern. To Ernst Rudorff, a former student and family friend who was helping with arrangements for seventeen-year-old Ferdinand in Berlin, she wrote: "I ask nothing more for him than a small room to sleep in and where he can also work on Sundays and evenings, and a simple but hearty diet; at noon he should regularly have as much meat as he wants, as he is growing frightfully fast." To the friend with whom fifteen-year-old Julie was staying she expressed concern about the kind of undergarment the girl should wear: "a proper corset, with whalebone in the back and wooden staves in front (not woven but sewn). . . . Have two bodices made to fit over the corset to keep it clean."[23]

A stream of instructions and admonitions flowed by mail to housekeepers, governesses, music teachers, and the children, but she was rarely with them for birthdays, confirmations, or even Christmas holidays, and they suffered grave illnesses, even death, without their mother's presence. Despite Clara Schumann's regular meticulous instructions concerning her children's physical well-being, she was not sensitive to their emotional needs. Her primary concerns were with their health and with her own professional tasks and the duties that supported the family: teaching, practicing, learning new works, keeping up with an enormous professional and personal correspondence, and, of course, her

Six Schumann children in 1855: Ludwig, Marie (holding Felix), Elise (standing), Ferdinand, Eugenie. Robert-Schumann-Haus, Zwickau.

concerts, which involved ten months of travel each year. Since she managed her own concerts, she was, in a sense, an entrepreneur. The extensive correspondence—sometimes as many as ten letters for each concert—left her no time for familial interaction.

Clara Schumann was proud to be an artist but did not encourage any of her children to follow in her footsteps. Gender had no place in this decision. Each child was given the best musical education Clara could afford; each daughter was given the opportunity to develop enough skill to be able to teach and support herself if necessary. Recalling her own years as a child prodigy, she felt strongly that her children should experience as normal a childhood, family life, and education as was possible under their peculiar circumstances. Moreover, she believed that if any of her children was to attempt a life as a professional musician, the burden would be especially great because of the Schumann name; for this reason, Clara discouraged—often tactlessly and sometimes callously—Felix's interest in a musical or literary career. She realized that she might be doing him an injustice and belatedly attempted to make up for her severity by teaching her grandson Ferdinand and offering to aid him in his ambition to become a music teacher. Three of her daughters and several grandchildren and great-grandchildren had careers as piano teachers, but none was a concert performer.

In the sorrowful days and months that followed Schumann's death, the young widow accepted—almost eagerly—the responsibility of providing for her family. Outsiders may have pitied her, but she soon realized that the life of an artist, even with all its trials and tensions, brought her a fulfillment that motherhood could not match. Most of her contemporaries assumed that financial need was her only reason for living as she did: the good mother was sacrificing her comfort to provide for her little ones. Only Joachim and perhaps a few others understood that concertizing brought this artist satisfactions she could never achieve by remaining at home with her children. Few considered what life was like for the daughters and sons of Clara Schumann.

Marie Schumann, 1841–1929

Marie, the firstborn, was the favorite of both her parents. Of all the children, Marie seems to have had the happiest and most secure early years. Schumann noted her musical skills and other charms in his "Little Book of Memories," and he spent more time with her than with any of the other children. Beginning at the age of five, she was often delegated to take her mother's place on daily walks with Schumann, especially when Clara was recovering from childbirth or otherwise indisposed. Clara, twenty-two when Marie was born, also felt exceptionally close to her eldest daughter and confided to her diary in June 1870 that she found her greatest happiness as a mother in the friendly relationship with Marie. When she was away from home, it was Marie she missed most. In 1868 she wrote in a memorable letter to her eldest daughter, "My dear, dear Marie, if you only knew how dear you are to me, how my whole existence is bound up with yours . . ."[24] The life of the favorite became consumed by her mother's life. Never marrying, she remained with her mother until Clara's death.

As the oldest, Marie began to take over household tasks early, but she also vacationed and toured with her mother more than did any of the other children. All major decisions were first discussed with Marie. When Clara accepted a teaching position in Frankfurt, Marie became her assistant; when her mother retired from teaching, so did Marie. Their students reported that Fräulein Marie (perhaps fifty years old at the time) sewed the collars on her mother's concert dresses; she also wrote most of the letters that Clara dictated during her recurrent attacks of rheumatism and bursitis. She accompanied Clara to Vienna in 1858 and 1860, to Paris in 1862, to The Hague in 1863, to Russia in 1864, and to England thirteen times. What Louis Viardot did for Pauline Viardot and Otto Goldschmidt did for Jenny Lind Goldschmidt, Marie did for her mother. In fact, Clara Schumann's career might not have survived without Marie's efficient, patient service. In 1871 Clara Schumann changed her will to reflect her appreciation of Marie's help, acknowledging the sacrifice that had prevented the eldest daughter from pursuing a career of her own. (The will was revised several times: in 1882, in 1889, and once again in 1891, after the death of Ferdinand.)

In addition to serving as assistant teacher, secretary, seamstress, and companion, Marie acted as surrogate mother; at the age of twenty she was put in charge of their Berlin apartment so that the younger children would have a home while their mother toured. Marie went to see Julie in Divonne in 1867 and to visit Ludwig in the mental hospital in 1870; she sat up with the dying Felix in 1879; she visited Ferdinand when he was hospitalized for morphine addiction in 1887 and represented her mother at his funeral in 1891. Clara bequeathed her diaries to Marie, and after Clara's death Marie became the guardian of the Schumann tradition and the Schumann legend.[25] Both of Berthold Litzmann's books (the biography of Clara and her correspondence with Brahms) were written under Marie's direct supervision. Marie Schumann sold the Frankfurt home on Myliusstrasse and moved to Interlaken, Switzerland, after the death of her mother. She resided there until her own death in 1929.

Elise Schumann Sommerhoff, 1843–1928

Elise, the most independent of all the Schumann children, had the most normal adult life. Always unfavorably compared with Marie in appearance, temperament, and character, Elise went her own way as early as 1863, when she left home to take a position as a governess. For many years she supported herself by working successively as governess, music teacher, and companion to wealthy or titled older women until in 1877 she met Louis Sommerhoff (1844–1911), a businessman with interests in the United States. They married on November 24, 1877, when she was thirty-four years old. They spent the next six years in the United States, and three of their four children were born there.

Clara Schumann with Marie, ca. 1845. Daguerreotype. Robert-Schumann-Haus, Zwickau.

Marie Schumann, age 28. Drawing by Eduard Bendemann, 1869. Robert-Schumann-Haus, Zwickau.

They then returned permanently to Germany. Three of the four children lived to adulthood; their descendants—none of them professional musicians—live in Germany and the United States.

Unlike Marie, Elise suffered many reproaches from her mother, the worst, perhaps, when she was singled out in the letter Clara wrote to the children after their father's death:

> I can say nothing else—only later will you feel what you have lost! He was a magnificent person—may you, whom he loved so deeply, be worthy of such a father, may you, especially you, Elise, change your character, may both of you, Marie and Elise, strive to please me as much as possible, not only by your diligence, but by mild, gentle behavior, modest, friendly, noble; may you be a person such as he was.[26]

The pressure of her mother's criticism may have quickened Elise's moves toward independence, leaving Clara with ambivalent feelings about the loss of the capable, strong-minded daughter. On September 10, 1865, when Elise went to Frankfurt to begin a career as a piano teacher, Clara wrote to Ernst Rudorff and to her friend Elisabeth Werner almost identical letters in which she declared she was very unhappy to see Elise leave because she would not have her with her when she wanted her.[27] Elise developed into an adequate pianist and appeared several times in public, though after a successful performance of Robert Schumann's Andante and Variations for Two Pianos with her mother in November 1865 she declared that playing in public made her too nervous to want a career. After her marriage and return from the United States, she and her family lived near her mother in Frankfurt, and a warm and cordial relationship with Clara Schumann gave the mother support and comfort in the last unhappy years.

Julie Schumann, Contessa Radicati di Marmorito, 1845–1872

Described by her father as "charming and graceful," Julie, always frail and yet the prettiest of all the Schumann daughters, was frequently separated from her family (even as a two-year-old) because of her fragile health. And despite constant medical care and her mother's well-founded anxiety, this delicate young woman was not discouraged from marrying, which at that time automatically implied childbearing. In 1869 she married an Italian count, a widower with two children, and bore two sons within three years. She died of tuberculosis at the age of twenty-seven, pregnant with her third child. Julie's son Eduardo died within a few years of his mother's death; descendants of her other son, Roberto, are living in Torino.

When Robert Schumann went to Endenich, Julie was sent to her grandmother Bargiel in Berlin, since Clara believed she needed special attention that she could not get in a household of seven children. Thereafter she lived with a succession of wealthy friends who could provide comfortable homes (among

Elise Schumann, age 20. Robert-Schumann-Haus, Zwickau.

Julie Schumann, age 19. Drawing by Eduard Bendemann, 1864, Robert-Schumann-Haus, Zwickau.

them Elise von Pacher, Emilie List's sister) and were happy to have the charming, lovable girl with them. She spent most Christmases and birthdays far from home because doctors advised southern climates or medicinal spas for the fragile girl's coughs and nerves. Clara wrote in her diary in July 1867, "I yearn so much for Julie's loving, tender glances; it is so typical of Julie that she shows me her love and it does me such good. I need love as much as I need air to breathe."[28] Because she was so affectionate and tender, Julie probably suffered from her mother's incessant touring more than any of the other children. Only once, in 1861, did Julie have an opportunity to be alone with her mother; she toured with her for a few autumn months in a short respite from illness when she was sixteen. They spent some time in Hamburg while Brahms was there, and it was shortly after this that he dedicated to Julie his Variations on a Theme by Robert Schumann, op. 23. She was the only Schumann child to whom Brahms dedicated a work.*

Her sisters—not her mother—kept her in contact with the other children. When Julie was confirmed in 1861, her sister Elise went to Munich to be with her, since Clara was on tour. In 1867, when Julie was too ill to come home for Christmas, Marie traveled to Divonne to see her and bring her home if possible, while Clara went to Karlsruhe to hear Hermann Levi conduct a performance of *Genoveva* before she began her winter tours. (At the time, Clara wrote to Brahms that she was very unhappy at her inability to fetch Julie herself, but explained, "I could not put such a tax on my strength in view of the exertions awaiting me."[29]† It was Elise who visited Julie before the birth of her first child on August 31, 1870. When Julie was pregnant for the second time, Marie and Felix went to see her in Turin on an impromptu visit. Clara denied herself the pleasure of joining them, because she thought Julie might be harmed by the excitement of an unexpected visit.[30]

Julie's married life was short but happy; the count, a music lover, was devoted to her and she was a great favorite in Turin society. Clara Schumann had had many qualms about Julie's marriage plans, partly because of the differences in class and religion and partly because of Julie's health. She gave her consent, she wrote in her diary in November 1868, because she believed that young true love should not—and indeed could not—be discouraged. Brahms and other close friends were informed of the engagement as soon as it was formalized. To her great surprise, she heard from Hermann Levi soon after that Brahms was in love with Julie. She confided her astonishment to her diary on July 16, 1869, and also noted in a letter to Rosalie Leser in August 1869 that Brahms had been totally changed by the unexpected news of Julie's engagement.[31] In a gesture that seemed to sum up his feelings about mother and daughter, he gave Julie a photograph of Clara as a wedding gift. When Brahms showed Clara his deeply

*Brahms did dedicate his Volks-Kinderlieder, WoO 31, "to the children of Robert and Clara Schumann."

†This comment may very well have prompted Brahms's letter of February 2, 1868, questioning her "way of life"; see p. 187.

sorrowful Alto Rhapsody a few weeks after the wedding, she was convinced that it was really a mourning piece for Julie. What Brahms's feelings were will never be known, of course, but Julie's engagement and marriage seemed to increase the tension between him and Clara.

Clara Schumann's emotional insulation from her children was shown most vividly when Julie died. On November 10, the day she was scheduled to give a concert in Heidelberg with the contralto Amalie Joachim, Joseph's wife, she received a telegram informing her of Julie's death a day earlier in Paris. She told no one and went ahead with the concert, she wrote Rosalie Leser, because changing the date would have caused great difficulties for everyone.[32] She was astonished by her own strength and explained her feelings in a revealing letter to Levi dated November 12, 1872:

> I am calm because, since the first day I saw the dear child again in Baden [in the summer of 1872], I was convinced that she would not live much longer. Our first embrace was like a blow to my poor heart; the worry did not leave me for an instant and that may well account, alas, for my calmness now. Another reason may very well be that I fought through the loss of the beloved child three years ago [at her marriage]; it seemed to me that I had already lost her at that time.[33]

The patterns of work Clara set for herself during Schumann's illness maintained her emotionally through his death, the institutionalization of Ludwig, and the death of Julie. The death of a child was, to her misfortune, a tragedy she had known before and was to endure again.

Emil Schumann, 1846–1847

The first son and fourth child of the Schumann family suffered from poor health and was described by his father in his "Little Book of Memories" as "miserable and ailing." Emil's death at sixteen months was attributed to a "glandular" condition.[34] Though the event could not have been unexpected, Clara was depressed during the summer after his death. Emil had been left in the care of a nurse for most of his short life, and his death seemed to be a blow from which it was difficult for her to recover. When Emil died, in June 1847, Clara Schumann was already pregnant with Ludwig.

Ludwig Schumann, 1848–1899

Of all the Schumann children, Ludwig had perhaps the unhappiest fate and caused his mother the most anguish. He entered a mental hospital at the age of twenty-two and died there, having outlived her by three years.

At the age of eight, Ludwig was packed off to boarding school with Ferdinand, a year his junior. The first signs of "oddness" were not perceived until Ludwig's early adolescence. When he was thirteen his teachers' verdict that he would not be able to attend a regular school required him to be separated from Ferdinand, who was going to attend a gymnasium in Berlin to prepare for a university and eventually a profession. Clara was of course disappointed, not only because she was faced with the problem of finding a suitable career for Ludwig but because she believed it was important for the family to be together as much as possible. Yet when Ludwig was confirmed in August 1862, she did not change her vacation plans to be with him. She noted the occasion in her diary, however: "Naturally my thoughts were with him."[35] By 1863 Ludwig was deemed mature enough to go to a special school (in effect, a trade school) in Karlsruhe—still away from the family—but within two years it was clear that he would never be able to hold more than a menial job.

Clara Schumann always felt inadequate in dealing with her sons, particularly Ludwig, and continually looked to a man to guide her. Time and again she appealed to Brahms for advice about her boys, but he wisely refused to offer anything but money and perhaps a listening ear.

Everyone who knew Ludwig spoke of his upright, loving nature—perhaps to soften their comments on his "original" personality, his lack of punctuality, and his irresponsibility, which cost him his jobs. Only later were these traits recognized as symptoms of mental illness. After many sleepless nights Clara decided in 1865 to apprentice the dreamy, unrealistic seventeen-year-old to a book dealer. When he was twenty he insisted he wanted to become a musician, and so for a short time Clara, at her wits' end, devoted herself to him: she gave him music lessons, something she never would have considered doing with any of the other children at that age: "I teach him for two hours every day and he is very zealous but . . . he has neither an ear nor rhythmic feeling. . . . His composing is simply dreadful, . . . yet he exerts himself to such an extent that I am always in a state of anxiety.[36]

In 1870 Ludwig was finally sent to a clinic for observation and diagnosis. On her return from an English tour, his mother received the news that his illness was incurable and that he had a spinal disease that presumably affected his brain. A letter dated June 8 to Rosalie Leser tells the story:

> I always told you that I had no hope [for Ludwig] but the confirmation struck my poor heart like a frightful blow—it is a pain like no other. To add to it, I am tormented by the reproaches [I leveled at him]. I would like to take back every word with which I reproached the poor boy; it is true that at the time I didn't know what the situation really was but it still hurt him. And none of us were there—that is so awful for me![37]

Ludwig's tragedy had a tremendous impact on Clara; it reminded her of the troubles with her husband: "I have not felt such pain since the misfortune with Robert," she wrote in her diary in June 1870. "The nights were often dreadful; for hours I would see the poor boy before me, looking at me with his good, honest eyes, which I never could resist." But as always, she marshaled her defenses by "playing industriously, wrote a good deal, and, in short, distracted myself in

Ludwig Schumann, age 18. Robert-Schumann-Haus, Zwickau.

any way I could." For years she was haunted by thoughts of Ludwig, but, as she wrote Rosalie Leser on September 16, 1871, "resolutely pushed them away."[38]

After much debate with friends and family, she committed Ludwig to a state mental hospital in Colditz, some thirty kilometers southeast of Leipzig. The buildings, erected in the thirteenth century, were rebuilt many times and over the years have served as a castle, a fortress, a poorhouse, an insane asylum, a Nazi concentration camp, and a prison for Allied prisoners of war during World War II.[39] Robert Schumann had visited the institution when he had been infatuated with Agnes Carus, the wife of the hospital's supervisor. (His fear of insane asylums may have stemmed from his youthful visits to Colditz.) Clara Schumann was probably unaware of the associations the place had for Ludwig's father, but she knew it was unlike the smaller, more personal sanatorium where Robert had been treated.

Julius Hübner, a painter and an old family friend in Dresden, was named Ludwig's official guardian. Clara kept in constant contact with the institution through the director and the pastor but did not visit Ludwig until 1875, some four years after he had been committed. She went only after he wrote that he wanted to see her. When she visited him, on June 3, she confided in her diary, she almost broke down:

> I finally saw my poor Ludwig again. . . . I felt as though I were being torn apart. He looked well, better than before, but something in his look was disconcerting, though kindly. . . . He was extraordinarily happy to see me, embraced me convulsively and begged me to take him away with me since he was quite well. What torment to have to tell him it was not possible. . . . It was all too horrible for me. To see my child as though he were in a prison, his imploring look as I left—I will never forget it.[40]

A year later she went to Colditz again in response to Ludwig's pleas to be released from the institution. She felt she had to make sure his confinement was really necessary and left convinced that he was more ill than before. In a letter to Friedrich Grössel, pastor of the institution, she wrote that she would like to visit, but that each visit left her feeling miserable for weeks.[41] She could not face the tragedy and never saw Ludwig again.

Ferdinand Schumann, 1849–1891

Ferdinand was born two months after the May uprising in Dresden, during which Clara had behaved so courageously; the story of his life is one of contrast between his human failings and his mother's great strength. Family talk of her heroism at that time and on later occasions may well have overwhelmed the boy. The one Schumann son who survived to a healthy adulthood also suffered a terrible fate: called up for army service in the Franco-Prussian War of 1870, he was not injured but incurred such painful rheumatism that it was treated with morphine, and he became addicted. He died of its effects at the age of forty-two. Clara assumed financial responsibility for his widow and six children.

Basically, Clara Schumann lacked faith in her children, particularly her sons, and Ferdinand undoubtedly suffered most from her attempts to control and dominate them. On April 16, 1863, she wrote to Ernst Rudorff, who had volunteered to give Ferdinand piano lessons, that she appreciated and accepted his offer but that he should give it up if it was "too dreadful." In an undated letter sent in April 1864 she thanked him again for his exertions on Ferdinand's behalf but added, "I am afraid he doesn't deserve what you have done."[42]

For a time Clara seemed proud of Ferdinand's accomplishments and choice of career: after studies in the Joachimsthaler Gymnasium, he took a position in a Berlin bank and seemed headed for a successful business career. But she disapproved of his marriage, in 1873, to Antonie Deutsch:

> I had always hoped that he would acquire more experience with other businesses, had hoped for a really good position in time and that he would continue to develop intellectually—now, with one stroke, all these hopes are in vain. . . . Yet the girl seems nice—they both believe they will love each other for all eternity—may God bless them! I could do nothing but remonstrate and finally gave them my consent.[43]

Ferdinand and his wife had seven children between 1874 and 1884; six survived. In 1884, when both parents were ill, three of his children lived with Clara in Frankfurt. When Ferdinand was still addicted to morphine at the age of thirty-eight and was unable to provide for his family, Clara agreed to take over the responsibility on condition that she be granted a decisive voice in his children's living arrangements. Ferdinand and Antonie had to agree; Ferdinand was on crutches, helpless, and moving from one institution to another in an attempt to cure his habit, and Antonie evidently had no other recourse. The determined Clara had the means, or would earn the means, to support the family, and she proceeded to arrange the lives of her grandchildren. The eldest child and only daughter, Julie (named for her aunt), became her special care.* Clara used her connections with Prussian royalty to secure a scholarship for thirteen-year-old Julie at the Luisenstift, an excellent and model girls' school in Berlin that prepared girls of the "higher classes" for independent lives as teachers, governesses, and other appropriate occupations. After three years, Julie briefly continued with her education in a *Hauswirtschaftsschule,* a school that gave young women the skills to run an upper-class home, and then was brought back to Frankfurt, where she studied piano with her grandmother and music theory

*Julie's letters to her grandmother and excerpts from the diary she kept during the years she lived with them offer a candid portrait of the elderly Clara Schumann and her daughters Marie and Eugenie. See Clara Schumann, *Mein liebes Julchen: Briefe von Clara Schumann an ihre Enkeltochter . . . ,"* ed. Dietz-Rüdiger Moser (Munich: Nymphenburger, 1990).

Ferdinand Schumann, about age 21. Robert-Schumann-Haus, Zwickau.

at the Hoch Conservatory and enjoyed the advantages of living in the Schumann home.

The oldest grandson, Ferdinand, lived in Frankfurt with his grandmother and aunts, and the younger boys were sent to Clara's niece in Schneeberg. This responsibility clearly strained Clara's financial resources. In July 1888 she wrote to Brahms, who had insisted on giving her 10,000 marks for her grandchildren:

> I cannot accept your friendly offer now; it wouldn't be right if I were to accept it without a really serious need. I still have a little sum available that I earned in England this year and last and it will suffice for this year. In addition, Elise also helps me somewhat, as she is paying for the education of one of the boys (her godchild).[44]

When Brahms, ignoring her letter, sent the money anyway, Clara accepted it. In May 1890 Ferdinand, "a totally broken man" at forty-one,[45] came to see his mother about plans for his family. She did not see him again before his death a year later, on June 6. Marie went to Gera, where he had been living, to take care of the funeral arrangements. Clara resumed teaching the day after the funeral. Though her students urged her to cancel the lessons, she did not do so. "Work is always the best diversion from pain," she wrote in her diary.[46]

After Ferdinand's death, Clara's relationship with Antonie deteriorated even further. Bitter feelings were exacerbated by family alignments: Marie Wieck, Clara's half sister, made Ferdinand's children her beneficiaries. Clara could not object to the arrangement but it did not please her. She became estranged from Julie, who was engaged to a young man Clara had not chosen and of whom she did not approve. With this Julie, "young true love" did not prevail, and the unhappy tale of the young Clara and Robert was recapitulated. In the end, Ferdinand's oldest son, who studied music with Clara and Marie Schumann, was the only grandchild who had close ties to his grandmother. He was with Clara when she died and his reminiscences of life in Frankfurt with her were later published.[47] His brothers were embittered by Clara's attitude toward their mother; the third child, Alfred Schumann, published (under a pseudonym) a scurrilous attack on his grandmother that Marie and Eugenie unsuccessfully attempted to buy up and destroy.[48]

Eugenie Schumann, 1851–1938

Thanks to Eugenie, the youngest Schumann daughter, we have a firsthand account of life in the Schumann family. Her first book, *Erinnerungen* (*Memoirs*) has been translated into English. A later biography, *Robert Schumann: Ein Lebensbild meines Vaters* (A Portrait of My Father), includes extensive excerpts from the marriage diaries of Robert and Clara Schumann (not published in their entirety until 1987), family documents, and other important material.[49]

Eugenie hardly knew her father and had limited contact with her mother, who was concertizing extensively during Eugenie's formative years. Raised successively by a housekeeper, by Elisabeth Werner (a family friend who acted as governess from 1858 to 1860), and by her older sisters, Marie and Elise, she was finally, at the age of twelve, sent off to boarding school in Rödelheim, where for almost three years she was isolated from her family and was desperately unhappy. According to Eugenie, the school combined the discomforts of a British public school with the brutal tyranny of a Prussian schoolmistress. At a smaller school near Wolfenbüttel that she subsequently attended, she had a far better experience. Despite the harshness of the years at Rödelheim, however, Eugenie had a better general education than any of her sisters.

Her musical education, too, was exceptional. In 1869 she was enrolled at the Königliche Hochschule für Musik in Berlin, directed by Joseph Joachim. Clara rarely asked for favors for her children (in fact, she bent over backward to avoid doing so) and Eugenie took the regular entrance examination, despite her family's friendship with Joachim. Her teacher there was Ernst Rudorff, her mother's former student, and though Clara trusted him as a friend and as a musician, she could not refrain from sending him advice on teaching Eugenie. Eugenie studied with Rudorff for about a year and a half and also had lessons with her mother and Brahms. (Her descriptions of their teaching are among the most vivid we have.)

From 1871 to 1891 Eugenie lived with her mother and Marie, acting as assistant hostess, companion, and teacher. In 1891, when she was forty, Eugenie decided to leave home and pursue a career of her own. Her mother did not discourage her decision, particularly because she felt that Eugenie was gifted and would be able to carry on the Schumann tradition.[50] As with Elise, however, her mother had mixed feelings. She never got along too well with Eugenie ("We unsettle each other"),[51] but she missed her companionship. The youngest daughter established herself as a piano teacher in England and remained there for many years, returning home for frequent visits. She was with her mother when Clara died.

In her younger years, Eugenie was outgoing, spirited, and sociable; she made many friends and always attempted to lead a more independent life than Marie. After the death of her older sisters, Eugenie, who lived on into the 1930s, took on some of the stern possessiveness of Marie and fought all attempts to tarnish the image of her parents.

According to Eugenie, all of the children, with the possible exception of Marie, regarded Clara Schumann as a kind of superbeing, seen occasionally and worshiped from afar. In her memoirs she wrote, "But one thing I know for certain, that wherever she might be, we were ever conscious of her loving care, her protecting hold over us, and that to us little ones, as well as to the elder sisters and brothers, she was the greatest thing we possessed in the world."[52]

Eugenie Schumann, age 20. Pencil sketch by Mrs. R. Lehmann, 1871. Robert-Schumann-Haus, Zwickau.

Felix Schumann, 1854–1879

Felix, the youngest and most gifted Schumann child—he had inherited his father's literary as well as musical ability—began to show symptoms of tuberculosis in adolescence and suffered for ten years before he died at the age of twenty-four. In her memoirs, Eugenie wrote that he had "brilliant gifts, a rare character, nobility, and kindness of heart, combined with a charming disposition and attractive appearance."[53] Felix's letters to his mother[54] reflect all these qualities and reveal that more than any of the other children, her youngest yearned to be with her and his older siblings, yet because of strict schoolmasters, Clara's career, and his ill health he was forced repeatedly to be separated from them.

This delicate and sensitive young man was orphaned in many senses: born after his father's hospitalization, he never knew the man he resembled, and his busy and practical mother had little sympathy for his poetic and musical aspirations. From birth to the age of four Felix was cared for by a housekeeper while his mother toured; then he and Eugenie lived in an apartment in Berlin with Elisabeth Werner—and later Marie—in charge; at nine he joined his older brother Ferdinand at a Berlin boarding school and saw his grandmother and sisters on Sundays. Although Felix spent some summers and vacations with his mother and siblings, he never had his mother's undivided attention until he came home to die in 1878.

He, like all the others, was very hurt and frightened when Ludwig was institutionalized. He yearned to go home and wrote to his mother:

> I have been a great expense to you this year, and have irritated you so much with my last letter that I can only ask in fear and trembling whether you are willing to let me come home for the holidays, which are beginning on July 9? I am afraid you will say, "He does not deserve it," but please let me hear soon, so that I can get over the shock. I have been looking forward so long to the coming weeks; when I was depressed I thought of them, and mind and heart, those heavy dull things, felt refreshed.[55]

His mother, totally involved with her own problems, seemed to have no conception of the depth of his feelings. He suffered a double burden when he read such words as these from her:

> Poor Ludwig's fate is terrible; I can find no words for grief such as this—it tears my heart. I could not bear it at all if I did not feel that I owe it to you to pull myself together.
>
> . . . Oh, dear boy, never give me trouble; this one is so great that it is almost unbearable. My dearest hopes are centered in you, and I am sure you will become a useful member of society if you fight against the faults which prevent you from doing your duty, especially your obstinacy. We can overcome much if we try, and I am sure, you mean to try, if only for love of me.
>
> You know how much we too are looking forward to your holidays, and

Felix Schumann, age 18. Robert-Schumann-Haus, Zwickau.

thank God I can afford to let you come; but it must be third class, dear boy! Take a cushion or rug with you.[56]

Felix was drawn to a musical career but his mother discouraged him. Still determined, he was finally forced to drop the idea because of his health and went to Heidelberg to study law. Like his father before him, he seemed to enjoy everything in Heidelberg but his legal studies. And like his father, the talented young man found it hard to settle down to one course of study. He wrote some poems that his mother, ever mistrustful of her children's talent, sent to Brahms with the request "Tell me frankly what you think of them. Don't think that I, like a weak mother, think him a genius. On the contrary, I have such fear of overrating the talent of his [Robert's] children that I probably sometimes demand too much of them."[57]

Brahms chose two of Felix's poems as texts for songs in his op. 63, "Meine Liebe ist grün" and "Wenn um den Holunder," and he used a third, "Es brausen der Liebe Wogen," in his op. 86. Fortunately Felix lived to hear some of his poetry in Brahms's settings. Yet in 1877 his mother asked him not to publish his poems under his own name; if his work were unsuccessful, she pointed out, a pseudonym would spare himself and his family discomfort. Though she was telling him, in effect, that she had no faith in the quality of his work, she was hurt when he answered with an "unloving" letter. She asked Brahms to visit Felix and try to set the situation straight.[58]

When Felix was dying in 1879, Clara, astounded by her own fortitude, wrote to Brahms:

Things are going very badly with us; Felix is visibly weaker every day though he still has not taken to his bed. The poor man suffers indescribably and we suffer with him. . . . I see him only for a few minutes at a time because it excites him too much, but my heart bleeds when I see him and no matter what I am doing, whatever it is, the poor sufferer is always before my eyes so that I must summon up all my strength to keep from being overcome by the pain. . . .

It was extraordinary to me that I was able to play with such freedom and strength at the concerts I gave while I was so unhappy that I could not forget my sorrow for one moment.[59]

In her diary she noted:

On the 14th [of February] I played in the Museum concert, an engagement promised some time ago. It was frightfully difficult, alas, and I wished I had not done it. Had I known how near the end was for our sufferer I would not have done it. My heart bled as I said good night to Felix and went to the concert. The contrast was so dreadful. Throughout the entire concert I saw only him, his emaciated body, his lifeless appearance, and alas, his lack of breath—it was horrible. And yet I played quite well, without even one wrong note![60]

Most poignant of all her diary entries is the final one on Felix:

> At three o'clock during the night between Saturday and Sunday [February 15–16] our Felix died in Marie's arms; she had not called me. . . . He suffered frightfully; it was a death struggle in the fullest sense of the term. . . . Marie, the loving one, always sacrificing herself, wanted to spare me this hour. . . . So I saw him in the morning, a corpse, and oh, I must confess I felt a release for which I had to thank heaven.[61]

The Wanderer

These tragic histories might have broken the spirit of another woman; Clara Schumann survived. As is often the case, this survivor had well-developed defenses against loss. She could not have gone on without her ability to set aside her anxiety and pain while investing all her energies in her work. Her career filled the lonely and frightening hours when she might otherwise have brooded or become unable to act; it provided a constructive outlet for her anxiety and tensions. Fortunately this means of self-preservation was accepted by society because of her position as an artist. It was generally conceded that her career—which enabled her to become the family provider—relieved her of the obligation to follow the conventional path of a middle-class German woman. During Schumann's lifetime she had accepted—with diminishing enthusiasm—the traditional role of mother. During his illness and after his death, acting as both mother and father to her children, she drew ever closer to the strongest and only parental model she had known: Friedrich Wieck. Like him, she set high standards of behavior and loyalty; like him, she was demanding and controlling. She was, of course, more reasonable than her father, certainly not so coarse, and never displayed the viciousness with which he conducted his affairs, but she lacked the tenderness and gentleness that Robert Schumann's nature had brought to parenthood. Propriety and self-restraint were among her highest priorities; her admonitions to her children and grandchildren stressed duty, thrift, discipline.

Clara Schumann's sorrow at the illnesses and deaths of Julie, Ludwig, Felix, and Ferdinand was deep and guilt-tinged and undoubtedly affected her own health. Yet it did not seem to occur to her that her living children also suffered losses and had as much need to mourn as she. Lacking the outlets she possessed, they suffered even more. After Julie died, Ferdinand took the long road to Vienna because he felt he had to see his mother, a natural gesture from a loving brother and son. Clara was surprised and touched, but troubled by the cost of the trip.

Money was, of course, a constant concern, and the fact that it was a real problem may have made it easier for her children to accept her solution. Eugenie wrote, "The thought that Mamma had to earn every penny I needed with the 'work of her hands' often troubled me when I was a mere child, and I hated to have to ask for new clothes."[62] She acknowledged that she often wished her home could be more like others.

> We knew that in our mother woman and artist were indissolubly one, so that we could not say this belongs to one part of her and that to another. We would sometimes wonder whether our mother would miss us or music most if one of the two were taken from her, and we could never decide.[63]

Clara knew well the value of a family life and in her own way tried to create a semblance of one. In 1857 she left her Düsseldorf apartment with all its sad memories and established a base in Berlin, which was more convenient for touring and close to her mother. Her two younger children remained there while the older children were scattered throughout Germany. The Berlin home, at 11 Unter den Zelten, only partially satisfied her restless spirit, and she was always considering other cities for permanent settlement. A summer house in Baden-Baden (actually Lichtenthal, an outlying area of that famed Black Forest resort) that she owned from 1863 to 1873 was the most successful in fostering family life, though even there it was rare to find everyone gathered at once. Too often her mothering was done through the mail. Restlessly Clara roamed the vacation resorts of Europe, even after she had bought the house in Baden-Baden. Inevitably she wanted to try a new spa, a new lake, a new mountain area. She needed rest from her winter tours but she also needed diversion and time with her friends. After she sold the Baden-Baden house and established another home in Berlin, she moved again, for the last time, to Frankfurt in 1878.

THE MUSICIAN

Clara Schumann's need to make music could never be quelled. This need extended to hearing music as well as performing. In 1873 she found she had to relinquish the opportunity of hearing Hermann Levi conduct a performance of Schumann's rarely performed opera, *Genoveva,* with which she had been intimately associated. There had been few opportunities to see the work, but Marie needed her urgently in Berlin. She wrote Brahms, "I cannot describe to you how *difficult* it was for me to give this up. The children hardly suspect what a proof of my love I have given them with this renunciation. Only someone who like us is an artist—body and soul—can understand the delight we feel."[64]

At times during and after her marriage Clara Schumann insisted that her love for Robert was the most important consideration in her life, exceeding even her art and career. On September 20, 1840, during the second week of their marriage, she wrote in their diary, "I live only in you," and added during that same week: "I was out of sorts because Robert was not feeling well. In the evening we took a little walk and Robert spoke to me in such a friendly way that I became quite cheerful again. I am so dependent on his mood; it may not be good but I cannot help myself." On February 5, 1860, when she was thinking about growing old and having to relinquish her art, she wrote in her diary, "Only for one, for Him, could I have renounced my life as an artist; my heart would have been completely fulfilled—with the understanding of his art and his whole being."[65]

But these statements give a false impression. More characteristic, and certainly more honest and consistent with her education and personality, are the many references to her own artistic sphere found throughout her letters and diaries. Perhaps the most telling is the letter she wrote to Joachim in September 1854, after Schumann was sent to the sanatorium and she was preparing to leave home and children in order to tour:

> I always pray to God to give me the strength to successfully overcome the frightful agitations that I have lived through and that still await me. My true old friend, my piano, must help me with this! Oh, dear Joachim, I always believed I knew what a splendid thing it is to be an artist, but only now, for the first time, do I really understand how all my pain and joy can be relieved only by divine music so that I often feel quite well again.[66]

If Clara Schumann felt any conflict between the roles of wife and mother and artist, it was almost always resolved in favor of the artist, though not untinged with guilt. So, for example, she hesitated—but only momentarily—before deciding to participate in the August 1873 Schumann festival in Bonn, which was organized to raise money for a new tombstone for Robert Schumann (and under which she, too, would eventually lie). "As a *wife*," she wrote in her diary in February, "my feelings were not [to play], but as an artist, I felt I ought not to absent myself."[67]

In a slightly defensive letter to Levi on May 22 she described her feelings more succinctly: "Shall I, who have been among the staunchest champions of his music all my life, be silent at this occasion in his honor? Should I relinquish to another that which is so entwined with my entire being and is, above all, my prerogative?"[68]

There were few women with whom Clara Schumann shared her feelings about art or with whom she collaborated. She had many women friends but only one or two women colleagues. She read through music with her daughters, played publicly with Julie von Asten, a Viennese pianist who had been her pupil, and Pauline Viardot, and worked with a few female singers, carefully chosen, such as Amalie Joachim, Mathilde Hartmann, Livia Frege, and Marie Fillunger. Otherwise her colleagues and associates were men—Julius Stockhausen, Hermann Levi, Brahms, Joachim, and the other leading male musicians and conductors of the day. Of the female artists, she regarded only Pauline Viardot as an equal.

There was no question of a "weaker sex" as far as Clara Schumann's musicianship was concerned. She had been trained as a professional, she was a figure of power and authority in the musical world before she was forty, and as an artist she was either extravagantly admired or fiercely criticized by both men and women. Cosima Wagner and Anton Schindler, for example, were exceedingly hostile, but not because she was a woman. She was generally regarded as unique, almost above gender.

In 1860 she wrote Joachim that she wanted to sign the militant declaration against the "new Germans" (Liszt, Wagner, and their school).[69] The document appeared prematurely and her name was not among the signatories, but it was clear that she fully expected to take a stand with Joachim, Brahms, and the two other male signers.*

Yet, like any other woman of her time, she turned to her men friends for advice, personal as well as professional. In 1870, when she was invited to participate in a Beethoven festival in Vienna but wanted no part of performances conducted by Liszt and Wagner, she found it difficult to face the problem squarely and asked Joachim for advice. "As a *woman*, I cannot act like you. It would seem very arrogant if I, a woman—as compared to a man—were to express my opinion openly. I must invent a lie! But what shall I say?" She went on to ask if he did not also think it right that she should refuse to play. Joachim's reply summed up what he and many others felt about her: "That you are a woman seems to me to have nothing to do with it, or perhaps it may be the very reason for you to stay away. In any case, you are, as far as art is concerned, 'man enough.'"[70]

Money

As a girl, Clara professed modesty about her accomplishments and was uneasy about competition from Liszt and Thalberg. As an adult, she had few reservations about her performances and could not abide the kind of false modesty that was expected of a woman of her time. She perceived herself as a professional and even during her married life took pride in the fact that she could earn money with her talent and skills, though to some extent she attempted to conceal it in deference to her husband's feelings and the tradition of male support of the family. Clara paid obeisance to this tradition but thought it was carried too far when, after her first concert in Düsseldorf, in October 1850, she was presented with nothing but a basket of flowers. Indignantly she wrote to Ferdinand Hiller, the previous music director, on whose recommendation Robert had been engaged:

> The directors [of the Düsseldorf Municipal Concert Society] invited me to play in the first concert without asking what I wanted for an honorarium. I assumed they had learned from you—since you knew from the Dresden days—that I never play for less than 10 louis d'or (in large cities like Bremen, Hamburg, etc. I always get 20 louis d'or). Now the concert is over, and, they say, a

*The declaration is discussed further on p. 181.

> brilliant success, and the directors send me—a basket of flowers! I was surprised at that, yet I still accepted it as a friendly gesture; now, however, they come and thank me for my courtesy and finally a light dawns. But it is simply incomprehensible that the gentlemen can think that for the first time here I will play gratis—moreover, I cannot understand the indelicacy of wanting this. Do they think we are rich people? or do they think I will play whenever they like for the salary my husband receives? Dear Herr Hiller, if I had no children or were rich, then I could play as often as the people wanted and I would be happy always to play gratis, but in my circumstances I cannot do so. . . . My playing is a separate matter, which they could not count on when they engaged my husband.[71]

After Schumann died, there was no need to tiptoe around this issue. Though friends offered money and established funds to help pay for Schumann's medical expenses, Clara was determined not to be dependent on anyone. Though she could support her family only by breaking it up, she did not hesitate. The situation was not uncommon: many widows in similar circumstances sent their children to friends or relatives or boarding schools or, if necessary, hired them out as apprentices. Clara Schumann did all these things. She was particularly incensed at the idea of benefit concerts for her, and in 1873 she was so insulted by a "horrible" announcement in a Graz paper of a benefit concert for the Schumann family that she wrote Brahms she was "beside herself." She denounced the concert givers and announced she would not accept money earned by other musicians.[72]

Her self-esteem equaled her pride; she knew her worth and demanded substantial fees. When she was negotiating for some concerts in Vienna in 1870, she asked Brahms to find out what they were thinking of paying: "They are asking me about the honorarium and I am perplexed about what to do—I don't want to ask too much, but on the other hand I don't want less than what they would give other artists."[73]

Her high fees and her great reputation led to the mistaken belief that she was wealthy. (Twice in her lifetime she was the victim of burglars who stole jewelry and valuable mementos—gifts from wealthy admirers of her artistry.) Only her intimate friends knew how she struggled to make ends meet. In 1864 she apologized to Brahms for playing in Hamburg under Stockhausen, who had been appointed to a position that Brahms had hoped to get, because, as she put it, "in my circumstances, I cannot afford to turn down any engagement."[74]

Earlier that year, she explained to Brahms why she had to work so hard and had been unable even to spend Christmas with her children: "Last summer I had many financial worries, had to take 1,000 taler from my capital,* but had the luck to make it up through the admittedly terribly strenuous concertizing I did before Christmas."[75]

*Probably for purchase of the house in Baden-Baden.

From a chatty letter from Amalie Joachim to her husband we learn of money problems again in 1872:

> I have just come from Frau Schumann. The poor dear woman made such a sad impression. That is not the worst sorrow for me—the burdensome cares are the worst—cares over her daily bread. It seems she has not yet received any money. . . . Imagine, Felix has incurred debts of 500 florins which Frau Schumann must now pay; besides that, all the money he received for the quarter was gambled away in Baden. But now she has still more grief on account of Elise, who has left her position [as a piano teacher] in Frankfurt in order to go and live as a companion to a friend. The manner in which she did this in opposition to her mother was totally horrendous. Enough—she has a lot to endure from her children. Poor Julie is doing very poorly and she awaits news of her death every day,* but she still wants to go to Vienna. She says she could not do otherwise and feels that art is the only thing and that, moreover, the work elevates and strengthens her. . . . The people who give money for Frau Schumann also believe she already has enough. . . . None of them know what it is like to really have sorrow and need.[76]

Until 1873, Clara Schumann toured from September to May with few stops in between and often did one-night stands, especially in England. In 1869 she gave concerts on February 1, 3, 4, 6, 8, 15, 17, 20, 22, 23, and 27. The schedule eased in March but she continued to perform in the British Isles until April. A trip to Russia in 1864 was particularly strenuous, concluding with a forty-four-hour train trip from St. Petersburg to Berlin. Correspondence regarding the tours went on all year long but major arrangements were made in the summers, which she devoted to practicing, teaching, and writing letters, sometimes as many as fourteen a day. During the concert season she snatched a day here or a week there to see any of her children who were within reach. After 1873 she was forced to slow down somewhat; plagued by pains in her arms and other incapacitating illnesses, she found huge expenses mounting. Julie had already died but Ludwig's sanatorium, Felix's treatment for tuberculosis, Ferdinand's treatment for drug addiction and rheumatism, and her own medical bills placed a heavy burden on her. Fortunately, gifts from foundations, royalties from performances and her editions of Schumann's music, and payments from the sale of his manuscripts became available about this time;† this was money that she had no qualms about accepting. Though these funds sufficed to meet basic financial needs, any year in which she did not give at least fifty concerts was a bad year as far as she was concerned. "I get so melancholy when I cannot be active,"

*Frau Joachim was unaware that Julie had died the day before the letter was written.

†Robert Schumann had suggested (probably in the Dresden years) that his musical autographs be used to sustain the family in the future. In 1887 Clara Schumann made up her mind to sell them, and after several years of negotiations they went to the Royal Library in Berlin for 15,000 marks. This sum was a major source of support for the Schumann family until well into the twentieth century (Eugenie Schumann, *Robert Schumann*, 386).

she wrote to Brahms on June 2, 1874. "I have no talent for lazing about [Zum Bummeln habe ich so gar kein Talent]."[77]

Winding Down

Among the highlights of the late years were the Bonn Music Festival of 1873 and her fiftieth and sixtieth jubilee concerts. The 1873 festival, where she played the Schumann Piano Concerto, was one of the few occasions when all the Schumann children gathered together to hear their mother perform. Close friends who attended included Jenny Lind and her husband and the Freges, and such colleagues as Brahms, Joachim, Stockhausen, Rudorff, Dietrich, Grimm, and Hiller.

A few weeks after she took a permanent teaching position at a Frankfurt conservatory in 1878, she was elated by surprise celebrations, first at the conservatory, where fellow faculty members performed an all–Clara Schumann program, and then at the Gewandhaus in Leipzig, where she had made her first appearance as a nine-year-old in 1828. In her diary she wrote of the "unforgettable" day in Leipzig—October 24, 1878—on which only compositions of her husband were played. Among the listeners were old friends who had been present fifty years earlier. She described the event:

> The entire hall was decorated with green and gold wreaths and garlands of oak leaves. As I entered, the whole audience stood and a rain of flowers began, under which I was literally buried. . . . It was a long time before I could seat myself at the piano. Several times I felt as though I would be overwhelmed by the emotions I was feeling; I shook violently but I controlled myself and played the concerto with perfect calm and it succeeded magnificently.[78]

Ten years later, in 1888, she was overwhelmed by more surprise concerts and tributes, this time accompanied by addresses, letters, telegrams, flowers, poetry, and wreaths from all over the world. "I never suspected how much love was bestowed on me, and I am often quite embarrassed. . . . The celebration brought many people closer to me, and I to them, and that is really gratifying; it gives me a feeling of being at home here [in Frankfurt]—something I had not felt in this way before."[79]

Throughout her years of concertizing, Clara Schumann was often in severe physical pain. Both as a young girl and as an adult woman, she drove herself relentlessly. Despite the regimen of daily walks and outdoor exercise established by Wieck, the young Clara was not always in the best of health. The tensions between her and her father took their toll: in Paris in 1839 she had headaches, severe anxiety, pains in her fingers; in January 1840 she had several fainting spells and severe facial neuralgia just before and even during concerts in Berlin. She was in such mental and physical pain at that time that she wrote Robert she

Clara Schumann, age 59. Portrait (pastel) by Franz von Lenbach, 1878. Robert-Schumann-Haus, Zwickau.

"sometimes wanted to lie down and die."[80] A few weeks after their wedding, Robert noted her "illness" in letters to friends and in his household books.[81*] Indeed, the surprisingly frequent reports of her indispositions are intermingled with Robert Schumann's meticulously kept records of his own ill health. Her symptoms are not spelled out, but the details of her complaints given in later letters suggest that they may have been psychosomatic in origin. We know that in the 1860s and later she suffered attacks of anxiety and fits of weeping, and before performances feared that she would forget her music or break down. At times she believed she could no longer play. Invariably she recovered, but the tension and fear affected her health.

When she resumed her full-time career after Schumann's illness, pains in her arms, hands, and fingers prompted visits to spas and other health resorts. Rheumatic attacks continued: on November 27, 1857, she wrote Joachim that several concerts had to be canceled; her pain was so intense that opium was prescribed, and she was forced to rest her arm in a sling for some time.[82] She was unable to perform for some eighteen months in 1874 and 1875. Over the years she tried many cures: water treatments, electric shock, "animal baths,"† massage, rest. The "rest cure," popular at that time, was the most difficult for her. She could ask her daughters to conduct her correspondence but no one could take her place at the piano. During the last decade of her life, she was plagued by arthritis in her hands, hearing difficulties, and growing infirmity. In February 1894, fearful of what the future held for her, she wrote in her diary, "What will become of me if I cannot play any more?"[83] She was desolate without her art.

By 1878, when she was fifty-nine, she found she needed a week to recuperate between concerts and recognized the necessity of cutting down on the number of engagements she accepted. In addition, she was having increasing difficulty hearing. These problems may have prompted her decision to accept the teaching position in Frankfurt. After twenty-five years of wandering, she rented—and eventually bought—a home for her family. The house, Myliusstrasse 32, which still stands, was to be hers until her death. The years of wandering were over, but professional concerns did not cease.

At her last public concert, in March 1891, the seventy-two-year-old woman joined with a colleague from the conservatory to perform Brahms's arduous Variations on a Theme by Haydn for Two Pianos, and until she was felled by a stroke in 1896, she played, taught, improvised, edited, arranged, and reveled in music.

As she lay dying, she asked her grandson Ferdinand to play for her. The music, from Schumann's Intermezzi, op. 4, and his F-sharp Major Romance, op. 28, was the last she heard.

*Many entries throughout the marriage diary remark on her indispositions, especially in the early months of the marriage.

†An archaic treatment in which the affected limb was placed in a cavity of a recently slaughtered animal to "absorb" the bodily heat. Robert Schumann took such *Tierbäder* in 1832 in an effort to cure his hand injury.

PART II

Themes from the Life of Clara Schumann

CHAPTER 9

Clara Schumann and Johannes Brahms

The friendship between Clara Schumann and Johannes Brahms has always been a subject of spirited speculation and even malicious gossip.[1] The frequent published accounts that emphasize the "passionate" friendship that developed between the thirty-four-year-old pianist and the twenty-year-old composer neglect the deeper personal and artistic bonds between them. Neither Clara Schumann nor Brahms ever denied the deep love they felt for each other, but a sexual liaison during the time Schumann was institutionalized would have been entirely out of character for the grieving, practical, conscientious woman. And in later years, all evidence points to a platonic relationship. The significance of their many-layered friendship, which began in 1853 and endured until her death in 1896, lay not in any sexual relationship but in the musical and personal interaction between them. As she had been for Schumann, Clara was the inspiration for much of Brahms's music and one of the first musicians to recognize his genius.

The second child of Johann Jakob Brahms, a Hamburg musician, and his wife, Christiane, Johannes matured in an atmosphere of financial insecurity.* Christiane Brahms was seventeen years older than her husband. With their children—Elise (born 1831), Johannes (born 1833), and Friedrich (Fritz), (born 1835)—they shared two rooms in an apartment in what is still a shabby district (but not a slum) of Hamburg. During Johannes's childhood his parents had great hopes and ambitions for him, for he showed unusual talents. He was given the opportunity to study piano and composition with Eduard Marxsen, probably the best teacher in Hamburg, but until he toured as an accompanist with the Hungarian violinist Eduard Reményi beginning in April 1853, Brahms had never been far from home. Through Joseph Joachim, a compatriot of

*The myths of extreme poverty and the boy Brahms playing piano in low-class dives in Hamburg have been thoroughly disproved by recent research. See Avins, 1–6.

Reményi, with whom the young pianist struck up an instant friendship, he met Liszt in Weimar and, a few months later, the Schumanns in Düsseldorf.

Only twenty years old when he arrived in Düsseldorf, Brahms was already an accomplished pianist and composer. At fifteen he had given his first solo concert, which, like the early programs of the young Clara Wieck, was a hodgepodge of songs and duets, solos for clarinet, violin, and cello, and several virtuoso piano pieces.[2] Works he had composed between the ages of seventeen and twenty included the bold, romantic sonatas for piano later labeled op. 1 and 2; the beginnings of the Sonata op. 5; the Scherzo op. 4; a violin and piano sonata, since lost; and a miscellany of songs, later published as opp. 3, 6, and 7. Marxsen's prize student, the young Brahms was well schooled in the techniques of composition and knew the work of his great predecessors, including Bach and Beethoven. A performance of *The Marriage of Figaro* at the Hamburg opera house had made an indelible impression on him and begun a lifelong fascination with Mozart.[3] But he knew very little of the work of Schumann, as it was rarely played outside of Leipzig and Dresden. The Schumanns had visited Hamburg in March 1850 and it is assumed that Brahms heard their programs, which included Schumann's Piano Concerto, Piano Quintet, and Variations for Two Pianos, op. 46. They did not meet on that occasion, however. Schumann had returned unopened a package of compositions that Brahms had sent to him at his hotel. When Brahms had an opportunity to study Schumann's music in the summer of 1853, he felt an immediate kinship with the older composer. At the urging of Joachim and other friends, the young man shyly approached the Schumann home in Düsseldorf. But he was not timid in regard to his music. Unlike Schumann at twenty, Brahms was confident of his future; there were no doubts in his mind—or in that of anyone who knew him—that he was a supremely gifted and creative musician.

Brahms's arrival coincided with a most difficult period in the lives of the Schumann family. Robert's position as municipal music director in Düsseldorf was threatened and his mental illness was progressing. His enthusiasm for Brahms's work was so overwhelming that the younger man, a typical North German who habitually understated his feelings, may well have been embarrassed by it.

During the month Brahms spent with the Schumanns, he accepted gratefully the help they offered. Leaving Düsseldorf on November 2 with Schumann's recommendations in hand, he proceeded to Leipzig, where he met and played for influential music circles. Several Leipzig publishers, including Breitkopf & Härtel and Senff, undertook to publish some of his works. Obviously seeing the Schumanns in a parental role, he wrote to them in December 1853, when the works appeared in print, "I am taking the liberty of sending you your first foster children, who owe to you their right to exist."[4]

During October 1853, Brahms, still beardless, with softly curling blond hair, a high forehead, and a voice barely changed, had at Schumann's request been sketched by Jean-Joseph-Bonaventure Laurens, a French admirer of Robert Schumann's music, who was visiting Düsseldorf at the time. During Schumann's confinement at the mental hospital in Endenich, he asked for the Lau-

Clara Schumann, age 35, in a photograph by Franz Hanfstaengl taken in 1854, after Robert Schumann's hospitalization. Robert-Schumann-Haus, Zwickau.

rens sketch so that he might view it daily. Even in the hospital he requested Brahms's works, played and analyzed them, and responded to them with joy and delight. He addressed Brahms now with the formal *Sie*, now with the intimate *du*. Respect—we may even say veneration—for his art is evident in all the letters Schumann wrote from Endenich.

The modern reader is inevitably troubled by such unselfish admiration. It is difficult not to assume that Schumann envied the boy who displayed his powers with a self-assurance in such marked contrast with the uncertainty of the young Schumann. It is sad to contemplate Schumann, only forty-three years old, weary and ill, already casting himself in the subordinate role of prophet. That there was an element of envy in his extravagant praise is suggested by his use of the term "demons" or "young demons" to characterize Brahms and Joachim.[5] The last few letters Schumann wrote to Joachim are fanciful, even irrational, and in retrospect are symptomatic of what was to follow in February 1854.

After Schumann's hospitalization, Clara turned for comfort and moral support to a group of young musicians (friends referred to them as "the young gentlemen")[6] who were devotees of her husband's music; the group included Albert Dietrich, Julius Otto Grimm, and Schumann's "demons," Joachim and Brahms. It must be remembered that Schumann was still virtually unknown, and Clara was deeply grateful for their advocacy. Of them all, Brahms was not only the most gifted composer but the one most available and devoted. He sped to Düsseldorf as soon as he heard of Schumann's suicide attempt and virtually sacrificed the next two years of his life for Robert, Clara, and their seven children. On his arrival he took over the keeping of Schumann's household books. Beginning with the entries for February 1854 and continuing until December 30, 1854, he noted down all the family's expenses, including postage stamps, servants' wages, rent, the girls' school tuition, and income from Schumann's publishers and investments.[7] By keeping such intimate records, he became a member of the family; with these entries he stepped into the shoes of the husband—an awesome responsibility for a young man of twenty.

Unlike Joachim and Dietrich, Brahms had no regular post, and though he had begun a career as a concert pianist, he abandoned it with few regrets; his real interest lay in composing. His parents approved of his decision to aid the Schumanns, but after a few months his mother wrote:

> June 15, 1854
> Schumann smoothed the way for you but you must do more. You cannot live by composing alone—the greatest masters were not able to do it. Hopefully, you would have undertaken something if Schumann had not fallen ill. For the moment you did the right thing in going there. But to remain? You are losing much money and time. . . . Like it or not, only the person who has money will be respected.[8]

His mother's advice was ignored. During the two years he remained in Düsseldorf, he eked out a meager living by teaching a few pupils and borrowing

Johannes Brahms, age 20, in Düsseldorf. Sketch by Jean-Joseph-Bonaventure Laurens, 1853. Schumannhaus, Bonn.

money from Joachim and Julius Otto Grimm, another young musician he had met in Leipzig and who came to join him in Düsseldorf. Letters from his mother continued exhorting him to seek other avenues:

> March 20, 1855
> That you're giving lessons is probably good; at least it's something. But you always disliked it and it brings in very little—I mean for you, who can do so much more. Frau Schumann also gives lessons, but she prefers concertizing. You think the returns [from the concerts] are not great. But she would not do it otherwise—turn her family and home over to strangers and travel about without a husband.
> ... When one has been so richly endowed by God with so many gifts, it is not right to remain sitting there so calmly.[9]

Again Brahms ignored her advice. He took lodgings near the Schumann home and settled into the family circle. When Clara resumed touring a few months after Felix's birth, he supervised the children's schooling and music lessons and assisted the housekeeper and the servants with the care of the younger children. When Clara and the children moved to a new apartment in 1855, he rented a room in the same house. He had the freedom of the Schumann apartment, used the pianos for practicing and composing, and arranged the library of books and music, a particularly grateful task for a young man who had a limited education, an avid thirst for literature, and no funds for scores or books.

After Schumann's death, Clara explained in a letter to her children what Brahms had meant to her during those two years: "Like a true friend, he came to share all my grief; he strengthened the heart that threatened to break, he uplifted my spirit; brightened my soul any way he could. He was, in short, my friend in the fullest sense of the word."[10] Brahms gave her his youth, his love for nature, consolation, passionate admiration, and above all, the opportunity to share the thinking and work of a creative genius.

The importance of this particular bond in their long relationship cannot be overestimated. As a child prodigy, Clara had been an active member of the most elite circles of Leipzig musical life; great men had rhapsodized about her artistry. Before she played Schumann's works, she was her father's right hand in the musical evenings at the Wieck home. Beginning at the age of twelve, she had introduced Schumann's works in Leipzig, Dresden, Vienna, and Paris. As an adolescent she had been honored with the friendship and respect of Mendelssohn, Liszt, and Chopin as well as Schumann. Clara's daughter Eugenie explained further:

> She once asked me if I could at all realize what it meant to have had a friend from childhood upwards who stimulated all your noblest and most artistic qualities, who in daily and hourly intercourse lavished pearls and jewels upon you; if I did not think it was natural that she felt she could not go on living de-

prived of such gifts, and that she clung to friends like Brahms and Joachim who could console her in some measure for what she had lost.[11]

Just as she could understand and interpret Schumann's genius before it was generally appreciated, so she could recognize Brahms's genius; she had the musical understanding to encourage the young man who was destined to be the leading instrumental composer of his age. Her friendship with him was in keeping with a lifelong pattern of close ties with the creative figures of her time. The appreciation and support of a Clara Schumann would have overwhelmed any twenty-year-old musician, but for Brahms, whose acquaintance with educated women was limited, and who (like the young Schumann) was inspired by the German Romantics—E. T. A. Hoffmann, Jean Paul, Joseph von Eichendorff—it was an almost shattering experience. Many years later, Brahms referred obliquely to the time in Düsseldorf as his "Werther years."[12]* Certainly there were many parallels between the young Brahms and Goethe's sensitive young hero, with his unrequited love for the beautiful, maternal Lotte, the betrothed of another man. Brahms wrote to Joachim in June 1854:

> I often have to restrain myself forcibly from just quietly putting my arm around her and even—I don't know, it seems to me so natural that she could not misunderstand. I think I can no longer love an unmarried girl—at least I have quite forgotten about them. They but promise heaven while Clara shows it revealed to us.[13]

Exactly what happened in Düsseldorf will never be known, but it is clear that from the beginning their relationship was far more than a mere infatuation; meeting and loving Clara Schumann was to affect the course of Brahms's life. The young Brahms was an extraordinary phenomenon; Clara Schumann was no ordinary woman. The commonly held notion of her as a combination of artist and *Hausmütterchen* (little housewife) is misleading.[14] She had entered marriage as a world-famous figure and, as we have seen, maintained her career as pianist and composer in a thoroughly professional way. While bearing and raising children, she was composing serious works, arranging, editing, and teaching. She was not merely Schumann's wife and partner; she was a colleague. As Schumann's breakdowns became more frequent, she was forced to make the decisions, musical and personal, which in that time and place were generally left to men. At the same time, she was still a young woman, and though perhaps not beautiful in the conventional sense (solemnity and melancholy had already settled on her features), she was attractive and she had a forceful personality.

*During the Düsseldorf years, Brahms composed, among other works, two movements of the Piano Quartet op. 60, which was published many years later. In statements and letters to friends and to Simrock, his publisher, he noted that the publication of his op. 60 could well be illustrated with a picture of the man "in the blue swallow-tailed coat and a yellow vest." Every literate German understood the reference to Goethe's *Der Leiden des jungen Werthers* (The Sorrows of Young Werther).

Her marriage to Schumann must have been a disappointment to her by this time: he was ill and getting worse, and even if he were to recover, there seemed to be no place for him in the musical world.

Whether Brahms's love, like Werther's, was unrequited cannot be established. Clara never minimized what his presence and friendship meant to her at the time. That the two were aware of raised eyebrows and gossip is certain; all but a few of her letters to him before 1858 (the responses to his passionate letters) were later destroyed. Moreover, she evidently felt it necessary to explain their relationship to her children. Brahms, conscious that their correspondence might be compromising, urged her in May 1856 to put a note on the packet of his letters to the effect that they belonged only to the two of them.[15] He was always concerned about the safekeeping of their letters, and this question arose many times in their long correspondence.[16] Though Clara Schumann generally observed all the conventions of her time, she disregarded comments made by close friends who believed that she permitted Brahms too many liberties and deplored her acceptance of the young man as a colleague and equal. She held firmly to her decision to call him *du*, declaring that she felt like a mother to him.* Her friends were evidently skeptical, and both she and Brahms were aware of the inevitable misunderstandings. In May 1856, when she was in England, he wrote, "How I would like to come! But would it be possible? . . . If Bargiel [Clara's half brother] went, nobody could say anything, but it would be too noticeable if I, who have nothing to do there, came."[17]

After Robert Schumann's death in July 1856, Clara invited Brahms and his sister Elise to join her and two of her sons for a month's vacation in the Rhine Valley and Switzerland. During that month, from August 14 to September 13, they may have discussed their future, perhaps even marriage, but just what was said will, of course, never be known.† It seems evident, however, that a decision was reached that they should part. By October 21 Brahms had left Düsseldorf and Clara had begun her first concert tour of the season, a wearying round of the concert halls of Europe and England to earn the money she needed to educate and raise her seven children, and eventually the six children of her son Ferdinand, who became incapacitated at the age of thirty-five. The concert circuit was to continue for thirty-five years. The correspondence between them went on, but the tone of Brahms's letters changed from impatient passion to a warm, resigned love. Though an almost desperate longing to see her still pervades the letters written between 1856 and 1860, it seems likely that they were slowly becoming reconciled to living apart and pursuing separate careers. Eugenie Schumann hints that the decision may not have been entirely mutual:

> But it was inevitable that he should recognize that the destiny he had to fulfill was irreconcilable with single-minded devotion to a friendship. To recognize

*At this time he was the only man outside her family whom she addressed in the familiar form.

†Despite persistent conjecture, I have never found any convincing evidence that they discussed marriage.

> this and immediately to seek a way out was the natural outcome of his virile nature. That he broke away ruthlessly was perhaps also an inevitable consequence when one takes his inherent qualities and the nature of his situation into account. But without doubt he had had a hard struggle with himself before he had steered his craft in a fresh direction, and he never got over the self-reproach of having wounded my mother's feelings at the time, and felt that this could never be undone.[18]

Though Brahms had several flirtations with suitable attractive musical young women, he avoided matrimony, and Clara Schumann never remarried. She always felt very possessive about her younger friend. In her diary Clara declared her wish to mother him, and though she expressed the conventional wish that he marry, she was unhappy when he showed an interest in younger women.[19] The thought that he might have loved Julie, the only one of her children who evoked such emotion, was so difficult for her to accept that she could not acknowledge it, even in her diary, until after Julie was engaged to someone else.[20] No matter where he was, she acted in a proprietary manner toward him. An unceasing stream of directions, admonitions, reproaches, requests flowed to him, and he accepted them with patience, though not always with grace.

The special quality of their friendship was recognized by everyone who knew them. They were "best friends" to each other, with all that the term implies in respect to emotional ties, understanding, mutual interests, and background. The friendship was sustained despite jealousies, reproaches, and frequent tiffs.

Their correspondence reflects a change in Brahms's feelings toward Clara after Schumann's death. Yet though the tone of his letters became more dispassionate after she was widowed, it is manifest that he loved her in his own way throughout his life. Brahms, though personally reserved (he was generally considered to be unusually secretive), had many close friends—Joachim, Grimm, Hermann Levi, the surgeon-pianist Theodor Billroth, the composer Heinrich von Herzogenberg and his wife, Elisabeth. Sooner or later, however, some disagreement always arose and the intimacy faded. His friends never doubted his integrity and genius but eventually his gruffness, lack of social skills, and blunt candor alienated many of his closest associates. The relationship with Clara, however, was unique: his letters imply a faith and trust he shared with no other person. It was one of the foundations of his life.

Brahms's interests ranged beyond music, and he forged friendships with such writers as Klaus Groth and Joseph Viktor Widmann and such artists as Anselm Feuerbach, Julius Allgeyer, and Max Klinger. Clara could not share these friendships: she was embarrassed about her lack of general education and told Brahms that she often felt uneasy in intellectual circles,[21] but she respected his insatiable appetite for reading. She delighted in presenting him with books. Her first gifts to him were literary works: twelve volumes of Jean Paul at Christmas 1854, Ariosto and Dante in May 1855, Schiller's works in June 1855, and the tragedies of Sophocles in July 1855.[22] He was encouraged, of course, to read everything in the rich Schumann library in Düsseldorf.

One of the most significant links in their friendship was their common economic situation. Unlike many of their friends, neither had inherited wealth or been given the advantages of a cultivated upper-middle-class home. Both depended on their musical activities to support themselves and their families: even during their adolescence, money they earned through professional activities was a welcome contribution to the family income. Both as a girl and as the wife of a composer, Clara was all too familiar with financial insecurity. Though she had not endured the difficulties Brahms had known as a boy, money was as great a concern to her as to him, and they discussed it without embarrassment. Poverty was not an experience Brahms could share with the aristocratic Elisabeth von Herzogenberg, for example. It would have been unthinkable for Frau von Herzogenberg to visit the humble apartment of the Brahms family in Hamburg, as Clara did.* And no other woman in Brahms's life would have invited his unsophisticated sister to join her for a vacation and offer advice about the kind of petticoats to pack.[23]

Nevertheless, their attitudes toward money differed considerably. Frau Schumann was practical and thrifty. As a child she had been rewarded with money for her efforts at the piano, and, as we have seen, probably equated it with love. The sums she earned as a child prodigy were invested by her father. Schumann's small inheritance was also carefully invested, and was the basic source of income throughout their married life, since Schumann did not earn a regular salary until 1850.

Brahms, whose family never had extra money to invest, knew nothing of the world of capital, investments, and interest, and alternately prized and disdained financial rewards. His ambivalence was evident in many other areas as well. Clara, who was free of such conflicts, functioned as his financial consultant when he finally began to earn the money he claimed to despise, and gave him basic advice:

> November 19, 1860
> Note well, tell Fritz and Elise that they should separate the coupons from the papers and secure each in different places. That is always done so that if one is stolen, one always has the other as a receipt. Also, they should write down the exact number in case of fire or theft.[24]

For many years Clara advised him on such practical matters as fees, salaries, and investments. She instructed him in the intricacies of coupon clipping, and from London she suggested when and how much he should be paying for lodgings in Baden-Baden.[25] By 1868 Brahms was receiving sizable sums for his music (he was one of the first composers to amass a small fortune from his pub-

*After one visit in August 1855, Brahms asked her how she had slept crowded together with the double bass, the horns, and the fiddles (Johannes Brahms, *Johannes Brahms in seiner Familie: Der Briefwechsel*, ed. Kurt Stephenson [Hamburg: Ernst Hauswedell, 1973], 63).

lished works) and simply sent his money to her to be banked and invested.[26] Later, when he realized the task was a burden to her, he asked his publisher, Fritz Simrock, to take it over.

In addition to discussions of music, friends, travel, money, and other mundane matters, Brahms expressed his feelings in his letters to Clara in a way he could not have done with anyone else. In December 1856, as he was working on his first piano concerto, he wrote that in the Adagio movement he was "painting a tender portrait of her." On March 19, 1874, after hearing of Felix's illness: "Permit my fervent love for you to be of some comfort—I love you more than myself and more than anyone or anything in the world." October 19, 1888, on the occasion of her sixtieth anniversary as a performer: "You, best of all women and artists . . ." September 13, 1892, in answer to a quarrel she had picked with him: "You, dearest to me of all persons . . ." On May 23, 1893, he wanted to send her, "foremost among my special friends," a gold medal that had been struck in his honor by the Gesellschaft der Musikfreunde.[27] In November 1889 he wrote her from Vienna:

> The thought of my D Minor Sonata proceeding gently and dreamily under your fingers is so beautiful. I actually put it on my desk and gently and deliberately accompanied you through the thickets of the organ point. For me, there is no greater pleasure than to be always at your side, to sit or, as now, to promenade with you.[28]

Clara was his confidante when he suffered disappointment; she offered emotional solace, particularly in the early years, when he could accept it from no one else. His successes and failures, depressions and triumphs were reported to her first. She was the first to know of his wounded feelings when he was passed over for a major position in Hamburg in 1862. (He asked her not to mention it to his parents.) For her part, Clara carried grudges on his behalf longer than he did, and turned down an engagement to play in Hamburg after he was passed over for the second time for a position in his native city. He turned to her as to a sister for comfort when he had bitter or melancholy moods, and gratefully accepted her maternal solicitude when she reminded him to take warm slippers on the trip back to Hamburg when his mother died.[29]

Brahms's frequent prickliness (of which Clara often complained) may have covered hurt feelings. He was and yet was not a family member, and his relationship with her children shows deep ambivalence. He betrayed a yearning for a place within the Schumann family as either husband or son, and his tactlessness may well have stemmed from resentment that he could be neither. It surfaced in 1892 when, soon after his sister died, they had a serious quarrel, ostensibly about music, in which, they later agreed, both had been at fault. In his letter written for her seventy-third birthday, Brahms expressed what were probably his true feelings when he termed himself an outsider:

> September 13, 1892
> Grant a poor outsider the pleasure of telling you today that he thinks of you with never changing veneration and that he wishes you, the person dearest to him, everything good, kind and beautiful from the fullness of his heart. I am, unfortunately, an outsider to you more than any other.[30]

While tensions and temporary estrangements were the unhappy aspects of their many-layered friendship, their musical association provided a supporting matrix that endured.

As Brahms himself was a pianist of concert caliber, Clara did not become the major interpreter of his works, the role she had performed for Schumann. The championship of his music by an artist of her prestige, however, was a significant aid to the young composer. She figured in both his earliest and his last piano works. Ten Brahms works were premiered by Clara Schumann, the first in Leipzig in October 1854, when she performed two movements of his Sonata in F Minor; two months later she played the entire sonata in Berlin. She also performed two movements from his Sonata op. 1, his Scherzo op. 4, and a Gavotte that year. In 1894, when she was no longer playing in public, her student Ilona Eibenschütz premiered his last works for piano, the *Klavierstücke*, opp. 118 and 119, in London.

Clara propagandized incessantly for his music among friends, musicians, conductors—more than she had for the young Robert Schumann, and to greater effect because her influence had grown. Some of her efforts caused strains between her and her colleagues. Verhulst could not warm up to the Brahms *Ballades*, op. 10, and Jenny Lind warned her against performing music that had what she described as "perverse tendencies."[31] Clara was triumphant when her old friend Livia Frege was won over and became a champion of Brahms's music. In 1860 Clara agreed to play at a benefit concert in Vienna on condition that Brahms's Serenade no. 1 would be played.[32]

Clara Schumann spoke and wrote to publishers on his behalf; she spoke to Simrock (toward whom she still harbored bad feelings on Robert's account) about the Harp Songs (op. 17) and recorded in her diary, "I would not do it for anyone else." She reminded the Härtel brothers, Raimund and Hermann (of Breitkopf & Härtel), of Brahms's music by speaking of it and playing it whenever they met. In a letter of August 9, 1854, Clara urged Hermann Härtel to publish Brahms's Variations on a Theme by Robert Schumann (on which she had also written variations):

> We have discussed publication of these works and find it most fitting that both (his and mine) appear at the same time. His are, according to everyone who has heard them (I have played them in Berlin too), the most beautiful he has composed, not too difficult and very accessible [*eingänglich*]—a true Beethovenian spirit wafts over them. I am sure you will make a good profit with these variations by Brahms—it cannot be otherwise![33]

She continued her efforts on his behalf even after his work began to be accepted by publishers. From Paris in 1862 she wrote to the Hamburg conductor Theodor Avé-Lallement:

> I have invited several musicians to a Brahms session here tomorrow; they should hear his Serenades and Händel Variations! Don't tell him about it; you know he doesn't take such efforts kindly. I am anxious, however, at least to inspire the musicians here to have respect for him; aside from my duty as a friend, I consider it my artistic duty.[34]

Her assistance extended to his concert work. She gave Brahms lessons during his first month in Düsseldorf, and in the early years of their friendship, when he especially needed the support of a prestigious performer, she appeared in concert with him and Joachim. The three shared the concert stage in Danzig in 1855 and in Altona (now part of Hamburg) in 1861.

As a result of her introductions to influential friends, Brahms was offered an official position at Detmold in 1857. During the 1855 Lower Rhine Music Festival, held in Düsseldorf that year, Clara saw to it that he met the leading critics of the day—Eduard Hanslick, Henry Chorley, Otto Jahn—as well as all the musical celebrities who crowded into the city for the event, which included a performance of Schumann's *Paradies und die Peri* with the universally popular Jenny Lind as the Peri.[35] He saw Liszt again (this time in the Schumann home) and renewed contact with Ferdinand David, Ferdinand Hiller, Stephen Heller, Hermann Härtel, and other eminent men of the musical world—all old friends of Clara's. She accompanied him to Cologne for his first hearing of the Beethoven *Missa Solemnis* in April 1855. In short, she left no stone unturned to expand his experiences.

In March 1860, the twenty-six-year-old Brahms and three other young musicians—Joseph Joachim, Julius Otto Grimm, and Bernhard Scholz—published a declaration in a Berlin newspaper protesting the "pernicious" influence of Liszt, Wagner, and their self-proclaimed *Zukunftsmusik* (music of the future). The Brahms-Joachim declaration was also directed against the *Neue Zeitschrift für Musik,* the journal Schumann had founded in 1834, which was now the organ of the Liszt group. Despite her former ties to the journal, Clara Schumann was prepared to align herself with the young musicians. The declaration was published before she had an opportunity to sign it, as she had intended to do. Her motives were musical as well as personal. In contrast to Liszt's music and showmanship, which filled her with distaste, the music of Brahms aroused her deepest sympathies. To Clara Schumann his masterful handling of form, his lyric gifts, his contrapuntal skills, his bold harmonies and rich rhythms were evidence of his genius. She and Joachim were his strongest champions in the dark days of January 1859, when his First Piano Concerto was virtually hissed off the stage in Leipzig.

Both publicly and privately, Brahms acknowledged his indebtedness for her support, advice, criticism, and friendship. Even as a young man, Brahms, who had little patience with lesser musicians, recognized and appreciated her unique qualities. It was far more than friendly admiration and adoration for an older woman: he valued her professionalism and respected her work as both performer and composer.

Brahms the pianist is often forgotten in the general admiration of the composer. Yet he earned his living as a pianist until fees from his compositions became a major part of his income. (In his later years he practiced little, and Clara frequently complained about his sloppy playing). He honored her by programming several of her works in the 1850s: he played her Trio op. 17 in Hamburg on December 17, 1854; he accompanied Livia Frege in a private Leipzig performance of Clara's unpublished "Volkslied" in January 1856; and he played her *Romanze* op. 21, no. 1, in Cologne on May 29, 1856, soon after it was published. In his Variations op. 9 he wove a theme from her *Romance variée* into one of the variations, symbolizing, as Schumann so often had done, the personal and musical relationship between them. In November 1853, very shortly after they met, Brahms asked Robert Schumann if he might dedicate his op. 2 (actually his first piano sonata) to Frau Schumann as a "small token of my esteem and gratitude." It was the first of many dedications to her.*

He wrote his most passionate letters to Clara from 1854 through 1856. As early as December 1854 the young Brahms wrote, in a style reminiscent of the young Schumann years before, "I often visualize you as if you were here in person; for example, in the trill of the closing passages of the Andante of the C Major Symphony, in the pedal points of great fugues, where you suddenly appear to me as the holy St. Cecilia."[36]

Brahms knew Clara as an artist who never stopped growing. Her repertoire expanded throughout her life, her appetite for new music was never sated, and, most telling of all, her responses to music never ceased to be immediate and total. In February 1861 he advised her to listen to two Mozart piano concertos previously unknown to her. After she heard and played them she wrote to him:

> . . . if I could only pour out my whole heart to you, face to face, you would have to listen for a long time, even though I would only be saying what you yourself already know very well. I think you can guess that I am speaking of the Mozart concertos, both of which I played with indescribable delight. My first reaction was to embrace you in thankfulness for providing me with this pleasure. What music this is—these adagios! I could not restrain tears as I played them both. The Adagio of the C Major was particularly affecting—heavenly bliss streams through one in that work. The first movement—how splendid; the last one in A major—doesn't it seem as though sparks were flying out of the instruments—how everything weaves and breathes together. But enough—I thought I could not stop talking about it and yet this is only a weak expression of what I feel.[37]

*Eric Sams also points out the use of "Clara themes" in these and a number of other Brahms works ("Brahms and His Clara Themes," *MT,* 112 [1971], 432–34).

Her comments on the music of Brahms are reminiscent of the terms in which she spoke of Schumann's creations: she perceived them as gifts for her. Her modesty prevented her from telling him what she confided to her diary: "I know that nobody else plays it [the Trio] as I do."[38] While regretting her inability to express in words how she felt about his music, she repeatedly wrote that the music "filled" her (the German *erfüllt* also implies fulfillment). The effect of his music on her was described in such phrases as "the pleasures you create," "the blissful hours," "treasures I am gathering," "my most beautiful hour," "the sunshine you have bestowed on me."[39] She described his Trio in C Major as "invigorating," "charming," "magnificent" and the Third Symphony as "such a wonderful creation," and though she claimed she could find no words for it, she rhapsodized about it for a page and a half.[40]

She felt that Brahms's music, like her husband's, was written for her, and that only she could truly feel and understand it: "Every tone in your Serenade [op. 11] has become part of me, just as everything you create is deeply and totally absorbed [by me]."[41] When, after an illness, she was finally able to play his Trio op. 101, she wrote, "If only your things were not so often beyond my physical strength. It is so painful for me because I know that I understand and feel them better than so many others do, and yet I must resign myself."[42]

Of the Violin and Piano Sonata op. 78 she wrote:

> After the first delicate enchanting movement, and then the second, you can imagine my delight when, in the third movement, I found my beloved melody again. . . . I say "*mine*" because I don't believe there is another person who can experience this melody as [both] blissful and melancholy as I do.[43]

And a few days later, after she had played it again, she wrote, "Many others could perhaps understand and speak about it better but no one could feel it more than I do—the deepest and most tender strings of the soul vibrate to such music."[44]

The sonatas for violin and piano and the Trio in C Minor, op. 101, were special favorites. When she first played through the A Major sonata, she wrote in her diary, "It was a joy that removed all my miseries for that evening." (She was plagued at the time by illness—her own and that of her son Ferdinand.) When, in 1887, she played through the "wonderfully gripping" Trio, she wrote in her diary, "No other work of Johannes's has transported me so completely. . . . How happy I was tonight, how long it has been!" Of the last movement of his *Regenlied* Sonata (op. 78) she wrote, "This last movement is what I would wish to accompany me on my journey to the other world." When, in 1894 (she was seventy-five years old), she played Brahms's Third Violin Sonata with Joachim, she told Brahms, "It was a pure delight—something one is rarely given. In the surging of harmonies in the first movement, I always have the feeling that I am soaring in the clouds. I love this sonata indescribably—each movement of it!" Earlier, after a performance she gave of this sonata, she wrote, "Again I felt sheer rapture and thought of you with a thankful heart. How magnificent this sonata is and how my pulse still throbs for something truly beautiful!"[45]

Such encomiums were not merely romantic or sentimental enthusiasms couched in extravagant phrases. Clara was forthright, and if something did not please her, she was quick to point out weaknesses. In his early years, Brahms found her ecstatic reactions embarrassing, and more than once asked her to tone them down.[46] She believed in him more than he believed in himself: "You are a man of genius and you know it well!"[47] As he gained self-confidence he was better able to accept her faith in his work, although he had self-doubts to the end of his life. When he wrote her about a new piece he had written in 1888, at the peak of his immensely successful career, he confided, "You may not believe why I did not send it to you first. The truth is I never have any faith that a new piece could please anyone."[48]

The close musical bonds continued to the end. In 1893 he referred to his op. 119 as "your and my little pieces."[49] In 1891, when Clara was preparing an edition of her cadenzas, she was suddenly overwhelmed by guilt when she realized that the cadenzas to the Mozart D Minor Piano Concerto that she had been playing as her own had been borrowed largely from Brahms.* She wrote to ask if she shouldn't put his name on it too. Brahms answered that in that case, he would have to put her name on all his loveliest melodies, for "I owe more melodies to you than . . . passages you could take from me."[50]

Soon after their parting in 1856, Brahms began to send her his manuscripts for comments, suggestions, advice, and criticism. Of his 122 compositions later published with opus numbers, he had asked for her advice, reactions, and comments on at least 82. Other pieces were dispatched to her immediately after publication. Op. 2 and op. 9 were officially dedicated to her, and the autograph of op. 24, the Händel Variations (written for her birthday in 1861), bears the inscription "For a beloved friend." Several works without opus number were also dedicated to her: Theme and Variations in D Minor, an arrangement of Gluck's Gavotte, and two Preludes and Fugues. Countless other works, though not expressly dedicated to her, were written for her birthday or as Christmas presents or simply with her in mind.

After 1882 Brahms was less punctilious about sending manuscripts to her, and she knew that some works went to other friends first. She did not hesitate to reproach him: "Do you want to slight your old friend entirely? Why are you not sending her anything?"[51] By this time Clara was sixty-seven and finding it increasingly difficult to play through his manuscript scores and send them back as promptly as he liked. (She complained that she could not sight-read through his full scores, especially since he persisted in using the old clefs, a source of

*The autograph of Brahms's cadenza for the first movement of Mozart's Concerto in D Minor, K. 466, now in the Library of Congress, bears a note from Clara Schumann in which she identified the passages she used. Her own cadenzas for this concerto are also in the Library of Congress. See Catalogue of Works, pp. 328–29.

difficulty for more than one later musician.) As she grew older, Brahms showed more consideration and awareness of her need for his music. During the last years of her life, when she was suffering from hearing problems, rheumatism, and stomach afflictions (all carefully reported to him), he wrote tenderly and solicitously, rushed published scores to her, and arranged for her to hear performances of his works in comfortable surroundings. After 1893 he visited Frankfurt often, particularly eager for her to hear his late chamber works with clarinet—the Trio, Quintet, and sonatas, played in her own home by Richard Mühlfeld, the clarinetist for whom he had written them.

Unlike Schumann, Brahms kept her informed of what he was writing and planning, and this may have been a trust she cherished above all others. Though he did not care to discuss works in progress, she was usually the first to know about a new project when he was ready to divulge his thoughts. Though she realized she might learn more if she did not ask too many questions, she could not always restrain herself; she came to feel it was her right to know and was indignant if word of his creations or performances reached her from other sources.[52] For the most part, Brahms respected, even welcomed, her interest. He sent her his manuscripts with such requests as "Write me in as much detail as you can; that is most agreeable and also most important to me. What do you say about the 'Wechsellied' [from op. 31]? Is it any good?" When he began work on the *Requiem,* he sent her the magnificent "How lovely is thy dwelling place, O Lord," along with several songs and piano works, and wrote, "Perhaps you will have a free hour to strum through these things and perhaps another to write me just a word as to whether there is any sense or purpose in my having two volumes of the Variations [op. 35] published. Please, just a word on that." And again, in 1865, in reference to the *Requiem,* "Please don't show Joachim the choral piece yet—it is probably the weakest. . . ." In the same letter he wrote out some of the texts he was using in his great masterpiece and ventured, "I hope that such a German text can please you as much as the customary Latin one."[53]

In June 1878 he sent her "a few duets that I intend to publish together with 'Edward.' Write me what you think of the idea, and also how you like the duets and also the songs. . . . If you wish it—and write good reviews—I'll send more."[54] A year earlier he had written:

> April 24, 1877
> I want to publish my songs [opp. 69–72] and I would really like it very much if you would first play through them sometime, and say a word to me about them. I would most prefer to be sitting beside you—but I really couldn't. . . . Write whether you like any of it—and if there are other things, perhaps, that you dislike intensely. . . . If possible, write me a *brief word* for each one.

In his usual self-deprecatory manner he added, "You might simply indicate opus or number: op. X, 5. bad; 6. shameful 7. preposterous. etc."[55]

Clara would have preferred to be his only critic but she accepted the fact that she was one of several, though admittedly it was a very elite group. Brahms customarily asked all of his intimate friends to comment on his works before publication. A continuous round robin of new works went from one friend to another and then often directly to the publisher. The circle included Joachim, Grimm, Dietrich, and Clara Schumann in the early years, Joachim, Levi, and Clara from about 1865 to 1875. It was enlarged to include Billroth and the Herzogenbergs a few years later. In the last eight years of his life, from 1888 to 1896, the inner circle included Hanslick, Joachim, Clara, and Eusebius Mandyczewski, the archivist of the Gesellschaft der Musikfreunde and later co-editor of Brahms's complete works. From time to time Brahms consulted Julius Stockhausen and George Henschel on vocal music, and from 1890 on he played over new works from manuscript with Ignaz Brüll, a Viennese pianist. None of his friends could resist Brahms's requests for criticism of his music, least of all Clara. When she heard of a work she had not seen or learned it had been sent to another friend first, she complained bitterly. Brahms sent the Third Violin Sonata, op. 108, to Elisabeth von Herzogenberg before Clara had seen it, and when she kept it longer than he expected, he wrote in alarm that it was to be sent to Frau Schumann *immediately*. Elisabeth von Herzogenberg commented, "Frau Schumann must be jealous of our having had the pleasure first." Brahms had no doubt about that. "You know Frau Schumann is very touchy," he wrote on another occasion.[56]

For the most part, Brahms disregarded the advice of his friends. Works that Clara praised were not necessarily published; others that she criticized as "ordinary" were retained. Although he always insisted he was shy about his work and lacked self-confidence, Brahms was always his own master, and his friends understood that he sought their comments in order to strengthen or confirm his own thoughts. (However, Brahms readily accepted recommendations from such conductors and instrumentalists as Joachim, to whom he sent almost all the chamber works, the Violin Concerto, and the Double Concerto, and he generally followed suggestions on range and transposition made by Stockhausen, Amalie Joachim, Henschel, and other singers.) Final decisions were his alone, and the works were often published in the form in which they were first cast.

Whether or not her advice was taken, Clara relished the opportunity to have her say. In answer to his request for her opinion on opp. 69–72, she carefully went through every song and made detailed comments on each. Despite her advice ("Only about half should be published; the others are not worthy of your name, etc."), all the songs were published. She described a motif from op. 25 as "too ordinary for Johannes Brahms," but he retained it. On the other hand, he agreed with her perception of his "Brautgesang" as "ordinary" (he had, in fact, used the same term earlier in a letter to Grimm about the work), and it was never published.[57] It would not be entirely accurate to describe Clara Schumann as Brahms's musical adviser, but it is certain that she remained longest as a member of that special circle of musicians and trusted intimates on whom he depended throughout his life.

Brahms was, in turn, Clara's "best friend." (This was a term they both used.) Besides deriving joy and solace from his music throughout her tragedy-ridden life, she turned to him for personal advice and became increasingly dependent on him. His opinion of her playing was crucial; compliments meant more from him than from any other musician.[58] Every decision, no matter how trivial, that had to be made about editions of Schumann's music or correspondence, letters from journalists and would-be biographers, moves to other cities, offers of teaching positions—all were discussed with Brahms. She had faith in his musical judgment and turned to him time and again, especially in her late years. Though she may not always have expressed her appreciation directly to him, she gratefully noted his help in her diary; on August 13, 1895, for example, she noted how "deeply moved" she was to see how carefully he had gone through her arrangement of Robert Schumann's Sketches for the Pedal-Piano.

As the years went on, Clara attempted to use him as a surrogate father, asking for his help particularly with decisions involving her sons. He generally refused to cooperate, though he evidently did help out with one difficult situation with Felix.[59]* He gave piano lessons to Eugenie for a short time, and never begrudged any effort or time when musical decisions were involved.

Though Brahms may have been reluctant to give advice about the education or rearing of her children, he was deeply concerned about her mental and physical health and well-being. This interest may have been responsible for their first major quarrel, in 1861. He tried to persuade her to cut down on her work. "You certainly have enough money," he wrote. "It would be far more reasonable and better if you cared for your health and your beautiful self."[60] Though the letter was couched in flattering terms, she found it offensive. She pointed out that her responsibilities included seven children whom she hoped to educate and for whom she wanted to provide a normal family life, and that she was, moreover, obliged to provide for her own future. She added a sentence that could well stand as her life's motto: "My health may well be better preserved if I exert myself less, but in the end doesn't each person give his life for his calling?" To the implied criticism of her playing, which certainly hurt most, she answered, "I am not doing too much for I feel no less freshness and warmth than I did twenty years ago. On the contrary, I feel younger and believe that a quieter life would leave me too much time to brood on my sorrows."[61]

The next time he chastised her for her "unsettled way of living," in 1868, she was puzzled and angry at what she took to be more criticism of her playing and the implication that it might be time to retire gracefully. She answered from London, where she was giving her usual season to warm applause and sold-out

*Among his songs are three with texts by Felix; see p. 157.

halls: "You actually seem to imagine that I really have enough money and travel merely for my own pleasure. . . . This is hardly the point at which I should retire from public appearances, as you advise."[62] The exchange of letters over the next few months skirted a possible break. There was talk of "hatred" and a wall that had grown up between them. Finally, in a letter of October 15, 1868, she revealed the full extent of her dissatisfaction with Brahms: he was rude and boorish, inconsiderate of her feelings and of those of her children. "One cannot have a friendly relationship with the mother which does not carry over to the children."[63]

Unfortunately, his hints that it was time to slow down had come at the worst possible time. In 1868 she was facing multiple catastrophes and feeling very much alone. None of her friends, not even Brahms, could help her shoulder the responsibilities facing her: the possibility that Felix's illness might be fatal, the continued ill health of Julie, and the mental symptoms that were to bring Ludwig to the institution where he was confined for the remainder of his life. Brahms was often brusque (she once begged him not to write when he was in an angry mood), and all his friends suffered from his tactlessness sooner or later. This time Brahms apologized, the breach was healed, and the correspondence continued (until the next quarrel), but with some resentment on Clara's part. Clara Schumann's letters had none of the delightful charm of those of Elisabeth von Herzogenberg. In her serious, solemn way, Clara could never respond adequately to his dry wit and humor; in fact, she was embarrassed by the realization that her letters were often nothing but recitals of family problems and illnesses. Brahms, however, never failed to be moved by her troubles, listened sympathetically, and responded with sympathy. He did not reject her trust as long as he could make his own decisions.

Clara Schumann was easily offended and never forgot slights, real or imagined. She did not conceal her feelings from Brahms. Fully aware of the contrast between herself and the childless, beautiful, wealthy, young, talented aristocrat to whom Brahms began sending manuscripts in 1877, Clara reminded him why she could not always return manuscripts as quickly as he would like: "I am not master of my time and energies so that I can burrow in a work for days, as Frau von H. does."[64] In her diary she wrote, "They [the von Herzogenbergs] have all the time in the world while I have lessons to give in the morning, am entirely exhausted in the afternoon, and continually have a piano loaded with proofs for Härtel, which also demands strength."[65]

The subject of money arose in almost every letter between Clara and Brahms. She reported to him how much she earned, how much she lost if a concert had to be canceled, how she lived from season to season, and never hesitated to ask frankly about his fees. By the 1870s Brahms was financially secure, making more money than he could spend—his tastes remained simple—and, knowing that she had accepted additional responsibilities for Ferdinand's children when he was ill, insisted on sending her a considerable sum of money. She had refused similar offers from other friends many times before, partly from a fear of losing her independence and partly because she was proud that she possessed the skills to support her family. Brahms's offer was made so discreetly and tactfully, however, that she could not refuse.[66] She felt comfortable enough with her old friend to accept, and, ever prudent, invested her money for her grandchildren.

After a tender exchange of letters on this subject, however, she was just as touchy as ever. He held his breath when he wrote to her, asked for forgiveness, and avoided the unthinkable. Their last argument (in 1891–92, over the publication of the original version of Schumann's D Minor Symphony and her omission of some of Brahms's editions of Schumann music from the *Collected Works*), to which he reacted with unwonted bitterness,[67] was resolved when they both realized that it was caused by extraneous considerations: her great age and forgetfulness were partly to blame, and his tactlessness may have been exacerbated by his unhappiness over his sister's illness and death. After that incident, Brahms's letters were unfailingly tender and solicitous. When Clara suffered a series of strokes in 1895, he realized that the woman he had always loved could not live forever. As her death approached, he wrote to her daughter Marie: "If you believe that the worst may be expected, be so kind as to send word to me so that I can come and still see those dear eyes—those eyes that, when they finally close, will close so much for me."[68]

His deepest feelings about her are revealed in his last great songs, the *Vier ernste Gesänge,* written in May 1896, as she lay dying in Frankfurt. Officially dedicated to the artist Max Klinger, the songs were first played to a group of close friends at a private gathering after Clara's funeral.[69] After publication in July, a copy was sent to Marie Schumann with the words:

> July 7, 1896
> I wrote them in the first week of May. . . . Deep inside a human being there is often something that speaks to us and germinates almost unbeknownst to us, and that occasionally may ring out as poetry or music. You cannot play through the songs, because the texts would affect you too deeply now. But I ask you to consider them quite literally a funeral offering to your beloved mother.[70]

Clara's death came on May 20, 1896. Brahms died eleven months later.

CHAPTER 10

Other Friends and Contemporaries

Clara Schumann found it essential to have people around her and cultivated friends and acquaintances assiduously. Her friendships sustained her musically and emotionally; her children could not fulfill this need. She explained to sixteen-year-old Felix when he questioned the necessity for her enormous correspondence, a daily task that he felt deprived him of her presence and care:*

> You have to consider how many people I get to know on my tours and how fond I become of them, how they always shower me with love and kindness, and all I can give them in return is constancy. . . . I do not like to offend people who have been close to me; there are so many now that even if I keep in contact with just some of them, my correspondence is still very large. Above all, however, it is naturally my deepest desire to communicate as regularly as possible with all of you—those dearest in the world to me.[1]

With her friends she played many roles: to such younger male associates as Brahms, Rudorff, Grimm, Joachim, and Stockhausen, musicians with whom she toured and performed, she was a comrade; to male musicians of her own age or older, such as Mendelssohn, Chopin, and Hiller, she was a professional colleague above gender; to Amalie Joachim, Clara Stockhausen, and the other wives of her colleagues she was a mother figure. And despite the devotion of her daughters, the adoring public, and her male colleagues, she also needed the sympathy and understanding of women friends. Her mother became a friend and confidante, and after her death, her daughter Marie took on this role. There were many other women with whom she had lifelong contact. Her correspondence with Emilie List,[2] for example, offered an opportunity for intimacy

*She spent several hours almost every day of her adult life writing letters. She often received more than a hundred letters on her birthday and on New Year's Day. Each was answered personally and usually at some length.

and understanding she could not find elsewhere. The friendship with Emilie dated back to 1833 and continued when the List family offered help and hope during the difficult days in Paris in 1839. Emilie List, the German-born daughter of the U.S. consul in Leipzig, was unusually mature and level-headed. An independent woman who had a career as a language teacher and governess, List was a brilliant linguist and Clara's first English teacher. She never married but had great empathy for Clara's family problems. Clara Schumann kept Emilie abreast of all her activities; intermingled with information on her concerts, repertoire, and audience reception were gossipy notes about people they both knew. Often years passed when they did not see each other, but Emilie was always there when Clara needed to pour her heart out and receive a sound and sympathetic response.

Some of the other women on whom she depended for support and comfort were Livia Frege, Rosalie Leser, Lida Bendemann, and Laura von Beckerath. With these friends she could express her feelings about her husband, her children, and her life. All were cultivated, well-educated women—not professional musicians but intensely interested in and knowledgeable about music. Clara Schumann also developed warm relationships with her students, beginning with Henriette Reichmann, the young woman who was with her in Paris in 1839 as both student and companion. Reichmann, who later moved to Hull, England, offered to come to London for Clara's first British concert tour (1856), extending friendship and support to the lonely and depressed pianist.[3]

Clara Schumann was a public figure and her professional relationships with the great musicians of her time were well known. One intimate relationship, however, was kept from public notice: in the 1860s she had a very brief and discreet liaison with Theodor Kirchner, a composer of the Schumann circle. Kirchner, a gifted student of Robert Schumann who wrote in the Schumann style, was said to have physically resembled Robert Schumann. In their correspondence (1857–64), parts of which have recently been published, Clara Schumann discussed her children, her housekeeping and parenting responsibilities, and her concerts, and made some trenchant comments on music and musicians.[4] In only two of the letters did she write to him in the familiar *du* form. Kirchner was an inveterate gambler; when she realized he was also a ladies' man,[5] she broke off the relationship in a letter of July 21, 1864, resumed the *Sie* form, and probably never saw him again. Indeed, she told Brahms that he was never to bring Kirchner to her house. Twenty years later, she explained to Elisabeth von Herzogenberg that she had lent Kirchner money and that he had gambled it away. It is highly unlikely that she had any other such affairs.

Frédéric Chopin (1810–1849)

At the age of twelve, Clara Wieck performed the works of Frédéric Chopin in private circles and at her public concerts to great acclaim. His Variations on

"Là ci darem la mano" became one of the staples of the young Clara's repertoire. Published in the spring of 1830 and first performed at the Gewandhaus on October 27, 1831, by Julius Knorr, a contemporary and friend of Robert Schumann, it was the subject of Schumann's first music review—"Hats off, gentlemen, a genius!"—and one of his best-known literary pieces.[6]

At his first hearing of the Chopin work, Wieck realized its potential as a vehicle for his daughter, and he set her to work on the piece during the summer before her big tour to Paris. An entry in her diary written by her father on June 8, 1831, reads, "Chopin's Variations, op. 2, which I learned in eight days, is the hardest piece I have ever seen or played till now. This original, brilliant composition is still so little known that almost every pianist and teacher considers it incomprehensible and impossible to play."

Emulating Schumann, Wieck, who believed he had something to say about piano playing—the fruits of twenty years of study and experience—penned a review of the work[7] and sent it to Eduard Fechner, his wife's brother and a well-established artist in Paris, asking him to give it to the composer. Chopin had his permission, he wrote, to edit the essay, translate it, and turn it over to François-Joseph Fétis, the powerful editor of the *Revue Musicale.* Wieck assumed that his essay would serve as a brilliant introduction for them in Paris.[8] He proudly called the review, written in a high-flown style (in unconscious imitation of Schumann?), "a rhapsody" and "a fantasy." (He sent a copy to Frau Wieck with a note: "Schumann may read it. . . . True, it is not so poetic as his, but it is clear, strong, and rough.")[9]

The fastidious Chopin was not impressed and wrote disdainfully to a friend, "One can die of the imagination of this German, who insists that his brother-in-law should send it to Fétis for the *Revue Musicale;* the good [Ferdinand] Hiller rescued me from this with difficulty by telling the brother-in-law that the thing is not clever at all but very stupid."[10]

Wieck had her play Chopin's op. 2 for Spohr and other notables on their way to Paris and put Chopin's name on the list of people to contact. They arrived in the French capital on February 15, 1832, left visiting cards at Chopin's on the 17th, and finally met him on February 21. Though Chopin scoffed at Wieck's review of his op. 2, he admired the playing of the twelve-year-old and sent her a manuscript copy of his E minor concerto with a note: "I am looking forward very eagerly to hear it performed by such a wonderful talent as yours."[11]

On March 14 Clara and her father heard Chopin play that same concerto (accompanied by a string group) and Wieck made the surprising comment in Clara's diary that if he had not known whose concerto it was, he would have taken it for a work by Schumann. Wieck believed Schumann's music to be too avant-garde for the concert public and he put Chopin's music in the same category, writing in the diary that Chopin's compositions were too difficult for an ordinary audience to understand.[12] Yet he recognized that Clara had a real affinity for the Polish composer's music and consistently programmed Chopin's works at his daughter's concerts.[13] Shrewd manager that he was, however, he also made certain that popular potboilers appeared on the same program.

Their first Leipzig meeting with Chopin in September 1835 was typical of Wieck's arrogance. The visit was recorded in the diary by both father and daughter:

> [CW] Chopin arrived here on the 27th, but was going to leave almost immediately, staying only one day. He came to see us only 2 hours before his departure and that annoyed Father so much that he left and sent me out too, so that I would not have to play something if Chopin should come. He did come, however, and waited an hour [FW] until I came. [CW] Now there was nothing for it: I had to go into the room and play. He listened to the Schumann sonata, the last movement of my concerto, and 2 of his Etudes.

The young Pole, just ten years older than Clara, showered her with compliments, and then played for her. She noted in her diary that he played with great artistry but that he seemed frail and ill and "was able to produce a forte only with a convulsive movement of his whole body." She added, however, that he was ever the "gallant Frenchman."

Chopin was returning to Paris the next day, and Wieck, placated by the young man's high regard for Clara's playing, went to see him off. When Chopin visited Leipzig again in September 1836, Wieck recorded the visit in the diary:

> Chopin surprised us; he listened to all of [Clara's] op. 5 and 2 Mazurkas and the Ballade from op. 6 as well as the concerto, op. 7. He was delighted, expressed himself enthusiastically and left us, very moved. . . . He took op. 5 with him then and there and left an Albumblatt for Clara.

The album leaf, dated Leipzig, 12 September 1836, was inscribed, "A Mlle Clara Wieck, par son admirateur," and signed, "F. Chopin."[14]

A survey of all the Clara Wieck Schumann programs makes it clear that the music of Chopin had a significant place in her repertoire. On the January 1833 program, in which she performed works of Robert Schumann in public for the first time, she also played eight mazurkas by Chopin, very likely the first performance of these works in Leipzig. Chopin's works were featured on her girlhood concerts and both Wiecks took pride in the fact that she introduced them at concerts in many cities and played them privately to musicians who did not know Chopin's music. In his discussion of the reception of Chopin's music, James Methuen-Campbell credits Clara Wieck and Franz Liszt with "being the two most notable champions of his music during his early period."[15]

At least one Chopin work figured on almost every one of her programs in later years as well. Although Robert Schumann's enthusiasm for Chopin's music waned over the years, Clara Schumann continued playing Chopin to the end of her concert life; the Concerto in F Minor was the last concerto the seventy-one-year-old pianist performed in public, on November 7, 1890.[16]

It is not generally known that Clara Schumann was involved with the Breitkopf & Härtel editions of Chopin's works. She and Robert Schumann began looking over the proofs of Chopin's works issued by Breitkopf in the 1840s,* and she expressed her delight with this task when she wrote to Hermann Härtel: "You are giving us the pleasure of doing this small service and also offering us an early acquaintance with the works." When she returned the corrections for Chopin's Sonata for Piano and Cello, she wrote that she hoped to have an opportunity to play this interesting piece with a cellist and get to know it better because "one cannot have a really clear impression of a work by merely reading it."[17]

Clara Schumann continued to work on the publications of Chopin's music, but when Breitkopf & Härtel published a German edition of Chopin's collected works between 1878 and 1880, her name did not appear among those of the editors.[18] She had made a point of requesting that her name not be mentioned, and when Härtel sent her a gift she answered: "Thank you for the gift. The little work I did on the Chopin edition was in the interest of art and I never thought of being paid to do it; on the contrary, I was happy to be able to do something helpful for you."[19]

A Chopin influence is clear in the young Clara's compositions, especially her op. 6. The national dance forms—mazurkas and polonaises—that color her early works, the narrative ballade in op. 6, the notturno with its songlike melody, the delicate melodic figuration, the abrupt and surprising harmonic changes, the operatic melodies transformed for the keyboard—all point to an intimate knowledge of Chopin on the piano. Though there is no record that Clara Schumann saw Chopin after 1836, his compositions were a mainstay of her professional life for sixty years.†

Franz Liszt, 1811–1886

Clara Schumann's deteriorating relationship with Franz Liszt tells us more about her than it does about the great virtuoso, who treated her with consistent courtesy and respect. Even at the very beginning of their acquaintance, in 1838, Clara was overwhelmed by and envied his technical prowess but felt uneasy

*Clara Schumann generally checked proofs of the German edition against the French edition rather than the manuscripts since the French editions were usually issued earlier than the German. Chopin's works were published by several German firms, among them Breitkopf & Härtel, Kistner, and Peters. Clara Schumann, who had a close relationship with the Härtels, worked on the B&H editions.

†Although Clara was in Paris from February to August 1839, she did not see Chopin. He was in Majorca, Marseilles, and then at Nohant, George Sand's estate, during those months.

about his flamboyant personal and musical style. By 1854, the year in which he sent her his B Minor Sonata, dedicated to her husband, she could barely disguise her hostility.

Liszt, like Chopin and Mendelssohn, had been in Paris in 1832, the year of Clara's first big concert tour, but he did not take cognizance of her until he heard her play in 1838; the glamorous young man, eight years her senior, was at the height of his performing career. Chopin had spoken highly of Clara's playing and Liszt was eager to meet her. In a letter to Friedrich Hofmeister, the Leipzig publisher, he expressed his hope of hearing soon the young woman who played with "energy, intelligence, and accuracy," declaring that such a pianist was "an exceedingly rare phenomenon in any country."[20]

In Liszt, showmanship and genius were combined with generosity. He heard Clara in Vienna in April 1838 and wrote glowingly about her in a letter that appeared in the Parisian *Revue et gazette musicale* and was reprinted in the *Neue Zeitschrift*. To the comtesse d'Agoult, the mother of his three children, he reported on April 13, 1838:

> Just one word about Clara Wieck—distintissimo [most distinguished]—(but not a man, of course). We are living in the same hotel, Zur Stadt Frankfurt, and after dinner we make as much music as possible. She is a very simple person, cultivated . . . totally absorbed in her art but with nobility and without childishness. She was astounded when she heard me play. Her compositions are really very remarkable, especially for a woman. There is a hundred times more ingenuity and true sentiment in them than in all the fantasies, past and present, of Thalberg.[21]

He showed his interest in many ways: Liszt's Paganini Etudes are dedicated to Clara; his letters to her are models of affectionate esteem; three of her songs figured in his famed song transcriptions. His article about her performances in Weimar in 1854 was published in the *Neue Zeitschrift für Musik* of December 1, 1854, and translated in *Dwight's Journal of Music,* a Boston music periodical that followed the careers of Clara Schumann, Joachim, Brahms, and others of that circle with great interest. In *Dwight's* translation, Liszt's comment "The lovely playmate of the Muses has become a consecrated, faithfully devoted, severe priestess" was often quoted.[22]

In 1838, at the end of Clara's Viennese tour, Liszt and the Wiecks spent ten whirlwind days together. His playing overwhelmed her and she wrote in her diary:

> We heard Liszt. He cannot be compared to any other player—he is absolutely unique. He arouses fear and astonishment and yet is a very kind artist. His appearance at the piano is indescribable—he is an original—totally involved with the piano. . . . His passion knows no bounds; he often injures one's sense of beauty by tearing the melodies apart and using the pedal too much so that his compositions must become even more incomprehensible, if

not to the connoisseur, then certainly to the layman. He has a great soul; one may say of him, "His art is his life."[23]

During the time they spent together, the two artists played with and for each other. She described his effect on her in a letter to Robert: "I receive as much applause as ever yet my playing seems so dull and I don't understand it, but I have almost lost the desire to continue to travel. Since I have seen and heard Liszt's bravura, it seems to me that I am only a schoolgirl."[24]

Wieck, of course, took a different view. He admitted that "the musical powers of this Liszt truly border on the incredible," but believed that he was hampered by lack of "proper training" and inability to "tame and control himself and his energy." After Wieck heard Liszt's big solo concert of April 18, 1838, however, he raved about him: "It was the most remarkable concert of our life—and will not be without influence on Clara, but the old schoolmaster is worried about her getting used to his bad habits and mannerisms."[25] His description of those "bad habits and mannerisms" makes clear the reason for his anxiety:

> The seriousness of the concert and his decidedly artistic appearance, combined with the greatest, most unbelievable mastery of every possible mechanical problem, aroused the stormiest applause. Who could describe his appearance as a concert artist? After he had destroyed Thalberg's Erhard [Erard piano] in the first piece, he played the Fantasie on a Conrad Graff [Graf], broke two middle strings, went and fetched the second Graff from the corner, and played his Etude. After he broke two strings again, he played it once more, but not before he had loudly proclaimed to the audience "he had not been successful; he would play it again." When he first appeared, he vehemently threw his gloves and handkerchief on the floor in front of the piano.[26]

Despite his showmanship, bordering at times on the eccentric, Franz Liszt was a great and genuine musician and proved to be a loyal friend to both Clara and Robert. The chill that descended later was not initiated by Liszt. As early as 1837, well before the two men met, Robert's spirits were lifted by Liszt's long article about Schumann's keyboard music in the *Revue et gazette musicale*. And after Clara had played privately for Liszt in Vienna, he wrote to Robert, "Your *Carnaval* and *Fantasiestücke* have interested me greatly. I play them with delight and God knows I cannot say that of most other things. To speak frankly and freely, only Chopin's compositions and yours have a strong interest for me." He then asked Robert to write some trios, quintets, or septets, since, as he put it, "it seems to me that you could do it admirably and nothing really interesting has been published in this genre for a long time. If you ever decide to do this, please let me know at once. I would like to have the honor of introducing it to the public."[27]

Less than a year later he reiterated his feelings about the German composer: "My friends . . . have often heard me say that Chopin and Schumann are the colleagues for whom I have always had the highest esteem, the greatest sympathy."[28] The correspondence between Liszt and Schumann continued for several years. Schumann's *Fantasie* op. 17 was dedicated to Liszt, and he acknowledged it with thanks on June 5, 1839: "The *Fantasie* that you have dedicated to me is a work of the highest rank. I am truly proud of the honor you have done me in dedicating so grand a composition to me. I intend to work at it and learn to know it thoroughly so as to make the utmost possible effect with it." He noted that the work would be "difficult for the public to digest," and added a tactful paragraph that must have pleased Schumann during the difficult months of Clara's stay in Paris:

> What you tell me of your private life has interested me and touched me deeply. If I could, I know not how, be agreeable or useful to you in the slightest way in these circumstances, I am completely at your service. Whatever happens, you can count on my absolute discretion and sincere devotion. If I am not asking too much, tell me if it is Clara of whom you speak. But if this question seems misplaced, do not answer it.[29]

The two young men finally met in Dresden in March 1840. At that time Clara was in Berlin with her mother, awaiting the outcome of the court hearings, practicing, performing, and studying French and English. Though Liszt arrived at a time when Robert was extremely busy, Schumann welcomed him: this was an event to which he had been looking forward for many years. On March 18 he wrote to Clara:

> Yesterday he said to me, "I feel as if I had known you for twenty years," and I feel the same. . . . And how extraordinarily he plays, daringly and madly, and then again tenderly and sweetly—I have heard it all. But Clärchen, this world, I mean his, is no longer mine. Art, as you practice it, and as I often do at the piano when composing—this beautiful intimacy [*Gemütlichkeit*] I would not give up for all his magnificence—and there is also some tinsel with it all—too much. No more today, you already know what I mean.[30]

But Liszt's wonderful good nature and extraordinary musicality triumphed over the "tinsel" and turned all heads, Mendelssohn's included. Robert's letters sang such praises of Liszt that on March 24, 1840, Clara lamented from her "isolation" in Berlin:

> Ah, unfortunate me, I am sitting here now and cannot have even a tiny part in all the pleasures you are giving each other! What would I not have given to have been in Leipzig yesterday, how happy I would have been; how I sighed! I was in the theater, but my thoughts were totally with you. I saw you in musical raptures and wanted so much to be at your side. For some time, I actually had the intention of coming with Mother, but then I thought I would just disturb you in your companionship with Liszt and wouldn't be as welcome as

> I would have liked. I believe it is better that we stayed here. . . . Does Liszt still yearn for aristocratic Vienna, for the countesses, etc.? I should think that he would not have time to think of such things with you. The Bach concerto, was it in D minor?* Oh, God, I could cry! I think it is a nice thought that Liszt seems to you to become more and more powerful—sometimes one would think it was a supernatural being sitting there at the piano.[31]

Even before Robert received this letter, however, he had urged her to come to Leipzig to hear Liszt play. She did go, with her mother. She confided her reaction to her diary on March 30, 1840:

> One could hear and see that he felt most comfortable in the *Hexameron* [his own work]. He did not play the things by Mendelssohn and Hiller as freely and it was disturbing to see that he always looked at the music. He did not play *Carnaval* to my satisfaction and altogether did not make the same impression on me that he had made in Vienna. I believe it was my own fault; my expectations were too high.

She also noted, with great disapproval, that he had performed a Mendelssohn concerto that he had learned at a rehearsal that same day. A day later she wrote:

> This morning Liszt spent several hours with us and endeared himself to us even more by his refined, truly artistic personality. His conversation is full of life and spirit; he is also quite a flirt, but one can forget this completely. . . . He played his arrangements of "Erlkönig," "Ave Maria," his own Etudes, etc. I had to play a few things for him too, which I did with real anxiety. Otherwise I didn't feel at all intimidated by his presence, as I had feared; he acts so naturally that everyone has to feel at ease in his company. But I could not be around him for long: this agitation, this restlessness, this enormous vivacity, these are all a great strain.

In the diary entry of April 4, a few days after Liszt had departed, Clara inadvertently contrasted the two composers:

> I went to Connewitz with Robert. I never feel so well, so comfortable, as when I am with him. He doesn't have to talk at all. I like it so much when he is just thinking and would like to be able to listen to each thought. And when he gently presses my hand, it makes me feel happy to the very core of my being. Then I feel so sure that I am his best beloved.

In the autumn of 1841, the Schumanns, now married, met Liszt in Weimar at their hotel, "where the champagne flowed like water,"[32] and he proposed joint concerts in Leipzig in December. He played as assisting artist at her December

*This was the work that Clara, Mendelssohn, and Louis Rakemann had premiered in Leipzig in 1835. She was to play it several more times in Leipzig.

6 concert and she did the same for him at his December 13 concert. Although the *Neue Zeitschrift* reported that the usual applause was replaced by a "transport of fanaticism" at the first concert, Clara wrote in her diary in December 1841 that she was unhappy about the concert: Robert's works had not been performed well and he had been dissatisfied with her playing. There were several reasons for Robert's reactions: David, the concertmaster, was substituting for Mendelssohn, the regular conductor, and the orchestra did not respond as Schumann had expected; moreover, the two new works that were premiered—the Overture, Scherzo, and Finale, op. 52, and the Symphony in D Minor—on a long, overfull program could hardly compete with the appearance of the reigning favorites of the concert stage: Franz Liszt and Clara Wieck Schumann playing a big bravura work—his *Hexameron* as a duo—together. Liszt brought Clara a bouquet and the audience went wild.

Though their unhappiness was not specifically with Liszt, it was certainly associated with the great virtuoso. In the excitement over Liszt's presence, Schumann's works were all too easily overlooked. Moreover, Schumann himself was not satisfied with his D Minor Symphony, which, unlike his first, the "Spring" Symphony, was coolly received. He revised it several times before he had a second version published in 1853. In addition, he may have felt some discomfort at seeing his wife and Liszt on the stage together.

The Schumanns had several more encounters with Liszt. At each Clara's esteem for him fell, and she made no attempt to conceal her feelings. The reasons are, as always, complex, and both personal and musical. Though Clara admired Liszt's playing and said so publicly and privately, some uneasy competitiveness was always mixed with her deference. Her competitiveness was no doubt fueled by an essay that had appeared in the *Neue Zeitschrift* in April 1838, in which she was favorably compared with three other pianists of the first rank: Liszt, Thalberg, and Adolph von Henselt. Thus from the beginning of their relationship she was publicly given a place in the constellation of the great performers of her time and greeted as an equal. A tribute at this level could only have intensified the inner tensions of the young woman who was struggling with divided loyalties to her father and Schumann. As we have seen, her letters to Schumann in 1839–40 reveal much self-doubt, and she was continually questioning whether she could sustain her position, whether she was intelligent enough to study fugue, if she could (and should) compose. She knew she could play as well as any woman but had recurring doubts that she could compete with men. Her confidence was shaken when she read Schumann's words of enthusiasm about other pianists, and she suffered severe pangs of jealousy over his reaction to Liszt. Moreover, Clara always felt proprietary about Robert's works and would have preferred to be their sole interpreter. Realistically, of course, she knew this was not possible, and that for Schumann's sake it was important to have such a performer as Liszt as a champion, since there was no doubt that his performances would have more impact than hers. Yet she was hurt when Schumann was ecstatic about Liszt's playing of his *Novelletten, Fantasie,* and sonata—"her" pieces.[33]

There were deeper reasons for her dislike of Liszt, some beyond her awareness. But she knew in December 1841 that her respect for him had been shaken. "Liszt likes to play the way he wants. It is always clever even though tasteless at times, and that is especially true of his compositions. I can only call them horrible." She found his compositions, she wrote in the marriage diary in December 1841,

> a chaos of the worst dissonances with an endless murmuring in the deepest bass and the highest treble at the same time, boring introductions, etc. I could almost hate him as a composer. As a performer, however, his concert on the 13th absolutely astounded me, especially in his *Don Juan* Fantasy, which he played overpoweringly—his performance of the Champagne Aria will remain unforgettable—the bravado, the pleasure with which he played was unique! One saw Don Juan with the popping champagne corks, in his wantonness, as only Mozart could have possibly imagined him. After the concert we all had supper together. . . . Of Liszt there was not much to be seen, since two women had attached themselves to him. I am convinced that the reason Liszt displays such arrogance at times is really the fault of the women, because they pay court to him everywhere in a way that is intolerable to me and that I also find highly improper. I venerate him too, but even veneration must have a limit. . . . On the 16th, Liszt played for the last time and performed Beethoven's E-flat Major Concerto masterfully, but then he played the *Robert-Fantasie* [on Meyerbeer's *Robert le Diable*] in dreadful taste, and after that, the *Galopp* [Liszt]. He seemed tired, which is not surprising, considering the way he lives—he had come early that day from Halle, where he had a wild night, and still had three rehearsals in the morning. . . . Liszt came to the soirée [at the Schumann house] late, as always. He seems to enjoy making people wait for him, which is something I don't like. He strikes me as a spoiled child, good-natured, tyrannical, amiable, arrogant, noble, and generous, often hard on others—a strange mix of characters. Yet we have become very fond of him and he has always treated us in the friendliest way.[34]

Yet Clara reciprocated this friendliness with coldness and eventually with outright hostility. Why? First, she was genuinely offended by his attitude toward the music he performed. From Wieck she had learned that her duty as an interpreter was to play in a manner as close as possible to the spirit and intention of the composer. This attitude was reinforced, of course, when she married Schumann. Liszt, though a composer himself, had no compunctions about embellishing the music he played, his own and that of others, adding trills and cadenzas, doubling octaves, exaggerating tempo changes, rolling arpeggios, "as he wanted," as Clara put it. Moreover, the serious young Leipziger probably resented his careless ease: he played in public without rehearsal, caroused half the night before a performance, canceled concerts at will—all without noticeable effect on his playing. In a sense, he dishonored her high musical ideals, and the conscientious Clara Schumann found such an attitude unforgivable.

Clara herself gave a clue to her antagonism when she described Liszt's verve, his zest for life and excitement, and what she sensed as his capacity for happiness. These characteristics were unnerving to the sober young pianist who still retained the "inclination to melancholy" that had struck observers of the adolescent Clara. All the sufferings and strains of the years of courtship took their toll, and the marriage brought its own problems. The portraits of the years 1840–50 show a sad, solemn woman. She was still slender and had the soulful eyes that were so remarkable in the child's face, but the responsibilities of marriage, motherhood, and career weighed heavily upon her. The continuing hostility between the Schumanns and Wieck was also an emotional burden. It must be remembered that Clara had never known the gaiety, flirtations, lightheartedness, spontaneous laughter—the excitement and carefree fun most girls experience in their teens. She always took herself seriously and carried out her duties and responsibilities gravely, even grimly as she grew older. Furthermore, she believed she was not pretty, found it difficult to understand that a man could find her attractive, was even overcome at times by doubts that she could keep Robert's love. The vivid, outgoing personality of the womanizing Liszt was profoundly disturbing to her—perhaps doubly so because he never paid court to her. While she scrupulously deplored his flirtations, she may have unconsciously resented his lack of attention.

The later contacts between the Schumann household and Liszt widened the gulf between them. When Liszt visited the Schumanns in Dresden in 1848, he outraged Clara by appearing two hours late for a dinner party, insulted Robert by pronouncing his Quintet "Leipzigerish," praised Meyerbeer at Mendelssohn's expense, and horrified both Schumanns by his "dreadful" playing. After an outburst from Schumann, Liszt is reported to have said to Clara, "Tell your husband that there is only one person in the world from whom I would take such words calmly."[35]

Despite this scene, Liszt generously presented Schumann's works in Weimar, attended premieres of his works in Leipzig, visited him in Düsseldorf in 1851 and Clara in 1855, invited Clara to play in Weimar in 1854, and dedicated his great Sonata in B Minor to Schumann. This act, too, annoyed Clara, who described the sonata in her diary on May 25, 1854, as "merely a blind noise—no healthy ideas anymore, everything confused, one cannot find one clear harmonic progression—and yet I must now thank him for it. It is really too awful."[36]

When Liszt came to Düsseldorf on September 1, 1851, with Princess Wittgenstein (supposedly soon to be his wife, Clara added in her diary), she noted, "He played, as always, with a truly demonic bravura and possessed the piano really like a devil (I cannot express it in any other way) . . . but oh, his compositions, that was really dreadful!" When she met and played with him in Leipzig in 1852, she raged, "Liszt at his piano . . . no longer music, but like demonic boozing and bluster." She objected not only to his compositions but also to his taste. After her performances in Weimar, to which she had come at his gracious invitation, she heard him play another composer's eight-hand arrangement of Berlioz's *Romeo and Juliet* with three of his students and wrote, "His playing sounded like truly hellish, devilish music."[37]

Her remarks must finally have reached his ears, for they saw each other infrequently after 1856.

Richard Wagner, 1813–1883

As a young student, Richard Wagner lived and studied in Leipzig. During those years he had contact with both Clara Wieck and Robert Schumann. Wagner borrowed music and books from Wieck's lending library, studied theory with Christian Weinlig about the same time as Clara, and was acquainted with Schumann. The acquaintance was renewed when the Schumanns moved to Dresden in 1844. There Wagner, an assistant director at the opera, saw Schumann more frequently: they enjoyed visits, walks, and talks together, discussed opera, libretti, and aesthetics. It is doubtful that Clara was present at these meetings. Though Wagner is rarely mentioned in her diary, the few notes she did make about him make clear that she not only disliked his music, but even in 1843 found the man offensive. On February 12, 1843, she saw *Rienzi,* "which drove everyone in Dresden crazy," and wrote that her feeling about it was that it was disagreeable. "The same feeling repeated itself when I became acquainted with Wagner personally; a person who never stops talking about himself, is highly arrogant, and laughs continually in a whining tone."[38]

After her husband's death, she saw Wagner now and again, but remarked in her diary after meeting him in Zurich in December 1857: "I can't say very much about him. He is certainly friendly to me and that makes me feel even worse because I cannot bring myself to feel the least spark of sympathy for him."[39]

Her comments on Wagner and his music became increasingly corrosive:

> I decided to go to see *Rheingold.* I felt as if I were wading in a swamp the whole evening. The one good thing about the opera is that one is not deafened by the brass as one is in his other operas. . . . The boredom that one must endure, however, is dreadful. In every scene the actors on stage are in a cataleptic trance in which they remain fixed for such a long time that one cannot look at them any more. The women have just a few measures to sing in the entire opera and stand around forever; in general they are all nothing but tattered, villainous gods.

Her reaction to *Die Walküre* was no kinder:

> There was much that interested me in *Walküre,* but boredom was the dominating feature. . . . The gods don't interest one in the slightest, they are all

such scoundrels; and this Wotan is the stupidest fellow. . . . Musicians are always talking about the interesting orchestration—I will try to hear the opera once more and pay special attention to that.

A few days later she went to hear *Das Rheingold* and *Die Walküre* again and did admit to hearing some sections that sounded quite beautiful, but also, she wrote, many harmonies that reminded her of Mendelssohn, Schumann, and Heinrich Marschner.[40] Her reaction to *Tristan und Isolde* is as revealing about herself as about its composer. In September 1875 she wrote in her diary:

> In the evening we went to see *Tristan und Isolde*. That is the most disgusting thing I have ever seen or heard in my life. To be forced to see and hear such crazy lovemaking the whole evening, in which every feeling of decency is violated and by which not only the public but even musicians seem to be enchanted—that is the saddest thing I have ever experienced in my artistic life. I remained to the end because I wanted to hear the whole thing. During the whole second act the two of them sleep and sing; through the whole last act—for fully forty minutes—Tristan dies. And that they call *dramatic*!!![41]

Wagner's music as well as his personality was the antithesis of everything Clara held sacred. Unlike Liszt, whose generosity of spirit Clara could acknowledge (however grudgingly), Wagner was supremely selfish and self-serving. She refused to play in Vienna in 1870 under Wagner and wrote Brahms that she could not play under the direction of a man who shamelessly spoke of Robert, Mendelssohn, and Brahms in such a scornful manner.[42] Her friendship with Hermann Levi was marred by Levi's Wagner worship, which she tried in vain to overlook. Levi, strangely enough, was able to forgive Wagner his violent anti-Semitism; Clara could tolerate neither the man nor the musician.

Richard and Cosima Wagner spoke of both Schumanns and the Schumann circle with crude contempt, and though Clara Schumann could not have been aware of the kind of spiteful gossip that seemed to be the daily talk in the Wagner home,[43] she had ample reason to despise the man and enough sense of history to fear his influence. She described his death as simply "an event."[44]

Felix Mendelssohn Bartholdy, 1809–1847

The elegant and worldly Felix Mendelssohn Bartholdy, already illustrious at twenty-six, arrived in Leipzig on the last day of August 1835 to take over the leadership of the Gewandhaus Orchestra. Soon after his arrival, he visited the Wiecks and heard more of Robert's works and some of Clara's own compositions.[45] He seemed to be more impressed by Clara's accomplishments than by those of her friend Robert Schumann. Schumann's position as editor and littérateur meant little or nothing to the brilliant pianist, conductor, and composer, who had little patience with critics and other writers about music. Clara, by contrast, was a respected colleague. Though they had met in Paris years before, there is little evidence that Felix had paid much attention to the awkward, serious child she then was. In 1835, however, the presence in Leipzig of the graceful and accomplished young pianist aroused the conductor's interest. At her sixteenth birthday celebration they played together and for each other: she performed a Bach fugue and, at his special request, the Scherzo from Schumann's unpublished sonata. He, in turn, played for her and a few days later gave her an autograph of his *Capriccio*, op. 5.[46*]

Within a few weeks, on November 9, 1835, Mendelssohn conducted the Gewandhaus Orchestra with Clara Wieck as soloist in the premiere of her Concerto for Piano and Orchestra. On the same program she played with Mendelssohn and Rakemann the Bach Concerto for Three Claviers in D Minor, the first performance of this work at the Gewandhaus. Clara Wieck performed under Mendelssohn's direction and played with him frequently, both in public and privately. Over the years Mendelssohn depended on her, asked her to substitute for him when he was unable to play, and obviously considered her to be a musician of the first rank.† In answer to a letter from Clara asking if he would like to play with her, he wrote on November 24, 1845, "You know I am *always* ready to do this and am *always* thinking of playing something with you whenever you want to give me that pleasure."[47] In August 1844 she joined the faculty of the Leipzig Conservatory, which he had established, but Schumann's illness and the subsequent move to Dresden prevented her from continuing that association.

Despite several misunderstandings and the anti-Jewish remarks in the marriage diary,[48] Schumann admired Mendelssohn tremendously. Unfortunately, it must be recorded that Robert Schumann was not immune to the anti-Semitism prevalent in Germany at that time. His remarks reflected the prejudices found even in enlightened European circles in the early nineteenth century.[49] When Robert Schumann was annoyed with Mendelssohn or envied his fame and success, he noted that Mendelssohn (though baptized) was born Jewish and should not be so greatly esteemed. Clara, like a dutiful wife, was quick to agree. Yet for all his extraordinary and numerous activities, Mendelssohn, generally known to be reserved and rather cool, proved himself a true friend when he came forward to testify for Schumann during Wieck's suit. Mendelssohn's death in 1847, at the age of thirty-eight, was a severe blow to both Schumanns. In his uncompleted memoirs of Mendelssohn, Schumann noted his many courtesies to Clara. Mendelssohn gave her small but cherished gifts and praised her playing both publicly and privately. Schumann took pride in Mendelssohn's high regard for Clara, though he may very well have had mixed feelings about it. "He always thought highly of her," he wrote, "and said, 'She really understands how to play the piano.' It always gave him great pleasure to take lively

*See letter to Emilie List, pp. 46–47.

†Mendelssohn conducted at twenty-one of her concerts.

tempos with her in the four-hand works they played together, especially when they were sight-reading."[50]

Despite Robert's warning in November 1840 not to put Felix Mendelssohn on a pedestal, Clara idolized Mendelssohn as pianist, composer, and conductor and considered his playing of Bach beyond compare. On December 30, 1838, after hearing Thalberg, Liszt's rival, she wrote in her diary, "As a player, he has a place among the greats, but towering above all others—stands Mendelssohn." In 1840 she described his performance of his Trio in D Minor and Mozart's G Minor Piano Quartet as so masterful and fiery that she was brought to tears. "Aside from the pleasure, I believe that I learn a great deal when I hear him."[51] One Mendelssohn work—and often more than one—appeared on the program of almost every recital she gave in her long years on the concert stage.

As conductor of the Gewandhaus Orchestra, Felix Mendelssohn was the leader of musical life in Leipzig, and both Clara and Robert were in awe of his talents, proud of his interest in their affairs, and also a bit jealous of his lofty position.* Robert Schumann valued Mendelssohn's opinions not only because of his powerful position but because he respected the experience and judgment of this creative genius who seemed to have everything in his favor—wealth, the best education, early experience, social and administrative talents, unflagging industry, and self-discipline. Clara, whom her husband described as "glowing for hours after a nice word from Mendelssohn,"[52] approached the director for help and advice several times without Robert's knowledge. In November 1843, for example, when Schumann was unable to make a decision about a trip to Russia—a journey on which she had long set her heart—she went to Mendelssohn for counsel. On December 9, 1843, she wrote to him:

> My husband is now talking seriously about the trip. I am very happy about this but I also know whom to thank. When I think of the morning when I came to you in such despair, I am embarrassed and realize that I must have seemed really childish to you, but I will never forget how kindly and patiently you listened to me, and how you met all my wishes with such sympathy.[53]

Apparently Clara was not troubled by the fact that she had gone behind her husband's back to a male friend, only by the fear that she might have appeared childish.

Clara visited Mendelssohn's mother when she was in Berlin and was greatly taken with Fanny Mendelssohn Hensel, Felix's sister. She found her so congenial that she noted in the marriage diary that the presence of such an accomplished woman who could be a real friend was a lure that made the thought of settling in Berlin an attractive prospect.[54] When Fanny Hensel died in May 1847, six months before her brother, Clara Schumann wrote to Emilie List:

*Though Schumann and Mendelssohn were about the same age, they were not on *du* terms, as Schumann was with Ferdinand David and Ferdinand Hiller, for example.

> The situation in regard to Mendelssohn's sister is very sad! I learned to know her better only recently and esteemed her highly. We saw each other daily and had already arranged between us that when we would come to Berlin we would see each other often and play music together. She was undoubtedly the most distinguished [woman] musician of her time and a very important person for musical life in Berlin—one heard only the best at her place. I had dedicated my trio, which I am awaiting from the printer daily, to her and now she is dead!* It affected my husband and me deeply.[55]

Clara Schumann maintained her close ties with Mendelssohn until his death and with other members of his family afterward. When Schumann was hospitalized, Mendelssohn's brother Paul offered help so tactfully that Clara accepted it though she had refused aid from others.[56] The youngest child of Clara and Robert Schumann was named in memory of their friend, the "unforgettable one," as Schumann wrote from the hospital.[57]

JOSEPH JOACHIM, 1831–1907

As a concert performer Clara Schumann was most closely associated with two artists, the violinist Joseph Joachim and the singer Julius Stockhausen, both considerably younger than she. They reached positions of eminence early in life and were regarded by Clara and the public alike as her equals in stature, rank, and musicianship.

Her long relationship with Joachim was particularly close: she gave over 238 concerts with him in Germany and in England, more than with any other artist.[58] She first met the violinist when he came to Leipzig as a boy of twelve to study with Ferdinand David, concertmaster of the Gewandhaus Orchestra. In May 1853 Joachim came to Düsseldorf, at Schumann's urging, to perform the Beethoven Violin Concerto at the Lower Rhine Music Festival, in which Schumann, as Düsseldorf's municipal music director, played an important role. Joachim's dazzling performance and sympathetic artistry impressed the Schumanns, and he visited Düsseldorf frequently in the following months. In August of that year he and Clara played chamber music together, and he returned for another public concert on October 27 (the last conducted by Robert Schumann), at which he premiered Schumann's new *Fantasie,* op. 131, which was dedicated to him.[59]

When Robert fell ill, Joachim and Brahms were the two friends on whom Clara most depended. She was never on *du* terms with Joachim, but in July 1854, soon after her husband went to Endenich, she wrote in her diary:

> He is as dear a friend as Brahms, and in him, too, I have the utmost confidence. He has such spirit and delicate perception that he understands my

*When published, the Trio had no dedication.

> slightest and most subtle feelings immediately. These two, Brahms and Joachim, seem made to be Robert's friends, but he does not know them yet as I do. One learns to know one's friends in adversity.[60]

Her first concerts after Schumann's hospitalization were with Joachim. They never missed an opportunity to make music together, at home or on the concert stage. She admired his playing and musicianship more than those of any other performer of her time. The two were particularly noted for their playing of Beethoven's sonatas for violin and piano. Clara Schumann and Joachim saw eye to eye musically and the collaboration gave them—and their audiences—unending joy. (She also toured extensively with his wife, Amalie, a mezzo-soprano. Frau Joachim was one of the few singers—Stockhausen was another—for whom she played accompaniments. Amalie Joachim and Julius Stockhausen, she felt, were colleagues, not assisting artists.) She played with Joseph Joachim in England as well as on the Continent from 1854 until the 1880s.

Clara Schumann was so fond of Joachim that she mentioned to him several times that she wished they could live in the same town. Soon after Schumann died, she thought of looking for a teaching position in a large city where she could be near Joachim and Brahms. In January 1858, she described what she would consider an ideal situation: "I want to go where I can be with both of you; where you can stand by me with counsel and help [*Rat und That*], uplift me through your music, and inspire me to self-study through your praise and reproof." Clara was obviously attempting to recapture the years with Robert. She went on, "You will smile when you think of my tears [when I am reproached] but it doesn't matter. Reproaches that come from true friendship are priceless and have already brought me many steps forward."[61]

Her dream was not realized, but they corresponded for forty years.[62] Since they were both basically performers, their letters centered on such common problems as conductors, orchestras, the scheduling of engagements, and touring, on questions of tempos and interpretation, and on the physical afflictions that trouble many performing artists. She also turned to Joachim for advice about her career, as one artist to another. Like Brahms, Joachim responded sympathetically; the most trivial questions were answered with respect for her feelings and with affirmation of his admiration for her artistry.

The separation of Joseph and Amalie Joachim in the early 1880s and their subsequent divorce caused Clara much anguish. The impending divorce may have brought back memories of the breakup of her own family so many years earlier, and she wrote with great emotion to a mutual friend that she hesitated to go to Berlin, even to perform, because she was so troubled by the Joachim situation.[63] Unlike Brahms, however, she did not take sides in the controversy and maintained her friendship with both Joseph and Amalie as long as she could.

As director of the Königliche Hochschule für Musik in Berlin, Joachim endeavored year after year to lure her to a faculty position at the school. Finally, however, he gave up: her conditions were always too demanding (one suspects she did not want to be tied down to a regular job) and he was never able to procure the necessary funds from the trustees. Though Joachim had the greatest respect for Clara Schumann, it seems that even her luster could not compete with prevailing attitudes toward women, and he may not have tried very hard to persuade his board to hire her. As he wrote to Ernst Rudorff, his assistant and head of the Piano Department, she could teach only girls, and as it was chiefly the men that needed a teacher at the time, he had given up trying to get a position for her. Rudorff, himself a Clara Schumann student, agreed.[64] Joachim was hurt when in 1878 she accepted a professorship in Frankfurt—where she taught both men and women—but the friendship continued nevertheless.

Among her last joys was Joachim's playing. In May 1890 she wrote to him that when he played, she forgot all her physical pains.[65] Joachim visited her in November 1894. At that time she wrote of the friend of her youth: "He brought his violin with him, but this time I wanted the human being [*Mensch*], the friend, rather than the violinist."[66]

Julius Stockhausen, 1826–1906

Clara Schumann met Julius Stockhausen during the first summer of her husband's hospitalization and after one hearing proclaimed him a "star in the artistic heavens." She dubbed him *Herrlicher Sänger* (glorious singer),[67] and he was referred to in the Schumann circle by that term ever after. Stockhausen, an Alsatian-born baritone trained in Paris, was one of the first great lieder singers of the nineteenth century. He gave the first complete performances of Schubert and Schumann song cycles: Schubert's *Schöne Müllerin* in 1854, Schumann's *Dichterliebe* with Brahms in 1861 and with Clara Schumann in 1862. Later he premiered complete performances of Robert Schumann's *Frauenliebe und Leben, Liederkreis,* and the *Spanisches Liederspiel.*[68] One of Stockhausen's great achievements was his championship of Schumann's *Faust* Scenes. Ferdinand Hiller, the conductor in Cologne, wanted to present only excerpts, but Stockhausen telegraphed him, "All or nothing," and Hiller capitulated. Stockhausen gave the first complete performance of this little-known work in Cologne in 1862.[69] In April 1855, knowing that Stockhausen's singing would give her husband great pleasure, Clara attempted to arrange a private concert at Endenich, but the plan did not work out and Schumann never heard the young man sing.[70]

Her delight with Stockhausen's voice and musicianship was equaled by his admiration for her. "Madame Schumann is one of those rare persons for whom I would go to the ends of the earth. . . . What an artist!" he wrote to his father in 1856.[71] After he met her, his circle of musical associates enlarged to include Brahms, Joachim, and later, in London—where he toured with Clara Schumann in 1859—her old friends Jenny Lind, Pauline Viardot, and Ferdinand Hiller.

Stockhausen's appointment in 1862 as music director in Hamburg was a blow to Brahms and to Clara Schumann as well, but the friendship and musical collaboration among the three of them survived. Soon after Clara Schumann moved to Frankfurt to teach at the Hoch Conservatory, Stockhausen followed to become the principal voice teacher. His years in Frankfurt were marked by great battles with Joachim Raff, the director, and he left for a time, but returned to the conservatory after Raff's death. Later he established his own voice school in Frankfurt. He and Clara Schumann remained friends and colleagues to the end.

Pauline Viardot, née García, 1821–1910

Clara Schumann first met Pauline García—actress, singer, pianist, composer, teacher, and talented painter—in Leipzig in June 1838 and recognized her genius instantly. She believed that Pauline was an exception among singers: "She has a lively interest in music," Clara wrote in her diary on June 25, 1838, "and is the most musical singer living today." The two girls—Clara almost nineteen, Pauline almost seventeen—became fast friends; indeed, fifty-four years later Pauline described them as "the two oldest friends of this century."[72]

When they first met, Clara, overwhelmed by the singer's mastery, intellectual skills (she read and understood Schiller and Goethe), her linguistic ability (she was fluent in five languages), and her many other talents, was envious and on the verge of losing her self-confidence. She was relieved by her father's reassurances and by Pauline's generous and unfailing admiration. Clara was captivated by Pauline's vivacity, temperament, and seemingly carefree ways. The earnest Clara alternated between envy and disbelief at the way Pauline, the youngest daughter of Joaquina Sitches de García and Manuel García, enjoyed life.[73*]

Despite the vast differences in personality, the two artists respected each other and relished the few opportunities they had to meet. After three hearings of a group of operettas that Pauline Viardot had composed, orchestrated, and produced, Clara Schumann wrote to Brahms, "Once more I have confirmation of what I have always said: she is the most gifted woman I have ever met."[74†]

The two women, so dissimilar in temperament, had much in common. Both were international concert stars who performed and composed; both were from professional families in which concertizing was the basic source of family

*The García family was internationally known: her father, Manuel García, the famed Spanish tenor, teacher, and impresario, was probably the most renowned vocal teacher in the nineteenth century. At the age of five Pauline had accompanied her parents to New York, where they established the first Italian opera company in the United States. Her fabled older sister, María, the soprano known simply as Malibrán, had a brilliant career cut short by a fatal riding accident when she was still in her twenties. Malibrán's second marriage was to Charles de Bériot, the violinist, with whom both Clara and Pauline concertized.

†After her marriage to Louis Viardot in 1840, she was known simply as Pauline Viardot.

income; both were career women, married with children.* Yet the ultimate destinies of the two differed widely. Pauline's husband, Louis Viardot, twenty-one years older than she, a successful French theatrical producer and entrepreneur, devoted himself to her career and acted as her agent and manager. Pauline never knew the financial insecurities that plagued the Schumann household, nor did she undergo one pregnancy after another. The disastrous illnesses and deaths that shadowed Clara's life were unknown to Pauline Viardot.

Over the years their paths crossed now and again: in Paris in 1839 Clara saw Pauline almost daily; in 1843 they appeared together in a concert with Mendelssohn in Leipzig; they met in London in 1856, in Pest in 1858, in Paris in 1862. With Pauline's encouragement, Clara bought her cottage in Baden-Baden; they were neighbors there for the ten summers Clara Schumann owned the house.

When the Schumanns arrived in Russia in 1844, Pauline Viardot was completing a triumphal tour. In her farewell press interview the singer announced, "I am leaving you Clara Schumann. Her singing on the piano is better than mine."[75]

*Viardot had four children. The eldest, Louise Viardot-Héritte, was also a professional singer, teacher, and composer.

CHAPTER 11

Clara Schumann as Composer and Editor

Clara Wieck Schumann's achievements as a composer and editor are not so well known as her accomplishments on the concert stage. Her compositions, published, reviewed, reprinted, and performed throughout the nineteenth century, were esteemed by Robert Schumann, Mendelssohn, Chopin, and Brahms, among others. For some time after her death, however, her compositions were all but forgotten; on the occasions when they were performed, they were generally considered interesting only in relation to those of her husband. The surge of interest in her works in the late twentieth century, fueled by the attention to women's history, has ensured that all but two or three of her known compositions are now available in print or on recordings. As a result, her works—both vocal and instrumental—are performed with increasing frequency and are gaining the respect and admiration they deserve.*

Although Clara Schumann was encouraged by the reception of her works during her lifetime, she expressed many doubts about the value of her creative work. Personal and social factors fed into her insecurities. The prevailing expectation that women should maintain a modest demeanor, cultivate humility, and avoid creative activities did not seem to affect her ambitions for a concert career but did add to her discomfort about composing. In addition, her marriage to a great but underappreciated composer had disturbing elements of competition on both musical and personal levels. Yet despite alternating feelings of despair, embarrassment, and exhilaration about her creative powers, she persevered and continued to compose music as long as her husband was alive. The question of why she gave up composing after 1856 can perhaps best be explained in the context of the astonishing number of her responsibilities as mother and musician.

*The Catalogue of Works gives the origin, descriptions of autographs, publication history, and comments on each composition and edition.

Education of a Composer

From her very first days at the piano, creative activities were integrated into Clara Wieck's daily routine. As a consequence of her father's innovative approach to the instrument, the five-year-old Clara played by ear before she could read notes, transposed little pieces, and improvised on her own or given themes, a skill she continued to develop throughout her life. Once she learned to read, sight-reading skills were encouraged.

Formal harmony, counterpoint, and composition lessons began when Clara was barely ten, and her own compositions appeared on her earliest programs, as was customary in the 1830s. Her musical education also included voice lessons, violin lessons, instruction in orchestration, score reading, and regular attendance at every musical event in Leipzig and the other cities where she performed.

Friedrich Wieck, her sole teacher and manager, directed every aspect of her education. He looked upon her not only as his possession but as an alter ego. His identity confusion is evident in the entries in Clara's diary in which he wrote in the first person.[1] Among many examples are:

Early July 1833: "This month I composed a great deal, finished—among other things . . . the first solo of a large Concert Rondo."

August 18, 1833: "My Romance, Opus 3, has just been published."

August 7, 1835: "The composer Herr Meyer is giving me lessons in orchestration. I completed the orchestration of my Waltzes on the 25th and wrote it out myself. Herr Meyer looked over the score."

Such entries and the canon that women were unable to compose may have contributed to a widespread assumption that Wieck wrote Clara's compositions. That Wieck did not write for her is certain. His own published works have neither the charm nor the skill of even her earliest attempts. Her continued growth as a composer and Wieck's own expressions of joyous surprise at her talent[2] give the lie to assertions that he composed her works. He must be credited, of course, for the creative music education and ambiance he provided, but her compositions were her own.

Clara Wieck's girlhood compositions were created to be performed at her concerts: an improvisation or an original work was included in almost every concert Clara gave between 1830 and 1838. Many of these works for voice, for solo piano, and for orchestra have disappeared; we know of them only through mention in the diaries and correspondence or in the programs of her concerts. If the extant works are a reliable guide, we may assume that the early lost works were popular crowd-pleasers in the style of the music she performed by Henri Herz, Johann Peter Pixis, and Friedrich Kalkbrenner. Three of her published works—op. 3, *Romance variée;* op. 8, *Variations de concert sur la Cavatine du Pirate de Bellini;* and op. 9, *Souvenir de Vienne*—are in this category. They are big virtuoso works, designed to show off her technical prowess.

Within a few years, however—and while she was still under Wieck's aegis—a new style began to emerge. In 1837, when Clara and her father were on their way to Vienna, a Prague newspaper, presumably with Wieck's consent, published an article describing her as a "member of the new romantic school,"[3] thus linking her with such young "modern" composers as Chopin, Mendelssohn, and Schumann. Wieck was receptive to the new music and included himself, and hence his daughter, among the avant-garde.

Most descriptions of her work, both then and later, refer to her compositions as "Chopinesque" or "Schumannesque," or note a resemblance to Mendelssohn, even to Brahms (though that was hardly possible, since she was almost fourteen years old when he was born). Although she was ten years younger than Chopin, Mendelssohn, and Schumann, she was aware of the musical currents of her time. Moreover, all three composers played their music for her themselves, and she, in turn, played her own works for them.

By the time Clara was fourteen years old, many features of the new romanticism could be heard in her compositions: the bravura technique; the lyrical aria-like middle sections; the miniature forms with extramusical associations; the loosening of regular phrase structure; the experiments with rhythm and meter and the use of such dance rhythms as the polonaise and mazurka. The young Clara Wieck, who saw herself primarily as a performer, may not have had the power or soaring ambition of the leaders of the "new romantic" school, but she was accepted as one of them.

The music she wrote in her girlhood shows many influences: the flashy keyboard works of such composers as Friedrich Kalkbrenner and Henri Herz; the piano works of Beethoven, Schubert, and Weber, composers whose music she heard and performed from her earliest years; and the music of the "new romantics"—Schumann, of course, but also Chopin and Mendelssohn. Other influences were the Italian operas of Vincenzo Bellini, Gaetano Donizetti, and Gioacchino Rossini; the national dances—polonaises, mazurkas—that she heard from Chopin; the German operas of Spohr and Heinrich Marschner; and the dazzling brilliance of Nicolò Paganini, which captivated Schumann, Liszt, and all their contemporaries.

Of all the new romantic composers, Robert Schumann—not surprisingly—had the greatest influence on the young girl. The influence turned very quickly into a musical partnership that continued on into their married life. In the songs as well as the instrumental works, we are struck by the continuing personal cooperation and interchange of musical ideas between the two composers. By 1832 Robert Schumann was already depending on the twelve-year-old girl to perform his music for him because of his hand injury. By 1833 their correspondence was filled with musical games, riddles, and secret messages referring to the music they both were creating. That same year, Clara asked Robert to orchestrate her *Concertsatz,* the piece that became the final movement of her Concerto, op. 7.

Beginning in 1839, they exchanged information about texts that could serve as song settings. Both Clara and Robert read poetry with an eye toward possible settings, and each brought poems to the attention of the other. We know that

Robert enlisted Clara's aid in finding song material for him. In May 1840, at the height of his "song fever," he requested, "Write to me often. And bring me poems to set to music."[4]

A notebook in the Zwickau archives titled "Abschriften von Gedichten zur Composition" (Copies of Poems for Composition) includes poetry written out by both husband and wife.[5] That Clara was involved in this activity even before her marriage is clear from the section of the book labeled "Gesammelt von Robert und Clara Schumann vom Jahre 1839 an" (Collected by Robert and Clara Schumann from 1839 on). Of the 169 poems in the book, 106 were written out by Clara. Some of the texts she used were copied by Robert Schumann, and conversely, many of the texts he used are in her hand.

After her marriage, Clara Schumann's composing efforts followed closely the patterns set by her husband in respect to the genres she chose, though the voice was distinctly her own. Robert Schumann had been concentrating on lieder in 1839 and 1840; her first works in 1840 were also songs. After their counterpoint studies in early 1845, both composers produced music that reflected these efforts: Robert Schumann's *Vier Fugen,* op. 72; *Sechs Fugen,* op. 60, for organ; and the *Sechs Studien für Pedal-Flügel,* op. 56, were composed at about the same time as Clara's op. 16 and the other preludes and fugues (not published at the time). All had their inspiration in the counterpoint studies of 1845. Her Sonata in G Minor and later the Trio for Piano, Violin, and Cello, op. 17, were informed by the studies of the symphonies and chamber music of the classical masters undertaken soon after their marriage.

Clara and Robert encouraged, criticized, advised, and dedicated important works to each other. Robert continually urged her to compose and to catalogue, organize, and preserve her manuscripts. He pressed her to treat her own work with care and respect: he urged her to make and keep fair copies of her songs; with his obsession for systematic order, he wrote out title pages and tables of contents of her manuscript collections. His hand can be seen on cover pages and in suggestions regarding tempo and naming of pieces.

As editor of the *Neue Zeitschrift für Musik,* Robert Schumann chose the works to be published in the musical supplements. He urged her to submit compositions and she did so, both before and after their marriage.[6] He corresponded and negotiated with publishers, and arranged for the publication of almost every work she composed, a mission she would not have undertaken on her own as a young married woman.

Although Robert Schumann encouraged and praised her original efforts and exerted his influence to have them published, he had mixed feelings about her creative activities. On the one hand, he took pride in her successes and acknowledged her talents. Among the reviews and articles that Robert Schumann carefully preserved was one in which he underlined phrases and made marginal comments. He underlined the following: "*The greater influence on his profession was his marriage to one of the greatest artists of our century, the admirable Clara Wieck.* Schumann lived in her father's house for many years." In the margin, he wrote, "1 year." The article continued: "In contrast to other virtuosas, she almost always avoided playing her own compositions, although she composed better and more solidly than many of the most famous artists of that time."[7] On the other hand, an entry in the marriage diary dated February 17, 1843, reveals his thinking:

> Clara has written a number of small pieces that show a musical and tender invention that she has never attained before. But to have children and a husband who is always living in the realms of imagination do not go together with composing. She cannot work at it regularly and I am often disturbed to think how many profound ideas are lost because she cannot work them out. But Clara herself knows her main occupation is as a mother and I believe she is happy in the circumstances and would not want them changed.[8]

Ambition, Ambivalence, and Women's Work

During the marriage Clara Schumann took on many of the traditional roles of a musician's wife: she copied music, she accompanied groups her husband conducted, she played and sang in performances of his works. But since she was a musician herself and a renowned pianist, she also premiered almost all his piano works during his lifetime (and after) and prepared piano arrangements of his instrumental works.

Reflecting the thinking of her time, this wife—despite her superior musical education and years of experience in the musical world—believed her husband to be the preeminent authority in all things, musical and otherwise. Thirteen years after they were married, she still awaited his judgment on each piece (and even her playing) with some apprehension. In 1853 Clara wrote to her sister, Marie Wieck: "To my great joy, all the pieces [opp. 20–23] were so well done that there was nothing that Robert wanted to change. So you see, as one gets older there are also many pleasures that only a more mature mind and feelings can bring."[9]

The couple began to study counterpoint and fugue together in 1845, and even though Clara had taken lessons in counterpoint in 1837 with Siegfried Dehn, a leading theorist of his time, performed Bach concertos with Felix Mendelssohn at the Leipzig Gewandhaus, and had played fugues from Bach's *Well-Tempered Clavier* in 1838 for the emperor and empress at the Burg in Vienna, she wrote in her diary: "I cannot thank Robert enough for his patience with me and am doubly happy when something is successful since he can view it as his work as well. He himself is in the midst of a fugue passion."[10]

Clara Schumann felt ambivalent about her creative work. On the one hand, composing brought a glow of satisfaction: "There is nothing that surpasses the joy of creative activity, even if only for those hours of self-forgetfulness in which one breathes solely in the realm of tones," she wrote after completing the six songs of op. 23 in 1853. And after her Trio was finished, she noted in her diary,

"There is really no greater pleasure than having composed something and then to hear it" and expressed confidence in its success. On the other hand, she never fully accepted that very success, writing later that it was "women's work, which always lacks force and occasionally invention."[11]

Other musicians enjoyed playing her Trio and were unaware of her conflicts. On March 13, 1860, Joachim wrote, praising the work, and added: "I recollect a fugato in the last movement and remember that Mendelssohn once had a big laugh because I would not believe that a woman could have composed something so sound and serious."[12]

Even praise from such an esteemed colleague, however, could not convince her of the Trio's worth. She played her husband's trios far more often than her own and seldom programmed her Trio. Contradictory feelings about her creative work appeared well before her marriage. On November 25, 1839, she confided to her diary:

> I once believed that I had creative talent, but I have given up this idea; a woman must not wish to compose—there never was one able to do it. Am I intended to be the one? It would be arrogant to believe that. That was something with which only my father tempted me in former days. But I soon gave up believing this. May Robert always create; that must always make me happy.[13]

Yet shortly before, she had written to Robert, "It is really sinful that I have not composed anything for such a long time. Father is beside himself and I too am often unhappy about it and in general more dissatisfied with myself than I can say."[14]

The correspondence with Robert about her *Trois Romances* further illustrates her mixed emotions about the creative act. On April 23, 1839, she wrote, "I have a peculiar fear of showing you my compositions; I am always ashamed." She asked him for criticism, but when Robert returned her work with alterations and suggestions, she objected strenuously, at the same time adding, "You are not angry with me, are you?"[15]

Her ambivalence, however, has another aspect: Clara evidently felt safe in derogating her own work but could express indignation at what she regarded as unwarranted criticism even from those she loved and trusted.[16] When Robert asked her, not too tactfully, "Do you always play your concerto of your own accord? There are brilliant ideas in the first movement yet it did not make a complete impression on me. When you are sitting at the piano, I no longer know you—my judgment is quite a different matter," she snapped back:

> You had Becker write about my concerto, and what did he write? "We forgive the young for the many tenth chords." I know quite well what is lacking in the concerto, and know that I would compose it differently now. I wouldn't play it so often in public here and in Prague if I had not pleased the experts and the nonexperts with it so much, here and in public recitals in Prague. How-

ever, I do know that it would have been worthy of a better review than the one Becker wrote.[17]

She resented Berlioz's review of her Scherzo, op. 10, in the *Journal des Débats* and found it "highly malicious."[18] And "malicious" is repeated in a letter to Robert of April 23 in which she writes that Berlioz called Anna de Belleville, a German pianist, "solid" but Clara "worldly," which she evidently interpreted as trivial or unimportant. She was also not above repeating some slanderous gossip: she was told, she wrote to Robert, "as soon as you offer him [Berlioz] money, he writes whatever you want. Döhler always invites him to dine and sets good wine, which he likes *very much,* before him." That, in her opinion, was why "Döhler's compositions get good reviews."[19]*

Clara Wieck eventually gained more confidence in her own work, but the apologetic inscriptions on the works she presented to her husband continued. The cover page of the three songs she gave him at Christmas 1840 is inscribed: "Composed and dedicated to her ardently beloved Robert with the *deepest modesty* from his Clara on Christmas 1840." She received the joint song cycle, op. 37/12, on her birthday in 1841 and wrote, "Robert surprised me with the published Rückert Lieder, among them several of my own weak products."[20] Her Sonata in G Minor, unpublished in her lifetime, bears this phrase on the cover page: "Accept it with love, my good husband, and be lenient with your Clara. Christmas 1841." Even the inscription on her op. 20, considered by many to be one of her finest works and one in which she seemed to take pride, gives evidence of self-doubt: "To my beloved husband on June 8, 1853; this renewed feeble attempt from his old Clara."[21]

She frequently expressed fears that her work might embarrass herself and him. Her moods fluctuated wildly. In May 1841 she wailed, "I can't compose any more. All poetry has abandoned me." Yet a month later she presented four songs to Schumann on his birthday, and was pleased, she wrote in the marriage diary, that he "wanted to publish them with several of his own." The first songs composed after her marriage elicited this note in the marriage diary: "I finally succeeded in completing *three,* which I will present to him at Christmas. If they are really of little value, merely a *very weak attempt,* I am counting on Robert's forbearance and [hope] that he will understand that it was done with the best will in the world in order to fulfill this wish of his—just as I fulfill all his wishes."[22]

Why? Why did this gifted, skilled, creative, successful woman write to her husband in such a self-effacing way? Why did she feel the need to demean herself and "fulfill all his wishes"? The answers may be found in the unique union of these two musicians. Clara Wieck Schumann was married to a great composer whose work she admired and loved. Even as a girl, she realized what few

*Theodor Döhler (1814–56) was a German pianist. The gossip was probably spread by Georges Onslow, the Anglo-French composer who had befriended Clara in Paris. He apparently had his difficulties with Berlioz as well.

of her contemporaries understood—that Robert Schumann belonged to the elect, that he would eventually be counted among the great composers of the ages. Any musician married to such a figure would find his stature intimidating; as the younger of the two, she asked for his criticism, but feared and resented it at the same time. She accepted fully the dictum that the husband was the dominating figure in a marriage, but in this case the situation was complicated by the fact that Clara Wieck Schumann was a celebrated performer and earned more money than her husband.* She may well have felt some guilt about her reputation and earning ability, especially in an age when women musicians routinely gave up careers when they married. As a young bride, she may have believed that his love for her might be jeopardized if she showed too much ambition, so it seemed wiser to profess humility. As she grew older and maintained a successful career, the inscriptions she continued to write to him and the entries in the marriage diary gave her a certain measure of protection in the event that her work might not please. Moreover, they eased the imbalance in their careers that might have affected the marriage.

Societal attitudes toward women composers, especially as revealed in newspaper reviews (which she read), played a large part in her feelings of discomfort about composing. Her improvisations and compositions were acclaimed by audiences and reviewers, but the praise was almost always for the work of a *woman* composer: critics compared her work with that of male composers or expressed surprise that a female could compose with such skill. In reviewing her Trio, the critic for the *Allgemeine musikalische Zeitung* wrote: "Women rarely attempt the more mature forms because such works assume a certain abstract strength that is overwhelmingly given to men." And though he went on to say, "Clara Schumann, however, is truly one of the few women who has mastered this strength,"[23] she continued to apologize to her husband for her work.

As the years went on she showed more self-confidence in her creative work. When the Leipzig music publisher C. F. Peters rejected Robert Schumann's offer of Clara's fugues (op. 16), she took pen in hand and offered them to Breitkopf & Härtel.[24]

She never hesitated to insist on more careful work from the printers, as is evident in the letters to her publisher.[25] Her husband, as was usual, negotiated with publishers for the fees and honoraria she was to receive. When he was ill, she took over these tasks. Though at first she prefaced requests for fees by saying, "Robert had such a sum in mind," she dropped this face-saving device after his hospitalization, and we note a decided change in letters to her publishers after he died. If any reluctance to discuss money was indicated in her letters to Dr. Härtel, it was primarily because of their friendship rather than feminine "modesty." On October 25, 1857, for example, she wrote to Härtel:

*Hanslick writes of the Schumanns' 1846–47 tour to Vienna, "Both works [Symphony in B-flat and the Piano Concerto in A Minor] conducted by Schumann himself were received in the Musikvereinsaal on January 1, 1847, with respectful silence; all the attention was given to—his wife" (*Geschichte des Concertwesens in Wien*, 371).

> As far as the honorarium [for her arrangement of Robert Schumann's Quintet] is concerned, I don't think it is immodest for me to ask for 8 louis d'or; it has cost me much time and great care; I am, moreover, convinced that it will be played a great deal so that you will not suffer any losses. It is so disagreeable for me to write about such business affairs though I know that you will separate it from our friendship so that I will always be able to approach you in an open manner.[26]

Clara Schumann's letters and diary provide much evidence that creativity did not come easily to her. Although her works were not rejected by publishers and received favorable reviews, she genuinely believed her primary field of competence was as a performer: an interpretive rather than a creative artist.[27] Her success as a concert artist had come early, was gratifying to her ego, and enabled her to contribute money to the family even when she was a young girl. As a widow with seven children to support, she was always thankful that she could rely on her two hands to earn the necessary funds and proud that she did not have to accept money from friends. When she composed, it was rarely of her own volition but because she was expected to do so; she had the talent, she had the training, and she composed with skill and elegance, fulfilling successfully the expectations of her father and the concert public.

When her relationship with her father weakened and she no longer had to please him by composing, she found that her husband—for whom composing was essential to existence—had similar expectations. In March 1840, before their marriage, he wrote her: "Clärchen, do you perhaps have something for my supplement. . . . Do compose a song! Once you begin, you cannot leave it. It is far too seductive."[28] Again in May 1840, when he was in the midst of a feverishly exalted creative period, he urged, "Write to me again of what you see and hear and compose. Try to compose a song; you'll see how well it will turn out."[29]

Robert Schumann had few distractions to interfere with his primary objective. His wife, on the other hand, had a performing career, a teaching career, and responsibilities for children and household. After her marriage, her compositions were almost always written for Christmas or birthdays or at her husband's special request. Despite his continued encouragement, the conflicts seen in her letters and diaries continued to the very end of her composing career, which, not unexpectedly, closed when her husband died.[30] After 1856, any time she found available after fulfilling family duties and concert responsibilities was devoted to her self-imposed obligation to promote her husband's works.

The Piano Music of Clara Wieck Schumann

An extraordinary flow of ideas between Robert Schumann and Clara Wieck is recognizable in the works of the years between 1830 to 1836. Beginning with his op. 2, *Papillons,* and her op. 2, *Caprices en forme de valse,* the two young musicians were working and playing in such close proximity that it is often difficult to determine the origin of many musical ideas they shared.

Robert Schumann used musical quotations, motifs, and words that symbolized Clara for him, incorporating her into his work, as it were. In 1839, he wrote to their old teacher Heinrich Dorn that Clara had been the inspiration for all of his greatest piano works. He often declared that he could feel her very presence as he composed.[31] And Clara, even as a young girl, used motifs and phrases of his, sometimes deliberately—paying homage to the man she loved and admired—and sometimes unconsciously taking in the musical ideas flowing from his fingertips.

It has long been known that Schumann, more than most composers of his age, used allusions, quotations, and self-quotations in his music.[32] The many ways in which Clara appeared in his music include direct quotations from her works as well as allusions to her person and her works. The best known of "her" themes, titled "Quasi Variazioni. Andantino de Clara Wieck" (Example 1), used in the slow movement of Schumann's Sonata in F Minor, op. 14, cannot be found as such in any of the autographs that survive.[33] It strongly suggests, however, a motif outlining a descending fifth that is found in a number of her works and that Schumann used many times as well. In describing the theme as an "Andantino by Clara Wieck," Schumann proclaimed the name of the sixteen-year-old girl to the world. The theme not only appears in the variation movement; it plays a major role throughout his sonata, beginning with the bold octaves in the opening measure of the first movement (Example 2). Schumann almost always modified Clara Wieck's motifs but clearly seems to be taking pleasure in revealing the special relationship between them.

Example 1. Robert Schumann, Sonata in F Minor, op. 14, third movement, "Quasi Variazioni. Andantino de Clara Wieck."

Example 2. Robert Schumann, Sonata in F Minor, op. 14, first movement, Allegro.

Similarly, Robert Schumann's name comes up in almost any discussion of Clara Wieck's music after her op. 1, as we shall see.

Op. 1, *Quatre Polonaises*

The first of Clara's works that Friedrich Wieck deemed worthy of an opus number and publication was her *Quatre Polonaises*, composed when she was eleven. Clara's gift for harmonic surprise (one reviewer considered it "too dissonant") and her keyboard facility are already evident. The review in *Iris,* a Berlin musical journal, found portions to praise but was in essence an indictment of her father: "What reasonable person wants to have school exercises printed, even if they turn out well? But that is the sorry fate of our time—not to take heed of art or the needs of the public, but only to pay allegiance to the purse or homage to vanity."[34]

Wieck paid no attention, of course, and Clara's op. 2 was published the following year.

Op. 2, *Caprices en forme de valse,* and Op. 4, *Valses romantiques*

Since Schumann was living in the Wieck home while he was working on *Papillons,* Clara must have heard the work in progress; her *Caprices,* op. 2, have a similar structure: each is a series of loosely related short works with a dance character, inspired by the waltzes of Schubert and Weber. In the opening measures of her Caprice no. 1 and in Caprices 3, 5, and 6, Clara used the ascending figure associated with Florestan in *Papillons* and *Carnaval.*

In their form and inspiration, the waltzes in Clara's op. 4, *Valses romantiques,* are similar to the waltzlike Caprices of op. 2. Here, too, Clara and Robert shared a musical idea that in all likelihood first appeared in her op. 4: the descending figure in measures 7–10 (Example 3) is repeated almost exactly in the "Valse allemande" of Schumann's *Carnaval* (Example 4).

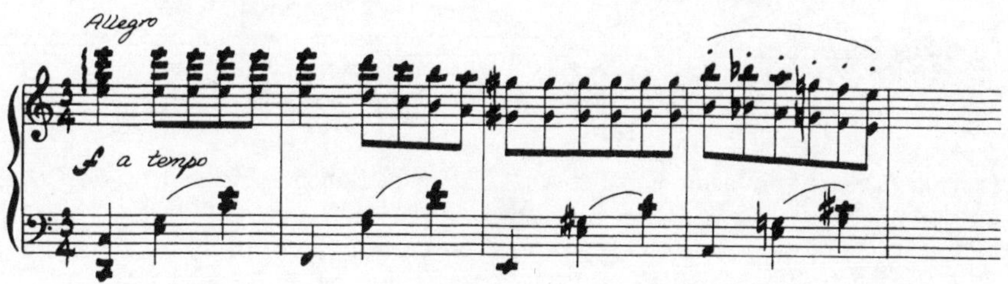

Example 3. Clara Wieck, *Valses romantiques,* op. 4, measures 7–10.

Example 4. Robert Schumann, *Carnaval,* op. 9, "Valse allemand," measures 9–12.

Op. 3, *Romance variée*

An examination of the history of her op. 3, *Romance variée*—the first of Clara's works to be dedicated to Robert Schumann—and the complex story of the origin of the theme (Example 5) further confirm the musical interaction between Clara, thirteen years old when she composed this work, and the twenty-three-year-old Robert Schumann. This work also reveals aspects of the three-sided relationship of Clara, Robert, and Friedrich Wieck and later between Clara, Robert, and Johannes Brahms. The mature Clara Schumann recalled this childhood work when, following the example of Johannes Brahms, she skillfully wove the theme from her op. 3 into the coda of her op. 20, the Variations on a Theme by Robert Schumann (Example 6). A version of her theme also appeared in Brahms's variations on the same theme by Robert Schumann (Example 7).

Example 5. Clara Wieck, *Romance variée,* op. 3, "Romanza."

Example 6. Clara Schumann, Variations on a Theme by Robert Schumann, op. 20, Coda, measures 9–10.

Example 7. Johannes Brahms, Variations on a Theme by Robert Schumann, Variation 10, measures 30–32.

Her Romance, op. 3, has always been of special interest to Schumann scholars because Robert Schumann's *Impromptus sur une romance de Clara Wieck* (his op. 5), dedicated to Friedrich Wieck, was supposedly based on the theme in Clara's Romance (Example 8). Both the *Romance variée* and Schumann's Impromptus were published in the summer of 1833, but the tangled history of the theme goes back to 1830, possibly even earlier.

It has always been assumed that the theme was Clara's own: Schumann him-

Example 8. Robert Schumann, Impromptus on a Romance by Clara Wieck, op. 5 (1833 version), "Romanza."

self labeled it hers; Berthold Litzmann reported that she played op. 3 in 1831; and in May 1833, just before Schumann began work on the Impromptus, he asked Clara to send him all her variations.[35] Two scholars working independently, however, have traced the first appearance of the theme to an entry in Schumann's diary for September 28/29, 1830 (Example 9), thus identifying it as Robert's rather than Clara's.[36] Again, as with so many other works, the two young musicians shared ideas and inspiration. We can speculate that Clara heard Schumann improvising on his melody and then incorporated it in her own daily improvisations and later in her op. 3. Schumann, on hearing her play it, may have forgotten the source and assumed it was her musical idea. In 1850, when Schumann revised his op. 5, he used a slightly different version of the theme (Example 10), changed "Romance" to "Theme," and—still angry at his father-in-law—dropped the dedication to Wieck.

Although Schumann's Impromptus paid tribute to the young girl, Clara's

Example 9. Robert Schumann, theme from *Tagebuch,* 1830.

Example 10. Robert Schumann, Impromptus on a Theme by Clara Wieck, op. 5 (1850 version), "Thema."

Romance variée is scarcely in a style of which he approved. The variations are replete with the musical clichés of the day, and it is precisely the kind of shallow work Robert Schumann was to hold up to ridicule in the *Neue Zeitschrift*.[37]

Op. 5, *Quatre Pièces caractéristiques*

The four "character" pieces that make up op. 5, typical of the new romantic school, were composed over a period of three years and have borne varying titles. They were much admired by contemporary composers; Spohr, Chopin, and Mendelssohn, among others, were impressed by and enthusiastic about the work. Numbers 1 and 4 were the best known and most frequently performed.

1. Impromptu: Le Sabbat

The tempo (allegro furioso), wide leaps, reiterated chromatic appoggiaturas that provide sharp dissonances, accents on weak beats, chromatically ascending bass passages in the middle section—all typical nineteenth-century "demonic" touches—contribute to the supernatural effect of "Le Sabbat," a reference to the witches' sabbath, a theme that intrigued many romantic composers.

The Impromptu began to appear on Clara's programs in November 1834 and, as *Hexentanz* (op. 5A), was published separately in Vienna in 1838. She played it for the royal family and Prince Esterhazy in Vienna and in her public concert there on January 7, 1838. It enjoyed enormous popularity and was performed more times than any other girlhood work (Example 11).

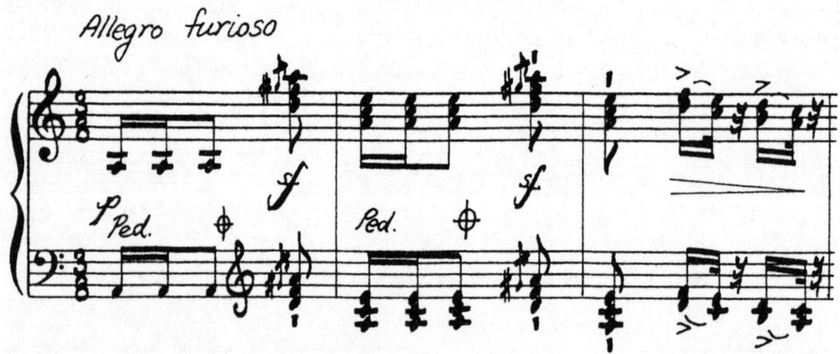

Example 11. Clara Wieck, *Quatre Pièces caractéristiques,* op. 5, no. 1, "Impromptu. Le Sabbat" ("Hexentanz").

4. Scène fantastique: Le Ballet des revenants

Because motifs from this piece figure in the first movement of Robert Schumann's great F-sharp Minor Sonata, "dedicated to Clara by Florestan and Eusebius," it is perhaps the best-known piece in Clara's op. 5. The "Scène fantastique" opens with a rocking motif using diminished fifths (Example 12). Schumann used this motif throughout the first movement of his sonata but altered it to perfect fifths. Although the second motif in Clara's "Scène fantastique" (Example 13) bears a great resemblance to a fandango theme in Schumann's sonata, this motif seems clearly to have originated with Robert Schumann. There is no question, however, that in combining the two figures (Example 14), Schumann was complimenting the young composer he loved.

Example 12. Clara Wieck, *Quatre Pièces caractéristiques,* op. 5, no. 4, "Scène fantastique."

Example 13. Clara Wieck, *Quatre Pièces caractéristiques,* op. 5, no. 4, "Scène fantastique," measures 44–47.

Example 14. Robert Schumann, Sonata in F-sharp Minor, op. 11, first movement, Allegro vivace.

Op. 6, *Soirées musicales*

Like op. 5, with which it is often grouped, op. 6 consists of character pieces in the new romantic tradition. Five of the miniatures in op. 6—a ballade, a nocturne, a polonaise, and two mazurkas—are reminiscent of Chopin and the musicians who influenced his work, John Field and Johann Hummel. Another influence, rarely mentioned, may have been the Polish composer Maria Szymanowska (1790–1832), whose polonaises and mazurkas were published in Leipzig and who performed in that city in 1823.

In a poetic and enthusiastic review in the *Neue Zeitschrift* dated September 12, 1837, Schumann described Clara's op. 6 as "like the buds before the wings of color are exploded into open splendor, captivating and significant to view, like all things that contain the future within themselves."[38] Two musical ideas from this work were incorporated into his oeuvre. The first, a melody hinted at in the Toccatina, appears in the Notturno (his "favorite piece," he wrote in February 1838)[39] and becomes the melody in Schumann's Novellette no. 8, labeled "Stimme aus der Ferne" (Voice from Afar) (Examples 15 and 16).

Example 15. Clara Wieck, *Soirées musicales,* op. 6, no. 2, "Notturno," measures 3–10.

Example 16. Robert Schumann, *Novelletten,* op. 21, no. 8, "Stimme aus der Ferne."

The second, the buoyant, surging theme of the Mazurka in G Major (Example 17), is the "Motto von C. W." (motto by Clara Wieck) that opens Schumann's *Davidsbündlertänze* (Example 18).

Example 17. Clara Wieck, *Soirées musicales,* op. 6, no. 5, "Mazurka."

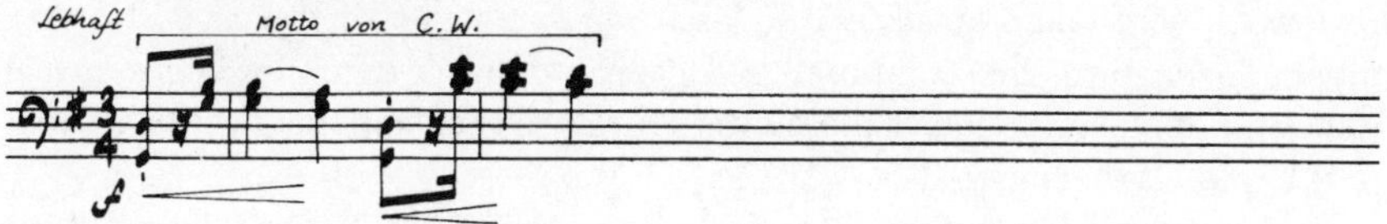

Example 18. Robert Schumann, *Davidsbündlertänze,* op. 6.

Op. 7, *Concert pour le Pianoforte*

The concerto that Clara began in January 1833, when she was thirteen years old, was first conceived as a *Concertsatz,* a one-movement work for piano and orchestra. This work eventually became the third movement, Allegro non troppo, of the concerto. Schumann scholars had not been aware of Robert Schumann's close involvement with this work until recently. Clara's diary and an existing score in Schumann's hand tell the story:[40] on November 22, 1833, Clara noted in her diary that she had asked Robert to orchestrate her concerto (actually the third movement was all that had been composed), perhaps because she considered him a close friend and an experienced orchestrator. The manuscript contains many erasures and alterations (Clara told Robert that she made some changes in the Tutti before publication), but his major ideas for the instrumentation were retained. She informed Robert in a letter of September 1, 1835, that she had orchestrated the other movements herself.[41]

After several performances and revisions, the complete concerto was given at the Gewandhaus under Mendelssohn's direction on November 9, 1835. It was revised again before publication in 1837. The copy for the engraver was discovered in 1999 in the Hofmeister archives in Leipzig. In accord with the custom of the time, the score consists of the piano part with instrumental cues. (A full orchestral score was not published until the twentieth century.) It is written in a copyist's hand with corrections, additions, and comments by Friedrich Wieck and Clara Wieck.[42]

The Concerto in A Minor is a remarkable achievement for an adolescent. Many of its stylistic features are typical of the concertos of such contemporaries as Kalkbrenner and Herz, those fashionable composers whose efforts Schumann so cleverly derided in his journal. But Clara also offers many innovative ideas, perhaps inspired by Mendelssohn's G Minor Concerto, written a few years earlier and performed in Leipzig by the composer on October 29, 1835. Clara's concerto, like Mendelssohn's, has no pauses between movements, no cadenzas in the classical tradition, nor does it have the expected orchestral exposition before the entrance of the soloist.[43] Unlike Mendelssohn, however, Clara was not greatly concerned about the conventional inner structure of the first movement: the development section in A-flat major leads directly to a coda that serves as a transition to the second movement. Also so unconventional that reviewers were taken aback is the A-flat major tonality of the second movement. To be sure, the composer had prepared the listener for this unusual tonality, but one critic found the move to A-flat so shocking that he attributed it to the "moods of women."[44]

In the second movement, a simple "Romanze" (sometimes referred to as "Notturno" on her programs) with a graceful, tender melody, the orchestra remains silent while a solo cello plays alone with the piano, foreshadowing the prominent cello parts in the Intermezzo movement of Robert Schumann's Piano Concerto (1845) and later, interestingly enough, a solo cello in the Andante of Brahms's Second Piano Concerto (1882).

In the first movement of Clara's concerto, the orchestra functions mainly as a support; there is little interplay between the soloist and the instrumental groups. In the much longer third movement (Schumann's orchestration), however, the orchestra plays a more significant part: tympani rolls beginning in the closing measures of the second movement are repeated just before the brass fanfares that open the third movement. They announce the entrance of the piano, which opens with the lively rhythmic polonaise figure; later in the movement, dialogues develop between the lower and upper instrumental groups and between piano and woodwinds.

Up until the Concerto, Clara had written only miniatures. Though continuous growth can be observed throughout her oeuvre from op. 1 on, the boldness and maturity of this work are unexpected; the listener is taken aback by the sweep of Clara Wieck's conception in this concerto and the skillful manner in which she now handles material on a large scale. A number of scholars have commented on the originality of the work and its influence on Robert Schumann's own concerto, composed only a few years later.[45]

Op. 8, *Variations de concert pour le pianoforte sur la Cavatine du Pirate de Bellini*

Staples of the repertory for the pianist-composers of Clara's day were works based on themes from operas by Bellini, Rossini, Donizetti, and other popular Italian composers. Variously titled "Impromptu," "Fantasia," "Variations," "Reminiscences," they had a clear function and predictable impact.[46] Clara's op. 8 was a piano work in this category. Dedicated to Adolph von Henselt, the composer-pianist whose popular works were often featured on Clara's concert tours, the Variations on Bellini's *Il Pirata* (an opera Clara saw in 1832) was played frequently and always elicited thunderous applause. In her diary Clara described the reactions of Gasparo Spontini, the popular Italian composer and kapellmeister in Berlin in 1837: "Spontini thinks the world of me; I had to play for him for two hours and he was entirely delighted, most of all with my Variations which he has now heard three times."[47]

The Variations were written during the months of Schumann's diatribes against the virtuosos and their "bungling, mediocre" variations on "vulgar" and "hackneyed" Italian themes—in contradistinction, Schumann wrote, to "good, boring German tunes."[48] Like Clara's *Romance variée,* the Bellini Variations contains many clichés: a grandiose introduction, diminished seventh chords, spectacular keyboard leaps, recurring thirds, sixths, and octaves, and a coda in which one brilliant coup succeeds another—running scale passages in sixteenth notes, ascending arpeggios, thundering bass rolls, and a spectacular closing section marked "Fortissimo" and "Presto."

Op. 9, *Souvenir de Vienne: Impromptu pour le pianoforte*

In the same tradition as Clara's op. 8, the *Souvenir* is a bravura work based on a good (but presumably not boring) German tune, Haydn's "Emperor" hymn. The work, in a free variation style, opens with an *Adagio quasi fantasia,* moves to an embellished presentation of Haydn's theme, and then proceeds to an exhibitionistic display à la Thalberg. The *Souvenir,* a tribute to the Vienna that had taken Clara up so warmly, was a showcase for the accomplished young pianist, who had just been named Royal and Imperial Virtuosa to the court of the Austrian emperor.

Op. 10, *Scherzo pour le pianoforte*

The independent spirit with which Clara, defying her father, prepared to go to Paris without him is evident in this first Scherzo in D Minor. It remains a display piece but offers more than the showy, ostentatious opp. 8 and 9. This was the work that occasioned the "malicious" review by Berlioz. Performed frequently by the composer, it must have been a favorite of hers; as "Erstes Scherzo," it was published in her *Pianoforte-Werke* (1879), the one work of her girlhood considered worthy of inclusion in Clara Schumann's collection of piano music.*

Op. 11, *Trois Romances*

The Romances were composed in Paris in 1839 and occasioned some excited and occasionally tendentious correspondence between there and Vienna, where Robert was living. He arranged for its publication by Mechetti in Vienna, where it appeared in the fall of 1839. Robert was particularly impressed by the second Romance. He wrote on July 18: "I like your Romance more and more, especially the idea in the allegro beginning in the third measure; it is like

*The collection, *Pianoforte-Werke zu zwei Händen,* presumably selected by the composer herself for reprinting, was published by Breitkopf & Härtel in 1879, V.A. 27. It includes the following works: *Erstes Scherzo,* op. 10; *Zweites Scherzo,* op. 14; *Vier flüchtige Stücke,* op. 15; *Drei Praeludien und Fugen,* op. 16; *Variationen über ein Thema von Robert Schumann,* op. 20; *Drei Romanzen,* op. 21.

Beethoven and very heartfelt and full of passion. Don't you want to compose a third piece to go with them?"[49]

But when he offered ideas regarding tonality and the title of an additional piece to complete the Romances or sent too many suggestions, she stood her ground, protesting (while she hoped he wouldn't be angry) that he had altered her piece and did not understand the effect it had on French audiences.[50]

The three miniatures, each in ternary form, are in E-flat minor, G minor, and A-flat major. The first, though probably written last, functions as a prelude to the other two. It is a slight work with much piano figuration. The second is the most expressive and the piece Robert Schumann chose to publish in the supplement to the *Neue Zeitschrift für Musik* in September 1839. One scholar has speculated that the opening of this Romance inspired the "innere Stimme" (inner voice) in Schumann's *Humoreske.* Others have pointed to the similarities between measures 53–54 of the Romance and measures 667–68 of *Humoreske*. The exact points of identification are less significant than Schumann's reaction. His emotional response to her Romance confirms, as Hans Joachim Köhler puts it, "Schumann's struggle toward an inner identity with Clara."[51]

The entire correspondence on op. 11 was conducted during a period of high tension over the marriage plans. Janina Klassen suggests that some of the touchy reactions and responses to the *Trois Romances* may have been provoked by the bitter conflicts with Wieck at this time.[52]

The next group of piano works was composed after Clara's marriage to Robert Schumann, when time and space for creative work became a problem. Nevertheless, some serious, mature, and distinguished works were born during this period, including the Preludes and Fugues, the Trio in G Minor, and the unpublished Sonata in G Minor. Although these works grew out of their joint studies, Clara Schumann created them on her own.

Op. 16, *Drei Praeludien und Fugen*

Op. 16, as well as the *Three Fugues on Themes of Sebastian Bach* and the F-sharp Minor Prelude and Fugue, was the culmination of studies undertaken by husband and wife in the early months of 1845. Clara's interest in fugue never became a "passion" (Robert described himself in the household book as being in a "Fugenpassion"), but she did continue her studies up to March 10, the day before the birth of Julie. There was a temporary cessation after the birth, but on April 7, the day before Julie's christening, mother and father resumed their studies.[53]

The fugues demonstrate her mastery of polyphonic writing. Robert Schumann's view of the romantic fugue as a character piece[54] may have been an influence, but Clara Schumann's major inspirations were probably her own performer's knowledge of fugues by Bach and Mendelssohn. The fruits of the contrapuntal studies can be seen and heard in many of the works that followed, notably in the final movement of her Trio.

Op. 17, *Trio für Pianoforte, Violine, und Violoncello*

The Trio was composed in Dresden during a difficult period in Clara's life. Though chamber music was a genre familiar to her, she had never before attempted to compose for any combination other than voice and piano. Soon after her marriage, she and her husband had studied together the chamber music of Haydn, Mozart, and Beethoven. She had often played the chamber music of the classical masters. As early as November 1834 she had performed Beethoven's "Archduke" Trio, op. 97—at the time a startling choice for audiences accustomed to showpieces.[55] During the Dresden years, Frau Schumann organized chamber music series—one of the first of its kind in that city—and played regularly with the Schubert brothers, Dresden court musicians.

Robert Schumann's Quintet, dedicated to her, became the cornerstone of her repertoire almost immediately after its composition in 1842. He had composed other works for chamber groups—string quartets (1842) and the Piano Quartet (1842)—but when Clara set out to write her Trio for Piano, Violin, and Cello, Robert Schumann had not yet published a full-fledged work for that particular combination.

Some months after Clara completed her Trio, Schumann noted in his household book, "Thoughts about a trio."[56] Entries on the days following show that he worked on his first trio (op. 63, in D minor) at his usual frenzied pace and had it performed on September 13, 1847, just at the time her work appeared in print. The expertise and quality of his D Minor Trio shook Clara's confidence in her own work, yet Schumann—and many other musicians—respected and admired it. Her Trio was often paired with Schumann's first trio in concerts during his lifetime and was frequently performed during the nineteenth century.

The Trio (and the Sonata in G Minor that preceded it) are her only published works in four-movement sonata form. The Andante in G Major, a three-part song form, is especially lovely: the lyrical, pensive melody and its return, led by the cello after the animato middle section in minor, is memorable. In the last movement, the fugato that so impressed Mendelssohn is heard in the development section. Chissell writes about the final movement:

> The G minor Finale, again in sonata form, shows Clara's craftmanship at its peak. Not only can the first theme be regarded as a metamorphosis of the opening phrase of the Andante, but in the development section its own rhythm is changed into a stern, quasi-fugal subject which, juxtaposed with the second subject, is explored with a contrapuntal cunning of which Mendelssohn would not have been ashamed even if a little too academic for Schumann.[57]

Not since the work on the Concerto did the composer attempt to carry out her musical ideas on such a large scale. Especially impressive is the fact that she was able to rise to these creative heights a few months after the death of her fourth child, Emil, and during a period when both she and her husband were ill and depressed. The Trio was completed during the hectic summer when the Schumanns traveled to Norderney in an effort to divert and cure Robert. While there, Clara suffered a miscarriage. It is possible that the creative activity served as a welcome outlet and relief during this period of extraordinary tension and pressure.

That the Trio was her own work (some critics expressed doubt that she could have produced such a skilled work and assumed her husband had a hand in it) is indisputable. Robert's household books document all of his activities during this period in obsessive detail. We know also that Clara had the talent, education, and experience to write this work. Moreover, the one surviving autograph, a draft with alterations, reinstrumentation, crossouts, and other emendations, shows Clara at work. Robert's participation is seen on the carefully written title page and in the penciled notes and directions that indicate that he may have made suggestions. Though Clara Schumann, with her characteristic self-abnegation, described her trio as "effeminate and sentimental," the work does not belong in that category. In a forthright and vigorous musical statement, the composer laid out her plans, carried them out with skill and ingenuity, and produced an eminently playable and delightful work.

In the list of Clara Schumann's compositions published in Berthold Litzmann's biography there is a gap between op. 17 and op. 20. Litzmann speculates that op. 18 may have been meant for the "Andante und Allegro" published by Schuberth in the 1860s and op. 19 for the song "Am Strande" (printed as "Am Strand") published by Schuberth about the same time. Why he was not aware of the publication of these two works in the supplements of the *Neue Zeitschrift für Musik* is a mystery. It is more likely that Clara was holding these opus numbers open for more extended works, such as her Sonatine (1841), published in 1991 as *Sonata in G Minor;* her unfinished concerto (1847), published in 1994 as *Konzertsatz,* or the choral works (1848) published in 1989 as *Drei gemischte Chöre*.

The Clara Schumann compositions for piano opp. 20 and 21 bear the imprint of her friendship with the remarkable visitor of that year: Johannes Brahms.

Op. 20, *Variationen über ein Thema von Robert Schumann*

Op. 20 is one of the works written in May and June 1853, Clara Schumann's final creative period. The theme, from the first "Albumblatt" in Robert Schumann's *Bunte Blätter,* op. 99, was the descending five-note motive (see Example 6) found in so many Robert Schumann and Clara Schumann works. She presented the autograph to her husband on the last birthday he was to spend with his family, but the work was not published until the fall of 1854, when he was already in Endenich.

By the time arrangements had been made for publication with Breitkopf & Härtel, Brahms had arrived in Düsseldorf to stay, and, undoubtedly inspired by Clara's example, he began his variations on the same Schumann theme. He sent his work, conceived as a tribute to both Schumanns, to Clara shortly after the birth of Felix, on June 11, 1854. In a graceful play on the dedication "To Frau Clara Schumann," Brahms wrote on his manuscript that his op. 9 was on "a theme by him" and "dedicated to her."[58]

Both Clara Schumann and Johannes Brahms wove into their published Schumann Variations the theme from Clara's childhood Romance, op. 3. For Clara, the quotation may have recalled the glowing days of her childhood; for Brahms, it was a gesture to honor both older composers. On September 25, 1854, Brahms wrote to Breitkopf & Härtel, who had accepted his work, requesting that his variations appear simultaneously with those of Frau Schumann. The proofs of her work were enclosed with his letter.[59]

Clara's op. 20 Variations, more structured and formal than such earlier variations as opp. 3, 8, and 9, which tended to be virtuosic and rhapsodic, explore many aspects of Robert's F-sharp minor theme: in the major mode, in a chorale-like version, as a canon, and, in the seventh variation, far-flying arpeggios ending, just before the Coda, with a Lisztian sweep and brilliance. Her op. 3 theme appears at the very beginning of the Coda, and is skillfully intertwined with Robert Schumann's theme (see Example 6) in measures 202-225.

Op. 21, *Drei Romanzen*

The Romances of op. 21 went through several transformations. The original Romance no. 1, composed in 1853 (later published as Romanze in A minor), was replaced by one composed in 1855 on a day when Brahms was visiting Robert Schumann at the sanatorium and she was, as she writes in her diary, "feeling so sad."[60] The first of the Romances has a poignant quality that contrasts strongly with the second, a short, scherzo-like interlude before the third and final "agitato" Romance. By the time negotiations for the publication of the Three Romances were completed, Brahms had become a close and trusted friend and the work was dedicated to him.

Op. 22, *Drei Romanzen für Pianoforte und Violine*

The Romances for Piano and Violin, Clara Schumann's only works for this combination, were composed in July 1853, the last music of her final creative period. The Romances reflect the increasingly important presence in her life of the other "young demon," Joseph Joachim. Conceived for and dedicated to Joachim, these lyrical character pieces were presented to the young violinist who was to become a devoted friend, and they played the Three Romances together on tours in Germany and in England. (Clara Schumann also played the Romances with Alfredo Piatti, the great cellist, but it is not known who arranged them for that combination.) They quickly won favor with the audiences of the day. In 1856, Joachim, then engaged at the Hannover court, wrote to Clara Schumann that the king was in total "ecstasy" over the Romances and could "hardly wait" to enjoy such "marvelous, heavenly pleasure again."[61]

Piano Works without Opus Numbers

All but one of the known piano works without opus numbers have been published within recent years. Among the major works, unpublished in her lifetime, that are now in print are the Sonata in G Minor, her Christmas present to Robert Schumann in 1841. Robert noted the completion of her sonata in his household book as well as the marriage diary but in the former added the word "first" in his description of the sonata.[62] Did he expect her to continue and write more in this form?

The *Konzertsatz* (published in 1994) is a completed version of a concerto movement that Clara Schumann began in 1847, ten years after the publication of her Concerto for Piano and Orchestra in A Minor. The fragment, clearly labeled "Concerto," consists of 175 measures of a first movement, with "Solo" and "Tutti" indicated. Why she did not finish the work is still a matter of speculation. It was completed and orchestrated by Jozef de Beenhouwer.

The Romance in A Minor, originally conceived as the first of the Three Romances, op. 21, was displaced by the Romance written in 1855 but not discarded. The composer presented the autograph to her friend Rosalie Leser and authorized publication of a version very similar to the Leser Romance in an English magazine for girls.

The appearance in 1885 of the Impromptu in E Major in a French publication, *Album du Gaulois,* a collection of unpublished or little-known piano works of eminent living composers, says a great deal about the reputations of both Schumanns in France. Clara Schumann was asked to contribute to the *Album* by Arthur Meyer, "Directeur du *Gaulois*." She chose the Impromptu, composed many years earlier but never published. In the preface to the collection Meyer explained: "Today, December 15 [1885], the journal *Le Gaulois* has among its offerings a collection of music it considers of admirable character and taste." The *Album* includes sixty-one works by, among others, Liszt, Tchaikovsky, Ambroise Thomas, and, interestingly enough, several women composers: Marie Jaëll, Cécile Chaminade, Augusta Holmès, and the vicomtesse de Grandval. In the brief biographies of the composers given in the table of contents we read:

> The name Schumann, usually referring to the glorious composer of *Manfred,* of *La Vie en Rose* [*Der Rose Pilgerfahrt*], of the Symphonic Etudes and the Symphony in B-flat, owes new honor to the noble woman whom the maestro had chosen and who is so fiercely devoted to his memory. We are proud to be able to write here this great name dear to artists, and to add our homage to all the other earnest praises.[63]

The Romance in B Minor, composed a few months after the death of Robert Schumann, was the last work composed until the March of 1879. The descending opening theme of this sorrowful, beautiful little piece, presented to Johannes Brahms at Christmas 1856, is closely related to the theme of the Intermezzo movement in Brahms's Piano Sonata no. 3, op. 5, a work Clara Schumann heard soon after the Schumanns met Brahms.

The March, written for the golden wedding anniversary of Pauline and Julius Hübner, was the one work Clara Schumann created long after the death of her husband. Julius Hübner (1806–82), an artist and director of the Dresden Gemäldegalerie, was the official guardian of Ludwig Schumann. The composer arranged it for solo piano and for four hands, and Julius Otto Grimm made an orchestral version to be performed at her sixtieth anniversary concert in Frankfurt on October 26, 1888. In this nostalgic work Clara Schumann includes the Grossvater melody used by Robert Schumann in his duet "Familiengemälde" (op. 34, no. 4) and alludes to themes from his *Manfred*.[64]

Among Clara Schumann's recently published works are a group of preludes. Some are simple exercises written for students, but the greater number are preludes that had their origin in improvisations. Improvisation, or "preluding," was expected of a concert pianist both at home and on the concert stage in the first part of the nineteenth century, and Clara Schumann never disappointed. Years later, in her seventies, she still began her daily practice sessions with improvisatory preludes. In 1895, a few months before her death, her daughters urged her to write them down and she reluctantly did so, explaining: "I would like to write out the preludes that I always play before my scales but it is so hard because I do it differently each time, as it occurs to me as I sit at the piano."[65] The act of fixing them on paper may have been antithetical to her purpose—to allow her imagination to roam freely and to maintain her inspiration at the keyboard. She was persuaded, however, and the preludes survive.

A note from Marie Schumann, Clara's eldest daughter, is attached to the autographs of the preludes and provides a fuller explanation:

> Interlaken, February 1929
> In the last year of her life, our mother, at our request, wrote out the exercises she played before her scales, with which she began her practice daily, as well as a few preludes of the kind she was in the habit of improvising before the pieces, quite freely on the spur of the moment; she also did this publicly, and one could get an idea of her frame of mind from the way in which the harmonies flowed into her work.

Marie mentions that her mother improvised publicly, a practice that was common in the nineteenth century. The preludes that preceded larger works were a regular feature of her concerts, from childhood to old age, and were noted in both programs and reviews. Valerie Goertzen points out that Clara Schumann was acclaimed as one of the greatest improvisers of her time.[66]

The Songs of Clara Wieck Schumann

From her earliest years, Clara performed, as singer and as accompanist, lieder of her own composition. Some songs mentioned in her girlhood diary and documented on her early concert programs have disappeared; the search for them continues.* Twenty-five of her songs have been published in recent years and eagerly taken up by singers.[67] Of these, all but two were composed after her marriage—between 1840 and 1853—and almost all were written for her husband as Christmas or birthday presents.

Sometime in 1843 Clara made fair copies of all the songs she had written since her marriage and assembled them in a notebook.[68] Robert, a great believer in systematic organization, wrote in their diary on June 28, 1843, "Clara is now setting her songs and several piano pieces in order."[69] Robert's contribution to the Liederbuch was the title page, "Lieder mit Begleitung des Pianofortes [Songs with piano accompaniment] von Klara Schumann, 1842," and a list of the contents. The composer evidently planned to include only songs written between 1840 and 1843, but she added others, and the notebook eventually included all the songs she composed between 1840 and 1853. Thus an authoritative record of the songs she thought worthy of preserving survives.

The songs of Clara Schumann contradict the common misconception that women write only light, sentimental "parlor" pieces. Her songs were written for concert performance as well as for more intimate settings and require a high level of artistry. During her lifetime Clara Schumann's songs were performed by the greatest singers of the nineteenth century in the great concert halls of Europe. Franz Liszt chose three of Clara Schumann's songs, "Warum willst du and're fragen," "Ich hab' in deinem Auge," and "Geheimes Flüstern," for volumes of piano transcriptions published in 1875.[70] (In view of her feelings about Liszt, the compliment may not have pleased her.)

Unlike Robert Schumann, one of the most lettered German composers,[71] Clara Schumann was not particularly well read. She stood in awe of educated people and those she considered intellectuals. The poets whose works she set—Friedrich Rückert, Emanuel Geibel, Heinrich Heine, Hermann Rollett, and Robert Burns (in translation)—were also favorite poets of Robert's, and he probably introduced her to them. Yet we know she had strong ideas about the

*Eighteen songs by Clara Wieck Schumann were published during her lifetime; seven others, preserved in archives, did not appear in print until 1992, although they were known to scholars. All known songs were finally made available in Draheim/Höft. Bernhard Appel has informed me that several songs were discovered in the summer of 1999. I have not had an opportunity to examine them.

performance of German lieder. She deplored the fact that many singers did not have a true understanding of the text. To her disappointment, even Pauline Viardot, a singer she greatly admired, showed more interest in vocal effect than in conveying the inherent emotion of the words when she sang Schubert.[72] At the same time, however, the musical effect was uppermost in Clara's mind. When necessary for musical or aesthetic purposes, she made small changes in the text: repeating words and lines ("Liebst du um Schönheit"), phrases ("Das Veilchen," "Er ist gekommen"), contracting words ("Lorelei," also "Loreley"), changing the order of words or dropping a verse ("Der Mond kommt still gegangen"), changing the title ("Am Strande" rather than the translator's title, "Sehnsucht am Strande").

Clara Wieck was familiar with the songs of her predecessors and contemporaries: Schubert's "Die Forelle" was performed at her first concert of 1828; "Gretchen am Spinnrade" and "Erlkönig" (of which she owned an autograph) and Liszt transcriptions of such Schubert lieder as the "Serenade," "Gretchen," and "Ave Maria" were on her girlhood concert programs. Songs by Felix Mendelssohn and his sister, Fanny Hensel, figured on her programs as well. Robert Schumann's lieder were, of course, an intimate part of her life, and one or two appeared on almost every one of her programs after her marriage.

For her own settings, Clara Schumann generally chose poems of two to three stanzas on such subjects as love, parting and rejection, springtime and nature, exploring the romantic themes of yearning, unrest, melancholy, foreboding, separation, death, and mystery. The lieder fall into several groups: the lyrical ("Die stille Lotosblume"), dramatic ("Er ist gekommen"), narrative ("Lorelei"), semi-declamatory ("Die gute Nacht" and "Oh weh des Scheidens"). Most are in varied strophic form.

Some of her songs—"Er ist gekommen," "Geheimes Flüstern," "Am Strande"—have the brilliant piano accompaniments that one might expect from a concert artist, but they do not overpower the voice. Her writing for piano is impressive; the preludes to the songs create a setting and mood; the accompaniments delineate a character or intensify an emotion. In all the songs, the piano works *with* the voice and text. A contemporary reviewer referred to the "charm" of the accompaniment to "Liebst du um Schönheit" as "embodying the perception of a sympathetic soul who is moved by the thoughts the voice expresses."[73] In such songs as "Volkslied," "Sie liebten sich beide," and "Ich stand in dunklen Träumen" the postludes are eloquent resolutions of the sorrows expressed in the songs. In "Lorelei" the repetitive triplets in the piano accompaniment create an atmosphere of intensity and fear that leads to a terrifying climax (reminiscent of Schubert's "Erlkönig"); in the virtuoso piano part we hear the master hand of the concert pianist. All the songs written after 1840 (with perhaps the exception of two settings of poems by Friederike Serre) are harmonically adventurous, emotionally powerful, and musically sophisticated.

Op. 12, *Zwölf Gedichte aus F. Rückert's "Liebesfrühling"*

Appropriately enough, the first of Clara Schumann's songs to be published after her marriage* were three songs in *Zwölf Gedichte aus F. Rückert's Liebesfrühling* (Twelve Songs from Rückert's *Liebesfrühling*), a joint project by husband and wife numbered op. 37/12. Friedrich Rückert's *Liebesfrühling*, a paean to conjugal love written in 1821, the year of his marriage, comprised about four hundred poems. After the publication of op. 37/12, the Schumanns sent Rückert a copy of the music and he reciprocated with a poem of thanks, which Clara promptly transcribed into their marriage diary.[74]

The three songs "Er ist gekommen in Sturm und Regen," "Liebst du um Schönheit," and "Warum willst du and're fragen" are often sung as a separate group, but beautiful as they are in themselves, they are most effective when sung as part of the entire cycle. Citing Schumann's letter to his publisher, Rufus Hallmark sets forth the premise: "The cycle . . . is to be understood as a dialogue."[75]

Robert Schumann negotiated for the publication of *Liebesfrühling* without Clara's knowledge. She received the first printed copy on her birthday in 1841, just thirteen days after the birth of her first child. The title page of the collection gives no inkling as to the authorship of each song, and reviewers were confused, probably to Robert Schumann's amusement. He identified Clara's songs on the flyleaf of his own copy of his works, and the extant autographs in Zwickau and Berlin confirm her authorship.[76] As early as 1833, Robert had expressed the hope that the union of their names on her op. 3 (dedicated to him) was a portent of the future; in 1839 he predicted: "We will publish many things under both our names; posterity shall see us as one heart and one soul and not learn which is yours and which is mine. How happy I am."[77] Op. 37/12 fulfilled his prophesy.

Op. 13, *Sechs Lieder*

Op. 13 was an independent publication, but the composer's husband urged and encouraged her in this effort, as in all her others. The songs, set to texts by Emanuel Geibel, Heinrich Heine, and Friedrich Rückert, were composed for various occasions between Christmas 1840 and the summer of 1843. The dedication to Denmark's queen Caroline Amalie was an acknowledgment of the warm hospitality extended to the composer on her visit to Copenhagen in 1842.

Op. 13 is a collection of six songs, not a song cycle. Included are her second versions of settings of two Heine poems: "Ich stand in dunklen Träumen" ("Ihr

*The songs composed and presented to Robert for their first Christmas together, "Am Strande," "Volkslied," and "Ihr Bildniss," were all published after 1841.

Bildniss" in the original version) and "Sie liebten sich beide."[78] In both cases, it is interesting to note, the earlier versions are bolder harmonically and more unconventional. The second versions (written out a year later) were chosen for publication (by Robert?). Many people regard the last song in the collection, "Die stille Lotosblume," a setting of Geibel's "Die stille Wasserrose," with its rhythmic irregularities, chromaticisms, and poignant melody, as a quintessentially romantic song, conjuring up such typical romantic images as the lotus flower, the sea, the moon, and the swan.[79]

Op. 23, *Sechs Lieder aus "Jucunde"*

The songs of op. 23 are settings of poems by Hermann Rollett, a little-known Austrian poet. When Robert Schumann was reading *Jucunde* in January 1853, he commented that the verses were "very musical,"[80] and this observation may have aroused Clara's interest.*

Though the texts are simple and rather sentimental, the settings are not. The piano and vocal lines in op. 23 show greater independence and the accompaniments have greater rhythmic variety and flexibility than those of many of the earlier songs. Several songs, notably "Was weinst du, Blümlein" and "Das ist ein Tag," display playfulness; the spirited evocations of forest, field, flowers, and birds stamp these lieder with a joyfulness rare in Clara Schumann's work.

Clara set "Am Strande," a Robert Burns poem translated by Wilhelm Gerhard and published in 1840, that same year, but since it was not among her numbered works, it was often overlooked. The virtuoso piano accompaniment portrays the swelling and rolling of the ocean and the growing agitation in the woman's heart as she waits for her beloved on the shore.

Songs Without Opus Numbers

The songs unpublished in the composer's lifetime are on a level with the published lieder and include some of her finest works. It is not known why publication was delayed for 140 years.[81] To be sure, one, "Abendstern," was a very early work, and neither Clara nor Robert took it very seriously or copied it into the Liederbuch. Two others, "Mein Stern" and "Beim Abschied," strophic songs written to sentimental verses by Friederike Serre, a friend of the Schumanns, have charm but are more predictable and regular than other songs by

*One of the last letters Schumann wrote before his hospitalization was to Hermann Rollett, who evidently believed that it was Robert Schumann who had set his poems to music. Schumann assured him that it was his wife who had composed the six songs from *Jucunde* and added that they were songs "that I would like very much even if they were not by my wife" (Robert Schumann to Hermann Rollett, February 7, 1854, Schumannhaus, Bonn). Clara Schumann spelled the poet's name Rollet.

Clara Schumann. She was fond of the Serre songs, however, authorized an English publication of "Mein Stern," and wrote it as an album leaf many times.

There are some great surprises among the lieder unpublished in her lifetime. "Lorelei" and "Das Veilchen" are works that can proudly take their place among the more familiar settings of these poems. "Volkslied" was the only poem set by both Clara and Robert Schumann. Soon after she presented it to him for Christmas 1840, he decided to write his own music for Heine's poem. They differ considerably: Clara Schumann's conception is dramatic and haunting, Robert Schumann's folklike (Examples 19 and 20).

Example 19. Clara Schumann, "Volkslied" ("Es fiel ein Reif in der Frühlingsnacht").

Example 20. Robert Schumann, "Es fiel ein Reif in der Frühlingsnacht." (op. 64, no. 3b)

Other songs unpublished in Clara Schumann's lifetime were two quite remarkable settings of Rückert poems from *Liebesfrühling,* the moving "Die gute Nacht, die ich dir sage" and the bold and disturbing "Oh weh des Scheidens, das er tat" (Example 21).

Example 21. Clara Schumann, "Oh weh des Scheidens, das er tat."

Edited Works: The Collected Works of Robert Schumann

On June 6, 1851, Robert Schumann wrote a document that clearly set forth his wishes regarding his unpublished works:

> Since all of us are mortal, I would like to arrange things —as regards the compositions that I leave behind—so that Gade or—in case he should be prevented—J. Rietz should decide on works possibly still to be published; this should, of course, be done with the consent of my dear Clara, and please, only after most severe critical evaluation.
>
> [Postscript] I especially want Faust and Manfred to be edited.[82]

Niels Gade, the Danish composer who succeeded Mendelssohn as conductor at the Gewandhaus, and Julius Rietz, cellist, composer, and conductor active in Düsseldorf, Leipzig, and Dresden, who edited Mendelssohn's collected works and works by Bach, Mozart, and Beethoven, were mature musicians and experienced editors. But despite the clearly written request, Clara turned neither to Gade nor to Rietz after Schumann's death. She consulted Brahms and Joachim, the two young musicians to whom her husband was closest at the time he was hospitalized. And although she discussed every detail with them ("You know, I have confidence only in you [two]," she wrote in 1860),[83] she ultimately assumed full responsibility for all decisions about the Robert Schumann editions.

After she died, and despite all efforts by her daughters, her wishes were ignored as zealous editors vied for rights to publish any available works by Schumann. While she was able, however, she made decisions about publication of such late Schumann works as the 1853 piano accompaniments for the Bach cello suites, the *Mass* (published in 1862), and the *Requiem* (published in 1864). Just as she had feared, many of the works whose publication she had opposed appeared in the twentieth century: the two Schumann movements of the FAE Sonata,* for example, were published in 1935; the variations for the theme he wrote in February 1854 appeared in 1941. The Violin Concerto remained unpublished until 1937, and was issued against the expressed desire of Eugenie Schumann, the sole surviving Schumann child. In an article in which she protested its publication, she wrote:

> Never shall I forget the moment in our home at Frankfurt am Main when my mother came in to see us and said with deep but suppressed emotion visible on her face, "I have just settled with Joachim and Johannes that the Concerto is not to be published, now or at any other time. We are quite agreed on the subject."[84]

Clara Schumann was always uneasy about the works of Schumann's last years, fearing that the music was weaker and showed signs of the mental confusion he suffered. In 1877 she wrote to Brahms that she was alarmed because Eduard Hanslick, who had requested copies of Schumann's letters from Endenich, seemed to be interested in writing only about Schumann's "sick years."[85]

On January 27, 1860, she wrote to Julius Schuberth about her decision not to publish the piano accompaniments for the Paganini Caprices that Schumann had written in 1853: "My husband is too dear to me to permit me to have something of his published that is trivial."[86] And from the household books we learn that she kept five Romances composed in November 1853 out of sight and destroyed them in 1893 because she feared they might be published after her death.[87]

Brahms and Joachim were aware of her anxiety over the late works; indeed, they shared it. She asked them to look at the unpublished Requiem and Mass and advise her about publication. In August 1860 Brahms responded that since these two works had been composed in 1852 and prepared for publication by Schumann himself, he and Joachim believed they had no right to withhold them even if they did not meet the standard set by earlier works. Some eleven months after receiving Brahms's letter, Clara went to Aachen to hear the Mass conducted by Franz Wüllner and was struck by the beauty of the work. She wrote Brahms that she no longer had any hesitation about its publication.[88] The work appeared in 1862.

All the decisions she made regarding Schumann's compositions —including the great critical *Werke* (Collected Works of Robert Schumann)—were made in conjunction with Brahms and other friends. The one Schumann edition that can truly be said to be hers was the so-called Instructive Edition, published in 1887.

Why did the widow not go to Gade or Rietz, as Schumann had requested? Why did she turn to the two "young demons"? In 1851, the year Schumann

*A sonata written in 1853 by Robert Schumann, Johannes Brahms, and Albert Dietrich for Joachim, whose motto was "*F*rei *a*ber *e*insam" (free but lonely).

wrote the testament regarding his works, he had not yet met Brahms; Joachim he knew only as a young violinist, the student of their old Leipzig friend Ferdinand David. But the friendship, almost a kinship, that developed as soon as these musicians met was immediate. The younger men loved and respected Schumann, referring to him in such terms as "honored master," "respected friend," "sir," and "Mynheer Dominie." The two young men who stood at Clara's side in the worst days of the troubled autumn in Düsseldorf and throughout the Endenich years were not only loyal friends; they were certainly the most gifted musicians of their generation. There were other men to whom she could have turned—Hiller, Dietrich, Reinecke, Woldemar Bargiel, all musicians who admired Schumann and in whom she had confidence—but none, as she well knew, of the caliber of Joachim and Brahms.

In May 1877 Clara Schumann asked Brahms for his opinion about an offer she had received from Breitkopf & Härtel to edit a critical edition of all the Schumann works.[89] She was in a potentially embarrassing position, since she was on the verge of signing a contract with the English firm of Novello for an edition of the piano works. By this time, Brahms, no longer a shy and inexperienced composer, was able to suggest a graceful way out of the situation. She decided to go ahead with the Collected Works, however, only after she was assured of Brahms's active assistance with the project. On his advice and with his backing, she signed with Breitkopf & Härtel on favorable terms.

The letter in which she asked for his counsel was the first of hundreds they exchanged about the edition, and although Clara Schumann is officially listed as the editor of the thirty-one-part series, it is clear it could not have been completed without the patient, guiding hand of Johannes Brahms.[90] Clara turned to him with questions ranging from the petty and trivial to the most significant; she made no move without him and sent him proofs of every work she edited. She begged him to take over the editing of the orchestral, choral, and ensemble works, as she did not feel confident about them and needed his help. She urged him to take half the money offered by Breitkopf & Härtel, but he refused, although he did eventually (and reluctantly) assume full responsibility for the supplementary volume (1893), in which his name and a brief preface appeared.[91]

A reading of the published Schumann-Brahms correspondence gives only a partial idea of Brahms's involvement, as Berthold Litzmann, the volume's editor, omitted many details, partly because of considerations of length and partly because of pressures from the Schumann family. But despite the precautions taken by Litzmann (and by Marie, who supervised his work), the correspondence does reveal the enormous tensions engendered by the edition. Several times, especially in 1891 and 1892, the long friendship almost foundered because of bitter disagreements over editions and versions of Schumann's works. On close examination, however, many of the arguments seem to be not necessarily products of musical disagreement but deflections of other anxieties. By 1892, Clara

Schumann, old, forgetful, and weary, begged him to take over the supplementary volume, writing, "Please tell me I can count on your old friendship."[92]

From the beginning Brahms had urged her to consult with other friends (as he did in regard to his own works), and sooner or later she solicited advice from all the Schumannians in Germany: Joachim, Heinrich von Herzogenberg, Philipp Spitta, Hermann Levi, Julius Otto Grimm, Ernst Rudorff, Franz Wüllner. Other musicians were paid for their efforts but neither their names nor their contributions were mentioned in the pages of the edition. She made no secret of the participation of such young musicians as Ernst Franck, Woldemar Bargiel, and Alfred Volckland. It must have seemed clear to her, her friends, and her publishers that the Collected Works of Robert Schumann would have most authority if hers were the sole name to appear, and Breitkopf acted accordingly.

Frau Schumann's willingness to embark on such a great responsibility when she was already burdened with so many duties is hard to understand until one realizes her motivations. The money was no doubt alluring to this woman with a large family to support, but the greater attraction was what she perceived as her duty to her husband. Annoyed by the proliferation of new Schumann editions—particularly in England—that she felt had no validity, convinced (and rightly so) that no one knew Schumann and his music as she did, determined to protect him (as she had done in his lifetime) and put the stamp of authenticity on what she perceived as a project for at least a century, she set to work. Having spent so many years in the service of his music, she saw the edition as a logical extension of her life's work.

Clara Schumann's efforts on the Collected Works have been severely criticized; many scholars consider them to be incomplete and inaccurate.[93] But her work must be seen in the context of her time and the special circumstances in which the edition was prepared. Standards of editing differed considerably from those of today. True, many of the critical editions published by Breitkopf & Härtel (the collected works of Beethoven, Mozart, Chopin, Schubert, Mendelssohn, Liszt, Wagner, and others) were edited by committees of musical scholars and included textual commentary, identification of sources, indexes, and other features of scholarly apparatus that confer credibility. But evidently Breitkopf & Härtel believed that the authority of Clara Schumann would be sufficient for the Robert Schumann edition (and a good selling point). As far as is known, she was never asked for, nor did she suggest, a critical commentary that might have given information on her sources or explained the rationale for her choices.

Clara Schumann chose to begin the Collected Works with the piano compositions. Conscientious and concerned, she followed the example of Schumann and the advice of Brahms,[94] requesting manuscripts that were no longer in her possession, examining carefully those autographs and proofs she retained, and consulting the first and second editions published during Schumann's lifetime.

She was well aware of Schumann's passion for good editions and studied the collection of his first editions, which he had had bound and in which he had entered comments and alterations. There is no doubt that she knew of the letter he had written to Härtel on January 31, 1845, in which he proposed a "really good edition" of Bach's *Well-Tempered Clavier:* "My object is to obtain as correct an edition as possible, based on the original manuscript and the oldest editions, and quoting the various readings."[95]

She searched her memory for comments Schumann had made about her performances and interpretations of his works.* Particularly sensitive to charges that her tempos were too fast, she made a special effort to determine exactly what the tempos should be. She wrote Brahms that she labored for months, timing her own performances with the second hand of a watch and attempting to take an average, although Brahms had warned her that such painstaking work would not be appreciated. She finally gave it up, admitting he was right, and besides, the work was "torture."[96]

The changes Clara Schumann made in metronome markings have occasioned more discussion and indignation than other aspects of her edition.[97] (These alterations were actually not so significant as many others she made.) Apparently she was convinced that Schumann's metronome was faulty; as early as 1855, an announcement appeared in the *Neue Berliner Musikzeitung* informing the public, on Frau Schumann's authority, that Schumann's metronome was incorrect and that many of the indicated tempos were faster than he meant them to be.[98] In 1863 she wrote Julius Stockhausen that she found that metronomes varied greatly and he should not be too concerned about the markings, since "a musician like you will not blunder."[99] Brahms expressed similar thoughts more than once.[100] Although she had advanced the "faulty metronome" theory in 1855 and subsequently vacillated on the question of the importance of metronome markings, she retained—contrary to popular belief—most of Schumann's metronome markings in the Collected Works.†

The Instructive Edition, 1887

In the Instructive Edition, often confused with the Collected Works, there is no question that Clara Schumann frankly expressed her own views.[101] Many twentieth-century musicians view her decisions as arbitrary, but her contemporaries—and her publishers—expressed no indignation at the liberties she took. Indeed, she was encouraged on all sides to take on this task, and the edition, of

*Some scholars have made much of the disagreements between husband and wife about interpretation and tempos. The Schumanns had their differences of opinion over the years, often expressed openly in the marriage diary, but as we shall see, Robert Schumann regarded his wife as the foremost interpreter of his music.

†Dietrich Kämper compared thirty-two Schumann first editions with the same works in the *Gesamtausgabe* and concluded that in the overwhelming majority of cases, Clara had remained true to the original metronome markings ("Zur Frage der Metronombezeichnungen Robert Schumanns," *AfMw*, 21 [1964], 145). Brian Schlotel came to the same conclusion ("Schumann and the Metronome," in *Robert Schumann: The Man and His Music*, ed. Alan Walker [London: Barrie & Jenkins, 1972], 111).

course, sold widely in its original form and in the numerous revisions and editions based on it.

Breitkopf & Härtel proposed an instructive edition of Schumann's piano works in May 1882, while Clara was still laboring on the Collected Works. This was the age of annotated editions of the classics, complete with analyses. Hans von Bülow was preparing volume after volume of works by Bach, Beethoven, Scarlatti, Mendelssohn, Schubert, Chopin, and Johann Baptist Cramer (150,000 copies of this minor master's work alone were sold, according to one publisher, Universal of Vienna). These heavily annotated, didactic editions, "as played by von Bülow in his concerts," directed the pianist's attention to every detail of performance: fingering, phrasing, tempos, accents, pedaling, embellishments, dynamics, voicing, emphasis. Bülow left nothing to the imagination of the performer; he altered the text freely, usually without acknowledgment. Clara Schumann disliked Bülow's editions,[102] and fearing that he or someone else might attempt something similar with Schumann's piano works, she agreed—after consultation with Brahms—to edit an instructive edition for Breitkopf & Härtel. She wrote in her diary, "It is clear to me that I must do it, so that at least one correct edition will be available for students."[103]

And so once more, and during the same year she and Brahms were correcting the last proofs of the Collected Works, she undertook a major editorial task. For the Instructive Edition she relied on the help of Marie, who had always acted as her assistant, and engaged in less frantic correspondence with Brahms and other friends. As a result, she left fewer records of how she arrived at her decisions.

The Instructive Edition differs from the Collected Works—and Schumann's early editions—in many ways: alterations in metronome markings and tempos (some faster, some slower);* the addition of tempo and expressive markings (grazioso, tranquillo, a tempo, ritenuto, etc.), fingerings, additional dynamic indications (sometimes in parentheses to distinguish them from Schumann's), and a particularly large number of additional pedal markings; deletion of Schumann's dedications—in the first printings only in the *Fantasie,* op. 17 (to Liszt), the *Fantasiestücke,* op. 12 (to Robena Laidlaw), and the G Minor sonata, op. 22 (to Henriette Voigt).† In later printings the dedications were restored, but other changes and errors made at the time reappear to this day.‡ In 1901 Marie Schumann asked the publisher to indicate which changes had been made by

*Kämper, 148, points out that 59 percent of the metronome markings in the Instructive Edition agree with Schumann's own first editions and 41 percent depart from the original scores.

†Alan Walker, in "Schumann, Liszt, and the C Major Fantasie, Op. 17: A Declining Relationship," *ML,* April 1979, 156–65, states: "When the Fantasie was prepared for re-publication, Clara had no hesitation in striking out the dedication to Liszt and substituting her own name instead." The dedication to Liszt was omitted in the first printing of the Instructive Edition only and was later restored. I have not found Clara Schumann's name substituted for Liszt's in any of the printings I have examined, including the first printing in RSH.

‡Some riddles (perhaps merely misprints or misunderstandings) in the Instructive Edition remain puzzling: the dedication of op. 58 to Comtesse Abegg (pointed out to me by Edwin M. Good), for example, and discrepancies in dates of composition.

her mother, but by this time the scores had been so thoroughly amended that Breitkopf & Härtel could not distinguish between those made by Clara Schumann and those made by Carl Reinecke, who—much to Marie Schumann's dismay—had been given the responsibility for the edition after Clara's death.[104]

There is no doubt that users of the Instructive Edition would have found a brief critical commentary useful, but like Bülow and other nineteenth-century editors of student editions, Clara Schumann chose not to explain her decisions, choices, or sources or to discuss Schumann's sometimes cryptic titles and mottoes, all of which would have been particularly appropriate and helpful.

Other Editions and Arrangements

Robert Schumann delegated the piano arrangements for several of his major works to his wife. Recognizing her talents and skills, he asked her to begin the piano arrangements of some of his large works, such as *Peri* and the *Faust Scenen,* when he was busy with other projects. He acknowledged his wife's assistance with the piano arrangements and piano-vocal scores in letters to his publishers. She also worked on piano arrangements of *Faust,* the Symphony in B flat, and the Symphony in C Major, but is credited only for the piano-vocal score of *Genoveva* and the four-hand arrangement of his Quintet, op. 44.

Her name stands alone on the title pages of the transcriptions for piano of thirty Robert Schumann songs and the arrangement for piano, two hands, of Schumann's opp. 56 and 58 (originally written for pedal piano), which was published in 1895, long years after she had performed them in concert halls throughout Europe.

Clara Schumann's name appeared also as editor of Czerny's *School of Fingering,* a manual she used throughout her teaching career, although this was one edition in which she did not have a hand; her daughter Marie, aided by Brahms, actually prepared the edition.[105] Almost unknown and still not published are arrangements for solo piano of a composition by William Sterndale Bennett and three Brahms works. Her name also appears on an edition of Scarlatti sonatas published by Breitkopf & Härtel, but confirmation of her participation is lacking.[106]

As early as 1874, when an arm injury gave her the time to reread her husband's correspondence, Clara Schumann began to consider an edition of his letters.[107] It was not until May 1885, however, that she began to read, select, and edit the letters of Schumann's youth. With the help of Marie Schumann and their friend Heinrich von Herzogenberg,[108] the task was completed within a few months. Unlike her editions of Schumann's music, the book included a preface (signed by Clara Schumann but actually written by Herzogenberg) that informed readers about omissions, deletions, changes, and sources. Few composers had written with the imagination and grace of the young Schumann; the very popular *Jugendbriefe* appeared in four German printings and was translated almost immediately into English as *Early Letters*. This project brought both sorrow and joy to its editor as she looked back on her own early years and the happiness for which the two young artists had hoped.

In undertaking the publication of his Collected Works, the Instructive Edition, and the *Jugendbriefe,* his wife and "creative partner" performed a heroic service and preserved Schumann's work in the best way possible at the time.

CHAPTER 12

The Concert Artist

Clara Schumann's life as a concert artist parallels the history of concert life in the nineteenth century. A study of her long and illustrious career, beginning with her first performance at the Leipzig Gewandhaus in 1828 and closing with her last public performance in Frankfurt in 1891, gives us an intimate knowledge of programming traditions, repertoire, concert arrangements, customs in various cities, the child prodigy phenomenon, women in concert life, and changes in musical standards and taste. In each of these spheres Clara Schumann had a decisive influence.

Her lengthy career on the concert stage—over sixty years—may be divided into three parts: 1828 to 1840, the years in which she concertized as Clara Wieck, first as a local prodigy and then as an international celebrity; 1840 to 1854, the years of her marriage and childbearing, during which her concertizing was somewhat curtailed, but not nearly to the extent that popular literature would have us believe; and 1854 to 1891, the years after Robert Schumann's hospitalization and death, when she toured the British Isles and the Continent, hailed as one of the top pianists of the world while supporting and supervising a household and seven children. Her perseverance and stamina throughout the trials of these years are legendary. That she was able to study and premiere works and maintain her position and popularity despite many tragedies was due to her talent, determination, and discipline, and in no small part to her father's genius as a teacher and his obsession with her career; this debt she always acknowledged.

Her first solo program, November 8, 1830 (she was eleven years old), was typical of those given in the 1830s by virtuoso pianists in all the major cities of Europe. Inherited from the late eighteenth century was a tradition of a diversified concert that would appeal to the new middle-class audiences that paid for an evening of musical entertainment. Whether the concert was arranged by the soloist or an organization such as the Gewandhaus board of directors, the soloist shared the program and alternated with a group of "supporting" artists—singers, instrumentalists, perhaps a small ensemble. Occasionally a monologist or a theatrical troupe varied the fare. The soloist made all arrangements, received the proceeds of the ticket sales, and was responsible for hiring and paying the supporting artists.

In small cities, such programs were truly a hodgepodge of events, musical and nonmusical. In Altenburg, for example, on May 18, 1831, Clara Wieck shared a program with a Dr. Langenschwarz, an "improviser and reciter." Members of the audience submitted topics—historical, philosophical, epic—on which the doctor would speak. His share of the evening included an improvisation in honor of the ladies of Altenburg and closed with a recitation in comic Austrian dialect. Between Langenschwarz's numbers, Clara played a concerto by Pixis and Herz's *Bravour* Variations.

On her first appearance in Hamburg, March 28, 1835, she performed Moscheles's Concerto in E-flat Major and Herz's "Bravour" Variations between two comedies, *Der Secretair und der Koch* and *Richards Wanderleben*.[1] And as late as February 13, 1864, in such smaller towns as Mitau, her performance was flanked by two theatrical works.

The tradition of playing with assisting artists is said to have ended officially when Liszt gave what is now considered to be the first solo "recital," in London in 1840. Soon after, Clara Schumann began to experiment with this concept. She decided to dispense with the assistance of an orchestra and supporting artists on her Russian trip of 1844 simply because it was so difficult to arrange. She wrote to her father, "I gave all my concerts alone, without any supporting artists, something I shall always do from now on; it is the best way."[2] She was not able to break entirely with the tradition, however, because audiences expected to hear a variety of performers, and Clara, like her father, always kept the demands of the public in mind.

By the 1870s, her reputation was secure enough, particularly in England, to ensure the success of solo recitals. She continued to work with other artists, however, choosing ranking musicians who were friends and colleagues rather than "supporting" artists. This decision may have been dictated by considerations of health and increasing family needs. For Clara Schumann's responsibilities, unlike those of most other working women, did not lessen as her children grew up; their illnesses and deaths and her assumption of responsibility for Ferdinand's children took their toll of her health and stamina. She probably accepted the fact that sharing a program was the only way she could continue to concertize. And so she appeared regularly with such congenial colleagues as Joseph and Amalie Joachim, Brahms, and Julius Stockhausen. The performers alternated solo and ensemble works and closed the program by playing together; interestingly enough, they sometimes shared the platform throughout the concert. A critic for *Dwight's Journal* described Clara and Joachim chatting between numbers and listening attentively to each other.[3]

Almost to the end of the century, audiences demanded singers at every concert. Arias and lieder alternated with instrumental numbers. Schumann often resented the presence of singers, but because of public pressure for the "glamorous" vocalists, she was forced to continue the tradition. More than once (in Vienna in 1847, Hamburg in 1850, Ems in 1855) Jenny Lind, the universally admired "Swedish Nightingale," a loyal old friend, rescued her from financial failure when she programmed concerts of new or unknown instrumental music.

Clara must have been taken aback by William Sterndale Bennett's warning in a letter dated January 26, 1855: "In England, they must always have so many expensive singers at concerts that they will not always give Pianistes as much as they deserve."[4] In her early years Clara accompanied all the singers herself; as her prestige grew, she was able to choose the singers (and the repertoire) to appear on her programs, and after 1860 she accompanied only vocalists of the stature of Julius Stockhausen and Amalie Joachim. Together with these singers, she gave some of the early performances of complete song cycles: Schubert's *Winterreise* and *Schöne Müllerin,* and Schumann's *Dichterliebe* and *Frauenliebe und Leben.* But even such works were interspersed with instrumental selections, a custom unthinkable today. On February 22, 1862, in Zurich, for example, three pieces from Schumann's *Kreisleriana* were performed between parts 1 and 2 of *Dichterliebe.* And in Hamburg on November 27, 1862, at a concert with Stockhausen in which, perhaps for the first time, *Die Winterreise* was performed in its entirety, the program was arranged as follows: I. Schumann, Piano Quintet; II. *Winterreise,* parts 1–4; III. Selections by Bach and Scarlatti; IV. *Winterreise,* parts 5–9; V. Mendelssohn, *Lieder ohne Worte;* VI. *Winterreise,* parts 10–13.

The tradition of using assisting artists in the early nineteenth century resulted in programs that were mixtures of many genres. A sonata or movements from one, variations on a theme (with applause after each variation), songs, a symphony, arias, declamations, instrumental and vocal duos were all thrown together like a musical variety show. By the middle of the century, Clara Schumann's programs show more integration. There was still a mixture of works on the orchestral programs in which she was an invited artist, but on her own programs of the 1850s and 1860s, works are grouped by composer and fewer genres were presented. By 1880, Schumann's programs were not only shorter—allowing for greater concentration on each work—but more homogeneous.

Repertoire

Until 1839, when Clara went to Paris alone, her father was responsible for all her concert arrangements and repertoire. Her debut program in 1830, an *Extra-Concert* for which the Gewandhaus directorate presumably had to give special permission, included Kalkbrenner's *Rondo Brillant*, op. 101; Herz's *Variations Brillantes*, op. 23; a *Quatuor Concertant* for four pianos, op. 230, by Czerny; and Clara's own Variations on an Original Theme (now lost). Clara had her own supporting artists: Henriette Grabau, a regular singer at the Gewandhaus, and Heinrich Hammermeister, a court singer. The three Leipzig pianists who played with her in the Czerny quartet—all of them ten to twelve years

Kleiner Saal des Saalbaues zu Frankfurt a. M.

Donnerstag, den 12. März 1891, Abends 7 Uhr:

Dritter Kammermusik-Abend

des Frankfurter Trio's

(die Herren **James Kwast, Fritz Bassermann** u **Hugo Becker**) unter freundlicher Mitwirkung der Frau **Clara Schumann** und des Herrn **E. Welcker.**

PROGRAMM.

1. **Quartett** (G-moll) für Pianoforte, Violine, Viola und Violoncell . . . . *W. A. Mozart.*
   a) Allegro.
   b) Andante.
   c) Rondo (Allegro).
2. **Variationen** für zwei Pianoforte über ein Thema v. J. Haydn, Op. 56, No. 6 (B-dur) *Joh. Brahms.*
   (Das Werk wurde ursprünglich für 2 Pianoforte componirt, und erst später instrumentirt.)
3. **Trio** für Pianoforte, Violine und Violoncell, Op. 70, No. 2 (Es-dur) . . . . . . *L. v. Beethoven.*
   a) Poco sostenuto. — Allegro ma non troppo.
   b) Allegretto.
   c) Allegretto ma non troppo.
   d) Finale (Allegro).

Die Instrumente (von Steinweg und Schiedmayer) sind aus dem Pianofortelager der Herren **L. Lichtenstein & Co.**, Zeil 69, Hier.

Einzelbillets à 3 Mark
in den Musikalien-Handlungen der Herren C. A. André, B. Firnberg, Schillerstr. 10, Th. Henkel und Steyl & Thomas, bei Herrn Richard Koch, Gutleutstrasse 103, sowie Abends an der Kasse.

Program of Clara Schumann's last concert, March 12, 1891. Robert-Schumann-Haus, Zwickau.

older than she—were Heinrich Dorn, composer and director of the Leipzig opera; Julius Knorr, a writer and piano teacher; and Emil Wendler, a medical student and ardent musical amateur.

The Paris concerts of 1832 featured two overtures by Weber arranged for six pianos—four hands at each—and singers, guitarists, and a cellist. These concerts lasted three to four hours. At private soirées the twelve-year-old girl waited her turn in an anteroom while all the "acts" went on, sometimes until one or two o'clock in the morning.

None of the works played were pieces that we would hear today, nor, as we shall see, were they works that Clara was likely to play even ten or fifteen years later. The choices reflected not her father's taste but what he deemed to be the popular taste of the 1830s. Wieck would not jeopardize her career by programming too much Bach or Beethoven.

This does not mean, however, that the Wiecks ignored "serious" music. Beethoven, Bach, Scarlatti figured on many of her programs in the 1830s. On the tour to Vienna in 1837–38, several J. S. Bach works were in her repertoire. One fugue was played at the December 26, 1837, concert at the Burg, the royal residence, at the special request of the empress. Her performance of the "Appassionata" Sonata was the one that elicited the Grillparzer poem described in Chapter 1.*

In Paris, at age nineteen, Clara planned her own programs. She found musical life in the French capital to be "frivolous and superficial" and discovered that she could not play anything serious (or anything she truly loved) at the aristocratic soirées unless it were perhaps at 2 A.M., when most of the guests had left and the real connoisseurs remained to hear her play Schumann, Chopin, and Scarlatti. She recognized that her own Scherzo, op. 10, which was so well received, was flashy enough to please the Parisian public. And though Robert Schumann was crusading against superficiality and "philistinism" in the columns of his *Neue Zeitschrift*, she did not hesitate to write and make a request:

> [April 4, 1839]
> Listen, Robert, won't you for once compose something brilliant and easy to understand, something that has no titles, but hangs together as a whole, not too long and not too short? I want so much to have something of yours to play publicly, something that suits the audience. It is indeed humiliating for a genius, but policy demands it for once.[5]

This hardheaded practicality was probably anathema to her fiancé; in any case, he ignored her request.

*On the Vienna tour from November 12, 1837, to April 30, 1837, Clara Wieck performed works by Adolph Henselt 38 times, Chopin 27 times, her own compositions 20 times; works by J. S. Bach appear 5 times, by Pixis 4, by Mendelssohn 3, by Liszt 2, and by Beethoven, Thalberg, Sechter, Spohr, and Tomaschek once each.

Clara soon realized to her dismay that fashion and coquetry played leading roles in Paris. After the dazzle of such players as Liszt and the coquettish ways of Camilla Pleyel, the serious German girl must have seemed dull to Parisian audiences. She reported that she had considered playing with Alexander Batta, a highly regarded cellist, but deplored the way he flirted with the ladies, "who adored it," while he played. "He plays delicately," she wrote, "but has an affected French soul." She abandoned the idea of playing with him after he treated her rudely at a rehearsal. The famous soirées at the home of Pierre Zimmermann, professor of piano at the Conservatoire, were attended by "50 ladies so closely packed together in a tiny room that they could not move, and then there is music until late at night, but what music! Nothing but badly sung arias, one after the other."[6]

But Clara wanted success in Paris, and though she could not afford to dress stylishly or bring herself to flirt with her audiences as Pleyel did, she valued the drawing power of a brilliant supporting artist. She was fortunate enough to secure the services of the violinist Charles de Bériot (brother-in-law of Pauline Viardot), and programmed works in which they could play together as well as works in which her splendid technique could be displayed. With Bériot she played a duet on themes from Bellini's *Sonnambula* and alone she played Liszt's transcriptions of Schubert's *Erlkönig* and *Ständchen,* a Chopin Etude, a Thalberg Caprice, and her own Scherzo. She chose wisely: the hall, Erard's Salon, was packed, and she wrote to Schumann, "Mein Renomme ist gemacht."[7]

The preferences of the Paris audiences reflected the great rage for vocal music; entire recitals consisted solely of arrangements and transcriptions of works derived from other genres, principally opera and song. Original works or improvisations by the performer were also basic fare. Thus every program of Clara's up to the time of her marriage included at least one composition of her own and at least one work derived from an opera. Robert Schumann's piano pieces were unknown in Paris, and though Clara had braved her father's wrath when she packed them with her other music, she did not attempt them in public. In Paris, as in Vienna, she played Schumann's works at small private soirées, and only for those connoisseurs who would appreciate them.

On her return to Germany, however, she offered programs more in keeping with her own sentiments, with Schumann's ideals, and with a presumably more serious German public. In Berlin on January 25, 1840, for example, she played Beethoven's Trio, op. 70, no. 2; solos by Henselt, Liszt, Mendelssohn, and Scarlatti; and her own Variations on a Theme by Bellini, op. 8. A few days later she gave a concert that included a Schubert trio (she wrote Robert that the audience understood it so little that they didn't know when to applaud), her own Scherzo, op. 10, and Robert Schumann's Sonata no. 2 (op. 22, in G minor), the first performance of a large Schumann work in Berlin.[8]*

*Questions have been raised about which sonata she played. The program, no. 165, lists only "Sonata," but Clara's diary entry of February 1, 1840, notes "second sonata."

The change in her programming became decisive after her marriage.[9] The display pieces by Herz and Pixis and her own bravura variations all but disappeared from her programs; fewer arrangements and variations show up; the dominating works are those written for the keyboard by Bach, Beethoven, Chopin, Mendelssohn, Mozart, Schubert, and Schumann.

Quite aside from her husband's influence, she loved and believed in Schumann's music, and she felt her primary mission was to present these works to the public, particularly inasmuch as Robert himself could not do so. This partnership was implicit in their marriage. Moreover, her sphere of knowledge was enlarged through their common studies of Bach's Well-Tempered Clavier, Beethoven's symphonies, and the chamber works of Mozart and Haydn. In August 1841, after one year of marriage, she wrote in the joint diary:

> I pity the musician who has no understanding of this magnificent art [Beethoven's sonatas]. The less I play in public now, the more I hate the whole world of mechanical virtuoso showpieces; concert pieces like Henselt's Etudes, Thalberg's Fantasies, Liszt, etc. have become completely repugnant to me. . . . I will play them only if I need to for a concert tour.[10]

Despite her protestations, she did play Liszt's *Hexameron* in December of that year and his *Lucia* Fantasy in Berlin in 1847, but this kind of work rarely appeared on her programs after 1850.

The friendship and close ties with Mendelssohn also stimulated changes in her repertoire. Mendelssohn's perfectionism had raised standards of playing and programming, and his revivals of the music of Johann Sebastian Bach prompted study and performances of the old Leipzig cantor. With Mendelssohn, Clara—as the young Clara Wieck and later as Madame Schumann (as she was generally known)—played several Bach works that had not been heard before at the Gewandhaus.[11]

By 1840, Schumann's editorials and reviews in the *Neue Zeitschrift* were affecting the thinking and taste of a large number of music lovers, particularly in northern Germany, and audiences were thus better prepared for a new repertoire.

The Influence of the "Priestess"

Clara Schumann was frequently described metaphorically as a "priestess" by Schumann, Brahms, Hanslick, Liszt, and many others—undoubtedly because of her devotion and quiet dignity. Her evolving repertoire may have contributed to the saintly aura. As she grew older and her reputation more secure, she programmed what she loved and her adoring audiences generally respected her choices, though as late as 1856 some heads were shaken in Budapest over her "serious" programming: Beethoven's "Waldstein" Sonata, a Chopin nocturne and impromptu, Mendelssohn's *Variations sérieuses* and a *Lied ohne Worte,* and two pieces from Schumann's *Fantasiestücke.*[12*]

Because of her great prestige and longevity on the concert stage, Madame Schumann had considerable influence on repertoire and programming throughout the nineteenth century. Though she was not the first pianist to play Bach fugues and Beethoven sonatas in public concerts, she was certainly one of the first to program such works consistently after 1840. The pattern still followed by recitalists today—a work by Bach or Scarlatti, a major opus such as a Beethoven sonata followed by groups of shorter pieces by Schumann, Chopin, Mendelssohn—was pioneered by Clara Schumann. The works she performed were generally new to audiences accustomed to opera transcriptions and flashy variations. Liszt, it is true, had a wide and varied repertoire that included ten Beethoven sonatas, the "Diabelli" Variations, concertos by Bach, Beethoven, Chopin, and Mendelssohn, and some Schumann works.[13] But it must be remembered that the great Hungarian pianist stopped concertizing in 1848. Thalberg, the other great rival of Clara's youth, rarely played Beethoven and certainly did not attempt Schumann; as late as 1849 he was still giving programs consisting solely of opera fantasies and overtures, almost always of his own composition. Mendelssohn and Chopin, two great composer-pianists whose musical ideals were similar to hers, died in 1847 and 1849. Thus of all her generation, she alone held sway on the concert stage to the end of the century.

In the 1850s a new generation of pianists—Carl Tausig, Hans von Bülow, Anton Rubinstein—emerged; their programs and repertoire were modeled after those that Clara had popularized in the 1840s. Meanwhile, in London, a young German immigrant who had changed his name from Karl Halle to Charles Hallé began to give all-Beethoven recitals in the 1850s. By the end of the century, the tradition of the assisting artist, the improvisations and fantasies, and the vaudeville aspects had all but disappeared from the programs of the leading European pianists, and at least one Beethoven sonata was obligatory. Following the example set by Clara Schumann, concerts were shorter and less varied, permitting greater concentration on each work.

A brief look at works included in a concert she gave in Paris on April 23, 1862 (program 615), indicates how drastically her programs changed. Her accompanying artists included her good friends Pauline Viardot, who performed on the piano and sang, and Julius Stockhausen, baritone. The instrumental works—Robert Schumann's Quintet, op. 44; Beethoven's "Eroica" Variations for piano; J. S. Bach's Prelude and Fugue in A Minor for Organ, arranged for piano; Schumann's Andante and Variations for Two Pianos, op. 46 (with Viardot); and two selections from Schumann's opp. 12 and 32—were interspersed

*The objections to her programming ceased after her first concert.

with arias by Rossini (Viardot) and Handel (Stockhausen), and Schubert and Schumann lieder (Stockhausen).*

Clara Schumann and the Music of Robert Schumann

One of Clara Schumann's great achievements was to bring the work of Robert Schumann to the attention of European concert audiences. There is no doubt that without her crusading performances it would have been many more years before his music was played and accepted. A study of piano programs in the nineteenth century makes it clear that Schumann's works began to appear regularly on programs of the leading pianists a few years after Clara first performed them.[14] Among the great pianists who were undoubtedly inspired by Clara Schumann's performances were Bülow, Tausig, and especially Anton Rubinstein. Though Liszt included the *Fantasie,* selections from *Carnaval,* and the F-sharp Minor Sonata in his repertoire of 1850, he wrote Wilhelm von Wasielewski that "they did not suit the public taste and most pianists did not understand them," and so, regretfully, he had given up the attempt, though he played Schumann's works in private circles.[15] Clara, of course, played almost every piano work Schumann had written, though she, too, sometimes waited for years until she considered the public ready for them. She premiered almost every one of Schumann's chamber and orchestral works that had a piano part. And most significant, his symphonies and many orchestral works (with a few rare exceptions) were first presented at concerts in which Clara was the soloist and leading attraction.† Almost every program she played after her marriage included at least one Schumann work—often three or four—for piano alone, orchestra, chamber combinations, or voice.

She considered it not only her sacred duty to play his music but her sacred right, and was jealous if his music was played by any other pianist, anywhere. "Robert wrote a very nice letter to Wilhelmine Claus in Paris today," she wrote in her diary on April 9, 1853, "but I was sad that she had to be the one to give the first performances of his works in Paris and London, when I am certainly the one who has the right to do this before anyone else."[16]

There are misunderstandings and some controversies about when and just how much of Schumann's music was performed by Clara Schumann. Table 1

*The program is reproduced in Désirée Wittkowski, "'In Paris hast Du doppelte Mühe in Allem . . .': Clara Wieck-Schumanns Parisreisen," in *Katalog*, 159.

†The first movement of Robert Schumann's early G minor symphony was performed at thirteen-year-old Clara's Zwickau concert of November 18, 1832, and again (after some revisions) at her Leipzig Gewandhaus concert of April 29, 1833. If she was unable to appear at premieres of Robert Schumann's orchestral works, her pupils performed in her stead. At the premiere of his Third Symphony, in Düsseldorf in 1851, for example, three of her students played a Bach Concerto for Three Claviers.

Zu einer

Musikalischen Unterhaltung

Sonntag den 13. Januar 1833

Vormittags präzis 9½ Uhr

wird ergebenst eingeladen

von

Friedrich Wieck.

(Reichsstrasse № 579.)

Erster Theil.

1.) *La belle Union*, Rondo à 4/m von Moscheles.
2.) Vier *Mazurkas* von Chopin, H. 1., für Pianoforte solo.
3.) Drittes *Trio* für Pianoforte, Violine & Violoncello von Pixis.
4.) *Romanze* für Physharmonica & Pianoforte.
5.) *Caprices en forme de Valse* von Clara.
6.) *Gesang*.
7.) Zwei *Studien* für die Violine von Paganini, für das Pianoforte bearbeitet von R. Schumann.

Zweiter Theil.

8.) Sechstes *Trio* von Reissiger.
9.) Vier *Mazurkas* von Chopin, H. 2.
10.) *Gesang*.
11.) *Notturno* von Chopin, für Pianoforte solo.
12.) Viertes *Trio* von Pixis.

Program of Clara Wieck's concert at her home, January 13, 1833, when she gave the first public performance of a work by Robert Schumann. Robert-Schumann-Haus, Zwickau.

Table 1. Piano works of Robert Schumann and years of first public performances by Clara Wieck Schumann

Opus no.	Title	Year	Comments
1	*Abegg* (Variations)		No public performance known
2	*Papillons*	1871	Place and date of concert unknown; played in Wieck home, 1832
3	(Paganini) *Etudes*	1833	Leipzig, Jan. 13; 2 selections played in Wieck home
4	*Intermezzi*		No public performance known
5	*Impromptus*		No public performance known
6	*Davidsbündlertänze*	1860	Vienna, March 27; 10 selections only at first performance
7	*Toccata*	1834	Leipzig, Sept. 11
8	*Allegro*		No public performance known
9	*Carnaval*	1856	Vienna, Feb. 7; many private performances beginning 1837
10	(Paganini) *Etudes*	1844	Place and date of concert unknown
11	*Sonate 1*(in F-sharp Minor)	1884	London, March 17; many private performances beginning 1835
12	*Fantasiestücke*	1838	3 played in Leipzig, August 12
13	*Etudes Symphoniques*	1837	3 selections played in Leipzig, Aug. 13; first complete performance, Rotterdam, Dec. 19, 1853
14	*Concert sans orchestre* (Sonata no. 3, in F Minor)		No performance known
15	*Kinderscenen*	1868	London, March 19; performed privately beginning 1840
16	*Kreisleriana*	1859	Vienna, Jan. 2, selections only; performed privately beginning 1840
17	*Fantasie*	1866	Leipzig, Dec. 15; performed privately beginning 1839
18	*Arabeske*	1867	London, Feb. 18
19	*Blumenstück*	1871	Place and date of concert unknown
20	*Humoreske*	1866	Vienna, Feb. 9
21	*Novelletten*	1839	Stettin, Nov. 7, probably no. 2 only; others played later
22	*Sonate 2* (in G Minor)	1840	Berlin, Feb. 1
23	*Nachtstücke*	1865	London, June 13; single pieces played beginning 1854
26	*Faschingsschwank aus Wien*	1860	Vienna, March 15
28	*Drei Romanzen*	1846	Norderney, August 18; selection only
32	*Scherzo, Gigue, Romanze und Fughette*	1856	London, June 30; Romanze only?
44	*Quintett*	1843	Leipzig, Jan. 8
46	*Andante und Variationen*	1843	Leipzig, Aug. 19
47	(Piano) *Quartett*	1844	Leipzig, Dec. 8
54	*Concert* (Piano Concerto)	1845	Dresden, Dec. 4
56	*Studien für den Pedal-Flügel*	1846	Vienna, May 3
58	*Skizzen für den Pedal-Flügel*	1863	Paris, March?
60	*Sechs Fugen* (Bach)	1849	Place and date of concert unknown
63	*Trio I* (in D Minor)	1849	Leipzig, Jan. 20
66	*Bilder aus Osten*	1850	Leipzig, February
68	*Album für die Jugend*	1849	Dresden, Feb. 7; 6 selections only
70	*Adagio and Allegro*	1850	Dresden, Jan. 26
72	*Vier Fugen*	1845	Leipzig, Oct. 5; 1 selection only

Table 1. (Continued)

Opus no.	Title	Year	Comments
73	*Fantasiestücke*	1853	Bonn, Feb. 24
76	*Vier Märsche*		No performance known
80	*Trio 2* (in F Major)	1850	Leipzig, Feb. 22
82	*Waldscenen*	1869	London, March 18; selections played beginning 1854
85	*Vier-Händige Clavier stücke*	1851	Düsseldorf, March 13; 2 selections only
88	*Phantasiestücke*	1866	Vienna, March 1
92	*Introduction und Allegro appassionato*	1850	Leipzig, Feb. 14
94	*Drei Romanzen*	1867	London, Feb. 4
99	*Bunte Blätter*	1862	Selections only
102	*Fünf Stücke im Volkston*	1855	Berlin, Nov. 11; 3 selections only
105	*Sonate I* (for Piano and Violin, in A Minor)	1852	Leipzig, March 21
109	*Ball-Scenen*		No public performance known
110	*Trio 3* (in G Minor)	1852	Leipzig, March 21
111	*Drei Fantasiestücke*	1857	Elberfeld, March 28; 1 selection only
113	*Märchen-Bilder*	1853	Bonn, Nov. 12
118	*Drei Clavier-Sonaten*		No public performance known
121	*Sonate 2* (for Piano and Violin, in D Minor)	1853	Düsseldorf, October 29
124	*Albumblätter*	1862	Rostock, Dec. 12; "Schlummerlied" played beginning 1854
126	*Sieben Clavierstücke*		No public performance known
130	*Kinderball*		No public performance known
132	*Märchenerzählungen*	1876	Leipzig, Jan. 9
133	*Gesänge der Frühe*		No public performance known
134	*Concert Allegro mit* Introduction	1853	Utrecht, Nov. 26

Sources: Litzmann; Program Collection, reviews, and diaries, RSH; RS/Tgb 3; Alfred Dörffel, ed., *Geschichte der Gewandhausconcerte zu Leipzig vom 25. November 1781 bis 25. November 1881* (Leipzig, 1884).

gives the dates on which Robert Schumann's works were first played publicly by his wife. These occasions were not always premieres; a few works were performed by other pianists before Clara played them. But she and her public always believed that her performances were definitive.

Clara was performing Robert's works even during the years when her father was planning her programs. Friedrich Wieck was an advocate of the music of the new romantic school and billed Clara as a representative of that style. She introduced many new Chopin works; his op. 2, as noted, became one of the staples of her repertoire. Mendelssohn's *Lieder ohne Worte* and Schumann's *Toccata* appeared on her programs even during the height of Wieck's fury at the young suitor. Wieck limited his daughter's performances of the music of Schumann, Chopin, and Mendelssohn primarily because of box office considerations, not necessarily because of his feud with Schumann. He permitted her to play Schumann's music privately in Vienna and even at home when they returned to Leipzig. She told Robert that her father objected to her taking his music with her to Paris but she packed it anyway.

The first Schumann works Clara played in public—the *Paganini Etudes* and the *Toccata*—were virtuoso pieces, not too different from the popular works of Clara's girlhood. Before her marriage she occasionally played sections of his *Novelletten, Fantasiestücke,* and *Etudes symphoniques.* The next group of Schumann works that she programmed consistently was made up of chamber and orchestral works in which the piano was prominently featured. Between 1840 and 1854 Clara premiered or performed the Piano Concerto, Quintet, Piano Quartet, trios, and sonatas for piano and other instruments. The great piano cycles of his youth—inspired by Clara, he always insisted—were almost totally neglected in public concerts. Schumann himself never heard his piano cycles performed in concert.[17]

Only after 1854, when Schumann was already hospitalized, did single pieces from the *Fantasiestücke, Novelletten,* and *Waldscenen* begin to appear regularly on Clara's programs. And finally, between 1864 and 1870, such works as *Kreisleriana, Davidsbündlertänze, Humoreske,* and *Arabeske* took their places in her concerts. Even a work as significant as *Kreisleriana,* however, was not performed in its entirety when she first played it. After some urging, she performed excerpts in Vienna in 1859, but she wrote Brahms that she did so reluctantly because she did not feel the work was "suitable for a concert."[18]

Audiences had to wait until 1866 for her public performance of the great Fantasie in C Major (Brahms had played it in Vienna in 1862). She did not perform *Papillons* in public until 1871. Once played, however, these works remained in her programs. Between 1864 and 1879, for example, she played the Concerto at least eighteen times, *Carnaval* fifteen times, the *Etudes symphoniques* twelve times. She performed the Quintet so regularly that it could almost be said to have been her signature piece.

Table 1 raises an important question: Clara Schumann, who repeatedly declared that her mission was to bring her husband's work to the attention of the public, did not, in fact, perform many of his works until years after his death; indeed, some of them she never played publicly at all. There may have been several reasons for this seeming paradox.

Clara Schumann reached the pinnacle of financial success early, and she was quite determined to stay there. She may have felt it her duty to the living—to herself and the children and grandchildren dependent on her—to do so. But for many years she must have felt as though she were treading a narrow line between conflicting goals: to make her husband's music known and to sustain her own popularity on the concert stage. Schumann himself agreed that his early works were particularly controversial; both he and Clara were aware that the public was not ready for these imaginative piano cycles with their autobiographical and esoteric literary allusions, innovative rhythms and harmonies, and experimental sounds (though we now see them as having a natural place in a particular German musical tradition). In his day Schumann was not generally perceived as a solid composer, and for many years his music was ignored outside of a small circle of enthusiasts. The correspondent for *Dwight's Journal of Music*, for example, wrote on March 24, 1855, "Some pillars of the musical world here [Berlin] seem to think that Joachim is injuring himself by the amount of study he bestows upon the works of Schumann and the school to which he belongs." Schumann's music was neither showy nor virtuosic; his variations were based on original melodies or motifs rather than on arias or popular tunes of the day; the very idea of the piano cycles was strange and unfamiliar; and the imaginative titles and title pages confused, even irritated the public.

Clara loved, indeed reveled in his compositions. As we know, she had grown with them and played them since she was twelve. Since Schumann was not a pianist of concert caliber, he depended on Clara to try out and perform his works for friends and other musicians. In Paris in 1839, Friedrich Kalkbrenner told her that he had heard that no one played Schumann's compositions as she did.[19] With appropriate girlish modesty, she demurred, but there is no doubt that she agreed completely. When she was sixteen, she played Schumann's First Sonata to Mendelssohn, Chopin, Ignaz Moscheles, and Ferdinand David in Leipzig, to Ernst Becker in Dresden, to Joseph Fischhof and Aloys Fuchs in Vienna, and to other friends and composers in Breslau and Paris. She played it again at home after their marriage, yet she delayed public performance of this difficult sonata until 1884, almost fifty years after it had been written. At that time Clara, now a widow of sixty-five, restudied the sonata and presented it to an enthusiastic British audience, an audience carefully educated, as it were, by her playing of selected Schumann works over the years.* It is interesting to note that this was one of the few piano works she did not premiere; Anton Rubinstein played it on October 30, 1883, in Frankfurt, then her home. It is possible that her first performance was given in an attempt to show audiences, as she wrote in her diary, the right way to play it, as she believed Rubinstein could not do it justice.[20]

Even *Carnaval,* today one of Schumann's best-known piano works, was carefully eased onto her concert programs. Clara had introduced it to Liszt in Vienna in 1838, and the great virtuoso chose to play ten of its movements at his Leipzig concert of 1839, an act of honor and respect for the hometown composer and editor. Clara played it for friends in Paris and Hamburg but did not perform it in public until 1856, after Schumann was ill. At that time, and for some thirty years thereafter, a statement headed "Zum besseren Verständnis" (For better understanding) was distributed with the program to familiarize the audience with the characters portrayed in this unknown piano cycle.

Clara and Robert engaged in much serious discussion about her playing of

*In 1871 she noted in her diary that a piece must be played frequently so that the audience can hear it and get used to it. "The right moment to introduce a whole new work must be carefully calculated" (Litzmann, 3:255).

his works. He gave her many suggestions about what and when to play to best effect, emphasizing the importance of making the right choices. On December 1, 1839, he wrote:

> I am totally opposed to your doing the Novellette in A [for a Berlin concert in January 1840]—that works only as part of the whole cycle. . . . You would certainly make the biggest impression with the second, in D. That has a beginning and an end, spins itself out nicely so that the public can follow it, and the Trio also has a really nice melody. Don't be angry at me because I always find fault with something, but *it is not unimportant.* I am not yet so well known or recognized that one could expect the public to accept *everything* just because it is mine. Therefore, playing the most original, the most clever works is not always suitable for the masses; instead, give them those things that are more pleasing and brilliant. . . . Just for a test, play the one in E, for my sake, and the one in D later, and notice which will have more effect. If you don't want to play either, then it would really be best to play the Sonata in G Minor [op. 22] (but *without* the Scherzo), because it develops a character that is comprehensible. Think about it, because, as I said, I do not consider it unimportant to have my music played by you in a city like Berlin. If it is not effective, I will be the one taken to account, no matter how well you play, and that does not make me unhappy, yet it does not make me happy either.[21]

In February 1838 he suggested that she might play "Traumeswirren" with "Des Abends" (from op. 12) but advised that "In der Nacht" was perhaps too long. From Leipzig he wrote that she should not expect applause for the Symphonic Etudes. "It's impossible for them to suit the public taste." He repeated the thought a month later: "You were right not to play my pieces—they are not suitable for the public."[22] In September 1839, on her return from Paris, she noted in her diary:

> I am often pained that Robert's compositions are not recognized as they deserve to be. I would gladly play them but the public doesn't understand them. I'm so afraid that someday Robert will have to witness the fact that his compositions arouse little interest in comparison with other works that are dull and insipid. I think this will be dreadful for him. He has much too deep an intellect for the world and because of this must he be misunderstood!? I believe that the best thing is for him to compose for orchestra; his fantasy is limited by the piano. The piano doesn't have enough scope; his pieces are all in orchestral style, and I think that is why they are so inaccessible to the public: the melodies and figures cross so much that it takes a great deal to discover all their beauties. I myself always find new beauties each time I play one of his works (I'm finding this to be the case with the *Novelletten* now). The *Novelletten* are really beautiful works. Intellect, soul, humor, the greatest tenderness, everything is united in it—there is no end to the most delicate features. One must know them as I do, and then will find his entire personality in his compositions. If Beethoven and Mozart were alive today, he would be the third in

> that trinity. The time will come when the world will recognize the third one, but it will come late. His improvisations hold such a wealth of fantasy that one can only be continually amazed. My greatest wish is that he compose for orchestra—that is his realm. If I could only succeed in persuading him![23]

These words have been criticized as a demonstration of Clara's ignorance and insensitivity.[24] They can also be viewed, however, as a rare statement of understanding from a young musician. Schumann himself was eager to write for orchestra and, as his 1839 letter indicates, was aware of the problems his music posed; he was quite resigned to wait for the judgment of posterity.*

Schumann rarely consulted Clara about his compositions, but he respected her judgment as a seasoned performer, and when he did turn to her with a question, he generally took her advice. She wrote from Vienna in 1838:

> I am looking forward to your Second [G Minor] Sonata; it reminds me of so many happy as well as painful hours. I love it, as I love you. Your whole being is expressed so clearly in it, and besides, it is not too obscure. Only one thing. Do you want to leave the last movement as it was before? Better to change it and make it a bit easier because it is much too difficult. I understand it already and can play it if necessary, but people, the public, even the connoisseurs for whom one actually writes, do not understand it. You won't take this badly, will you?[25]

There were times when Robert reacted angrily, as when she questioned his ability to write a string quartet, but he seemed to have no qualms about accepting her suggestions for the G Minor sonata. On December 29, 1838, he wrote that he had composed another, simpler final movement, thought it went well with the first movement, and was sending it to the printer.[26]

It has been suggested that Clara did not understand his titles and objected to them because of her own lack of sensitivity, but Schumann himself knew that his fanciful title pages and headings might be a deterrent to audiences unaccustomed to fantasy and imagination. In January 1840 he asked Clara what she thought of the proposed titles for *Nachtstücke,* his op. 23: "1. 'Trauerzug' [Funeral Procession] 2. 'Kuriose Gesellschaft' [Strange Company] 3. 'Nächtliches Gelager' [Nocturnal Revels] 4. 'Rundgesang mit Solos' [Round with Solo Voices]."[27] The young lady answered in her confident, practical way that "the public will not know what you mean . . . and will just take offense at it. I think you should leave the general title, *Nachtstücke.*"[28] Here, too, he took her advice.

*This is not to imply that Schumann was passive about promoting his works; he made every effort to have them performed but was realistic about the difficulties he might encounter. In 1843 he explained to Carl Kossmaly, composer, conductor, and writer on music, that his piano works (especially opp. 12, 16, 21, and 28) were not too well known because "1. There are difficulties in form and content; 2. I am not a virtuoso who could perform them publicly; 3. I am the editor of my journal, in which I cannot mention them; 4. Fink is the editor of the other journal and does not want to mention them" (Boetticher/1942, 391).

In 1838 he suggested to Friedrich Kistner, the publisher of his first sonata, which had originally appeared under the pseudonym "Florestan and Eusebius": "Wouldn't it be better for you and for me if you had a *new* title page prepared with my real name without the romantic appendage?"[29] The second, *"nouvelle"* edition was published under his name. In January 1839 he asked Clara's advice about writing to Heinrich Probst to discuss reprinting a number of works, including *Davidsbündlertänze* and *Kreisleriana*—"the latter," he wrote, "perhaps *with different titles*."[30] And a few years later, on November 5, 1842, he offered the *Davidsbündlertänze* to Friedrich Hofmeister and proposed that instead of, or perhaps in addition to, the "mystic" title, the explanatory phrase "*12 Charakterstücke*" (12 character pieces) should appear.[31] (Hofmeister rejected the offer and a second, revised edition was published as *Davidsbündlertänze, 16 Charakterstücke* in 1850–51 by Schuberth in Leipzig.)

Schumann's response to Clara's playing is revealed in these words:

> [February 6, 1838]
> I have heard you play only twice in two years. . . . It seemed to me, however, as though it were the most perfect playing one could imagine; I will not forget how you played my [Symphonic] Etudes [August 1837]. The way you portrayed them, they were absolute masterpieces—the public cannot possibly understand how to value them—but there was one person sitting in the audience—and though his heart was pounding with other feelings, at that moment his whole being paid homage to you as an artist.[32]

Occasionally Schumann reproached her, but mildly. When he chastised her for not wanting to play his works in Paris in 1839, she answered that it was too painful for her to play for people who did not understand him.[33] Difficult as this judgment was for a composer, Schumann could accept it.

From their inception, Schumann's concerted and chamber works were less problematical than the early piano cycles. The Quintet, the trios, the sonatas, the Concerto were played frequently during Schumann's lifetime. Critical reception of Clara's playing of these works was almost invariably enthusiastic; the same, however, could not be said for his music. As far as we know, Schumann did not begrudge her the praise. He more than merely approved: he admired and loved her performances. For the most part, he delighted in her interpretations and rarely criticized her playing. (She found *any* criticism from him hard to take, and could barely tolerate his praise of any other pianist, male or female.)

Thus his criticism of her playing in 1854 was particularly devastating. Though she must have recognized that he was not himself, this world-famous artist still trembled at any criticism from her husband. She may have found some belated comfort in the praise he sent from Endenich. On September 14, 1854, he wrote, "Oh, how I would love to hear your glorious playing just once." And on October 12, after receiving her published variations (op. 20) on his theme, he wrote, "Now I must tell you how your variations enchant me more and more and remind me of your magnificent playing of this and of my work."[34]

Table 1 makes it clear that the first Schumann works that Clara played in public were those that could not fail to appeal to audiences. As Martin Schoppe has pointed out, the excerpts from opp. 12 and 13—carefully chosen, brief, simple works—prepared the audiences for such larger works as *Carnaval* and *Humoreske*.[35] This strategy was clearly pursued with Schumann's approval. It is interesting to note, however, that sections of certain works were always excluded. Clara never played *Carnaval* or *Waldscenen,* for example, in its entirety. She always omitted "Estrella" (supposedly a portrait of Ernestine von Fricken), "Florestan," and "Eusebius" from *Carnaval* and "Verrufene Stelle" (with its accompanying macabre poem) from *Waldscenen.* Perhaps they evoked painful memories; perhaps they were too surrealistic, too fanciful, too extravagant for this practical, down-to-earth woman.

Reception in Foreign Countries

The nineteenth-century virtuosos with international reputations achieved their stature by dint of tireless traveling. This circumstance may explain the large number of divorces among women artists and the fact that many dropped out of the competition after they married and had children. Clara apparently never considered leaving the concert stage for any reason. Table 2 shows the concert tours she made before, during, and after the years of her marriage to Robert Schumann.

From her first trip after her marriage, it was obvious that Clara found touring exhilarating. Thus in Moscow in 1844, while Robert, ill and depressed, retired to their hotel room, Clara trotted round to play, made calls, visited institutions, and enjoyed her fame. All in all, Clara Schumann made thirty-eight journeys outside of Germany. In each foreign land she made a point of performing her husband's music and was often surprised and delighted by its reception. Writing to her young friend Ernst Rudorff from Paris on March 19, 1862, she reported on an altogether new attitude among French audiences:

> I received such pressing invitations to come here and they wanted so much to hear me, especially to hear my husband's works, which are becoming widely known here, that I decided to come, partly because I regarded it as a duty to my husband. I wouldn't have thought of coming for that reason alone—to popularize his music among the French—because I never would have believed that such a thoroughly German nature as his could become so greatly appreciated in another country. I still don't believe it, but considering the heartfelt reception that I have had for his works here, it would have been wrong to say no.
>
> You really would have enjoyed seeing the enthusiasm with which they were received by the public. It's peculiar; in one's heart one thinks little of

Table 2. Countries where Clara Schumann performed on foreign tours, 1832–1888

Year	Country
1832	France
1837–38	Austria, Hungary
1839	France
1842	Denmark
1844	Russia
1846–47	Austria
1853	Holland
1854	Belgium
1855	Holland
1856	Austria, Hungary, England, Denmark
1857	England, Switzerland
1858	Switzerland, Austria, Hungary
1859	Austria, England
1860	Holland, Austria
1861	Belgium
1862	Switzerland, France, Belgium
1863	Holland, France, Belgium
1864	Russia
1865	Bohemia, England
1866	Austria, Hungary
1867	England
1868	Belgium, England, Austria, Hungary
1869	Holland, England, Austria
1870	England
1871	Holland, England
1872	England, Austria, Hungary
1873	Belgium, England
1876	Holland, England
1877	Holland, England, Switzerland
1879	Switzerland
1880	Switzerland
1881	England
1882	England
1883	Holland
1884	England
1886	England
1887	England, Switzerland
1888	England

Source: Gerd Nauhaus, RSH.

> the public, yet in the concert hall their interest is really needed. It stimulates one and, for the moment, heightens the performance.[36]

In Paris the Schumann works she played were indeed enthusiastically received by audiences, but—and this she did not write to her friends—the critics' reviews were mixed.[37] In general, however, her Paris reception in 1862 contrasted greatly with the difficult experiences of 1832 and 1839. This time Madame Erard, of the Erard piano manufacturing family, provided Clara and her daughter Marie with an escort and made housing arrangements for them; the leading French artists came to pay their respects; she was invited to play at the Conservatoire (a signal honor) and was overwhelmed by the enthusiasm her playing provoked. Her opinion of the French public softened, though she remained critical of the "cold perfectionism" of the Conservatoire orchestra, with which she played Beethoven's E-flat Piano Concerto. Practical and cautious as always, she charged Brahms not to repeat her words to anyone because the Conservatoire was a "musical shrine" to the French, and if word of her criticism were to get out, it would be most damaging to her.[38]

Clara Schumann is also credited with influencing the taste and standards of music in Russia. Before her 1844 tour, the music of Robert Schumann and her standards of programming and playing were unknown in that country. Commenting on that trip, Daniel Wladimirowitsch Shitomirski wrote, "Clara's successful appearances ensured significant success for a serious repertoire and a deeper, concentrated interpretation."[39] In 1844 her playing in Moscow inspired the following remarks:

> We have had an abundance of famous pianists here, but what have we heard? Frightful noise, cannon salvos, difficult things that merely astounded; and what touched the heart? In point of fact, very little . . . we soon forgot that they had ever visited Moscow and not one of us remembers their playing. Can we say the same of Clara Schumann? Absolutely not! The "Spring Song" of Mendelssohn, the nocturnes of Field, a presto by Scarlatti, fantasies by Liszt and Thalberg, fugues by Bach, masterpieces by Beethoven—these works have been so vividly impressed in our hearts and memory that henceforth they will hold us captive with their sweet fetters.[40]

Another Russian critic described the effect of her playing thus:

> Who would have thought this possible ten years ago? Who would have believed that this music [Scarlatti and Bach] would have made such an extraordinary impression and that Frau Schumann would have had to repeat works several times? This is a noteworthy lesson for every artist who believed, up to now, that one could please the public only by performances of variations on the one and only Bellini motif.[41]

Once the critics had been won over, she cautiously introduced a few Robert Schumann works in her public concerts in Russia and played more of them at private parties. These performances turned the tide for Schumann in tsarist Russia. Prominent Russian composers, among them Anton Rubinstein (who premiered several Schumann works) and Tchaikovsky, became great adherents of Schumann's music then and later. On her second and last Russian tour, in 1864, Clara Schumann was again greeted with wild enthusiasm. César Cui pointed out in a review of her concerts, "During the first sojourn of Clara Schumann with her husband in Petersburg, people said, 'Monsieur Schumann, the husband of Clara Schumann'; now people say, 'Madame Schumann, the wife of Robert Schumann.'"[42]

Clara Schumann crossed the English Channel nineteen times to play in the British Isles, an adventure not always to be undertaken lightly.* The impetus to visit England the first time came from William Sterndale Bennett, Robert's old friend, who had been issuing invitations to the Schumanns for years. Though they had considered such a trip, they were never able to carry out their intentions. In January 1856, however, much to the consternation of Brahms and other friends, renewed correspondence with Bennett led to Clara's first concert with the Philharmonic Society, on April 14, 1856. This premiere tour set the pattern for those that followed, though her association with Bennett was of short duration. From her late thirties onward, she was to spend more time concertizing in London than in any other city in Europe.† She also played in Liverpool, Manchester, Bath, Bristol, Dublin, Edinburgh, and Glasgow.

Concert arrangements in England were generally made by professionals (often a music publisher, such as William Chappell) and thus were not burdensome, so that the pleasures of touring were considerably enhanced. On most trips, she and her traveling companion—usually one of her daughters—lived with well-to-do English friends, music lovers such as Arthur Burnand, who delighted in providing warm hospitality. After some initial difficulties, she became immensely popular in England and was gratified not only by the money she earned but also by the unanticipated warmth she experienced in the traditionally chilly British Isles. On March 3, 1884, she wrote in her diary that news of political events in England had led her to fear an explosion, but instead she had received a "Blumenexplosion": flowers had rained down on her from the balconies and galleries of the concert hall.[43]

She used the English tours as opportunities to play and popularize the music of her husband and also the "serious" music of Beethoven and Brahms.[44] Clara Schumann always gave lessons in England, and her reputation drew many English students to work with her in Germany. In 1888, after she had almost ceased concertizing on the Continent because of her health, she was persuaded to come to Britain once more. After her final concert, she wrote in her diary: "The last 'Popular.' I was very nervous again but made a brilliant closing with *Carnaval*. I believe I never played it as I did today and yet I have decided that this shall be the finale for England and was sadder than I can say."[45]

Her reputation spread across the Atlantic, and invitations came from the New World several times. Although Jenny Lind, Thalberg, and other friends had made brilliant and lucrative tours in the Western Hemisphere, she declined the offers. It was not only fear of the voyage or reluctance to leave her

*Karl Geiringer speculates that Brahms never visited the British Isles because he feared seasickness while crossing the narrow waterway between Europe and England (*Brahms: His Life and Work*, 2d ed. [New York: Doubleday/Anchor, 1961], 115).

†See Janet Ritterman, "'Gegensätze, Ecken, und scharfe Kanten': Clara Schumanns Besuch in England, 1856–1888," in *Katalog*, 235–61. Many thanks to Janet Ritterman for permitting me to use her original English version.

children that accounted for her rejection; rather she felt the tours might not be financially feasible for an artist with expenses as great as hers. American interest in her playing grew, however, stimulated by glowing reviews in such journals as the Boston-based *Dwight's Journal of Music*, which mentioned her name in almost every issue. Many ambitious young American pianists traveled to Frankfurt to study with her, and some of her students (Leonard Borwick, her favorite student, among them) made successful tours in the United States.[46]

The Press and Public Opinion

Long before her marriage Clara's relationship with the press was well established. Because German nouns have genders, the perennial phrase *die erste Pianistin,* for example, is ambiguous; it is never clear whether she is being called first among all pianists or first among women pianists. But there is no mistaking her stature when she is ranked with Liszt, Thalberg, and Henselt,* or when "Clara Schumann" is listed, in a review of a Thalberg concert in 1847, along with "Liszt, Döhler, Litolff, . . . Dreischock," among the "most distinguished names of the day."[47]

In 1841 she joined the glamorous Liszt in two concerts in Leipzig. The *Allgemeine musikalische Zeitung* concluded:

> We have already spoken about his exaggerations and also about *Hexameron,* which Frau Dr. Clara Schumann performed with Herr Liszt for the second time. We do not like to compare . . . but we must admit that the quiet, beautiful, correct, and refined playing of Frau Dr. Schumann was more effective than the stormy extravagances of Herr Liszt.[48]

It is difficult to locate outright hostility in reviews of Clara Schumann's performances. Of some 200 reviews examined, 10 were unfavorable. Anton Schindler was one of the few critics who detested her performances, calling her "infinitely overrated" and complaining that she had "sorely maltreated" Beethoven.[49] Occasionally she was faulted for poor programming, but the major complaint related to fast or erratic tempos—comments about which she was very sensitive.

Like most artists, she was not fond of critics, and she kept her distance even from Eduard Hanslick, who was her great admirer. But she never lost a sense of proportion about her playing and was her own severest critic. In a remarkable letter to the critic Selmar Bagge she wrote on March 29, 1856:

*An article by the Viennese correspondent to the *NZfM* (1838) included Clara Wieck among "the four greatest pianists" of the day. Of them all—Henselt, Liszt, Thalberg, and Wieck—she was the only one who continued her career to the end of the century. Henselt retired to Russia, Liszt left the concert stage in 1847, and Thalberg died in 1853.

> But, dear friend, why do you wish to deny that I have occasionally taken tempos that are somewhat too fast?
>
> . . . I believe that now and then this reproach may have been justified. You know that I rarely play without inspiration—it just seems to happen of itself—but it is so easy to allow oneself to be carried away so that one loses one's sense of judgment as to whether it was too fast or not. This does happen to me, particularly with the very pieces that I love so much that I lose myself in them and forget myself completely. Of course, that should not happen—the artist should always be master of his feelings, just as a calm and composed person is in ordinary life. Well, now—I will strive to do better and the reproach will certainly be useful to me.[50]

On the whole, press reports ranged from approbation to raving enthusiasm. In later years there were grumbles that she always played the same pieces,[51] but neither her interpretation nor her artistry was ever questioned. Terms commonly used to describe her performances were "elegant, solid playing," "clarity and solidity," "extraordinary accomplishment," "incomparable," "clear," "pure," "deeply artistic nature." After a Gewandhaus concert on January 1, 1842, in which Clara, now married and the mother of one child, played Mendelssohn's G Minor Concerto and Thalberg's "Moses" Fantasy, a local journal (not Robert's) reported: "Again we come to the conclusion that there is scarcely a virtuoso living today who might stand beside her in terms of virtuosity as well as in genuine artistic development."[52]

In October of that year the same journal reported:

> In general, Clara Schumann is more remarkable in the performance of compositions in which, from the intellectual point of view, there is something worth working out than she is in the execution of purely one-sided virtuoso pieces . . . although one cannot deny that Frau Dr. Schumann can also achieve recognition as a pure virtuoso.[53]

And in 1865, in a review of a concert with Julius Stockhausen, a critic wrote, "There are many virtuosos who are not inferior to her in technique or general interpretation, but she distinguishes herself from all the rest through her high level of musicality, which gives her performances the stamp of a divine summons."[54]

In her late forties, as family problems and physical ailments multiplied, she became very anxious about performing and fearful of forgetting the music. Clara Wieck had been one of the first pianists to play from memory. When she played in Berlin in 1837, Bettina von Arnim is reputed to have remarked, "How pretentiously she seats herself at the piano, and without notes, too. How modest, on the other hand, is Doehler, who placed the music in front of him."[55] Under Wieck's thorough tutelage, Clara had learned to memorize as a child, and she never found it a problem. Reviewers commented on this feat when she was only thirteen, an indication of how exceptional this practice was.[56] But with age and heavy responsibilities she found playing from memory increasingly difficult.*

In 1871 she wrote to Brahms from London:

> God knows how I can begin to control the anxiety that is attacking me. . . . Though I am often so nervous from one piece to the next, I cannot make the decision to play from the music; it always seems to me that it is almost as though my wings were clipped—and yet they still retain some buoyancy—more for art than for life, which never ceases to bring me new trials.[57]

She played without music as long as possible, despite the anxiety that assailed her as she mounted the platform.

What did she sound like?[58] Several of her contemporaries—Joachim, for example—recorded performances to be played on the recently invented phonograph, but Clara never did so. We have only a few recordings by her students—Fanny Davies, Adelina de Lara, Ilona Eibenschütz, and Nathalie Janotha†—and descriptions of her playing by contemporaries.[59] In German discussions of her artistry, the term *werktreu* (true to the text) was invariably used. Because of her personal severity, her loyalty to Schumann, and her reputation for integrity, it is natural to assume that she never tampered with the music, as so many other respected nineteenth-century pianists did. Yet even the "priestess" was known to play too fast, double an octave, or add an occasional embellishment. Unlike Liszt, however, she was never guilty of adding effects to gain attention. Reviewers universally remarked on her masterful technique and her deep respect for and understanding of the music; particularly striking was the quality of her beautiful, full, "singing" tone, an aspect of her art carefully cultivated by her father.

Concert Management

When Clara Wieck toured with her father, he attended to the hundreds of details of concert giving: he rented the halls and instruments, hired the supporting musicians, had the tickets printed and distributed, arranged for refreshments to lure the reluctant, peddled Clara's picture, set up advertisements in the papers and posters on the streets, collected and counted the money. All these tasks became Clara's from 1839 to the close of her performing career. Though she advised her students to hire professional managers (infrequent in Germany until

*As early as October 1850 she commented that only the young had the confidence to play from memory (Litzmann, 3:229).

†*The Pupils of Clara Schumann* has been issued by Pavilion Records, along with a booklet featuring interviews with several of the artists. Although the recordings were generally made long after the pianists had studied with Schumann and were well along in years, they are nonetheless fascinating documents. See note 59.

the 1880s), she herself did not do so. She had developed a network of friends throughout Europe, and in letters filled with requests and directives she enlisted their help. Flattered and proud to assist the great artist, they never failed her. But her greatest aid came from her daughters, who were pressed into service as soon as they were old enough to help. One daughter saw to her clothes, another made arrangements for the shipping of her instruments and music, a third arranged for transportation and housing for the artist and her traveling companion or helped with the selling and distribution of tickets. Each daughter took her turn as traveling companion, but in the end it was Marie who became her constant attendant.

In the early part of the century, few halls existed for the sole purpose of concerts, and most cities had no box offices. Tickets were bought from local music dealers or directly from the artist. In these days of international contracts prepared five years in advance, it is astonishing to read of the speed with which concerts were announced and arranged. Cities were smaller, music lovers were known to each other, and interested parties could easily be reached through the reliable mail service. Concerts were announced in the newspapers, on placards posted around the city, and by word of mouth only two or three days before they took place.

Clara Schumann insisted on making all her own arrangements, necessarily a tedious and thankless job, and over the years wrote thousands of letters regarding details that she would not entrust to her daughters, associates, or friends. In their obsessive and meticulous attention to minutiae, the letters resemble those written by her father to Clementine Wieck.[60]

Much thought and energy went into the planning of Madame Schumann's concerts. Often ten or more letters were exchanged before final agreement could be reached on ticket prices, hall, and program. She always kept in mind the works that she and other artists had performed in a particular city and the size and interests of the potential audience; she juggled rehearsals so they would not interfere with the busy lives of her fellow artists and her own schedule of teaching, mothering, and traveling. A letter sent to Wilhelm Joseph Wasielewski when she was arranging a concert in Bonn in November 1853 indicates the style of her management:

> I am sending you 200 tickets as well as 20 free tickets. I will bring tickets for the box office with me. The program remains as described earlier: 1. Quartet no. 1 [Schumann, op. 47], II. Vocal works, III. Beethoven C Major [*Waldstein*] Sonata. Second half: IV. Three *Märchenbilder* with you [Schumann, op. 113], V. Vocal works, VI. Etude in C Major and B Major Nocturne by Chopin, *Lied ohne Worte* by Mendelssohn. We leave here [Düsseldorf] tomorrow, Friday afternoon, at 3 and will arrive, I believe, in Bonn at 6 or 7. Would you reserve a room in the Stern for us, but please, not the same one where my poor husband was sick. I saw some very nice rooms on the other side facing the court; we do not like to face the street—it is too noisy. On account of the tickets, I am sending this letter separately so there will be no

extra delay. Also I am sending this unfranked, it is safer, also because of the tickets. Add it up with the concert costs.[61]

WUNDERKINDER

One of the unforgettable comments about Clara Wieck was Hanslick's "kein Wunderkind—und doch noch ein Kind und schon ein Wunder" (not a wonder-child—and yet still a child and already a wonder).[62]

Wunderkinder were not uncommon in eighteenth-century Europe. Vienna had its share well before Clara appeared on the scene; Wolfgang Amadeus Mozart made a dazzling impression when he played there in 1762, at the age of six. As early as 1736 the Hamburg and Frankfurt papers published reports of child performers; a 1756 advertisement read: "A child of six years, of the female sex . . . will perform publicly on the violin."[63] So popular were the wunderkinder that in 1792 it was said that over half the concert artists in Vienna were under fourteen. Though Hanslick claimed that this was an exaggeration, he admitted that Vienna was an important marketplace for wunderkinder, who were "by no means all Mozarts."[64]

There is general agreement that the young Mozart received a valuable musical education on his concert tours: the varied musical styles and techniques that he heard were integrated into and enriched his music. This was not his father's primary concern, however; Leopold Mozart was hoping for money, fame, and eventually a secure position for his son at a prestigious court. In the late eighteenth century, a virtuoso without a city or court appointment was dependent on private appearances at courts or homes of music-loving noblemen; the elder Mozart bowed, scraped, and petitioned, courting connections and the goodwill of influential aristocrats and wealthy music-loving merchants who might arrange a concert for a larger audience.

Fifty years later, Friedrich Wieck faced a different situation. From the beginning of her career, his daughter gave public concerts to which admission was charged, and he could and did pocket the profits. He did, however, have to act as his own manager and accept all the attendant commitments and anxieties.

The glamour of presenting a wunderkind proved irresistible. Wieck, usually honest about Clara's achievements and genuinely concerned about her welfare, followed the example of other stage fathers and deducted a year or two from her age when he could. Schumann noted in his diary in July 1831 that Wieck swore that Clara was ten and half when she was almost twelve.[65]

Yet Wieck was convinced (and on the concert trips his opinion was confirmed by Louis Spohr and others) that Clara was no mere wunderkind. Knowing that the general opinion of child prodigies was not high, he wrote his wife that the combination of Clara's age and skills presented an obstacle: "Most have had a few pieces crammed into them and they're not musical—nothing can come of them and nothing will." He worried about the response to his daughter's genuine talent. "Where are the cognoscenti and the pianists who will recognize Clara's extraordinary training and know how to examine it without prejudice?"[66] Wieck's own prejudices aside, it was generally agreed that Clara's playing was extraordinary. Her name became a byword for child prodigies, just as Mozart's had been before her. In 1839 Hector Berlioz, in his role as music reviewer, wrote about a Mlle Emilie Pousseze, "a nice child of eleven years who plays the piano in a way that raises hopes of a new Clara Wieck."[67]

Women Artists

At eighteen, Clara Wieck ranked with the principal artists of the day. When she resumed active concert life at the age of thirty-five, she was hailed once again as one of the two or three leading pianists of Europe. She plunged into public concerts with such difficult and unfamiliar works as Beethoven's "Hammerclavier" Sonata and C Minor Variations, neither of which she had performed before. No other woman achieved the eminence she did on the concert stage, nor did any other pianist, male or female, maintain a like position for so long a time. She was not a feminist and it is doubtful that she sympathized with the views of those few women who were just beginning the struggle for equal rights in nineteenth-century Germany. She assumed her position as a premiere pianist without self-consciousness. From her birth it had been understood that she would be an artist, and she seldom doubted her success. Several times in her life she wrote that she regretted not having learned any "feminine skills," such as cooking and household management, but these moments were rare. Though Robert presented her with a cookbook inscribed "To my little housewife" when they were first married, she never did cook. Such tasks were left to servants—as was the custom even in lower-middle-class families—or to her daughter Marie, who from the age of twenty supervised the Schumann household and younger children and did the cooking when servants were unavailable.

In planning a concert career for his young daughter, then, Wieck was not treading an unknown path. When Clara was a child, there were no stage mothers, only stage fathers. In almost every case of a young musician in the eighteenth and early nineteenth centuries, it was the father—usually a musician himself—that stood behind the artist. Many ambitious fathers had attempted to carve careers for their daughters, and indeed, almost as many female as male wunderkinder were touring Europe, among them pianists, violinists, singers, and harpists. The music journals reviewed a surprisingly large number of concerts given by women artists and compositions by female composers, often without comment on the gender of the musician. Those who continued past the child prodigy stage generally concertized until marriage and then settled down to court appointments (in the eighteenth century) or teaching (in the nineteenth), situations that did not require travel and were more compatible with family life.

In any discussion of women musicians of the early nineteenth century, a distinction must be made between professional musicians who, like Clara Wieck, performed in order to earn money and those highly proficient performers of the upper classes and aristocracy who, like Elisabeth von Herzogenberg, Henriette Voigt, and Fanny Mendelssohn Hensel, had received professional training but never performed for a fee.[68] Such artists as Livia Frege, who married into the upper middle class, were forced by convention or the insistence of their husbands to discontinue their professional activities. This situation prevailed well into the twentieth century; some of Clara Schumann's best students (Ilona Eibenschütz, for example) who married into the moneyed classes gave up performing careers. These women carried on significant musical lives from their own homes, building music rooms large enough for audiences of a hundred or more connoisseurs in the tradition of the great music-loving aristocrats of the eighteenth century. They did not simply run salons, nor did they necessarily serve as the proverbial feminine inspiration for composers. They sang, played, made suggestions, and performed a valued service, providing a stage, even a forum for such composers as Beethoven, Mendelssohn, Brahms, and the young Schumann. But these gifted amateurs did not perform in public and so did not undergo the scrutiny of reviewers or have to battle for the attention and money of the public. As a professional, Clara Schumann competed with men on an equal footing.

When Clara Wieck first made her entrance into the concert world, she was favorably compared with other young women pianists of her generation, notably Leopoldine Blahetka and Anna de Belleville.* Another name to be reckoned with was Maria Moke, later Marie Pleyel but better known as Camilla Pleyel (1811–75). Like Clara Schumann, these women were all survivors of the child prodigy experience. Of the three women rivals, Marie Pleyel had the longest career and the only one that rivaled Clara's in any way. Born in Paris in 1811, she was eight years older than Clara. A student of Henri Herz, Ignaz Moscheles, and Friedrich Kalkbrenner, she created a European sensation when she began to concertize at the age of fifteen. Berlioz was madly in love with the very beautiful Marie, but she spurned him and in 1831 married Camille Pleyel, of the Paris piano manufacturing family. The French were very proud of Marie Pleyel, and François-Joseph Fétis, the reigning Parisian music critic, declared that among the many famous pianists he had heard, "no other gave the feeling of perfection that her playing created."[69]

Pleyel performed in Leipzig in 1839. Clara, then living in Berlin, suffered needless torment at the thought of Pleyel in *Leipzig*. Pleyel, whose marriage lasted only four years, concertized until 1848 and then retired to a life of teach-

*Leopoldine Blahetka (1811–87) studied with Friedrich Kalkbrenner and Ignaz Moscheles, toured successfully, and was very popular in Vienna in the 1820s. She composed an opera and many works for piano. Anna de Belleville (1808–80) studied with Carl Czerny in Vienna before she settled in London and married James Oury, a violinist, with whom she toured. Clara met her in Paris in 1839 and reported her to be disagreeable and vain.

Table 3. Number of performances given at Gewandhaus, Leipzig, by male and female piano soloists, 1794–1881

Men	Number of performances	Years	Women	Number of performances	Years
Felix Mendelssohn	47	1835–45	Clara Schumann	74	1828–81
Carl Reinecke	46	1843–81	Elisabeth Catharina Müller	17	1794–1810
Ignaz Moscheles	20	1816–61	Louise Hauffe	12	1854–70
Friedrich Schneider	16	1809–23	Marie Wieck	7	1845–56
Hans von Bülow	15	1857–80	Charlotte Fink	7	1835–38
Alexander Dreyschock	12	1838–61	Wilhelmine Clauss-Szárvády	6	1850–60
Anton Rubinstein	10	1842–79	Emilie Reichold	5	1826–29
			Anna de Belleville	3	1830–31

Note: Of the 261 pianists who appeared at the Gewandhaus in these years, 84 were women.

Source: Alfred Dörffel, ed., *Geschichte der Gewandhausconcerte zu Leipzig vom 25. November 1781 bis 25. November 1881* (Leipzig, 1884).

ing in the Brussels Conservatory. Clara met her for the first time in 1854 but never heard her play.

From time to time Clara Schumann acknowledged jealousy of another female pianist in her diary, but in each case it was clearly based on the rival's youth or beauty or on attentions bestowed by Wieck, Robert, or Brahms. In 1841, for example, she wanted to be present during Robert's lessons with Amalie Rieffel, ostensibly to learn from Robert's teaching but more likely because she feared her husband might prefer the girl's playing to hers.[70] She envied Camilla Pleyel not because of her playing but because of her flirtatious manner and the attention she received from Wieck at a time when Clara was estranged from him. She had no doubts that her own playing was superior to Pleyel's: in 1838, just before her trip to Paris, she heard Thalberg play and wrote Robert, "If I were not a woman, I would have said farewell to the life of a virtuoso long since, but I can calm myself a little—I can surely cope with the ladies."[71]

As her career advanced, younger women took their places on the concert stage—Wilhelmina Clauss-Szárvády (1834–1907); Arabella Goddard (1836–1922); Sophie Menter (1846–1918), a Liszt protégée; Annette Essipof (1851–1914); and eventually her own students—but there was general agreement that she was more than a match for them. No other pianist, male or female, appeared at the Gewandhaus as a soloist more frequently than she (see Table 3).

The goals, desires, and needs of the woman artist in the nineteenth century differed in no substantial way from those that confront women in every era. She was aware of the extra efforts that women had to make to achieve success, efforts entirely unknown to their male counterparts; at nineteen, she wrote Robert that she would love to play at the Paris Conservatoire but that it was very difficult for a woman because there were "many cabals."[72] Clara Schumann knew well the stresses and strains of the life of a concert artist, yet again and again she confessed that her music brought her fulfillment that she could not live without. In 1853, for example, when she finally had her own room and could practice without disturbing her husband, she wrote in her diary:

> When I am able to practice regularly, then I really feel completely in my element; it is as though an entirely different mood comes over me, much lighter, freer, and everything seems to be happier and more gratifying. Music is, after all, a goodly portion of my life, and when it is missing, it seems to me that all my physical and spiritual elasticity is gone.[73]

In a memorable exchange with Brahms, who had urged her to give up her strenuous life as a performer, she wrote: "You regard it *only* as a way to earn money. I do not. I feel a calling to reproduce great works, above all, also those of Robert, as long as I have the strength to do so. . . . The practice of art is, after all, a great part of my inner self. To me, it is the very air I breathe."[74]

CHAPTER 13

Clara Schumann as Student and Teacher

As pianist and as teacher, Clara Schumann followed the precepts taught her by Friedrich Wieck. She retained the greatest respect and admiration for his guidance and instruction despite his irrational intrusions into her personal life. Friedrich Wieck had many successful students and took great pride in them, but his daughter Clara was by far the most outstanding pianist he ever produced. In typical Wieck fashion, he dismissed any influence other musicians might have had on his daughter. This proscription included Robert Schumann, of course.

How did Wieck teach? Frederick Niecks, who spoke with many students of Wieck, including Clara Schumann herself, reported:

> In spite of much inquiry, I have never yet succeeded in meeting a fairly adequate presentation of Wieck's method by himself, by his pupils, or by his critics. . . . I am quite sure that when I questioned Madame Schumann—the most carefully, patiently, lovingly and perfectly trained pupil that ever went through his hands—about her father's method she was taken aback and really puzzled. She said her brother Alwin Wieck's Materialen [finger exercises] gave an idea of it. Of course they do nothing of the kind. Then, trying as it were to seize the main features of the method, Madame Schumann remarked [conversation at Frankfurt on June 12, 1889]: "He aimed especially at equality of touch, and the cultivation of right feeling for the use of the soft pedal."[1]

Both Marie and Alwin Wieck edited versions of their father's work; each purported to give the pianist the key to the method of this remarkable teacher and each claimed that these were the studies from which Clara Schumann had learned.

In the preface to her edition of her father's works, Marie Wieck wrote:

> These have been published because I have never met with this kind of rhythmic exercise, united with the first rudiments of theory, in any pianoforte method. These exercises, taught and played in the manner my father intended, are designed to produce a fine touch, to encourage playing from memory and transposing, and to cultivate a taste for the more refined style of piano playing.*

Wieck's method is difficult to describe, not because it is complicated but because he did not use a uniform approach; he attempted to give each student what was needed for individual growth and development. He used the best of several systems, notably that of Johann Bernhard Logier, a music teacher born in Germany but trained in England.

The major elements of Logier's teaching consisted of (1) the use of a "chiroplast," a device placed over the keyboard to aid (actually to enforce) the development of correct finger, hand, and wrist positions (Wieck never used one); (2) group instruction of pupils at various levels of proficiency simultaneously: he arranged works so that beginners, for example, could play a basic theme while at the same time more advanced students played variations on it; and (3) incorporation of music theory and harmony in basic piano instruction, with the aim of fostering knowledgeable musicianship. This method, enthusiastically endorsed by such influential musicians as Louis Spohr, who saw Logier in action in England, became very popular in Germany, and though this approach was not used universally, aspects of Logier's method, such as group instruction and the combining of theory with piano lessons, are used in music instruction today and in many quarters are still considered innovative.

Though many features of his method were sensible and effective, Logier acquired a reputation as a charlatan, probably because he instituted a successful public relations campaign and earned a great deal of money. (Spohr noted that he was charging 100 guineas a lesson to impart his "secrets" to London teachers.)[2]

Wieck was teaching piano before Logier's method was well known in Germany, but he admitted that he learned a great deal from him. Clara's instruction actually began before she left for Plauen with her mother in the spring of 1824, but Wieck began to teach her (and two other girls) by the Logier method in September, when she returned to his home. By Easter he was giving her lessons privately, according to his own system.

*In the preface, dated Summer 1875, Marie Wieck also wrote: "These are the celebrated studies used by the composer in teaching his two daughters, Madame Clara Schumann and Marie Wieck" (Friedrich Wieck, *Pianoforte Studien,* ed. Marie Wieck [Leipzig: C. F. Peters, 1875)]. The title page of Alwin Wieck's edition, titled *Materialen zu Friedrich Wieck's Pianoforte Methodik* (Berlin; Simrock, 1875), states: "Friedrich Wieck instructed his daughter, Frau Clara Schumann, née Wieck, according to this method." Clara, who had a more cordial relationship with her brother than with Marie, helped contact a publisher for his edition and supported it to the best of her ability. Both editions are undoubtedly authentic representations of Wieck's work.

There is no doubt that this harsh, opinionated, and often crude man had immense gifts as a teacher. Even without Clara and her signal success—which he admitted to his wife surprised him as much as it did the rest of the world—he would have enjoyed a reputation as an outstanding piano teacher. His philosophy was expressed in an inimitable style in his 130-page treatise, *Clavier und Gesang* (Piano and Song). Most of the chapters are written as dialogues in which Wieck appears as "DAS" (*Der alte Schulmeister:* the old schoolmaster); others are in the form of letters or lectures—one might even call them harangues.

Wieck insisted that the accomplishments of Clara and her half sister Marie were the best proof of the superiority of his system. Despite the five-year-old Clara's supposed deafness, she was taught to play dance tunes and accompaniments to them by ear. She developed an extraordinary memory for musical phrases and could play a short piece after a single hearing. All of Wieck's students were taught to play first by ear so that they could concentrate on producing a good, full tone. All understood tempo and meter, and all played scales and cadential progressions of I, IV, and V chords in every key before they could read music. They were expected to find and practice triads and dominant seventh chords with inversions in all keys, and then to use what they had learned in new ways by improvising and composing their own little pieces.[3] Improvisation was a skill that Clara began to develop as a young child and it remained an integral part of her daily practice. Wieck wrote individual exercises for each student in a sequential order of difficulty; thus each could reach his or her potential in a natural way.

The title of his book indicates his concern with the art of singing—the basis, he believed, of beautiful, refined piano playing. All of his students were required to study voice; recall that Clara studied voice with Johann Aloys Miksch (the teacher of the famous soprano Wilhelmine Schröder-Devrient and the man with whom Wieck himself later studied).

Wieck's approach was inherently musical and demonstrates the kind of understanding of the learning process outlined by many twentieth-century music psychologists. As early as 1853 we find him writing:

> As a psychologist, thinker, man, and teacher, I have striven to work for all-around development and have been especially concerned in many ways with the art of song as an indispensable basis for beautiful and refined piano playing. I never stood still, learned daily as I taught, and always sought to improve myself. My direction was determined, as far as was possible, by the mood of the pupil at the time. With each child and at each lesson, I presented myself in a new and different guise and in a cheerful and happy state of mind and this was effective because it came from the heart. Moreover, I was never one to follow convention, never behaved like a pedant with fixed ideas and opinions.[4]

Wieck did not believe in overpracticing: he expected his students to practice every day, but only when they were fresh. Even ten minutes of practice could be effective, he believed, if the student practiced frequently and made the most of each minute. Children should begin piano instruction, he believed, about age six, and to maintain correct habits three lessons a week with a cheerful, devoted, energetic teacher were optimal. Two cornerstones of his method were his beliefs that musical education was nourished by listening to good music and that outdoor exercise was essential for health. As we know, Wieck could be sarcastic, insensitive, even cruel, but be brought an abundance of humor and common sense to his teaching.

When Clara's father left Leipzig to settle in Dresden, he set out to learn as much as possible about singing and then took up the teaching of singing, though he continued to teach piano as well. Some pupils came to study both. Amy Fay described an evening in the Wieck household in Dresden in 1872. After Marie Wieck had played,

> the old Herr then said, "Now we'll have something else," and got up and went to the piano, and called the young girls. He made three of them sing, one after the other, and they sang very charmingly indeed. One of them he made improvise a cadenza, and a second sang the alto to it without accompaniment. He was very proud of that. He exercises his pupils in all sorts of ways, trains them to sing any given tone, and "to skip up and down the ladder," as they call the scale.[5]

Wieck believed that every virtuoso should know how to teach. In his letter of August 9, 1830, to Robert Schumann's mother, he made a special point of the fact that he was educating his eleven-year-old daughter to be a teacher even though, he claimed, she was already the best female pianist in the world.[6] At twelve Clara began to teach her brother Alwin (Wieck paid her several groschen for her work), and she continued to teach throughout her life.

The experience she gained by teaching her brother under Wieck's guidance served her well. When Clara went off to Paris alone at nineteen, she paid her way by giving lessons to aspiring pianists in every city in which she performed. Indeed, Henriette Reichmann, the young woman she met in Stuttgart who accompanied her to Paris, was both companion and student. In the French capital Clara taught wealthy French and English women who were eager to study with the young virtuosa.

Clara Schumann appreciated her father's talents and his total devotion to her career. Many years after Wieck's death she wrote to an Englishman who had studied with her, Dr. Richard Wilkinson, a letter that tells us much about the relationship between daughter and father, student and teacher. She was worried, she wrote, about the health of one of her students:

> She does not have—as I did—the good fortune to have a wise father at her side, a father who guarded her health, saw to it that she went walking, that she did not accept invitations to late parties, that she did not practice without

> a stop, and that in the afternoon before an evening concert she never did anything but rest; in short, a father who stood guard. Indeed, people would call him a tyrant, a term my father had to accept—but I still thank him daily; the freshness I have retained even at my great age (at least as far as art goes)—for that I have him to thank! It was also a blessing for me that he was extremely strict, rebuked me when I deserved it and thus prevented the praises from making me insolent. Sometimes the rebuke was bitter, yet it was good![7]

Though the daughter lacked her father's humor and instincts as a teacher, she had the advantage of years on the concert stage. Moreover, she displayed warmth toward her students, a quality that Wieck lacked (and that was not always apparent in her relationships with her own children and grandchildren). She followed each student's career with great interest, was saddened by poor reviews, rejoiced at triumphs. Like all great teachers, she became a parental figure to her students, and young women and men flocked to study with her wherever she was—in Berlin, Frankfurt, Baden-Baden, and on summer vacations in Austria and Switzerland.

An examination of a collection of letters of Clara Schumann to Ilona Eibenschütz, one of her favorite pupils, is illuminating. Thirteen-year-old Ilona came to study with Madame Schumann in Frankfurt in 1886 and stayed with her until 1890. Clara Schumann had advice to give about every aspect of Ilona's life—health, partying, friends, dress, repertoire, fees, and agents. She introduced her to Brahms (for whom Ilona became a favorite as well),* gave her letters of introduction to patronesses, well-to-do friends, and conductors. She was often critical but always added words like: "Let me hear from you soon and think of me always as your true motherly friend, who follows your career with deepest interest and who, as you know, will always do everything she can to help you, with all her heart, Your loving Clara Schumann."[8] A typical letter written soon after Ilona left Frankfurt to begin her concert career:

> Frankfurt a/Main, January 24, 1891
>
> Dearest Ilona,
>
> Just a few words at once to send you my warmest congratulations on your lovely debut in London! You must heed very carefully: BE PRECISE AND METICULOUS about everything even to the smallest detail. The public expects this of you and must never be disappointed.
>
> How charming Mr. Chappell has been and how fortunate that you have so entirely won his interest, as he has great influence. Is he going to act for you at the Crystal Palace? For the Bach concert I would advise the C Major Concerto (the same one the two young men (M & W) played last winter). I, for my part, prefer the C minor (I played it in Leipzig with Mendelssohn in past years quite often), but the C Major is more suitable for the big Hall. It must

*Brahms entrusted Ilona Eibenschütz with the premieres of his op. 116, no. 6 (1893), op. 118 (1894), and op. 119 (March 1894) in London.

however, be studied and WORKED OUT very CONSCIENTIOUSLY and carefully between you both, especially in the PHRASING, because only then is it effective. Do not take it too lightly because it does not present technical difficulties for you! I hope you will be paid for this performance? Leave it all to Mr. Chappell and rely on him in every way as you have done already.

I hope, dear Ilona, you are very sensible in your daily routine, quite dutifully take walks in one of the parks, for at least an hour every day, or your nerves will not be strong enough to bear the strains and particularly the exertions.

How much I think of you always, and wish I could protect you from everything that could harm you, and from taking things too lightly where music-making is concerned.

I am writing hastily, as I am so terribly busy, however, I hope you can read this. Between the lines you will read many things, loving and caring—From yours, Clara Schumann.

March 1, 1891

Dear Ilona,

. . . Since yesterday you are in a lodging; that is a great difference from a private family, but it has advantages in so far as you can live at your own pace, and have privacy and rest whenever you wish.

ARE YOU BEING SENSIBLE AND NOT GOING OUT TO LATE PARTIES? You must be very careful now as you have so many acquaintances, sometimes even refuse an invitation, and you must particularly not go out on an evening before a concert, and always go to bed early. That is of the utmost importance and it is really what matters most. Furthermore, do you always study everything scrupulously? I read in the Times that you played the Chopin concerto beautifully but that in the solos you made some mistakes. In which piece was that? And why did you go wrong? Did you perhaps not follow the music? I have repeatedly told you always to do so. You see how people take note of these things.

When Clara Schumann accepted a position as principal teacher in the Hoch Conservatory* in Frankfurt at the age of fifty-nine, it was the first time she had ever committed herself to a full-time teaching position. In Frankfurt, Frau Kammervirtuosin Schumann, as she was named in the conservatory's first annual report, taught in her own home and was permitted much free time for touring. She was the only woman on the faculty when the school opened in 1878 and was accorded this privilege because of her unique position in the German musical world. Once again her talents and reputation placed her above considerations of gender. In 1879 Joachim Raff, the first director, wrote to another woman who was seeking a position: "With the exception of Madame Schumann there is no woman and there will not be any

*The Hoch'sche Conservatorium, founded by Dr. Joseph Hoch, a wealthy Frankfurt music lover, was headed first by Joachim Raff, then from his death in 1882 until 1908 by Bernhard Scholz.

women employed in the Conservatory. As for Madame Schumann, I count her as a man."[9]*

Raff knew Madame Schumann would draw students; her presence in Frankfurt was an asset to the conservatory and to the musical life of the city. She taught at the Hoch Conservatory until the end of the school year of 1892, when she was almost seventy-three. The roster of students she attracted included pianists from Chicago, New York, Florence, London (she had an unusually large group of students from Great Britain), Vienna, and every city in Germany.†

As Raff was a prominent Lisztian, Clara Schumann had many qualms about him. Her doubts were stilled by Brahms, who encouraged her to take the position and time and again helped her to unravel the intricacies of academic politics. Madame Schumann was treated royally by the director and governing board, and in return was the model of a conscientious teacher. She pondered questions of curriculum, standards, auditions, scheduling, examinations, and similar educational issues—some petty, some serious—with interest and concern.[10]

Reports by many of her former students indicate that although Clara Schumann based her technique on Wieck's principles, she developed her own style of teaching. As a working artist, she was forced to limit her teaching time, and accepted only advanced students who had mastered basic piano technique and had already studied theory. She taught mainly by example, though she did not expect her students to follow slavishly. Her daughters Marie and Eugenie (and later her students Nathalie Janotha, Lazzaro Uzielli, and others) acted as assistant teachers and coached less advanced pupils who sought admittance to her classes. Some never achieved this distinction. One young English student, Clement Harris, noted his triumph when he was accepted by Clara Schumann in 1889: "At home I was overwhelmed by congratulations. . . . Telegraphed London, 'It is done; I finally made it. Hurrah. Long live seven hours of daily practice.'" A few days later he wrote: "I am proud to be a Schumann scholar now. I would never have dreamed how difficult it would be to be accepted in her class. Everyone in my generation is trying for it. I believe that fortune really favored me, but I also certainly worked hard enough to earn it."[11]

Her carefully chosen students took their lessons, usually two a week, in the presence of other students so that they benefited doubly. Less advanced students listened in from other rooms. All of her students were invited to musicales at her home to hear her play with Brahms, Joachim, Stockhausen, and other artists. They were expected to attend opera, orchestral, and chamber

*Raff soon changed his mind: by 1880 two other women had joined the school's faculty. And from that year on, Raff established composition classes for women, probably the first of their kind in Germany.

†During the first school year, 1878–79, the class included Edward MacDowell of New York. See Peter Cahn, *Das Hoch'sche Konservatorium in Frankfurt am Main* (1878–1978) (Frankfurt am Main: Waldemar Kramer, 1979).

music performances, and generally to participate in the musical life of Frankfurt. The diary entries of her granddaughter Julie, who lived with "Grossmutter" and Aunts Marie and Eugenie, reported with great excitement on the Christmas parties to which all the students were invited as well as on the student recitals held at the Myliusstrasse home Clara Schumann bought soon after her move to Frankfurt.[12] Tante Marie kept a *Vorspielbuch*, a performance book in which every recital was recorded with the name of the student, the works performed, and Madame Schumann's comments on the playing. From the *Vorspielbuch* we can see that the repertoire her students were expected to know included piano works of Bach, Beethoven, Scarlatti, Haydn, Mozart, Beethoven, Schumann, Mendelssohn, Chopin, and Brahms—all composers heard on her own programs.* In addition, she expected them to be familiar with chamber music: trios, piano quartets, and violin and piano sonatas that she taught in the Ensemble Class required of all her students.

In Frankfurt her loyalty to her students was legendary. Mathilde Verne, one of her students at the conservatory, wrote, "To her, each pupil represented a sacred trust, not only in music, but as a character, and she influenced us for good in every way."[13] Audiences and admirers always expressed interest in her teaching techniques, and many of her English students described their lessons with Clara Schumann in English-language newspapers and journals. Marie Fromm, a Hoch Conservatory student, reported in the *Musical Times*, "The very foundation of her training was that the arm must be absolutely loose, not a single muscle in upper or lower arm or wrist strained or forced, the fingers kept loose in the knuckle-joints, all power and quality coming from the back muscles."[14]

Though she did not insist, as her father had done, that her students study voice in order to learn the essence of the bel canto legato style, she did teach her students to "caress" or press the keys in order to produce the singing tone for which she was noted. Franklin Taylor told Sir George Grove that "nothing ever sounded harsh or ugly in her hands" and that

> the peculiarly beautiful quality of the tone she produced, which was rather vigorous without the slightest harshness, was obtained, even in the loudest passages, by pressure with the fingers rather than by percussion. Indeed, her playing was particularly free from violent movement of any kind; in passages, the fingers were kept close to the keys and squeezed instead of striking them, while chords were grasped from the wrist, rather than struck from the elbow.[15]

Other students also recorded their reactions to her emphasis on a loose wrist; Eugenie Schumann writes of her first lesson with her mother:

*Dietz-Rüdiger Moser, a great-grandson of Clara and Robert Schumann's son Ferdinand and editor of Clara Schumann, *Mein liebes Julchen: Briefe von Clara Schumann an ihre Enkeltochter Julie Schumann* . . . (Munich: Nymphenburger, 1990), reports (74) that when one of Schumann's English students played Liszt's *Rhapsodie espagnole* on December 9, 1893, she commented that she was not responsible for the choice; it was "a dreadful piece that he himself chose."

> She played the first eight bars [of a Czerny étude] from the wrist with all the notes of equal strength, forte, yet exquisitely mellow in tone, never stiffening the wrist for an instant, and knitting the chords rhythmically together so that the simple piece suddenly took on life and character. It was a revelation to me; my feeling for beauty of touch and rhythm was stirred into life from that moment.[16]

Though her own position at the piano was often characterized as "hunched over," her students remember that she insisted on an air of seeming relaxation at the keyboard. She taught that the arms should fall easily from the shoulders, Carl Friedberg reminisced, but never pressed against the sides of the body.[17] The pressure from the fingers may have contributed to the control of tone and expressiveness that was the hallmark of her playing and of that of many of her pupils.

In her typical conscientious fashion, she meticulously observed every note and marking and, according to Eugenie, never allowed "the smallest inexactitude to pass."[18] Adelina de Lara also noted her patience with details. "Her vigilance never relaxed in matters of tone-quality, rhythm and phrasing; in short, she treated the pianoforte as an orchestra and required her pupils to consider every minute phrase and to express it as though it were given to a separate instrument."[19]

No one dared question Clara Schumann's authority; indeed, she was perceived as having a direct link not only to Schumann, Mendelssohn, Chopin, and Brahms but to Bach and Beethoven as well. "Do you think Beethoven would have taken the trouble to write all this notation, dots, ties, crotchets here, quavers there, if he had meant it to be otherwise?" she asked Eugenie.[20] Fanny Davies, another English student, wrote, "Clara Schumann summed up the essentials in these words, 'Play what is written; play it *as* it is written. It all stands there.' "[21] At the same time, however, she was never loath to correct an edition if she believed it to be faulty. And because of her firsthand experience with early editions of Bach, Beethoven, and the early romantic masters, she never doubted that she was in the right.

All of her students knew that she deplored ostentation in any form: no exaggeration of dynamics, of tempo or change of tempo, or of pedaling, no trick that might detract from the purity of the interpretation was permitted. Lara's description of Clara Schumann's admonition to students delineates her position vis-à-vis technical prowess: " 'Keine Passagen' [No passages], she would cry out in despair if one tried to rattle through any rapid figuration with mere empty virtuosity . . . she would tolerate nothing that was done for mere brilliance and pace."[22]

Her feeling that technique should serve the composer was characteristic of the "priestess," and was reflected in the music she chose to play and to teach. Though she had a magnificent technique at her disposal, she selected her repertoire for its intrinsic beauty, style, and musical qualities and not necessarily because its difficulty might impress audiences. She expected her students to adhere to the standards of technique and repertoire she set for herself. Scales, arpeggios, and exercises by Clementi, Cramer, and Czerny (in her edition) were included in every lesson, along with piano works by Bach, Beethoven, Brahms, Chopin, Haydn, Heller, Mendelssohn, Mozart, Schubert, Schumann, and Weber. A collection of music belonging to Emma Schmidt, a Schumann pupil, includes a few pieces by little-known contemporaries—Nicolai von Wilm, Eduard Strauss (brother of Johann)—but no showpieces by Liszt or Thalberg.[23]

In many letters and diary entries Clara Schumann expressed (with some envy) her conviction that only a composer—a creator—could achieve immortality; the interpretive artist would soon be forgotten. As a performer she was only too well aware of the younger stars waiting to take their places in the spotlight and of the evanescence of an interpreter's career, no matter how brilliant. As a teacher, however, she did achieve some degree of immortality: her influence extends to this day. Many of her pupils concertized; others became prominent teachers and thus passed on her philosophy. The Schumann tradition colored the playing of such pianists as Fanny Davies, Leonard Borwick (her favorite student), Nathalie Janotha, Adelina de Lara, and Mary Wurm. Mathilde Verne (sister of Mary Wurm), though not a well-known performer, was the teacher of Harold Samuel and Cutner Solomon, eminent English pianists; Carl Friedberg brought the tradition to the United States, where during his many years at the Institute of Musical Art (later the Juilliard School) he taught such artists as Malcolm Frager, William Masselos, Bruce Hungerford, and Yaltah Menuhin.[24]

As a teacher Clara Schumann demonstrated the same qualities that made her a great artist. Her teaching style, infused by her resolute and determined spirit, combined her high ideals and scrupulous attention to details, her emphasis on expression and tone, her insistence that technique be cultivated to serve the music, and her demand that the performer honor, above all, the composer—the creator. This was her legacy to the future.

Catalogue of Works

In this catalogue of works the reader will find the genesis and history of each of Clara Schumann's known compositions, arrangements, and editions. Information about lost or missing works is also provided. Particular attention to contemporary reviews has been given and excerpts from reviews are translated to enable the reader to gauge the reception of her works.

Selections from the composer's diary and correspondence document her ideas, sympathies, responses, sensibilities, and susceptibilities as she progresses from the Four Polonaises, published when she was a child of eleven, to the arrangements for piano of Robert Schumann's opp. 56 and 58, published in the last year of her life.

Works are listed in chronological order by opus number or, if they have no opus number, by date of composition, as far as is known.

Opus number and title: Opus number as given by the composer. Works without opus numbers are listed by title. Title as given in first edition. The titles of unpublished works are determined by reference to autographs, diaries, letters, or other pertinent sources, identified in parentheses.

Dedicatee:

Text (for vocal works): Author/translator, dates; other pertinent information.

Origin of work: Date, place, history of work.

Autographs: Locations and call numbers of all autographs known to date. Inscriptions on the autograph, distinctive features, and variants are briefly described, with excerpts from correspondence and diary entries concerning the autograph.

First edition: City: publisher, date, plate number (PN). Excerpts from correspondence and diary entries about history and progress of publication. Selected excerpts from correspondence and diary entries referring to publication.

Performances: Performances by Clara Schumann with date, place, and documentation. For works frequently performed, only selected dates are given with an indication of the total number of performances. Program numbers are from the collection of programs (*Programm-Sammlung* [PS]) in Robert-Schumann-Haus. These data by no means represent the total of Clara Schumann's performances. The composer/pianist played in more than the 1,299 programs in the collection; many of her performances were undocumented.

Reviews: Citations; selected excerpts and commentary.

Later editions, facsimiles, reprints: Selected editions (other than the first) are cited with title, editor, place, publisher, year, and plate number. Particular attention is given to twentieth-century editions. Facsimiles and reprints are also noted. Abbreviations are listed on page xxiv; works cited by short title are listed in the bibliography.

Arrangements, transcriptions, translations:

Literature: Citations of literature that offers significant information, discussion, analysis of work. Facsimiles and reprints are also noted. Abbreviations are listed on page xxv; works cited by short title are listed in the bibliography.

Commentary:

PUBLISHED WORKS WITH OPUS NUMBERS

Op. 1. QUATRE POLONOISES POUR LE PIANOFORTE

Origin of work: 1829–30, Leipzig.

CW/Diary, October 4, 1829 (FW): "We went to see Paganini at 10:30 in the morning. . . . I had to play my Polonoise in E Flat for him on an old, very poor piano with black keys (left behind by a student). He enjoyed my playing very much and told my father that I had a calling for art because I had feeling."

CW/Diary, September 2–4, 1830: "While father was away, I composed a variation and 1 polonaise."

Autograph: Not found.

First edition: Leipzig: Hofmeister, 1831. PN 1590.

Hofmeister printed 200 copies on February 4, 1831; 300 copies in all were printed by Hofmeister between 1831 and 1884.

CW/Diary, March 10, 1831 (FW): "My first work, *4 Pol[onoisen] p[our] Pianoforte,* is ready at Hofmeister's. I am sending copies to Dresden—to Kraegen, Dem. Veltheim and Carus, to Graf Baudissin etc. I gave copies to Herr Kegel and Herr Schumann (who has been living with us since Michaelmas 1830 and is studying music) and also to Henriette Weick[e]."

Performances: Probably played on the trip to Paris in 1831.

FW to his wife, Nov. 14, 1831: "Clara's compositions and the 4 Polonaises—which no one in Leipzig can—or will—judge in an unbiased way, will be heard in the right way here [Cassel]" (Wieck/*Briefe*, 38).

Reviews:

Iris, June 17, 1831, 96: "From a woman? No; this time from a little girl who is yet to become a woman. As far as we know, the young composer is just ten or eleven years old and already a very accomplished pianist. Early accomplishments are no barrier to future performance; in fact, it is certain that those who are early achievers generally accomplish later on as well. The polonaises that lie before us are quite artful; at times the harmonies are a bit forced, often too dissonant, yet not without talent and with a good rhythm. Small details are very likable. Yet there remains a question of how much of it was the child's own work and how much contributed by another. In any case, we would have considered it better if this publication had not appeared. Not on account of the compositions—these are no better and no worse than many other modern piano pieces—but for the child's own sake. What reasonable person wants to have school exercises printed, even if they turn out well? But that is the sorry fate of our time—not to take heed of art or the needs of the public, but only to pay allegiance to the purse or homage to vanity."

Allgemeiner Musikalischer Anzeiger [Vienna], 4 (1832), 143: "These pieces are good; indeed better than so many of her colleagues, and that pleases us doubly."

Allgemeiner Musikalischer Anzeiger [Vienna], 5 (1833), 66: "Nicely devised and effectively carried out. Despite the existing national characteristics, a gentle breath of tender feminine grace still prevails."

Later editions, facsimiles, reprints: (1) Op. 1/2, titled "Polonaise de Bohemia," appeared in *Musical Bijou*, 20 (1848), 60–61; (2) *Quatre Polonaises für Klavier*; (3) facsimiles of op. 1/1 and 2 in Wieck/*Briefe*, Appendix; (4) op. 1/2 in *Keyboard Classics*, September/October 1985, 26–27; (5) CW/Early Works, FH 2324.

Literature: Chissell, 11; Klassen/1990, 16–18; De Vries, 159, 178; CW/Early Works, "Vorwort"; Rehberg, 662–63.

Commentary: The plates of op. 1 were sold to Whistling sometime between 1832 and 1838 and then resold to Hofmeister.

CW/Diary, July 5, 1838 (FW): "In June I took the plates of the Polonaises Op. 1, plates and 54 copies of the Valses Op. 4, plates and 77 copies of Op. 5, back from Whistling and sold everything to Hofmeister today for 50 rt. Pr. Courant. This will count as the honorarium for Op. 4 and 5 since the proceeds and expenses from Whistling come to the same as the production of opus 4 and 5, namely 75 rt. 5 gl."

Op. 2. CAPRICES EN FORME DE VALSE POUR LE PIANO

Dedicatee: Madame Henriette Foerster née Weicke (dates unknown). Henriette Weicke Foerster was one of the two girls with whom Clara had begun piano lessons in 1825.

CW/Diary, August 25, 1832 (FW): "I was at Henriette Weicke's on the eve of her marriage and brought her the dedication of my Caprices which have been published by Hofmeister."

Origin of work: 1831–32, Leipzig and Paris.

Autograph: SBPK, Mus. ms. autogr. K. Schumann 3. (Autographs of Caprices 3 and 6 only.) The two autographs (unnumbered) are in a folder marked "3 Klavierstücke." The first (Caprice 6) is marked in upper left "Allegro risoluto" and in upper right "Caprice en forme de Valse par Clara Wieck." The second autograph (Caprice 3) is marked "Andantino . . . Caprice par Clara Wieck." (For the third autograph, see "Etude," below.) See illustration of Caprice 6 in *Katalog*, 25.

First edition: Leipzig: Hofmeister; Paris: Stoepel, 1832. PN 1675.

CW/Diary, May 10, 1832 (FW): "Shortly before our return from Paris, my Caprices were printed by Stoepel and Father received 10 copies. Now he will have Hofmeister print them here."

The Leipzig print (100 copies) appeared on August 22, 1832. The edition is referred to as "Op. 2, Cah[ier] 1." No copies of Cahier 2 have been found. In all, 325 copies of op. 2 were printed by Hofmeister between 1832 and 1874.

Performances:

January 13, 1833, Leipzig (PS 28). Private concert in Wieck home, Reichstrasse 578. See program, p. 258.

CW/Diary, January 1833, (FW): "On the 13th, my father gave a big morning musicale for which he had made up printed programs. 60 people were there. . . . Among other pieces, I played my Caprices."

January 27, 1835, Hanover (PS 62).

CW/Diary, January 27, 1835 (FW): "For the third time, Clara played at court where the entire nobility was gathered and the Duke and Duchess very gracious. [Among other things] she played the Caprice in A Flat at the request of the Ducal family."

March 24, 1836, Breslau (PS 95). Program lists "Two Caprices by Clara."

Reviews: NZfM, 2 (May 12, 1835), 154–55.

Later editions, facsimiles, reprints: CW/Early Works, FH 2325.

Literature: Chissell, 26; De Vries, 159; Hohenemser, 117–18; Klassen/1990, 18–19; Rehberg, 663.

Commentary: Franz Stoepel, 1794–1836, piano teacher, advocate of the Logier method, and friend of Friedrich Wieck, directed a school in Paris where Clara gave a concert in April 1832.

Although Robert Schumann noted in his diary on May 13, 1832: "Clara wants to dedicate her Caprices to me" (RS/Tgb 1:388), the work was published in Paris with the dedication "Aux Elèves de l'Academie de Mons. F. Stöpel" (RS/Tgb 1:469n400) and in Leipzig to Madame Foerster.

Op. 3. ROMANCE VARIÉE POUR LE PIANO

Dedicatee: Robert Schumann, 1810–1856. Schumann was no longer a student of Friedrich Wieck or living in the Wieck home when this work was composed. He saw the Wieck family almost daily, however, and a lively friendship between the 14-year-old Clara Wieck and 23-year-old Robert Schumann was well under way.

Origin of work: 1831–1833, Leipzig.

Autograph: Not found.

First edition: Leipzig: Hofmeister; Paris: Richault, 1833. PN 1897.

First print run of 150 copies on July 22, 1833; a total of 350 copies were printed by Hofmeister between 1833 and 1854.

Performances: No known public performances. Clara performed several of her own variations in 1831 and 1832 for Goethe, Moscheles, Spohr, and others; op. 3 may have been among them.

CW/Diary, October 22, 1832 (FW): "In the evening [Moscheles with] his wife was also at our home. I played my Variations in C [Op. 3?] and Father performed on the Physharmonica for her."

Reviews: *AmZ*, 35 (1833), 616–17.

Later editions, facsimiles, reprints: (1) CS/Goebels, 2:2–11; (2) CW/Early Works, FH 2326.

Literature: Chissell, 31–32; Daverio, 100, 107–9, 520; De Vries, 164; Klassen/1990, 23–24, 70; Rehberg, 663.

Commentary: See Literature for opp. 3 and 20 for discussions of the origin of the melody and its use in Clara Schumann's op. 20 and Johannes Brahms's op. 9. See also pp. 222–24 and 232–33.

Op. 4. VALSES ROMANTIQUES POUR LE PIANOFORTE

Dedicatee: Emma Eggers née Garlichs (dates unknown). Emma Eggers, the wife of a Bremen schoolteacher and music lover, was particularly helpful to the Wiecks on their 1835 trip to Bremen.

CW/Diary, January 9, 1836 (CW): "I received a letter from Madam Eggers thanking me for dedicating the Waltzes to her."

Origin of work: 1835, Leipzig.

Autograph: Not found. It is known that the Valses were orchestrated but neither score nor parts are extant.

CW/Diary, August 7, 1835 (FW): "I completed the orchestration of my Waltzes on the 25th and wrote it out myself. Herr Meyer looked over the score. (The composer Herr Meyer is giving me lessons in orchestration.)"

First edition: Leipzig: F. W. Whistling, 1835. No PN.

[Bottom right, p. 2] NB. Diese Walzer sind auch für Orchester in sauber geschriebenen Stimmen für 2 Thlr. zu haben. [These waltzes are also available in neatly written parts for orchestra for 2 taler.]

The plates of op. 4 were sold to Hofmeister in 1838 (PN 2307). Hofmeister's first print run of 54 copies was on June 30, 1838. A total of 104 copies were printed by Hofmeister between 1838 and 1851.

Performances: As far as is known, only the orchestrated Valses were performed publicly.

CW to Emilie List, September 8, 1835: "I have been playing very little. My piano has slept for three weeks. I have done much work, however. . . . Composed and orchestrated a group of Waltzes and they have already been played and received with much applause in the Kuchengarten and the Hotel de Prusse." (Wendler, 55)

Reviews: *NZfM*, 4 (February 23, 1836), 69–70.

Later editions, facsimiles, reprints: CW/Early Works, FH 2327.

Literature: De Vries, 159; Hohenemser, 118–19; Klassen/1990, 20–22; Rehberg, 663.

Commentary: CW/Diary, July 5, 1838, (FW): "In June I took the plates of the Polonaises Op. 1, plates and 54 copies of the Valses Op. 4, plates and 77 copies of Op. 5, back from Whistling and sold everything to Hofmeister today for 50 rt. Pr. Courant. This will count as the honorarium for Op. 4 and 5 since the proceeds and expenses from Whistling comes to the same as the production of opus 4 and 5, namely 75 rt. 5 gl."

Op. 5. QUATRE PIÈCES CARACTÉRISTIQUES POUR LE PIANOFORTE: 1. "Impromptu. Le Sabbat"; 2. "Caprice à la Boleros"; 3. "Romance"; 4. "Scène fantastique: Le Ballet des Revenants."

Dedicatee: Sophie Kaskel (1817–1894). A girlhood friend of Clara's, later Gräfin von Baudissin.

Origin of work: 1833–36, Leipzig.

CW/Diary (FW): July 1833: "I composed many things this month. . . . Chor der Doppelgänger . . ."

CW to RS, September 1, 1835:"I wrote out a fair copy of my Variations in F[?] for the printer and also my Danse de Fantomes (Doppelgängerchor) and Une nuit de Sabbat (Hexenchor)" (*Briefwechsel,* 1:17).

Autographs:

1. SBPK, Mus. ms. autogr. K. Schumann 1 (Romance [No. 3] only). One page, first five measures crossed out. Top right: "Leipzig. Im Juni 1836./Clara Wieck." Below: "Sempre pedale. Andante. Romanze." See illustration in *Katalog,* 29. Verso of autograph has a 42-measure fragment labeled "Concerto." See Op. 7 for fuller description.
2. Wgm, VII.64.289 (Romance [No. 3] only). One page; top left: "Andante con sentimento."; top right: "componirt von Clara Wieck"; bottom right: "zu Wien im April 1838." See illustration in *Katalog,* 118.

First edition: Leipzig: Whistling, September 1836. PN 2308.

The plates of op. 5 (PN 2308) were sold to Hofmeister in 1838. Hofmeister's first print run of 77 copies was on January 6, 1838; 252 copies were printed between January 1838 and November 1889.

CW/Diary, August 18, 1836 (FW): "Clara's three new works, Op. 5, 6, 7 were finished."

September 10, 1836 (FW): "The first eight copies of Op. 5 are ready. Hofmeister is working on Op. 6."

Performances:

May 24, 1834, Dresden.

CW/Diary (CW): "I dined with [Graf] Baudissin and after dinner played . . . my Hexenchor which he liked very much."

June 24, 1836, Cassel.

CW/Diary, July 17, 1836 (CW): "I played four of my newest Characterstücke for him [Spohr]. (I had just written them out in order to give them to the printer.) They pleased him so much that his cold but otherwise pleasant face beamed with joy and he kept nudging his wife with great delight while I played."

September 12, 1836, Leipzig.

CW/Diary, September 12, 1836 (FW): "Chopin surprised us; he listened to all of Op. 5. . . . He was delighted, expressed himself enthusiastically and left us, very moved."

As far as is known, CW did not play the entire work in public. Movements from Op. 5 were played February 25, 1837 (Bolero) (PS 103), and April 26, 1837, Bremen (Bolero) (PS 114). For performances of "Impromptu. Le Sabbat," see Op. 5A.

Later editions, facsimiles, reprints:

1. "Hexen-Tanz." Vienna: Haslinger, 1838. See Op. 5A.
2. Op. 5 was reprinted with op. 6 by Hofmeister in 1837 or early 1838 as *Soirées musicales: 10 Pièces caractéristiques.* PN 2148/2308. Prints of the combined work were issued throughout the nineteenth century.
3. Da Capo.
4. Klassen/1987, 2–21.
5. CW/Early Works, FH 2328.
6. CS/Goebels 2:112–14. Romance only. Based on the Vienna autograph and titled by Goebels "Andante con sentimento."

7. Marciano, 14–16. Romance only. Based on the Vienna autograph and titled by Marciano "Andante con sentimento."

Evidently Goebels and Marciano did not realize that the "Andante con sentimento" was the "Romance" from op. 5.

Literature: Chissell, 44–46; De Vries, 160; Hohenemser, 119–20; Klassen/1990, 31–46; Rehberg, 663–64 .

Commentary: CW/Diary, July 5, 1838 (FW): "In June I took the plates of the Polonaises Op. 1, plates and 54 copies of the Valses Op. 4, plates and 77 copies of Op. 5, back from Whistling and sold everything to Hofmeister today for 50 rt. Pr. Courant. This will count as the honorarium for Op. 4 and 5 since the proceeds and expenses from Whistling comes to the same as the production of opus 4 and 5, namely 75 rt. 5 gl."

Op. 5A. HEXENTANZ for Piano

Origin of work: Op. 5, no. 1, "Impromptu. Le Sabbat," published separately as "Hexen-Tanz."

Autograph: Not found.

First edition: Vienna: Haslinger, 1838. PN 7548.

CW/Diary, April 5, 1838, (FW): "Haslinger sent 25 rt. for the Variations Op. 8 and 20 Species for the Hexenchor, which he is printing separately."

Performances: Between 1834 and 1839, Clara gave at least 15 public performances of the Hexenchor (op. 5/1), variously referred to as "Hexentanz," "Doppelgänger Chor," and "Impromptu."

January 22, 1835, Hannover (PS 60).

December 26, 1837, Vienna (PS 124).

CW/Diary, December 26, 1837 (FW): "Performance in the Burg for the entire imperial family. Duet with Blagrove—the piano stands on thick rugs. . . . Clara, the person, pleases the Empress even more than Clara the virtuosa. Everyone conversed with Clara. The Empress let her deepest satisfaction be known and sent 50 gold ducats."

January 4, 1838, Vienna (PS 125).

CW/Diary, January 4, 1838 (FW): "In the evening, performance at Prince Esterhazy's, the Ambassador to England, for 200 diplomats. . . . The Prince was discreet enough not to have her play too much. The honorarium—25 ducats in a beautiful little box."

January 7, 1838, Vienna (PS 126). See program in *Katalog*, 34 and 112.

March 21, 1839, Paris (PS 154).

Later editions, facsimiles, reprints: Berlin: Robert Lienau, 1993 (reprint).

Op. 6. SOIRÉES MUSICALES: 1. Toccatina; 2. Notturno; 3. Mazurka (G Minor); 4. Ballade; 5. Mazurka (G Major); 6. Polonaise

Dedicatee: Henriette Voigt (1808–39), wife of a well-to-do Leipzig merchant, gifted pianist, good friend of the Wieck-Schumann circles.

CW/Diary, September 30, 1836 (FW): "Madame Voigt bought the Tomaschek-Wieck piano and Clara dedicated Op. 6 to her to thank her."

Origin of work: 1834–36, Leipzig.

Autograph: Not found.

First edition: Leipzig: Hofmeister; Paris: Richault, 1836. PN 2148.

In all, 425 copies of *Soirées musicales,* Clara's most popular early work, were printed by Hofmeister between 1836 and 1873.

CW/Diary, August 18, 1836 (FW): "Clara's three new works, Op. 5, 6, 7 were finished."

CW/Diary, September 10, 1836 (FW): "The first eight copies of Op. 5 are ready. Hofmeister is working on Op. 6."

CW/Diary, September 12, 1836 (FW): "Hofmeister is paying 40 rt. Pr. C. for Op. 6."

CW/Diary, November 6, 1836 (FW): "Clara's Soirées musicales were published today. She is receiving an honorarium of 40 rt. and 12 free copies."

CW/Diary, February 2, 1837 (FW): "Hofmeister paid me 40 rt. for my op. 6 and 80 rt. for my concerto op. 7 in addition to 12 free copies of the first and 24 free copies of the concerto. This is the first honoraria I have received for my compositions."

Performances: Single movements only.

May 24, 1834, Dresden.

CW/Diary, May 24, 1834 (CW): "I dined with [Graf] Baudissin and after dinner played several Mazurkas . . . which he liked very much."

September 12, 1836, Leipzig.

CW/Diary, September 12, 1836 (FW): "Chopin surprised us; he listened to . . . the 2 Mazurkas and Ballade from Op. 6. . . ."

There were at least five additional performances of a "Mazurka" between 1836 and 1838.

Selected reviews: *NZfM,* 7 (September 15, 1837), 87 (signed "Am 12 September 1837/ Florestan und Eusebius"); *Morgenblatt,* Vienna (cited in Wieck/*Briefe,* 87).

Later editions, facsimiles, reprints: (1) Reprinted with op. 5 by Hofmeister in 1837 or early 1838 as *Soirées musicales. 10 Pieces caractéristiques* (see Op. 5); (2) Da Capo; (3) Klassen/1987, 22–37 (includes only Toccatina, Notturno, Ballade, Mazurka (G major); (4) CW/Early Works, FH 2329.

Literature: Chissell, 44–46; Hohenemser, 120–21; Klassen/1987, "Vorwort"; Klassen/1990, 46–57; Rehberg, 664.

Commentary:

RS to CS, February 11, 1838: "Do you know what I love best of yours—your Notturno in F Major in 6/8? What were you thinking of [when you wrote it]? . . . And next is the Trio from the Toccatina" (*Briefwechsel,* 1:100).

Op. 7. PREMIER CONCERT pour le Piano-Forte avec Accompagnement d'Orchestre (ou de Quintour): 1. Allegro maestoso; 2. Romanze, Andante non troppo con grazia; 3. Finale, Allegro non troppo

Dedicatee: Louis [Ludwig] Spohr (1784–1859).

Instrumentation: Solo piano, 2 flutes, 2 oboes, 2 clarinets, 2 bassoons, 2 horns, 2 trumpets, 1 trombone, tympani, 2 violins, viola, violoncello, bass.

Origin of work: 1833–36, Leipzig.

CW/Diary, January 13, 1833 (CW): "I have begun to compose a concerto."

The third movement was the first composed and was variously titled "Concertsatz" and "Concert-Rondo."

CW/Diary, Early July 1833 (FW): "This month I composed a great deal, finished—among other things . . . the first solo of a large Concert Rondo. . . ."

CW/Diary, November 22, 1833 (CW): "I finished my Concerto and Schumann will orchestrate it now so that I can play it in my concert."

CW/Diary, May 17, 1834 (CW): "[Dresden] In the afternoon, there was a little gathering at Kraegen's (Kaskels among them), who had wanted to hear me. I played the Concerto, the Notturno and the Etudes of Chopin, my Concertsatz, and sang a song."

CW/Diary, June 17, 1834 (CW): "On the 17th, before Father came, I quickly composed the first solo for the first movement of my concerto."

CW/Diary, June 22, 1835, (CW): "The son of the famous Mozart visited us. I played the Adagio and Finale from my Concerto for him."

CW to Emilie List, August 6, 1835: "My concerto is finished. The Adagio is played without orchestra and only with a solo cello obbligato. It works very well" (Wendler, 51).

CW/Diary, August 25, 1835 (FW): "The composer Herr Meyer is giving me lessons in orchestration. . . . I am now preparing for the printer . . . the first movement of the concerto—and thus—the entire concerto."

CW to RS, September 1, 1835: "You will smile, but it is true: 1. I finished my score. 2. wrote out all the parts myself—and that in two days; 3. . . . I have begun orchestrating the concerto but have not written it out yet. I changed the Tutti a bit" (*Briefwechsel,* 1:17).

CW/Diary, August 18, 1836 (FW): "Clara's three new works, Op. 5, 6, 7, are finished. The instrumental parts of her revised Concerto are being copied out."

CW/Diary, October 1836 (FW): "This month, Clara rehearsed her revised Concerto with Queiser's ensemble. It took ten bottles of wine to get things started."

CW/Diary, November 4, 1836 (FW): "Banck, Hofmeister and Louis Spohr dined with us; before dinner, I played my concerto which Hofmeister is now printing."

Autographs:

1. SBPK, Mus. ms. 20 427. A draft of the Finale, full score, 26 pages, in the hand of Robert Schumann. A penciled notation, top right, p. 1, in RS's hand, reads: "Concertsatz von Clara, von mir instrumentirt. (1836)" (Clara's Concertsatz, orchestrated by me). At the bottom of the page are three boxed statements in black ink, each one carefully crossed out, which appear to be sketches for the placement of the composer's name on the title page. Some tempo indications and changes are in red ink; other changes are in red-orange pencil and still other emendations are in pencil.

   Instruments are written in the following order: "Tympani 1. 2., Trombe in C, Corni in C, Flauti, Oboi, Clarinetti in A, Fagotti, Tromboni, Violino 1., Violino 2., Viole, Bassi, Pianoforte."

   RS probably dated the manuscript several years after he worked on the orchestration; hence the incorrect date. See illustration in Klassen/1990, 136.
2. Staatsarchiv Leipzig, Bestand Hofmeister. *Stichvorlage* (engraver's copy) of solo part with instrumental cues of Clara Wieck's Concerto op. 7 in hand of copyist with additions in the hands of CW and FW.
3. SBPK, Mus. ms. autogr. K. Schumann 1. What may be a sketch for the first movement of the concerto is on the verso of Romance (Op. 5/3) in CS's hand. The sketch consists of 42 measures not used in the concerto, but in the same key (A Minor), with the same time signature, and headed "Tutti." The top of the page has been cut off but "[Apr?]il 35 Concerto" remains.

First edition: Leipzig: Hofmeister; Paris: Richault; Hamburg: A. Cranz, 1837. PN 2169.

[Bottom p. 1 of each string part] When accompanied by [string] quintet all the small notes marked "with quintet" are to be played omitting the others where necessary.

Hofmeister printed 200 copies of the solo piano part (with instrumental cues) and instrumental parts on January 1, 1837. In all, 350 copies of the solo piano and instrumental parts were printed between 1837 and 1888. The full score was not published during the nineteenth century.

CW/Diary, November 10, 1836 (FW): "The first pages of Clara's Concerto were given to Hofmeister. She will receive an honorarium of 80 rt. and 20 free copies for piano solo and 4 with orchestra."

CW/Diary, January 27, 1837 (FW): "My concerto, op. 7 has been published."

CW/Diary, February 2, 1837 (FW): "Hofmeister paid me 40 rt. for my Op. 6 and 80 rt. for my concerto Op. 7 in addition to 12 free copies of the first and 24 free copies of the concerto. This is the first honorarium I have received for compositions."

Selected performances:

As "Concertsatz":

May 5, 1834, Leipzig (PS 43).

CW/Diary, May 5, 1834 (FW): "My own concert in the Gewandhaus. Chopin's Concerto got less applause than his Etudes and my Concertsatz." Mendelssohn conducted with the composer at the piano.

September 11, 1834, Leipzig (PS 44).

November 26, 1834, Magdeburg (PS 49).

February 27, 1835, Bremen (PS 68). Listed as "Concert Rondo mit Orchester"

As "Concerto":

November 9, 1835, Leipzig (PS 80). Mendelssohn conducted with the composer at the piano.

CW/Diary, November 9, 1835 (FW): "I gave a concert in the Gewandhaus . . . [it] was very well attended for an Extraconcert. I played my Concerto (of which the first movement had just been completed). . . . My Concerto received much applause from the connoisseurs."

December 1, 1835, Plauen (2d and 3d movements) (PS 81). Second movement given as "Notturno in A flat Major" in program.

March 28, 1836, Breslau (2d and 3d movements) (PS 96).

February 16, 1837, Berlin (PS 102).

April 1, 1837, Hamburg (PS 110).

CW/Diary, April 1, 1837 (CW): "My concerto was liked but probably applauded out of respect. It was the first time [they heard it] and they did not understand it. (Yet it met with great approval.)"

October 8, 1837, Leipzig (PS 117).

November 23, 1837, Prague (PS 120).

December 21, 1837, Vienna (PS 123). Titled "Concertino."

February 18, 1838, Vienna (PS 129). Titled "Concertino."

April 5, 1838, Vienna (PS 141). Titled "Concertino."

Reviews:

Der Komet, September 26, 1834, p. 510: "The Concertsatz in A Minor in the modern-romantic style, full of lovely, melancholy, and impassioned ideas, delightful because of the varied and inspired treatment of the theme and above all, because of an original, wistful main theme that winds its way through the whole. Clara received the most enthusiastic applause both as composer and as virtuoso."

NZfM, 3 (December 8, 1835), 182–83.

Breslauer Zeitung, March 31, 1836.

NZfM, 6 (February 17, 1837), 56–57.

Allgemeiner Musikalischer Anzeiger (Vienna), 10 (September 16, 1838), 143: "Here the famous North German pianist has dared with extreme boldness to take flight poetically; and that with such compelling energy as is customarily never displayed by gentle femininity. When one examines this work with all seriousness, one has to marvel approvingly at the masculinity of the spirit that pervades it, and the technical difficulties leave absolutely no doubt about the widely admired virtuosity of the composer.

"But what surely strikes one as strange is the A-flat Major of the middle movement, squeezed between the two exoteric A Minor keys of the Allegro and the Finale; on the other hand, ladies have their moods to which they are entitled and are their privilege; who can argue with that? If the daughters of Eve would only make no greater leaps, digressions, or modulations than such a tiny semitone in our cherished domestic and matrimonial affairs, all would be well and the sharpest dissonances in matrimonial matters would always resolve themselves into purely harmonic triads."

AmZ, 39 (March 22, 1837), 193–94.

AmZ, 39 (October 18, 1837), 686–87: "The 'Concertino' received moderate applause; op. 8 was enthusiastically praised."

Later editions, facsimiles, reprints, arrangements:

1. Reprint of first edition, piano solo only. Amsterdam: A. J. Heuwekemeijer-Uitgeverij, 1970. Musica Revindicata series.
2. CS, *Konzert für Klavier und Orchester,* ed. Klassen. Study score. First scholarly publication.
3. CS, *Konzert für Klavier und Orchester,* ed. Erber. Arranged for two pianos.
4. CS, *Concerto for Piano and Orchestra,* ed. Smith. Arranged for two pianos.
5. CW/Early Works (based on 1st ed. for piano and strings), piano (with instrumental cues), FH 2538; string parts, FH 2539.

Literature: Chissell, 37–39; Daverio, 237–38; De Vries, 166–67; Hohenemser, 122–23; Janina Klassen, "Vorwort," in Clara Schumann, *Konzert für Klavier und Orchester;* Klassen/1990, 112–79; Klassen, "'Schumann will es nun instrumentieren'"; Stephan D. Lindeman, "Clara Wieck—Piano Concerto in A Minor," in *Structural Novelty and Tradition,* 129–40; Claudia Macdonald, "Critical Perception and the Woman Composer"; Macdonald, review of Clara Schumann, *Konzert für Klavier;* Rehberg, 664–65.

Commentary: A lithograph by J. Giere, Hannover, 1835, shows the composer seated at the piano with score of solo piano part of the third movement titled "Concerto." See p. 36.

Op. 8. VARIATIONS DE CONCERT POUR LE PIANOFORTE SUR LA "CAVATINE DU PIRATE" DE BELLINI

Dedicatee: Adolph von Henselt (1814–89).

Origin of work: Leipzig, 1837.

CW/Diary, February 2, 1837 (FW): "My Concert Variations Op. 8 were finished today. They will be dedicated to Adolph Henselt."

Autograph: Not found.

First edition: Vienna: Haslinger, 1837. PN 7368.

CW/Diary, October 13, 1837 (FW): "I received the Variations, which had just been finished, from Haslinger. Nicely engraved."

CW/Diary, April 5, 1838 (FW): "Haslinger is sending 25 rt. for the Variations, Op. 8. . . ."

Selected performances:
March 1, 1837, Berlin (PS 105).
FW to his wife: "Triumph, Triumph. Last evening Clara completed the conquest of the same elite music-loving public with her Concerto and her thundering Bravour-Variations. Again, the applause was like thunder with the most tremendous Bravissimo." (Wieck/*Briefe,* 65).
At least twelve performances between March 11, 1837, and May 16, 1839, followed; among them these four:
August 13, 1837, Leipzig (PS 115).
January 7, 1838, Vienna (PS 126). See program in *Katalog,* 112.
May 16, 1839, Paris (PS 156).
Emilie List to RS, May 17, 1839: "Clara played her Pirat-Variations to enormous applause in yesterday's concert. The audience was captivated by the composition, not to speak of the performance" (Wendler, 67).
January 25, 1840, Berlin (PS 164).

Reviews:
NZfM, 7 (September 1, 1837), 71–72: "Clara's Variations certainly throw her great bravura prowess into bold relief."
NZfM, 8 (January 2, 1838), 3–4 and 6–7.
AmZ, 39 (October 18, 1837), 687.
Hamburger Musikalische Zeitung, February 28, 1838, 72: ". . . a dull and disordered composition" (quoted in Klassen/1990, 89).
Iris, February 1, 1840, 20: "her own, brilliant Variations."
Iris, February 7, 1840, 24.
NZfM, 12 (February 28, 1840), 70: ". . . we heard her own Variations on a theme from Bellini's Pirate, which made such a grand furore earlier here [Berlin], and after that in Paris."

Later editions, facsimiles, reprints: Da Capo.

Literature: Chissell, 43–44; Klassen/1990, 87–89; Rehberg, 449, 665.

Commentary:
FW to his wife, March 20, 1837: "Gasparo Spontini . . . considers Clara's Variations to be the greatest and most beautiful work of musical bravura in recent times" (Wieck/Briefe, 68).

Op. 9. SOUVENIR DE VIENNE. IMPROMPTU POUR LE PIANOFORTE

Origin of work: Spring 1838, Vienna.
CW/Diary, April 11, 1838 (FW): "Clara finished the Souvenir a Vienne today."
CW to FW, July 12, 1838: "It [Op. 9] should have been a little less monotonous. In a word, it was composed too quickly" (quoted in Klassen/1990, 86).

Autograph: SBPK, Mus. ms. autogr. K. Schumann 2. *Stichvorlage* (copy for the engraver), 7 pages, with penciled corrections, erasures, and cross-outs in composer's hand. See illustration in *Katalog,* 119.

First edition: Vienna: Diabelli, 1838. PN 6530.
RS to CW, July 13, 1838: "I received your souvenir a few days ago; it made me very happy, my dear girl. It has several bride-like places and in between them that prosaic song—you seemed to me to be quite roguish" (*Briefwechsel,* 1:201).

Selected performances:
April 30, 1838, Graz (PS 143).

CW/Diary, April 30, 1838 (FW): "Last performance in the theater and first performance of Souvenir à Vienne. Received with furore."

CS to RS, April 30, 1838: "I played, among other things, a Souvenir à Vienne that I had begun in Vienna and finished here [Graz]. It is just a little Impromptu, but pleased the audience immensely; the Austrians go into raptures over their national hymn and that happened here today" (*Briefwechsel,* 1:162).

Leipzig, August 12, 1838 (PS 144).

Leipzig, December 16, 1838.

CW/Diary, December 16, 1838 (CW): "Morning musicale at Ferdinand David's. . . . I played my Souvenir à Vienne."

Reviews: None found.

Literature: De Vries, 164–66; Klassen/1990, 79–87; Klassen, *"Souvenir de Vienne";* Rehberg, 665.

Op. 10. SCHERZO POUR LE PIANOFORTE (D minor)

Origin of work: Summer 1838, Maxen (near Dresden).

CS to RS, July 9, 1838: "Today I finished a Scherzo but I believe it would be too long for the [*NZfM*] Supplement; I am sending it to Father and will have him ask you to look at it and to say whatever you don't like about it. I promised it to Härtels for the Album which is coming out for Christmas" (*Briefwechsel,* 1:193).

CW to FW, July 13, 1838: "I don't believe it is too long because it goes very fast 'appassionato que possible.' I like the last repetition of the theme to the end of the piece best of all. . . . Don't strike out the misterioso as this is the most beautiful part of the whole piece." (Quoted in Klassen/1987, "Vorwort")

Autograph: Not found.

First edition: Leipzig: B&H, 1838. PN 5987.

Album edition: The Scherzo was also published in the B&H *Album für Pianoforte und Gesang für das Jahr 1839*, which appeared a few weeks before the official first edition, probably in December 1838. Other composers in the *Album* included Chopin, Mendelssohn, Spohr, and Meyerbeer.

Performances: Selected performances between 1838 and 1846:

CW/Diary, July 27, 1838, CW: "I played the Scherzo I composed in Maxen for him [the violinist Charles de Bériot], and he was very pleased with it."

August 12, 1838, Leipzig (PS 144).

September 8, 1838, Leipzig (PS 145). See program in *Katalog,* 35. This concert inspired the RS poem "Als Du gespielt hattest," published in *NZfM,* September 21, 1838, as "Traumbild am 9ten [*sic*] Abends. An C.W." (Date was in error.)

April 16, 1839, Paris (PS 155).

CW/Diary, 16 April 1839 (CW): "I gave my concert in Érard's Salon; the room looked nice, it was very full and I received (as they told me) extraordinary applause; the entire audience was moved to the greatest enthusiasm. I was most delighted with Onslow. Berlioz, Döhler etc. seem to want to form a faction against me."

November 4, 1839, Stettin (PS 158).

April 14, 1842, Copenhagen (PS 199).

March 17, 1844, St. Petersburg (PS 222).

Reviews:

NZfM, 9 (December 25, 1838), 204 (review of the *Album* edition): "The Scherzo by

Clara Wieck is a Humoreske that reveals to us all the treasures of a rich artistic temper, a fantastic magic kingdom enlivened by mocking gnomes amidst the soft murmurings of fairies, while gentle nightmares from infancy peep out of the alien underbrush. A properly critical person must, however, acknowledge that in the artistic weavings of the principal melodies the rules of double counterpoint are nonetheless actually very intelligently employed."

Journal des Débats, April 18, 1839, p. 2: "Mlle Wieck is another big talent, accurate, elegant, spirited, playing equally well the most challenging works, but a little more worldly, if I may express myself thus; that is not to say that Mlle Wieck gives in to bad taste in playing music of the antechamber [i.e., trivial music]; far from it: her Scherzo is a piece of much merit that demonstrates her knowledge of composition, and that suffers less than many others by comparison with the admirable etudes of Chopin. . . ." (Hector Berlioz)

CW/Diary, April 18, 1839: "Berlioz composed an article about me in the *Journal de Débats* that was highly malicious; I admit, I don't play up to him the way Herr Döhler and others do, so that their compositions then become the most beautiful. I had a visit from [Georges] Onslow, a genuine musician, who is all fire and flame when he hears music. He encouraged me to write more despite the cabals."

NZfM, 10 (May 17, 1839), 159–60: "Clara Wieck demonstrated in the various pieces she performed that she is a master [Meisterin] of the piano. The Caprice by Thalberg, performed with admirable power and exceptional perfection, provided sufficient evidence of that. But what matters even more than all dexterity is the life, spirit, character, expressiveness, light and shadow, melancholy, humor and caprice that unfolded with maidenly purity and charm in the performance of the Chopin Etude, of her own Scherzo, and the very expressive songs by Schubert." (Carl Mangold)

Gazette musicale de Paris, April 1839, 125. (Henri Blanchard)

CW/Diary, April 23, 1839: "In the *Courier Française, Commerce, Gazette musicale,* there are very nice reviews about me, as well as more in other papers which I don't even know."

Iris, October 4, 1839, 159: ". . . because she was always in the wrong environment and she herself presented in the wrong light, and because one can do no greater and more damaging harm to the talent than when it is received from outside oneself and is deprived of its own reality. This has always been the lot of the virtuosa in question, in the beginning at the hand of her father, whose overestimation bordered on the comical, but much may be excused in a father; later by another musician also driven by forgivable motives (how can reason cope with a reluctant or seductive heart). . . . For her Scherzo we therefore give our best thanks and hope to hear it soon performed by the composer. We only regret that the Scherzo is not provided with the serious substance, namely the rest of the sonata of which one may consider it to be part."

Iris, February 7, 1840, 24 (review of concert of February 1, 1840): "She performed compositions by various masters, such as F. Schubert, Robert Schumann, Chopin, Liszt, and also her own Scherzo. The artist's solid, elegant playing deserves the fullest recognition. But her selection of pieces seems to us to have been somewhat unfortunate."

Later editions, facsimiles, reprints: (1) CS/Piano Works, "Erstes Scherzo," 2–9 (the only work of her girlhood years to appear in this collection); (2) Da Capo; (3) Klassen/1987, 38–47.

Literature: Hohenemser, 121–22; Klassen/1987, "Vorwort"; Klassen/1990, 89–92.

Commentary: Excerpts from *Briefwechsel* about op. 10:

RS to CW, August 31, 1838: "I like the character and the structure of the Scherzo and find it very nice but then it becomes too free for me." (1:229)

CW to RS, April 4, 1839: ". . . yesterday [at a private musicale] I really created a furore. It is strange to me that my Scherzo is so well liked here. I always have to repeat it." (2:469)

CW to RS, April 9, 1839: ". . . publishers can print anything they like here; my Scherzo, for instance, was published here without my knowing it." (2:476)

RS to CW, April 17, 1839: "Which Scherzo is it they like so much?" (2:489)

CW to RS, April 23, 1839: "The Scherzo that everyone likes so much is the one in the Härtel Album that you didn't like." (2:500)

CW to RS, October 9, 1839: "Have you read that exceedingly malicious essay about my Scherzo in . . . *Iris*? [Review of October 4, quoted above.] I am usually indifferent about such things but the article was too offensive." (2:732)

RS to CW, October 13, 1839: "Now, tell me, how shall I deal with Rellstab? I was quite beside myself at his insolence. Should I box his ears by letter?" (2:741)

RS to CW, October 30, 1839: "Don't forget to play your Scherzo here and there; nobody can play it the way you do." (2:771)

RS to CW, December 1, 1839 [re programming]: "Don't leave your Scherzo out, either." (2:810)

Op. 11. TROIS ROMANCES POUR LE PIANO: 1. Andante; 2. Andante; 3. Moderato

Dedicatee: Robert Schumann.

Origin of work: 1838–39. Romance II begun in 1838 in Maxen. Romances I and III, Spring 1839, Paris.

CW to RS, July 9, 1838: "I began a Romance for you a long time ago and it sings powerfully in my head but I can't get it down on paper. And the instrument here is completely without tone for that. However, I will do it very soon." (*Briefwechsel,* 1:193)

CW to RS, April 18, 1839: "Yesterday evening I was very happy—I had a nice idea for a little Romance, but I am dissatisfied with it today." (*Briefwechsel,* 2:490)

CW/Diary, April 18, 1839 (CW): "I played a (unfinished) Romance for him [Georges Onslow] and he made a few comments about it."

CW/Diary, April 20, 1839 (CW): "I composed a small, dramatic Andante."

CW to RS, April 23, 1839: "I wrote a little piece but don't know what to call it. I had so many feelings as I wrote it—so intimate and heartfelt—won't you find a name for it for me? one that the French will understand—also, I will wait for your opinion; I am sending it to you and you write and tell me what I should change." (*Briefwechsel,* 2:500)

CW to RS, June 6, 1839: "I have received the Idylle [Romance no. 3?] and thank you for it, my dearest, but you will surely forgive me if I tell you that there are some things in it I do not like. You have completely altered the ending, which was always my favorite part and precisely the one that made the biggest impression on everyone to whom I played it. . . . You are not angry with me, are you?" (*Briefwechsel,* 2:577)

CW to RS, July 2, 1839: "The Romance is coming. You must play it very freely, at times passionately, then melancholy again—I like it very much. Please, send it right back to me, and don't be embarrassed to criticize it—that can only be helpful to me" (*Briefwechsel,* 2:617).

RS to CW, July 10, 1839: "In your Romance I heard anew that we are destined to be man and wife. You complete me as a composer just as I do you. Each of your thoughts comes from my very soul; indeed it is you I have to thank for all my music.

There is nothing to change in the Romance; it must remain exactly as it is." (*Briefwechsel,* 2:629)

Autograph: Not found. An *Albumblatt,* with the first six measures of op. 11, no. II, signed "Clara Wieck, Dresden 26.XI.1838," is in SBPK Mus. ms. autogr. K. Schumann 11.

First edition: Vienna: Mechetti, 1840. PN 3391.

RS, October 17, 1840: "On the 17th, I received 34 Th. Pr. Cour. for Clara's Romances from Mechetti through Hofmeister and gave it to Clara" (RS/Tgb 3:164).

Op. 11 no. 2 appeared as "Andante und Allegro" in the September 1839 supplement to *NZfM*.

Later editions, facsimiles, reprints:

1. Op. 11 no. 2 appeared in Aus den Muster-Beilagen der von Rob. Schumann s.Z. redigirten Zeitschrift für Musik (Leipzig: Schuberth & Co., ca. 1867). PN 4106. Works in this collection were also issued individually by Schuberth in the 1870s.
2. Da Capo.
3. CS/Goebels, 1:15–27.
4. Klassen/1987, 48–61.

Literature: Chissell, 66–68; De Vries, 170–71; Hohenemser, 122; Klassen/1987, "Vorwort"; Klassen/1990, 93–105; Rehberg, 665.

Commentary: There are slight differences in Romance no. 2 between *NZfM*, the Mechetti edition, and the Schuberth editions. See Klassen/1987, "Vorwort."

Op. 12. ZWÖLF GEDICHTE AUS F. RÜCKERT'S LIEBESFRÜHLING für Gesang und Pianoforte: 2. "Er ist gekommen"; 4. "Liebst du um Schönheit"; 11. "Warum willst du and're fragen"

The three songs of Clara Schumann's op. 12 are part of a joint cycle of twelve songs by Clara (her op. 12) and Robert Schumann (his op. 37), designated by the publisher as op. 37/12. The CS songs are numbered according to their position within the joint work.

Text: Friedrich Rückert (1788–1866).

Origin of work: 1841, Leipzig.

After immersing himself in Rückert's *Liebesfrühling,* RS wrote in the marriage diary, January 3–11, 1841: "The idea of publishing a volume of songs together with Clara inspired me to go to work. From Monday to Monday the 11th, nine songs from Rückert's Liebesfrühling were completed, and I believe I have found a special tone again for them. Now Clara should also compose some songs from the Liebesfrühling. Oh, do it, Klärchen!" (RS/Tgb 2:139).

At Robert's urging, CS set four Rückert poems and presented them to RS on June 8, 1841. Entries in the marriage diary refer to the progress of her work:

June 2, 1841: "My composing is simply not going anywhere. Sometimes I would just like to strike my dumb head!" (RS/Tgb 2:167).

June 3, 1841: "I sat down many times this week to compose and then brought four Rückert poems to completion for my dear Robert. If he should enjoy them just a little, my wish would be fulfilled" (RS/Tgb 2:167).

June 6–21, 1841: "I could give my Robert little, yet he always smiled in such a friendly way because he knew well with what love it was given. He was delighted with the four Rückert lieder, and treated them so indulgently, even wants to publish them with some of his own, which makes me very happy" (RS/Tgb 2:168).

RS chose three songs for the joint collection. The fourth song, "Die gute Nacht," remained unpublished until 1992.

Autographs:

1. RSH 5985-A1. The three songs of op. 12 and "Die Gute Nacht" are bound together as a presentation copy in a booklet of 20 pages. The cover page is inscribed: "Vier Gedichte von Rückert/meinem geliebten Manne/zum 8ten Juni 1841/componirt/von seiner Clara" (Four poems by Rückert for my beloved husband composed on June 8, 1841, by his Clara). The songs, untitled, are written in the following order: Pp. 1–4: "Warum willst du and're fragen." Pp. 5–10: "Er ist gekommen." Pp. 11–15: "Liebst du um Schönheit," with many cross-outs and emendations; three measures crossed out, one measure substituted. Pp. 16–19: "Die gute Nacht." P. 20 is blank.
2. SBPK, Mus. ms. autogr. K. Schumann 5. no. 5, "Er ist gekommen"; no. 7, "Liebst du um Schönheit"; no. 4, "Warum willst du and're fragen."

RS made several efforts to have the songs published. On April 22, 1841, he wrote to Friedrich Kistner, the music publisher: "My wife has composed some very interesting songs, which have inspired me to compose a few more from Rückert's *Liebesfrühling*. Together they form a very nice whole, which we should like to publish in *one* book. . . . As I should like to give my wife a surprise, I should prefer to keep the matter private for the present." (RS/Jansen, 430–31)

After what may have been a rejection, Robert wrote to B&H on June 23, 1841, and that firm published the songs.

First edition: Leipzig: B&H, 1841. PN 6596/97.
[See illustration of title page in *Katalog*, 51.]
The songs were published in two parts; Part I: PN 6596; Part II: PN 6597.

Performances:
April 10, 1842, Copenhagen: "A Rückert Lied" (PS 198),
February 2, 1844, Königsberg: "Er ist gekommen" (PS 207).
"Warum willst du and're fragen" January 8, 1843, Leipzig/(PS 202).
Performed at least 10 times between January 8, 1843, and January 30, 1882, Stuttgart (PS 1221).

Reviews: *AmZ*, 44 (19 January 1842), 61–62: "According to the title, we are dealing here with songs not only by Robert Schumann but also by his wife. Since no further information about the part played by each is provided, we cannot take this into account, but can only discuss the collection in general terms, keeping our conjecture to ourselves and letting everyone form his or her own opinion."

Later editions, facsimiles, reprints: (1) RS and CS, *Lieder und Gesänge;* (2) Draheim/Höft, 1:10–17.

Arrangements, transcriptions, translations:

1. "Déclaration," French trans. by Victor Wilder of "Warum willst du and're fragen" in *Album du Gaulois; Oeuvres 1869 inédites,* ed. Eugène Tarké, vol. 2. Paris, 1869. Words in French and German.
2. "Warum willst du and're fragen" transcribed for piano in Liszt, *Lieder von Robert und Clara Schumann* and *42 Lieder.*

Literature: Appel/Katalog, 177–79; Draheim/Höft, vol. 1, "Vorwort" and "Revisionsbericht"; Fricke, "Rückert, das Kunstlied und die Schumanns"; Hallmark, "Rückert Lieder"; Hohenemser, 124–25.

Commentary: The copy of Rückert's poems used by the Schumanns and presented by RS to CW in 1837 is in RSH, 7901-A4/C1.

Op. 13. SECHS LIEDER MIT BEGLEITUNG DES PIANOFORTE: 1. "Ich stand in dunklen Träumen"; 2. "Sie liebten sich beide"; 3. "Liebeszauber"; 4. "Der Mond kommt still gegangen"; 5. "Ich hab' in deinem Auge"; 6. "Die stille Lotosblume"

Dedicatee: Queen Caroline Amalie of Denmark (1796–1881).

Origin: Op. 13 was assembled from songs composed between 1840 and 1843.

Texts and dates of composition:

1. "Ich stand in dunklen Träumen." Heinrich Heine (1797–1856). No title; poem known by first lines: "Ich stand in dunklen Träumen/Und starrte ihr Bildniss an." Composed December 1840, Leipzig.
2. "Sie liebten sich beide." Heinrich Heine. No title; poem known by first line: "Sie liebten sich beide . . ." Composed June 1842. Presented to RS on June 8, 1842, together with "Liebeszauber."
3. "Liebeszauber." Emanuel Geibel (1815–84). No title; poem known by first line: "Die Liebe sass als Nachtigall." Composed June 1842. Presented to RS on June 8, 1842, together with "Sie liebten sich beide."
4. "Der Mond kommt still gegangen." Emanuel Geibel. Titled "Nachtlied." Composed July 1843.
5. "Ich hab' in deinem Auge." Friedrich Rückert (1788–1899). Composed June 1843, Leipzig. Presented to RS as a birthday gift together with "Lorelei" and "Oh weh des Scheidens."
6. "Die stille Lotosblume." Emanuel Geibel. No title; poem known by first line: "Die stille Wasserrose . . ." Composed July 1843.

Autographs:

1. "Ich stand in dunkeln Träumen."

a. RSH 5984-A1. Written on presentation paper and bound together with "Am Strande" and "Volkslied." Cover page inscribed: "Am Strande/von/R. Burns./Ihr Bildniss/von Heine. Volkslied/von/Heine./ componirt/und/in *tiefster Bescheidenheit*/ gewidmet/ihrem innigstgeliebten Robert/zu Weihnachten 1840/von seiner/Clara" (Composed and dedicated to her ardently beloved Robert with the *deepest modesty* from his Clara on Christmas 1840). See illustration of cover page in *Katalog*, 59.

b. SBPK, Mus. ms. autogr. K. Schumann 5 no. 2. (Titled "Ich stand in dunklen Träumen" by RS in Table of Contents.)

Autographs 1a and 1b vary considerably. See Draheim/Höft, 2:24–26, for a second version based on autograph 1a.

2. "Sie liebten sich beide."

a. RSH 7311-A1. "Sie liebten sich beide" and "Liebeszauber" are written on presentation paper and bound together with a cover page inscribed: "Wenig, mit Liebe/meinem guten Robert/zum 8ten Juni 1842/von seiner Clara" (A little thing with love to my good Robert on June 8, 1842).

b. SBPK, Mus. ms. autogr. K. Schumann 5, no. 9.

Autographs 2a and 2b vary considerably. See Draheim/Höft, 2:32–33, for a second version based on autograph 2a.

3. "Liebeszauber."

a. RSH 7311-A1 (see 2a, above).

b. SBPK, Mus. ms. autogr. K. Schumann 5, no. 8.

4. "Der Mond kommt still gegangen."
a. SBPK, Mus. ms. autogr. K. Schumann 5, no. 11. Working copy with many alterations and emendations. Verses 1 and 2 under staff; verse 3 written over staff but discarded in published version; verse 4 (published as "3") is written out after the double bar.
b. Universitätsbibliothek Leipzig, Rep. III, fol. 15. See facsimile in *Musikalischen Albumblätter der Luise Avé- Lallemant zu Leipzig* (Leipzig: Edition Leipzig, 1981).
5. "Ich hab' in deinem Auge."
a. RSH 5987-A1. Bound with green ribbon together with "Lorelei" and "Oh weh des Scheidens"; cover page inscribed: "An meinen lieben Mann/zum 8ten Juni 1843" (To my dear husband on June 8, 1843).
b. SBPK, Mus. ms. autogr. K. Schumann 5, no. 13.
6. "Die stille Lotosblume," SBPK, Mus. ms. autogr. K. Schumann 5, no. 10.

Selected performances:
1. "Ich stand in dunklen Träumen":
March 21, 1881, London (PS 1210).
March 22, 1884, London (PS 1249).
March 5, 1887, London (PS 1271).
2. "Sie liebten sich beide":
February 3, 1844, Königsberg (PS 208).
November 1, 1856, Karlsruhe (PS 417). See program in *Katalog*, 295.
October 21, 1862, Winterthur (PS 625).
October 23, 1862, Zurich (PS 626).
3. "Liebeszauber": January 8, 1843, Leipzig (PS 202).
4. "Der Mond kommt still gegangen":
January 24, 1860, Cassel (PS 531).
November 9, 1875, Cologne (PS 1104).

First edition: Leipzig: B&H, December 1843/January 1844. PN 6996.
See reproduction of title page in *Katalog*, 52. "Liebeszauber" appeared in *Album für Gesang*, ed. Rudolf Hirsch, 2:48–51 (Leipzig: Bösenberg, 1843), earlier than the B&H publication of op. 13 but with identical plate numbers.

Reviews:
AmZ, 46 (April 1844), 254–55: "[With this collection] the famous virtuosa presented to song lovers a most aimiable, welcome offering, a delightfully fragrant garland of flowers. Its colors do not dazzle or shimmer, but each of the flowers speaks with warm and gentle earnestness and we cherish them more the more closely and longer we gaze at them. . . . To sum up, the volume of songs that was examined here with genuine sympathy, albeit only fleetingly, is an interesting one in its own right, but it becomes doubly appealing because of the individual relationship to the presenting artist, so famous for her rare performance talent."
NZfM, 20 (March 25, 1844), 97: "Tender, gracious outpourings of a bounteous heart, quiet and unadorned, but conceived as warmly and sincerely as they are expressed: simply, clearly, unpretentiously. In addition, the songs have both a deliberately simple harmonic structure and melodies in keys that make them accessible to most voices."

Later editions, facsimiles, reprints: (1) RS and CS, *Lieder und Gesänge;* (2) "Die stille Lotosblume," in Stephenson, *Romantik in der Tonkunst;* (3) Draheim/Höft, 1:18–32.

Arrangements, transcriptions, translations: "Ich hab' in deinem Auge," transcribed for piano in Liszt, *Lieder von Robert und Clara Schumann* and *42 Lieder.*

Literature: Appel/Katalog, 177, 183; Chissell, 81–82; Draheim/Höft, 1:3–8; Hohenemser, 125–26; Rehberg, 666.

Op. 14. DEUXIÈME SCHERZO POUR LE PIANOFORTE (C minor)

Dedicatee: "Peppina" Josepha Tutein (1806–66), daughter of Giuseppi Siboni, the Italian singer and vocal pedagogue who founded the first music conservatory in Denmark. Mme Tutein, a good amateur pianist, was helpful to the composer on her trip to Copenhagen in March 1842.

Origin of work: After 1841, Leipzig.

Marriage diary, September–October 1841: "Clara has completed a small composition; it has a truly lovely character" (RS/Tgb 2:187).

Autograph: Not found.

First edition: Leipzig: B&H, 1845. PN 7214.

RS to B&H, January 9, 1845: "Keeping in mind your earlier invitation to submit works, she [Clara] is just copying out several shorter piano compositions, which she hopes to send to you as soon as possible. The compositions are a little Impromptu, a Scherzo [op. 14], and a volume of four short movements [op. 15]. A word from you as to whether these things could be published soon would, I believe, inspire her to a speedier completion" (RS/Jansen, 439–40).

B&H accepted the Scherzo [op. 14] and the volume of four short pieces [op. 15] but not the Impromptu. Soon after the acceptance, RS wrote to B&H: January 31, 1845: "With regard to the honorarium for my wife's two small works [Scherzo, op. 14, and *Pièces fugitives,* op. 15], she has given me these instructions: that you should decide on it with reference to the number of plates of her Scherzo [op. 10] that you have already published, and that she thanks you for your recent kind lines" (RS/Jansen, 441).

Selected performances:

November 16, 1846, Leipzig (PS 238).

December 15, 1846, Vienna (PS 240).

January 12, 1868, Brussels (PS 862).

March 30, 1878, Berlin (PS 1170).

At least ten programs list "Scherzo," with opus number unspecified. Because op. 14 was published and reviewed in 1845, it is probable that this was the Scherzo played from 1845 on.

Reviews:

AmZ, 47 (October 1, 1845), 676: "The composer preserves in all of her works that tender, poetic aura that raised her above the position of a virtuoso . . . and has earned her many friends. On the other hand, the old adage that in artistic endeavors of the female gender, replication is more apparent than individualism, also applies to her to some extent. Her appealing and tender sensitivity for the truly poetic in art prevents this artist from standing firmly on her own feet, as it by the same token raises her above the mere technician and music fabricator.

"We have noticed her adherence to models, indeed even to varying them somewhat, while talented men generally stick to a single model and are drawn into monotony and mannerism. Clara Schumann's writings nevertheless contain much of her own characteristic style. She is a long way from copying Chopin, Mendelssohn, or Robert Schumann. These masters are apparent only in the tone color that all of Clara Schumann's piano pieces preserve, at times throughout.—The Scherzo, C minor, 3/4 time, moves with a lively motif until it is transformed to 6/8 time by rhythmic displacement and adopts a songlike character, before returning to the first motif. The 'Alternativ' [Trio] in A-flat sounds somewhat empty; it would probably be better suited for wind instruments."

Wiener allgemeine Musik-Zeitung, 6 (December 17, 1846), 618.

Later editions, facsimiles, reprints: (1) CS/Piano Works ("Zweites Scherzo," 10–17, mistakenly lists composer as "Clara Wieck"); (2) CS/Goebels, 2:28–35.

Literature: Chissell, 96; De Vries, 172–73; Hohenemser, 168; Klassen/1990, 91–92.

Op. 15. QUATRE PIÈCES FUGITIVES for Piano: 1. Larghetto; 2. Un poco agitato; 3. Andante espressivo; 4. Scherzo

Dedicatee: Marie Wieck (1832–1916), half sister of CS; daughter of Friedrich Wieck and his second wife, Clementine, née Fechner.

Origin of work: 1841–44, Leipzig.

RS in marriage diary, February 1843: "Clara has written a group of smaller pieces [probably op. 14, op. 15, and Impromptu] that are more tenderly and musically conceived than any she has succeeded in doing before" (RS/Tgb 2:255).

Autograph: RSH 5986-A1. The Scherzo was originally intended to be one of the movements of the *Sonate für Klavier, g-moll* (Sonata in G Minor), composed in December 1841 but not published until 1991. In 1845 the Scherzo was published (with some slight changes) as the final movement of op. 15. See Instrumental Works without Opus Numbers, *Sonate für Klavier, g-moll*, for description of autograph.

First edition: Leipzig: B&H, 1845. PN 7215.

RS to B&H, January 9, 1845: see Op. 14 for text of letter.

CS to B&H, February 25, 1845: "I am returning the proofs [of op. 15]. . . . Because of the many errors, I want a complete revision. You too would certainly prefer to have the pieces appear as free from errors as possible" (Steegmann, 16).

Performances: Not known.

Reviews: *AmZ*, 47 (October 1, 1845), 676 (continuation of review of opp. 14 and 15): "Nr. 4, Scherzo, simple and innocent, is reminiscent of older periods of keyboard playing, of the smaller Beethoven sonatas."

Later editions, facsimiles, reprints: (1) CS/Piano Works, "Vier flüchtige Stücke," 18–27; (2) CS/Goebels, 2:38–48; (3) CS, *Quatre Pièces fugitives*, ed. J. Draheim.

Literature: De Vries, 172–73; Draheim, Preface to CS, *Quatre Pièces fugitives;* Hohenemser, 168; Nauhaus, "Preface" and "Textual Commentary" to CS, *Sonate für Klavier, g-moll;* Rehberg, 667.

Op. 16. DREI PRAELUDIEN UND FUGEN FÜR DAS PIANOFORTE: Praeludium I; Fuga I; Praeludium II; Fuga II; Praeludium III; Fuga III

Origin of work: February and March 1845, Dresden.

RS, February 2, 1845: "Diligently studying fugues with Clara" (RS/Tgb 3:379).

CS, January 23, 1845: "Today we began counterpoint studies, which I enjoyed greatly despite the effort, for I soon beheld what I had never believed possible, a fugue of my own making—and before long, several others, for we continued the studies regularly every day" (Litzmann 2:131).

Autographs: RSH 5982-A1. Autographs of preludes and fugues (Prelude II is missing) in a music notebook that also includes Three Fugues on Themes of Sebastian Bach (see below). Label pasted on cover in CS's hand: "Notiz-Buch." Below that, in RS's hand: "Praeludien u. Fugen/z. Th. gedruckt" (Preludes and fugues, printed in part). The op. 16 fugues are numbered 4, 5, and 6 and dated by CS. Fugue 1 is written on two staves; fugues 2 and 3 are written on four staves with four clefs (treble, alto, tenor, bass).

"Nr. 4. *Praeludium*" [Prelude I]. Für Pianoforte"; bottom: "Attacca Fuga" and "D. 28 Febr: 1845."

"*Fuga a 3 voci.*" [Fugue I]; top right: "(Thema von Robert Schumann.)"; "Clara Schumann/ D. 1*ten* März 1845."

"Nr. 5. *Fuga a 4 voci* [Fugue II]; top right: "(Thema v. Robert Schumann.)"; "Clara Schumann/D. 2*ten* März 1845."

"*Praeludium zur Fuga Nr. 6* [Prelude III]. Pianoforte"; bottom: "Attacca/Fuga Nr. 6."

"Nr. 6 *Fuga a 4 voci.* [Fugue III]; top right: "(Thema von Robert Schumann.)"; left: "Auch für die Orgel. Clara Schumann/D. 2*ten* März 1845."

RS to C. F. Peters, May 27, 1845: "Since this is probably the first time that a woman artist is attempting this beautiful but difficult genre, the work may well attract the interest of music lovers" (Hirsch and Roeser, *Erst- und Frühdrucke von Robert Schumann,* 46).

Peters evidently rejected the offer.

CS to B&H, July 1, 1845: "I have recently written a collection of fugues and intend to select for publication four [that were] written chiefly for public performance. I am taking the liberty of inquiring if you might be inclined to publish them? They would fill up about 15 or 16 plates and the volumes would, accordingly, not be too large. I would naturally like to see them printed by October, before our next trip, since I am considering playing some of them in my concerts. My most esteemed Herr Doctor, would you kindly let me have an answer about this soon" (Steegmann, 17).

When B&H accepted the fugues, RS wrote on August 17: "I would like to surprise my wife with the Preludes and Fugues for her birthday on September 13. Would it be possible to complete the volume for that occasion? If it is indeed possible, then I beg you not to send the last final proofs directly to me, but to send them to my father-in-law, so that my wife will not learn of them" (RS/Jansen, 444).

First edition: Leipzig: B&H, 1845. PN 7334.

Reviews:

AmZ, 48 (February 4, 1846), 74: "To encounter Clara Schumann in this domain [preludes and fugues] is indeed a surprise and one all the happier since the feminine mind is prone to abandon itself solely to lyrical expression, while such earnestness is the surest guarantee for the continued development of her considerable talent."

NZfM, 24 (April 2, 1846), 105: "Old Papa Counterpoint, hand in hand with a delightful woman artist, is once again entering the modern world, where he has not been seen for some time. . . . Whoever knows how to honor art that is serious and thoughtful while being distanced equally from pedantry and superficiality will bid him welcome."

Later editions, facsimiles, reprints: (1) CS/Piano Works, "Drei Praeludien und Fugen," 28–39; (2) Da Capo; (3) CS/Goebels, 1:3–15; (4) CS, *Preludes and Fugues,* ed. Barbara Harbach; (5) CS, *Preludes and Fugues,* ed. Sylvia Glickman.

Arrangements, transcriptions:

1. *Praeludium I and II.* Arranged and edited for English Horn und Organ by Jürgen Schwab. Kassel: Furore, 1986.
2. *Praeludium und Fuge d-Moll, Opus 16, Nr.* 3. Arranged for Organ by Joachim Dorfmüller. Kassel: Furore, 1988.

Literature: De Vries, 173–74; Goertzen, "Clara Schumann"; Hohenemser, 168–69; Klassen/1990, 58–67; Litzmann, 2:131; Rehberg, 667; Steegmann, 17, 30.

Commentary: RS to Gustav Keferstein, Dresden, October 26, 1845: "I am also enclosing the fugues of my Clara; I admit to being very fond of them; in the recent past they were preceded, as were my Pedalflügel pieces [opp. 56 and 58], by sustained and exacting studies. I hope that you will again detect in both volumes [CS, op. 16, and RS, opp. 56 and 58] progress in our artistic endeavor" (Oberlin College Library, Special Collections).

Op. 17. TRIO FÜR PIANOFORTE, VIOLINE UND VIOLONCELLO: 1. Allegro moderato; 2. Scherzo. Tempo di Menuetto; 3. Andante; 4. Allegretto

Origin of work: 1846, Dresden. CS worked on the Trio from May 1846 to September 1846.

CS to B&H, October 27, 1846: "You were kind enough to request my Trio for publication, but if it is to be published, I very much want it to happen soon so that I could play it in Vienna this winter. I am, therefore, enclosing it herewith, after having looked through it carefully one more time" (Steegmann, 39).

Autograph: RSH 12897-A1. A working draft differing in some details from the first edition, written on 37 pages bound into a hard-cover music notebook. The title: "Trio/für/Pianoforte, Violine und Violoncello./Cl. Schumann." is in RS's hand. Many corrections, cross-outs, paste-overs. Some annotations and dynamic and tempo markings in pencil are also in RS's hand; some may have been made after first rehearsal. See illustration in *Katalog,* 62.

First edition: Leipzig: B&H, 1847. PN 7562.

The cello part is shown in *Katalog,* 63.

CS to B&H, September 14, 1847: ". . . I received my Trio yesterday and was happy to see it finished at last; we played it right away with Schubert and Kummer last night as well as a Trio of my husband's that he just finished and gave to me as a birthday gift" (Steegmann, 51).

Selected performances:

October 2, 1846, rehearsal at home (Dresden).

January 15, 1847, Vienna (farewell matinee).

March 8, 1847, Berlin (matinee for friends) (PS 247a).

September 13, 1847, Dresden (rehearsal at home).

January 15, 1852, Düsseldorf (soirée).

March 8, 1860, Vienna (PS 547).

CS to Joachim, March 3, 1860: "My second concert is on the 8th—my Trio!!! what do you say to such courage? I am playing it in public for the first time and truly, only because of urgent persuasion from all sides" (JJ/*Briefe,* 2:76).

Reviews:

NBMz, 1 (March 10, 1847), 88.

Monatsschrift für Dramatik, Theater, Musik, March 1847, 47: "The concert closed with a Trio by Frau Clara Schumann, which received exceptional applause. The composition had something melancholy about it and had a few brighter moments only now and then, which were all the more effective since the entire work seems to be veiled."

NBMz, November 17, 1847, 384: "The work is clear, something rarely seen; it demonstrates a calm mastery of the formal artistic medium that we would not have expected of a woman composer."

AmZ, 50 (April 5, 1848), 232–33: "Women rarely attempt the more mature forms because such works assume a certain abstract strength that is overwhelmingly given to men. Clara Schumann, however, is truly one of the few women who has mastered this strength. . . . We would wish that we might meet her [as a composer] more frequently than has happened in the past."

NZfM, 28 (May 27, 1848), 253–54: "This trio deserves a place in the forefront of the new works in this genre."

Breslauer Zeitung, December 23, 1877: "The qualities that characterize this artist as a pianist also bestow considerable merit on her compositions. They reflect the same mixture of genuinely male earnestness and mental sharpness with feminine feeling and graciousness, which is typical of Frau Schumann."

Schlesische Zeitung, December 23, 1877: "Does not the Trio of Clara Schumann give us a lightly veiled picture of her husband as a youth? Except that all coarseness and energy of that striking head has been softened into feminine features. Schumann, as a 19-year-old composer, began very differently and with all the decisiveness of his sharply etched nature; but had that G-minor Trio turned up posthumously, half of us would have considered it to be one of his earliest works. Every creative mind has two sides, a male, giving one and a female, receiving one; the Trio points predominantly in the latter direction and hence to its true origin."

Later editions, facsimiles, reprints: (1) Munich-Gräfelfing: Walter Wollenweber, 1972, 1989. Reprint of 1st ed. 1989 printing: "Nach dem Erstdruck revidiert und neu herasugegeben"; (2) Winterthur: Amadeus, 1989. "Nach dem Erstdruck herasugegeben." PN: BP 2610.

Transcriptions: HHI/Dickinson: manuscript arrangement for two pianos, 2d piano part only. Signed Emilie [illegible]. May have been arranged by Emilie Heydenreich, née Steffens, a CS student.

Literature: Chissell, 96–97; Hohenemser, 169–71; Klassen/1990, 206–48; Rehberg, 667.

Commentary: In a letter of June 15, 1847, CS wrote to Emilie List that she was shocked by the news of the death of Fanny Hensel (sister of Felix Mendelssohn) and added that she had dedicated her Trio, which she was awaiting daily from the printer, to Fanny Hensel (Wendler, 148). The Trio was published without any dedication.

Clara Schumann's friends and colleagues were enthusiastic about the Trio. Brahms performed it in Hamburg on December 17, 1854, and Joachim wrote that it was a great favorite at the court of his employer, the king of Hannover. (JJ/*Briefe*, 2:79)

Op. 20. VARIATIONEN FÜR DAS PIANOFORTE ÜBER EIN THEMA VON ROBERT SCHUMANN

Dedicatee: Robert Schumann.

Origin of work: May–June 1853, Düsseldorf.

CS diary, May 29, 1853: "Today I began to compose again for the first time in several years; I want to work on variations on a theme from his *Bunte Blätter* for Robert's birthday; it is very hard for me, however—I have paused for too long" (Litzmann, 2:273).

CS diary, June 3, 1853: "It seems to me that I have not been unsuccessful" (Litzmann, 2:273–74).

Autographs:

1. RSH, 5989-A1. Fourteen pages bound with red ribbon; first page inscribed: "Meinem geliebten Manne/ zum 8ten Juni 1853/ dieser schwache Wieder-Versuch/ von seiner Alten Clara" (To my beloved husband on June 8, 1853; this renewed feeble attempt from his old Clara). The theme from Clara Wieck's op. 3 that is quoted beginning at measure 202 of the first edition is missing from this autograph. See Commentary below. The autograph is illustrated in *Katalog*, 209.
2. Wgm, VII 65.501. Ten pages bound with white ribbon and written on presentation paper; cover page inscribed: "Dem verehrten Johannes Brahms/auf freundliches Verlangen/von/ Clara Schumann./Düsseldorf July 1854" (To the esteemed Johannes Brahms at his kind request). The theme from Clara Wieck's op. 3 that is quoted beginning at measure 202 of the first edition is also missing in this autograph. See Commentary below.

First edition: Leipzig: B&H, Autumn 1854. PN 8944.

CS to B&H, 17 July 1854: "In the past few days, I wrote out a set of variations on a beautiful theme of my husband's (in the Mendelssohnian variation form). My husband was about to offer it to you for publication when he became ill. So now I am doing it myself, and inquire if you are perhaps inclined to do it? I am enclosing them for you to look over—I would of course have preferred to play them for you myself" (Steegmann, 123).

Selected performances:

December 9, 1853, Rotterdam (PS 314).
December 21, 1854, Leipzig (PS 342).
February 7, 1856, Vienna (PS 379).
June 17, 1856, London (PS 408).
April 5, 1886, London (PS 1264).

While rehearsing for the London concert of April 5, CS wrote in her diary (April 1, 1886) that she would be playing her Variations in public for the first time (Litzmann, 3:476). This was, of course, a case of forgetfulness.

Reviews: *NZfM*, 42 (January 1, 1855), 8.

Later editions, facsimiles, reprints: (1) CS/Piano Works, 40–51 (differs from 1st ed.; error in measure 6); (2) CS/Goebels, 1:16–25 (repeats error in measure 6); (3) Klassen/1987, 62–73.

Literature: Chissell, 116–18, 195; De Vries, 174–76; Hohenemser, 172; Klassen/1973; Klassen/1987, "Vorwort"; Klassen/1990, 67–71; Rehberg, 667–69.

Commentary: Johannes Brahms's op. 9, Variations on a Theme by Robert Schumann, composed June–August 1854 and dedicated to CS, is based on the same theme as CS's op. 20. The theme from Clara Wieck's op. 3 was woven into his 10th variation, which was added to the autograph in August. On September 12 Brahms wrote Joachim: "Clara *speaks* through one of them [var. 10]" (Brahms and

Joachim, *Briefwechsel,* 1:56). CS also added her version of her op. 3 theme to her manuscript (beginning measure 202) before it was sent to the printer. It is not known whose idea this was. Both works were published by B&H in November 1854 and CS sent both prints to RS in Endenich. See RS to Brahms, December 15, 1854, in Avins, 76.

Op. 21. DREI ROMANZEN FÜR PIANOFORTE: 1. Andante; 2. Allegretto; 3. Agitato

Dedicatee: Johannes Brahms. Op. 21 was presented to Brahms on his twenty-second birthday, May 7, 1855.

Origin of work: 1. April 2, 1855, Düsseldorf; 2. June 25, 1853, Düsseldorf; 3. end of June 1853, Düsseldorf. CS composed three Romanzen in June 1853 but decided in 1855 to substitute for the first the Romanze in the same key of A Minor composed on April 2, 1855, while Brahms was visiting RS in Endenich. Although the work was intended as a birthday gift for Brahms, she wrote in her diary: "The mood [of the Romanze] is really sad; I myself was so sad as I wrote it" (Litzmann, 2:370). The 1853 A Minor Romanze, not published until 1891, was given to Rosalie Leser. See Instrumental Works without Opus Numbers, Romanze in A Minor.

Autographs:

1. RSH 5990-A1. Op. 21, no. 1 only. Written on presentation paper; cover page inscribed: "Dem geliebten Manne am/8ten Juni 1855./Seine Clara" (To my beloved husband . . .).
2. SBPK/Mus. ms. autogr. K. Schumann 10. Op. 21, nos. 2 and 3, the Romanzen op. 22, and the A Minor Romanze for Rosalie Leser are bound into a notebook labeled, in CS's hand: "Compositionen/von/Clara Schumann." The two Romanzen of op. 21 are in a copyist's hand but dated by CS: Romanze 2: "Componirt/d. 25 Juni/1853"; Romanze 3: "Componirt Ende Juni 1853." Romanze 3 has a few emendations by CS.
3. Wgm, VII.64.288, Op. 21, no. 1 only. Written on presentation paper; cover page inscribed: "Meinem lieben Freunde Johannes/componirt/d. 2ten April 55/Clara Schumann" (To my dear friend Johannes . . .). P. 1 is illustrated in Draheim, *Brahms und seine Freunde,* after p. 130.

First edition: Leipzig: B&H, 1855. PN 9200.

CS TO B&H, 28 SEPTEMBER 1855: "I would have answered you long ago if I had not wanted to include at the same time the volume of songs you requested and also a few small works; these are 3 Romances for piano and violin [op. 22] and three of the same for piano alone [op. 21]. Should you be inclined to publish both these things as well, I would be most pleased, but only if you really wanted to. I am enclosing them for your inspection and ask for their return if you do not feel like publishing them" (Steegmann, 148).

CS TO B&H, NOV. 22, 1855: "I am returning everything to you today and request (if it is possible) another set of proofs for the two volumes of Romances since I had still found many errors" (Steegmann, 153).

Performances: None known. Brahms performed Op. 21, no. 1 in Cologne on May 29, 1856 (*CS/JB Briefe,* 1:189).

Reviews: Not found.

Later editions, facsimiles, reprints: (1) CS/Piano Works, 52–67; (2) CS/Goebels, 2:49–53 (no. 1), 1:26–32 (no. 2); (3)Draheim, *Brahms und seine Freunde,* 14–29;

(4) Klassen/1987, 74–89; (5) Marciano, 3–8 (though not labeled as such, this is op. 21, no. 1).

Literature: Chissell, 117; De Vries, 176; Draheim, "Biogaphische Notizen . . . ," in *Brahms und seine Freunde;* Hohenemser, 172; Klassen/1987, "Vorwort"; Klassen/1990, 105–8; Rehberg, 669.

Op. 22. DREI ROMANZEN FÜR PIANOFORTE UND VIOLINE: 1. Andante molto; 2. Allegretto; 3. Leidenschaftlich. Schnell

Dedicatee: Joseph Joachim (1831–1906). Joachim's performance of the Beethoven Violin Concerto at the Niederrheinische Musikfest in Düsseldorf in May 1853 initiated a lifelong professional and personal friendship between the two musicians. The Romanzen were written for Joachim soon after the festival.

Origin of work: July 1853, Düsseldorf.

Autographs:

1. SBPK, Mus. ms. autogr. K. Schumann 4. Score for violin and piano in CS's hand on presentation paper with elaborate gold borders. Cover page is inscribed: "Dem verehrten Musiker und Freund/Joseph Joachim/zu freundlichem Erinnern/von/Clara Schumann./Düsseldorf im October 1853" [To the esteemed musician and friend . . .]. Individual violin parts are in a copyist's hand. The page is illustrated in *Katalog*, 82.
2. SBPK, Mus. ms. autogr. K. Schumann 10. Opp. 21/1 and 2, the entire op. 22, and the A minor Romanze for Rosalie Leser are bound into a notebook labeled, in CS's hand: "Compositionen/von/ Clara Schumann." Each piece in op. 22 is dated by CS: Romanze 1: "Componirt d. 14 July 1853"; Romanze 2: "Componirt d. 18 July/1853"; Romanze 3: "Componirt d. 4 July 53."
3. HHI, 71.25, Romanze I only. Score for violin and piano on four sides of presentation paper with elaborate gold borders on each page. P. 1, tempo: "Langsam." Last page inscribed: "Herrn Joseph v. Wasielewsky/zu/freundschaftlicher Erinnerung/von/Clara Schumann/Düsseldorf/ im July 1853." Violin part not in CS's hand.

First edition: Leipzig: B&H, December 1855/January 1856. PN 9201.

CS to B&H, July 17, 1854: "I also have three Romances for Violin and Piano (not difficult) and 6 Songs [op. 23] ready for printing" (Steegmann, 123).

CS to B&H, October 7, 1855: "With regard to our business affairs, I am pleased to let you have the three things for the honorarium you offered me, and would like to ask you kindly for a speedy publication, particularly of the Violin Romances, which Joachim is fond of playing with me" (Steegmann, 150).

CS to B&H, November 22, 1855: "I am returning everything to you today but request, if possible, one more set of proofs of both volumes of Romances [opp. 21 and 22] since I have still found many mistakes—I could make these corrections myself when I am in Leipzig but if that should be too troublesome, I will ask only that the typesetter pay close attention to the errors" (Steegmann, 153).

Performances:

January 28, 1854, Hannover (private performance at court).
March 8, 1855, Danzig (PS 353).
November 20, 1855, Berlin (PS 370).
February 18, 1859, Vienna (PS 500).
June 14, 1865, London (PS 751).
April 7, 1869, London (PS 931).

Two Romanzen, arranged for cello and piano, were performed with Alfredo Piatti on April 7, 1869.

Reviews:

NBMz, 10 (July 9, 1856), 218: "The violin melodies are very simple in themselves but are treated most effectively and without any exaggeration because of the very interesting harmonies and support of the accompaniment as well as because of the countermelodies. When performed with thoroughgoing artistry—a prime requisite for all three numbers—these Romances should always be assured of the most auspicious success."

Later editions, facsimiles, reprints: Wiesbaden: B&H, 1983. Edition Breitkopf Nr. 8383. Reprint of 1st ed. with preface in German and English by Brigitte Höft.

Literature: Chissell, 118; Hohenemser, 172–73; Klassen/1990, 249–55. See also CS to B&H, September 28, 1855, under Op. 21 above.

Op. 23. SECHS LIEDER AUS JUCUNDE FÜR EINE SINGSTIMME MIT BEGLEITUNG DES PIANOFORTE: 1. "Was weinst du, Blümlein"; 2. "An einem lichten Morgen"; 3. "Geheimes Flüstern hier und dort"; 4. "Auf einem grünen Hügel"; 5. "Das ist ein Tag"; 6. "O Lust, o Lust"

Dedicatee: Livia Frege, neé Gerhardt (1818–91).

Text: Hermann Rollett (1819–1904), Austrian poet and writer. *Jucunde* (Leipzig: Otto Wigand, 1853) is a novel with lyrics interspersed throughout.

Origin of work: June 1853, Düsseldorf.

Autographs: SBPK Mus. ms. autogr. K. Schumann 5. On each song CS wrote: "Hermann Rollett. [or Rollet.]/(Jucunde)." and the date of composition.

1. "Was weinst du Blümlein?" no. 17 in SBPK: "Componirt d. 9 Juni/1853." P. 2 crossed out and replaced by p. 3.
2. "An einem lichten Morgen," no. 19 in SBPK: "Componirt d. 13 Juni/1853."
3. "Geheimes Flüstern hier und dort," no. 18 in SBPK: "Componirt d. 10 Juni/1853."
4. "Auf einem grünen Hügel," no. 20 in SBPK: "Componirt d. 16 Juni/1853."
5. "Das ist ein Tag, der klingen mag," no. 22 in SBPK: "Componirt d. 21 Juni/1853." Some modifications in last four measures of piano part; conforms to 1st ed.
6. "O Lust, o Lust," no. 21 in SBPK: "Componirt d. 19 Juni/1853."

First edition: Leipzig: B&H, 1856. PN 9202.

Performances:

October 13, 1853, Barmen: "O Lust, o Lust" (PS 306).
December 13, 1853, Amsterdam: "O Lust, o Lust" (PS 316).
November 28, 1868, Vienna: "Jucunde Lieder" (PS 899).
January 30, 1882, Stuttgart: "Das ist ein Tag" (PS 1221).
March 23, 1882, London: "O Lust, o Lust" (PS 1226).

Reviews: Not found.

Later editions, facsimiles, reprints: (1) RS and CS, *Lieder und Gesänge;* (2) Draheim/Höft, 1:33–47.

Arrangements, transcriptions: "Geheimes Flüstern hier und dort," transcribed for piano in Liszt, *Lieder von Robert und Clara Schumann* and *42 Lieder.*

Literature: Chissell, 117–18; Draheim/Höft, vol. 1, "Vorwort" and "Revisionsbericht"; Hohenemser, 166–67.

Vocal Works without Opus Numbers

DER ABENDSTERN for Voice and Piano

Text: Unknown.

Origin of work: Unknown, probably 1830–33.

Autograph: RSH 11-A1, written on one page of presentation paper with raised decorative border; manuscript pasted on larger sheet of paper. Top center: "Der Abendstern." First verse written under voice part; second and third verses written sideways in right margin.

First edition: Draheim/Höft, 2:18.

Literature: Draheim/Höft, vol. 2, "Vorwort" and "Revisionsbericht."

WALZER for Voice and Piano

Text: Johann Peter Lyser (1803–70), novelist, music journalist, and artist, friend of RS, contributor to *NZfM*, and member of the *Davidsbund*.

Origin of work: 1833, Leipzig.

Autograph: RSH 10935-A1, a fair copy, probably *Stichvorlage* (copy for engraver), only partly in CW's hand. Written on four sides of coarse paper. P. 1, top left and center: "Zu den Lieder eines wandernden Malers" (Lyser's hand); top right: "Composé par Clara Wieck" (CW's hand); below composer's name: "Gedichtet von/ J. Lyser" (Lyser's hand). bottom p. 4: crossed out but still legible: "Diese Handschrift erbit ich mir zurück wenn sie gedruckt ist sowie auch die/von Dorn. Es sind Originale./Lyser" (I request that this autograph, and also that by Dorn, be returned to me when it is printed. They are originals).

First edition: Leipzig: Gustav Schaarschmidt, 1833.
CW/Diary, December 3, 1833 (CW): "Lyser brought me his Liedersammlung in which the lied [lyric] that he wrote and I composed appears. It was printed by Schaarschmidt."

Reviews: *NZfM*, 1 (May 29, 1834), 68.

Performances: Not known.

Later editions, facsimiles, reprints: (1) Reprint of "Walzer" (described as "a lost composition by Clara Wieck") as supplement in Hirschberg, "Robert Schumann und der Davidbündler Fritz Friedrich"; (2) Draheim/Höft, 2:10–15.

Literature: Draheim/Höft, vol. 2, "Vorwort"; Hirschberg, "Robert Schumann und der Davidsbündler Fritz Friedrich."

AM STRANDE for Voice and Piano

Text: Robert Burns (1759–96), Scottish poet, "Musing on the Roaring Ocean," translated by Wilhelm Gerhard (1780–1858) as "Sehnsucht am Strande" in *Robert*

Burns Gedichte/deutsch von/W. Gerhard./Mit des Dichters Leben und erläuternden Bemerkungen./Leipzig: 1840./Joh. Ambr. Barth.

Origin of work: December 1840, Leipzig. One of three songs (the others were "Ich stand in dunklen Träumen," op. 13, no. 1, and "Volkslied") presented by CS to RS, Christmas 1840.

Marriage diary, October 1840, RS: "I gave Clara a poem by Burns to set but she doesn't trust herself to do it" (RS/Tgb 2:107).

Autographs:

1. RSH 5984-A1. See autograph and description for Op. 13, no. 1. "Am Strande" has some variants from 1st ed.
2. SBPK, Mus. ms. autogr. K. Schumann 5, no. 1, "Componirt/ Weihnachten 1840"; some variants from 1st ed.

First edition: "Am Strand" first appeared in a musical supplement to *NZfM*, July 1841.

Performances: March 31, 1841, Leipzig (PS 183).

CS to Emilie List, April 10, 1841: "The lieder [two by RS and 'Am Strande' by CS] were definitely very successful and [Sophie] Schloss had to repeat the last one because of the general enthusiasm" (Wendler, 100).

Reviews: *AmZ*, 43 (1841), 317–18, 330–34.

Later editions, facsimiles, reprints:

(1) *Aus den Muster-Beilagen der von Rob. Schumann s.Z. redigirten Zeitschrift für Musik* (Leipzig: Schuberth & Co. [ca. 1867]). PN 4268. Works in this collection were also issued individually by Schuberth in the 1870s; (2) Draheim/Höft, 2:17–23.

Literature: Draheim/Höft, vol. 2, "Vorwort" and "Revisionsbericht"; Whitton, "Robert Schumann, Robert Burns, und der Myrthen-Zyklus."

Commentary: Although the composer titled the song "Am Strande," it was printed in the *NZfM* supplement and later Schuberth editions as "Am Strand."

VOLKSLIED for Voice and Piano

Text: Heinrich Heine (1797–1856).

Origin of work: December 1840, Leipzig. One of three songs (the others were "Ich stand in dunklen Träumen," op. 13, no. 1, and "Am Strande") presented by CS to RS, Christmas 1840.

Autographs: (1) RSH 5984-A1 (see autographs for Op. 13, no. 1, and illustration in *Katalog*, 59); (2) SBPK, Mus. ms. autogr. K. Schumann 5, no. 3.: "Componirt zu/ Weihnachten 1840."

Performances: No public performances known. Brahms wrote to CS about a private performance of "Volkslied" sung by Livia Frege in January 1856 (*CS/JB Briefe*, 1:168).

First edition: Draheim/Höft, 2:27–29.

Later editions: Norderval, 11–12.

Literature: Draheim/Höft, vol. 2, "Vorwort"; Norderval, "Introduction."

Commentary: "Volkslied" is the only song set for voice and piano by both RS and

CS. The second song of RS's trilogy *Tragödie,* op. 64, no. 3b, it is known by its first line: "Es fiel ein Reif." RS's version, composed on October 27, 1841, was published in 1847. CS's version remained unpublished until 1992.

The poem first appeared in *Taschenbuch für Damen* (Stuttgart and Tübingen: J. G. Cotta, 1829) and was later included in Heine's *Neue Gedichte* (1844). In the final line of the 1829 version, Heine wrote "gestorben, verdorben" but reversed the two words in the later edition. Both CS and RS used the version that appeared first in the *Taschenbuch für Damen*.

DIE GUTE NACHT for Voice and Piano

Text: Friedrich Rückert (1788–1866).

Origin of work: 1841, Leipzig (see Op. 12).

Autographs: (1) RSH 5985-A1 (see Autographs, Op. 12); (2) SBPK, Mus. ms. autogr. K. Schumann 5, no. 6: "Componirt/d. 8 Juni 1841."

First edition: Draheim/Höft, 2:29–31.

Later editions: Norderval, 21–22.

Literature: Appel/Katalog, 177–79; Draheim/Höft, Vol. 1, "Vorwort" and "Revisionsbericht"; Fricke, "Rückert"; Hallmark, "Rückert Lieder"; Norderval, "Introduction."

Commentary: "Die gute Nacht" was set by RS for SATB in his *Vier Gesänge,* op. 59, no. 4 (1846). The poem appears twice in the *Abschriftenbuch*. See Kaldewey, 94.

LORELEI for Voice and Piano

Text: Heinrich Heine.

Origin of work: June 1843, Leipzig. Composed as a birthday gift for RS in June 1843 together with "Ich hab' in deinem Auge" (op. 13, no. 5) and "Oh weh des Scheidens."

Marriage diary, June 28, 1843: "Clara, as always, bestowed gifts upon me on my birthday, June 8" (RS/Tgb 2:266).

Autographs: RSH 5987-A1 (see Autographs, Op. 13 no. 5); SBPK, Mus. ms. autogr. K. Schumann 5, no. 12: "Componirt im/Juni 1843." (Spelled "Loreley" by RS in table of contents.)

First edition: Draheim/Höft, 2:34–39 ("Lorelei").

Later editions: Norderval, 13–18.

Literature: Appel/Katalog, 183; Draheim/Höft, vol. 2, "Vorwort"; Norderval, "Introduction."

OH WEH DES SCHEIDENS for Voice and Piano

Text: Friedrich Rückert.

Origin of work: June 1843, Leipzig. Composed as a birthday gift for RS in June 1843 together with "Lorelei" and "Ich hab' in deinem Auge" (op. 13, no. 5).

Marriage diary, June 28, 1843, RS: "Clara, as always, bestowed gifts upon me on my birthday, June 8" (RS/Tgb 2:266).

Autograph, "Volkslied," p. 1. Robert-Schumann-Haus, Zwickau.

Autographs: RSH 5987-A1 (see Autographs, Op. 13, no. 5); SBPK, Mus. ms. autogr. K. Schumann 5, no. 14. CS: "Componirt/im Juni 1843." Some cross-outs and variants from RSH copy.

First edition: Draheim/Höft, 2:40–41.

Later editions: Norderval, 19–20.

Literature: Draheim/Höft, vol. 2, "Vorwort"; Fricke, "Rückert," 59–63; Norderval, "Introduction."

MEIN STERN for Voice and Piano

Text: Friederike Serre (1800–1872). Friederike and Major Friedrich Anton Serre (1789–1863) had known CS since childhood and were admirers and supporters of both Schumanns.

Origin of work: June 1846. The Schumann family spent that month near the Serre estate, a center of artistic and cultural life in Maxen, near Dresden.

Autographs:

1. RSH 7261-A1. "Mein Stern" and "Bey'm Abschied" are bound together in a booklet of eight pages tied with yellow ribbon and are written on presentation paper. Cover page is inscribed: "Zwei Gedichte von Friederike Serre/für die Verfasserin/zu/freundlicher Erinnerung/componirt/von/Clara Schumann." Bottom: "Maxen/im/Monat Juni/1846." In 3/8. See illustration in *Katalog*, 46.
2. SBPK, Mus. ms. autogr. K. Schumann 5, no. 15. CS: "Componirt im/Monat Juni/1846." In 3/8.
3. HHI 53.78. Written on presentation paper with rose-colored decorative border. Inscribed at end: "Madam Decker/bittet um ein freundliches Erinnern./Clara Schumann/geb. Wieck." Bottom left: "Berlin d. 17. März 1847." In 6/8. Facsimile issued by HHI. (Pauline Decker, née Schätzel (1811–82), was a leading Berlin soprano.)

First edition: Draheim/Höft, 2:42–45 (with English translation of "O Thou My Star").

Later editions: Norderval, 25–26.

Literature: Draheim/Höft, vol. 2: "Vorwort" and "Revisionsbericht."

Commentary: An English translation of "Mein Stern" was published in London in 1848 (PN 6945). In 6/8. The German text is given under the English. Title page:

"O Thou My Star",/Mein Stern—Gedicht von Fred. Sarre [*sic*]./Lied./Composed and Presented to/THE GERMAN HOSPITAL,/at Dalston,/(On the occasion of the First Fancy Fair held in aid of the Funds of that Institution. May 1848.) BY/CLARA SCHUMANN./(NÈE WIECK.)/Ent. Sta. Hall. Copyright. Price 2–/Wessell & Co. Publishers of German Music TO HER MAJESTY./HRH THE DUCHESS OF KENT (BY SPECIAL APPT.) THE COURT & ARMY/220 Regent Street. Corner of Hanover Street. London.

Although the correspondence and other sources give no indication of the origin of the English translation, Draheim/Höft, 2:60, "Vorwort," have identified the translator's name, Leopold Wray, as a pseudonym for the author and composer Clara Chatelain, née Clara de Pontigny (1807–76).

BEIM ABSCHIED for Voice and Piano

Text: Friederike Serre. See "Mein Stern."

Origin of work: June 1846. See "Mein Stern."

Autographs: (1) RSH 7261-A1 (see "Mein Stern"); (2) SBPK, Mus. ms. autogr. K. Schumann 5, no. 16. CS: "Componirt/im Juni/1846."

First edition: Draheim/Höft, 2:46–47.

Later editions: Norderval, 23–24.

Literature: Draheim/Höft, vol. 2, "Vorwort" and "Revisionsbericht"; Norderval, "Introduction."

Commentary: Song is titled "Bey'm Abschied" in RSH; "Letzten Abschied," by composer, in SBPK; and "Zum Abschied" in the table of contents written by RS.

DAS VEILCHEN for Voice and Piano

Text: Johann Wolfgang von Goethe (1749–1832).

Origin of work: July 1853, Düsseldorf. As far as is known, this was the last song composed by CS.

Autograph: SBPK, Mus. ms. autogr. K. Schumann 5, no. 23. CS: "Componirt d. 7 July/1853."

First edition: Draheim/Höft, 2:48–50.

Later editions: Norderval, 27–29.

Literature: Draheim/Höft, vol. 2, "Vorwort"; Norderval, "Introduction."

Commentary: Litzmann (2:274) wrote that CS did not know Mozart's setting of "Das Veilchen" when she composed the piece in 1853 and that RS laughed at her ignorance but liked her setting. In view of the reports that she had heard Mozart's song in 1841 (RS/Tgb 2:145) and accompanied a performance of it on March 3, 1853 (Draheim/Höft, 2:8n49), either Litzmann or CS was in error.

DREI GEMISCHTE CHÖRE for Unaccompanied Voices (SATB): 1. Abendfeier in Venedig; 2. "Vorwärts"; 3. Gondoliera

Text: Emanuel Geibel (1815–84).

Origin of work: June 1848, Dresden. Composed for the Dresdner Chorgesangvereins, founded by RS in January 1848. CS, the accompanist for rehearsals and concerts, composed and secretly rehearsed these choruses to surprise RS on his birthday, June 8.

Autograph: RSH 10427-A1. Eight pages bound with pink ribbon. Emendations in ink and pencil; many cross-out and corrections, some by RS. On p. 7, sketch of a variant of the closing of "Vorwärts" in pencil and several measures of "Gondoliera" (RS?). See illustration of p. 5 in *Katalog*, 47.

First edition: Leipzig: B&H, 1989. Ed. Gerd Nauhaus. Partitur-Bibliothek 3521.

Performances: Private performances only.
June 8, 1848 Dresden (morning serenade for RS).
September 13, 1848 Dresden (surprise performance for CS's birthday).

Reviews: *Notes,* December 1993, 747–49; *Neue Musikzeitung* 39 (October–November 1990).

Literature: Nauhaus, "Vorwort" to CS, *Drei gemischte Chöre.*

Commentary: Notes concerning rehearsals and performances are in RS's notebook "Notizbuch, Chorgesang Verein Dresden und Musikverein Düsseldorf," RSH, 4871-VII C7, and in RS/Tgb 3 for June, July, and August 1848.

Piano Works without Opus Numbers

ETUDE (A FLAT MAJOR)

Origin of work: Ca. 1831–82, Leipzig.

Autograph: SBPK, Mus. ms. autogr. K. Schumann 3. Written on one page, marked "Etude" (not in CW's hand) at left top. Music written in a childish hand on paper with ten hand-ruled staves. One of three pieces in a folder marked "3 Klavierstücke," which includes two caprices from op. 2.

First edition: Unpublished. Recorded by Jozef De Beenhouwer in *Clara Schumann: Complete Works for Piano,* vol. 1. Partridge, 1129-2, 1990.

Commentary: Very little is known about the Etude. It was probably written soon after op. 1.

SONATE FÜR KLAVIER, G-MOLL: 1. Allegro; 2. Adagio; 3. Scherzo; 4. Rondo

Origin of work: December 1841 and January 1842 Leipzig. The Allegro and Scherzo were composed for Christmas 1841 as a gift for RS. The other two movements were written in January.

Marriage diary, December 1841, CS: "I tried to compose something for Robert and amazingly, it worked! I was delighted to be able to complete a first and second sonata movement, and I don't suppose that it failed in its purpose—namely to prepare a little surprise for my dear husband" (RS/Tgb 2:198–99).

RS to Marianne Bargiel, December 31, 1841: "Clara gave me two movements of a sonata for Christmas—very tender and written with much clearer structure than anything she has written up to now. I also like her songs very much" (Schumannhaus, Bonn, Nachlass Kaufmann).

January 15, 1842:"Clara's first sonata finished" (RS/Tgb 3:205).

January 15, 1842:"Clara's sonata finished" (RS/Tgb 2:199).

Autograph: RSH 5986-A1. Nineteen pages, including a cover page, which is inscribed in center: "Sonatine./Allegro und Scherzo."; bottom left: "Der letzte Satz, vielleicht auch noch/ein kleines Andante, soll,/denke ich, später nachfolgen./Einstweilen bitte ich für diese/zwei Sätze um Gnade" (The last movement, and possibly a small Andante as well, will probably follow later. Meanwhile, I ask your forbearance for these two movements). Bottom right: "Nimm es mit liebe auf, mein guter Mann, und schenke Nachsicht Deiner Clara./Zum Weihnachtsfest 1841" (Accept it with love, my good husband, and be lenient with your Clara. Christmas 1841).

The manuscript consists of all four movements. A detailed description is given in the Textual Commentary of the 1991 edition.

After the Adagio and Rondo movements were composed, in January 1842, the order of the movements was changed and the Scherzo designated the third movement.

First edition: Wiesbaden–Leipzig: B&H, 1991. Edition Breitkopf 7445. Preface and Textual Commentary in German and English.

Reviews: Not found.

Later editions, facsimiles, reprints: The Scherzo movement was published in 1845 as the final movement of op. 15/4. See Op. 15.

Literature: De Vries, 171–72; Nauhaus, "Vorwort" and "Revisionsbericht," in CS, *Sonate für Klavier, g-moll*.

Commentary: Litzmann (2:23) was apparently unaware that the two final movements had been composed and that the entire autograph, described above, was preserved.

IMPROMPTU (E Major)

Origin of work: Composed before 1844. The Impromptu was one of the "smaller" works about which RS wrote to B&H in January 1845. See Op. 14, above.

Autograph: Not found. May have been the Impromptu, SBPK Mus. ms. autogr. K. Schumann 6, reported "lost."

Reviews: Not found.

First edition: Paris: *Album du Gaulois,* 1885, 64–69.

Later editions, facsimiles, reprints: *Keyboard Classics,* September–October 1985, 20–24.

Literature: De Vries, 172–73; Reich, "Clara and Robert Schumann," 12.

THREE FUGUES ON THEMES OF SEBASTIAN BACH

Origin of work: February 1845, Dresden. The fugues on Bach themes were composed during the months when the Schumanns were studying counterpoint and fugue together. See Op. 16 and Prelude and Fugue in F-sharp Minor, below.

Autographs: RSH 5982-A1. The fugues are in the same notebook as the op. 16 preludes and fugues. See Op. 16, Autographs. The three fugues were dated, numbered, and marked by CS: "Fuga a 4 voci" and "Thema von Bach." Each fugue is written on four staves in four clefs. The subjects are from Book II of the *Well-Tempered Clavier:*
Fugue 1: "D. 11 Febr: 1845. Clara Schumann." Subject from E flat major fugue.
Fugue 2: "Clara Schumann/D. 17 Febr: 1845." Subject from E major fugue.
Fugue 3: "Clara Schumann/D. 22 Febr: 845." Subject from G minor fugue.

First edition: *WCMA*, 6:54–80.

Performances: Not known. (Recorded by Jozef De Beenhouwer in *Clara Schumann: Complete Works for Piano,* vol. 3. Partridge, 1131-2, 1991.)

Reviews: Not found.

Literature: Goertzen, "Clara Schumann."

PRAELUDIUM UND FUGA IN F# MOLL

Origin of work: 1845, Dresden. See Op. 16 and Three Fugues on Themes of Sebastian Bach. A version of this prelude in F Minor is also extant. See below.

Autograph: Sächsische Landes- und Universitätsbibliothek Dresden Mus. Sch. 267. On the first page of a small booklet of nine pages CS wrote: "Meinem lieben

Manne/zum 8ten Juni 1845." When the autograph was restored, probably after World War II, the sheets were sewn together with the pages in the incorrect order, so that it appeared that the manuscript broke off after measure 12 of the fugue. See Commentary below.

First edition: *WCMA*, 6:81-87.

Literature: Goertzen, "Clara Schumann."

Commentary: Although the F-sharp Minor Prelude and Fugue was a birthday gift to RS in 1845, no record of the gift was found in his household books or in his *Tagebücher*. For many years the fugue was presumed to be unfinished. Jozef De Beenhouwer, who examined the manuscript, found the piece to be complete when the pages were properly rearranged. He premiered the Prelude and Fugue in F-sharp Minor in 1998.

PRAELUDIUM IN F MOLL

Origin of work: 1845, Dresden. A version of the F# Minor Prelude (see above).

Autograph: SBPK, Mus. ms. autogr. K. Schumann 8. P. 1: "Präludium" (RS's hand); "Im lebhaften Tempo" (CS's hand?); top right: "Clara Schumann" (RS's hand).

First edition: Unpublished. Recorded by Jozef De Beenhouwer in *Clara Schumann: Complete Works for Piano*, vol. 1. Partridge 1129-2, 1991.

Literature: Goertzen, "Clara Schumann."

Commentary: See Goertzen's edition of the F# Minor Prelude in *WCMA* for additional information.

KONZERTSATZ FÜR KLAVIER UND ORCHESTER F MOLL (Concerto Movement [F Minor] for Piano and Orchestra)

Origin of work: May–June, 1847, Dresden. The work, presented to RS on his birthday, June 8, was not completed by CS.

Autograph: RSH 5988-A1. Eight pages bound with white silk ribbon, inscribed on cover page: "Meinem geliebten Robert/zum/8ten Juni 1847/von seiner/Clara."; p. 2: "Concerto"; over upper staff: "Tutti"; left of staff: "Pianoforte." "Solo" and "Tutti" are indicated throughout. Autograph breaks off on p. 7. A fair copy, no corrections, no cross-outs.

First edition: Wiesbaden: B&H, 1994. Studien partitur PB 5280.
Completed and orchestrated by Jozef De Beenhouwer.
The study score of the "Konzertsatz" is scored for piano solo, two flutes, two oboes, two B-flat clarinets, two bassoons, two horns in F, two trumpets in F, tympani, and strings. A "Vorwort" (translated into English, pp. 7–9) has been provided by Gerd Nauhaus for the edition. Photographs of the entire autograph appear on pp. 10–15.

Reviews: Not found.

Literature: Klassen/1990, 185–86; Nauhaus, "Vorwort" to CS, *Konzertsatz*, 3–6.

ROMANZE (A Minor)

Dedicatee: Rosalie Leser (1812?–96), Düsseldorf neighbor and close friend of CS.

Origin of work: June 1853, Düsseldorf. Written the same month as op. 21, nos. 2 and 3. Originally conceived as the first of the three Romanzen of op. 21. See Op. 21 above.

Autographs:

1. SBPK, Mus. ms. autogr. K. Schumann 7. Four pages, 69 measures; cover page inscribed: "Meiner theuren Rosalie/componirt/und zu liebreicher Pflege/empfohlen./Clara Schumann/Düsseldorf im July 1853" (Composed for my dearest Rosalie and commended to her loving care).
2. SBPK, Mus. ms. autogr. K. Schumann 10. Two pages (in copyist's hand with corrections by composer), 84 measures. Top left, first page inscribed: "Componirt d. 23 Juni 1853." Bound into a notebook labeled "Compositionen von Clara Schumann," which includes op. 21/2 and 3 and op. 22.

First edition: "Romance" in *The Girl's Own Paper,* 13 (October 17, 1891), 44–47. The version follows 2 above with some variants and many more markings for dynamics, tempo, pedal, articulation, and phrasing indicating extra care as composer readied the *Romanze* for publication. The first edition varies considerably from the autograph (SBPK, Mus. ms. autogr. K. Schumann 7) inscribed to Leser.

Later editions, facsimiles, reprints: (1) Klassen/1987, 90–92 (based on SBPK Mus. ms. autogr. K. Schumann 7 and 10); (2) *Keyboard Classics,* September–October 1989, 19–22 (reprint of first edition in *The Girl's Own Paper*).

Literature: Klassen/1987, "Vorwort"; Klassen/1990, 105–6; Reich, "Clara Schumann's *Romance*."

ROMANZE (B Minor)

Origin of work: Probably 1856.

Autograph: Wgm, VII 65.502. Eight pages, tied with pink ribbon, written on presentation paper with red geometric border; p. 1, top center: "Romanze"; top right: "Weihnachten 1856."; p. 7, bottom right: "Liebendes Gedenken!/Clara." (Loving memories). See illustration in *Katalog,* 122.

First edition: CS/Goebels, 2:54–57.

Later editions, facsimiles, reprints: Marciano, 9–13, titled "Romanze."

Literature: Klassen/1987, 105.

MARSCH (E-Flat Major) for Piano Four Hands

Dedicatees: Julius (1806–1882) and Pauline 1809–1895 Hübner.

Origin of work: 1879, Frankfurt.

CS diary, May 1879: "The Hübners in Dresden are celebrating their golden wedding anniversary. There were no good ideas about a gift for them and then it occurred to Marie that I could compose a march for them and weave Robert's "Grossvater und Grossmutter" duet into it. I went to work on it and after a few days, it succeeded." (Litzmann 3:400–401).

Autographs:

1. RSH 11712-A1. Ten pages including elaborately decorated cover page with inscription pasted on: "Den lieben Freunden—/Julius und Pauline Hübner/als/Festgruss/zum 21 Mai 1879/von Clara Schumann" (To my dear friends Julius and Pauline Hübner, as a festive greeting . . .). See reproduction of cover and p. 3 in *Katalog,* 322.
2. RSH 5994-A1. Music in copyist's hand with notations by composer. Cover page: "Marsch à 4 M. Clara Schumann" and note by CS: "nicht so zu drucken, soll noch anders werden. De. 1891" (Do not print this version. It is to be changed).

3. SBPK: Mus. ms. autogr. Klara Schumann 13. Music in copyist's hand with notations by composer. Eight pages and cover page in CS's hand: "Marsch à 4 mains"; bottom p. 1: "nicht so wie hier zu drücken, soll noch geändert werden. Dec. 1891."

First edition: Ed. Gerd Nauhaus. Wiesbaden: B&H, 1996. Edition Breitkopf 8161. Preface in German and English.

Literature: Nauhaus, "Vorwort" (translated in "Preface"), in CS, *Marsch*, 3–4.

Commentary: Several other manuscripts of the Marsch exist but have not been published. Two copies of an arrangement for two hands made by CS for her daughter Elise are in RSH: RSH 5993-A1 is in CS's hand; RSH 10824-A1 is in a copyist's hand with an inscription by CS: "An meine theure Elise!/Juni 1879/Clara Schumann." In 1888 an orchestration of the march by Julius Otto Grimm was performed at CS's sixtieth anniversary concert in Frankfurt on October 26. The orchestration, RSH 5995-A1, is a twelve-page score in a copyist's hand(?): "Marsch von Clara Schumann" for two flutes, two oboes, two clarinets, two bassoons, four horns, three trumpets, three trombones, three tympani, and strings, and signed at the end "Orch. J.O.G. 2 März 88."

PRAELUDIEN UND VORSPIELE for Piano

Origin of work: October, 1895, Frankfurt.

Autographs:

1. SBPK, Mus. ms. autogr. K. Schumann 9. The Berlin autographs, titled "Praeludien," consist of "Vorspiele" (Preludes), and "Einfache Praeludien für Schüler" (Simple Preludes for Students). The works are duplicated, with different numbering, in the Präludien und Vorspiele in RSH.
2. RSH 11514-A1. Copies, in CS's hand, of four of the introductory preludes in Berlin with slight variants. Four pages; top, p. 1: "Diese 4 Vorspiele befinden sich auch in der Kopistenhandschrft Nr. 7486.5" (These four Vorspiele can also be found in the copyist's hand No. 7486.5).
3. RSH 7486.5. Preludes and Preludes for Students, most in a copyist's hand, titled "Praeludien." Note in copyist's hand: "Die Vorspiele Nr. 1, 3, 4, 5, auf den Seiten 10ff befinden sich in Handschrift von Clara Schumann in Nr. 11514-A1" (Preludes 1, 3, 4, 5 are to be found in the hand of Clara Schumann on pp. 10ff. in no. 11514-A1).

First edition: *WCMA*, 6:88-104. The editor, Valerie Goertzen, selected eleven preludes for publication; four are preludes to RS's works: (1) third movement ("Quasi Variazioni. Andantino de Clara Wieck") of RS's Sonata in F minor, op. 14; (2) "Des Abends"; (3) "Aufschwung"; (4) "Schlummerlied."

Literature: Eugenie Schumann, *Erinnerungen*, 33–34; Goertzen, "By Way of Introduction"; Goertzen, "Clara Schumann"; Goertzen, "Setting the Stage."

Commentary: The published preludes were generally improvised by CS, privately and for concerts. They were used to frame short pieces, to join a series of pieces into a more substantial number, or to prepare the audience for the next work by weaving the themes into an improvisation.

CADENZAS FOR BEETHOVEN'S PIANO CONCERTO OP. 58

Origin of work: 1846. Composed for Gewandhaus concert on October 22, 1846.

Autograph: Not found.

First edition: Leipzig: Rieter-Biedermann, 1870. PN 636a and b.

Performances: October 22, 1846, Leipzig (PS 237).

Later editions, facsimiles, reprints: CS, *Fünf Kadenzen* (New York: C.F. Peters, 1952.)

Literature: De Vries, 168–69; Klassen/1990, 183–84; Litzmann, 2:140; Rehberg, 670.

CADENZA FOR BEETHOVEN'S PIANO CONCERTO OP. 37

Origin of work: 1868.

CS diary, November 3, 1868: "I played Beethoven's C minor Concerto for the first time (almost unbelievable) with real delight. I composed a cadenza for it and I believe it is not bad" (Litzmann, 3:225).

Autograph: Not found.

First edition: Leipzig: Rieter-Biedermann, 1870. PN 636a and b.

Performances: November 3, 1868, Bremen.

Later editions, facsimiles, reprints: CS, *Fünf Kadenzen* (New York: C. F. Peters, 1952).

Literature: De Vries, 168–69; Litzmann, 3:225; Rehberg, 670.

CADENZAS FOR MOZART'S PIANO CONCERTO IN D MINOR, K. 466

Origin of work: Not known. CS performed Mozart's D minor Concerto for the first time on January 1, 1857, at a Gewandhaus concert, playing cadenzas written by Brahms. (Litzmann, 3:17) See Commentary below.

Autograph: Washington, D.C., Library of Congress, ML96. W56 S4 (case).

First edition: Leipzig and Winterthur: Rieter-Biedermann, 1891. PN 1770.

Later editions, facsimiles, reprints: CS, *Fünf Kadenzen.* (New York: C.F. Peters, 1952.)

Performances: CS performed this concerto many times but dates of performances of her own cadenzas are not known.

Literature: De Vries, 168–69; Litzmann, 3:17 and 543; *CS/JB Briefe,* 2:461–63; Rehberg, 670.

Commentary: While correcting the proofs of her cadenzas in 1891 CS suddenly realized how much had been taken from Brahms's cadenzas for the same piece. Very disturbed, she wrote to Brahms on September 29, 1891, telling him she would place "J.B." and a note in the music to indicate she had used his work. He wrote back immediately: "I beg you very sincerely to let the cadenzas go into the world with your name. . . . Even the smallest J.B. would only look peculiar. . . . What's more, by rights I would then have to add to my loveliest melodies: actually by Cl. Sch.!

"For after all, if I think of myself, nothing clever, let alone beautiful, could occur to me! I owe more melodies to you than there are passages or suchlike that you could take from me" (Trans. Avins, 687).

CS, who owned a copy of Brahms's autograph of the Mozart cadenzas, left the following note on p. 1 of his manuscript (now in the Library of Congress): "Brahms's cadenza for the D minor Concerto by Mozart, which makes use of a cadenza by me. In the cadenza I published later, on the other hand, I used several passages from

Brahms's cadenza, which I have indicated by "A-b, C'D" in the enclosed copies. The passage from A-b in the second cadenza for the last movement is by Brahms. This comment is to my children, in order to avoid possible misunderstandings. Clara Schumann. 1891."

Published Editions, Arrangements, and Transcriptions

GENOVEVA: Piano-Vocal Score of Robert Schumann's op. 81

Origin of work: 1850–51, Düsseldorf.

Autograph: RSH 5983-A1 (partial autograph).

First edition: Leipzig: C. F. Peters, 1851. PN 3388.

Literature: Kurt Hofmann, *Erstdrucke der Werke von Robert Schumann,* 179.

Commentary: Full score was not published by C. F. Peters until 1880.

QUINTETT: Arrangement for Piano Four Hands of Robert Schumann's op. 44

Origin of work: Ca. 1857, Düsseldorf.

CS to Hermann Härtel, October 25, 1857: "I had mentioned to you once before that I wanted to simplify the arrangement of my husband's quintet. I have done so now and it cost me no little effort to do it without doing any harm to the composition. Happily, I believe that I have succeeded—I have played it myself with several people and nobody found it difficult. Would you like to have a look at it now or have some competent players play it for you, or would you rather wait until I myself come and then play it for you with somebody?" (Steegmann, 173)

First edition: Leipzig: B&H, 1858. PN 9643.

See facsimile of title page in Kurt Hofmann, *Erstdrucke der Werke von Robert Schumann*, Bildanhang.

CS to B&H, March 26, 1858: "Herewith is the score of the Quintet, which I am returning—only a few mistakes turned up" (Steegmann, 174).

Literature: Steegmann, 173–74; Hofmann, 103.

Commentary: Brahms had offered a four-hand arrangement of the Quintet to B&H in February 1855 but it was deemed too difficult and rejected. See letter from B&H in Avins, 88–89. CS may have been referring to Brahms's arrangement in her letter of October 25, 1857, to Dr. Härtel.

30 MÉLODIES DE ROBERT SCHUMANN TRANSCRITES POUR PIANO

Origin of work: 1873.

In May 1873, CS received an offer from Gustave Alexandre Flaxland, a French publisher, to transcribe some of RS's songs for piano. After some hesitation, she decided to accept the offer, fearing someone else might transcribe them and not do it as well.

CS diary, June 1873: "The work has affected me as none other before. Throughout the nights, I heard the song passages in the songs, especially those I had thought about and tried out the most, and to my despair, I couldn't escape them" (Litzmann 3:293).

Autograph: See Unpublished Transcriptions, p. 333.

First edition: Paris: Maison G. Flaxland, Durand, Schönewerk & Cie [1873?]. PN 1700.

Songs are titled in French, German, and English. Bromen, "Clara Schumann," gives 1875 for date of publication.

Later editions, facsimiles, reprints: RS, *Dreissig Lieder und Gesänge.*

Literature: Bromen, "Clara Schumann," 106–36; Litzmann, 3:291–2; *CS/JB Briefe*, 2:27–29.

Commentary: CS was uneasy about her transcriptions and consulted Brahms and Hermann Levi, among others, about them. Both encouraged her to go ahead with the work. Some transcriptions of RS's lieder remain unpublished.

FINGERÜBUNGEN UND STUDIEN AUS CZERNY

Origin of work: 1880, Frankfurt.

First edition: Hamburg: Cranz, 1880. PN 5455.

The introductory note (printed in English and German) by CS reads as follows (CS's italics): "I have been induced to edit the following finger exercises and studies from Czerny's Great Pianoforte School for the convenience of those students who do not wish to purchase the whole of that costly work; and have selected those parts that appear to me *most conducive to the development of technical proficiency*.

To save space most of the exercises are given on one stave only; the fingering for the right hand being placed above the notes, and that for the left below them.

It will naturally be understood that the left hand is to play the notes an octave lower.

Frankfurt, November 1880. CLARA SCHUMANN"

Commentary: Though the title page carried the name of Clara Schumann and she wrote the introductory note on p. 1, the edition was actually prepared by Marie Schumann, Clara's eldest daughter. Johannes Brahms also had a hand in the edition.

CS to Brahms, July 8, 1880: "On your advice, I have looked through the Czerny Schule (Pianoforte Schule, op. 500) carefully and find it outstanding. . . . Some time ago, Cranz came from Hamburg and told me that Peters had spoken with him about it, and that he would *very much* like to take over such an edition if he might put my name on it" (*CS/JB Briefe*, 2:214–15).

CS to Brahms, August 13, 1880: "From the very beginning, I told Marie that I could take only a small part in the work. . . . However, I don't want to undertake something of this kind without your advice since my name is supposed to be on it" (*CS/JB Briefe*, 2:220).

FOUR STUDIES FOR THE PEDAL PIANOFORTE, OP. 56, NOS. 2, 4, 5, AND 6, ARRANGED FOR PIANOFORTE SOLO

Origin of work: 1895, Frankfurt.

Robert Schumann's op. 56, *Studien für den Pedal-Flügel,* were written in April and May 1845 for the pedal piano, an instrument with a pedal keyboard like that of an organ. His six studies were published by Whistling in 1845. CS performed them in arrangements for piano beginning in 1846 but did not write them out until 1895.

CS diary, January 11, 1895: "Today I began to arrange some of Robert's *Pedal-Stücke* in the way I have always played them. I have often been asked for this and now it is Eugenie who urged me to do it" (Litzmann, 3:593).

Autograph: SBPK, Mus. ms. autogr. KS 20438 (Studien 4, 5, and 6 only)

First edition: London: Novello, Ewer & Co., 1896.

Performances:
May 3, 1846, Dresden (PS 234).
October 22, 1846, Leipzig (PS 237).
December 10, 1846, Vienna(PS 239).
October 19, 1854, Leipzig(PS 324).
January 7, 1856, Vienna (PS 376).
December 19, 1861, Leipzig (PS 597).
February 14, 1863, Paris (PS 647). Listed as "Deux Canons (études pour le Piano à pédales, op. 36 [*sic*])."

Literature: *CS/JB Briefe,* 2:588–609 (August 2 to December 19, 1895); Daverio, 306–8.

THREE SKETCHES FOR THE PEDAL PIANOFORTE, OP. 58, NOS. 1, 3, AND 4, ARRANGED FOR PIANOFORTE SOLO

Origin of work: January 1895, Frankfurt.
Robert Schumann's *Skizzen für den Pedal-Flügel,* op. 58, were composed in April and May 1845 and published in 1846 by Kistner. CS performed the *Sketches* in arrangements for piano beginning in 1863 but did not write them out until 1895.
CS diary, January 11, 1895: "Today I began to arrange some of Robert's *Pedal-Stücke* in the way I have always played them. I have often been asked for this and now it is Eugenie who urged me to do it" (Litzmann, 3:593).

Autograph: HHI/Dickinson. *Stichvorlage* (copy for engraver); eight pages in CS's hand.

First edition: London: Novello, Ewer & Co. 1896. PN 10143.
CS to Brahms, Interlaken, August 2, 1895: "First of all my belated thanks for your last letter, belated only because I wanted to enclose my Sketches which you had promised to look over. . . . You were kind enough to offer me your help, which gives me great peace of mind, for what matters most to me is that the Sketches (which every artist could actually arrange for him- or herself) can be played as easily and conveniently as possible. . . . Please, dear Johannes, tell me very frankly what you don't approve of. I will spare no pains, for I would feel terrible if they found fault with it. Eugenie has sold them to Novello, to whom I promised to send them by the end of this month. Here and there you may disagree with the somewhat chaotic markings, but I had primarily amateurs in mind to whom I wanted to make the voice-leading clear. Also, should I provide pedal markings throughout or only occasionally, where it is absolutely necessary? So then, please, please, your friendly advice! Should I use German or Italian markings?" (*CS/JB* Briefe, 2:588–89).
CS diary, August 13, 1895: "Johannes has returned the Skizzen arrangement and I am deeply moved to see how carefully he has gone through them" (Litzmann 3:598).

Performances: February or March 1863, Paris (PS 651). Listed in program as "Esquisse pour le Piano à pédales (op. 58)."

Literature: *CS/JB* Briefe, 2:588–609; Daverio, 306–8.

Commentary: The letters about the *Sketches* exchanged by CS and Brahms between August 2 and December 19, 1895, indicate how much she depended on his judgment at this point in her life and how responsive he was to her needs.

Unpublished Works

Arrangement of Andante Cantabile, op. 17/2, für Klavier zu Vier Händen von William Sterndale Bennett Bearbeitet für Klavier zu Zwei Händen

Origin of work: Ca. 1841, Leipzig. "Andante Cantabile," the second piece in *Three Diversions for the Pianoforte, à quatre mains,* was composed by William Sterndale Bennett (1816–75) in 1838 and published in 1839.

Autograph: HHI/Dickinson.

Performances:

October 25, 1841, Leipzig (at home of Ferdinand David).

CS, marriage diary: "I played several solos—*Diversions* by Bennett with which Robert was very satisfied, which made me quite happy—his praise was so rare" (RS/Tgb 2:189).

Leipzig, December 6, 1841 (PS 186). The program lists "Allegretto" from "Bennett's *Diversions*" but this may have been an error. No CS manuscript of the Allegretto movement from Bennett's op. 17 has been found. Williamson, *William Sterndale Bennett,* 79, cites a letter from Kistner, the music publisher, to Bennett: "Mrs. Clara will play one of your Diversions for 2 hands at concert of 6 December 1841."

February 28, 1842, Bremen. "Andantino" von Bennett (PS 192).

June 17, 1856, London. "Two Diversions, Op. 17" (PS 408). Perhaps performed as a gesture of thanks to Sterndale Bennett, who had invited her to England and was helpful, especially on this 1856 visit, her first, to that country. There is no information available about a second Diversion.

Literature: RS, *NZfM,* 6 (January 3, 1837), 2–3; RS, *Gesammelte Schriften,* 3:119–20 (review of *Diversions* on its first publication); Williamson, *William Sterndale Bennett,* 78–79.

Commentary: On his 1836 visit to Leipzig, where he remained from October to June 1837, William Sterndale Bennett met RS and his circle of friends, which included Clara Wieck. The three *Diversions* are titled, according to Williamson, I. "Allegretto semplice; II. Andante cantabile; III. Allegro agitato.

Menuettos i and ii from Serenade, No. 1 Op. 11, by Johannes Brahms Arranged for Piano

Origin of work: Not known.

Autograph: Brahms-Haus, Baden-Baden.

First edition: Not published. Recorded by Ira Maria Witoschynskyj, in *Clara Schumann and Her Family*. MDG Scene MDG 604 0729-2. Dabringhaus & Grimm.

Serenade No. 2, Op. 16, by Johannes Brahms, Arranged for Piano

Origin of work: Not known.

Autograph: RSH 5997-A1. Twenty-four numbered pages tied with brown thread. P. 1, top left: "Allegro moderato"; top center: "Serenade"; top right: "J. Brahms"/"Arrangement v. Clara Schumann."

Performances: Not known.

Commentary: Brahms sent the *Serenade,* which he composed in 1858–59, in sections to CS for comments (as he did almost all his works). CS was totally delighted with it. When he requested the return of the Adagio (which he had sent with several other movements for her birthday in 1859), she wrote that she could hardly bear to part with it:

CS to Brahms, September 18, 1859: "But what can I tell you about your Adagio? The proverb "When the heart is full, the mouth runs over" doesn't always hold true. It makes me feel powerless to find any words to express the joy this piece gives me" (*CS/JB Briefe,* 1:278).

Unpublished Transcriptions for Piano of Robert Schumann's Lieder

Origin of work: Probably 1873, while CS was working on *30 Mélodies.*

Autographs: RSH 5991-A1 and 5992-A1.

RSH 5991: Notebook titled "10 Lieder arrangirt f. Pianoforte." Six songs in copyist's hand with corrections and annotations by CS. All are marked "nicht gedruckt" (not published) except the last two: "Du bist wie eine Blume" and "Nichts schöneres," both published in *30 Mélodies*. Included in the notebook are "Lied der Braut" (RS op. 25); "Frühlingsfahrt" (RS op. 45); "Loreley" (RS op. 53); "Frühlingslust" (RS op. 125); "Du bist wie eine Blume" (RS op. 25); and "Nichts schöneres" (RS op. 36).

RSH 5992-A1: All in hand of copyist. All are marked "nicht gedruckt" except "Dem rothen Röslein gleicht mein Lieb" (RS op. 27), published in *30 Mélodies.* Included are "Dem rothen Röslein gleicht mein Lieb" (RS op. 27); "Mädchen Schwermut" (RS op. 142); "Lust der Sturmnacht" (RS op. 35); "Wanderlied" (RS op. 35); "Sehnsucht nach der Waldgegend" (RS op. 35); "Stille Thränen" (RS op. 35); "Die Soldatenbraut" (RS op. 64); and "Schöne Wiege meiner Leiden" (RS op. 24).

Commentary: Another piano transcription from 1895 is mentioned by Litzmann, 3:602. He described it as the duet "Am Bette meines kranken Kindes," but he may have been referring to a transcription of RS's op. 78/4, "Am Lager eines kranken Kindes," which has not been found.

Arrangements of Robert Schumann's Works to Which Clara Schumann Contributed

SCENEN AUS GÖTHE'S FAUST: Piano-Vocal Score of Robert Schumann's WoO 3

Origin of work: 1847–58.

RS diary, May 1, 1847: "Klara continually working on Faust, I am working on the Symphony [op. 61]" (RS/Tgb 3:347).

Commentary: According to the Household Book entry of May 1, 1847, CS worked on the piano-vocal score of portions of *Faust* at its inception. RS took over the work later, according to entries on October 31 and November 13, 1852, and May 24, 1853 (RS/Tgb 3:606, 607, 625).

SYMPHONY IN C MAJOR: Arrangement of Robert Schumann's op. 61 for Piano, Four Hands

Origin of work: March–April 1847. After several short trips at the beginning of 1847, CS noted in her diary: "As happy as I was to be with the children again, the sudden quiet after so many exciting days was difficult but I soon grew accustomed to it and began to arrange Robert's latest Symphony (C major, op. 61) for four hands" (Litzmann, 2:163).

RS, March 31, 1847: "Clara's arrangement of my symphony" (RS/Tgb 3:344).

RS took over when CS began to work on the piano arrangement of the *Scenes from Faust* (RS/Tgb 3: 467-68).

Commentary: The piano arrangement was published at the end of 1847 under Robert Schumann's name (RS/Tgb 3:739n454).

SYMPHONY IN B-FLAT MAJOR: Arrangement of Robert Schumann's Op. 38 for Piano, Four Hands

Origin of work: January 1842.

RS, Household Book, January 17, 1842: "Clara is arranging the symphony" (RS/Tgb 3:205).

And on the same day he wrote in the marriage diary: "Began the piano arrangement of the Symphony—horrible days and vexation with it" (RS/Tgb 2:199).

Commentary: The four-hand arrangement was completed on February 11, 1842, and published in June 1842 under Robert Schumann's name (RS/Tgb 2:520n507).

DAS PARADIES UND DIE PERI: Piano-Vocal Score of Robert Schumann's op. 50

Origin of work: Summer 1843, Leipzig.

CS, marriage diary, August 1, 1843: "I began working on the piano score of Peri at the end of July; it is a task that I greatly enjoy" (RS/Tgb 2:268–69).

RS, marriage diary, November 21, 1843: "Clara has prepared the piano score of Peri with great devotion and love and I have given her scant thanks for it. But I know how to appreciate her efforts and her love and was often so moved that I had to turn away when I saw her working so eagerly at the piano"(RS/Tgb 2:270).

RS to Dr. Härtel, December 1843: "Publication of the pianoforte score, the parts and the full score, for the sum of one hundred Louis d'or, for which sum you will receive the *complete* pianoforte score at once. It has been finished by my dear wife, who is most anxious to be of use to me."

CS, marriage diary, January 1844: "Robert still has much work to do on the *Peri*, which he wanted to deliver before our trip [to Russia]. In the piano score he still found much that could be improved and he did so with tireless diligence. He delivered it to Härtel the day before our departure—how I look forward seeing it in print!" (RS/Tgb 2:275–76).

Commentary: The piano score appeared in September 1844 under Robert Schumann's name (RS/Tgb 2:536n607).

PROBLEMATICAL WORKS

DER WANDERER: For Voice and Piano

Text: Justinus Kerner (1776–1862).

Origin of work: 1832(?), Leipzig.

Autograph: Not found.

First edition: Draheim/Höft, vol. 2, Appendix.

Literature: Draheim/Höft, vol. 2, "Vorwort"; Kaldewey, 89.

Commentary: "Der Wanderer" was published as an appendix to FW's *Musikalische Bauernsprüchen*. Draheim/Höft chose to include the song in their edition because of strong evidence that the work was by Clara rather than her father. The 12-year old-Clara mentioned the song in her diary, March 10, 1831: "I also sent along a song, "Der Wanderer," to Graf Baudissin." She is named as the composer of the song in the *Abschriftenbuch* with the annotation "[CS, lost.]"

DER WANDERER IN DER SÄGEMÜHLE: For Voice and Piano

Text: Justinus Kerner (1776–1862).

Origin of work: 1832(?), Leipzig. Written for the album of Heinrich Dorn (1804–92), with whom Clara studied theory beginning June 20, 1832.

Autograph: RSH 4407-A1. Eleven measures, "Leipzig dem 28ten Juli, 1832"; lower right: "Ihre dankbare Schülerin./Clara Wieck" (Your grateful student). Verso: "Komposition stammt von F. Wieck" (Composition by F. Wieck). See illustration in *Katalog*, 328.

First edition: Draheim/Höft, vol. 2, Appendix.

Literature: Draheim/Höft, vol. 2, "Vorwort"; *Katalog*, 328; Kaldewey, 90.

Commentary: "Der Wanderer in der Sägemühle" was published as an appendix to FW's *Musikalische Bauernsprüchen.* The editors of Draheim/Höft chose to include the song in their edition because of the evidence of the autograph.

Lost or Missing Works Cited in Diaries, Programs, Correspondence

Vocal

"Schwäne kommen gezogen." Four-part song written for composition lessons (CW/Diary, September 12, 1830). Other two- and four-part chorales written for lessons are mentioned in CW/Diary, October 1830.

"Der Traum" (1831). Text by Christoph August Tiedge. Performed in Frankfurt, according to a letter by FW, January 27, 1832 (Wieck/*Briefe*, 40).

"Alte Heimath," with text by Justinus Kerner, and other songs described simply as "Lied" or "Lieder," are cited in CW/Diary and in Wieck/*Briefe*.

Instrumental

Waltz, composed as a Christmas gift for Clara's old nursemaid, Hanne Strobel (CW/Diary, December 31, 1828).

"Three Waltzes for Violin, Glockenspiel, and Piano"

CW/Diary, December 26, 1829: "We had guests, for whom I played my own Variations and with Alwin (violin) and Gustav (glockenspiel) performed my 3 Waltzes for the three of us."

"Variationen über ein Originalthema" (1830)

Performances:

At Wieck home musicale (CW/Diary, January 30, 1830; "Solo-Variations").

November 8, 1830, Leipzig (Gewandhaus) (PS 2).

"Variationen über ein Tyrolerlied" (1830[?]). Cited in CW/Diary, February 15, 1830, and repertoire list for 1830 (Litzmann, 3:616).

"Phantasie-Variation über ein Wieck Romanze" (1831)
Performances:
January 27, 1831, Leipzig (PS 5).
October 26, 1831, Leipzig (PS 9).
December 13, 1831 (PS 13).
January 13, 1832 (PS 15).

Commentary: This work was titled variously "Variationen" and "Variationen und Finale über ein Romanze." The "Wieck Romanze" was probably Friedrich Wieck's composition for physharmonica featured on several of Clara Wieck's programs between 1830 and 1832.

"An Alexis" (1832–33).
Commentary: FW wrote (January 27, 1832) that Clara was composing variations on her own "An Alexis" for performance in Paris (Wieck/*Briefe*, 41). "An Alexis," the piano solo, was not completed until July 1833 (CW/Diary, July 1833).

Other "Variations" by Clara Wieck are noted in CW/Diary. One was played for Goethe on October 9, 1831.

"Rondo in H Moll" (1833)
CW/Diary, June 6, 1833: "My Rondo on the Theme by Reissiger (B minor) is finished."

"Capriccio" (1834[?])
Performances:
January 31, 1835, Hannover ("Capricio") (PS 63).
CW/Diary, Jan. 31 (FW): "Concert in the large Haustein Hall with an overflowing audience of 450 listeners. . . . The Duke was very excited and Clara received much applause."
March 20, 1835, Hamburg (PS 70).

Commentary: An *Albumblatt* titled "Capricio" in the Hannover Stadtarchiv, no. 4786, is a four-measure fragment in C minor inscribed "Wer sein Leben höher achtet als seiner Kunst, wird nimmermehr ein Künstler" (Whoever holds his life higher than his art will never be an artist"). Dated February 1, 1835, and signed "Clara Wieck."

"Duo für zwei Pianofortes über ein Thema aus dem Maskenball" by Clara Wieck and Antoine Gerke
Performances: September 16, 1837, Leipzig (PS 116).

Commentary: CW/Diary entries of September 11–17, 1837, cite Antoine Gerke's visit to Leipzig and their work together. In June 1839 she described the Duo to RS as "mechanical" and said she was ashamed of it (*Briefwechsel,* 2:597). Wieck described the Duo, composed in two days, as "one-eighth Czerny, one-eighth Kalkbrenner, one-eighth Herz, one-eighth *nothing,* one-eighth Gerke, and one-eighth Clara" (CW/Diary, September 16, 1837).

Works for Orchestra

"Scherzo für Orchester" (1830–31)
Performances:
May 18, 1831, Altenburg (PS 7).
November 18, 1832, Zwickau (PS 26).

November 24, 1832, Schneeburg (PS 27).
March 11, 1833, Dresden (PS 30).
August 13, 1833, Chemnitz (PS 34).

Other works are mentioned in Clara Wieck's diary between 1828–38 but because they are cited in such general terms as "a waltz," "a scherzo," "lieder," and "variations," it has not been possible to identify them. A number of *Albumblätter* of lost works from these years are also extant.

Notes

Chapter 1. *Prelude: The Wiecks of Leipzig*

1. Clara Schumann always treasured the autograph of the poem (RSH 5973-A3). The German text can be found in Litzmann, 1:170–71. A creditable translation is in Litzmann, *Clara Schumann: An Artist's Life, Based on Material Found in Diaries and Letters,* trans. Grace E. Hadow, 2 vols. (London: Macmillan, 1913), 1:136.

2. *AmZ,* 40 (1838), 164–65.

3. CW/Diary, December 26, 1837.

4. Eduard Hanslick, *Geschichte des Concertwesens in Wien* (Vienna: Wilhelm Braumüller, 1869), 332.

5. CW/Diary, March 8 and 21, 1838.

6. For information on Wieck I have relied on three biographies: Anna von Meichsner, *Friedrich Wieck und seine beiden Töchter, Clara Schumann, geb. Wieck, und Marie Wieck* (Leipzig: Heinrich Matthes, 1875); Adolph Kohut, *Friedrich Wieck: Ein Lebens- und Künstlerbild* (Dresden: Pierson's, 1888); Victor Joss, *Der Musikpädagoge Friedrich Wieck und seine Familie* (Dresden: Oscar Damm, 1902). The Schumann family papers (RSH 2174-A3 and A3b) and Cathleen Köckritz's articles, especially "Ausgewählte Aspekte der Klavierausbildung Friedrich Wiecks," in *Schumann Studien,* ed. Gerd Nauhaus (Sinzig: Studio, 1997), 6:41–54, have also been consulted.

7. See Hans Eberhardt, *Die ersten deutschen Musikfeste in Frankenhausen am Kyffhäuser und Erfurt, 1810, 1811, 1812, und 1815* (Jena: Frommann, 1934).

8. Meichsner, 15–21. Weber's letter is dated August 13, 1815.

9. *AmZ,* 17 (1815), 673.

10. Joss, 7.

11. Carl Ramshorn, *Leipzig und seine Umgebungen* (Braunschweig: George Westermann, 1841), 146.

12. Hajo Holborn, *A History of Modern Germany, 1648–1840* (New York: Knopf, 1964), 309.

13. Description in CW/Diary, June 24, 1840.

14. Excerpts from a letter Wieck wrote after meeting Beethoven in 1826 were published in Dresden in 1873 and have been translated in Oscar Sonneck, ed., *Beethoven: Impressions of Contemporaries* (New York: G. Schirmer, 1926), 207–9.

15. See Fritz Demmler, *Johann George Tromlitz (1725–1805): Ein Beitrag zur Entwicklung der Flöte und des Flötenspiels* (Buren: F. Knuf, 1985).
16. *AmZ*, 19 (1817), 158, 355, 357.
17. Meichsner, 14.
18. *AmZ*, 26 (1824), 489.
19. Rudolf Huebner, *A History of Germanic Private Law*, trans. Francis S. Philbrick (Boston: Little, Brown, 1918), 664. Further to confound the modern reader, the diary entry on the fourth page, written by Wieck as if Clara herself were writing, states: "Das Recht mich vom 5ten Jahre an zu besitzen stand ihm zu" (He had the legal right to take possession of me beginning in my fifth year).
20. Joss, 13–15.
21. Wieck correspondence, RSH 5967-A2; also Litzmann, 1:4n.
22. CW/Diary, December 1, 1825, and May 1, 1826 (FW).
23. Ibid., June 1827 (FW). See also Meichsner, 34.
24. See Friedrich Wieck, *Clavier und Gesang* (Leipzig: F. Whistling, 1853), iv, in which he refers to his "caustic brevity and bluntness."
25. RS/Tgb 1:364.
26. CW/Diary, November 12, 1839.
27. Ibid., June 1827 (FW).
28. Ibid., July 3, 1828 (FW).
29. Many of the letters have been published in Wieck/*Briefe*.

Chapter 2. *Clara's Career Begins*

1. Litzmann, 3:194.
2. Wieck/*Briefe*, 34.
3. Wieck, *Clavier und Gesang*, 60.
4. Ibid., 23.
5. CW/Diary, November 16, 1828 (FW).
6. Quoted in Meichsner, 69.
7. *Quellenwerk*, 1:100.
8. *AmZ*, 30 (1828), 805–6.
9. Wieck/*Briefe*, 24.
10. Ibid., 27.
11. *AmZ*, 32 (1830), 752–53.
12. CW/Diary, October 11, 1831 (FW).
13. *AmZ*, 34 (1832), 196–97.
14. Eugenie Schumann, *Robert Schumann: Ein Lebensbild meines Vaters* (Leipzig: Koehler & Amelang, 1931), 225.
15. *Caecilia*, 1 (1833), 253–58. In the diary, January 26, 1833, Wieck wrote, "There is a singular article about me and my special qualities in Lyser's *Caecilia* which was taken, most likely, from a letter by Heine in Paris."
16. Litzmann, 1:44.
17. Wieck/*Briefe*, 44.
18. Ibid., 45–46.
19. See "Musical Life in Paris, 1817–1848: A Chapter from the Memoirs of Sophie Augustine Leo," trans. Oliver Strunk, *MQ*, 17 (1931), 259–71, 389–403.
20. CW/Diary, August 10, 1832 (FW).
21. Eda Sagarra, *A Social History of Germany* (New York: Holmes & Meier, 1977), 406.
22. *Briefwechsel*, 2:575.
23. The insulting and unreasonable demands continued to throw a shadow on the

marriage. References to Major Serre and his efforts to mediate between Wieck and the Schumanns can be found in RS/Tgb 2:132, 147, 150, 160, 170, 177–78, 154.

24. CW/Diary, October 29, 1828 (FW).

25. RS/Tgb 1:364. Schumann wrote: "Bin ich unter Menschen?"

26. Ibid., 362, 402.

27. Wieck/*Briefe*, 51.

28. Ibid., 48–49.

29. CW/Diary, December 12, 1834 (CW).

Chapter 3. *Robert Schumann and the Wiecks*

1. RS/Tgb 1:382.

2. *Jugendbriefe*, 117.

3. Wilhelm Joseph von Wasielewski, *Robert Schumann: Eine Biographie*, 3d ed. (Leipzig: Breitkopf & Härtel, 1880), 60–61.

4. Litzmann, 1:21–24.

5. Eugenie Schumann, *Robert Schumann*, 223–24.

6. *Quellenwerk*, 1:44.

7. RS/Tgb 1:334.

8. *Jugendbriefe*, 138.

9. RS/Tgb 1:371, 364, 389.

10. *Quellenwerk*, 1:66.

11. *Jugendbriefe*, 161–62, 181.

12. *Briefwechsel*, 1:64.

13. *Jugendbriefe*, 134.

14. See Peter Ostwald, "Florestan, Eusebius, Clara, and Schumann's Right Hand," *Nineteenth-Century Music*, 4 (Summer 1980), 17–31; and for another opinion, see Daverio, 77–79.

15. *Jugendbriefe*, 149, 151.

16. RS/Tgb 1:358, 371; *Quellenwerk*, 1:75–76.

17. RS/Tgb 1:398.

18. *Briefwechsel*, 1:307.

19. RS/Tgb 1:419.

20. Ibid.

21. See Leon B. Plantinga, *Schumann as Critic* (New Haven: Yale University Press, 1967).

22. *Jugendbriefe*, 243.

23. *Briefwechsel*, 1:12.

24. RS/Tgb 1:420.

25. *Briefwechsel*, 1:111.

26. Niecks, 144.

27. Eugenie Schumann, *Robert Schumann*, 227. The book she was referring to was Philipp Spitta, *Ein Lebensbild Robert Schumanns* (Leipzig: Breitkopf & Härtel, 1882).

28. *Briefwechsel*, 1:9–10.

29. Ibid., 1:4–5.

30. Wendler, 57–59.

31. RS/Tgb 1:421.

32. Litzmann, 1:92.

33. *Briefwechsel*, 1:148.

34. CW/Diary, February 14–April 1836 (FW). See also Litzmann, 1:99.

35. Leopold Hirschberg, "Robert Schumann und der Davidsbündler Fritz Friedrich:

Mit einer Auswahl bisher unveröffentlicher Briefe J. P. Lysers an Schumann," *Velhagen & Klasings Monatshefte*, 24 (1909–10), 90.

36. Wasielewski, 342, 349.
37. CW/Diary, February 8, 1837 (FW).
38. Ibid., March 22, 1837 (FW).
39. All quotations on pp. 50–52 are from Wieck/*Briefe*, 58–69.
40. Wasielewski, 348–49.
41. *Briefwechsel*, 1:67–68.
42. RS/Tgb 1:422.
43. *Briefwechsel*, 1:21.
44. RS/Tgb 1:422.
45. Litzmann, 1:123–26.
46. Boetticher/1942, 28–29.
47. *Briefwechsel*, 1:24.
48. Ibid., 26.

Chapter 4. *The Break with Wieck*

1. CW/Diary, October 9, 1831 (FW).
2. This and subsequent references to the Viennese tour are from Wieck/*Briefe*, 75–97.
3. *Briefwechsel*, 1:88.
4. The autograph of "Erlkönig" that she received is now in the Pierpont Morgan Library, New York. See Franz Schubert, *Erlkönig: Facsimile of the Autograph Manuscript*, with introduction by Rigbie Turner (New York: Pierpont Morgan Library, 1978). According to CW/Diary, December 22, 1837 (FW), Antonio Diabelli published Schubert's Duo in C Major for Four Hands (D. 812, old op. 140), the so-called Grand Duo, dedicated it to Clara Wieck, and presented her with the autograph.
5. *Briefwechsel*, 1:164 (May 2, 1838). She informed Robert of the honor as soon as she heard and added that it meant little to her at that point; all that mattered was her longing for him.
6. Ibid., 58–59.
7. Ibid., 37, 61.
8. Ibid., 46. The remainder of this line was crossed out and is illegible.
9. Ibid., 48.
10. Ibid., 108, 110.
11. Ibid., 118, 121.
12. Ibid., 135.
13. Ibid., 177.
14. Ibid., 179.
15. Ibid., 140, 168.
16. Ibid., 181.
17. Ibid., 181–82.
18. Ibid., 183.
19. Ibid., 191.
20. Ibid., 197.
21. Ibid., 215, 223.
22. Ibid., 184.
23. Ibid., 195–96.
24. Litzmann, 1:230–31.
25. *Briefwechsel*, 1:234–35.

26. See "Nachwort," in Robert Schumann, *Humoreske,* ed. Hans Joachim Köhler (Leipzig: Peters, 1981), 41.
27. Litzmann, 1:233n.
28. *Briefwechsel,* 1:250.
29. Ibid., 272.
30. Ibid., 301.
31. Ibid., 230.
32. CW/Diary, January 8, 1839 (CW).
33. *Briefwechsel,* 2:425. Berlioz took another view of the opera. In a letter to Liszt dated January 22, 1839, he wrote, "The revival of *Benvenuto* was a great success" (*Hector Berlioz: A Selection from His Letters*, ed. and trans. Humphrey Searle [New York: Vienna House, 1973], 75).
34. *Briefwechsel,* 2:484, 501.
35. Ibid., 388.
36. For a full account of Clara Wieck's stay in Paris, her concerts and press reception, see Désirée Wittkowski, "'In Paris hast Du doppelte Mühe in Allem . . .': Clara Wieck–Schumanns Parisreisen," in *Katalog,* 137–56.
37. *Briefwechsel,* 2:387.
38. Ibid., 446–47.
39. Ibid., 443.
40. Ibid., 510.
41. Ibid., 571.
42. Ibid., 499–500.
43. Ibid., 512.
44. Wendler, 62–72 (three previously unpublished letters from Emilie List to Robert Schumann); see also Litzmann, 1:322–26.
45. *Briefwechsel,* 2:519–20.
46. Ibid., 524–25.
47. Ibid., 565. She quoted her letter to Wieck in her June 11 letter to Robert.
48. Litzmann, 1:342.
49. Ibid.
50. RS/Tgb 3:72.
51. CW/Diary, October 18, 1839 (CW). She asked for Clara's help in getting a position as a companion.
52. *Briefwechsel,* 2:650.
53. Ibid., 657.
54. Ibid., 747.
55. RS/Tgb 3:116, 700n129.
56. CW/Diary, October 13, November 11, 12, 1839; April 2, 1840 (CW).
57. Ibid., November 12, 1839 (CW).
58. Litzmann, 1:413; CW/Diary, March 11, 1840 (CW).
59. CW/Diary, September 26, 1839, and May 11, 1840 (CW).
60. Litzmann, 1:399.
61. Ibid., 395.
62. Ibid., 408, 410–11.
63. *Briefwechsel,* 1:304.
64. See, for example, his letter of August 29, 1840, in Boetticher/1942, 344.
65. CW/Diary, September 12, 1840 (CW).

Chapter 5. *The Marriage*

1. RS/Tgb 2:100 (September 13, 1840).
2. Ibid., 160, and 3:700n129. Wieck was actually sentenced to eighteen days in jail, but there is no record of the sentence being carried out.
3. RS/Tgb 3:175.
4. Siegfried Kross, ed., *Briefe und Notizen Robert und Clara Schumanns* (Bonn: Bouvier, 1978), 59.
5. In the CW/Diary, November 12, 1839, Clara wrote that he had already resettled in Dresden. See also Marie Wieck, *Aus dem Kreise Wieck-Schumann,* 2d enl. ed. (Dresden: Zahn & Jaensch, 1914), 231–34, 244.
6. Although Litzmann, 2:9, refers to this letter, Nauhaus (RS/Tgb 3:193 and 713n263) reports that it has disappeared.
7. See Schumann's letter to Clara of April 22, 1842, p. 92.
8. RS/Tgb 2:177–78, 164.
9. Wendler, 98–100.
10. Joss, 79–80. See also RS/Tgb 3:725n351.
11. Litzmann, 2:10–11.
12. RS/Tgb 3:254.
13. RS/Tgb 2:258 (February 14, 1843; February 1843).
14. Ibid., 264.
15. Gustav Jansen, *Die Davidsbündler: Aus Robert Schumanns Sturm- und Drangperiode* (Leipzig: Breitkopf & Härtel, 1883), 184. Schumann almost always spelled his wife's name Klara.
16. Litzmann, 2:13. The letter from FW to RS is in RSH 6940-A2.
17. RS/Tgb 2:190.
18. Ibid., 251.
19. Schumannhaus, Bonn.
20. RS/Tgb 2:150.
21. Ibid., 144.
22. Ibid., 149.
23. Ibid., 143.
24. *Briefwechsel*, 1:108.
25. RS/Tgb 2:148–49.
26. Ibid., 157.
27. Wendler, 98.
28. RS/Tgb 2:162.
29. Ibid., 166.
30. Ibid., 167.
31. Wendler, 110.
32. RS/Tgb 2:200. Also see, for example, RS/Tgb 3:206–7: "Immer krank und melancholisch," and just before the Russian tour: "Ewige Melancholie wegen d. Reise."
33. Boetticher/1942, 359.
34. RS/Tgb 2:209.
35. Wendler, 111.
36. RS/Tgb 2:213.
37. Ibid., 254.
38. Ibid., 3:209–12.
39. Excerpts from all letters from March 13 to April 22 are from Boetticher/1942, 364–69.
40. Joan Bulman, *Jenny Lind* (London: James Barrie, 1956), 226.
41. Boetticher/1942, 364.

42. Wendler, 118.
43. See also RS/Tgb 3:239–40 (March 8, 9, 13, 1843).
44. Ibid., 2:254.
45. Niecks, 211.
46. RS/Tgb 2:263.
47. Litzmann, 2:57, 58.
48. Boetticher/1942, 392–93.
49. Ibid., 395–96.
50. Ibid., 399.
51. Ibid., 396, 397.
52. Litzmann, 2:85.
53. RS/Tgb 2:120 (November 6, 1840). Clara had received similar advice in 1839 when she contemplated a trip to Russia.
54. *Quellenwerk*, 1:142–43.
55. Litzmann, 2:62.
56. RS/Tgb 2:327.
57. Ibid., 3:268. An accounting of earnings and expenses on the Russian tour is given.
58. *Quellenwerk*, 1:138.
59. Ibid., 144.
60. Daverio, 289.
61. Robert's comment (RS/Tgb 2:294) was entered in April. Clara saw it on their return to Germany and commented on it in June as she was reviewing his travel notes (see ibid., 356).
62. Wendler, 127–28.
63. Litzmann, 2:76.

Chapter 6. *The Dresden Years*

1. Wendler, 152.
2. Litzmann, 1:416.
3. Henry F. Chorley, *Music and Manners in France and Germany*, 3 vols. (London: Longman, Brown, Green & Longmans, 1844), 3:86.
4. RS/Jansen, 244.
5. Ibid., 519n, 327.
6. Ibid., 246.
7. Litzmann, 2:125; RS/Jansen, 247.
8. RS/Jansen, 249.
9. Ibid., 322–23.
10. Ibid., 302.
11. RS/Tgb 3:284, 285.
12. Ibid., 418, 419.
13. Ibid., 676.
14. Litzmann, 2:174.
15. RS/Jansen, 251.
16. Boetticher/1942, 412.
17. Ibid., 413.
18. Karl Laux, "Dresden ist doch gar zu schön," in *Robert Schumann*, ed. Hans Joachim Moser and Eberhard Rebling (Leipzig: Breitkopf & Härtel, 1956), 32, 33.
19. Wilhelm Löhner, ed., "Clara Schumann: Unbekannte Briefe an Emilie Steffens," *Zeitschrift für Musik*, 97 (1930), 177–79.
20. Quoted in Litzmann, 2:145–46.

21. RS/Jansen, 311–12.
22. Litzmann, 2:219, 220.
23. Ibid., 97.
24. RS/Jansen, 256, 273.
25. Ibid., 251, 242, 249.
26. Ibid., 318.
27. Litzmann, 2:164.

Chapter 7. *Düsseldorf and the Death of Robert Schumann*

1. Paul Kast, ed., *Schumanns rheinische Jahre* (Düsseldorf: Droste, 1981), 29. See also Irmgard Knechtges-Obrecht, "Clara Schumann in Düsseldorf," in *Katalog*, 189–229, for a comprehensive overview of the years in Düsseldorf.
2. Clara Schumann to Pauline Schumann, April 10, 1851, HHI/Dickinson.
3. Clara Schumann to Pauline Schumann, January 7, 1851, HHI/Dickinson. In a letter to Emilie List (Wendler, 166), she mentions seven students, one of whom came from England to study with her.
4. Renate Federhofer-Königs, *Wilhelm Joseph von Wasielewski im Spiegel seiner Korrespondenz* (Tutzing: Schneider, 1975), 39–40.
5. Niecks, 302.
6. Litzmann, 2:241.
7. Ibid., 245.
8. RS/Jansen, 302.
9. Quoted in Niecks, 274.
10. Litzmann, 2:242.
11. Wasielewski, 284.
12. Ibid., 285–86.
13. Litzmann, 2:253.
14. Niecks, 270–71.
15. Litzmann, 2:254–55.
16. Ibid., 264–66.
17. Ibid., 265.
18. Ibid., 277.
19. Ibid., 279.
20. RS/Tgb 3:637.
21. Quoted in Eugenie Schumann, *Robert Schumann*, 357.
22. RS to Joachim, October 7, 1853, in JJ/*Briefe*, 1:84.
23. *NZfM*, 39 (1853), 185–86.
24. RS/Tgb 3:639.
25. Niecks, 272–82, offers what seems to be a reasonably complete and fair discussion of these events.
26. See excerpts in Kast, 130.
27. Ibid., 129, 130.
28. Litzmann, 2:291.
29. *Quellenwerk*, 1:190–91.
30. Litzmann, 2:299–300.
31. Quoted in Eugenie Schumann, *Robert Schumann*, 391–92. Clara Schumann gave a similar but more detailed account in her letter of March 15, 1854, to Emilie List. See Wendler, 178.
32. Franz Hermann Franken, "Robert Schumann in der Irrenanstalt in Bonn-Endenich: Zum aufgefundenen ärztlichen Verlaufsbericht 1854–1856 von Doktor Franz Richarz," in

Brahms-Studien (Tutzing: Hans Schneider, 1997), 11:107–20, esp. 110–11. The symptoms were given in Richarz's log, parts of which were published in *Robert Schumanns letzte Lebensjahre: Protokoll einer Krankheit,* Archiv-Blätter 1 (Berlin: Stiftung Archiv der Akademie der Künste, 1994). Franken tones down the horrifying details of Schumann's illness.

33. *CS/JB Briefe,* 1:13.

34. The letters were published in Eduard Hanslick, *Am Ende des Jahrhunderts 1895–1899, Die Moderne Oper*, pt. 8, 2d ed. (Berlin: Allgemeiner Verein für deutsche Literatur, 1899), 317–42, and in RS/Jansen, 397–409. Note that the letters did not appear during Clara's lifetime.

35. Clara Schumann to Bettina von Arnim, April 13 and May 25, 1855, Biblioteka Jagiellońska, Krakow.

36. Franken, 111–12. See also Kast, 161, 164, and Brigitte Berenbruch and Helmut Helberg, *Robert Schumann und Bonn* (Bonn: Stadt Bonn, 1980), 8.

37. The thought was repeated, "Completely away from here!" in a letter to Brahms dated March 11, 1855. See RS/Jansen, 406, and Hanslick, 339, for Brahms's letter; Hanslick, 333, describes the letter to Joachim.

38. Johannes Brahms, *Johannes Brahms in seiner Familie: Der Briefwechsel*, ed. Kurt Stephenson (Hamburg: Ernst Hauswedell, 1973), 63, 68.

39. Kalbeck, 1:271–72.

40. JJ/*Briefe,* 1:165.

41. Federhofer-Königs, *Wasielewski im Spiegel seiner Korrespondenz*, 69–70.

42. Kalbeck, 1:168–69.

43. Federhofer-Königs, 72.

44. Wendler, 180, 182.

45. Steegmann, 142. A letter of March 9, 1855, to Dr. Härtel explains why she canceled her plans.

46. For details of her first visit to England, see Janet Ritterman, "'Gegensätze, Ecken, und scharfe Kanten': Clara Schumanns Besuch in England, 1856–1888," in *Katalog,* 235–61. Many thanks to Janet Ritterman for permitting me to use her original English version.

47. Litzmann, 2:387.

48. Clara Schumann to Pauline Schumann, March 23, 1856, HHI/Dickinson.

49. *CS/JB Briefe,* 1:96.

50. Litzmann, 2:309.

51. The complete letter is translated in Nancy B. Reich, "The Correspondence between Clara Wieck Schumann and Felix and Paul Mendelssohn," in *Schumann and His World,* ed. R. Larry Todd (Princeton: Princeton University Press, 1994), 225–26.

52. Litzmann, 2:308, 336.

53. Ibid., 415.

54. Ibid.

55. *Robert Schumanns letzte Lebensjahre.* The full report has not been made available to the general public but a publication with excerpts from the doctor's notes has been released. The document includes a commentary by Dr. Franz Franken, physician and medical historian, and an introduction by Aribert Reimann, who inherited the document and placed it in the Akademie der Künste for study. Richarz had requested that the medical log be kept in private hands, probably because Schumann was one of Germany's musical heroes and because he wanted to spare the family any possible embarrassment. Reimann made the decision to disclose the document in order to clear up misunderstandings and falsehoods that had been circulating in recent years.

56. Franken, 115.

Chapter 8. *The Later Years*

1. *Briefwechsel,* 1:114.
2. Litzmann, 2:48n.
3. CW/Diary, December 1839 (CW).
4. Sir George Henschel, *Musings and Memories of a Musician* (New York: Macmillan, 1919), 41.
5. Amy Fay, *Music Study in Germany*, 18th ed. (New York: Macmillan, 1903), 26.
6. *Dwight's*, 7 (April 1855), 9.
7. Quoted in Gordon S. Haight, *George Eliot: A Biography* (New York: Oxford University Press, 1968), 156–57.
8. Litzmann, 3:230–31.
9. Ibid., 231.
10. *Dwight's*, 8 (December 1855), 77.
11. *Memoirs,* 93.
12. Litzmann, 3:285.
13. *Briefwechsel,* 2:575.
14. See April Fitzlyon, *The Price of Genius: A Life of Pauline Viardot* (New York: Appleton-Century-Crofts, 1964), 11.
15. RS/Tgb 2:184–5.
16. Litzmann, 2:125.
17. Ibid., 180.
18. RS/Tgb 3:284–85.
19. RS/Jansen, 250, 294, 321.
20. Published in *Memoirs*, 206–18.
21. Litzmann, 3:15.
22. Wendler, 228.
23. Clara Schumann to Ernst Rudorff, September 4, 1866, Rudorff-Archiv; Clara Schumann to Elise von Pacher, December 19, 1860, in Wendler, 233.
24. Litzmann, 3:240, 220.
25. See the first footnote in Chapter 2.
26. Martin Schoppe and Gerd Nauhaus, *Das Robert-Schumann-Haus in Zwickau* (Zwickau: Robert-Schumann-Haus, 1973), 55.
27. Clara Schumann to Ernst Rudorff, September 10, 1865, Rudorff-Archiv; Clara Schumann to Elisabeth Werner, September 10, 1865, in Litzmann, 3:183.
28. Litzmann, 3:206.
29. *CS/JB Briefe*, 1:573.
30. Ibid., 644.
31. Litzmann, 3:230n.
32. Ibid., 278n.
33. Ibid., 279.
34. Ibid., 2:125n.
35. Ibid., 3:125.
36. Ibid., 228n.
37. Ibid., 238.
38. Ibid., 238, 263.
39. Wolfgang Stadler, *Colditzer Geschichten, 1265–1990: 725 Jahre Stadt Colditz* (Colditz: Stadt Colditz, 1989).
40. Litzmann, 3:322.
41. Clara Schumann to Pastor Friedrich Grössel, May 5, 1877, Stadtarchiv und Wissenschaftliche Stadtbibliothek, Bonn.
42. Rudorff-Archiv.

43. Clara Schumann to Ernst Rudorff, February 1, 1873, Rudorff-Archiv.

44. *CS/JB Briefe*, 2:355.

45. Litzmann, 3:528n.

46. Ibid., 537.

47. Ferdinand Schumann, "Brahms and Clara Schumann," *MQ*, 2 (1916), 507–15, based on his "Erinnerungen an Johannes Brahms," *NZfM* 82 (1915), 225–28, 233–36, 241–43.

48. The title page reads: "Johannes Brahms, der Vater von Felix Schumann: Das Mysterium einer Liebe. Eine sehr ernste Parodie auf die Erinnerungen von Eugenie Schumann [Johannes Brahms, the Father of Felix Schumann: The Mystery of a Love. A Very Serious Parody on the Memoirs of Eugenie Schumann]. By Titus Frazeni."

49. The marriage diaries, first published in their entirety in RS/Tgb 2, have been translated into English by Peter Ostwald as *The Marriage Diaries of Robert and Clara Schumann from Their Wedding Day through the Russia Trip*, ed. Gerd Nauhaus (Boston: Northeastern University Press, 1993).

50. Litzmann, 3:424.

51. *CS/JB Briefe*, 2:474.

52. *Memoirs*, 9.

53. Ibid., 72.

54. See ibid., 74–86.

55. Ibid., 83.

56. Ibid., 84.

57. *CS/JB Briefe*, 2:25–26.

58. Ibid., 109–10.

59. Ibid., 165–66.

60. Litzmann, 3:396.

61. Ibid.

62. *Memoirs*, 47.

63. Ibid., 152.

64. *CS/JB Briefe*, 2:30.

65. Litzmann, 3:70.

66. JJ/*Briefe*, 1:211.

67. Litzmann, 3:286.

68. Ibid., 291. She wrote in a similar vein to Emilie List. See Wendler, 309.

69. JJ/*Briefe*, 2:85–86.

70. Ibid., 3:42–43.

71. Ferdinand Hiller, *Aus Ferdinand Hillers Briefwechsel (1826–1861)*, ed. Reinhold Sietz (Cologne: Arno Volk-Verlag, 1958), 1:85–86.

72. *CS/JB Briefe*, 2:20.

73. Ibid., 1:623.

74. Ibid., 458.

75. Ibid., 436.

76. Amalie Joachim to Joseph Joachim, November 11, 1872, transcription, Newberry Library, Chicago.

77. *CS/JB Briefe*, 2:52.

78. Litzmann, 3:389.

79. Ibid., 509–10.

80. Ibid., 1:391.

81. RS/Tgb 3:165.

82. JJ/*Briefe*, 1:463–64.

83. Litzmann, 3:578.

Chapter 9. *Clara Schumann and Johannes Brahms*

1. See, for example, Alfred Schumann, *Johannes Brahms, der Vater von Felix Schumann*. Though Marie and Eugenie Schumann attempted to suppress this malicious document written by a son of Ferdinand Schumann under the pseudonym Titus Frazeni, it was published and circulated. It is, of course, totally specious. Other writings, not so vicious but equally free of documentary proof, have appeared in the popular press.
2. Kalbeck, 1:44.
3. Florence May, *The Life of Johannes Brahms*, 2d ed., 2 vols. (London: William Reeves, 1905), 1:83.
4. *CS/JB Briefe*, 1:3.
5. JJ/*Briefe*, 1:154.
6. Eugenie Schumann, *Robert Schumann*, 358.
7. RS/Tgb 3:649–55, 683–84.
8. Brahms, *Johannes Brahms in seiner Familie*, 56.
9. Ibid., 60–61.
10. Litzmann, 2:337.
11. *Memoirs*, 152.
12. Kalbeck, 1:231–32. See also Avins, 483–84.
13. Artur Holde, "Suppressed Passages in the Joachim-Brahms Correspondence, Published for the First Time," *MQ*, 45 (1959), 314.
14. See Kalbeck, 1:115.
15. *CS/JB Briefe*, 1:187.
16. See ibid., 2:300–301 (May 14, 1886), 315–16 (May 1887), 321 (August 1887).
17. Ibid., 1:186.
18. *Memoirs*, 154.
19. Litzmann, 2:354. See also Avins, 39–40, and Michael Musgrave, "Brahms and Women," in *A Brahms Reader* (New Haven: Yale University Press, 2000), 45–56.
20. Litzmann, 3:230.
21. In 1890 Clara commented to Brahms, "I always feel shy in relation to clever people" (*CS/JB Briefe*, 2:411). See also Litzmann, 3:455.
22. See Karl Geiringer, "Schumanniana in der Bibliothek von Johannes Brahms," in *Convivium Musicorum: Festschrift Wolfgang Boetticher*, ed. Heinrich Hüschen and Dietz-Rüdiger Moser (Berlin: Merseburger, 1974), 79–82. See also Kurt Hofmann, *Die Bibliothek von Johannes Brahms* (Hamburg: Wagner, 1974).
23. Karl Geiringer, *Brahms: His Life and Work*, 2d ed. (New York: Anchor Books, 1961), 45.
24. *CS/JB Briefe*, 1:339.
25. Ibid., 506.
26. See, for example, ibid., 337.
27. Ibid., 198; 2:45, 362, 476, 510.
28. Ibid., 2:396.
29. Ibid., 1:413–14, 560, 217, 493.
30. Ibid., 2:476 (translation from Avins, 696). My thanks to Styra Avins for reminding me that Brahms often referred to himself as an "outsider." In a private communication, Avins writes:

> "The Outsider" refers to Goethe's poem, "Harzreise im Winter" [text of Brahms's Alto Rhapsody, op. 53]. To many people, not only to Clara, Brahms referred to himself . . . as "The Outsider," sometimes humourously, sometimes grimly. I have no doubt that he always meant it, and that this is the reason Goethe's poem had touched such a responsive chord in him in the first place.

31. Litzmann, 2:365–66, 381.

32. Ibid., 3:53, 72.
33. Ibid., 88, and Steegmann, 124.
34. Litzmann, 3:120.
35. See Kalbeck, 1:241–47.
36. *CS/JB Briefe*, 1:50. Avins points out (76) that he is referring to the slow movement of Robert Schumann's Symphony no. 2.
37. *CS/JB Briefe*, 1:353–54.
38. Litzmann, 3:498.
39. *CS/JB Briefe*, 2:128; Litzmann, 3:498; *CS/JB Briefe*, 2:526, 530, 516.
40. Ibid., 258, 273.
41. Ibid., 1:300.
42. Ibid., 2:317.
43. Ibid., 177.
44. Ibid., 179.
45. Litzmann, 3:490; *CS/JB Briefe*, 2:415, 541–42, 395.
46. See, for example, her letter to him of July 1, 1858, in *CS/JB Briefe*, 1:223, in which she defends her enthusiasm.
47. Ibid., 226.
48. Ibid., 2:363.
49. Ibid., 517.
50. Ibid., 463.
51. Ibid., 308.
52. Ibid., 1:560.
53. Ibid., 323, 504–6.
54. Ibid., 2:144.
55. Ibid., 94–96 (translation from Avins, 509–10).
56. Brahms, Heinrich von Herzogenberg, and Elisabeth von Herzogenberg, *Johannes Brahms im Briefwechsel mit Heinrich und Elisabeth von Herzogenberg*, ed. Max Kalbeck (Berlin: Deutsche Brahms-Gesellschaft, 1907), 2:217, 221, 220.
57. *CS/JB Briefe*, 2:96–98; 1:370, 234; Brahms and Julius Otto Grimm, *Johannes Brahms im Briefwechsel mit Julius Otto Grimm*, ed. Richard Barth (Berlin: Deutsche Brahms-Gesellschaft, 1907), 78.
58. Litzmann, 3:367.
59. *CS/JB Briefe*, 2:109–10.
60. Ibid., 1:356.
61. Ibid., 357.
62. Ibid., 576, 579.
63. Ibid., 598–99.
64. Ibid., 2:307.
65. Litzmann, 3:481.
66. *CS/JB Briefe*, 2:353–60.
67. Ibid., 464–77.
68. Ibid., 617.
69. May, *Life of Johannes Brahms*, 2:658–59.
70. *CS/JB Briefe*, 2:623 (translation from Avins, 738). Though Kalbeck (4:443) insists that the songs were not written for Clara, Brahms's letter to Marie indicates otherwise.

Chapter 10. *Other Friends and Contemporaries*

1. Litzmann, 3:247–48.
2. In *"Das Band der ewigen Liebe": Clara Schumanns Briefwechsel mit Emilie und*

Elise List Eugen Wendler presents previously unpublished letters that had been in private hands as well as biographical sketches of members of the List family.

3. Ibid., 190 (letter of March 3, 1856).

4. See Renate Hofmann, *Clara Schumanns Briefe an Theodor Kirchner* (Tutzing: Hans Schneider, 1996). In addition to the (remaining) letters from Clara Schumann to Kirchner, Hofmann includes carefully documented biographical sketches of Kirchner and Clara Schumann, excerpts from Kirchner letters to other friends, and detailed notes on the music they discussed.

5. Ibid., 16, describes him as a "Frauenliebling und Charmeur."

6. *AmZ*, 33 (1831), 805–8. See also the discussion in Plantinga, 34–35.

7. Wieck's article appeared in *Caecilia* (Mainz), 14 (1832), 219–23. The review is followed by a testimonial by Gottfried Weber, the editor, on Clara's brilliant playing of the Chopin work and Wieck's role in developing her artistry.

8. CW/Diary, November 14, 1831. Clara copied Wieck's long letter to Fechner into the diary.

9. Wieck/*Briefe*, 36, 38.

10. Frédéric Chopin, *Chopin's Letters*, ed. Henryk Opieński, trans. E. L. Voynich (New York: Knopf, 1931), 155–56.

11. Quoted in Ernst Burger with Gerd Nauhaus, *Robert Schumann: Eine Lebenschronik in Bildern und Dokumenten* (Mainz: Schott, 1999), 111.

12. CW/Diary, March 14, 1832 (FW).

13. She premiered the last two movements of the E minor concerto at the Leipzig Gewandhaus on September 29, 1833 (PS 36), and the entire concerto on May 5, 1834 (PS 43).

14. The album leaf is now in the Heineman Collection in the Pierpont Morgan Library in New York. A facsimile can be found in Mieczysław Tomaszewski and Bożena Weber, *Fryderyk Chopin: A Diary in Images,* trans. Rosemary Hunt (Warsaw: Arkady, 1990), 138.

15. James Methuen-Campbell, "Chopin in Performance," in *The Cambridge Companion to Chopin,* ed. Jim Samson (Cambridge: Cambridge University Press, 1992), 196–97.

16. Her nervousness and anxiety about this performance are described in Litzmann, 3:530–31.

17. September 14 and October 9, 1847 (Steegmann, 51–53).

18. Bargiel, Brahms, Liszt, Reinecke, and Rudorff—all close friends—were named as the editors of the B&H Chopin *Gesamtausgabe*.

19. January 8 and August 28, 1867 (Steegmann, 204, 213). Härtel offered her a choice of editions instead of money.

20. Quoted in *Briefwechsel,* 1:72: Hofmeister sent the letter to Robert Schumann, who copied it out for Clara.

Je suis ravi de ce que vous me dites du talent de Mlle. C.W. Une jeune personne sachant exécuter avec energie, intelligenze et précision des morceaux de ma façon, est un phenomène excessiment rare à tout pays, et tout à fait introuvable je crais dans celui que j'habite à present. Chopin et plusiers autres artistes m'en ont deja beaucoup parlé, Je desire vivement la conaître et malgré ma paresse de locomotion *je ferai presque un voyage pour l'entendre*.[sic]

21. Franz Liszt, *Correspondance de Liszt et de Madame d'Agoult*, ed. Daniel Ollivier, 2 vols. (Paris: Grasset, 1933), 1:217.

22. *Dwight's*, 7 (1855), 9.

23. Litzmann, 1:199.

24. *Briefwechsel*, 1:159.

25. Wieck/*Briefe*, 93, 94.

26. Ibid., 93–94.
27. Boetticher, *Briefe und Gedichte*, 109–10.
28. Ibid., 111 (March 1, 1839).
29. Franz Liszt, *Franz Liszts Briefe*, ed. La Mara, 2d ed., 8 vols. (Leipzig: Breitkopf & Härtel, 1893), 1:26–27.
30. Litzmann, 1:413.
31. Ibid., 417–18. She expressed similar emotions in her diary on March 23, 1840.
32. RS/Tgb 2:194.
33. Litzmann, 1:414, 417.
34. RS/Tgb 2:196–98.
35. Litzmann, 2:122.
36. Ibid., 317.
37. Ibid., 263, 268, 351.
38. RS/Tgb 2:257.
39. Litzmann, 3:29.
40. Ibid., 425–27.
41. Ibid., 326.
42. *CS/JB Briefe*, 1:622.
43. See, for example, Cosima Wagner, *Cosima Wagner's Diaries*, ed. Martin Gregor-Dellin and Dietrich Mack, trans. Geoffrey Skelton, 2 vols. (New York: Harcourt Brace Jovanovich, 1978, 1980), 1:170, 555, 763, 824, 838–39; 2:110, 203, 317, 355, 441, 609, 812.
44. Litzmann, 3:443.
45. CW/Diary, September 12, 1835.
46. Ibid., September 16, 1835.
47. Felix Mendelssohn Bartholdy to Clara Schumann, November 24, 1845, Staatsbibliothek zu Berlin, Preussischer Kulturbesitz, Musikabteilung; translation in Reich, "Correspondence," 220–21.
48. RS/Tgb 2:122–23, for example.
49. See Schmuel Ettinger, "The Origins of Modern Anti-Semitism," *Dispersion and Unity*, 9 (1969), 23, for a discussion of this mind-set during the romantic period. I am grateful to Robert Seltzer for referring me to this article.
50. Robert Schumann, *Erinnerungen an Felix Mendelssohn Bartholdy: Nachgelassene Aufzeichnungen*, ed. Georg Eismann (Zwickau: Predella, 1947), 70–71.
51. Litzmann, 1:423.
52. RS/Tgb 2:113.
53. Litzmann, 2:85.
54. Ibid., 161–62.
55. Wendler, 148–49.
56. See Reich, "Correspondence," 225–27.
57. RS/Jansen, 398.
58. Ute Bär, "Zur gemeinsamen Konzertätigkeit Clara Schumanns und Joseph Joachims," in *Clara Schumann: Komponistin, Interpretin, Unternehmerin, Ikone*, ed. Peter Ackermann and Herbert Schneider (Hildesheim: Georg Olms, 1999), 46.
59. RS/Tgb 3:809n916.
60. Litzmann, 2:321.
61. JJ/*Briefe*, 2:4–5.
62. Many of the several hundred letters appeared in JJ/*Briefe*.
63. Clara Schumann to Ernst Rudorff, January 17, 1882, Rudorff-Archiv.
64. JJ/*Briefe*, 3:24. See also Nancy B. Reich, "Women as Musicians: A Question of Class," in *Musicology and Difference: Gender and Sexuality in Music Scholarship*, ed. Ruth Solie (Berkeley: University of California Press, 1993), 144–46, for a translation of the Joachim-Rudorff correspondence.

65. JJ/*Briefe*, 3:370.
66. Litzmann, 3:590.
67. Ibid., 2:326.
68. Julia Stockhausen Wirth, ed., *Julius Stockhausen, der Sänger des deutschen Liedes: Nach Dokumenten seiner Zeit* (Frankfurt am Main: Englert & Schlosser, 1927), 489–98.
69. Litzmann, 3:114.
70. Wirth, 150.
71. Ibid., 155.
72. Litzmann, 3:556.
73. See Beatrix Borchard, "Zwei Musikerinnen—zwei Kulturen: Unveröffentliche Briefe von Clara Schumann und Pauline Viardot-García," in *Clara Schumann: Komponistin. . . Ikone*, 59–92.
74. *CS/JB Briefe*, 1:565.
75. Fitzlyon, 166.

Chapter 11. *Clara Schumann as Composer and Editor*

1. The diary entries in the Catalogue of Works marked "(FW)" were written by Friedrich Wieck. See also Nancy B. Reich with Anna Burton, M.D., "Clara Schumann: Old Sources, New Readings," *MQ*, 70 (Summer 1984), 332–54.
2. Wieck/*Briefe*, 27: "Nobody would believe that she could compose because there had never been a girl of that age who could do it."
3. "Klara Wieck die Pianoforte-Virtuosin aus Leipzig und Mitglied der neu romantischen Schule daselbst ist hier angekommen um 3 Concerte zu geben" (quoted in CW/Diary, November 20, 1837 [CW]; also Litzmann, 1:139).
4. Boetticher/1942, 339.
5. RSH, 4871/VIII, 4-5977-A3. Kaldewey, 88–99, discusses the notebook and describes its contents in detail.
6. Clara's works were published along with those of such composers as Johann Sebastian Bach, Mendelssohn, Ignaz Moscheles, Robert Schumann, Pauline Viardot, and lesser known composers. The works in the supplements were collected and published again individually by Schuberth & Co. ca. 1867.
7. "Robert Schumann. 2," in *Die Grenzboten: Zeitschrift für Politik, Literatur, und Kunst*, September 27, 1850, 521–22.
8. RS/Tgb 2:255.
9. Marie Wieck, *Aus dem Kreise Wieck-Schumann*, 38 (letter of August 16, 1853).
10. Litzmann, 2:131.
11. Ibid., 274, 139–40.
12. JJ/*Briefe*, 2:78–79.
13. CW/Diary, 118 (CW).
14. Litzmann, 1:355–56.
15. *Briefwechsel*, 2:500, 577.
16. See the excerpts from their correspondence about op. 11 in Catalogue of Works, pp. 303–4.
17. *Briefwechsel*, 1:53, 57. Robert Schumann had assigned Carl Friedrich Becker, a colleague, to write the review of Clara's concerto.
18. CW/Diary, April 18, 1839 (CW). Excerpts from the review are in the Catalogue of Works, p. 302.
19. *Briefwechsel*, 2:501.
20. RS/Tgb 2:186.
21. RSH 5984-A1, 5985-A1, 5986-A1, 5989-A1.

22. RS/Tgb 2: 162, 168, 134.

23. See reviews of Clara Schumann's Trio in *NBMz,* November 17, 1847, 384, and *AmZ,* 50 (April 5, 1848), 232–33.

24. Steegmann, 17. Although Clara Schumann mentioned four fugues for possible publication, only three (selected by her husband) were included in op. 16. See her letter to Breitkopf & Härtel in Catalogue of Works, p. 310.

25. See her letter to Dr. Härtel in Steegmann, 16 and 153. Excerpts are in the Catalogue of Works, pp. 309, 314, 315.

26. Steegmann, 173.

27. See, for example, her letter to Joachim in JJ/*Briefe*, 2:86: "Bin ich auch nicht producierend, so doch reproducierend" (I may not be a creative artist, but still I am re-creating).

28. Litzmann, 1:411.

29. Boetticher/1942, 338.

30. She did, however, compose the Romance in B Minor in 1856, a few months after his death, and a march for the wedding anniversary of close friends in 1879.

31. RS/Jansen, 170.

32. See R. Larry Todd, "On Quotation in Schumann's Music," in *Schumann and His World,* ed. R. Larry Todd (Princeton: Princeton University Press, 1994), 80–112.

33. Klassen/1990, 166–70, presents several hypotheses on the derivation of the Andantino.

34. *Iris*, 2 (June 17, 1831), 96. The entire review is in Catalogue of Works, pp. 290–91.

35. *Briefwechsel,* 1:6.

36. See Claudia Stevens Becker, "A New Look at Schumann's Impromptus," *MQ*, 67 (October 1981), 568–86, and Robert Schumann, Op. 5 [Klavierwerke], ed. Hans Joachim Köhler, 27–31. Both refer to an entry in RS/Tgb 1:321.

37. See Plantinga, chap. 10.

38. Robert Schumann, *Gesammelte Schriften,* 2:98.

39. *Briefwechsel,* 1:100.

40. SBPK, Mus. ms. autogr. K. Schumann 20 427.

41. *Briefwechsel*, 1:17.

42. Many thanks to James Deaville, who found the manuscript and brought it to my attention.

43. See Stephan D. Lindeman, "Clara Wieck, Piano Concerto in A Minor, op. 7," in his *Structural Novelty and Tradition in the Early Romantic Piano Concerto,* 133–38 (Stuyvesant, N.Y.: Pendragon Press, 1999).

44. *Allgemeiner musikalischer Anzeiger* [Vienna], 10 (September 16, 1838), 143.

45. See Daverio, 237–38; Lindeman, 139; Macdonald, "Review," *Notes,* 48 (December 1991), 676.

46. See Charles Suttoni, "Piano and Opera: A Study of the Piano Fantasies Written on Opera Themes in the Romantic Era," Ph.D. dissertation, New York University, 1973.

47. CW/Diary, March 22, 1837 (CW).

48. Plantinga, 197.

49. *Briefwechsel,* 2:653.

50. Ibid., 577.

51. Robert Schumann, *Humoreske* [Klavierwerke], 40–44; Chissell, 67.

52. Klassen/1990, 97.

53. "Fugenpassion" recorded in RS/Tgb 3:381. According to ibid., 385 and 749, the text they used was Cherubini's *Theorie des Contrapunktes und der Fuge.*

54. See Daverio's discussion of Schumann fugues, 306–12.

55. Concert in Magdeburg, November 25, 1834 (PS 50).

56. RS/Tgb 3:429.

57. Chissell, 97.

58. *CS/JB Briefe*, 1:6n2.

59. Kalbeck, 1:176–77. Brahms obviously treasured Clara Schumann's Variations. He owned two copies: one was the inscribed autograph she gave him in July 1854 and the other the printed copy that he received in November 1854. Both are part of his legacy to Wgm.

60. Litzmann, 2:371.

61. JJ/*Briefe*, 1:380 (November 12, 1856).

62. RS/Tgb 3:205 and 2:199.

63. A portion of the correspondence with Arthur Meyer is in SBPK, Briefe an Clara Schumann (translation by Adrienne Fried Block).

64. In the preface to his 1996 edition, Nauhaus points out that the Grossvater theme appeared in other Robert Schumann works, among them *Papillons* and *Carnaval*.

65. Litzmann, 3:601.

66. Valerie W. Goertzen, "Setting the Stage: Clara Schumann's Preludes," in *In the Course of Performance: Studies in the World of Musical Improvisation,* ed. Bruno Nettl with Melinda Russell (Chicago: University of Chicago Press, 1998), 237; see also Goertzen, "By Way of Introduction: Preluding by 18th and 19th Century Pianists," *Journal of Musicology,* 14 (Summer 1996), 299–337.

67. Draheim/Höft, 1:5, includes two additional songs, originally attributed to Friedrich Wieck, that the editors believe were composed by the young Clara Wieck.

68. Liederbuch.

69. RS/Tgb 2:267. The remainder of his entry reads: "She wants always to move forward but Marie is grasping her dress on the one side, Elise also creates much to do, and the husband sits deep in thoughts of Peri [his oratorio]. So, forward, always forward through joy and sorrow, my Clara, and love me always as you have always loved me."

70. Franz Liszt, arr., *Lieder von Robert und Clara Schumann für das Pianoforte übertragen* (Leipzig: Breitkopf & Härtel, 1875) and *42 Lieder von Ludwig van Beethoven, Robert Franz, Felix Mendelssohn Bartholdy, Robert und Clara Schumann für das Pianoforte übertragen* (Leipzig: Breitkopf & Härtel, [ca. 1879]).

71. See Appel/Katalog.

72. RS/Tgb 2:105.

73. The unidentified reviewer (*AmZ,* 44 [January 19, 1842], 62) did not know whether the song was by Robert or Clara Schumann. Translation here adapted from Rufus Hallmark, "The Rückert Lieder of Robert and Clara Schumann," *Nineteenth-Century Music,* 14 (Summer 1990), 16.

74. Rückert's poem is printed in full in RS/Tgb 2:230–31 and Litzmann, 2:22–23. It also appeared in several periodicals in 1843.

75. Hallmark, "Rückert Lieder," 3–30.

76. RSH 4501-D1/A4: bound volumes of editions of Robert Schumann works in which he made notes regarding various pieces; e.g., "Op. 37/12/Gedichte aus der Liebesfrühling/ von Rückert./Leipzig, 4–11 Januar/1841./(2, 4, & 11 sind von Klara)."

77. *Briefwechsel*, 1:10, 2:571.

78. Draheim/Höft includes both versions, the first in vol. 1, the second in vol. 2.

79. It appeared in *Romantik in der Tonkunst,* ed. Kurt Stephenson (Cologne: Arno Volk Verlag, 1961), 47–48.

80. RS/Tgb 3:802.

81. All the known unpublished songs appeared for the first time in Draheim/Höft, vol. 2 (1992). Seven were published in Norderval.

82. Martin Schoppe and Gerd Nauhaus, *Das Robert-Schumann-Haus in Zwickau,* rev. ed. (Zwickau: Robert-Schumann-Haus, 1978), 52.

83. *CS/JB Briefe*, 1:315.

84. Eugenie Schumann, "Über das letzte Werk ihres Vaters Robert Schumann," *Schweizerische Musikzeitung*, 78 (January 1, 1938), 9. The Concerto was published by Schott; the movements of the FAE Sonata were issued by Heinrichshofen; and the Variations were published by Hinrichsen, London. See Robert Schumann, *Robert Schumann: Thematisches Verzeichnis* . . . , ed. Kurt Hofmann and Siegmar Keil (Hamburg: J. Schuberth, 1982).

85. *CS/JB Briefe*, 2:90–91.

86. HHI. The Caprices were published by C. F. Peters of Leipzig, 1941.

87. RS/Tgb 3:641n920.

88. *CS/JB Briefe*, 1:318, 372.

89. Ibid., 2:100–101.

90. The first complete edition was published between 1879 and 1893. The 31 parts are usually bound in 14 volumes. See the valuable discussions of this and the *Instruktive Ausgabe* in "Die Herausgeberin," in De Vries, 279-303.

91. *CS/JB Briefe*, 2:209, 119, 121, 480–88.

92. Ibid., 484.

93. See, for example, Wolfgang Boetticher, "Neue textkritische Forschungen an R. Schumanns Klavierwerk," *AfMw*, 25 (1968), 46–76; Edward A. Lippman, "Robert Schumann," *MGG*, 12:320; and William Newman, *The Sonata since Beethoven*, 2d ed. (New York: W. W. Norton, 1972), 264. A new edition, *Robert Schumann: Neue Ausgabe sämtlicher Werke* (Mainz: Schott, 1991–), is currently under way. Encompassing 63 volumes in 8 series, it will incorporate contributions by a group of international scholars and will include works, sketchbooks, other previously unpublished materials, a *Lebenschronik* (1999), and a two-volume thematic catalogue that will be published by Henle Verlag.

94. See, for example, *CS/JB Briefe*, 2:135, 169.

95. RS/Jansen, 440.

96. *CS/JB Briefe*, 1:359–69, 2:142–43.

97. Several scholars have dealt with the question of Schumann's metronome markings and Clara Schumann's editions. See Dietrich Kämper, "Zur Frage der Metronombezeichnungen Robert Schumanns," *AfMw*, 21 (1964), 141–55; Brian Schlotel, "Schumann and the Metronome," in *Robert Schumann: The Man and His Music*, ed. Alan Walker (London: Barrie & Jenkins, 1972), 109–19. See also De Vries, 287–94.

98. *NBMz*, 9 (December 19, 1855), 407.

99. Wirth, 253. Her letter was a reply to one in which Stockhausen had written that he found the metronome markings for Schumann's Third Symphony "frighteningly" fast and wondered if Schumann's metronome was correct.

100. See, for example, Sir George Henschel, *Personal Recollections of Johannes Brahms* (Boston: R. G. Badger, 1907), 78–79.

101. Titled in German *Klavierwerke von Robert Schumann: Erste mit Fingersatz und Vortragsbezeichnung versehene Instruktive Ausgabe. Nach den Handschriften und persönlicher Überlieferung*. After Clara's death it was revised by Carl Reinecke but continued to carry her name on the title page for many years. The Instructive Edition is best known to English-reading pianists as Robert Schumann, *The Complete Works for Piano Solo, Edited According to Manuscripts and from Her Personal Recollections by Clara Schumann*. See "Die Herausgeberin" in De Vries, 279–303, for a discussion of both Robert Schumann editions from the point of view of Clara Schumann as pianist and teacher.

102. *CS/JB Briefe*, 2:252.

103. Litzmann, 3:442.

104. B&H to Marie Schumann, January 96, 1901, RSH.

105. Clara Schumann, ed., *Fingerübungen und Studien aus Carl Czerny's grosser Pianoforte Schule, Op.* 500 (Hamburg; Cranz, [1880]). See also *CS/JB Briefe*, 2:219–20.

According to a footnote to the correspondence (217n), this work was evidently the inspiration for Brahms's own *51 Übungen für das Pianoforte* (1893).

106. The B&H catalogue of 1902, 901, lists "*Domenico Scarlatti. 20 ausgewählte Sonaten.* V.A. 432. (Cl. Schumann)."

107. In a letter to Philipp Spitta dated September 1874, Brahms inquired, on Clara Schumann's behalf, whether Spitta could offer any advice on the subject (Johannes Brahms and Philipp Spitta, *Johannes Brahms im Briefwechsel mit Philipp Spitta*, ed. Carl Krebs [Berlin: Deutsche Brahms-Gesellschaft, 1920], 61).

108. Litzmann, 3:466–47.

Chapter 12. *The Concert Artist*

1. Frank Munte, "Robert und Clara Schumann in Hamburg," in *Brahms-Studien,* ed. Helmut Wirth (Hamburg: Wagner, 1977), 2:9–10.

2. Litzmann, 2:62.

3. *Dwight's,* 6 (March 24, 1855), 196.

4. SBPK, Briefe an Clara Schumann.

5. *Briefwechsel,* 2:469.

6. CW/Diary, March 7, 1839.

7. *Briefwechsel,* 2:484. This was the concert reviewed by Berlioz, discussed in Chapter 4.

8. Litzmann, 1:392–93.

9. See Pamela Susskind Pettler, "Clara Schumann's Recitals, 1832–1850," *Nineteenth-Century Music,* 4 (1980), 70–76.

10. RS/Tgb 2:181.

11. She played Bach's Concerto in D Minor for Three Claviers with Mendelssohn and Rakemann on September 11, 1835, and again with Mendelssohn and Hiller on October 30, 1843. On December 19, 1861, she premiered, with Moscheles and Reinecke, Bach's Concerto in C Major for Three Claviers.

12. Litzmann, 2:401.

13. See Humphrey Searle, "Franz Liszt," *Grove,* 11:33, for "Programme général des morceaux exécutés par F. Liszt à ses concerts de 1838 à 1848," compiled by A. Conradi and Franz Liszt.

14. See George Kehler, ed., *The Piano in Concert,* 2 vols. (Metuchen, N.J.: Scarecrow Press, 1982).

15. Wasielewski, 318.

16. Litzmann, 2:273.

17. Martin Schoppe, "Schumann-Interpretation Clara Schumanns (Tageskritik und Konzertbericht)," in *3. Schumann-Tage des Bezirkes Karl-Marx-Stadt, 1978* (Zwickau: Robert-Schumann-Gesellschaft, 1978), 20.

18. *CS/JB Briefe,* 1:237, 246.

19. *Briefwechsel,* 2:419.

20. Litzmann, 3:448.

21. *Briefwechsel,* 2:809–10.

22. Ibid., 1:105, 93, 126.

23. CW/Diary, September 29, 1839.

24. Robert Haven Schauffler, *Florestan: The Life and Work of Robert Schumann* (New York: Henry Holt, 1945), 147. Schauffler knew only the abridged version of her words in Litzmann, 1:372–73, where the three sentences beginning "If Beethoven and Mozart were alive today" are omitted.

25. *Briefwechsel,* 1:108.

26. Ibid., 126, 333. The original last movement was published in the Supplement (vol. 14) of the Collected Works.

27. Robert Schumann, *Jugendbriefe*, 309.

28. Boetticher/1942, 320.

29. RS/Jansen, 422–23.

30. *Briefwechsel*, 2:368.

31. RS/Jansen, 434.

32. *Briefwechsel*, 1:98–99.

33. Ibid., 2:424.

34. RS/Jansen, 397, 401.

35. Schoppe, 17, 20.

36. Rudorff-Archiv.

37. See Désirée Wittkowski, "'In Paris hast Du doppelte Mühe in Allem . . .': Clara Wieck-Schumanns Parisreisen," in *Katalog*, 160. Several French critics were virulently anti-Schumann.

38. *CS/JB Briefe*, 1:395.

39. Daniel Wladimirowitsch Shitomirski, "Schumann in Russland," in *Sammelbände der Robert-Schumann-Gesellschaft* (Zwickau, 1961), 21.

40. Quoted ibid., 22.

41. Quoted ibid.

42. Quoted ibid., 28.

43. Litzmann, 3:452.

44. See Ritterman, "'Gegensätze, Ecken, und scharfe Kanten,'" Table 2, in *Katalog*, for complete list of repertory and performances in England.

45. Litzmann, 3:500.

46. See Reich, "Clara Schumann and America," in *Clara Schumann: Komponistin . . . Ikone*, 195–203.

47. Litzmann, 1:202; *Neue musikalische Zeitung für Berlin*, 1 (April 21, 1847), 141.

48. *AmZ*, 44 (1842), 16–18.

49. Anton Schindler, *Beethoven as I Knew Him*, ed. Donald W. MacCardle, trans. Constance S. Jolly (New York: W. W. Norton, 1966), 434, 433.

50. Martin Kreisig, "Einige Briefe Clara Schumanns," *Neue Musik-Zeitung*, 41 (1919), 35–36.

51. Budapest, 1872 (personal communication from Mariá Eckhardt).

52. *AmZ*, 44 (1842), 80–81.

53. Ibid., 804–5.

54. *NZfM*, 61 (1865), 57.

55. Litzmann, 1:107.

56. *AmZ*, 34 (1832), 532.

57. *CS/JB Briefe*, 1:636.

58. De Vries offers a valuable and detailed study of Schumann's career as concert pianist.

59. *The Pupils of Clara Schumann*, Pavilion Records (Wadhurst), presenting recordings of music by Robert Schumann, Brahms, and others played by Ilona Eibenschütz, Fanny Davies, and Adelina de Lara, has record liner notes by Jerrold Northrop Moore. Unfortunately, no compositions by Clara Schumann are included. Spoken commentary by Ilona Eibenschütz and Fanny Davies can also be heard.

60. See, for example, the letters to Emilie Steffens written in 1850 (Chapter 6), which are surprisingly similar to the Wieck letters cited in Chapters 2 and 4.

61. Federhofer-Königs, 67.

62. Hanslick, *Geschichte des Concertwesens in Wien*, 332.

63. Arthur Loesser, *Men, Women, and Pianos: A Social History* (New York: Simon & Schuster, 1954), 93.

64. Hanslick, *Geschichte des Concertwesens in Wien*, 224.

65. RS/Tgb 1:337–38.
66. Wieck/*Briefe*, 39.
67. *Journal des Débats*, March 22, 1839.
68. See Nancy B. Reich, "Women as Musicians: A Question of Class," in *Musicology and Difference: Gender and Sexuality in Music Scholarship*, ed. Ruth Solie (Berkeley: University of California Press, 1993), 125–46.
69. Rita Benton, "Pleyel," in *Grove*, 15:11.
70. RS/Tgb 2:104, 180.
71. *Briefwechsel*, 1:328.
72. Ibid., 2:592.
73. Litzmann, 2:273.
74. *CS/JB Briefe*, 1:599.

Chapter 13. *Clara Schumann as Student and Teacher*

1. Niecks, 71–72.
2. Louis Spohr, *Lebenserinnerungen*, ed. Folker Göthel (Tutzing: Schneider, 1968), 2:87–90.
3. Litzmann, 1:4–6.
4. Wieck, *Clavier und Gesang*, 7. Translation modified from Wieck, *Piano and Song*, trans. Pleasants, 18.
5. Fay, 166.
6. Litzmann, 1:23.
7. Ibid., 3:585.
8. July 4, 1890. Translation of this and letters of January 24 and March 1, 1891, by Elizabeth Derenburg, daughter of Ilona Eibenschütz Derenburg. I am grateful to Oliver and Anthony Robinow, grandsons of Ilona Eibenschütz, who have generously given me access to Clara Schumann's letters to Ilona Eibenschütz Derenburg and related materials.
9. See Peter Cahn, *Das Hoch'sche Konservatorium in Frankfurt am Main (1878–1978)* (Frankfurt am Main: Waldemar Kramer, 1979), 51.
10. Her correspondence with Raff concerning conservatory matters is preserved in the Bayerische Staatsbibliothek, Munich.
11. Quoted in Claus Victor Bock, "Pente Pigadia und die Tagebücher des Clement Harris," *Castrum Peregrini*, 50 (1961), 15. I am indebted to Peter Cahn for bringing this article to my attention.
12. See Clara Schumann, *Mein liebes Julchen: Briefe von Clara Schumann an ihre Enkeltochter Julie Schumann . . .*, ed. Dietz-Rüdiger Moser (Munich: Nymphenburger, 1990).
13. Mathilde Verne, *Chords of Remembrance* (London: Hutchinson, 1936), 55.
14. Marie Fromm, "Some Reminiscences of My Music Studies with Clara Schumann," *MT*, 73 (1932), 615.
15. Quoted in Sir George Grove, "Clara Schumann," in *Grove's Dictionary of Music and Musicians*, 3d ed., ed. H. C. Colles, (New York: Macmillan, 1935), 4:647.
16. *Memoirs*, 97.
17. Julia Smith, *Master Pianist: The Career and Teaching of Carl Friedberg* (New York: Philosophical Library, 1963), 58.
18. *Memoirs*, 98.
19. Adelina de Lara, "Clara Schumann's Teaching," *ML*, 26 (1945), 145.
20. *Memoirs*, 98.
21. Fanny Davies, "On Schumann—and Reading between the Lines," *ML*, 6 (1925), 215.
22. Lara, 146.
23. See Siu-Wan Chair Fang, "Clara Schumann as Teacher," DMA thesis, University

of Illinois, 1978. This dissertation, a study and analysis of the Schmidt Collection, formerly housed at Butler University, Indianapolis, confirms what many Schumann students have written. The editions used by Emma Schmidt still bear Schumann's decisive notes and comments on fingering, phrasing, articulation, pedaling, accents, and other aspects of piano performance.

24. De Vries, 254–79, 383–401, gives biographies of Schumann students and discusses their recordings. Smith lists many of Friedberg's students. The late Rosalie Marshall, a Friedberg student, kindly shared her recollections of his teaching with me.

Bibliography

Archival Sources

Major Collections of Letters*

Bayerische Staatsbibliothek, Munich, Handschriftenabteilung.
Heinrich-Heine-Institut, Düsseldorf.
Robert-Schumann-Forschungsstelle, Düsseldorf.
Robert-Schumann-Haus, Zwickau.
Rudorff-Archive: Privatarchiv v. Gottberg.
Staatsbibliothek zu Berlin Preussischer Kulturbesitz, Musikabteilung.
Stadtarchiv und Wissenschaftliche Stadtbibliothek, Bonn.
Stadt- und Universitätsbibliothek, Frankfurt am Main, Musik- und Theaterabteilung.
Universitätsbibliothek, Leipzig, Handschriftenabteilung.

Music Autographs of Clara Schumann

Heinrich-Heine-Institut, Düsseldorf.
Robert-Schumann-Forschungsstelle, Düsseldorf.
Robert-Schumann-Haus, Zwickau.
Staatsbibliothek zu Berlin Preussischer Kulturbesitz.

Other Sources

Robert-Schumann-Haus, Zwickau.
Diaries *(Tagebücher)* of Clara Wieck, catalogue no. 4877-A3, and transcription by Gerd Nauhaus. The diaries date from June 7, 1827, to September 13, 1840.
Family papers *(Familien-Urkunde)*, catalogue nos. 2174-A3 and A3b. Birth, baptismal, marriage, and death certificates of the Wieck, Tromlitz, and Schumann families.

*Fifty or more Clara Schumann letters.

Legal papers *(Prozessakten)*, catalogue no. 5725-A3c, and transcriptions by Georg Eismann. Copies of originals in Staatsarchiv Dresden, Bestand Landgericht Leipzig, no. 1.
Program collection *(Programm-Sammlung)* of Clara Schumann, catalogue no. 10463. The 1,299 programs, numbered and the city in which the performance took place noted on each, are bound into five volumes: I, nos. 1–320, 1828–53; II, nos. 321–484, 1853–58; III, nos. 485–709, 1858–64; IV, nos. 710–1188, 1864–80; V, nos. 1189–1299, 1881–91.

Published Sources

Selected Music Editions*

Draheim, Joachim, ed. *Brahms und seine Freunde.* Wiesbaden: Breitkopf & Härtel, 1983; Clara Schumann, op. 21, reissued separately 1996.
Liszt, Franz, arr. *Lieder von Robert und Clara Schumann für das Pianoforte übertragen.* Leipzig: Breitkopf & Härtel, 1875.
—— arr. *42 Lieder von Ludwig van Beethoven, Robert Franz, Felix Mendelssohn Bartholdy, Robert und Clara Schumann für das Pianoforte übertragen.* Leipzig: Breitkopf & Härtel, ca. 1879.
Schumann, Clara. *Concerto for Piano and Orchestra.* Ed. Kile Smith. Arranged for two pianos. Bryn Mawr, Pa.: Hildegard, 1993.
——. *Drei gemischte Chöre.* Ed. Gerd Nauhaus. Leipzig: Breitkopf & Härtel, 1989.
——. *Konzert für Klavier und Orchester.* Ed. Victoria Erber. Arranged for two pianos. Wiesbaden: Breitkopf & Härtel, 1993.
——. *Konzert für Klavier und Orchester.* Ed. Janina Klassen. Wiesbaden: Breitkopf & Härtel, 1990.
——. *Konzertsatz für Klavier und Orchester.* Ed. Jozef De Beenhouwer. Wiesbaden: Breitkopf & Härtel, 1994.
——. *Marsch Es-Dur für Klavier zu vier Händen.* Ed. Gerd Nauhaus. Wiesbaden: Breitkopf & Härtel, 1996.
——. *Pianoforte-Werke.* Leipzig: Breitkopf & Härtel, 1879.
——. Preludes and Fugues, op. 16. Ed. Sylvia Glickman. Bryn Mawr, Pa.: Hildegard, 1997.
——. Preludes and Fugues, op. 16. Ed. Barbara Harbach. Pullman, Wash.: Vivace Press, 1994.
——. *Quatre Pièces fugitives.* Ed. Joachim Draheim. Wiesbaden: Breitkopf & Härtel, 1994.
——. *Quatre Polonaises für Klavier.* Ed. Babette Hierholzer. Berlin: Ries & Erler; New York: Carl Fischer, 1987.
——. *Romantische Klaviermusik.* Ed. Franzpeter Goebels. 2 vols. Heidelberg: Willy Müller Süddeutscher Musikverlag, 1967, 77. (Now Kassel: Bärenreiter.)
——. *Sämtliche Lieder für Singstimme und Klavier.* Ed. Joachim Draheim and Brigitte Höft. 2 vols. Wiesbaden: Breitkopf & Härtel, 1990, 92.
——. *Seven Songs.* Ed. Kristin Norderval. Bryn Mawr, Pa.: Hildegard, 1993.
——. *Sonate für Klavier, G-Moll.* Ed. Gerd Nauhaus. Wiesbaden/Leipzig: Breitkopf & Härtel, 1991.
Schumann, Clara Wieck. *Selected Piano Music.* New York: Da Capo, 1979.
Schumann, Robert. *30 Mélodies de Robert Schumann transcrites pour piano.* Arr. Clara Schumann. Paris: Maison G. Flaxland, Durand, Schönewerk [1873?]. Published in German as *Dreissig Lieder und Gesänge von Robert Schumann. Für Clavier übertragen von Clara Schumann.* Berlin: Ries & Erler, 1886; reprint, 1991.

*Major editions and reissues only. Other first editions, later editions, facsimiles, reprints, arrangements, transcriptions are noted in the Catalogue of Works.

Schumann, Robert, and Clara Schumann. *Lieder und Gesänge für eine Stimme mit Begleitung des Pianoforte.* Leipzig: Breitkopf & Härtel (ca. 1872). Also issued for low voice as *Lieder und Gesänge für eine Stimme mit Begleitung des Pianoforte. Ausgabe für eine tiefere Stimme*. Leipzig: Breitkopf & Härtel (ca. 1873).

Stephenson, Kurt, ed. *Romantik in der Tonkunst.* Cologne: Arno Volk Verlag, 1961.

Wieck-Schumann, Clara. *Ausgewählte Klavierwerke.* Ed. Janina Klassen. Munich: Henle, 1987.

Wieck, Clara. Frühe Klavierwerke. Ed. Joachim Draheim and Gerd Nauhaus. Hofheim: Hofmeister, 1996, 1997. (Opp. 1–7, based on first editions.)

Books and Articles

Abraham, Gerald, ed. *Schumann: A Symposium.* London: Oxford University Press, 1952.

Appel, Bernhard R., and Inge Hermstrüwer, eds. *Robert Schumann und die Dichter: Ein Musiker als Leser. Katalog zur Ausstellung.* Düsseldorf: Droste, 1991.

Avins, Styra. *Johannes Brahms: Life and Letters*. Selected and annotated by Styra Avins. Trans. Josef Eisinger and Styra Avins. Oxford: Oxford University Press, 1997.

Bär, Ute. "Zur gemeinsamen Konzertätigkeit Clara Schumanns und Joseph Joachims." In *Clara Schumann: Komponistin, Interpretin, Unternehmerin, Ikone*, ed. Peter Ackermann and Herbert Schneider, 35–57. Hildesheim: Georg Olms, 1999.

Bary, Helene de. *Museum: Geschichte der Museumsgesellschaft zu Frankfurt am Main.* Frankfurt am Main: Brönners, 1937.

Barzun, Jacques. *Berlioz and the Romantic Century.* 2 vols. Boston: Little, Brown, 1950.

Becker, Claudia Stevens. "A New Look at Schumann's Impromptus." *Musical Quarterly,* 67 (1981), 568–86.

Benton, Rita. "Pleyel." In *The New Grove Dictionary of Music and Musicians,* ed. Stanley Sadie, 20 vols., 15:10–11. London: Macmillan, 1980.

Berenbruch, Brigitte, and Helmut Hellberg. *Robert Schumann und Bonn.* Bonn: Stadt Bonn, 1980.

Berlioz, Hector. *Hector Berlioz: A Selection from His Letters.* Ed. and trans. Humphrey Searle. New York: Vienna House, 1973.

Beschreibung von Leipzig für Fremde und Reisende. Leipzig: Baumgärtnersche Buchhandlung, 1816.

Bock, Claus Victor. "Pente Pigadia und die Tagebücher des Clement Harris." *Castrum Peregrini,* 50 (1961), 5–31.

Bodsch, Ingrid, and Gerd Nauhaus, eds. *Clara Schumann, 1819–1896: Katalog zur Ausstellung.* Bonn: Bonn Stadtmuseum, 1996.

Boetticher, Wolfgang. "Neue textkritische Forschungen an Robert Schumanns Klavierwerk." *Archiv für Musikwissenschaft,* 25 (1968), 46–76.

——. *Robert Schumanns Klavierwerke: Neue biographische und textkritische Untersuchungen.* Pt. 1, Opp. 1–6. Wilhelmshaven: Heinrichshofen, 1976.

——. "Robert Schumann und seine Verleger." In *Musik und Verlag: Karl Vötterle zum 65. Geburtstag am 12. April 1968*, ed. Richard Baum und Wolfgang Rehm, 168–74. Kassel: Bärenreiter, 1968.

——. "Zur Zitatpraxis in R. Schumanns frühen Klavierwerken." In *Speculum Musicae Artis: Heinrich Husmann zum 60. Geburtstag,* ed. Heinz Becker and Reinhard Gerlach, 63–73. Munich: Wilhelm Fink, 1970.

——, ed. *Briefe und Gedichte aus dem Album Robert und Clara Schumanns.* Leipzig: Deutscher Verlag für Musik, 1979.

——, ed. *Robert Schumann in seinen Schriften und Briefen.* Berlin: Hahnefeld, 1942.

Borchard, Beatrix. *Clara Schumann: Ihr Leben*. Frankfurt am Main: Ullstein, 1991.

——. "Zwei Musikerinnen—zwei Kulturen. Unveröffentliche Briefe von Clara Schumann und Pauline Viardot-Garcia." In *Clara Schumann: Komponistin, Interpretin, Unternehmerin, Ikone,* ed. Peter Ackermann and Herbert Schneider, 59–92. Hildesheim: Georg Olms, 1999.

Boyd, Melinda. "Gendered Voices: The Liebesfrühling Lieder of Robert and Clara Schumann." In *Nineteenth-Century Music,* 23 (Fall 1999), 145–62.

Brahms, Johannes. *Johannes Brahms in seiner Familie: Der Briefwechsel.* Ed. Kurt Stephenson. Hamburg: Ernst Hauswedell, 1973.

Brahms, Johannes, and Theodor Billroth. *Letters from a Musical Friendship.* Trans. and ed. Hans Barkan. Norman: University of Oklahoma Press, 1957.

Brahms, Johannes, and Julius Otto Grimm. *Johannes Brahms im Briefwechsel mit Julius Otto Grimm.* Ed. Richard Barth. Berlin: Deutsche Brahms-Gesellschaft, 1907.

Brahms, Johannes, Heinrich von Herzogenberg, and Elisabeth von Herzogenberg. *Johannes Brahms im Briefwechsel mit Heinrich und Elisabeth von Herzogenberg.* Ed. Max Kalbeck. Berlin: Deutsche Brahms-Gesellschaft, 1907. 2 vols. Published in English as *The Herzogenberg Correspondence.* Ed. Max Kalbeck. Trans. Hannah Bryant. London: John Murray, 1909.

Brahms, Johannes, and Joseph Joachim. *Johannes Brahms im Briefwechsel mit Joseph Joachim.* Ed. Andreas Moser. 2 vols. Berlin: Deutsche Brahms-Gesellschaft, 1908.

Brahms, Johannes, and Philipp Spitta. *Johannes Brahms im Briefwechsel mit Philipp Spitta.* Ed. Carl Krebs. Berlin: Deutsche Brahms-Gesellschaft, 1920.

Brody, Elaine. "Schumann's Legacy in France." *Studies in Romanticism,* 13 (1974), 189–212.

Bromen, Stefan. "Clara Schumann." *Studien zu den Klaviertranskriptionen Schumannscher Lieder von Franz Liszt, Clara Schumann und Carl Reinecke,* 106–36. Sinzig: Studio, 1997.

Burger, Ernst, with Gerd Nauhaus. *Robert Schumann: Eine Lebenschronik in Bildern und Dokumenten.* Mainz: Schott, 1999.

Bulman, Joan. *Jenny Lind.* London: James Barrie, 1956.

Burk, John. *Clara Schumann: A Romantic Biography.* New York: Random House, 1940.

Burton, Anna. "A Psychoanalyst's View of Clara Schumann." In *Psychoanalytic Explorations in Music,* ed. Stuart Feder, Richard L. Karmel, and George H. Pollack, 97–113. Madison, Conn.: International Universities Press, 1990.

——. "Robert Schumann and Clara Wieck—A Creative Partnership." In *Music and Letters,* 60 (1988), 211–28.

Cahn, Peter. *Das Hoch'sche Konservatorium in Frankfurt am Main (1878–1978).* Frankfurt am Main: Waldemar Kramer, 1979.

Callomon, F. T. "Unbekannte Briefe Robert und Clara Schumanns." *Neue Zeitschrift für Musik,* 118 (1956), 396–400.

Chissell, Joan. *Clara Schumann: A Dedicated Spirit.* London: Hamish Hamilton, 1983.

Chopin, Frédéric. *Chopin's Letters.* Ed. Henryk Opieński. Trans. E. L. Voynich. New York: Knopf, 1931.

Chorley, Henry F. *Music and Manners in France and Germany: A Series of Travelling Sketches of Art and Society.* 3 vols. London: Longman, Brown, Green & Longmans, 1844.

Citron, Marcia. "Women and the Lied, 1775–1850." In *Women Making Music: The Western Art Tradition, 1150–1950,* ed. Jane Bowers and Judith Tick. Urbana: University of Illinois Press, 1986.

Clara und Robert Schumann: Zeitgenössische Porträts. Düsseldorf: Heinrich-Heine-Institut, 1994.

Daverio, John. *Robert Schumann: Herald of a "New Poetic Age."* New York: Oxford University Press, 1997.

Davies, Fanny. "On Schumann—and Reading between the Lines." *Music and Letters,* 6 (1925), 214–23.

Demmler, Fritz. *Johann George Tromlitz (1752–1805): Ein Beitrag zur Entwicklung der Flöte und des Flötenspiels*. Buren: F. Knuf, 1985.

Deutsch, Otto Erich. *Mozart: A Documentary Biography.* 2d ed. London: Adam & Charles Black, 1966.

De Vries, Claudia. *Die Pianistin Clara Wieck-Schumann: Interpretation im Spannungsfeld von Tradition und Individualität*. Mainz: Schott, 1996.

Dörffel, Alfred, ed. *Geschichte der Gewandhausconcerte zu Leipzig vom 25. November 1781 bis 25. November 1881*. Leipzig, 1884. The second section of this book, "Statistik," pp. 1–100, is not found in every copy.

Eberhardt, Hans. *Die ersten deutschen Musikfeste in Frankenhausen am Kyffhäuser und Erfurt, 1810, 1811, 1812 und 1815*. Jena: Frommann, 1934.

Eismann, Georg. "Robert Schumanns Ehetagebücher entsiegelt." *Musik und Gesellschaft,* 9 (1951), 279–84; 10 (1952), 7–9.

——, ed. *Robert Schumann: Ein Quellenwerk über sein Leben und Schaffen.* 2 vols. Leipzig: Breitkopf & Härtel, 1956.

Ettinger, Schmuel. "The Origins of Modern Anti-Semitism." *Dispersion and Unity,* 9 (1969), 17–37.

Fang, Siu-Wan Chair. "Clara Schumann as Teacher." DMA thesis, University of Illinois, 1978.

Fay, Amy. *Music Study in Germany.* 18th ed. New York: Macmillan, 1903. First published 1880.

Federhofer-Königs, Renate. "Der Briefwechsel von Wilhelm Joseph von Wasielewski (1822–1896) in seiner Bedeutung für die Schumann-Forschung." In *Convivium Musicorum: Festschrift Wolfgang Boetticher,* ed. Heinrich Hüschen and Dietz-Rüdiger Moser, 52–67. Berlin: Merseburger, 1974.

——. *Wilhelm Joseph von Wasielewski im Spiegel seiner Korrespondenz.* Tutzing: Schneider, 1975.

Fellinger, Imogen. "Clara Schumann." In *Die Musik in Geschichte und Gegenwart,* ed. Friedrich Blume, 12:261–69. Kassel: Bärenreiter, 1965.

Fiske, Roger. "A Schumann Mystery." *Musical Times,* 105 (1964), 574–78.

Fitzlyon, April. *The Price of Genius: A Life of Pauline Viardot.* New York: Appleton-Century-Crofts, 1964.

Frager, Malcolm. "The Music of the Schumann Piano Concerto." *Current Musicology,* 15 (1973), 83–87.

Franken, Franz Hermann. "Robert Schumann in der Irrenanstalt in Bonn-Endenich: Zum aufgefundenen ärztlichen Verlaufsbericht 1854–1856 von Doktor Franz Richarz." In *Brahms-Studien,* 11, 107–20. Tutzing: Hans Schneider, 1997.

Fricke, Harald. "Rückert, das Kunstlied und die Schumanns." In *Robert Schumann und seine Dichter. Almanach, 4. Schumannfest 1991,* 59-63. Düsseldorf: Robert-Schumann-Gesellschaft, 1991.

Fromm, Marie. "Some Reminiscences of my Music Studies with Clara Schumann." *Musical Times,* 73 (1932), 615–16.

Fuller Maitland, John Alexander. *Masters of German Music.* London: Osgood, McIlvaine, 1894.

Gal, Hans. *Johannes Brahms: His Work and Personality.* Trans. Joseph Stein. New York: Knopf, 1963. First published in German, 1961.

Geiringer, Karl. *Brahms: His Life and Work.* 2d ed., rev. and enl. New York: Anchor/Doubleday, 1961.

——. "Schumanniana in der Bibliothek von Johannes Brahms." In *Convivium Musico-*

rum: Festschrift Wolfgang Boetticher, ed. Heinrich Hüschen and Dietz-Rüdiger Moser, 79–82. Berlin: Merseburger, 1974.

Gerber, Ernst Ludwig. *Neues historisches biographisches Lexikon der Tonkünstler.* 4 vols. Leipzig: Kühnel, 1812–14.

Gerig, Reginald. *Famous Pianists and Their Techniques.* 2d ed. Washington, D.C.: R. B. Luce, 1974.

Goertzen, Valerie W. "By Way of Introduction: Preluding by 18th and 19th Century Pianists." In *Journal of Musicology,* 14 (Summer 1996), 299–337.

——. "Clara Schumann." In *Women Composers: Music through the Ages,* 6:44–53. New York: G. K. Hall, 1999.

——. "Setting the Stage: Clara Schumann's Preludes." In *In the Course of Performance: Studies in the World of Musical Improvisation,* ed. Bruno Nettl with Melinda Russell, 237–60. Chicago: University of Chicago Press, 1998.

Greene, Harry Plunkett. "Leonard Borwick: Some Personal Recollections." In Music *and Letters,* 7 (1926), 17–24.

Grove, Sir George. "Clara Schumann." In *Grove's Dictionary of Music and Musicians,* ed. R. C. Colles, 3d ed., 6 vols., 4:645–48. New York: Macmillan, 1935.

Gutman, Robert. *Richard Wagner: The Man, His Mind, His Music.* New York: Harcourt Brace Jovanovich, 1968.

Haight, Gordon S. *George Eliot: A Biography.* New York: Oxford University Press, 1968.

Hallmark, Rufus. *The Genesis of Schumann's Dichterliebe: A Source Study.* Ann Arbor, Mich.: UMI Research Press, 1979.

——. "The Rückert Lieder of Robert and Clara Schumann." In *Nineteenth-Century Music,* 14 (Summer 1990), 3–30.

Hanslick, Eduard. *Am Ende des Jahrhunderts 1895–1899.* Die Moderne Oper, pt. 8. 2d ed. Berlin: Allgemeiner Verein für deutsche Literatur, 1899.

——. *Aus neuer und neuester Zeit.* Die Moderne Oper, pt. 9. 3d ed. Berlin: Allgemeiner Verein für deutsche Literatur, 1900.

——. *Concerte, Componisten und Virtuosen der letzten fünfzehn Jahre, 1870–1885.* Berlin: Allgemeiner Verein für deutsche Lituratur, 1886.

——. *Geschichte des Concertwesens in Wien.* Vienna: Wilhelm Braumüller, 1869.

Harwood, Gregory. "Robert Schumann's Sonata in F# Minor: A Study of Creative Process and Romantic Inspiration." *Current Musicology,* 29 (1980), 17–30.

Henschel, Sir George. *Musings and Memories of a Musician.* New York: Macmillan, 1919.

——. *Personal Recollections of Johannes Brahms.* Boston: R. G. Badger, 1907.

Hiller, Ferdinand. *Aus Ferdinand Hillers Briefwechsel (1826–1861).* Ed. Reinhold Sietz. Cologne: Arno Volk-Verlag, 1958.

Hirsch, Ferdinand, and Ellen Roeser, eds. *Erst- und Frühdrucke von Robert Schumann in der Musikbibliothek Leipzig.* Leipzig: Bibliographische Veröffentlichungen der Musikbibliothek der Stadt Leipzig, 1960.

Hirschberg, Leopold. "Robert Schumann und der Davidsbündler Fritz Friedrich: Mit einer Auswahl bisher unveröffentlicher Briefe J. P. Lysers an Schumann." *Velhagen & Klasings Monatshefte,* 24 (1909–10), 85–91, 241–47.

Hofmann, Kurt. *Die Bibliothek von Johannes Brahms.* Hamburg: Wagner, 1974.

——. *Die Erstdrucke der Werke von Johannes Brahms.* Tutzing: Schneider, 1975.

——. *Die Erstdrucke der Werke von Robert Schumann.* Tutzing: Schneider, 1979.

Hofmann, Renate. "Clara Schumann und ihre Söhne." In *Schumann Studien,* ed. Gerd Nauhaus, 6:27-40. Sinzig: Studio, 1996.

——, ed. *Clara Schumanns Briefe an Theodor Kirchner, mit einer Lebensskizze des Komponisten.* Tutzing: Hans Schneider, 1996.

Hofmann, Renate, and Harry Schmidt, eds. *Das Berliner Blumentagebuch der Clara Schumann, 1857–1859.* Wiesbaden: Breitkopf & Härtel, 1991.

Hohenemser, Richard, "Clara Wieck-Schumann als Komponistin." *Die Musik,* 5 (1905–6), 113–26, 166–73.

Holborn, Hajo. *A History of Modern Germany, 1648–1840.* New York: Knopf, 1964.

Holde, Artur. "Suppressed Passages in the Joachim-Brahms Correspondence Published for the First Time." *Musical Quarterly,* 45 (1959), 312–24.

Holoman, D. Kern. *Berlioz.* Cambridge: Harvard University Press, 1989.

Huebner, Rudolf. *A History of Germanic Private Law.* Trans. Francis S. Philbrick. Boston: Little, Brown, 1918.

Jahresbericht des Dr. Hoch'schen Conservatoriums zu Frankfurt am Main. Frankfurt am Main: C. Adelmann, 1879–1921.

Jansen, F. Gustav. *Die Davidsbündler: Aus Robert Schumanns Sturm-und Drangperiode. Ein Beitrag zur Biographie R. Schumann's nebst ungedruckten Briefen, Aufsätzen und Portraitskizzen aus seinem Freundeskreise.* Leipzig: Breitkopf & Härtel, 1883.

Joachim, Joseph. *Briefe von und an Joseph Joachim.* Ed. Johannes Joachim and Andreas Moser. 3 vols. Berlin: Julius Bard, 1911–13. Published in English as *Letters from and to Joseph Joachim.* Trans. Nora Bickley. London: Macmillan, 1914.

Joss, Victor. *Der Musikpädagoge Friedrich Wieck und seine Familie: Mit besonderer Berücksichtigung seines Schwiegersohnes Robert Schumann.* Dresden: Oscar Damm, 1902. 2d enl. ed. of *Friedrich Wieck und sein Verhältnis zu Robert Schumann.* Dresden: Oscar Damm, 1900.

Kalbeck, Max. *Johannes Brahms.* 4th ed. 4 vols. Berlin: Deutsche Brahms-Gesellschaft, 1921. Used here are reprints (Tutzing: Hans Schneider): vol. 1, 4th ed. (1921); vol. 2, 3d ed. (1921); vol. 3, 2d ed. (1912); vol. 4, 2d ed. (1915).

Kaldewey, Helma. "Die Gedichtabschriften Robert und Clara Schumanns." In *Robert Schumann und die Dichter: Ein Musiker als Leser,* ed. Bernhard Appel and Inge Hermstrüwer, 88–99. Düsseldorf: Droste, 1991.

Kämper, Dietrich. "Zur Frage der Metronombezeichnungen Robert Schumanns." *Archiv für Musikwissenschaft,* 21 (1964), 141–55.

Kast, Paul, ed. *Schumanns rheinische Jahre.* Düsseldorf: Droste, 1981.

Kehler, George, ed. *The Piano in Concert.* 2 vols. Metuchen, N.J.: Scarecrow Press, 1982.

Kinsky, Georg, ed. *Manuskripte, Briefe, Dokumente von Scarlatti bis Stravinsky: Katalog der Musikautographen-Sammlung Louis Koch.* Stuttgart: Hoffmansche Buchdruckerei, F. Krais, 1953.

Klassen, Janina. *Clara Wieck-Schumann: Die Virtuosin als Komponistin.* Kassel: Bärenreiter, 1990.

——. "'Mach doch ein Lied einmals': Clara Wieck-Schumanns Annäherung an die Liedkomposition." In *Schumann Studien,* ed. Gerd Nauhaus, 6:13–25. Sinzig: Studio, 1997.

——. "Recht Brahms, ernst und humoristisch: Noch ein paar Bemerkungen zu Clara Schumann und Johannes Brahms." In *Brahms-Phantasien: Johannes Brahms-Bildwelt, Musik, Leben, 18. September bis 26. Oktober 1983,* 7–10. Catalogue, Kunsthalle, Christian-Albrechts-Universität, Kiel, 1983.

——. "'Schumann will es nun instrumentieren': Das Finale aus Clara Wiecks Klavierkonzert, op. 7 . . ." In *Schumann Studien* 3/4, ed. Gerd Nauhaus, 291–99. Cologne: Studio, 1994.

——. "*Souvenir de Vienne:* Künstlerische Präsentation und musikalische Erinnerung." In *Ich fahre in mein liebes Wien: Clara Schumann—Fakten, Bilder, Projektionen,* ed. Elena Ostleitner and Ursula Simek, 61–72. Vienna: Löcker Verlag, 1996.

Knechtges-Obrecht, Irmgard. "Clara Schumann in Düsseldorf." In *Clara Schumann, 1819-1896: Katalog zur Ausstellung,* ed. Ingrid Bodsch and Gerd Nauhaus, 189–229. Bonn: Bonn Stadtmuseum, 1996.

Kneschke, Emil. *Das Conservatorium der Musik in Leipzig: Seine Geschichte, seine Lehrer und Zöglinge.* Leipzig: Breitkopf & Härtel, 1868.

Köckritz, Cathleen. "Ausgewählte Aspekte der Klavierausbildung Friedrich Wiecks." In *Schumann Studien,* ed. Gerd Nauhaus, 6:41–54. Sinzig: Studio, 1997.

——. "So strebe darnach ein Lehrer Ersten Ranges zu werden—Die beginnende Unterrichtstätigkeit Friedrich Wiecks." In *Clara Schumann: Komponistin, Interpretin, Unternehmerin, Ikone,* ed. Peter Ackermann and Herbert Schneider, 151–63. Hildesheim: Georg Olms, 1999.

Köhler, Karl-Heinz. "Felix Mendelssohn (Bartholdy)." In *The New Grove Dictionary of Music and Musicians,* ed. Stanley Sadie, 20 vols., 12:134–59. London: Macmillan, 1980.

Kohut, Adolph. *Friedrich Wieck: Ein Lebens- und Künstlerbild.* Dresden: Pierson's, 1888.

Krebs, Carl. "Clara Schumann." In *Allgemeine Deutsche Biographie,* 54:262–68.

Kreisig, Martin. "Einige Briefe Clara Schumanns." *Neue Musik-Zeitung,* 41 (1919), 35–36.

Kross, Siegfried, ed. *Briefe und Notizen Robert und Clara Schumanns.* Bonn: Bouvier, 1978.

Kruse, Joseph, ed. *Robert und Clara Schumann: Dokumente zum Düsseldorfer Musikleben.* Düsseldorf: Heinrich-Heine-Institut, 1976.

Lara, Adelina de. "Clara Schumann's Teaching." *Music and Letters,* 26 (1945), 143–47.

Lara, Adelina de, with Clare H. Abrahall. *Finale.* London: Burke, 1955.

Laux, Karl. "Dresden ist doch gar zu schön." In *Robert Schumann: Aus Anlass seines 100. Todestages,* ed. Hans Joachim Moser and Eberhard Rebling, 25–42. Leipzig: Breitkopf & Härtel, 1956.

Leo, Sophie Augustine. "Musical Life in Paris, 1817–1848: A Chapter from the Memoirs of Sophie Augustine Leo." Trans. Oliver Strunk. *Musical Quarterly,* 17 (1931), 259–71, 389–403.

Leven, Louise W. "Clara Schumann's First Visit to England." *Musical Times,* 97 (1956), 190–91.

Lindeman, Stephan D. *Structural Novelty and Tradition in the Early Romantic Piano Concerto.* Stuyvesant, N.Y.: Pendragon Press, 1999.

Lippman, Edward. "Robert Schumann." In *Die Musik in Geschichte und Gegenwart,* ed. Friedrich Blume, 12:272–326. Kassel: Bärenreiter, 1965.

Liszt, Franz. *Correspondance de Liszt et de Madame d'Agoult.* Ed. M. Daniel Ollivier. 2 vols. Paris: Grasset, 1933.

——. *Franz Liszts Briefe.* Ed. La Mara. 2d ed. 8 vols. Leipzig: Breitkopf & Härtel, 1893–1902.

Litzmann, Berthold, ed. *Clara Schumann: Ein Künstlerleben nach Tagebüchern und Briefen.* 3 vols. Leipzig: Breitkopf & Härtel, 1902–8. Abr. ed. published in English as *Clara Schumann: An Artist's Life, Based on Material Found in Diaries and Letters.* Trans. Grace E. Hadow. 2 vols. London: Macmillan, 1913.

Loesser, Arthur. *Men, Women, and Pianos: A Social History.* New York: Simon & Schuster, 1954.

Löhner, Wilhelm, ed. "Clara Schumann: Unbekannte Briefe an Emilie Steffens." *Zeitschrift für Musik,* 97 (1930), 177–79.

Lossewa, Olga. "'Zwanzig Jahre später'—Clara Schumann in Petersburg und Moskau, 1864." In *Schumann Studien,* ed. Gerd Nauhaus, 6:147–64. Sinzig: Studio, 1996.

Lowder, Jerry. "Friedrich Wieck as a Teacher." *Clavier,* 8 (1969), 42–43.

Lyser, Johann Peter. "Clara Wieck." *Caecilia* (Hamburg), 1 (1833), 253–58.

Macdonald, Claudia. "Critical Perception and the Woman Composer: The Early Reception of Piano Concertos by Clara Wieck Schumann and Amy Beach." *Current Musicology,* Summer 1994, 24–55.

——. Review of Ernst Burger, *Robert Schumann: Eine Lebenschronik in Bildern und Dokumenten. Notes,* 56 (December 1999), 409–11.

——. Review of Clara Schumann, *Konzert für Klavier und Orchester,* ed. Janina Klassen. *Notes,* 48 (December 1991), 674–76.

May, Florence. *The Girlhood of Clara Schumann: Clara Wieck and Her Time.* London: Edward Arnold, 1912.
——. *The Life of Johannes Brahms.* 2d ed. 2 vols. London: William Reeves, 1905.
McCorkle, Margit L. *Johannes Brahms: Thematisch-bibliographisches Werkverzeichnis.* Munich: Henle, 1984.
Meichsner, Anna von. *Friedrich Wieck und seine beiden Töchter, Clara Schumann, geb. Wieck, und Marie Wieck: Biographische Notizen über dieselben nebst ungedruckten Briefen von H. v. Bülow, Czerny, R. Schumann, Carl Maria von Weber usw.: Ein Familiendenkmal.* Leipzig: Heinrich Matthes, 1875.
Mendelssohn, Felix. *Felix Mendelssohn Bartholdy: Briefe aus Leipziger Archiven.* Ed. Hans-Joachim Rothe and Reinhard Szeskus. Leipzig: Deutscher Verlag für Musik, 1972.
——. *Felix Mendelssohn-Bartholdys Briefwechsel mit Legationsrat Karl Klingemann in London.* Ed. Karl Klingemann. Essen: Baedeker, 1909.
Methuen-Campbell, James. "Chopin in Performance." In *The Cambridge Companion to Chopin,* ed. Jim Samson, 191–205. Cambridge: Cambridge University Press, 1992.
Moser, Andreas. *Joseph Joachim: Ein Lebensbild.* Rev. and enl. ed. 2 vols. Berlin: Deutsche Brahms-Gesellschaft, 1908.
Müller-Reuter, Theodor. *Bilder und Klänge des Friedens: Musikalische Erinnerungen und Aufsätze.* Leipzig: Wilhelm Hartung, 1919.
Munte, Frank. "Robert und Clara Schumann in Hamburg." In *Brahms-Studien,* ed. Helmut Wirth, 2:7–45. Hamburg: Wagner, 1977.
——. *Verzeichnis des deutschsprachigen Schrifttums über Robert Schumann.* Hamburg: Wagner, 1972.
Musgrave, Michael. *A Brahms Reader.* New Haven: Yale University Press, 2000.
Nauhaus, Gerd, with Annette Müller. *Robert-Schumann-Haus Zwickau.* Munich: Deutscher Kunstverlag, 2000. Text in German and English.
Newman, William. *The Sonata since Beethoven.* 2d ed. New York: W. W. Norton, 1972.
Niecks, Frederick. *Robert Schumann.* London: J. M. Dent, 1925.
Ostleitner, Elena, and Ursula Simek, eds. *Ich fahre in mein liebes Wien: Clara Schumann—Fakten, Bilder, Projektionen.* Vienna: Löcker Verlag, 1996.
Ostwald, Peter. "Florestan, Eusebius, Clara, and Schumann's Right Hand." *Nineteenth-Century Music,* 4 (1980), 17–31.
——. *Robert Schumann: The Inner Voices of a Musical Genius.* Boston: Northeastern University Press, 1985.
Perenyi, Eleanor. *Liszt: The Artist as Romantic Hero.* Boston: Little, Brown, 1974.
Pettler, Pamela Susskind. "Clara Schumann's Recitals, 1832–50." *Nineteenth-Century Music,* 4 (1980), 70–76.
Plantinga, Leon B. *Schumann as Critic.* New Haven: Yale University Press, 1967.
Ramshorn, Carl. *Leipzig und seine Umgebungen.* Braunschweig: George Westermann, 1841.
Rehberg, Paula, and Walter Rehberg. *Robert Schumann: Sein Leben und sein Werk.* 2d ed. Zurich: Artemis, 1969.
Reich, Nancy B. "Clara and Robert Schumann: A Musical Partnership." *Keyboard Classics,* September–October 1985, 11–12.
——. "Clara Schumann." In *New Grove Dictionary of Women Composers,* ed. Julie Anne Sadie and Rhian Samuel, 411–16. London: Macmillan, 1994.
——. "Clara Schumann and America." In *Clara Schumann: Komponistin, Interpretin, Unternehmerin, Ikone,* ed. Peter Ackermann and Herbert Schneider, 195–203. Hildesheim: Georg Olms, 1999.
——. "Clara Schumann and Johannes Brahms." In *Brahms and His World,* ed. Walter Frisch, 37–47. Princeton: Princeton University Press, 1990.

——. "Clara Schumann's *Romance* Discovered in an 1891 London Weekly." In *Keyboard Classics,* September/October 1989, 19–22.

——. "The Correspondence between Clara Wieck Schumann and Felix and Paul Mendelssohn." In *Schumann and His World,* ed. R. Larry Todd, 205–32. Princeton: Princeton University Press, 1994.

——. "Women as Musicians: A Question of Class." In *Musicology and Difference: Gender and Sexuality in Music Scholarship,* ed. Ruth Solie, 125–46. Berkeley: University of California Press, 1993.

Reich, Nancy B., with Anna Burton, M.D. "Clara Schumann: Old Sources, New Readings." *Musical Quarterly,* 70 (Summer 1984), 332–54.

Reimann, Ute, and Joachim Draheim. *Clara und Robert Schumann in Baden-Baden und Carlsruhe*. Munich: Emil Katzbichler, 1996.

Ritterman, Janet. "'Gegensätze, Ecken, und scharfe Kanten': Clara Schumanns Besuch in England, 1856–1888." In *Clara Schumann, 1819–1896: Katalog zur Ausstellung,* ed. Ingrid Bodsch and Gerd Nauhaus, 235–61. Bonn: Bonn Stadtmuseum, 1996.

Robert Schumanns letzte Lebensjahre: Protokoll einer Krankheit. Archiv-Blätter 1. Berlin: Stiftung Archiv der Akademie der Künste, 1994.

Roesner, Linda Corell. "Studies in Schumann Manuscripts: With Particular Reference to Sources Transmitting Instrumental Works in the Large Forms." Ph.D. dissertation, New York University, 1973.

Rudolphi, Caroline. *Gemälde weiblicher Erziehung.* Heidelberg: Mohr & Winter, 1815.

Sagarra, Eda. *A Social History of Germany.* New York: Holmes & Meier, 1977.

Sams, Eric. "Brahms and His Clara Themes." *Musical Times,* 112 (1971), 432–34.

——. "Schumann and the Tonal Analogue." In *Robert Schumann: The Man and His Music,* ed. Alan Walker, 390–405. London: Barrie & Jenkins, 1972.

——. "Schumann's Hand Injury." *Musical Times,* 112 (1971), 1156–59.

——. *The Songs of Robert Schumann.* 2d ed. London: Eulenburg, 1975.

Schauffler, Robert Haven. *Florestan: The Life and Work of Robert Schumann.* New York: Henry Holt, 1945.

Schindler, Anton. *Beethoven as I Knew Him.* Ed. Donald W. MacArdle. Trans. Constance S. Jolly. New York: W. W. Norton, 1966.

Schlotel, Brian. "Schumann and the Metronome." In *Robert Schumann: The Man and His Music,* ed. Alan Walker, 109–19. London: Barrie & Jenkins, 1972.

Schonberg, Harold C. *The Great Pianists from Mozart to the Present.* New York: Simon & Schuster, 1963.

Schoppe, Martin. "Schumann-Interpretation Clara Schumanns (Tageskritik und Konzertbericht)." In *3. Schumann-Tage des Bezirkes Karl-Marx-Stadt, 1978,* 17–24. Zwickau: Robert-Schumann-Gesellschaft, 1978.

Schoppe, Martin, and Gerd Nauhaus. *Das Robert-Schumann-Haus in Zwickau.* Zwickau: Robert-Schumann-Haus, 1973.

Schubert, Franz Peter. *Erlkönig: Facsimile of the Autograph Manuscript.* New York: Pierpont Morgan Library, 1978.

Schumann, Alfred (under pseud. Titus Frazendi). *Johannes Brahms, der Vater von Felix Schumann: Das Mysterium einer Liebe. Eine sehr ernste Parodie auf die Erinnerungen von Eugenie Schumann.* Bielefeld: Manfred, 1926.

Schumann, Clara. *Lettres autographes conservées à la Bibliothèque royale de Belgique,* ed. Gerd Nauhaus. Brussels: Bibliotheca Regia Belgica, 1999.

——. *Mein liebes Julchen: Briefe von Clara Schumann an ihre Enkeltochter Julie Schumann mit Auszügen aus Julie Schumanns Tagebüchern und einem Bericht über ihre Begegnung mit Johannes Brahms.* Ed. Dietz-Rüdiger Moser. Munich: Nymphenburger, 1990.

Schumann, Clara, and Johannes Brahms. *Clara Schumann–Johannes Brahms Briefe aus den Jahren 1853–1896*. Ed. Berthold Litzmann. 2 vols. Leipzig: Breitkopf & Härtel, 1927. Abr. ed. published in English as *Letters of Clara Schumann and Johannes Brahms, 1853–1896*. Trans. Grace Hadow. London: Edward Arnold, 1927.

Schumann, Clara, and Robert Schumann. *Briefwechsel.* Ed. Eva Weissweiler. Critical ed. Vol. 1, *1832–1838*. Vol. 2, *1839*. Basel: Stroemfeld/Roter Stern, 1984, 1987. Published in English as *The Complete Correspondence of Clara and Robert Schumann.* Trans. Hildegard Fritsch and Ronald L. Crawford. 2 vols. New York: Peter Lang, 1994–96.

Schumann, Eugenie. *Erinnerungen*. Stuttgart: Engelhorn, 1925. Translated into English by Marie Busch and published as *The Memoirs of Eugenie Schumann* (London: William Heinemann, 1927) and as *The Schumanns and Johannes Brahms: The Memoirs of Eugenie Schumann* (New York: Dial, 1927). References in this book are to the translation, for several reasons: the book is not abridged, Eugenie Schumann knew English well, and since the translation was completed during her lifetime, I believe it to be a reliable version.

——. *Robert Schumann: Ein Lebensbild meines Vaters*. Leipzig: Koehler & Amelang, 1931.

——. "Über das letzte Werk ihres Vaters Robert Schumann." *Schweizerische Musikzeitung*, Jan. 1, 1938, 8–10.

Schumann, Ferdinand. "Brahms and Clara Schumann." *Musical Quarterly*, 2 (1916), 507–15. A translation of Ferdinand Schumann, "Erinnerungen an Brahms," *Neue Zeitschrift für Musik*, 82 (1915), 225–28, 233–36, 241–43.

——. *Reminiscences of Clara Schumann as Found in the Diary of Her Grandson Ferdinand Schumann of Dresden*. Ed. June M. Dickinson. 2d ed. New York: Musical Scope, 1973. A translation probably based on Ferdinand Schumann, "Erinnerungen an Clara Schumann," *Neue Zeitschrift für Musik*, 84 (1917), 69–72, 77–80, 85–88, 93–96, 101–4.

Schumann, Robert. *Erinnerungen an Felix Mendelssohn Bartholdy: Nachgelassene Aufzeichnungen*. Ed. Georg Eismann. Zwickau: Predella, 1947.

——. *Gesammelte Schriften über Musik und Musiker*. 4 vols. Leipzig: Wigand, 1854. Reprint with "Nachwort" by Gerd Nauhaus and index. Leipzig: Breitkopf & Härtel, 1985.

——. *Jugendbriefe von Robert Schumann: Nach den Originalen mitgetheilt*. Ed. Clara Schumann. 2d ed. Leipzig: Breitkopf & Härtel, 1886. Published in English as *Early Letters*. Trans. May Herbert. London: G. Bell, 1888.

——. [Klavierwerke]. Ed. Hans Joachim Köhler. Leipzig: C. F. Peters, 1973–. The piano works of Robert Schumann issued in separate volumes with extensive commentary.

——. *Robert Schumanns Briefe*. Neue Folge. Ed. F. Gustav Jansen. Leipzig: Breitkopf & Härtel, 1904.

——. *Tagebücher*. Pt. 1, *1827–1838*, ed. Georg Eismann. Pt. 2, *1836-1854*, ed. Gerd Nauhaus. Pt. 3, *Haushaltbücher (1837–1856)*, ed. Gerd Nauhaus, 2 vols. Leipzig: Deutscher Verlag für Musik, 1971–87. Pt. 2 includes marriage diaries and other entries by Robert and Clara Schumann.

——. *Thematisches Verzeichnis sämtlicher im Druck erschienenen musikalischen Werke mit Angabe des Jahres ihres Entstehens und Erscheinens*. Ed. Kurt Hofmann and Siegmar Keil. 5th ed., enl. and rev. Hamburg: J. Schuberth, 1982.

Schumann, Robert, and Clara Schumann. *The Marriage Diaries of Robert and Clara Schumann from Their Wedding Day through the Russia Trip*. Ed. Gerd Nauhaus. Trans. Peter Ostwald. Boston: Northeastern University Press, 1993.

Searle, Humphrey. "Franz Liszt." In *The New Grove Dictionary of Music and Musicians*, ed. Stanley Sadie, 20 vols., 11:28–74. London: Macmillan, 1980.

Shitomirski, Daniel Wladimirowitsch. "Schumann in Russland." In *Sammelbände der Robert-Schumann-Gesellsehaft*, 19–46. Zwickau, 1961.

Slater, Eliot. "Schumann's Illness." In *Robert Schumann: The Man and His Music,* ed. Alan Walker, 406–17. London: Barrie & Jenkins, 1972.
Smith, Julia. *Master Pianist: The Career and Teaching of Carl Friedberg.* New York: Philosophical Library, 1963.
Smyth, Ethel. *Impressions That Remained.* New York: Knopf, 1946.
Sonneck, Oscar, ed. *Beethoven: Impressions of Contemporaries.* New York: G. Schirmer, 1926.
Spohr, Louis. *Lebenserinnerungen.* Ed. Folker Göthel. 2 vols. Tutzing: Schneider, 1968.
Stadler, Wolfgang. *Colditzer Geschichten, 1265–1990: 725 Jahre Stadt Colditz.* Colditz: Stadt Colditz, 1989.
Stargardt-Wolff, Edith. *Wegbereiter grosser Musiker.* Berlin: Bote & Bock, 1954.
Steegmann, Monica, ed. *". . . dass Gott mir ein Talent geschenkt": Clara Schumanns Briefe an Hermann Härtel und Richard und Helene Schöne.* Zurich: Atlantis Musikbuch-Verlag, 1997.
Stephenson, Kurt. *Clara Schumann, 1819–1969.* Bonn/Bad Godesberg: Inter Nationes, 1960.
Susskind, Pamela. "Clara Schumann as Pianist and Composer: A Study of Her Life and Works." Ph.D. dissertation, University of California, Berkeley, 1977.
Suttoni, Charles. "Piano and Opera: A Study of the Piano Fantasies Written on Opera Themes in the Romantic Era." Ph.D. dissertation, New York University, 1973.
Todd, R. Larry. "On Quotation in Schumann's Music." In *Schumann and His World,* ed. R. Larry Todd, 80—112. Princeton: Princeton University Press, 1994.
Tomaszewski, Mieczysław, and Bożena Weber. *Fryderyk Chopin: A Diary in Images.* Trans. Rosemary Hunt. Warsaw: Arkady, 1990.
Verne, Mathilde. *Chords of Remembrance.* London: Hutchinson, 1936.
Wagner, Cosima. *Cosima Wagner's Diaries.* Ed. Martin Gregor-Dellin and Dietrich Mack. Trans. Geoffrey Skelton. 2 vols. New York: Harcourt Brace Jovanovich, 1978, 1980.
Walker, Alan. *Franz Liszt.* Vol. 1, *The Virtuoso Years, 1811–1847.* Rev. ed. Vol. 2, *The Weimar Years, 1848–1861.* Ithaca: Cornell University Press, 1987, 1989.
——. "Schumann, Liszt, and the C Major Fantasie, Op. 17: A Declining Relationship." *Music and Letters,* 60 (1979), 156–65.
Wasielewski, Wilhelm Joseph von. *Robert Schumann: Eine Biographie.* 3d enl. ed. Leipzig; Breitkopf & Härtel, 1880. Published in English as *Life of Robert Schumann.* Trans. A. L. Alger. Boston: Ditson, 1871.
Wendler, Eugen. *Friedrich List: Eine historische Gestalt im deutsch-amerikanischen Verhältnis.* Munich: Moos, 1989. Text in German and English.
——, ed. *"Das Band der ewigen Liebe": Clara Schumanns Briefwechsel mit Emilie und Elise List.* Stuttgart: J. B. Metzler, 1996.
Whitton, Kenneth S. "Robert Schumann, Robert Burns, und der Myrthen-Zyklus." In *Robert Schumann und seine Dichter: Almanach, 4. Schumannfest 1991,* 64–69. Düsseldorf: Robert-Schumann-Gesellschaft, 1991.
Wieck, Friedrich. *Briefe aus den Jahren 1830–1838.* Ed. Käthe Walch-Schumann. Cologne: Arno Volk-Verlag, 1968.
——. *Clavier und Gesang: Didaktisches und Polemisches.* Leipzig: F. Whistling, 1853. Published in English as (1) *Piano and Singing: Didactical and Polemical for Professionals and Amateurs.* Trans. H. Kreuger. Aberdeen: H. Krueger, [1875]. (2) *Piano and Song: How to Teach, How to Learn, and How to Form a Judgment of Musical Performances.* Trans. Mary P. Nichols. Boston: Ditson, 1875. Reprint New York: Da Capo, 1982. (3) *Piano and Song: Didactic and Polemical.* Trans. Henry Pleasants. Stuyvesant, N.Y.: Pendragon Press, 1988.
——. *Musikalische Bauernsprüchen.* Leipzig: Leuckardt, 1875.

Wieck, Marie. *Aus dem Kreise Wieck-Schumann.* 2d rev. and enl. ed. Dresden: v. Zahn & Jaensch, 1914.

Williamson, Rosemary. *William Sterndale Bennett: A Descriptive Thematic Catalogue.* Oxford: Oxford University Press, 1996.

Wirth, Julia Stockhausen, ed. *Julius Stockhausen, Der Sänger des deutschen Liedes: Nach Dokumenten seiner Zeit.* Frankfurt: Englert & Schlosser, 1927.

Wittkowski, Désirée. "'In Paris hast Du doppelte Mühe in Allem . . .': Clara Wieck-Schumanns Parisreisen." In *Clara Schumann, 1819–1896: Katalog zur Ausstellung,* ed. Ingrid Bodsch and Gerd Hauhaus. Bonn: Bonn Stadtmuseum, 1996.

Index

In this index, t stands for table.